Comparative Politics of Latin America

Students will explore and understand the evolutions and revolutions that have brought the region to where it is today in the fully-updated new edition of Daniel Hellinger's *Comparative Politics of Latin America*. This text offers a unique balance of comparative politics theory and interdisciplinary country-specific context, of a thematic organization and in-depth country case studies, of culture and economics, of scholarship and pedagogy. No other textbook draws on such a diverse range of scholarly literature to help students understand the ins and outs of politics in Latin America today.

Insightful historical background in early chapters provides students with a way to think about how the past influences the present. However, while history plays a part in this text, comparative politics is the primary focus, explaining through fully integrated, detailed case studies and carefully paced analysis such concepts as democratic breakdown and transition, formal and informal institutions, the rule of law, and the impact of globalization. Country-specific narratives integrate concepts and theories from comparative politics, leading to a richer understanding of both.

Several important features of the second edition ensure student success:

- Dramatically reorganized text now with 16 chapters
- Focus Questions at the start of every chapter
- "For Review" boxes interspersed in every chapter to ensure comprehension
- New "Punto de Vista" boxes in every chapter, showcasing competing perspectives on democratization and development throughout the region
- Country locator maps spread throughout the book to help students orient themselves in the region
- "Democracy Snapshot" graphics show support for democracy in each Latin American country
- Bolded key terms focus attention on important concepts and a glossary at the end of the book provides a useful reference
- Discussion Questions and Further Resources at the end of each chapter
- Integrated Case Studies on most countries in the region
- A companion website (www.routledge.com/cw/hellinger) with discussion questions and other useful study aids.

Daniel C. Hellinger is a Professor of International Relations and has been teaching at Webster University for over 30 years. He also serves on the Advisory Board of the Center of Democracy in the Americas (a Washington DC-based NGO) where he supports efforts towards a better understanding between the U.S. and Latin America. He is an authority on the politics of Venezuela.

Comparative Politics of Latin America

Democracy at Last?

Second edition

Daniel C. Hellinger

Routledge
Taylor & Francis Group

NEW YORK AND LONDON

Commissioning Editor: Michael Kerns
Textbook Development Manager: Rebecca Pearce
Production Editor: Alf Symons
Cover Design: John Maloney
Companion Website Manager: Natalya Dyer
Typesetter: Apex Covantage, LLC

Second edition published 2015
by Routledge
711 Third Avenue, New York, NY 10017

and by Routledge
2 Park Square, Milton Park, Abingdon, Oxon, OX14 4RN

Routledge is an imprint of the Taylor & Francis Group, an informa business

First edition published by Routledge 2011

Library of Congress Cataloging-in-Publication Data
Hellinger, Daniel.
    Comparative politics of Latin America : democracy at last? /
    Daniel C. Hellinger.
        pages cm
    Includes bibliographical references and index.
    1. Latin America—Politics and government.   2. Comparative government—
Latin America.   I. Title.
    JL960.H45 2014
    320.3098—dc23
    2014020620

ISBN: 978-0-415-82761-4 (pbk)
ISBN: 978-0-203-52244-8 (ebk)

Typeset in Minion Pro
by Apex Covantage, LLC

Dedication

To my good friends Steven Ellner, María Pilar García Guadilla,
Raúl Rodríguez, Bernard Mommer, Bernardo Álvarez, Angelo Rivero Santos,
and Eduardo Cavieres.

Contents

List of Punto de Vista Feature Boxes

Preface

Perhaps the world's most exciting and controversial experiments in democracy are underway in Latin America. Neither liberal nor Marxist orthodoxy has much appeal to most people in the region today, and perhaps that explains why Latin America has been a hothouse for democratic experimentation. As I explore these transitions to democracy throughout the text, the question is less about whether or not democracy is the best form of government and more about what form of democracy makes the most sense for today's world. I believe that the answer is not wildly different for Latin America than for other parts of the world, including the United States. In my personal view, democracy must not only embrace choice, equality before the law, and civil liberties; it must also be participatory, be socially and economically inclusive, and extend deeply into social and economic structures. It cannot be limited to affairs of government.

I suspect that attentive teachers and students will recognize that this agenda for democracy puts me somewhere on the left of the political spectrum, but I hope they will feel this text has not failed to fairly represent arguments drawn both from the liberal tradition of democracy and from the orthodox pluralist views that dominate the field of comparative politics. I would like comparative political scientists whose work reflects different views on democracy to feel that this book is passionate and intellectually honest, not polemical or deliberately selective in its treatment of the issues.

My goal in writing this text was to provide students with a method for exploring the politics of Latin America through a specific lens, with which they are free to agree or disagree. Ideally, each student will reach his or her own conclusions about what "democracy" means and what forms of government appear best suited to the countries explored in the text. Because Latin America contains a large number of diverse countries, each with its own challenges to address, I believe a thematic framework is the best method to help students organize the massive amount of information typically provided in courses of this nature. As someone who has been teaching the course for many, many years, I am fully aware of the challenges students face with grasping and organizing its content, and with this book I hope to provide them with a better tool for learning about—and thinking about—politics in Latin America.

As Latin America continues to expand its presence in the global economy and leaders from regimes of old begin to fade away, it is an exciting and important time to be studying Latin American politics. Arguably, the worldwide human rights movement began in Latin America during its last transition from military rule to electoral democracy. In Latin America today, social movements are re-conceptualizing the state, civil society, and the market. Social movements throughout the region are attempting to tame both the centralized power of states and the tyranny of market forces.

Brazilians started experimenting 25 years ago with participatory budgeting, a practice now spreading to other parts of the globe. Indigenous Andeans have gone farther than anyone else in promoting responsible stewardship of the earth on a world stage, insisting that we can have the *buen vivir* without the materialism and consumption of unbridled capitalism. Venezuelans have provided the world with its first constitution written in gender-neutral language. Though deeply divided about what democracy should look like, they have taken the lead in insisting that democracy cannot exist without social and economic inclusion. Cubans now wrestle with how to open their economy and politics without losing the values of solidarity, facing the challenge of a transition from the old Leninist model of the state.

Changes from the First to Second Edition

I have thoroughly updated and revised the text from the first edition. A few changes are especially worth highlighting:

- Reorganized chapter structure from 19 down to 16 chapters so that the text fits more easily with the traditional semester-long course.
- An all-new final chapter (chapter 16) where instead of covering the consequences of U.S. hegemony (chapter 19 in the previous edition), I discuss the consequences of weakening U.S. hegemony and new diplomatic initiatives by Latin Americans.
- Topical updates, including the Pink Tide, social movements' uneasy relationship with leftist parties, the expansion of the middle class, new hemispheric diplomatic organizations and initiatives for economic integration, post-Chávez Venezuela, post-Lula Brazil, the student movement in Chile, the revival of Mexico's PRI, the economic reforms launched by Raúl Castro, the impact of Chinese markets and investments and many other contemporary developments.

New Learning Aids in this Edition

In response to feedback from instructors, some new pedagogy has also been introduced, and existing pedagogy has been improved to help students better engage with the text.

Thumbnail "locator" maps are strategically placed throughout the text to help geographically challenged students develop familiarity with the location of countries. "Democracy Snapshots" of the 2013 Latinobarómeter poll results on attitudes toward democracy for various Latin American countries are also included where each country is discussed in depth. These "snapshots" provide instructors with an interesting talking point in class as the figures reveal a wide (and often surprising) gap between the degrees of support for democracy, from the highest (Venezuela) to the lowest (Mexico), in the region. Last, one of the most exciting new features to this edition is the "Punto de Vista" debate box. These boxes appear in nearly every chapter and ask students to debate issues facing citizens in Latin American countries, including affirmative action programs in Brazil, Ecuador's regulation of the media, Uruguay's amnesty for human rights abuses, and the U.S.-promoted drug war in the region.

Improved Learning Aids from the Last Edition

Changes to existing pedagogy in the new edition include the following:

- Revision of the introductory *Focus Questions* to make sure they correspond more closely to the chapter organization.
- *For Review* questions that appear throughout the text so that students can quickly check their comprehension. (Instructors might also utilize the *For Review* questions to get a pulse on their class's comprehension of the reading through classroom discussions, homework assignments, or quizzes.)
- *Discussion Questions* at the end of the chapter that encourage students to think critically about what they've read.
- Expansion of the glossary and number of key terms.
- Expansion of the *Resources for Further Study*, including more suggestions for readings (fiction and nonfiction), websites, films, and videos.

Companion Website

Routledge hosts a companion website that includes a number of useful resources for both students and instructors. Students looking for extra study aids will find chapter summaries, country profiles from Europa World, and web links to online resources. We are fortunate to be able to partner with Europa because they have a wealth of information available on the countries of Latin America. The inclusion of select Europa World content enables teachers to combine the thematic approach of this book with assignments to help provide students with a coherent narrative of the history, the social and economic features, and the recent development of individual nations in the region. It is also a good resource for students to have on hand if they are not familiar with the region or if they are researching a country-specific topic for the course. To help instructors with classroom preparation, the companion website includes PowerPoint lecture slides, suggestions for exam questions, suggestions for classroom activities, and more. The accompanying website has been thoroughly updated and revised by my colleague, Dr. Philip Meeks, professor at Creighton University. Phil brings a substantial and distinguished résumé in Latin American politics to this task. The companion website can be found at www.routledge.com/cw/hellinger.

Acknowledgments

In addition to all of those who helped with the first edition, I especially want to thank several people whose work has helped enormously in this second edition. I always must start with my love and life-partner, Joann Eng-Hellinger, whose patience and support is invaluable. Once again I want to thank especially commissioning editor Michael Kerns at Routledge for his faith in this book. Also deserving of my thanks is Phil Meeks for taking on development of a website that I hope teachers and students will find to be an invaluable resource. When Sawyer Judge, a high school junior, approached me about helping do research for this book, I was skeptical she would have the background and skills at such a young age. I put her to work finding new entries for "Resources for Further Study," and she did a fine job. As I was drowning in deadlines due to overcommitment to various projects, I received a lifeline in the form of Jake Seifert, who not only helped me compile the glossary and references, but who also read every chapter carefully with the eye of a student, identifying unclear and confusing passages in need of re-drafting, and culled out many of the mistakes in the penultimate draft of the book. And I save for last my thanks to Rebecca Pearce, the textbook development manager at Routledge. Among many examples of good judgment and suggestions is the inclusion of the "Puntos" sections in the chapters, which I hope teachers and students find allows them to enter into dialogue with Latin Americans about the issues that confront them. Of course, the success of this innovation depends on my execution of the idea. Any shortcomings or mistakes in this text are ultimately my responsibility. A special thank-you to the reviewers, anonymous and otherwise, whose insights and recommendations have helped to improve this edition:

Jeff Harmon, *University of Texas–San Antonio*
Philip Kelley, *Emporia State University*
Michael Fleet, *Marquette University*
Diana Kapiszewski, *Georgetown University*
Tony Spanakos, *Montclair State University*
Rick Coughlin, *Florida Gulf Coast University*
Diane Johnson, *Lebanon Valley College*
Philip Meeks, *Creighton University*
Marieke Reithof, *University of Liverpool*
Jennifer McCoy, *Georgia State University*
Damon Coletta, *U.S. Air Force Academy*

Introduction

Latin American Studies and the Comparative Study of Democracy

Focus Questions

► Why should we focus on democracy as the theme for an introduction to Latin America, a region long associated with political instability, military coups, and dictatorships?

► What do opinion polls tell us about support for democracy in Latin America today?

► Why does the study of Latin America fall into the field called "comparative politics"?

AS THE FIRST decade of the twenty-first century drew to a close, most of the political scientists, journalists, and policy makers following Latin American affairs seemed optimistic that the countries of the region were finally, after nearly 200 years of political independence, on track to enter a new era of stability, economic development, and democracy. The military were staying in the barracks, the students were studying, rebels were laying down their arms and founding political parties, poverty rates were falling, and the United States was no longer supporting dictatorships. Of course, just about everyone tempered this optimism with recognition of risks and concerns, but few doubted that progress had been made, and few doubted that the model of democracy preferred by Latin Americans was liberal, representative democracy.

Among the positive signs, they could point to the rising percentage of Latin Americans expressing confidence in democracy in surveys. Latinobarómetro, an annual poll of more than 20,000 Latin Americans in 18 countries, found in 2011 that 58 percent agreed that "democracy is preferable to any other form of government" (see Figure 0.1). Although almost everyone recognized some serious shortcomings, it seemed that regular elections where incumbents face loyal opposition and where governments accept basic human rights had become permanent features of the region's politics. Democracy had come to Latin America—at last and for good.

The two principle threats to liberal democratic rule seemed to have receded. Between 1968 and 1990, almost all Latin American countries experience a prolonged period of harsh military rule. Two that escaped this fate (Mexico and Cuba) were dominated by a single political party. Central America was wracked by three civil wars involving leftist insurgencies against brutal military regimes. Two others, Venezuela and Costa Rica, remained liberal democracies, but they did not entirely escape social and economic forces eroding confidence in their political systems. The fierce dictatorships of the period produced several effects that were felt even in those countries not under the rule of generals and admirals: the reputation of militaries was severely tarnished, and in the struggle to send the soldier back to the barracks, a strong, internationally supported human rights movement developed throughout the hemisphere. On the left, with only a few exceptions, few parties or movements seemed ready anymore to pursue revolution through armed struggle or guerrilla warfare.

Jorge Castañeda, a prominent Mexican intellectual who had once identified with the revolutionary movements, authored a widely read book, *Utopia Unarmed* (1993), proclaiming that Latin American leftists were no longer inspired by Fidel Castro's revolutionary experiment in Cuba. They had now, he thought, turned primarily to elections and other peaceful strategies to seek power—and mainly for reform, not revolution. Encouraging this development was the emergence of new social movements in the form of worker democracy organizations, neighborhood groups, women's organizations, indigenous peoples, and environmental groups, among others.

Nearly 20 years after Castañeda's book appeared, Michael Shifter (2011) of the Washington-based Inter-American Dialogue argued along similar lines that overall Latin America had experienced a "surge" in the pragmatic center, with both leftist and right-wing politicians moving toward more moderate positions. However, Shifter was less optimistic about the direction of Latin America's left. Castañeda (2006) had already expressed his misgivings. Both now began to warn that a new threat to democracy had emerged in the form of left, **populist** leaders. Until his death in 2013, the main target of criticism was Venezuela's president Hugo Chávez. Shifter warned that Chávez (and now Nicolás Maduro, his successor), along with Bolivia's Evo Morales, Ecuador's Rafael Correa, and Nicaragua's Daniel Ortega, represented the tendency toward "autocratic concentration of vast power into the hands of a single person," even though that person was elected.

Shifter, Castañeda, and other analysts express a viewpoint common among those who make or influence U.S. foreign policy, seeing these presidents as the radical, undemocratic part of a political tendency called the "**Pink Tide**." "Pink" here serves partly as a way to suggest that the leftist leaders and parties are diverse, ranging from moderate social democrats such as Chile's Michelle Bachelet to more militant leaders such as Venezuela's Chávez. But even the firmest supporters of Chávez, who called themselves *rojo rojito* (loosely, "red through and through"), do not think of themselves as "reds" in the sense of being committed to communism as it was associated with the Russian Revolution and the Soviet Union in the twentieth century. All of these leftist presidents, though friendly to Cuba, have said that they do not want to replicate the Cuban example. More specifically, they refer to the Soviet single-party state model as "twentieth-century socialism," and they express their preference, without much detail, for a new model of "twenty-first-century socialism." And all of them have been elected. But this does not mean in the eyes of critics that all of them are democrats. Chávez, Argentina's Cristina Kirchner, Ecuador's Rafael Correa, and some others are seen by some commentators as authoritarian populists, in contrast to other Pink Tide presidents, such as the former and still influential president of Brazil, Inácio Lula da Silva (Lula) and Bachelet.

But there is significant dissent about this perspective among those who study Latin America. Steve Ellner (2012), an American historian who has lived in Venezuela for over 40 years, argues that this is a simplistic division. What separates the more radical leaders from the moderates has been advancement of reform of Latin America's highly unequal economic order and experimentation with new participatory institutions. For Ellner, this is not a return to stale populism or an authoritarian tendency but a commitment to construction of a more profound form of democracy better suited to Latin America's needs.

Argentine political scientist Atilio Borón (2005) objects that the United States should not be preaching about democracy to Latin America, given its own problems conducting clean elections, as the 2000 presidential election showed. Unlike Venezuela, he points out, the United States does not permit its people the right to vote by referendum on important national issues or to recall a president through a popular vote. As for human rights, the United States repeatedly violated the human rights of prisoners held at its base in Guantánamo Bay. Borón also argues that the kind of **liberal democracy** (discussed in chapter 1) promoted by the United States seeks to instruct Latin Americans to "accept meekly our ineluctable neocolonial destiny under the dominion of the American Rome."

By 2010, there were already doubts about just how broadly and deeply democracy had been consolidated throughout the region. New social movements were raising questions about the appropriateness of liberal democratic institutions for dealing with economic inequality and persistent social problems. More ominously, between 2009 and 2014, some storm clouds began to gather over a few countries. Sabers were rattling in places like Honduras and Ecuador; mass protests in Chile challenged what seemed to be a model of success for combining a market economy with electoral democracy; Venezuela's future lay in doubt as the country relapsed into polarized conflict after the death of President Hugo Chávez; Brazil, the region's great economic "success story," experienced mass protest over lavish spending to host soccer's World Cup and the Olympic Games; Mexico's government seemed to be losing control of swaths of territory to drug gangs or vigilantes fighting them.

In this introduction to the politics of Latin America, we take a closer look at the strengths and weaknesses of democracy in Latin America in what is undoubtedly—given the end of the **Cold War** (1948–1991), the rising concern with terrorism, and unprecedented globalization—a new era. To accomplish this task, we need to study the history and culture of the region and to draw upon the many different academic disciplines that contribute to the study of Latin America as a unique area of the world. Some questions we will want to address include the following:

- Did the shift to more market-friendly economic policies and free trade in the final 20 years of the last century encourage or discourage democracy?
- Have popular demands for more influence of common people, economic justice, and defense of human rights strained or enriched the practice of democracy and its institutions?
- Has the left given up armed insurgency and the right given up coup-making, both committed now to contesting politics through constitutional processes?
- Has globalization weakened or strengthened democratic institutions?

To address these questions we will draw in depth upon **comparative politics**, that field within political science that provides tools and theories relevant to our quest to evaluate the democratic condition in the region. But if we are to address whether or not democracy has arrived there "at last," we need to think about what democracy means to us and also what it means to Latin Americans.

For Review

What were the reasons that observers like Castañeda and Shifter were relatively optimistic about democracy? What is the Pink Tide? How do critics, like Castañeda and Shifter, of the Pink Tide's more radical leaders see them differently than do observers like Ellner and Borón?

▉ What Is Democracy?

So where do I come down in this debate? I prefer to let my answer unfold as we go through the chapters, and I hope to offer you a fair summary of the contrasting views. However, it is customary in such introductions for the author to reveal his own values so that the reader may be aware of biases that influence the book. Just about every political scientist will profess his or her allegiance to democracy, but that usually takes the form of expressing a commitment to democratic values and institutions, such as regularly scheduled elections, respect for minority and individual rights, and some system of checks and balances.

Although I too believe in these democratic principles, such statements are not very enlightening about what other kinds of opinions about democracy the author holds. Is a capitalist economic system a prerequisite for democracy? Should "economic freedom," usually meaning a less regulated market and inviolable property rights, be included? Or, on the contrary, does democracy seem to be compatible with other kinds of economic systems? If people have the right to participate but do not, can the political system still be regarded as democratic?

The question "what is democracy?" is deceptively simple. In chapter 1 we explore some of the different answers that have been given as far back as the ancient Greeks, as well as today. Here I offer my preferred definition: *Democracy is a system whereby ordinary people in a society have the ability to participate as equals in the major decisions that shape the future of their nation and communities.*

A *necessary* condition for democracy is that people have the ability to hold government accountable for its policies through periodic elections and that there exist protections of civil liberties (i.e., freedom of speech and association) that guarantee the ability of loyal opposition to contest incumbents. However, this is not a *sufficient* condition for democracy because extreme inequalities in wealth and income translate into great differences in real power in a society. Such inequalities limit the ability of people to participate as equals in shaping the future of their societies. Besides class differences, so also do differences arising from racial, ethnic, religious, and gender prejudices hinder democracy, even if discrimination is illegal. Real equality in a democracy involves more than just legal, civic equality. Many of the fundamental decisions about the future of a society take place beyond the reach of government, most importantly under the powerful influence of enormous global corporations.

Many political scientists would regard my view as idealistic or wrongheaded. Most in the mainstream of political science focus much more narrowly on what I have just called the *necessary* conditions—elections, civil liberties, and opposition. I will not say that most

Latin Americans would agree with my conception of democracy, but I do think most are dissatisfied with these more limited conceptions associated with liberal or representative democracy. I hope that this book allows you to think through your own position by exposing you to issues of democracy in Latin America.

Another way that political scientists differ from one another on the question "what is democracy?" involves the amount of weight we place on each of three characteristics of democracy: choice, participation, and equality. Indeed, we all think these are good values, but we do not agree on how much the latter two matter, and we do not agree on what each of them means. A theme of this text is that liberal democracies, which today are sometimes called **polyarchies** (defined and explained in chapter 1), generally score well on "choice," meaning that elections and civil rights ensure the ability of citizens to choose who governs them. Some theorists of liberal democracy would even go further and argue that societies that minimize the state control over the market maximize economic choice, something that the organization Freedom House calls "economic freedom" (see www.freedomhouse.org; also www.heritage.org/index/ranking, accessed November 4, 2013).

"Participation" here refers to more than just rates of turnout in elections. Participation can also mean extension of democracy into social and economic life—for example, encouraging more forms of direct democracy (referendums, citizen meetings to decide directly on public spending, and worker ownership and control over factories and farms). Many liberal democrats see such forms of participation as intrusions on property rights or unrealistic expectations of citizens, but as we shall see, many Latin American countries are experimenting with participatory democracy. Finally, some theorists of democracy think that civil rights and elections laws have little meaning in societies with great social and economic inequality, where the ability, for example, to buy expensive media time gives some people more louder voices than others.

We will draw upon the literature in comparative politics for some definitions, theories, and data, but we also will consider perspectives from within the region and from other traditions of democracy. Along the way, then, we will find ourselves examining our own values and ideas about democracy. For North Americans, Latin America represents something of a mirror in which our notions of democracy are reflected, testing our true degree of commitment to it.

For Review

How might two or more political scientists vary in how they define "democracy"?

What Do Latin Americans Tell Pollsters about Democracy?

Let us shift our attention from what intellectuals think about democracy in Latin America to the attitudes of the people in the region. In its 2013 report, Latinobarómetro, an international polling organization based in Santiago, Chile, summarized the findings of its annual survey of 20,204 people throughout the region as follows: "There are now two Latin Americas, one which enjoys the benefits of economic growth and one which watches while the other enjoys. We are seeing more and more protests as an expression of citizens' awareness of the deficiencies of the economic, political and social system. There is demand for more democracy" (1).

Figure 0.1 compares levels of support for democracy to levels of satisfaction with democracy registered in surveys carried out in 2013 in both Latin America and Europe. You can see that satisfaction varies greatly from country to country, but Uruguay is the only country where satisfaction (the darker of the two bars) really seems to be a consensus, and in only four other countries does it hover near 50 percent. On the other hand, perhaps we should not be too alarmed because the overall rate of satisfaction in Europe is nearly the same as for Latin America (or should we worry more about Europe?). More worrisome is the low score for Mexico, which has the largest Spanish-speaking population in the world. The level of satisfaction with democracy in the region's largest country, Brazil, is merely 25 percent.

Although satisfaction scores may be low in most places, the responses of Latin Americans to another question are a little more encouraging. Seventy-nine percent told Latinobarómetro that "democracy may have its problems but is preferable to any other form of government. (See the lighter bar in Figure 0.2.) As you can see from the darker bar in Figure 0.2, however, almost half believe that their democracy "has major problems."

This raises a question: why would satisfaction be so much lower than support for democracy? Of course, we can simply think that people are being inconsistent, but the

FIGURE 0.1   Support for Democracy and Satisfaction with Democracy

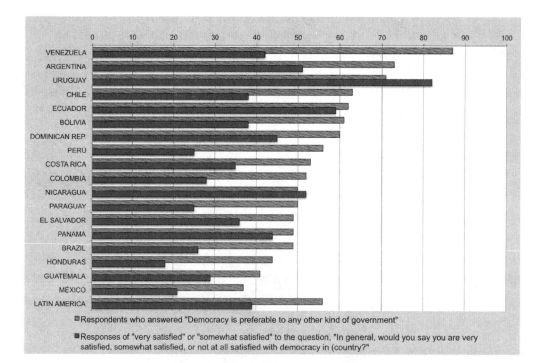

■ Respondents who answered "Democracy is preferable to any other kind of government"

■ Responses of "very satisfied" or "somewhat satisfied" to the question, "In general, would you say you are very satisfied, somewhat satisfied, or not at all satisfied with democracy in (country?"

answer suggested by Latinobarómetro makes more sense. Perhaps people are discontented with social and economic conditions and think that the best answer is more democracy. One finding in the figures consistent with this theory is the case of Venezuela, where only 25 percent of respondents expressed satisfaction with democracy, but where support for democracy far exceeds the average for Latin America, topping all the other countries. The country is highly polarized, and a year after this survey was published, violent clashes between predominantly middle-class citizens and the government broke out, with many of the protestors calling for the resignation of President Nicolás Maduro, the successor to the deceased Hugo Chávez. There seems to be a significant gap in the country between what the middle class expects of democracy and what the poorer classes expect; there also may be a gap between how they conceive of democracy.

"Why" will have to await further analysis; here we merely note that there is bad and good news on each side of the argument about Latin Americans' views on democracy.

The numbers might indicate broad support for democracy, but they do not address how deep support may go. Some political scientists think support is superficial and temporary (see chapter 1). The transitions to civilian rule from military regimes that dominated the region in the 1970s were negotiated in a way that limited majority rule; few human rights abusers were held accountable for their actions. Some argue that acceptance of democracy is not firmly rooted in society (i.e., there is little **deepening of democracy**) and that many important issues have been walled off from democratic decision-making (i.e., little **broadening of democracy**).

FIGURE 0.2   Churchillian Democracy and Self-Evaluation of Democratization

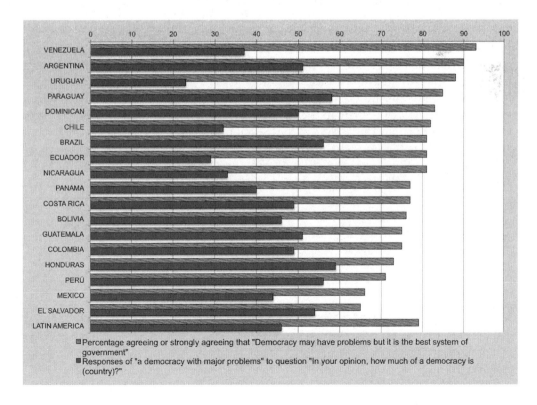

■ Percentage agreeing or strongly agreeing that "Democracy may have problems but it is the best system of government"
■ Responses of "a democracy with major problems" to question "In your opinion, how much of a democracy is (country)?"

DEMOCRACY IN COLOMBIA

MEAN SUPPORT	48%
SUPPORT 2013	52%
SATISFACTION 2013	28%

Throughout this book we have inserted "Democracy Snapshots" for each country in Latin America. These snapshots give you a quick, thumbnail reference to the degree of support and satisfaction with democracy for each country in the region, taken from Latinobarómetro's 2013 report. For example, the figure on the left is a large version of the snapshot for Colombia. You will see three bars. The top one, "Mean Support," shows the average percentage of Colombians, for the years 1995 to 2013, who said that they agreed with this statement: "Democracy is preferable to any other kind of government." (They could have chosen instead to agree either with "Under some circumstances, an authoritarian government can be preferable to a democratic one" or with "For people like me, it doesn't matter whether we have a democratic or non-democratic regime.") The second bar shows the results for the same question, only for 2013. This gives you a rough measure of whether support has fallen, risen, or stayed the same in recent years. The third bar, "Satisfaction," gives the percentage of Colombians who answered in 2013 that they were "satisfied or somewhat satisfied" in response to the following question: "In general, are you satisfied, somewhat satisfied, not very satisfied, or not at all satisfied with the working of democracy in Colombia?"

As you can see, only about half of Colombians are supportive of democracy without reservation. Only about 28 percent are satisfied at all with how democracy is working. This happens to be low, compared to most other countries in the region. We can speculate on why, but Colombians are only beginning to emerge from a long civil war in which politics has been mixed with drug trafficking and serious atrocities. Perhaps personal security takes precedence for many people under such circumstances.

Political leaders of Latin American countries all say they believe in democracy. The list includes (now retired) Fidel Castro and Raúl Castro of Cuba, seen by Washington as the region's "only remaining dictatorship." Castro insists that Cuba's political system is truer to democracy than others in the hemisphere. No Latin American leaders today say that they want to adopt Cuba's system, but several (e.g., in Bolivia, Ecuador, Nicaragua, and Venezuela) say they are experimenting with new forms of democracy. Their admirers see them as a breath of fresh air; critics dismiss their rule as merely a more popular version of dictatorship. By the end of this book, you should be better prepared to draw your own conclusions.

For Review

Looking at Figures 0.1 and 0.2, what does the Latinobarómetro poll indicate regarding popular support for democracy in Latin America? For which countries does support seem weakest, and for which does it seem strongest?

■ What Defines Latin America as a Geographic Area?

So far, we have been considering democracy in Latin America without thinking about just what countries should be included in our analysis. Exactly which parts of the Western Hemisphere should be included is not a settled question. There are regions north of the Rio Grande River, the modern boundary between the United States and Mexico, where the majority language is Spanish, not English. California, Nevada, and the states in the southwestern United States were once part of Spain's empire, and many Hispanic families there can trace their roots back well before settlers from the eastern states began arriving.

South of the Rio Grande, not all Latin Americans regard a language derived from Latin (mainly Portuguese or Spanish) as their native tongue. Many—a majority in some regions—speak an indigenous language. Wherever the European conquerors established plantation agriculture (sugar, cotton, cacao, etc.), people are predominantly descendants of enslaved Africans. Some countries (Belize, Jamaica, Haiti, the Guyanas, etc.) were colonized by the British, Dutch, and French and not by the Iberians. The late nineteenth and twentieth centuries saw important immigrations to South America from places such as Japan, China, Palestine, Germany, and other parts of the world. Are these people Latin?

The idea of "Latin America" was conjured up by the government of France, under the dictator Louis Napoleon III, around 1865. Napoleon III had designs to incorporate parts of the region into a new French empire. Aware of growing British and U.S. influence, the emperor enlisted French geographers to propagate the idea that these Spanish- and Portuguese-speaking countries had more in common culturally with his French-speaking country than with North America and Britain, the "Anglo" countries. The French designation became more firmly established as universities created area studies programs that baptized the region "Latin America."

We will consider Latin America to include those countries that were once colonies of Portugal and Spain and where one of the Iberian languages predominates or coexists with indigenous languages. We will find it useful at times to refer to countries such as Haiti, Belize, the three Guyanas, and Jamaica that share some history and culture. We consider Puerto Rico, though ruled by the United States, to be part of Latin America. As a practical matter, we will not include areas of the United States with significant Hispanic populations as part of Latin America for the simple reason that these regions lie north of the internationally recognized border between the United States and Mexico.

For Review

How did the name "Latin America" come about? Why is it not clear that the name adequately describes what countries do or do not lie within the region?

◼ Why Is a Comparative Approach Needed to Understand Latin American Politics?

Comparative politics is identified not only as a methodology or approach to studying politics but also as the branch of political science where those with an interest in or love of a particular area of the world develop specialized expertise. As a methodology, "comparative" refers to a way to test theories about politics by comparing cases to one another. This methodology might just as well be applied to the study of state and local politics. However, comparative political science is usually identified with the work of those who specialize in developing in-depth knowledge of a particular geographic area.

This kind of specialized knowledge became important to the U.S. government during World War II (1939–1945), when the U.S. military and diplomatic establishment competed for the loyalty and support of people all over the world against the Axis powers—Germany, Italy, and Japan. This attitude carried over into the Cold War, when the United States and the Soviet Union competed to integrate other parts of the world into the capitalist or communist bloc of nations. The U.S. government turned to foundations and universities to fill in the gap in expertise about the rest of the world, promoting area studies centers, an investment by American taxpayers in increased knowledge of the cultures and languages of other cultures (Lewis and Wigen 1997: 163–167, 181–182). This support gave a major boost to comparative politics.

Although in this text we draw upon comparative political science to gain insight, we cannot neglect the insights of other disciplines—such as anthropology, history, economics, and sociology—into the study of politics. In fact, many comparative political scientists identify their subfield with the development of expertise about the history and culture of a particular region of the world. For many political scientists in other fields, foreign language study is often merely a required formality, but most **comparativists** would agree that competence in the language of a region is essential to qualify as an expert.

After the collapse of communism in Eastern Europe (1989–2001), some sources of funding for comparative political studies began to divert money from area studies to projects and institutions that focus on "transnational themes"; that is, they want "cross-national" studies that attempt to understand the causes of corruption, roots of terrorism, effectiveness of courts, human rights, and so on. One of the main themes is "democratization"—transitions from authoritarian systems to democracy. Research proposals usually assume that "democracy" is associated primarily with the kind of economic and political system found in the United States and its allies.

This book assumes that understanding Latin America requires a comparative approach that embraces both transnational and area studies. I assume that there are some constants in politics across cultures. However, I also believe that an adequate understanding of politics must take into account cultural diversity, historical inheritances, and the specific challenges that confront particular societies. Transnational specialists lacking background in the history and culture of a particular region are usually less familiar with its political peculiarities than are area studies specialists. They risk choosing and interpreting cases in a manner that fits preconceived ideas. How does this affect understanding? To take an example, many comparativists who study democratization date the transition process in Nicaragua from the defeat of the Sandinistas (FSLN), who came to power through a revolution in 1979, in the 1990 presidential elections. On the other hand, the Latin American Studies Association (LASA) observed the election of 1984, won by the FSLN, and generally found it free and fair.

For their part, area studies specialists might be too focused on the particular region or country to see broader global forces at work or to take into account the commonalities in politics that cut across cultures. Consider, for another example, the question of what role the surge in social movements in Latin America over the past two decades might play in the region's democratic future. Might we not gain some insights from the experience of Eastern Europe's social movements? Strong, civic-minded organizations and movements are important features of a healthy democracy, say theorists (Grugel 2002: 92–115, 209–211). Such associations, often called "**civil society**," allow citizens to satisfy social and economic needs and to band together to promote their interests to government. We might learn more about democratization by comparing the role of social movements in two different regions of the world, rather than concentrating on one country or area.

Of course, there is a lot of variation and cultural difference within Latin America itself. In some respects, individual Latin American countries may have more in common with countries in other regions of the world than with each other. Cuba, by virtue of its language, colonial past, and so on, clearly belongs to the family of Latin American nations. On the other hand, alone in the hemisphere since the 1959 revolution, its government has emulated many of the political structures characteristic of communism as it emerged in Eastern Europe and Asia. In assessing Cuba's political future, would we not profit from studying the successes and failures of the post-communist era in Eastern Europe? Raúl Castro, since succeeding his brother Fidel, has seemed more open to economic liberalization (introduction of more room for market forces), Asian-style, so we might want to compare Cuba's economic reform measures to those implemented in Vietnam or China.

Will Cuban communism collapse entirely, as occurred in Eastern Europe? Will it evolve into "market-Leninism"—that is, a single-party system that allows the market to operate, as it has in China? We need to apply lessons learned from the experience of others, but with caution. In Eastern Europe, **nationalism** was usually at war with **communism**, closely associated with foreign domination. Communism in Cuba emerged from a national revolutionary process that asserted Cuban self-determination against historic intervention in its affairs by the United States. On the other hand, Cuba still has strong ties to Europe through Spain, and a huge proportion of the Cuban population living in the United States will press for a more liberal order after the Castro brothers are gone (if not before). We are seeing changes in Cuba, but where they will lead is harder to predict.

Defense of democracy has often served to obscure darker motives for intervention in Latin America. Simón Bolívar, the great liberator of much of the continent, is reputed to have said, "The United States seems destined by Providence to plague America with misery in the name of liberty." Early 2013 saw conservative presidents in important countries, such as Chile and Colombia; more radical populist regimes in Venezuela and Bolivia; and center-left regimes in Argentina, Brazil, and Peru. Yet all of these countries were cooperating with each other to create new regional economic, diplomatic, and security organizations and, for better or worse, were asserting their intention to make their own decisions on human rights, democracy, and global issues (see chapter 16). Still, in Latin America itself, no head of government and few political leaders openly espouse a preference for any form of government other than democracy.

For Review

What is the difference between a transnational approach and an area studies approach in comparative politics? What advantages and disadvantages does each approach offer for studying democracy in Latin America?

Preview of the Chapters

One of the challenges of introducing this subject matter to students is how to make a text engaging and thematic on the one hand, but a useful reference and guide to the field on the other. The first task requires a lively style; the other demands the dry and passionless prose of an encyclopedia. Addressing the question of whether democracy is finally, at last, taking root in Latin America permits us, I hope, to avoid draining the lifeblood out of politics while providing the comprehensive coverage one needs in a text.

As indicated previously, Latin Americans generally believe in democracy, but they are not always satisfied with how their existing democracies are working. Chapter 1 examines controversies over what "democracy" itself means, offering readers alternative ways of thinking about and evaluating democracy. Chapter 2 looks at the social and cultural context of Latin American politics, with stress on equality and the importance of personal and family relationships in the region.

In chapters 3 through 5 we provide historical background. Often this means a forced march through more than 500 years of post-Columbus history. Understandably, students may ask at the end, "So what is the connection with politics today in Latin America?" To start with, every country's history has its villains and heroes. These stories give modern citizens a sense of who they are and what binds them together, at least in their imaginations, as a nation. However, the same history that provides us stories about what we have in common is laden with other stories that make us question whether current social arrangements are fair, or even whether we all belong together in a single nation. Furthermore, history, colonialism in particular, has left a legacy of deep divisions and issues—social cleavages—that democracy, like any other form of state, must mediate.

Spanish and Portuguese—European languages in their origins—are the predominant languages in the region, but most Latin Americans are descended fully or partly from indigenous people or African slaves. Still others are immigrants who came long after the Spanish or Portuguese; they too have influenced the region. We will see that ethnic tensions are sources of political conflict in many parts of Latin America today, especially where racial or ethnic populations feel excluded from economic, social, and political participation. Exclusion and democracy are incompatible; disputes over who has the right to participate in democratic politics can undermine democratic stability by creating explosive resentment among those excluded.

Democracy can hardly be complete without the freedom of citizens to decide their own destiny, to effectively exercise sovereignty. Independence came to most of Latin America in the 1800s, but in many ways the social and economic arrangements of the colonial era remained intact. We explore why in chapter 4, which also looks at the attempt to modernize and build coherent states in the second part of the nineteenth century.

Chapter 5 examines the twentieth century, the period in which the masses began to assert their right to participate in politics—clearly an important stage in any progress toward democracy. The second half of the twentieth century saw the emergence of competing theories to explain "underdevelopment"—why Latin America had failed to achieve the economic prowess and material wealth of the "developed" nations. In chapter 6 we look at how the relationship between the state and market has evolved and how this relates to issues of economic development in the region today.

The mass democracies of the twentieth century did not produce economies capable of including many citizens (most, in some countries) in the enjoyment of a dignified standard of living. If that is the object of "economic development," we must then consider how and why Latin America has failed in this respect. To some degree, this failure to develop accounts for why the first experiences with democracy did not survive the end of the twentieth century in most of the region. Beginning with a coup in Brazil in 1964, harsh dictatorships emerged in all but a few countries. Chapter 7 explores the breakdown of democracy and the theories developed by political scientists to explain and predict this phenomenon.

The military ruled most of the region for much of the late twentieth century, only to return to the barracks, usually under pressure, well before the century closed. The generals did not retreat before leaving an imprint still felt in the present. The repressive years created the context for a return to economic development policies that were more market oriented and export oriented—more "neo" liberal (a new version of the market- and export-oriented policies of the nineteenth century). Chapter 8 looks at the transitions back to civilian rule and electoral democracy, again placing this experience in the context of theories developed by political scientists.

Not all of the most recent political transitions in Latin America took place in countries that fell under military rule after 1964. Chapter 9 looks closely at Venezuela and Mexico to examine the process by which systems dominated by political parties unable or unwilling to adapt to new demands for participation by citizens were challenged by new forces within society. This helps us to see that reaction to harsh military rule, though important, was not the only factor shaping Latin American politics in recent years. Although the two countries under examination pursued quite different paths, what they had in common was that their citizens came to feel that their votes had little real impact on the decisions made by their elected leaders. In Venezuela, this "crisis of representation" resulted in the election in 1998 of the charismatic Hugo Chávez, the first president in the region to benefit electorally from a shift to the left called the "**Pink Tide**." This tide has not engulfed the entire region or eliminated other tendencies; nor do its member parties and politicians all agree on foreign, economic, and social policies. But they all do share some degree of commitment to fostering greater social and economic inclusion, and all have come to power through electoral means rather than insurgencies or coups.

One of the other factors at work in the resurgence of the left was the end of the Cold War with the fall of the Soviet Union in 1991, which in turn has somewhat separated the theme of anticommunism from another persistent theme in Latin American politics—revolution, which we take up in chapter 10. The elite's fear of revolution was especially heightened by the Cuban Revolution of 1959. Revolutions are exceptional events, but they are, as the Nicaraguan Omar Cabezas once said, the "fire in mind" of many fighters for justice.

Given that the revolutions in Nicaragua and Mexico left those countries facing challenges similar to others in the hemisphere, is there any basis for believing that revolutions produce progress? Revolutionaries always speak the language of democracy, but often the result of revolution has been some kind of system of authoritarianism. Is that inevitable? Has it happened again in Cuba?

The next four chapters explore how democracy is shaped by social structures, by political parties, by formal institutions, and by constitutions. Chapter 11 looks closely at social classes, movements, and groups (unions, peasant movements, urban neighborhood movements, the middle class, landowners, and business groups). Social movements in particular are clamoring for policies to achieve inclusion, fostering new forms of participatory democracy and carving out a new relationship with the market and the state. This prepares us to understand a political reality that Latin America shares with most of the rest of the world: people have grown deeply suspicious of political parties and frustrated with corruption. We examine the consequences for Latin America in chapter 12.

Specialists on Latin America have often regarded the study of economic, cultural, and social processes as more promising for understanding Latin American politics than the study of institutions, law, and constitutions. With most of the transitions to democracy now several decades old, some political scientists have decided that we have neglected this area for too long. Furthermore, we have seen some interesting innovations recently in the region's constitutions. Human rights and respect for the rule of law have become explicit goals for many new social movements. In chapter 13, we examine how well various institutions are functioning in Latin America. In chapter 14 we focus on **rule of law** (criminal justice and the issue of corruption) and respect for human rights.

The last two chapters look at how Latin America's place within the international order affects the prospects for democracy. Globalization, at least as it has unfolded so far, has challenged the sovereignty of the state throughout the world, including Latin America. However, it has also brought a degree of economic diversification with the rest of the world and new communication tools to press for democracy. Chapters 15 and 16 bring us to issues of how Latin American countries relate to each other, the United States, and the rest of the world. It probably would surprise few students that Washington has often intervened in Latin America in ways that have set democracy back—from invasions of weak countries in the Caribbean area to use of the Central Intelligence Agency (CIA) to destabilize regimes it dislikes. However, we seem to have entered an era of declining U.S. influence. Increased trade and investment with other parts of the world is a clear tendency, one that some people in the United States see as a threat. There have also been several fragile but innovative steps toward more economic and political cooperation among Latin American countries, independent of the United States.

Land and People

Just what lands and what peoples properly should be regarded as "Latin America" is just one of many questions on which experts, you will find, disagree. This is an important political issue in some countries, as we will see in chapter 2, but here we will just sketch in a preliminary way some of the major demographic and geographic features of this region. For our purposes, we will consider Latin America to embrace the continent of South America;

FIGURE 0.4   Map of Latin America

Mesoamerica, or the isthmus between the continents (beginning at Colombia's border with Panama and ending at the border with the United States); and those islands in the Caribbean that were part of the Spanish Empire in the centuries following Columbus's voyages and the Conquest.

Scholars will never agree to what extent "geography is destiny," but most area experts agree that there are and have been some formidable natural obstacles to easy travel, certainly before the advent of air travel. The Andes are not the highest mountains in the world, but they are the densest, with several parallel ranges. They run like a spine down the back of the continent, toward the Pacific side, making travel and communication difficult not only between east and west, but also between north and south. Today one can travel by good highways and air routes (but only rarely by good trains) from one capital to another, but to travel from one major city to another as recently as 100 years ago meant several days. Most of the population lives in highland areas, especially in the tropics, so it might be necessary to descend from your home, perhaps in Mérida in the Venezuelan Andes, by some combination of mules and river traffic, to catch a steamer from Maracaibo, which would then take you to La Guaira, the Caribbean port for Caracas. Caracas lies only a few miles inland—but on the other side of a mountain, Ávila, which rises approximately 9,000 feet straight out of the sea. So you would go by horse and carriage (until the late 1800s, when rail became available) to reach the capital of your country.

The Amazon River is not as long as the Nile, but it carries by far the most water of any river in the world. It empties over 200,000 cubic meters of water per second on average into the Atlantic Ocean; the Nile empties only a little more than 5,000, the Mississippi a little over 1,600. Several of the Amazon's tributaries themselves are among the 25 longest rivers in the world. Other rivers in South America among this group are the Oronoco (Venezuela), Paraná (Brazil), and three other Brazilian rivers. All carry vast amounts of water compared to rivers in North America. The continent boasts the highest waterfall (Angel Falls, in Venezuela), the driest desert (the Atacama, in northern Chile), the largest rainforest (mostly in Brazil), the highest capital city (La Paz, in Bolivia), and the highest lake that is navigated for commerce (Titicaca, in Peru).

The climate varies enormously because the region is aligned more on a north-south than an east-west axis. The equator runs through Ecuador, Colombia, and northern Brazil. However, the climate can be quite pleasant and spring-like year round in the highland regions. In the Southern Cone region of Argentina, Chile, Uruguay, Paraguay, and southern Brazil, the climate is temperate, excellent for growing many different kinds of grains, soy, and grass for livestock. Most people in this region experience winter, though generally mild. However, in the far south—toward an area revealingly named Tierra del Fuego (land of fire), the cold becomes increasingly more forbidding.

The Central American region, Mexico's Yucatán Peninsula, and the Caribbean islands are all in the tropics, but Mexico's topography and climate vary as one moves north to the capital city, the largest metropolitan area in the world, with more than 20 million inhabitants. As one moves farther north, the area becomes drier, with desert bordering much of the frontier with the United States.

For reasons we review in chapter 3, Latin Americans live in societies where ethnicity, race, and social class interact in ways that generate both conflict and pride. We can divide the population very broadly and imprecisely into an indigenous population that is most numerous in the highland areas and almost extinct in the Caribbean; Afro-descendant people who were enslaved and transported from Africa; and descendants of European people, not just ancestors from Portugal and Spain, the colonial powers, but also immigrants from other regions from just about every part of Europe. For example, a province in Chile is named O'Higgins after Bernardo O'Higgins, son of an Irish employee of Spain's colonial administration. Many more Europeans came after 1850 when governments of the day sought to "whiten" their populations, believing this would spur economic development (see chapter 4). Asian and Middle Eastern immigrants have also populated some regions—though it seems other Latin Americans often lump them together as, respectively, "Chinos" (Chinese) or "Turcos" (Turks), regardless of their origins.

But the largest sectors of the population have heritage that is a mixture of all these different groups; these Latin Americans are often called "mestizos" (if they or their ancestors have indigenous physical characteristics) or "mulattos" (for those with some African ancestry). But there are many other terms for differentiating race and ethnic composition, varying with the country and the mixture.

Social and economic conditions vary tremendously among countries and often within countries. We focus on poverty and inequality in the next chapter and also in chapter 11, which in part deals with class. The Socio-Economic Database for Latin America and the Caribbean (SEDLA) data for 2013 (see the "Resources for Further Study" section at the end of this chapter) indicate that the last 20 years have seen a significant fall in poverty. In 1992, 45 of 100 Latin Americans lived on $4 per day (even taking different purchasing power into account); today that ratio is 25 of every 100. The United Nations Economic Commission for Latin America (ECLAC 2012) estimates a slightly higher rate of poverty, but more importantly has expressed concern that the rate by which it has fallen has slackened in recent years. Brazil, Chile, Colombia, Chile, Uruguay, Mexico, and Argentina are all middle-income countries, though all are afflicted with some of the highest rates of inequality. Bolivia, Honduras, and Nicaragua are among the poorest countries.

We would be remiss if we did not recognize the remarkable contributions by Latin Americans to global culture in the form of vibrant music, modern art, philosophy (see the section of chapter 3 on the *buen vivir* conception of indigenous peoples), and award-winning novels. The region was once known in the North American media for "coups, Castro, and catastrophe," but in the sixteenth and last chapter, we take a look at how that stereotype is less accurate than ever before. Latin America is stepping forward with political as well as cultural innovation, and if deep economic problems remain, it seems to have gained in recent decades a greater capacity to share in shaping our common future on the planet.

An Invitation

This book is an invitation to students not only to learn about the politics, history, and culture of a fascinating part of the world but also to reflect on what democracy ought to mean. It is an invitation to study issues of social justice in a world where nations have in recent decades yielded some part of their sovereignty to the forces of globalization. My own encounter with Latin America has caused me to examine the values and motives behind U.S. foreign policy. I also wonder whether democracy at home would be durable if we faced the economic challenges and social inequalities that characterize Latin America. To have a global perspective requires not only understanding others but also understanding ourselves.

Throughout this book you will find "Puntos de Vista." These short sections introduce you to the kinds of issues that Latin Americans themselves are debating. For example, there is a "Punto" about Brazil's use of quotas for university admissions for people of African descent, in recognition of slavery and its negative legacy. This is an issue in the United States as well. I hope you will find in taking a position yourself that you can on the one hand clarify your own values about some important issues, but on the other hand simultaneously put yourself in the shoes of people living in another part of the world, for whom the question might have some different meaning or consequences.

Routledge hosts a companion website that includes a number of useful resources for both students and instructors. Students looking for extra study aids will find flash cards, chapter summaries, and links to online resources. To help instructors with classroom preparation, the companion website includes a test bank with a range of question types. The companion website can be found at www.routledge.com/cw/hellinger

Discussion Questions

1. Why do you think that to study politics we rely so much on comparison of countries?
2. What are your initial ideas about whether democracy can exist in Latin America (or anywhere) alongside high levels of poverty and inequality?

Resources for Further Study

For Basic Information: Do you need a primer on Latin America's geography—capitals, rivers, mountains, and so on? Sheppard Software has a briefing page consisting of map games that are easy to play and will bring you up to speed quickly: www.sheppardsoftware.com/South_America_Geography.htm

Help Teaching provides a good self-quiz at www.helpteaching.com/questions/South_American_Geography.

Several sources are available for basic demographic and geographic facts about Latin America. The Socio-Economic Database, http://sedlac.econo.unlp.edu.ar/eng/institutional.php, provides information gathered about the region by the World Bank and Universidad de La Plata.

Reading: Few Latin American politics courses are required, so presumably you chose to study this topic and therefore bring an interest. You can do no better than the *NACLA Report on the Americas*, which comes out four times per year and, though it draws heavily on academic specialists, is written for a general audience. *Latin American Research Review* is the most prestigious area-study journal. Among many other good journals, *Latin American Perspectives* differs in dedicating itself more to Latin American views, particularly radical ones. Among several other good journals on Latin America, *Latin American Politics and Society* and the *Journal of Latin American Politics* (published in Great Britain) are frequently cited.

Video and Film: A list of hundreds of Latin American films with English translation can be found at Steve Volk's resource page: www.oberlin.edu/faculty/svolk/latinam.htm. A recent look, sympathetic to more radical leftist leaders, is *South of the Border*, Oliver Stone's 2009–2010 documentary. Icarus Films is a repository of hundreds of documentaries; for Latin America, you can find them listed at www.icarusfilms.com/subjects/latin_am.html. Another source of good documentary material is http://www.journeyman.tv, which seems to add five or six high-quality videos of varying length every week and which can be streamed for free (and sometimes downloaded for free).

On the Internet: The Latin American Network Information Center (http:// lanic.utexas.edu) is the best general portal, with links categorized by theme and by country. More diverse is the portal *Zona Latina* (www.zonalatina.com/), which contains innumerable resources, systematically listed by type and then broken into country or region. The site treats a wide range of types and subject matters, with many English-language articles; the site is very eclectic ideologically and especially good on cultural topics. The Library of Congress offers the *Handbook of Latin American Studies* (HLAS) online, provides the titles and annotations of all sorts of articles and books concerning the region. Using the website's search engine, a student can find citations of documents for further study on any specific topic found in this textbook. The main page is located at http://lcweb2.loc.gov/hlas/hlashome.html.

Following News: The Center for Economic Policy Research (CEPR), a Washington-based think tank, provides a valuable compilation three to five days per week of English-language news. You can sign up to receive the digest (links to articles divided by region) via e-mail at the organization's website, www.cepr.net.

PART I

Comparative Politics, Democratic Theory, and Latin American Area Studies

1 Conceptions of Democracy

Focus Questions

▶ When we speak of a "third wave of democracy," what do we mean, and what kind of democracy do we envision? Are there alternatives?

▶ What is "polyarchy" as a model of democracy? How does it compare to other conceptions of democracy?

▶ Should we consider social and economic equality to be a measure, an outcome, or a precondition of democracy?

▶ What are some alternative views on liberal democracy and polyarchy in Latin America?

A S WE SAW in the introduction, judging the condition of democracy in Latin America may depend on how we understand the meaning of democracy. The United States, the most powerful nation in the world, promotes "liberal democracy," a version that most political scientists take almost for granted today. But democracy as it is defined in the United States does not necessarily reflect what democracy means to Latin Americans. Most of this chapter is devoted, however, to the U.S. conception and a model, called "**polyarchy**," that emerged as the orthodox (main) way that political scientists conceive liberal democracy. Of course, we do not use "polyarchy" in everyday speech, and rarely do we find it in news. But the model, if not the term, has migrated from academia to the world of policy.

In the late 1970s, beginning with the formal commitment of President Jimmy Carter (1977–1980) to promotion of human rights, followed by the creation of a federally funded **National Endowment for Democracy** (**NED**) by President Ronald Reagan (1981–1988), the United States made defense of democracy a professed goal of its foreign policy. (Keep in mind that a "professed" goal is not necessarily consistent with reality.) During this same period, most of Latin America, especially South America, was emerging from harsh military dictatorship, and the transition to civilian rule was welcome but still fragile. On the international stage, the years 1989 to 1991 saw the collapse of the Berlin Wall and the Soviet Union. Liberal democracy and capitalism seemed triumphant.

The international impact of this came to Latin America in a historical moment when authoritarian regimes were giving way to liberal democracy and when communism was coming to an inglorious end. In 1994, at the Summit of the Americas in Miami, all countries in the hemisphere (excluding Cuba, which was not invited) proclaimed a "consensus" to commit themselves to defense of this model—and not coincidentally, to a free-market economic system. On democracy, the summit's Statement of Principles (1994) pronounced that

> representative democracy is indispensable for the stability, peace and development of the region. It is the sole political system which guarantees respect for human rights and the rule of law; it safeguards cultural diversity, pluralism, respect for the rights of minorities, and peace within and among nations. Democracy is based, among other fundamentals, on free and transparent elections and includes the right of all citizens to participate in government.

This political model was tied explicitly to an economic model, capitalism, and more specifically a capitalism based on a reduced role for government and an expanded role for the market, both nationally and internationally.

> A key to prosperity is trade without barriers, without subsidies, without unfair practices, and with an increasing stream of productive investments. Eliminating impediments to market access for goods and services among our countries will foster our economic growth . . . Free trade and increased economic integration are key factors for raising standards of living, improving the working conditions of people in the Americas and better protecting the environment.
>
> We, therefore, resolve to begin immediately to construct the "Free Trade Area of the Americas" (FTAA), in which barriers to trade and investment will be progressively eliminated. . . . [We] are committed to create strengthened mechanisms that promote and protect the flow of productive investment in the Hemisphere, and to promote the development and progressive integration of capital markets.

Later, this commitment to liberal democracy and **laissez-faire** capitalism was reinforced at other hemispheric meetings. In late 2001, the governments (again, not including Cuba) of the hemisphere formally adopted the Inter-American Democratic Charter, stating, "Essential elements of representative democracy are the holding of free and fair elections as an expression of popular sovereignty, access to power through constitutional means, a pluralist system of political parties and organizations, and respect for human rights and fundamental freedoms." Take note of "pluralist," a term closely connected to polyarchy.

As you move through the rest of the book, you will find that there are many ways in which Latin Americans have questioned various aspects of the "Washington Consensus," as these agreements came to be known. Even as the ink was drying on the Democratic Charter, social movements in Latin America were already challenging its emphasis on representative democracy and free-market capitalism. They began to stress vesting decision-making not just in the institutions of government but also in many other places—communities, the workplace, ethnic groupings, and so forth.

The swing toward liberal economic policy produced economic growth. It also produced a political reaction. Popular discontent grew in the 1980s and 1990s as growth accentuated inequality and failed to alleviate poverty sufficiently. This nurtured the rise of social movements and an electoral swing toward the left—the **Pink Tide**, first evident in the election of Chávez in Venezuela in 1998. These developments, especially those of social movements, put back into debate questions about the adequacy of liberal democracy, but few saw the type of socialism practiced in the Soviet Union, Cuba, or East Asia as a desirable political alternative to liberal democracy.

The rules of the game in Latin America's new democracies had been negotiated among politicians, the military, businessmen, bishops, and other members of the elite—in many ways a top-down process influenced by but not usually determined by popular pressure (see chapter 8). By the early 2000s, a bottom-up process had begun to press for a democracy of participation, social equality, and inclusion. Whereas for pluralists the multiple interests of society seek to influence the state, where the power is, for Latin American social movements the objective was to transfer power and control over decisions to citizens in civil society, especially to empower women, people living in poverty, indigenous and Afro-descendent people, and others who felt excluded from the benefits of economic growth and dissatisfied with the quality of representative democracy.

▉ Liberal Democracy in the Real World of Latin America

In the United States we often associate the term "liberal" with politicians who favor government regulation of the economy and welfare rights, but in its original form **liberalism** refers to a political ideology that sees individual choice as the essence of freedom. To elaborate, liberal democracies assume the following:

- The individual takes priority over the community and the state—that is, the foundation of society and the state is a decision taken by individuals to form associations. Some other political theories would say that this way of thinking fails to consider how much the individual is a product of human society—of the family and groups that naturally make up a political community.
- The market is preferred over government planning or other forms of allocating economic resources and resolving economic conflict. Government action is reserved for exceptional circumstances—severe economic crisis, megaprojects that only the state can afford, threats to national security, key areas of human welfare (such as education and health), and so on. Most liberals today do see some need for government regulation and moderation of the market's flaws, but liberalism still prefers the market to government regulation.
- The right to private property is a "natural right"; that is, property, including wealth, is accumulated mostly as a result of some combination of hard work, creativity, and risk on the part of individuals. Property rights are extensions of individual human rights.
- Because liberals mistrust government, they seek to limit the power of the state through constitutions that (1) keep many social and economic questions off-limits to government and (2) divide the powers of government against one another—what is known as "checks and balances."

Is it possible for a government to be "liberal" without being democratic? The Canadian political philosopher C. B. MacPherson (1972) pointed out the historical fact that liberal democracies established limited government, individual property rights, and a market economy *before* all citizens had obtained the right to vote or enjoyed equal rights before the law. For example, Jefferson, Washington, and other founders were liberals but saw little problem with slavery and barring women from voting. Laws in many states in the liberal United States limited the vote to landowners until the 1830s. In Europe, industrialization and **capitalism** struck deep roots well before workers achieved the right to vote. In Latin America some of the most lasting dictatorships of the late 1800s were imposed by factions of elites who created liberal parties (see chapter 4). Nearly 100 years later, some of the region's fiercest dictatorships (e.g., in Chile between 1973 and 1989) adopted liberal (market-oriented) economic policies. Their economic philosophy came to be known as **neoliberalism**, "neo" meaning "new form of."

Neoliberal ideas resembled those that had defined "liberalism" in the early days of European capitalism, when industrial capitalists were attempting to shake off the legacy of strong monarchies and to do away with laws that protected big landowners from cheaper agricultural imports. Liberals advocated free trade and other economic policies called *laissez-faire* ("let do" or "allow to happen"). Instead of monarchs and blue-blooded aristocrats, the target of neoliberal plans was a state that had for much of the 1900s sought to promote economic development by protecting and subsidizing industrialization, often seeing itself, not the private sector, as the main force for economic development (see chapter 5).

For Review

What does the term "liberal" signify in "liberal democracy"? What does "neoliberal" signify?

Liberalism, Pluralism, and Polyarchy

Perhaps the political scientist who most influenced how we think about democracy following World War II was Robert Dahl. Dahl tried to develop a concept of democracy that was real, as opposed to "ideal." He coined the term **"polyarchy"** to describe his vision of "real democracy."

Dahl (1971: 7–8) defined polyarchy as a political regime in which elites, by which he meant leaders drawn from different sectors (labor, business, education, religion, etc.), compete with one another for influence in a system characterized by liberal freedoms (freedom of expression, right to assembly, fair elections) and extension of citizenship, especially the right to vote, to everyone. Dahl derived his views from the pluralist school of thought in American sociology. Pluralists argue that the real "stuff" of politics is found in group life, where citizens band together to promote their points of view. Pluralists recognize that many interest groups do not form from the bottom up but are instead either formed or eventually taken over by elites, the leaders in society. This does not matter as long as new groups can be formed freely. Groups and elites compete for power to advance their interests. A market economy is conducive to this kind of competition and thus supportive of democracy.

Pluralists were responding in part to political theories that were pessimistic about democracy. One such school of thought, elitism, argued that any political organization, even those that started out as highly democratic, inevitably would give way to a concentration of power in the hands of a few leaders. The most famous theory is Robert Michels's (1915) "iron law of oligarchy"—"He who says organization says oligarchy." Sociologists, such as C. Wright Mills (1956) and G. William Domhoff (1967), in the United States have argued that polyarchy is not really a democracy because there exist powerful networks of decision makers—elites, both in government and in society—that are the real "invisible government" lying behind the elected one.

Democracy must be, says Dahl (1971: 1), "a regime in which the opponents of the government [can] openly and legally organize into political parties to oppose the government in free and fair elections." When such conditions are met, the decision makers—that is, the elites of a society—must compete with one another for political power, and competition forces them to be responsive to public opinion. Perfect democracy may be unattainable, given that power is unequally distributed in all societies; however, the combination of elections and political rights gives people a chance to air grievances and hold elites, and government, responsible.

The result of liberal rules of the game and mass voting rights is what Dahl called *polyarchy*. Instead of one unified elite ruling class, polyarchies have a ruling class composed of many ("poly" means "many") elite actors relying on a variety of organized groups and political parties to compete for influence. Pluralism is the theory; polyarchy refers to the political system. Elitism, pluralism, and polyarchy are represented graphically in Figure 1.1, "Models of Democracy."

Elections are the crucial mechanism of polyarchy; they are supposed to function somewhat like a market does in a capitalist economy. In going to the polls, much like going to a supermarket, a voter makes individual choices among candidates or parties much like a consumer "votes" for products with his or her money. Liberal democratic theory, including pluralism, says that what is good for society as a whole emerges out of widespread individual choice—but only

Elitist Model: Mass, not Civil Society

- "Iron Law of Oligarchy"
- Policy is result of decisions made by political elites
- Elites have little accountability to masses

Pluralist Theory of Group Politics

- Emphasis on competition between groups of citizens
- Policy is the result of interest group competition

Pluralist Model of Democracy: Polyarchy, or "Democratic Elitism"

- Blending of Elite and Pluralist models
- Policy is the result of competition and bargaining among group elites

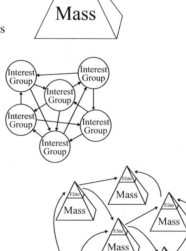

FIGURE 1.1   Models of Democracy, Relationships between Mass and Elite

if the rules of competition are fair. Minimally, this would include respect for civil rights, such as freedom of speech and association, and respect for the right of opposition. But there is a crucial difference between the market and an election. Consumers go to market with different amounts of buying power (wealth and income); in elections they all go with one vote.

However, in the broader political game, including election campaigns, wealthier individuals bring more resources and power to the competition. Even in the wealthier democratic states, this social and economic inequality raises questions about how much government should limit the influence of private wealth (e.g., limits on campaign contributions, rules on lobbying legislators, and other regulations); in poorer and highly unequal societies, this question takes on even greater significance.

For Dahl, a key characteristic of democracy is the continuing responsibility of government "to the preferences of its citizens, considered as political equals." All citizens should have "unimpaired opportunities" to formulate their preferences, signify them, and have them weighted equally in the conduct of government (1971:1–2). Dahl believes that no actual, existing political system will ever fully measure up to this ideal, but neither does any political system ever really reach its opposite, **totalitarianism**. A totalitarian system is one in which elites are entirely united about significant issues; instead of competing with one another, they are unified and maintain a monopoly of power.

To Dahl, all systems fall somewhere between these two polar opposites: at one end, airtight dictatorship by an oligarchy, and at the other, fully participatory democracy. Pluralists believe that even within the highly dictatorial systems of the Soviet Union under Stalin and Germany under Hitler, elites competed with one another for influence, and government had to pay some attention to the demands of citizens. This is worth our attention since Cuba is often described in the media as a "totalitarian" society.

Optimism about the most recent wave of liberal democracy was generated in the 1990s by the turn toward markets in economic policy and an apparent strengthening of constitutional processes in Latin America. A school of **new institutionalists** began to argue that the time was ripe to pay closer attention to formal constitutional arrangements among branches and levels of government (Mainwaring and Scully 1995; Mainwaring and Shugart 1997). This was somewhat of a departure from the tendency in Latin American area studies to place more emphasis on highly unequal social class structures, the raw power of military establishments, and the frequency with which constitutions come and go. Through the 1980s, political instability and dictatorship seemed chronic. So emphasizing the study of institutional **checks and balances**, legislative and judicial policies, or the functioning state and local governments, as political scientists do in studying Europe and North America, seemed misplaced. In Part IV, we will look more closely at the institutions in Latin America to assess how much emphasis to place on them today.

For Review

On what basis do pluralists maintain democracy is possible, even though they admit that in all societies elites have more power than ordinary people? How do the concepts of "oligarchy" and "polyarchy" differ? Why might pluralists reject terming Cuba a "totalitarian" society? Why would they also reject calling it a "democracy"?

Latin America and the "Third Wave" of Liberal Democracy

If we consider only **liberal democracy**, we can say that there has occurred a great **third wave** of democratization since 1970. The prior waves occurred in the early 1800s after the American and French revolutions and after World War II in places such as Germany and Japan. Figure 1.2 reproduces the way two political sociologists, Ronald Inglehart and Christian Welzel (2005), chart the wave that occurred in the second half of the twentieth century. Notice the spike between 1987 and 1996, when nations in Eastern Europe cast off communism and also when several Latin American countries held elections after years of military dictatorship. In the minds of some Western intellectuals, the third wave was a step toward liberal democracy becoming the world's only form of state (Fukuyama 1992; Huntington 1991).

The reestablishment of civilian governments in Latin America in the last quarter of the twentieth century reinforced this idea of a third wave. Between 1964 and 1980, governments

FIGURE 1.2   Number of Nations Shifting toward Democracy

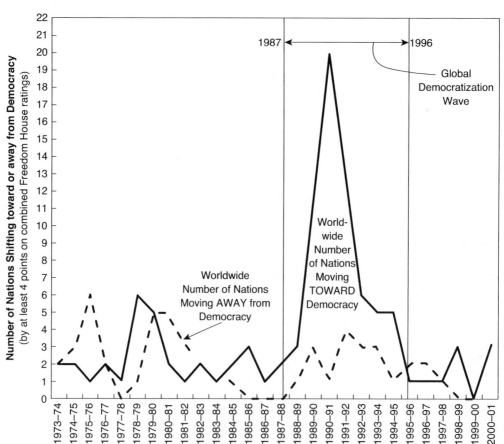

chosen by direct, opposition-contested, popular elections had been rare—Colombia, Costa Rica, and Venezuela. The late 1980s and the 1990s saw "transitions to democracy"—or at least the retreat of the military from presidential palaces to the barracks. Two political systems born in radical revolution were evolving toward liberalism. The Sandinista Front for National Liberation (FSLN) in Nicaragua and the Institutional Revolutionary Party (PRI) of Mexico, parties that had seemed impervious to defeat, both lost elections (in 1990 and 2000, respectively) and turned the presidency over to the opposition. Within a quarter century, elected governments had become the norm and not the exception throughout the hemisphere. By 1990, only Cuba remained outside the club of liberal democratic nations.

The third wave peaked with the **Washington Consensus**, a term that first arose in the 1990s to describe the set of market-friendly economic policies and commitment to liberal democracy formally adopted at the hemispheric summit meeting in Miami in 1991 (as mentioned in the opening of this chapter). Its originator, the economist John Williamson (2002), has said in a retrospective essay, "The three big ideas here are **macroeconomic** discipline, a market economy, and openness to the world (at least in respect of trade and FDI [foreign direct investment])." Williamson (2002) says that by "economic discipline" he meant balancing exports and imports and also making changes in budgeting. He insists that he did not mean cuts in programs that defend human welfare, but his list did include a list of measures that would at least in the short run be painful to the poorest sectors.

We will look more closely at the economic side of the consensus when we examine the impact, for better and worse, of **neoliberal** policies, which admittedly include some measures that Williamson did not recommend (but were much in the spirit of his overall recommendations). What is important to underscore in this chapter is that the Miami summit not only endorsed market-friendly economic policies, mainly reducing the state's influence over the economy, but also expressed the commitment of all countries in the hemisphere to electoral democracy and individual rights.

In Latin America, most political leaders and many intellectuals fell in step with the trend to see liberal democracy as the inevitable and sole legitimate form of government. To give some examples, Mario Vargas Llosa made his reputation with brilliant novels criticizing the race and class system of his native Peru, but he turned to politics in the 1980s espousing free-market capitalism. Mexico's Jorge Castañeda, whom we met in the introduction, started political life as a communist but in a popular book (1993) pronounced the traditional left in Latin America as "utopian." He ultimately became foreign minister in the conservative government (2000–2006) of President Vicente Fox. Venezuela's Teodoro Petkoff was a Marxist guerrilla in the 1960s and then founded the Movement to Socialism (MAS) party to advance revolutionary goals in a more democratic way. However, as the minister of planning under President Rafael Caldera (1993–1998), he backed privatizing state-owned companies and cutting back social security and unemployment benefits. Joaquín Villalobos, the most important leader of the Salvadoran guerrillas in the civil war of the 1980s, later took up residence at Oxford University in England and endorsed the U.S. proposal for a Free Trade Area of the Americas, which would commit all member countries to open their markets to global competition. Fernando Henrique Cardoso, once a leading leftist critic of capitalism, moved to the center and entered politics in Brazil. As minister of finance and then president (1995–2002), he implemented economic policies designed to put Brazil in step with capitalist globalization. Although Cardoso has denied saying it, he was reported once to have told a group of Brazilian businessmen, "Forget what I wrote" (Kane 2005).

We should not exaggerate and say these prominent Latin Americans have become right-wing advocates of unrestricted markets. Most endorse a strong welfare safety net and criticize some of the conservative economic policies that governments adopted under pressure of the **International Monetary Fund** (**IMF**; see chapter 6). In fact, Williamson himself argued for increased spending on health and education for the poor. What the Washington Consensus said at the time was that democracy can only be liberal and flourish in association with a free-market economic system.

A **Pink Tide** (see the introduction) of electoral victories in the 2000s has brought this consensus into question, but pushback in Latin America was not limited to the left. Noberto Ceresole, a right-wing Argentine nationalist, contended that the "third wave" of democracy is little more than an attempt to reinforce the subordination of underdeveloped countries of the periphery to wealthy ones. By "countries of the **periphery**," we mean those parts of the world that in both political and economic terms have relatively little power compared with wealthy, **core nations**, such as the United States, Europe, and Japan. For Ceresole (1999), liberal democracy in Latin America and the poorer countries of the world reinforces rule by an elite who function as subordinate partners of their counterparts in the wealthy countries, especially the United States. He urged resistance to economic globalization and promotion of third-wave liberalism. Though he was otherwise reviled by Latin America's democrats, Ceresole's nationalist views resonated favorably with some leftists.

Globalization advocates believe that market economies reinforce democracy by (1) promoting individual freedom, (2) decentralizing economic power, and (3) encouraging people with common interests to form groups to influence politics. (We return in depth to this theme in chapter 15.) In this way, free markets promote a more vigorous **civil society**. By "civil society," advocates of a market economy mean groups, movements, and organizations formed voluntarily by individuals. Overall, the guiding rule is that the best government is the one that governs least. In this liberal tradition, in a democracy individuals remain "free" to interact with each other. This is true liberty—freedom from the power of government.

Today's neoliberals—again, the "new liberals"—argue, like their predecessors of the 1800s, for reducing the influence of government over market forces. They also think that a reduced state creates more "space" for a strong civil society. Hernando De Soto (1989), a Peruvian entrepreneur and head of the Instituto Libertad y Democracia, introduced a version of neoliberalism with his influential book *The Other Path*. De Soto argues that the main obstacle holding back the huge sector of "informal" workers (itinerant vendors, sidewalk merchants, day workers, unlicensed repair shops, etc.) is their lack of secured property rights and legal status. Less government regulation combined with policies designed to encourage competition would unleash the entrepreneurial energies of this strata of the population. Few leftists would agree, as they see competition from global corporations (e.g., Walmart and McDonald's) squeezing out street vendors and small stores. Smaller enterprises have a difficult time competing with big companies' modern technology, marketing power, and ability to sell cheap long enough to drive out competitors. However, there is some common ground here between left and right on the desirability of strengthening the legal security for the homes and small businesses (microenterprises) of workers in the informal sector.

How might neoliberalism promote liberal democracy? Free-trade policies and globalization facilitated outside scrutiny of human rights conditions. Fiscal austerity may have caused hardship, but it also reduced the patronage resources available to politicians to reward friends and punish enemies. In other words, in certain ways liberal policies did widen the spaces for political participation that had been limited in an earlier era (roughly 1930–1970) of electoral democracy and that were closed off completely in most countries during years of harsh military rule. There was more room for **civil society** to exert itself.

At the same time, however, the economic policies associated with neoliberalism began to lose their luster in part because of the growth of economic inequality during the 1990s, despite the decade being one of economic growth. The privatization (selling off of government-owned businesses and services to private investors) of the 1980s and 1990s was rife with corruption that allowed a handful of businessmen to make huge profits. For example, Mexico's Carlos Slim benefited from the privatization of communications and media companies to become an overnight billionaire. Implementation of laissez-faire policy, called "**structural adjustment**," often resulted in higher unemployment, difficulties for small farmers, and reductions in social services. Critics began to see electoral democracy—something that Latin Americans had had to win in bitter struggles to send military regimes back to the barracks—as but a corrupt process of transferring public resources to private control and exposing the poor and less powerful to the rapaciousness of the wealthy. In the face of mounting hardships, especially those felt in the family, where women bore the brunt of the costs of "adjustment," social movements began to exert themselves in a way suggesting a different conception of civil society.

Liberal democrats see **civil society** as a sphere of social life where individuals freely cooperate and compete with each other. "Freely" here means they do so without interference by the state. It implies that governments not only will respect civil liberties but also will refrain from attempting to organize social life and the economy from above. This includes respect for the independent force of the market and property. Private rather than state ownership and limited control over wealth production and the means of producing it, the theory goes, contribute to freedom by limiting the power of the state. The authoritarian character of the communist states in the twentieth century reinforced these ideas but is out of fashion in Latin America today, even on the left. Without describing very clearly what it means, the left now commonly speaks of "**twenty-first-century socialism**," a new model distinct from what emerged in the Soviet Union after the 1917 Russian Revolution, and for that matter, from the one-party state and state-run economy that emerged in Cuba after its 1959 revolution.

As an alternative, many Latin Americans want to build a civil society that stands between the market and the state. As Carlos Vilas (1993: 38) puts it,

> The concept of civil society refers to a sphere of collective action distinct from both the market and "political society"—parties, legislatures, courts, state agencies. Civil society is not independent of politics, but clearly, when people identify themselves as "civil society," they are seeking to carve out a relatively autonomous sphere for organization and action.

The political left, on the defensive for most of the period between 1970 and 2000, took advantage of the popular discontent with neoliberal economic policies and scored a wave of electoral successes that became the **Pink Tide**. The tide rose along with social movements that are wary of being captured or manipulated by any politicians, leftist or otherwise. This has created some tensions because, as we'll see in Part IV, the perspective of those in government is not always in harmony with the perspective of the movements.

◼ How Comparativists Apply Polyarchy to the Study of Latin America

In the past 30 years, comparative political scientists have used a pluralist framework to analyze three phases in Latin America's recent political evolution: **breakdown, transition to democracy**, and consolidation, or **deepening of democracy**. (In chapters 8 and 9 we look closely at these phases.) The "breakdown of democratic regimes" refers to the economic crises, violence, and political polarization that afflicted Latin America beginning in the mid-1960s (starting with a coup in Brazil in 1964). In all of three of these processes, it is Dahl's notion of polyarchy that defines the kind of political system that broke down and the kind that later was the goal of a transition process.

Although Latin America has a long history of military intervention, the period after breakdown was marked by especially harsh repression. Similar events had transpired in a number of Mediterranean countries, attracting the attention of an international team of comparative political scientists. With support from several large foundations, they began to search for common causes. Although they identified multiple causes of crisis and breakdown, they placed greatest emphasis on the inability of elites to continue to respect each other's vital interests within the framework of constitutional democracy (Linz and Stepan 1978).

By the mid-1980s, Latin Americans had endured 20 years of brutal military rule. The decade saw the beginning of the end of communism in Europe, a new emphasis (at least in rhetoric) on democracy and human rights in U.S. foreign policy, and intensified pressure to end racial **apartheid** in South Africa. In Latin America, opposition movements placed pressure on the generals to return to the barracks. These protestors often braved imprisonment, torture, and death squads in the process. The persistence and growth of this movement, along with the changed international climate, induced politicians and business elites to negotiate a transition to democracy through elections before popular pressure assumed revolutionary proportions.

Just as most political scientists, as pluralists, stressed elite failure in explaining the breakdown of democracy elsewhere, their theories about transitions to democracy emphasized, not surprisingly, a process of elite compromise. That is not to say that these analysts ignore common people's resistance to dictatorships, but more often they see mass action as the context or the catalyst for the more important actions and decisions of elites. Pluralists tend to see regime transitions as a kind of game in which the elites negotiate with one another to arrive at a pact about the future after the civilians return and elections are allowed to go forth. The pact is an agreement among political, business, military, and economic elites to make sure that the vital interests of each group will not be at risk in the new democracy. Pluralists see this process as a way of building a political consensus and preventing conflict from destroying a new, fragile democracy. The people in the streets are a reminder to the negotiators that failure to reach agreement risks a more radical outcome or a new round of repression.

In the most influential study of this type, the authors define democracy as "the *right* to be treated by fellow human beings as equal with respect to the making of collective choices and the obligation of those implementing such choices to be equally accountable and accessible to all members of the polity" (O'Donnell et al. 1986: 7). However, it seems logical to ask whether a democracy created by a pact really results in a system where everyone enjoys such rights equally. After all, by negotiating a pact, elites seek to limit what can be changed. Think, for example, of the U.S. Constitution. It includes many provisions designed to prevent government from being too responsive to popular opinion. Some of these limits were originally put in place because of a pact among the founding fathers to protect the institution of slavery from being abolished by the central government. A key issue was thus taken out of the realm of democracy, eventually being resolved through civil war 75 years later.

Most of the "transitions" literature gave way to yet another wave of studies about a new task: consolidation or **deepening of democracy**. One prominent school of thought, **institutionalism**, emphasizes the importance of institution building (Linz and Stepan 1996; Linz and Valenzuela 1994; Mainwaring and Scully 1995; Mainwaring and Shugart 1997). This approach stresses the importance of developing the **rule of law**—that is, ensuring that all citizens are procedurally treated the same and can rely on the state to guarantee justice and security for both persons and property. More optimistic scholars now see hope for the establishment of stable democratic institutions in what they perceive to be an abandonment of extra-constitutional, violent challenges from both the political left (Castañeda 1993) and the right (Chalmers et al. 1992). More pessimistic scholars, as we have already seen, worry that social inequality and/or tendencies toward **personalism** remain too strong to inspire confidence in democratic stability. We look more closely at institutions and rule of law in Latin America in chapter 14.

One important aspect of "deepening" democracy in Latin America involves doing away with legal and constitutional principles that limit the full exercise of civic rights and protect the interests of landowners, the military, and other elites. Transitional pacts have often included immunity from prosecution for human rights violators, severe limits on the ability of the government to tax wealth, limits on the rights of labor, and systems of representation guaranteeing conservative parties votes in the legislature in excess of their share of the electoral vote. Perhaps the best-known case where all these elements were present was that of Chile, where General Augusto Pinochet, dictator between 1973 and 1989, incorporated limits on democracy into the country's present constitution, which dates from 1980. After Pinochet was forced out of the presidency, his constitution functioned just as he had designed it—posing severe obstacles to any attempt to legislate changes in the social and economic direction he had set in motion. Some of these limits have been lifted since 2000, but many Chileans have been disappointed that a return to democracy did not bring much change in the inherited economic model or cause rapid progress on human rights issues.

Although the scholars responsible for most of the literature on the "breakdowns, transition, and consolidation" of democracy have been guarded in their conclusions, there is a general tone of optimism in their work consistent with Huntington's (1991) third-wave thesis. For example, in his review of debates and recent research on democratic politics in Latin America for the *Annual Review of Political Science*, Gerardo L. Munck (2004) writes,

> Latin American politics has recently undergone a fundamental transformation. For many decades prior to the 1990s, most elected leaders could not discount the possibility of military coups, and most authoritarian rulers could not ignore the actions of antiauthoritarian movements. Now, in contrast, elections are held regularly, winners take office and make legally binding decisions, and losers and new players prepare for the next election. Latin America has made a clear break with its past.

This optimism has not gone unchallenged. George Philip (1996: 34–35), an English political scientist, expresses a more pessimistic view of how well democracy has been institutionalized: "The point is simply that Latin American elites have so far been more successful at holding elections than at creating state institutions which work well. This situation holds out the permanent threat of state failure." Philip sees the threat emanating from three sources: (1) capitalism and globalization have accentuated inequalities; (2) those losing out are resentful; and (3) a society remains weak and "patrimonially structured." With this last phrase, Philip refers to a state where "who you know" means more than your right as a citizen to be treated equally by the bureaucracy under law.

For Review

When we study democracy, what do we mean by "breakdown," "transition," and "consolidation" or "deepening"? According to pluralists, what role does a "pact" play in the transition to democracy? What might be some problems with pacts?

Political Culture in Latin America

Philip is just one of many political scientists who see an obstacle to democracy in Latin American culture, which they see as more traditional and personalist than developed, wealthier countries. In a modern culture, the argument goes, favoritism toward relatives or friends may occur, but it is regarded as an abuse of authority and source of corruption. In traditional cultures, such behavior is much more a norm—that is, not deviant. One example is the persistence of **compadrazgo**, which refers to the special relationship between a godparent and godchild in Catholic cultures. Latin Americanists use the term more broadly to refer to the importance of family ties. Such a culture, some argue, favors the formation of a **patrimonial state**, referring to a type of political system where personalism and patronage prevail. Within such a system, politics mostly involves leaders (patrons) who offer resources provided by the state—anything from a water pump for a poor village to multimillion-dollar construction contracts—in exchange for political support (e.g., votes). This practice is known as **clientelism**—and when practiced to an extreme, including outright corruption, it sometimes is called "crony capitalism."

O'Donnell (1994:164) fears that Latin Americans have a predilection for rule by a strongman. **Delegative democracies**, as he calls them,

> rest on the premise that whoever wins election to the presidency is thereby entitled to govern as he or she sees fit, constrained only by the hard facts of existing power relations and by a constitutionally limited term of office. The president is taken to be the embodiment of the nation and the main custodian and definer of its interests. Governmental policies need bear no resemblance to campaign promises.

Fareed Zakaria (1997), an influential journalist, coined the phrase "**illiberal democracy**" to refer to situations where concentration of executive power is combined with more serious abuses of human rights or limitations on civil freedoms. His article cited strongmen of the time, such as Argentina's president Carlos Menem and Peru's president Alberto Fujimori, along with a number of presidents of Eastern and Central European countries, as examples of this phenomenon. More recently, critics of Venezuelan president Chávez (1999–2013) have said that he made Venezuela into such an illiberal democracy, but his defenders deny the charge and say that he breathed life into a moribund democracy by giving poor Venezuelans a new sense of empowerment.

Comparative political scientists use the term "**hybrid regimes**" to describe some of the regimes that have emerged in Eastern Europe, the Middle East, and Latin America. This concept recognizes that most of these regimes that have emerged from an authoritarian past have not completely discarded past patterns but do show many hallmarks of pluralism. Although the term originally may have been meant to imply that hybrid regimes are transitional, moving toward democracy, other political scientists now see hybrid regimes as a type of state, one that may be stable and persist over time. So a question for us, then, is whether we should see "illiberal" or "delegative" democracies as flawed and temporary or as a form of state unlikely anytime soon, if ever, to become simply "polyarchies."

Not all comparativists see tradition as something to be overcome. Howard Wiarda (1981) believes that personalism simply reflects a cultural difference that inclines Latin America toward "**corporatism**," a type of society where the state treats society as a family. Pluralists tend to see corporatism as a distortion of democracy; corporatists, however, see it as an alternative ideology promoting a state that seeks to harmonize parts of society in conflict, to ameliorate the worst characteristics of capitalism, and to promote common effort toward economic development. We look more closely at corporatism in the next chapter.

For Review

What do we mean by "corporatism" in Latin American political culture? What is a "hybrid regime"—and how is "delegative democracy" an example?

Strong Presidents, Personalism, and "Illiberal Democracy"

Latin America might be seen as a museum of politics, having experienced just about every form of state categorized by political scientists. Military governments, electoral democracies, revolutionary regimes, charismatic dictatorships, and even monarchies have existed, sometimes side by side, in its history. However, there are several features of Latin American political culture and its social structure that have been visible in just about all types of regimes in the region: a tendency toward personalism in leadership styles and relationships of power; more pronounced inequality than in other parts of the world, even poor regions; and concern about external intervention, often manifest in attempts by leaders to rally people around defense of national sovereignty.

Distraught about the blatant theft of an election by President Alberto Fujimori in Peru (in 2000) and alleging that his country's president (Chávez) was embarked on a similar route, the Venezuelan political scientist Aníbal Romero (1999) once complained,

> We are dealing, in truth, with toy democracies, attached as we are to the erroneous belief according to which the temporary support of the masses justifies for the *caudillo* practically anything he wants to do, violating most of time judicial procedures and making a mockery of any notion of a state of law. . . . They are poor imitations of another reality, of true liberal democracies that protect the rights of minorities, maintain inviolable the sphere of individual rights, administer justice impartially, and balance powers.

The term **caudillo** literally means "man on horseback," an allusion to the strongmen, sometimes illiterate, who assumed regional or national leadership as a result of their fighting ability and leadership skills during the violent, anarchic nineteenth century (see chapter 4). As we shall explore later, at this time the ability to fight on horseback with great skill and courage could inspire the loyalty of men who joined the irregular armies that fought each other for control of territories in the 1800s when national armies and states had not yet fully formed after independence from Spain and Portugal. Caudilloism may be one of those tendencies that define Latin America as an "area study," which implies that there are some commonalities in its history and culture that stamp the people's way of life in ways distinctive from other parts of the world. Many area specialists think that caudilloism reinforces personalism—a tendency to place loyalty to a leader above other values, such as law, qualifications, or need.

Studies of Latin America that emphasize personalism and clientelism (discussed later) tend to stress political culture, rather than social class or foreign intervention, as the most important factors explaining why the region is economically "underdeveloped" and politically unstable. We will take up the question of economic development more fully in chapter 5.

We should also note that some analysts see this cultural legacy in positive terms. Norberto Ceresole, whom we met earlier in this chapter, was an admirer of the complex and controversial Argentine leader Juan Perón, whose rule he defended (Ceresole 1999) as embodying the will of the Argentine people and forging a unity between popular aspirations and the military. More recently, Diane Raby (2006), a British political scientist, has argued that highly centralized, personalized leadership can be democratic. Strong, popular leaders, she claims, may undermine the power of oligarchies, challenge the power of dominant countries (e.g., the United States), and thereby enable new forms of mass participation to arise.

More often, analysts on both the left and right sides of the political spectrum see caudilloism as an obstacle to democracy, even when the caudillo's power is ratified through elections. Zakaria (1997) put it this way in an article for the influential magazine *Foreign Affairs*:

> Democratically elected regimes, often ones that have been reelected or reaffirmed through referenda, are routinely ignoring constitutional limits on their power and

depriving their citizens of basic rights and freedoms. From Peru to the Palestinian Authority, from Sierra Leone to Slovakia, from Pakistan to the Philippines, we see the rise of a disturbing phenomenon in international life—illiberal democracy.

The tendency toward personalism reinforces a style of politics known as "populism." **Populism** might be described as the practice of appealing for mass support by championing the causes of ordinary people against powerful elites. We will look more closely at the history of populism and assess its relationship to democracy in Latin America in chapter 5. For now, we will only note that the caudillo often practices populism in the ascent to power and sometimes to hold onto it, but often populists are co-opted by the elites they initially challenged.

Ceresole (1999), a controversial figure accused of neo-Nazi tendencies (which he adamantly denied), viewed liberal democracy as antithetical to Latin American traditions that are "underestimated and denigrated by Anglo-North American sociological thought." The Argentine went on to justify not only personalist leaders but also military rule. He saw the military as the only institution capable of representing the entire nation in an era of crumbling political parties and other organized groups. The modern caudillo must unite the military with the masses and lead them on a crusade for sovereign, independent development. "The result of this confluence of factors," he wrote, "is a revolutionary model that pivots on the basic relationship between a national *caudillo* and an absolute popular mass majority that designates him personally as its representative to bring about broad and above all deep change." The theory is not new. For example, in 1919, a Venezuelan intellectual made a similar argument to justify the harsh, personal dictatorship (1908 to 1935) of Juan Vicente Gómez, which he called "democratic caesarism" (Lanz 1919).

Ceresole was a rabid anticommunist, but his theory of leadership in some ways seems to apply to the style of rule (1959–2008) that Fidel Castro brought to Cuba. The Cuban leader was the indirectly elected head of state and general secretary of the Cuban Communist Party (PCC), the only legal party in the country. But his longevity, in the face of 40 years of attempts by the United States to dislodge him from power, stemmed from his unusually personal and close relationship with the Cuban people themselves. Fidel, as his admirers refer to him, is also familiarly known by the military term "*el comandante*" by the millions who supported him enthusiastically throughout his rule. No other person or institution in Cuba could match his ability to call people into the streets, set agendas for debate, and make policy. He made unity in defense of Cuba's sovereignty a higher value than tolerance of opposition, much like Ceresole described the role of the caudillo. However, Castro and Ceresole loathed one another.

For Review

Why is personalism in Latin America often called "caudilloism"? Can you explain, even if you disagree, how Ceresole might justify his claim that a populist dictator or military regime could be considered democratic?

Clientelism and Corruption

The tendency toward personalism in Latin American politics is reinforced by the strong ties that can develop between leaders with resources at their disposal and those who need these resources. **Clientelism** involves an unequal exchange between people and public officials who can provide a benefit of some kind. The benefit might be anything from a subsidy for an industrialist to milk for desperate mothers, from a bag of cement for a poor person trying to repair a home to a license for a trader to import food at a more favorable exchange rate than others pay. In return, the person enjoying this benefit offers political support, often in the form of votes or financial contributions.

To some extent, these practices are rooted in the very nature of politics. For example, everywhere in the world winners of elections appoint people to office through a kind of spoils system—rewarding those who have worked on campaigns or provided money. However, this practice does seem more pervasive in Latin America, especially because, in general, government employees are not as well protected from losing their jobs as they are in countries with laws and courts that protect them. Often, the political appointee seems not just less qualified but even unqualified for a position. For example, someone who cannot type might get a job requiring the ability to enter data on a computer keyboard.

Political pull (*palanca*—i.e., leverage) is an asset in any society, but it sometimes seems that in Latin America even the most ordinary and routine service requires one to have *palanca*. Perhaps the person in charge of processing applications for unemployment looks favorably only on applicants who carry the same party ID card; renewing a passport can be a nightmare. The company dispatcher who schedules a phone or cable installation just can't find a free crew until you make it worth his while. A job collecting highway tolls is a license to keep some of the receipts—provided you pass along a percentage to your superior. A job as a policeman is also a license to collect little bribes from drivers (the *mordita*, or "little bite," as Mexicans call it). A permit to operate a taxi might require a bribe to a bureaucrat. All these acts of petty corruption are sustained in part because further up the social pyramid, more lucrative and serious corrupt practices are tolerated, such as major kickbacks on construction projects.

Politicians have long exploited the needs of the poor—and of other people—by promising and delivering something the community needs in return for the loyalty of its leaders and their willingness to deliver votes to the politicians' party. It may be as simple as providing cement to build concrete steps to replace the muddy, winding paths leading high up into a poor **barrio** (neighborhood). Residents may be appropriately grateful and reward parties with votes, but often the relationship goes further. Only with the right party membership card can a taxi driver expect to get a license. Only after the "right" election outcome can a neighborhood expect to receive services that many of us expect from government whether or not we voted for the winner. As our examples indicate, the process is not limited to the poor. Is this corruption or clientelism? The line blurs.

Clientelism, this exchange of material benefits for political loyalty, may not be all bad. It ensures that at least some economic benefits trickle down to the masses. Still, clientelism reduces the capacity of citizens to exercise effective control over public officials and to run local affairs in their best interests. **Patronage** politics take precedence over debate about policies and programs, and this is economically inefficient.

And it can frustrate those who want to make positive change. Álvaro García Linera, vice president of Bolivia, told an interviewer of the challenges posed by clientelism to Evo Morales, Bolivia's first indigenous president, and his party, the Movimiento al Socialismo (MAS):

> People believe that if they have worked for the party, they deserve something in return—a job or access to certain privileges. Evo has said repeatedly to social-movement leaders that they should not expect anything from the government, and this often provokes disgruntlement and questioning. He insists that they need to deepen their commitment to the process of social changes without seeking personal gain. This is hard for many to accept because that is not the way things have ever been done here. So of course corruption and clientelism continue, and addressing it repeatedly takes up an enormous amount of our time and energy. We have no choice but to stay on top of it all the time.
>
> (Farthing 2010: 32)

There is not much evidence that democracies are less corrupt than dictatorships. Indeed, mainstream parties may compete intensely for control of government but cooperate in limiting possibilities for new competitors to emerge. Such behavior is not limited to Latin America. For example, the Democratic and Republican parties in the United States have controlled the National Electoral Commission, which has consistently interpreted electoral laws in ways that reinforce the dominance of the two-party system. In Venezuela, two parties dominated politics until 1998 and competed fiercely with one another for votes, giving the appearance of a well-institutionalized, stable polyarchy. But they would cooperate with one another at the polling tables to steal votes from smaller parties (Buxton 2001) that were threatening to break their joint monopoly over politics. Better to slough a few votes off to a cooperative rival than to allow a troublesome opponent to get a foot in the door!

Alma Guillermoprieto (2000:30), covering Mexico's July 2000 election for the *New Yorker*, described how Mexico's PRI exercised "prestidigitation" to make up electoral deficits. Such efforts included

> the *ratón loco*, or crazy mouse, in which a group of hired voters was sent to one polling station after another to cast ballots for the PRI; the *urna embarazada*, or pregnant urn, in which a ballot box lost its way on the road to the counting station and was found again, mysteriously fuller of PRI votes than when it started out; and the *voto comprometido*, in which even before voting day the Party was able to tally millions of votes that had been promised—sometimes in writing—by labor and peasant unions, small businesses, street vendors, and the garbage pickers of every town.

During the middle decades of the last century, much of Latin America experienced mass democracy for the first time (the main theme of chapter 5). This era was strongly marked by populism and strong, personalist leadership. Populists rallied public support with inflammatory rhetoric against imperialism and the local oligarchy. Leaders such as Juan Perón of Argentina, Getúlio Vargas of Brazil, and Rómulo Betancourt of Venezuela were not as radical as their rhetoric implied, but they did mobilize new sectors of the population into political life. At the peak of power, these parties evolved into networks of power brokers who distributed patronage resources—hence the deep reliance on **clientelism**.

One way to think about political culture is the idea of "elective affinity." That is, culture is not just a set of intangible ideas in our heads. It is a set of practices and ideas that are rooted in history, passed along from generation to generation. To take an example from outside Latin America, individualism is strongly rooted in U.S. political culture in part because of the way Americans think of our history as one of pioneers moving westward into an "empty" continent and of immigrants forging a new life in a land of opportunity. What matters less than whether these beliefs—myths—are true or false is the way they are passed along, even if many historians challenge myths about the past or if economic, social, or international events force a society to rethink its values.

And before we leave the topic, it's important to remember the discussion here is at a very high level of generalization that does not reflect the diversity of countries or, for that matter, the diversity within countries. To take an example, indigenous peoples have extensive experience with economic cooperatives; Venezuelans do not. Countries of the Southern Cone experienced more European immigration from areas outside Iberia than countries further north. The influence of Catholicism is greater in Chile, Colombia, and Nicaragua than it is in Cuba (even before the revolution) or Venezuela. Northern Mexico is the land of Pancho Villa, whose followers were small independent landowners; southern Mexico is the land of Emiliano Zapata, whose followers worked lands collectively controlled by villages. The Mexican Revolution (1910–1920) may have forged a new national identity out of these different peoples, but to this day we can observe marked differences among north, south, and Mexico City.

Even a revolution does not fully change elective affinities, but neither is political culture fixed in stone. The notion of an "elective affinity" allows for us to see continuities without simply concluding, "The more things change, the more they remain the same," in Latin America or anywhere else.

For Review

Can you explain how the practice of clientelism is different from corruption—or do you think there is no difference? How might clientelism and corruption erode popular confidence in democracy? What is an "elective affinity"?

Other Kinds of Democracy

C. B. MacPherson (1972: 25) argued that liberal democracy and its economic companion, market capitalism, have been less appealing to cultures that rate community and equality more highly than individual freedom. MacPherson noted that the communists claimed to be democrats too. Communists interpreted the "common people" to mean the working class, or **proletariat**, whose "dictatorship" was democratic because workers were, presumably, the majority. Even if we were to adopt this idea, the idea of a proletariat as used by Karl Marx never applied very well to Latin America. Unlike Europe, Japan, and North America, Latin America has never been through an era when most workers were employed in manufacturing or mining. Rather than being paid wages for their work, even peasants today in many places work not for wages but on large, landed estates (**haciendas** or **latifundia**) in exchange for access to their own small plots of land (**minifundios**). Today most Latin Americans live in urban areas, but the cities are heavily populated with people who are unemployed or barely eking out a living on the streets (Stavenhagen 1966–1967; 1974).

From China and Vietnam to Cuba and Chile, Marxists in the **Third World** have had to adapt the master's theories to take into account their own histories and social reality. Their solution has often been to broaden the idea of the "oppressed class"—the "demos" in democracy—to a coalition of social classes from the poor, the peasantry, the working class, and even, sometimes, the middle class. Rather than a "working class," leftist politicians often refer to the "popular sector," vaguely defined to include all people who favor a national program of economic development and oppose foreign economic exploitation, which they identify with imperialism. Closely related to this is the frequent reference to *el pueblo*, "the people," which is perhaps best understood as a term suggesting that the common people or masses are in a power struggle with an elite that defends its own interest, often in common with imperialists from other countries.

This way of thinking about the "demos" is close to what MacPherson (1972: 24) saw as the third conception of democracy in the "real world"—the notion of democracy broadly as "rule of the oppressed." In many countries, the struggle to wrest control over the nation's destiny from colonial powers and foreign economic interests required national unity. In those parts of the world the twentieth-century struggle for independence required not just political sovereignty but something larger, called "national liberation." Most of Latin America had achieved political sovereignty a hundred years earlier, but the theme of "national liberation" ran through the great social revolutions in Latin America in Mexico (1910), Cuba (1959), and Nicaragua (1979). These revolutions gave rise, for at least some time (10 years in Nicaragua, decades for Mexico and Cuba) to governments dominated by a single party whose main goal was to unite the country for economic and social advancement and for "liberation" from foreign domination. All proclaimed themselves "democratic," but liberal critics claimed that they failed a key test—the possibility for an opposition to win a fair election. We look at this idea more closely in chapter 10.

With the collapse of communism in Eastern Europe between 1989 and 1991, the liberal concept seemed to have achieved worldwide **hegemony**, meaning that liberal democracy would be taken for granted, taken as common sense, as the only true kind of democracy. After 1989, Eastern European countries soon opened their economies to market forces, transformed state property into private property, and began a process of incomplete political liberalization. Elsewhere—for example, in China and Vietnam—political liberalization has been more limited, but governments opened their economies to market forces and private ownership, creating "market-Leninism," a one-party system with a capitalist economic system. Cuba resisted this tendency, but with economic reforms since the retirement of Fidel Castro from political leadership, analysts wonder whether the Chinese model might take root there. Throughout Latin America, countries swung away from economic development policies that relied heavily on the state and toward neoliberal economic policies and free trade.

Although this swing toward liberal economic policy produced economic growth, it also produced a political reaction. Popular discontent grew in the 1980s and 1990s as growth accentuated inequality and failed to alleviate poverty sufficiently. This nurtured the rise of social movements and an electoral swing toward the left—the **Pink Tide**, first evident in the election of Chávez in Venezuela in 1998. These developments, especially those of social movements, put back into debate questions about the adequacy of liberal democracy, but few saw the type of socialism practiced in the Soviet Union, Cuba, or East Asia as a desirable political alternative to liberal democracy. This has led to some interesting new democratic experiments that we examine in Part IV, but the most we can say is that although liberal democracy, communism, and single-party systems remain unsatisfactory, the shape of the alternative is far from clear. This discussion goes on annually in the **World Social Forum**, first held in Brazil in 2001 and held in Tunisia in 2013. In other words, many politically active Latin Americans have now joined with counterparts around the world to search for an alternative to the "liberal" brand of democracy—though not necessarily to reject liberal values, such as rights, tolerance, equality, and so on.

For Review

What do politicians and analysts mean by the "popular sector" in Latin America? How is this idea different from the idea of the "proletariat," or "working class"? What is the difference between "national liberation" and simply fighting for independence from colonialism?

In Cuba, only one party exists legally, but candidates need not be Communists. They run for office as independents and cannot campaign beyond making their backgrounds and views known, as you see here in a local community office. In other countries, candidates run with the support of one or more parties. As in the United States, they need to raise and spend lots of money to have a chance to win. What do you think of Cuba's claim to have a more democratic system?

PUNTO DE VISTA: FIDEL CASTRO ON DEMOCRACY

Given that the concept of democracy seems subject to interpretation in other areas of the world, one might be surprised to learn that staunch Communist leader Fidel Castro believes democracy exists in Cuba. Fidel Castro, who served first as premier (head of government) after 1959 and then as president of Cuba from 1976 until 2008, always rejected the claim he was a dictator. He insists that Cuba, which constitutionally is a single-party state, is a democracy suited to the country's needs. Fidel's brother, Raúl Castro, has introduced economic reforms widening space for a market in Cuba; so far he has adhered to Fidel's position on democracy.

Consider the following interview with the Nicaraguan leader Tomás Borge (1992), where Fidel was asked to define what democracy meant to him. He replied,

> Democracy, as Lincoln defined it, is the government of the people, by the people, and for the people. To me democracy entails the defense of all the rights of citizens, including the rights to independence, freedom, national dignity, and honor. To me democracy is the brotherhood of men.

We might ask whether Cuba has created such a brotherhood. What is Cuba's claim to call itself democratic?

> We have found our form of democratic expression and believe it suits our conditions ideally. Its efficacy has been proven for over 30 years because I think no country could have resisted the [U.S. imposed] embargo, threats, aggressions, and tremendous blows entailed by . . . the disappearance of the Soviet Union if the people were not united and aware of our democracy.

Castro went on:

> I am not going to say that our democracy is perfect. We cannot afford to commit errors of idealism within our current situation that entails more risks than ever before. We are not going to play with the independence and security of the country.

Groups such as Amnesty International and the Watch Committee have reported that dissidents in Cuba are harassed, often with short-term detention and intimidation. Fidel Castro replied that the country must be on guard against U.S. attempts to overthrow his government and especially against the right-wing Cuban community in Miami. He also pointed out that Cubans have never lived under a state of siege or military rule, unlike almost every other Latin American country.

Challenged by American reporter Robert MacNeil (1985) to defend his record on human rights, a free press, and legal opposition, Castro argued that public (state) ownership of the media is a more democratic arrangement than one where wealthy private owners of the media have the last word. "We do not have a multiparty system either, nor do we need it," he claimed.

> The political level of our people, the information level of our people is much greater. In surveys that have been made in the United States, an astonishingly high number of people do not know where Nicaragua is, where the countries of Latin America are. They don't know what countries belong to Africa, what countries belong to Asia. There is an incredible ignorance, astonishing. That does not happen here.

In a 2000 interview (www.workers.org/ww/2000/fidel1005.php), Castro contrasted the system of elections still used today in Cuba, whereby candidates are nominated at grassroots assemblies, are not allowed to campaign but are also not allowed to be supported by or to be identified with a party (including the Communist Party, the only legal one in the country), and are then elected by secret balloting by all citizens:

"Nobody needs to spend a penny, not a single one. The district candidates campaign together as a group, as do the candidates to the National Assembly, who are nominated in every municipality, proportionally to the size of each municipality, although [each] one must have a minimum of two deputies in the National Assembly. This is the procedure, the method we have developed to guarantee the democratic principle."

Point/Counterpoint

Do you see any merit in Castro's claim that Cuba is a democracy?

a. If you say yes, how do you respond to the criticism that the Communist Party is the only one legally allowed to exist?
b. If you say no, how would you respond to Castro's claim that Cuban elections result in voters choosing representatives closer to their interests and less dependent on money and advertising than in liberal democracies?

For more information

Reuters journalist Marc Frank has lived most of the last 30 years in Cuba and gives incisive analysis in his book *Cuban Revelations* (University Press of Florida, 2013). The Washington-based Center for Democracy in the Americas maintains a blog and numerous other good online resources at www.democracyinamericas.org/cuba. *Havana Times* (www.havanatimes.org/) is a terrific resource that is hard to pin down as either pro- or anti-revolution.

Democracy without People?

You are likely to find a broad range of views about the meaning of democracy among Latin Americanists. A sizable number, especially among political scientists, equate polyarchy with democracy. Others believe that only revolution and some radical alternative to capitalism and liberal democracy can ever truly bring justice to the region. Many Latin America area specialists think that polyarchy is a conception of democracy too much in the service of U.S. **hegemony**—that is, that polyarchy is "exported" to Latin America and keeps the region in a **neocolonial** status, ensuring that only ruling elites acceptable to American corporate and political interests hold power.

William Robinson contends that polyarchy is "low-intensity democracy"; that is, it limits popular participation and weakens the state, so that Latin America remains business-friendly for **transnational corporations** (big businesses that operate across national boundaries). According to Robinson (1996: 6), the United States promotes polyarchy "to achieve the underlying objective of maintaining essentially undemocratic societies inserted into an unjust international system."

Most critics of polyarchy argue that real democracy requires direct participation of citizens not only in government but also in social and economic realms. We will use the phrase "popular democracy" to refer to this broad tendency. Most commonly, this view is associated with socialism and communism, but it is also attractive to various social movements that are not exclusively focused on social class issues. On the more conservative side of the spectrum, and very often among Catholic thinkers, one finds those who argue that Latin America has a distinctive "corporatist" tradition of democracy. This tendency questions whether the competition among individuals and groups fostered by polyarchy and the marketplace can produce social good without the state taking a strong hand to guide and organize the resulting conflict.

Robinson (1996) is among those who pose the notion of popular democracy as an alternative to polyarchy. The concept is vague, but several Latin American governments have experimented with the idea. For example, after the 1979 revolution, which expelled the 35-year, U.S.-supported dictatorship of the Somoza family, the Sandinistas of Nicaragua attempted in the early years to set up a system allowing direct representation of social groups (women, unions, small farmers, etc.) in the legislature. Sergio Ramírez, then vice president, said at the time,

> For us, the efficiency of a political model depends on its capacity to resolve the problems of democracy and justice. Effective democracy, like we intend to practice in Nicaragua, consists of ample popular participation—a permanent dynamic of the people's participation in a variety of political and social tasks . . . For us democracy is not merely a formal model but a continual process capable of giving people that elect and participate in it the real possibility of transforming their living conditions, a democracy which establishes justice and ends exploitation.
>
> (quoted in Ruchwarger 1985: 4)

The Sandinistas (FSLN) encouraged all citizens to join and become actively involved in mass organizations representing businessmen, women, students, workers, small ranchers and farmers, peasants, and others. The mass organizations, in turn, would be represented in the Council of State, where important decisions would be made. Most of the leaders would coordinate their work through the FSLN, just as they had worked together to overthrow the dictatorship. (We will look more closely at the Central American revolutions of the 1980s in chapter 10.)

In 1984, the Sandinistas abandoned the Council of State and replaced it with a more typical legislature chosen directly by elections. Threatened by the U.S.-armed and trained *contras*, the Sandinistas hoped that a more typically democratic system would help them attract international support. Instead, Robinson argues, the Sandinistas' shift toward polyarchy made them vulnerable to intervention by the United States. That is not to say that the Sandinistas cannot be faulted for abuses of power and mistakes, but their problems were made worse when the United States continued the war even after the 1984 election was judged fair by all observers but those sent by the U.S. State Department. The United States continued the *contra* war and, in addition, by Robinson's estimate, spent US$18.7 million openly and even more clandestinely to influence the outcome of the 1990 elections (Robinson 1992: 136). The Sandinistas had made a Faustian bargain—that is, had sold their souls. To gain international **legitimacy**, they had accepted the precepts of polyarchy, but by doing so, they had also undermined the participatory and egalitarian goals of the revolutionary agenda.

The Sandinista experiment in some ways resembled the original, Aristotelian conception of democracy as rule by the ordinary people, by the poor. For all of its flaws and its vulnerability, it represented a serious attempt to build a democratic alternative to polyarchy without rejecting some of its key principles, such as legal opposition and civic freedoms (see La Ramée and Polakoff 1997; Prevost and Vanden 1997). But the notion of popular democracy presents its own problems. To participate, citizens must join and be active, but constant involvement in politics can take its toll. How much time can people devote to democracy in their day-to-day lives—especially poor people who often must worry simply about survival? In the Cuban and Nicaraguan models, people are expected to participate in **mass organizations** that are represented in government and that become their main channels of access to government. More recently, President Chávez and his followers began an experiment with participatory democracy in the Bolivarian Republic of Venezuela. Chávez hoped that networks of grassroots communal councils would be engines of direct popular participation in government in Venezuela, but skeptics believe that these organizations will serve as little more than instruments of political control and not grassroots democracy.

Revolutionary leaders, such as Fidel Castro or Hugo Chávez, tend to see themselves as entrusted with a mission to transform a society, but this attitude can encourage the formation of a new elite that sees itself as guardians of the process. Transformation of political culture is a long, difficult process. How should revolutionary leaders react when the people themselves threaten to betray the democratic principles of the revolution? **Machismo**, racism, economic exploitation, violence, and myriad other social problems are hard to overcome, and even harder to overcome when a powerful neighbor wants you to fail.

As MacPherson (1972: 19) put it,

> If you believe, as the makers of all these revolutions have believed, that the very structure of the society, the dominant power relations in it, have made people less than fully human, have warped them into inability to realize or even to see their full human potentiality, what are you to do? How can the debasing society be changed by those who have themselves been debased by it? . . . The debased people are, by definition, incapable of reforming themselves *en masse*. They cannot be expected to pull themselves up by their own bootstraps.

This dilemma will not be resolved in this book. If it is ever overcome, it probably will be through continued experimentation by the world's people and not through classroom discussion or on the pages of a book. As for myself, as stated in the introduction, I believe democracy is a system whereby ordinary people in a society have the ability to participate as equals in the major decisions that shape the future of their nation and communities.

Perhaps it is worth emphasizing here that regardless of the discontent with liberal democracy, especially its failure to address social and economic exclusion, in the 1970s many Latin Americans living today experienced life under military regimes that literally terrorized major parts of the population and stripped citizens of all the protections from arbitrary repression that are associated with liberal democracy. And if capitalism has not fulfilled its promises, few Latin Americans see communism today as a viable alternative. If nothing else, in this minimal way liberal democracy retains some appeal.

For Review

How might a "popular democracy" differ from a polyarchy? Why might a popular democracy end up producing a new elite rather than the intended goal of more power in the hands of people?

Not Taking Democracy for Granted

As we examine Latin American politics, I urge you not to take democracy for granted. However much it seems that everyone agrees today that it is the *only* legitimate form of government, remember that this notion of universality is historically unprecedented. Furthermore, the definition of democracy is contested. Most political scientists define democracy in the real world as polyarchy and see capitalism and globalization as desirable and encouraging of democracy. This text also takes seriously doubts about this notion of democracy. In this way, I hope that you, like me, will find in studying the democratic condition in Latin America a rich and rewarding path to reflect on our own systems of government.

Discussion Questions

1. Do you think that democracy is mainly a matter of elections, of making sure that a government holds fair elections, respects civil rights, and applies laws impartially? Do you think that democracy can function in conditions of social and economic inequality?
2. Increasingly, in this age of globalization, it seems that democracy is becoming the only form of government that is accepted as legitimate. Do you think this is a good trend—or should we accept that there are other legitimate forms of state that are not democratic?
3. At this point in your readings, and presumably your class experience, if you were evaluating the condition of democracy for each country of the world, would you focus, as many indices do, on factors that affect "choice," such as elections, civil rights, and free markets, or would you include some attention to participation (e.g., rates of voting, extension of democracy to social and economic spheres of life) and to socioeconomic equality (e.g., wealth and income equality)? Gapminder, at gapminder.org, is a good place to find comparative data, and it comes with an easy-to-use interface to compare countries of the world on animated graphs.

Resources for Further Study

Reading: Robert Dahl's most accessible work for newcomers to the pluralist approach is the hard-to-find *Pluralist Democracy in the United States: Conflict and Consent* (Chicago: Rand-McNally, 1968), a textbook on U.S. politics but a good overall introduction to his ideas. C. B. MacPherson's very readable *Real World of Democracy* (CBC Enterprises,

1965) argues that liberal democracy is but one form of democracy. It is a good explanation of liberalism, and it is online at http://books.google.com/books.

Video and Film: Political philosopher Benjamin Barber and host Thomas Watson produced *The Struggle for Democracy*, a 10-part series produced for PBS and CBS in 1998, exploring the idea from the ancient Greeks until modern times. You can find a debate that took place at an Australian University on the topic, "Is Democracy Not for Everyone?," at http://fora.tv/2009/10/04/Is_Democracy_Not_For_Everyone.

On the Internet: See the AmericasBarometer Insights Series of the Latin America Public Opinion Project (LAPOP), located at Vanderbilt University: www.vanderbilt .edu/lapop/insights.php. Several different nongovernmental organizations rank the world's countries on democracy using liberal criteria. See, for example, World Audit at www.worldaudit.org/democracy.htm and Freedom House, which is partly funded by the U.S. government, at www.freedomhouse.org. One of the few rankings to include social and economic criteria is at http://democracyranking.org. Upside Down World, at http://upsidedownworld.org, carries news reports from a social movement perspective. As just mentioned, http://gapminder.org is a great place to go for comparative data and historical trends about economic and social progress in countries of the world.

2 The Few and the Many: Inequality in Latin American Politics

Focus Questions

▶ How much inequality is there in Latin America, and what are the social and historical roots of inequality in the region?

▶ How does inequality in Latin America relate to how the region's people evaluate democracy?

▶ What is social "exclusion"? Why has it become an issue in the region in recent decades?

▶ What is corporatism? Why do some political scientists think that for cultural and historical reasons it is more pronounced in Latin America than elsewhere?

HOW MUCH SHOULD we measure democratic progress in Latin America according to the model provided by **polyarchy**—that is, in terms of elections, rights, and rule of law, regardless of what kinds of social and economic conditions exist in a country? In other words, how much should the procedures, such as elections and checks and balances, of liberal democracy, and civil liberties, such as freedom of speech and equality before the law, be valued for themselves? Alternatively, how much should we judge democratic progress by the difference democracy has made (or not made) in people's lives, the real world where they live?

We also need to concern ourselves with how equality affects democracy. Long before Karl Marx expressed skepticism about liberal democracy, Aristotle thought democracy was best defined in terms of the distribution of power between the wealthy and ordinary people. He did not really think much of democracy, thinking it, like oligarchy, a perverted form of rule and not in the best interest of the whole society. But he thought that the difference between oligarchy and democracy was a question of which social class holds power:

> The real ground of the difference between oligarchy and democracy is poverty and riches. It is inevitable that any constitution should be an oligarchy if the rulers under it are rulers in virtue of riches, whether they are few or many; and it is equally inevitable that a constitution under which the poor rule should be a democracy.
> (quoted in Barker 1962: 116)

In those countries that suffered dictatorships and civil wars, Latin Americans might reasonably have expected a return to democracy to bring about a more egalitarian society. But though the record here is mixed, I think we can safely say that most Latin Americans were disappointed with democracy. Some progress was registered in the 2000s, but poverty and inequality remain issues throughout the region. And there are some ways in which the political culture can be related to the lack of progress.

Later in this book we will look much more closely at **neoliberalism** (see chapter 1, for now), which saw greater reliance on the market and less on the state in the quest for economic development. The many critics of neoliberalism believe it sharply increased inequality and poverty in Latin America, leading to the emergence of social movements that challenged what seemed to be a consensus about liberal democracy. In this chapter we will examine more broadly how social and economic inequality have shaped Latin America's political culture and social structures.

Inequality, Poverty, and Democracy

The last quarter of the twentieth century saw not only a wave of democratization in the form of elected civilian governments replacing military regimes but also a sharp increase in inequality and poverty. The Organization of American States (OAS) estimates conservatively that 39 percent of all households in Latin America and the Caribbean were poverty-stricken in the mid-1990s, up from 35 percent found 15 years earlier (see Lustig 1998). But this modest increase tells only part of the story. Industrial workers in most large countries saw their real wages plummet in the last part of the twentieth century. They fell 16 percent in Brazil and 45 percent in Mexico between the late 1970s and late 1990s. An International Labour Organization study (Van der Hoeven 2000) estimated that the percentage of Latin Americans who were self-employed in activities (e.g., selling toys, cosmetics, lottery tickets, and smuggled clothing on sidewalks) outside the formal labor force rose from 51.6 percent to 57.7 percent. These members of the **informal sector** inhabit the sprawling slums of Latin America's cities. Some have recently migrated from rural areas, but many workers and some middle-class people have fallen into their ranks as well.

During the earlier part of the twentieth century in most Latin American countries, the "many"—that is, the peasants, workers, and urban poor—gained influence in politics. (We review this in chapter 5.) They were incorporated into politics, in most cases between 1930 and 1960, under the leadership of **populist** leaders and political parties. Although populist politics was deeply flawed, in most countries (with important exceptions—e.g., parts of Central America), ordinary Latin Americans gained not only political rights but also important social rights and benefits, such as unemployment and retirement insurance, access to social welfare (education, affordable food, etc.), and union rights.

Another common way of stating this is to say that masses of Latin Americans were "incorporated" into the social and economic life. But the period between 1970 and 1990 saw them "de-incorporated." First, military regimes in most of the region smashed unions, outlawed political parties, and took away many of the social and economic rights achieved under populism (we look at this process in chapters 6 and 7). Employees who had once belonged to unions, built up pensions, were protected by health and safety laws, received unemployment compensation if discharged, were protected from arbitrary firings, and so on now found themselves working on their own account or unemployed with little hope of finding new work. Residents of poor neighborhoods and sometimes of middle-class areas saw services like regular garbage collection, access to health care, and schooling shrink.

When Latin America's economies began to grow again, even though these were years in which almost all countries were electoral democracies, those suffering this deterioration in their political, social, and economic conditions began to demand inclusion in a variety of movements, some of which we analyze in Part IV. In contrast to the 1980s, often called the "lost decade" in Latin America, when the economies of the region showed little (sometimes negative) growth rate, the 1990s were years of recovery and growth in most of Latin America. But the benefits of this growth were concentrated in just a few parts of the population. Politicians and academics began to speak of "**exclusion**" as an emerging issue. Beginning with the election of the populist Hugo Chávez in Venezuela in 1998, leftist politics and parties of the **Pink Tide** began having success by criticizing the economic model (based on free-market capitalism) that was delivering growth but not adequately addressing poverty and inequality.

We explore the meanings of "left" and "right" in more depth in chapters 12 and 13, but we should note here that the meaning of both terms can change over time as politicians, movements, and parties confront the particular problems of their era. The "right" today in Latin America is often identified with **neoliberalism**; the "left" with the Pink Tide and socialism and populism. However, these categories gloss over a vast range of ideologies, parties, and leaders on both sides. Any other definition I could offer would fail to take into account the enormous variety. Conflicts within each wing seem more intense at times than conflict between the two.

Table 2.1 lists the countries of Latin America (and some others) in the order they appear in World Audit's ranking of nations by how well they fit liberal criteria for democracy. In the last column, you will find for each country the **Gini coefficient** for income inequality. This statistic can vary from 0, which is perfect equality, where everyone has the same income, to 100, the maximum level of inequality, where one person has all the income. As you can see, Latin America's "democracies" tend to have indices well over 40—and many considerably higher. The U.S. record is really not much better than Latin America on the whole. Were we to look at inequality in the distribution of land and other forms of wealth, we would find even more discouraging news.

Equality, Poverty, and Attitudes about Democracy

Guillermo O'Donnell (1999: 196), an Argentine who was among the most influential comparative political scientists of his generation, once commented that "extensive poverty and deep social inequality are characteristics of Latin America that go back to the colonial period. We have not overcome these conditions; we have aggravated them." He connected this condition to a weakness in democracy.

> This weakness opens ample opportunity for manifold tactics of co-optation, selective repression, and political isolation. Democracy makes a difference, in that the poor may use their votes to support parties that are seriously committed to improving their lot. But, if elected, these parties face severe economic constraints. In addition they must take into account that determined pro-poor policies will mobilize concerns not only among the privileged but also among important segments of the middle class who, after their own sufferings through economic crises and adjustments, feel that it is they who deserve preferential treatment.
>
> (O'Donnell 1999: 197)

TABLE 2.1 Liberal Democracy Ranking in 2012 and Income Inequality (Gini index, 2006 and later)

Country	Democracy rank	Press freedom rank	Corruption rank	Gini index of inequality
Sweden	1	1	3	26
Denmark	1	6	1	25
Canada	10	17	9	32
United States	13	13	15	38
Uruguay	18	26	15	45.3
Portugal	19	11	25	35
Chile	20	35	18	52
Costa Rica	21	13	33	50.7
Poland	22	26	28	31
Spain	25	30	29	32
Japan	28	23	14	33
Taiwan	29	26	26	N/A
Israel	30	35	32	37
South Korea	31	35	32	31
Panama	37	60	79	51.9
Jamaica	40	13	62	46
Trinidad and Tobago	42	26	62	N/A
India	52	46	73	38
El Salvador	53	49	62	43.3
Brazil	54	57	53	54.7
Peru	55	55	62	48.1
Dominican Rep.	58	47	100	47.2
Bolivia	61	60	85	56
Argentina	63	73	85	44.5
Ecuador	68	94	81	49.3
Mexico	69	94	85	47.2
Paraguay	70	94	126	52.4
Colombia	83	76	75	55.9
Nicaragua	89	70	105	40.5
Thailand	97	100	81	39
Guatemala	103	62	100	55.6
Haiti	103	62	138	N/A
Honduras	108	100	116	57
China	118	135	62	42
Cuba	122	144	47	N/A
Venezuela	133	125	135	44.8
North Korea	150	149	148	N/A

Sources: WorldAudit.org (accessed May 13, 2014); *OECD Factbook* 2013; www.quandl.com/demography/gini-index-by-country (accessed May 13, 2014).

FIGURE 2.1   Responses to: "How fair do you think income distribution is in (country)?"

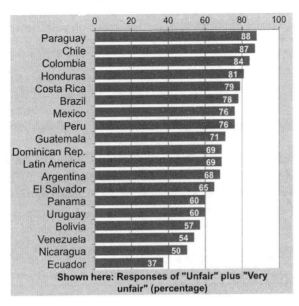

Shown here: Responses of "Unfair" plus "Very unfair" (percentage)

Latinobarómetro surveys give some indication of the interaction between inequality and democracy. As we can see from Figure 2.1, only about one-fifth of Latin Americans in most years believe that income distribution is "very fair" or "fair" in their country, and in some years and in many countries, the pattern varies. There is some evidence that poverty has declined in the post-2000 era (see Table 2.2), but again, the pattern varies considerably.

Some of the results in these figures are not very surprising. For example, only 12 percent of Hondurans answered "very fair or fair." Honduras is the only country in the region that has suffered an outright military coup recently; President Manuel Zelaya was seized and expelled by the military on June 28, 2009. Among Central Americans, data from the annual Latinobarómetro poll showed that in 2008 Hondurans also had the highest (48 percent) level of support for a military coup and the highest level of agreement that their country needs "a strong leader who does not need to be elected." Likely more relevant is the fact that nearly two-thirds of them live below the poverty line, nearly a quarter on less than US$1 per day. Seligson and Booth (2009: 5) found Hondurans had the highest ratio of citizens most dissatisfied—relative to those most satisfied—with democracy in the region. In the Latinobarómetro poll for 2013, Hondurans showed the lowest level of satisfaction with democracy in the region (see the snapshot Democracy in Honduras).

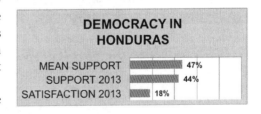

Although this data points toward the conclusion that inequality undermines democratic stability, we should take note that only 6 percent of Chileans, living in a country that ranks relatively high in terms of expression of support for democracy (see Figures 0.1 and 0.2 in the introduction), say that income distribution in their country is "fair" or "very fair"—lower than the percentage of Hondurans. In many ways Chile has been the model, not just in Latin America but in the world, of a country that has moved toward a free-market economy. This economic transition, however, was largely carried out first under a dictatorship (1973–1989) and then under a liberal democratic regime that was established with more checks on majority rule than in other cases of transitions from military to civilian rule (see chapters 8 and 13). This situation has become a major issue today in that country's

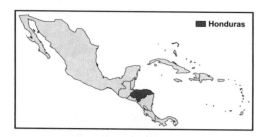

politics, with President Michelle Bachelet promising to convene a constitutional assembly to make changes in the rules of the political game so that her government can respond to large demonstrations protesting inequality.

In 2009, Chileans elected their first conservative president since the military years, but around the same period, a student movement protesting unequal treatment of public versus private education emerged and spread to other sectors. Inequality spurred the movement, but the spread to other sectors, the persistence of protest, and the significant fall in the Chilean perceptions of fairness may have had something to do with the change in political leadership. Indeed, the 2011 Latinobarómetro report (p. 35) found a drop of 26 percentage points—from 55 to 29 percent—in Chileans agreeing that the country is governed for the common welfare of all versus for powerful groups.

Figure 2.2 and Table 2.2 show the trajectory of economic change in the region. One can see that in the decade of the 1990s, the first full decade of democratic government for most of the region, the percentage of those living in poverty and indigence hardly fell. The absolute number of poor actually increased. Average real wages increased, but far below the rate of increase of gross domestic product. It is not likely that electoral democracy *caused* this pattern, but certainly those who had hoped it would bring more fairness have cause to be disappointed.

We should not overlook the simple fact that overall Latin American society remains highly unequal and poor. The causes of this condition are intensely debated, especially between those who use a framework called "modernization" and those who use one called "dependency theory." We will look closely at these and other conflicting perspectives in chapter 6, after we have charted the impact of colonialism, the interplay of foreign and domestic actors in the first century after independence, and the twentieth-century attempt to "catch up" to already industrialized countries.

For Review

What is meant by those who claim that the 1970s and the 1980s were marked by the "de-incorporation" of large numbers of people in Latin America and by "exclusion"? How have inequality and issues of democracy been linked in the cases of Honduras and Chile?

Race and Ethnic Inequality

So far, we have concentrated on Latin America's poverty and economic inequality, which have resulted in large sectors of the society being marginalized from dignified, sustainable

FIGURE 2.2   Latin America: Poverty and Indigence, 1980–2012 (Percentages and millions of persons)

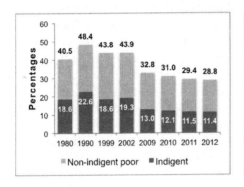 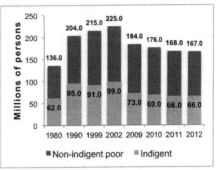

TABLE 2.2   Real Wages and Economic Growth, 1980–2010 (percentages)

	1981–1990	*1991–1997*	*1998–2002*	*2003–2010*	*1980–2010*
Change in GDP	14.4	26.2	8.9	35.6	113.2
Change in real wages					
Latin America	−37.5	14.9	3.1	14.3	−15.3
South America*	−24.0	5.0	−1.9	18.7	−7.1
Central America	−49.1	19.5	7.2	0.6	−34.4
Mexico	−22.1	1.7	20.2	7.3	2.2
Brazil	N/A	6.0	−11.9	1.5	N/A
Average annual rates					
Change in GDP	1.4	3.4	1.7	3.9	2.6
Change in real wages					
Latin America	−6.5	2.0	0.6	1.7	−0.6
South America*	−3.8	0.7	−0.4	2.2	−0.2
Central America	−9.2	2.6	1.4	0.1	−1.4
Mexico	−3.5	0.2	3.8	1.0	0.1
Brazil	N/A	0.8	-2.5	0.2	N/A

Source: Economic Commission for Latin America and the Caribbean (ECLAC), on the basis of data from CEPALSTAT.
* South America includes Brazil.

living conditions. However, social class is not the only source of exclusion from full benefits of citizenship. Race, ethnicity, and gender differences are also sources of exclusion.

Just as Europeans and North Americans often regard Latin cultures as inferior, so also have many in the Latin American ruling class viewed Indians and the descendants of slaves as less than equal. Under Spanish and Portuguese colonialism, Indian and African peoples were often regarded as children to be baptized and brought into the Christian family, all the while, of course, providing labor for their masters. After independence, for decades many new Latin American countries maintained laws reserving important positions in government, the military, and the Catholic Church for people who could prove their blood was "pure"—that is, "uncontaminated" with Indian or African ancestry. Intellectuals and government officials later in the century promoted European immigration to "improve" the genetic stock and to overcome the presumed cultural deficiencies inherent to the tropical climates.

The deep economic inequalities in Latin America are felt more intensely because of their relationship to race and ethnic patterns. Simply put, lighter-skinned descendants of Europeans tend to occupy the ranks of the upper class; Indians and descendants of African slaves tend to occupy the bottom rungs; and mixed-race people tend to be in the middle. But we must caution here that the relationship is not one-to-one, and in several ways race relations have been less bitter and more flexible in Latin America, for reasons we explore more closely in chapter 3.

Latin Americans, especially those with darker skin, have experienced racism in the United States and Europe. Many recent immigrants are excluded from legal rights by their undocumented status. This form of discrimination up north draws protests from Latin America, but it exists in the south as well. Guatemalans suffer political exclusion in Mexico; Bolivians share the same fate in Argentina; Haitians face pogroms periodically in the Dominican Republic; and many other examples could be cited as well.

Issues regarding race and gender to some extent also involve identity—the question as to just what defines a person as "Latin," "Brazilian," "Colombian," "Chilean," and so on. We live in a world where that question is answered by lines on a map defining borders between **nation-states**. For large numbers of Latin Americans, the existence of territorial states ruled by predominantly European-speaking peoples is nothing they or their ancestors have never fully accepted. Many indigenous people still feel like a conquered people and are demanding changes not only in the distribution of benefits but also in how they are treated and regarded by their fellow citizens. Many of African descent now demand government action to remedy the inheritance of slavery. In some countries, descendants of Asians also suffered from historical exploitation and captive labor. Meanwhile, other Latin Americans insist that to make distinctions by race or ancestry not only is impractical but also sows dangerous divisions in societies that have struggled to find identity in the idea that all are part of one common "new race."

The latter position is often called the "myth of *mestizaje*" (loosely translated, the "mixed-race myth"). Latin Americans often contend that racial prejudice has been surmounted because intermarriage and less rigid legal and social hierarchies have permitted more assimilation among races than in the United States. Anyone who has visited Latin America will acknowledge that cultural and racial divides seem much less rigid there than in the north. Latin Americans take great pride in seeing themselves as sharing a birthright, all members of **la raza**, a "new race" that has given the world distinctive achievements in music, dance, literature, art, and so forth; think, for example, of Latin music. These accomplishments do not mean, however, that racism has been eradicated. The last part of the twentieth century saw the emergence of movements inspired to some degree by the great civil rights movements in the United States and southern Africa. These movements often seek to address economic inequalities linked to historic discrimination and persistent racial prejudices, and they encounter critics, especially from those who identify more with European and North American cultural norms.

Latin America's "first Americans" (as they are known in Canada) have been victims of prejudice and exploitation. In a few countries, the indigenous population may be a majority, but few public officials or economic elites have come from their ranks. Their ways of thinking, speaking, and doing things are often regarded as primitive. Consider, for example, the argument made by Andrés Sosa Pietri, a former president of Venezuela's national oil company, for why the country should leave the Organization of the Petroleum Exporting Countries (OPEC), whose members are all Third World countries.

> Our country never was a colony, not of Spain or any other power. We are sons of the transcendental occurrence, without historical precedence, that some call the "Discovery" and others, the "Encounter." We were a practically unpopulated territory were it not for a few small indigenous tribes that live (and some continue to do so) in a "state of nature," that is, precariously in the midst of a more advanced civilization. Our nation was made, founded and forged after the Discovery and as a corollary of it. Almost all of us have to a greater or lesser degree European blood and are undoubtedly, from a cultural point of view, a European nation, although new and with specific, individual characteristics. Our language, our main religion, our ethical values, our morality, our legal and political institutions, all come from our European heritage.
>
> (Sosa Pietri 1998)

To Sosa Pietri, Venezuela, despite having been governed by Spain for 300 years, was never a colony! He was horrified by the new Venezuelan constitution drafted in 1999 because (among other things) it granted a degree of autonomy and independence to Venezuela's Indian peoples:

> We Venezuelans, who take pride in being an amalgamation of races, rooted in Western culture, now find ourselves in two categories: Those who came before, the "indigenous," "ethnics," and those who came later, "immigrants." . . . We presumed we were a mixed race nation. We were proud of being a society with open doors for good, working people with good customs, independent of their [national] culture.
>
> (Sosa Pietri 1998)

The motives for Sosa Pietri's view are not hard to discern. As an oilman, his perspective is that the national laws exist to protect and facilitate the right of the oil companies to drill and find more oil, the lifeblood of the Venezuelan economy. As the last frontiers in remote parts of Latin America (in its highlands, deserts, and rainforests) recede, in the face of migrants, oil and mining companies, missionaries, and soldiers, indigenous people have organized themselves throughout the hemisphere and won, in some cases, considerable political autonomy. However, because they live within the territorial boundaries of a nation dominated by European values, including a system of private ownership of land, the indigenous population finds itself continually in conflict with governments—democratic or dictatorial. Should they have to respect a majority decision to open their territories to foreign investors? A majority of whom? From Sosa's perspective, acknowledging the right of ethnic minorities to protect their land from such incursions is undemocratic and a compromise of Venezuela's national sovereignty. From the perspective of Venezuela's Indians, this is the first time in 500 years that they have achieved any control over their own affairs. Nothing, from their perspective, could be more "democratic," unless it was full sovereignty.

In 1993, Latin American anthropologists meeting in Barbados declared, "Democracy, as the philosophy of a Western social system, is centered on the individual and excludes collectivities like indigenous peoples." The new, fragile democracies deny indigenous people the ability to organize their linguistic, social, economic, and cultural affairs because these systems are "still monopolized by the interests of conservative sectors who in their majority descend from old European and colonial elites" (Barbados Group 1993).

The distinctively indigenous perspective on democracy is expressed in the Declaration of Quito, a statement issued in 1990 at a hemispheric meeting of Indian peoples called together to respond to and protest plans to celebrate the 500th anniversary of Columbus's "discovery" of the Americas for the Europeans. Indian organizations from all over the hemisphere declared,

> Our organizational, political, economic and production forms, in fact, all the elements that form our cultures, are rooted in, and oriented by, communitarianism. Out of this we believe that the ownership of the land should be collective . . . It is this value of the communitarian by which we understand the meaning of that which is human and the possibility of each and every one of us to achieve a harmonious life.
>
> (Declaration of Quito 1990)

Although indigenous peoples find the Western concept of territorial ownership and territorial states alien to their experience and values, they are forced to contend with a world dominated by Westerners. In defending their lands and communities, Indians are forced to speak in terms of ownership and sovereignty. To defend their right to construct alternative, communitarian systems, they declare their objectives in terms of "rights," "ownership," "self-determination," and so on. Still, indigenous **communitarianism** remains a major source of ideological inspiration for an alternative to liberal democracy in Latin America today.

Any overall assessment of democracy must take into account the very complex question of how greatly skin color matters in determining the distribution of wealth and power in Latin America today. How does this play out concretely? Consider one example, the rise of Alberto Fujimori, a Peruvian of Japanese descent, to become president of his country in 1990. His Asian ancestry might have been considered a disadvantage given the small percentage of Asians in Peru, where half the population self-identifies as Indian. However, he consistently ran strongest among rural Indians precisely because of his Asiatic appearance. The evident disdain for the predominantly white oligarchy made him more attractive to descendants of the Incas, who have been dominated by Europeans for 500 years.

Since 1990 Latin America has seen a surge of social movements addressing issues of race and ethnicity, and this goes far in explaining why more leaders with African and indigenous heritages are appearing. This is another reason for the appearance of the **Pink Tide** after 1998, the year after Hugo Chávez, whose physical appearance in many ways embodied racial and ethnic mixing, was elected president of Venezuela, followed in 2002 by Lula in Brazil. In 2006, Evo Morales, an Aymara speaker, achieved the presidency in his native Bolivia, with his base largely in the country's indigenous majority.

For Review

What is the "myth of *mestizaje*"? How might Latin Americans of European origin—or who identify more with their European heritage—differ from those with indigenous or African roots in how they understand their own history?

Women, Gender, and Exclusion

Women are a majority on the planet today, and this fact, plus disadvantages facing women in almost all societies, means that they are disproportionately part of the "many" who were de-incorporated, or excluded, in the last part of the twentieth century.

Democracy is "gendered" in several senses. Although there have been notable advances in recent decades—including in Latin America, which has seen the rise of several women to presidencies—women remain less wealthy and powerful than men in proportion to their numbers in the population. As those most often responsible for care of families, women disproportionately bear the costs of economic deprivation and inequality. As in other cultures, men often tend to regard women as more emotional and less rational—certainly ironic, given that outside the region both Latin men and women are both often stereotyped as more "fiery" and emotional. Also, like in many other male-dominated cultures, women's "proper" domain of influence is often defined to be "domestic." This does not mean, however, that Latin Americans are uniformly more sexist than most people of most other cultures. For example, Latin Americans are more likely to elect women to their legislatures than most of the rest of the world (United Nations 1999: 142–145). By 2010, Chile, Brazil and Argentina had already elected women to be president—whereas in the United States no woman has ever been nominated by a major political party.

According to the Gender Equality Observatory of the United Nations Economic Commission for Latin America, in 2012 women had attained a little more than 23 percent of seats in the lower house in the national legislatures in the region. But there was tremendous variation. In Brazil, for example, women held only 9 percent of seats; the three highest percentages were for Costa Rica (39 percent), Nicaragua (40 percent), and Cuba (46 percent). The same report (2012) found that although rates of poverty and indigence have fallen overall in Latin America and the Caribbean, the proportion of women living in such conditions has actually risen. Although many more women than men have no independent wage or salaries of their own, in the seven countries studied women actually worked more than men, from a minimum of 8 hours more per week in Brazil to a maximum of 23 hours more per week in Uruguay—the latter regarded as having one of the most liberal democratic cultures in Latin America.

Everywhere in the world, politicians seek popular support on the basis of beliefs about sexual mores, family matters, life cycle issues (e.g., abortion and euthanasia), and the kinds of jobs suitable for men versus women. Leftist movements and governments often favor reproductive rights, as well as greater educational and job opportunities for women. Such changes are often resisted by religious conservatives and exploited by right-wing movements that link economic difficulties or violence to moral decay or erosion of "family values." Conservative forces often rally opposition to reform or revolutionary change by mobilizing resistance to changes in the traditional relationship between men and women. In the face of such opposition, even revolutionary governments put women's issues on the backburner, much to the dismay of women who have fought in their ranks. The same happens with other gender issues. Homophobia (hatred and fear of gays) is hardly limited to Latin America, but sometimes it seems especially virulent in a society from which we derive the slang term *macho*. Still, some Latin American societies defy the stereotype. Brazil, for example, is known for its liberal attitudes about sexuality.

In times of war and economic distress, women tend to suffer the most because of the burden of family responsibilities. A common form of protest against economic conditions is the ***cacerolazo***. This form of protest is characterized by the massive and loud banging of empty pots at an appointed hour, mostly by women. The earliest use of *cacerolazo* was during the administration (1970–1973) of socialist Salvador Allende in Chile, when the United States worked with Allende's opponents to "make the economy scream," as former secretary of state Henry Kissinger put it. Women, mostly from the middle class, created a deafening din by clanging empty pots along their parade route and in their neighborhoods. The tactic was repeated by middle-class opponents of Venezuelan president Chávez between 2001 and 2004 and again during protests against his successor, President Nicolás Maduro. However, *cacerolazos* have also been used against targets other than the left. In December 1991, Argentine women used them to protest the freezing of savings accounts by banks during an economic protest.

Women were mobilized as part of the opposition to the Sandinista revolution in Nicaragua. During the 1980s, the revolutionary government tried to defend itself against the *contras* (right-wing guerrillas organized and financed by the U.S. Central Intelligence Agency) by implementing a military draft (see chapter 16). The terrorist tactics of the *contras* did little to make them popular, but the draft and the toll in deaths and injuries cost the Sandinistas valuable political capital. Mothers of the draftees organized resistance that contributed to the eventual defeat of the Sandinistas in the election of 1990. The opposition candidate in that election was Violeta Chamorro, widow of a newspaper editor killed by the dictatorship overthrown by the Sandinistas. Her appeal, ***marianismo***, was based in part on her image as a mother who could heal the rifts in Nicaragua, seen as a family divided.

Gender divisions can work against dictators and market democracies too. After Allende's overthrow in Chile, the wife of General Pinochet attempted to garner support for the dictatorship by promoting programs to teach poor women to repair clothing or stretch meager budgets, but the program had little success. The severe hardships imposed on the poorest Chileans induced women to organize soup kitchens in the poorest *barrios*. They raised money and consciousness about the dictatorship by making *arpilleras*, colorful textiles that dramatized disappearances.

The maternal role deeply influenced the development of a human rights movement in the region. Mothers felt most deeply the loss of loved ones kidnapped or murdered by the harsh military dictatorships of the 1970s and 1980s. During Argentina's harsh military rule in the 1970s, mothers known as the Madres de la Plaza de Mayo (Mothers of the Plaza de Mayo) were the first to stand up against the torturers and death squads. The community organizations that had begun mainly as ways to survive evolved into movements offering mass resistance to the dictatorships.

When the generals gave way to elected civilian governments, the economic policies that generated women's political movements often remained in place. With the return of "democracy" also came the return of traditional politicians, who tend to be male. However, a major breakthrough for women occurred in Chile in 2006 when the Socialist Party candidate, Michelle Bachelet (mentioned earlier), who had been tortured under Pinochet and had then served as defense minister under President Ricardo Lagos (2000–2005), won a four-year term as president.

Gender politics refers not only to **patriarchy** and women's rights. Paradoxically, considering the macho culture in the region, gays, lesbian, bisexual, and transgender peoples have emerged from the shadows. One might think that their struggle has largely been with cultural conservatives and Catholic bishops, but like women they have had to deal with gender prejudices across society. James Green (2012) tells of how prejudice against those with "homosexual desires" manifested itself within the left in the protests in the 1960s and 1970s. Although prejudice has hardly disappeared, the personal relationships between this sector and heterosexuals in struggles against the military dictatorship brought the LGBT movement more into the open, as they became part of the array of social movements that helped float Lula to the Brazilian presidency on the Pink Tide.

Machismo surfaces in political discourse (style of speech) even among leaders who have a progressive record in many respects. The late Hugo Chávez is a good example. The Venezuelan president aligned with women's organizations in demanding that the new Bolivarian constitution of 1999 have gender-neutral language. Thus, the constitution refers to "citizens" not with an all-inclusive masculine word, *ciudadanos*, but with the masculine and feminine forms of the word: *ciudadanos y ciudadanas*. And his government implemented many new programs aimed at addressing exclusion among the country's female population. His record on issues of concern to the LGBT population was mixed; he expressed no approval of legal rights but disapproved of repression.

However, Chávez also showed little consciousness about gender when he said of Condoleezza Rice, then secretary of state in the Bush administration, "Remember, little girl, I'm like the thorn tree that flowers on the plain . . . Don't mess with me, girl." In his 2012 campaign Chávez kept silent while the popular host of a program on state television spread rumors that Henrique Capriles, the opposition candidate for president, had been caught in a sexual liaison with a young man. Capriles denied being gay but, to his credit, also said he saw no problem if the rumor had been true. However, the opposition to Chávez did not always behave so responsibly. None of its members objected when an anonymous person, who was later discovered to be a prominent lawyer, sent women's panties to the male chiefs of the country's armed forces. "If you don't act promptly in an organized and effective way," the pamphleteer declared, "then you should put on these panties we're sending you. From that moment on, we will call you panty-wearers and cowards."

For Review

Why might women in Latin America as a group see things differently from men in terms of politics? How does Latin America's record in presidential voting for women compare to the United States? How are attitudes about gender and power reflected in political language (discourse)?

▉ Corporatism: A Latin American Way of Politics?

One way that modern market societies attempt to reconcile conflict between different social classes and groups is through **corporatism**. As we briefly discussed in chapter 1, corporatism seems to have especially deep roots in Latin American political culture.

In some ways, corporatism seems to contradict the pluralist view of democracy because corporatism as an ideology advocates that the state take responsibility for regulating the formation of interest groups—whereas pluralists believe that the right of individuals to voluntarily form groups to advocate and defend their interests is at the heart of democracy. The best example of this difference relates to relations between employers and workers. For the pluralists, workers have the right to form unions and also dissolve unions through processes ("collective bargaining rights") defined by law. Employers in different economic sectors may form organizations (e.g., chambers of commerce; organizations grouping different kinds of enterprises, such as insurance companies, steel corporations, and so on) and, similarly, have the right to form and dissolve organizations. Corporatists go further: through laws, workers are required to join unions, and unions are grouped into higher-level federations; employers are required to join "syndicates" of companies in the same economic sector. When it is time to negotiate a contract, the state sits at the bargaining table to represent the larger interest of society.

Howard Wiarda (1981) and some other political scientists in this school of thought see corporatism not as a perversion of pluralism but as a theory more consonant with Latin American traditions. They argue that behind the facade of liberal constitutions lies a society based on deeply rooted practices such as *compadrazgo*. The traditional emphasis on family and solidarity among friends and relatives dictates a different style of economic and political life, they argue. Economic development requires that the nation put aside conflicts that weaken the interest of the nation as a whole. In a society with tremendous gaps between rich and poor, the state must take an active role in improving the condition of the poor and ensuring that benefits of economic growth are shared.

Corporatist practices extend beyond labor relationships. For example, in Mexico, until recently almost all peasants belonged to a single Confederación Nacional de Campesinos (National Confederation of Peasants—CNC) formally linked to the Partido Revolucionario Institucional (PRI), which controlled the presidency and monopolized Mexican politics from 1928 to 2000. The CNC's access to the state bureaucracy meant that it was the privileged channel for distributing benefits critical to the well-being of peasants—land, credit, subsidies, transportation, water projects, and so on. Peasants received a piece of the economic pie, but they had little real influence over the leaders and groups representing them. They depended on the CNC more than the CNC depended on them. The leaders of the federation kept their jobs because they faithfully protected the interests of the PRI and not because they defended the interests of the peasants.

Corporatists justify this relation between the state and society because they believe that competing interests can and should be harmonized and be made to serve the interest of the nation as a whole. In contrast, liberal democrats admire individualism, competition in the market, and a state that respects the autonomy and independence of groups in civil society. Marxists believe that class conflict is inevitable and reject the view that the state can reconcile capitalists' and workers' interests with one another.

Both photos are taken in San Miguel de Allende, Mexico. Do you think that their lives are in any way connected to each other?

Corporatist philosophy often sees the relationship of the state to society much like the relationship of the head to the rest of the body. Just as all the organs of the body have a specific role and must function together for the benefit of the whole person, so too, according to corporatists, the different parts of society must work together. They believe that governments need to reconcile social and economic conflicts to make progress toward common goals. Corporatists advocate creation of official channels of representation for groups organized according to their function. European fascism was predicated on this idea, but most corporatists are not fascists. For example, corporatism is commonly found in papal encyclicals and other religion-based theories of justice that urge the state to defend society's weaker members. This example is especially relevant here because Catholic social doctrines have been influential in Latin America. A good example can be found in the social thought of the late Pope John Paul II and his successor, Pope Francis (see the Punto de Vista).

Like most "isms," corporatism is a social theory and not just an ideology. Pluralist thinkers use the term sometimes in warning against allowing organizations, once established, to gain a monopoly over group life. This happens when an organization, even if founded with little involvement of the government, gains an advantage over any rivals that later emerge because they already have won privileged access to the state (Schmitter 1974). For example, once a national organization exists to represent the interests of teachers, it is hard for a new organization to take its place.

To take again the example of labor unions, a corporatist might advocate state subsidies of labor unions as a desirable way to ensure that workers have representation and influence in the system. In fact, in Latin America, it has been quite common for unions, often through their association with political parties, to receive subsidies, to be given a share of power in management (e.g., the right to fill some percentage of jobs), and to benefit from laws requiring membership and facilitating collection of dues. Usually, there are strings attached. For example, laws typically have required unions to get certification from the labor ministry showing that certain requirements have been met before they can legally strike. Pluralists would contend that such subsidies and requirements undermine the relationship between union members and officials. Officially or unofficially, they give the state and political parties too much control over leadership and decision-making (Collier 1995), and they limit political competition. If a rival organization attempts to replace the already existing, well-connected organization favored by the government, politically connected bureaucrats can help maintain the status quo. A rival labor union may find its petitions dismissed on technical grounds or because of tiny discrepancies. Perhaps the government will work with employers to negotiate a highly favorable contract just before a crucial vote.

I witnessed an example of union co-optation while doing research on labor unions in Ciudad Guayana, in eastern Venezuela. In 1984, workers in a small but important company, Hornos Eléctricos de Venezuela (HEVENSA), which produced manganese and ferro-silicate for the nearby steel industry, voted to replace its union leadership. The workers were unhappy with the conditions in the plant, where they worked with hazardous materials in 125-degree (F) heat. The management hired a powerful local labor leader as its personnel director, a clear conflict of interest. He proceeded to fire the new labor leaders, provoking a strike, which in turn resulted in more firings. The National Confederation of Venezuelan Workers, closely associated with the Acción Democrática party, invited a few of the rebel workers to Caracas to be "trained" to assume positions in the labor movement. Some accepted, and others declined, dividing the strikers. After one year of struggle, workers settled the dispute, were reemployed, and received back pay. A victory? Only 30 of the original 108 workers made it through the long struggle and received benefits from the settlement (Hellinger 1991: 184–188). Corporatism is not found only in Latin America. Even in the United States, where individualism, consumerism, and suspicion of government are deeply ingrained, organized ("special") interest groups interact with each other and with government in ways that seem to be permanent. A revolving door among the government regulators, lobby groups, and Congress gives privileged access to some, while limiting the access of others. Japan and Germany are very different culturally, but in both, the state took on a leadership role in the process of industrialization and labor relation, and both are known for accepting corporatism as a positive feature of their societies, much in contrast to the more market-oriented societies of the United States and Great Britain.

In its more extreme forms, corporatism seems to merge with **fascism**, where the state is glorified as the supreme expression of the nation, and citizens are forced into syndicates and official state organizations (youth, women, etc.). The fascist state seeks to organize society completely from the top down. In Italy, France, and Spain in the 1930s, fascist states were one-party regimes marked by extreme militarism. After 1968, the military government in Brazil attempted to implement a variation on this theme by abolishing all the old political parties and permitting only two parties to contest elections and hold offices. One was an official party of government (the Alliance for National Renovation, ARENA) and the other an official party of opposition (Brazilian Democratic Movement, MDB). Ultimately, however, the generals eventually gave up and under pressure permitted parties to form freely again in a "transition to democracy" after 1982 (see chapter 8).

There is a tension today between corporatism and the goals of social movements that have formed in Latin America over the past 30 years. As we shall see in chapter 11, some of these movements emerged in resistance to authoritarianism and in reaction to increased economic inequality, which they often attribute to **neoliberalism**. However, they also have shown resistance to being subordinated to the interests of politicians, parties, and government. Take note: it is not necessarily the case that they have no relationship to political action or that they prefer the economy to be less guided by government and more market-oriented. However, they want to retain their autonomy, even in relationship to the political organizations and policies they support.

But it can be difficult to achieve this goal. Consider two cases, Brazil and Venezuela. In Brazil, a huge movement of landless workers, the MST, has demanded land reform and has had some success. In doing so, however, it has supported the presidential candidates of the country's Workers' Party. Not only does the MST help determine who settles on redistributed land, but it also is instrumental in administering the financial resources to make new settlements viable—50 million dollars by one account (Mark 2001). So far, most observers think the MST has done relatively well in balancing autonomy versus cooperation, but there is an evident danger of the MST becoming over time an intermediary funneling resources from the top down—corporatist style—rather than a bottom-up movement pressuring the state to keep its promises.

In Venezuela, the rise of Hugo Chávez to the presidency largely can be attributed to his ability to crystallize the hopes of a surge of participatory movements and organizations that emerged in the 1980s and 1990s. These movements were instrumental in rescuing Chávez when they took to the streets to reverse a coup that removed him from power for 48 hours in April 2002. Subsequently, Chávez instituted a number of programs attempting to directly funnel super-profits from the country's oil industry to local communal councils. These programs helped in many ways to reduce poverty in the country, and the councils were often led by ordinary residents of poor neighborhoods—often women and others who came out of these social movements. However, in Venezuela's volatile, highly conflictive politics, these leaders often found themselves diverting their efforts to supporting candidates of Chávez's United Socialist Party of Venezuela (PSUV), which despite its founder's intention included many career politicians (García-Guadilla 2011; Schiller 2011). This combination of a powerful state in control of the country's main source of wealth (oil exports) and the constant battle by Chávez (and after his death, President Nicolás Maduro) to keep the opposition at bay has led many critics, including many from within the PSUV, to fear that the old patterns of top-down corporatism have been reasserting themselves.

For Review

How does a corporatist image of the role of the state differ from one typical of a liberal democratic or pluralist perspective? Why do some Latin Americans think corporatism is stronger in Latin America than in the United States? Why might there be a tension between corporatism and participatory social movements?

PUNTO DE VISTA: CORPORATISM—THE POPES ON CAPITALISM

Although the influence of Catholicism varies in Latin America from country to country and also coexists with strains of Protestantism, indigenous and African belief systems, and other religious traditions (Jewish, Muslim, and so forth), Latin America is the home of a majority of the world's Catholics, and what popes think about issues of economic justice has some significant weight. Though not the only influence in the Church (**laissez-faire** capitalism and even Marxism in the form of **liberation theology** have influence as well), the influence of **corporatism** has most strongly marked the social doctrines emanating from the Vatican.

John Paul II, a native of Poland and pope from 1978 until 2005, was stridently anti-communist but also skeptical about free-market capitalism. He lashed out at unbridled "savage capitalism" on a visit to Cuba in 1994, criticizing concentrated ownership and control of wealth, whether private capitalists or the state is responsible. The pope had written earlier that

> each person is fully entitled to consider himself a part-owner of the great workbench at which he is working with everyone else. A way towards that goal could be found by associating labor with the ownership of capital, as far as possible, and by producing a wide range of intermediate bodies with economic, social and cultural purposes; they would be bodies enjoying real autonomy with regard to the public powers, pursuing their specific aims in honest collaboration with each other and in subordination to the demands of the common good, and they would be living communities both in form and in substance, in the sense that the members of each body would be looked upon and treated as persons and encouraged to take an active part in the life of the body.
>
> (quoted in Perone 2000)

More recently, Pope Francis, the first pope from Latin America (Argentina, specifically), addressed inequality directly in his 2014 encyclical *Evangelii Gaudium*, though he has been less specific so far about solutions than was John Paul in his Cuba speech. Said Francis,

> The need to resolve the structural causes of poverty cannot be delayed, not only for the pragmatic reason of its urgency for the good order of society, but because society needs to be cured of a sickness which is weakening and frustrating it, and which can only lead to new crises. Welfare projects, which meet certain urgent needs, should be considered merely temporary responses. As long as the problems of the poor are not radically resolved by rejecting the absolute autonomy of markets and financial speculation and by attacking the structural causes of inequality, no solution will be found for the world's problems or, for that matter, to any problems. Inequality is the root of social ills.

Though he represents a religion often criticized for its stance on women's issues, Francis related economic **exclusion** to gender: "Doubly poor are those women who endure situations of exclusion, mistreatment and violence, since they are frequently less able to defend their rights. Even so, we constantly witness among them impressive examples of daily heroism in defending and protecting their vulnerable families."

The papal critiques of capitalism are similar to that of the first pope to address modern social issues. In 1891, Pope Leo XIII was worried about the rise of Marxism and socialism in Europe. In *Rerum Novarum* he condemned socialism and class warfare and defended private property, warning that it would be a mistake to adopt Marxist analysis.

He denied that "class is naturally hostile to class, and that the wealthy and the working men are intended by nature to live in mutual conflict. So irrational and so false is this view that the direct contrary is the truth." He went on then to make a comparison frequently found in corporatist thought. (Keep in mind that the word "corporatism" is derived from the Latin world "corpus," meaning "body.")

> Just as the symmetry of the human frame is the result of the suitable arrangement of the different parts of the body, so in a State is it ordained by nature that these two classes should dwell in harmony and agreement, so as to maintain the balance of the body politic. Each needs the other: capital cannot do without labor, nor labor without capital. Mutual agreement results in the beauty of good order, while perpetual conflict necessarily produces confusion and savage barbarity.

Leo's ideas contributed to the eventual emergence of Christian Democratic political parties, which continue to be influential in some Latin American countries.

Corporatism is not just a religious idea. Juan Perón, president of Argentina from 1946 to 1955, championed an ideology that he called *justicialismo* (Ameringer 2009). Perón condemned both free-market capitalism and socialism. *Justicialismo*'s cardinal principles were to be "social justice, economic independence, and political sovereignty." He defined "the just state as one in which each class or element [like the human body] exercises its functions and its special abilities for the benefit of all."

Perón married corporatism to nationalism, a marriage uncomfortably close to the philosophy of European fascism. Perón greatly admired the Italian fascist dictator Benito Mussolini. He told the Argentine Congress in 1950,

Perhaps in our land there remains an old exploiter of human labor who cannot conceive of a socially just Argentine nation; or some astute Marxist in the pay of foreign interests to whom our *justicialismo* is not convenient because we have caused him to lose all the arguments he previously had; there remains perhaps some old foreign company that dreams of [the past] when traitors could profit and [that] does not want to know that we proclaim this new Argentina to be free.

Referring to communists and anarchists, whom Perón saw as competitors for working-class support, he added, "Perhaps there remains some group of men without a country and without a flag who does not want to see the nation politically sovereign . . . But no Argentine of good will can deny agreement with the basic principles of our doctrine without first renouncing the dignity of being Argentine" (Perón 1950).

Certainly, Pope John Paul II was not a fascist; nor is Pope Francis. Catholic thought is not fascist simply because it is corporatist. But corporatism is found in fascist ideology. Italian fascism in the era (1922–1943) of Benito Mussolini crushed unions and opposition parties in the name of social cohesion. "It is the State which educates its citizens in civic virtue, gives them a consciousness of their mission and welds them into unity," Mussolini once said.

Perón never proclaimed himself a fascist; unlike Mussolini, he built a working-class base and found himself opposed by the military. But the Argentine leader's philosophy, policies, and use of repression resembled fascism enough to raise the specter and make one wonder whether corporatism itself is compatible with democracy.

Point/Counterpoint

Does corporatism, as found in *justicialismo*, offer an alternative democratic ideology to liberalism and socialism?

  a. If you answered yes, how would you respond to those who argue that corporatism has been part of fascist ideology?

  b. If you answered no, how do you respond to Perón and the popes John Paul and Leo, all of whom gave reasons that a corporatist philosophy was preferable to liberalism or Marxism, theories based on social conflict?

For more information

A short explanation of corporatism and an argument that it is well-suited to Latin America is Howard Wiarda, "The Political Sociology of a Concept: Corporatism and the 'Distinct Tradition,'" *The Americas* 66, no. 1 (July 2009): 81–106. A broader examination of corporatism is Roland Czada, "Corporativism (Corporatism)," *International Encyclopedia of Political Science* (London: Sage, 2001), available at www.academia.edu/555951/Corporativism_Corporatism. You can find Francis's pronouncement on capitalism and inequality in *Evangelii Gaudium* (2013; www.vatican.va/holy_father/francesco/apost_exhortations/documents/papa-francesco_esortazione-ap_20131124_evan-gelii-gaudium_en.html#The_Church%E2%80%99s_teaching_on_social_questions).

Liberation Theology—Religion Addresses Inequality

Liberation theology emerged out of forces unleashed by the great Vatican II council called by Pope John XXIII in 1962. Though less committed to change than John XXIII, Pope John Paul II ratified the notion that Catholicism would have to address the concerns of the Third World, where a majority of its faithful lived. Latin American bishops at Medellín, Colombia, and at Puebla, Mexico, proclaimed their adherence in 1968 and 1979, respectively, to the doctrine of a "preferential option for the poor," a concept that gave momentum for clergy to work on behalf of social reform, even revolution.

  Liberation theology grew out of the experience of clergy who came to identify with the needs of the poor as they carried out pastoral work. Their experiences and others shaped the development of the theological movement, not vice versa. Bishops attending the Latin American Episcopal Conference in Medellín endorsed the concept of *concientización*—the responsibility of clergy and delegates to educate the poor to their political rights. Although the earliest developments took place within Catholicism, the movement also gained a foothold within the swelling Protestant missionary movement and spread to Africa and Asia.

  One of the central insights that liberation theologians, using Marxism as a tool of analysis, brought to the Church was recognition that, as an institution, it is shaped by social class conflict. More Catholics live in Latin America than anywhere else in the world. Because it is one of the poorest areas (only Africa is poorer) and the one with the widest gap between rich and poor, the shift in the Church inaugurated by Pope John made its greatest impact there. Some priests, nuns, and brothers adopted Marxism as a tool to understand how to put the preferential option into practice. Liberation theologians turned to Marxist analysis because it seemed pertinent to what their brethren were doing in the field, often drawing a violent reaction from oligarchs and generals.

In Central America, hundreds of clergy and lay "delegates of the word" worked to raise the consciousness of the poor and helped them self-organize, a process replicated in many other countries. These grassroots leaders formed "Christian base communities" where people met to discuss both the Bible and their local problems. Although some bishops were sympathetic, after 1980 the Church hierarchy began to assert opposition and roll back the movement somewhat. Catholicism stresses the role of ordained (male) priests as intermediaries between the faith and God. Only priests can say Mass and perform "transubstantiation"— the transformation of bread and wine into the body and blood of Christ, the central ritual of the Catholic Mass. The emergence of base communities led by lay "delegates," basing their understanding of scripture on discussions rather than received wisdom from clerics, threatened the patriarchal authority of the hierarchy.

Radical Christians often participated in developing a broad network of women's organizations, indigenous groups, human rights organizations, and other groups whose practices informed the development of liberation theology. More and more, they interpreted the Bible as a mandate to struggle for social justice. The inspiration often came from peasants themselves who, having been taught to read by using the Bible as a text, often interpreted its stories quite differently from the standard, middle-class, developed worldview. They looked to stories of Jesus driving moneylenders out of the temple as condemnation of rapacious businessmen. If it was harder for a rich man to get into heaven than for a camel to pass through the eye of a needle, then quite clearly God has a preference for the poor. In the Old Testament, prophets from God often appeared when his "chosen people" had gone astray from the principles of social justice, such as worshipping a golden calf.

The great example of the "praxis"—that is, the relationship between practice and social theory—advocated by liberation theology can be seen in the evolution of the greatest martyr of this movement, El Salvador's Archbishop Oscar Arnulfo Romero. Romero was assassinated for condemning repression in El Salvador in 1980, telling soldiers in his Sunday homily that they did not have to follow orders to kill in violation of God's law.

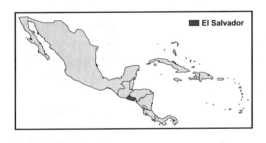

Romero assumed his position in 1977. The Salvadoran oligarchy was somewhat relieved that a more radical priest had not been appointed. Weeks later, Romero found himself officiating at the burial of his friend, Father Retulio Grande, who had been killed by landowners. Grande's murder led Romero to learn about and appreciate the courage of those clergy working with the poor to raise their material—not just spiritual—well-being. Father Grande was not organizing a peasant revolt but teaching peasants to read and dig wells, but in doing so, he was helping them reduce their dependence on landowners. The murder of Grande and others set Romero on the road that led to his martyrdom at the hands of Salvadoran soldiers using U.S.-supplied weapons.

Faith-motivated activists often exerted a humanizing influence over their secular, revolutionary brethren. The Nicaraguan Sandinistas, for example, were as much influenced by changes in the Church as by any explicit Marxist doctrine. Tomás Borge, a communist and atheist and one of the founders of the Sandinista guerrilla movement, kept a crucifix on the

Roger comments on bishops and business interests.

wall of his office and wrote a book titled *Christianity and Revolution*. Borge said that his encounter with radical Christians helped him forgive a torturer who had brutally maimed him and raped his wife. The Somoza guardsman had fallen into his hands after the Sandinista triumph. Borge wrote a poem expressing how he would "take revenge" by insisting on the right of his torturer's "children to school and flowers" and would "show you the good in the eyes of my people," who although "always unyielding in combat" are also "most steadfast and generous in victory" (Borge n.d.).

To some clergy, Vatican II's call for the Church to adopt a preferential option for the poor was a call to revolution. To others, it was not just religious insubordination but a heresy to suggest that the Church should profess one social philosophy more holy than another. Revolutionaries in Central America portrayed the opposition of conservative bishops in Nicaragua to the revolutionary Sandinista government of the 1980s as hypocritical, charging that the hierarchy had itself taken sides, aligning with the business community.

As the conflicts in Central America were becoming more intense, more conservative members of the Catholic hierarchy were laying plans to roll back the influence of liberation theology. They were heartened when Bishop Karol Wotyla, a Pole from communist Eastern Europe, assumed the papacy as John Paul II in 1978. Aided by conservative Cardinal Joseph Ratzinger, who would himself accede to the papacy as Pope Benedict XVI in 2005, the new pope began to discipline leftist theologians and radical bishops. The new pope, though he considered neoliberalism to be "savage capitalism", had experienced the repressive communist regime in his native Poland and had little sympathy for democratizing the Church's hierarchical structure. To hasten the exit of leftist bishops, John Paul instituted mandatory retirement of bishops at the age of 75 years (though he did not follow his own policy in this regard). For example, he forced Bishop Samuel Ruiz's resignation from the Chiapas diocese in 1999 and appointed a less outspoken successor.

Still, the institutional Church is unlikely to return entirely to its traditional position as defender of the privileges of the local oligarchy. Many clergy who do not fully embrace the philosophy of liberation theology have lent the authority and resources of the Church to defense of human rights. Also, Catholicism faces intense competition from Protestantism in Latin America, so it can no longer take the adherence of the poor majority in Latin America for granted. Religion and Catholicism shape Latin American social struggles, but the reverse is also true.

PUNTO DE VISTA: LIBERATION THEOLOGY AND THE LATIN AMERICAN CHURCH

Pope Francis, since his ascension in 2013, has said little directly on liberation theology, but his actions and willingness to meet with some prominent liberation theologians have encouraged many Latin American clergy.

A document titled "Peace" issued by Latin American bishops meeting in Medellín, Colombia, in 1968 was a major statement on this movement. Following are excerpts. You can find the whole document at www.shc .edu/theolibrary/resources/medpeace.htm.

> As the Christian believes in the productiveness of peace in order to achieve justice, he also believes that justice is a prerequisite for peace. He recognizes that in many instances Latin America finds itself faced with a situation of injustice that can be called institutionalized violence, when, because of a structural deficiency of industry and agriculture, of national and international economy, of cultural and political life, [quoting Pope Paul VI] "whole towns lack necessities, live in such dependence as hinders all initiative and responsibility as well as every possibility for cultural promotion and participation in social and political life," thus violating fundamental rights. This situation demands all-embracing, courageous, urgent and profoundly renovating transformations. We should not be surprised therefore, that the "temptation to violence" is surfacing in Latin America. One should not abuse the patience of a people that for years has borne a situation that would not be acceptable to anyone with any degree of awareness of human rights. . . .

> Also responsible for injustice are those who remain passive for fear of the sacrifice and personal risk implied by any courageous and effective action. Justice and therefore peace conquer by means of a dynamic action of awakening (*concientización*) and organization of the popular sectors, which are capable of pressing public officials who are often impotent in their social projects without popular support. . . .

> We address ourselves finally to those who, in the face of injustice and illegitimate resistance to change, put their hopes in violence. With Paul VI we realize that their attitude "frequently finds its ultimate motivation in noble impulses of justice and solidarity." . . .

> If it is true that revolutionary insurrection can be legitimate in the case of evident and prolonged "tyranny that seriously works against the fundamental rights of man and which damages the common good of the country," whether it proceeds from one person or from clearly unjust structures, it is also certain that violence or "armed revolution" generally "generates new injustices, introduces new imbalances and causes new disasters; one cannot combat a real evil at the price of a greater evil." . . .

> To us, the Pastors of the Church, belongs the duty to educate the Christian conscience, to inspire, stimulate and help orient all of the initiatives that contribute to the formation of man. It is also up to us to denounce everything which, opposing justice, destroys peace.

In 2009, Pope Benedict (Joseph Ratzinger) sent a letter to a gathering of Brazilian bishops warning them about embracing liberation theology. He reminded them of an earlier pronouncement he had made:

> It stressed the danger that is entailed in an a-critical acceptance on the part of certain theologians of theses and methodologies that derive from Marxism. Its more or less visible consequences consisting of rebellion, division, dissent, offence, and anarchy make themselves felt, creating in your diocesan communities great suffering and a serious loss of vitality. I implore all those who in some way have felt attracted, involved and deeply touched by certain deceptive principles of Liberation Theology to consider once again the above-mentioned Instruction, perceiving the kind light with which it is proffered. I remind everyone that "'the supreme rule of her [the Church's] faith' derives from the unity which the Spirit has created between Sacred Tradition, Sacred Scripture and the Magisterium of the Church in a reciprocity which means that none of the three can survive without the others" (John Paul II, *Fides et Ratio*, n. 55); and that in the context of Church bodies and communities, forgiveness offered and received in the name of and out of love for the Most Blessed Trinity, whom we worship in our hearts, puts an end to the suffering of our beloved Church, a pilgrim in the Lands of the Holy Cross.

Point/Counterpoint

Should the clergy restrict its work to pastoral mission, or should it denounce social injustice? Do you agree that *concientización* should be a responsibility of clergy?

a. If you believe that the clergy should take a position on social injustice and raise consciousness among the poor, then how do you respond to those who would argue that democracy requires separation of religion and politics? What answer would you give to a bishop who said that the Church should not discriminate against the rich? Finally, if the clergy takes on this role, would the Church not lose some of its ability to mediate on human rights issues?

b. If you answered that the clergy should limit itself to pastoral work, how would you respond to a member of the clergy who pointed out that Christ was born a poor carpenter? How would you respond to the argument that the majority of the world's Catholics are found in Latin America, and they are poor? Finally, how would you respond to the argument that without social consciousness, religion would just become the "opiate" of the masses?

For more information

On liberation theology, a good source is Robert McAfee Brown, *Liberation Theology: An Introductory Guide* (Westminster/Know Press, 1993). Pope Benedict's full letter on liberation theology can be found at www.vatican.va/holy_father/benedict_xvi/speeches/2009/december/documents/hf_ben-xvi_spe_20091205_ad-limina-brasile_en.html.

For Review

What does liberation theology stand for, and why was it controversial inside the Catholic Church? What is the cartoonist, Roger, trying to say about the Catholic Church's role in Nicaraguan politics in the 1990s?

Class, Culture, and Politics

Much of this chapter has described how social and economic inequalities, political practices, and gender and racial differences manifest themselves in Latin American politics. Those who study Latin America generally agree that class inequality is more pronounced, and just about everyone agrees that there are culturally distinctive traits that define "Latin American." However, there are widely divergent views on how inequality and cultural traditions relate to democracy. You may have formed some answers already, but we will want to return to this issue when we look at the impact of **neoliberal** economic policies since 1980 (chapter 6), globalization (chapter 15), and social movements (chapter 11). By now you should realize that many of the inequalities are rooted in the legacy of the colonial era, and the same can be said of the independence era. Therefore, we now turn to examining how "existing" democracy has evolved over the region, including how pre-Columbian patterns and colonialism have left their mark on the region's contemporary culture, class structure, and politics.

Discussion Questions

1. Should we treat the degree of inequality among social classes, men and women, and different ethnic groups as a test of how democratic a nation is? Or should we limit the idea of democracy to procedures and the form of government, looking at equality as something that might be an outcome of democracy?

2. Do you find it surprising that Latin America, often stereotyped for its **machismo**, has produced several women presidents, whereas the United States (at least as of 2014) has yet to produce one?

3. What are the most important ways we might measure the extent to which someone, not only in Latin America but wherever we may live, is part of those "excluded," as we have used the term here?

4. Has anything in this chapter about equality and political culture changed your thinking or reinforced your earlier response to the question of how much we should take equality into account in evaluating the democratic condition of Latin American countries?

Resources for Further Study

Reading: The World Bank publishes the annual *World Development Report* with an appendix filled with comparative economic statistics, including measures of inequality.

Clientelism in Everyday Latin American Politics, edited by Tina Hilgers (London: Palgrave MacMillan, 2012), gives well-supported insight into the relationship between democracy and clientelism.

Video and Film: "In Women's Hands," in the *Americas* series, explores the role of women in politics through the tumultuous years of revolution, dictatorship, and re-democratization in Chile. *Las Madres: Mothers of the Plaza del Mayo* (1986) exemplifies the powerful influence of women in the human rights movement. *Black Orpheus* (1959) is now a classic, a great film about the life of African descendants in the *favelas* of Rio de Janeiro. On the same subject, a more recent film is *City of God* (2002). See also *The Maid* (2002). *Romero* (1989) is a powerful biography of the Salvadoran archbishop.

On the Internet: The United Nations Development Project has a page devoted to the Millennium Project, which has much information on trends regarding poverty. See www.undp.org/mdg. The emergence of indigenous and Afro-descendant identity is very evident on the Indigenous Peoples page of the Latin American Network Information Center portal (http://lanic.utexas.edu/la/region/indigenous) and the African Diaspora page at the same site (http://lanic.utexas.edu/la/region/african). A wiki page with extensive information on class in Latin America can be found at http://uclast203.wikispaces.com/CLASS%2C+INEQUALITY.

PART II

History: Colonial Legacies, Mass Politics, and Democracy

3 Democratic and Autocratic Threads before Columbus and in Colonial Latin America

Focus Questions

▶ How do the legacies of the pre-Columbian and colonial eras exert influence over Latin American politics today?

▶ How did colonialism shape ethnic diversity and national identity in Latin America?

▶ What kinds of issues about national identity, sovereignty, and rights are still contested politically and pose challenges for democracy in Latin America today?

▶ How did colonialism influence the role that Latin America came to play in the global economy?

▶ How do attitudes about race in Latin America compare to those in the United States? How do race and social class relate to each other in the region?

HISTORY PROVIDES RAW material for advancing and retarding struggles for democracy in this region today. Like other peoples, Latin Americans often romanticize their heroes and vilify those "on the wrong side of history." For this reason, this chapter is less a chronology than a broad, interpretative account of Latin America's history, leavened with commentary about the relevance of this account to the present.

In particular, I want to address two themes about the legacy left by colonialism and the tumultuous first century after independence, covered in the next chapter. First, colonialism drastically impacted the social and economic structures of the people who were in the Americas before Columbus. At the same time, the history of Latin America does not begin with the Portuguese and Spanish conquest. In various ways, the way of life of indigenous peoples continues to resonate in Latin American society and politics, more so where they are found in greater numbers, but even in places (like the Caribbean) where they disappeared in the face of the forces of biology and conquest. Indigenous peoples, enslaved Africans, and immigrants (covered more in the next two chapters) shaped a Latin American identity and specific national identities that vary from country to country. This story cannot be told without taking gender relationships, especially the role of women, into account. Nor can we understand how issues of identity influence Latin America today without understanding pre-Columbian and colonial history.

Second, colonialism shaped the class structure of Latin American societies, interacting as it did with racial and ethnic factors. Colonialism in a related way shaped the way that Latin

America would be integrated into the global economic and political order. We will touch on this issue in this chapter but reserve much of the discussion about it for the next chapter, where we deal with the question of whether political independence really changed much about social class patterns and economic underdevelopment and dependency.

Narrating and interpreting history for such a large region risks simplification and over-generalization. The climate and the social characteristics of the conquered lands differed. The colonial history was greatly shaped by, among other things, the degree to which indigenous cultures survived and the extent to which immigrants and African slaves followed the Iberian conquerors into the region. Although northern Latin America is tropical, the Southern Cone has a temperate climate. Indigenous people were more numerous—and their cultures tended to survive more—in the highland regions than in lowlands. Indian wars comparable with those fought in North America were common until the late 1800s in the Southern Cone. Slavery was more prevalent in tropical regions. These are only a handful of factors that have shaped cultural diversity in the region.

The region's largest country, Brazil, which borders on every other South American country except Ecuador and Chile, was colonized by Portugal, which along with Spain makes up the Iberian Peninsula in Europe. As a result, Portuguese is Brazil's main language, whereas Spanish has been the native tongue of most other Latin Americans. Also, Brazil's path to independence in the 1800s was quite different from the path of most of the Spanish colonial empire. Portugal's American empire did not fracture into smaller nation-states, and for several decades of the nineteenth century, it was a monarchy.

For many historians of the colonial era (roughly from 1500 to 1800), the period "signifies economic backwardness; political arbitrariness, corruption, and nepotism; a hierarchical social order and attitudes of condescension and contempt on the part of elites toward the masses" (Keen and Haynes 2000: 2). For most indigenous peoples, the colonial period signifies conquest and the subordination of their societies to other nations. The descendants of African slaves see little to celebrate in colonial history. However, Latin American history is also about the struggles of ordinary people and innovative leaders to overcome autocratic traditions, to replace hierarchical structures with democratic practices, and to achieve economic development, providing inspiration to democratic movements today.

The Pre-Columbian Legacy

In large parts of the Andes and **Mesoamerica**, which includes Central America and Mexico, the conquistadors encountered settled populations with great cities and impressive accomplishments in art, architecture, science, and so on. Central Mexico was more densely populated than was Europe at the time. Indian settlements were also relatively dense in the Andean highlands. This includes large parts of present-day Peru, Bolivia, Ecuador, Colombia, western Venezuela, and northern Chile. Pre-Columbian populations were also dense in the Yucatán Peninsula and surrounding regions, as well as in the Mexican highlands. Most of the Southern Cone (Chile, Argentina, Paraguay, Uruguay, and part of Brazil) has a more temperate climate. The indigenous people have histories as well as social and economic structures more like those found in North American indigenous communities.

In the Caribbean, the Amazonian region, and other tropical regions at low elevations, it was once thought that the indigenous peoples were primarily fishers, hunters, and gatherers. More recent anthropological evidence (Mann 2005) suggests that the societies were much more complex, populous, and sophisticated. The Spanish and Portuguese may have found these societies in a "primitive" condition not because they lacked technology or more complex culture but because the ravages of disease, including smallpox brought by Columbus and earlier conquistadors, had already traveled to the area and decimated their social structures.

Did democracy exist in pre-Columbian America? The very notion seems anachronistic, but the democratic and egalitarian spirit of indigenous peoples often impressed European philosophers. The fruits of labor (e.g., the bounty from the hunt) were usually shared, and extremes of power and wealth were narrow in comparison with so-called advanced civilizations. The French philosopher Michel de Montaigne painted a portrait of a noble savage, and Rousseau warned that the advance of "civilization" tended to reduce and not enhance the freedom these people enjoyed. These accounts seem hopelessly romanticized, but surviving communities of indigenous people often fight today to preserve humanitarian values that we "civilized" peoples may have lost in the quest for progress. One such value in the Andean region is that of *buen vivir*, "living well," referring to the idea of living a simpler live, less focused on material consumption and more conscious of sustainable environmental practices. It is possible that indigenous cultures also shaped the values associated with democracy in the United States. Charles Mann (2005), reviewing recent and surprising insights from anthropology and archeology, suggests that in North America the "liberal values"—the ones that undergird the concept of **polyarchy**—were not simply imported from Europe but learned by North American colonists from Algonquin peoples' notions of egalitarianism and of freedom from constrictive social hierarchies.

Before Columbus, many civilizations and empires of indigenous peoples rose and fell (Table 3.1), but nothing could match the scale of social devastation wrought by the arrival of the Europeans. Whatever democratic and egalitarian practices existed were suppressed or practiced in modified forms within a ruthless and culturally aggressive imperial system. The Europeans exploited ethnic rivalries and resentment of conquered peoples. Still, indigenous groups resisted the imperial ambitions of militarily powerful peoples like the Aztecs and Incas; so too did they often rise up against European colonialism. This suggests a persistent desire for self-determination, if not democracy.

The Mayan region (mostly modern-day Yucatán and Guatemala) never was fully subordinated to one ruler before colonialism (Figure 3.1). Other indigenous peoples lived even closer to nature in highly decentralized communities where political structures were not distinct from religious and family structures, and these were less influenced by European culture (though unfortunately, they did not escape disease). Authority often tended to flow to men (but not always) from fighting prowess or some other ability, such as hunting.

The Aztecs were in reality not one but three warrior groups gathered into a coalition by the largest and most powerful group, the Mexica people. In the mid-1400s they came to dominate the central and northern part of what today is Mexico and ruled from their capital Tenochtitlán, a city of 150,000–200,000 people and site of present-day Mexico City. In the Andean region, the Inca Empire arose in the early 1400s; its emperor ruled from Cuzco in the Peruvian highlands.

On one hand, the two empires that confronted the Spanish were highly centralized, with a king and imperial court living off the tribute contributed by other regions. On the

TABLE 3.1 Chronology: Pre-Columbian Era and Conquest

Formative Era	30,000 BCE*	Hunter/gatherer groups migrate across the Bering Strait; second wave around 10,000 BCE.
	3500 BCE	Formative, pre-classic era begins; ceramic arts and figures appear.
	2000 BCE	By this time village life and agriculture have taken root in many regions.
Classic Era	200 BCE	More sophisticated technical achievements in ceramics, art, and weaving in middle Andes.
	200 BCE–1000 CE	Cities and more complex social structures appear.
	300–900 CE	Classic Mayan era. Peak of achievements in astrology/astronomy, calendars, mathematics, writing, and architecture. For example, Monte Albán is built in Mexico.
	200 BCE–600 CE	On southern Peruvian coastal desert. Hundreds of huge figures (Nazca lines) drawn in desert without the benefit of perspective from a height. Realistic painting on pottery in northern Peru.
	450–750 CE	Teotihuacán pyramids, near modern Mexico City, center of empire 900 years before Aztecs.
	600–1000 CE	Rise of urban centers and new empires in highlands of Peru and Bolivia.
Post-Classic Era	1000–1492 CE	Most regions experience development of more complex societies, with new economic classes (including merchants). Mexico experiences warfare, emergence and disappearance of cities, and political variations, but no great leaps in technology or artistic expression.
	968 CE	Toltecs, seen by some as ancestors of Aztecs, establish capital at Tula in central (modern Hidalgo) Mexico.
	1000–1476 CE	Chimú empire in Peru.
Aztec Era	1345 CE	Aztecs, coalition of three warrior groups, the largest of which was the "Mexica" group, found an empire based on tribute.
	1325 CE	Founding of Aztec capital of Tenochtitlán, site of modern-day Mexico City.
	1440–1487 CE	Aztecs expand under Emperor Moctezuma I; great temple (on site of modern-day Cathedral) dedicated in 1487.
	1502 CE	Moctezuma II becomes emperor of Tenochtitlán and rules until 1520, year after arrival of Hernán Cortés.
Inca Era	1200–1532 CE	Incas, beginning with founding of Cuzco, form the Tawantinsuyu empire based on tribute, outstanding administrative system.
	1438–1471 CE	Inca expansion toward south of Cuzco.
	1471–1493 CE	Tupac Inca conquers further south, into modern Chile, and west to coast.

(Continued)

TABLE 3.1 (Continued)

	1493–1527 CE	Huayna Capac expands north into Ecuador and Colombia, dies in smallpox epidemic, a disease brought by Europeans. Civil war breaks out; two sons battle for succession.
	1532	Atahualpa wins civil war, is leader of Tawantinsuyu, in same year that Francisco Pizarro arrives.
Conquest	1479	Ferdinand II and Isabella I unite Aragon and Castille to form Spanish monarchy.
	1492	Catholic monarchs expel last of Muslims and Jews from Spain, completing the Reconquista, setting a pattern for the "conquest" (e.g., rewarding warriors with grants of control, encomienda, over land and people).
	1492	Financed by Spain, the Italian Christopher Columbus accidentally finds a "New World" in the Western Hemisphere. Columbus makes three more voyages (last in 1502), takes part in establishing the Atlantic slave trade.
	1493	Alarmed by Portuguese and Spanish competition, Pope mediates conflict and divides control along a north-south longitudinal line—the Treaty of Tordesillas, dividing Portuguese- and Spanish-speaking America.
	1500	Pedro Álvares Cabral claims eastern extension of Brazil for Portugal.
	1511	Treatment of Indians draws criticism from Church; Atuey leads indigenous revolt against Spanish in Cuba.
	1512–1513	Large-scale enslavement and transport of Africans to the Americas begins.
	1513	Ponce de Leon begins eight-year exploration of Florida; Balboa sees Pacific from Panamá.
	1519–1522	Cortés conquers Tenochtitlán after death of Moctezuma II (1520); his successor, Cuitláhuac, dies of smallpox, a new European disease, after only 80 days; Cuauhtémoc, last Aztec emperor, is captured, tortured, and eventually put to death in 1525 as Cortés extends the conquest south, into Mayan regions and beyond.
	1532	Pizarro captures the Inca Atahualpa, puts a puppet ruler in Cuzco. Conquest is consolidated militarily around 1534 after Inca resistance leader, Rumiñahi, is defeated.

*"BCE"—"before the Common Era"—is used here in place of the more common "BC" ("before Christ") and "CE" instead of "AD" (*Anno Domini*, "year of our Lord") in recognition of the cultural and religious diversity in the region.

FIGURE 3.1   Map of the Pre-Columbian Empires of the Americas

other hand, typical of empires based on tribute, local communities retained considerable autonomy and were led by local chiefs, called **caciques**. Within the less-centralized Mayan culture of modern-day Central America and southern Mexico, even more political variation existed. A priestly caste ruled larger units, but much local and regional life was organized on a communitarian basis, with land collectively owned and often worked through a system of mutual aid, a tradition that persists in many indigenous communities and influences ideas of political and economic life today. Within the empires, there existed smaller communities and villages with chiefdoms. Even today, a powerful local political boss is often called a *cacique* (chief), a term not limited to indigenous communities.

At risk of exaggerating how women faired in pre-Columbian America, we can see some ways that they may have enjoyed higher status than after the Europeans arrived. In some Mesoamerican (Mexican and Central American) monarchies, women rose to the office of queen. Within Inca society, a kind of "gender parallelism" prevailed. Lines of descent were traced through both male and female ancestry. Irene Silverblatt (1987) has documented how women had a birthright through their mothers to land, livestock, water, and other resources. Women and men performed different tasks by tradition, but relatively equal status was accorded to men's work and women's work. Under the Spanish conquest women lost much of their influence, although the blame cannot be laid entirely on the Iberians. The rise of the militarist, exploitative Inca imperial system had already undermined gender equity (Keen and Haynes 2000: 5–36; Schroeder 2000; Schwartz 2000; Silverblatt 1987).

To some degree the pattern of Iberian conquest, as opposed to settlement, produced a paradox: a society where for 400 years proving your "whiteness" legally was a prerequisite for holding positions of power, yet the relatively small number of Iberian immigrants made intermarriage and miscegenation (sexual relationships between people of different races) essential for population growth. Hence, we can speak of the birth of a "new race," *la raza*, as some Latin Americans call it, that can proudly draw upon three cultures (Iberian, indigenous, and African); yet we can also speak just as accurately of the "rape of a continent" not only as a figure of speech for the pillaging of its gold, silver, and other natural resources but also literally in reference to the sexual relationships that gave birth to this new people.

"In a way," wrote historian Magnus Mörner (1967), "the Spanish Conquest of the Americas was a conquest of women." By this, he meant that the Spanish— and Portuguese

Here are two views of Cortés conquering the Aztec empire. The great Mexican muralist Diego Rivera depicted the first around 1930. The second is a Spanish painting done around 1520, ten years after the conquest. How does Rivera see the conquest differently than the Spanish painter? Which do you think better represents what happened?

too—used degrees of force to extract sexual and economic labor from Indian women. Hernán Cortés, conqueror of the Aztecs, had all Indian slaves branded, and by one account his men were extremely angered to learn their commander had claimed all the pretty women. Sometimes indigenous *caciques* bestowed women on the Spanish as gifts or were willing to sell them. Many women were forced to enter the conquerors' households as domestic servants and were subjected to sexual domination. Writing back to their homeland, the Iberians praised the extraordinary beauty and sexual prowess of Indian women. In this way, the sexual stereotypes of *machismo*, hot Latin lovers, and sexually alluring women were implanted during the conquest. Unlike the case in North America, many fewer women than men migrated from Europe to Latin America.

It is unlikely that Iberian cultural and political norms could have been so deeply implanted in Latin America without the rape of the continent taking a somewhat literal form. Understanding gender relationships in the colonial era is crucial to understanding how race, class, and gender interact with one another even today in Latin America.

For Review

What were the most important indigenous civilizations at the time of Columbus, and where were they located? In terms of the ethnic profile of Latin America today, what difference did it make in Latin America that, unlike in North America, the Europeans came as conquerors, not settlers, with few women?

The Colonial Era

The Iberians justified their conquest and continued domination of Latin America as a mission entrusted to them by God. In the first few decades after Columbus's so-called discovery, under the **encomienda** system (*encomendar* means to "entrust"), the king entrusted to his conquerors the responsibility to Christianize the Indian population; the conquistadors in turn received the right to extract tribute from the Indians. This usually meant that the Indians were required to work a certain number of days laboring in mines, constructing roads and buildings, doing domestic labor in the home, or working in the fields. Fray Bartolomé de las Casas, a bishop justly famed for entreating the Crown to defend the Indians from ruthless exploitation by the conquistadors, once remarked that it would have been better for the Indians to have gone to hell with their heresies than to have been Christianized by the Spanish. Fray de las Casas mused about importing African slaves and Moors to replace the Indians in their labor (Galeano 2001: 45). (The Moors were Muslim people who had lived in Spain for 800 years before being expelled by Ferdinand and Isabella in their "reconquest" of Iberia.) Las Casas and other religious protestors managed to persuade the Crown to repeal the *encomienda* system, but the systems that came later never truly freed the Indians from the yoke of the landlords (Table 3.2).

TABLE 3.2 Chronology: Colonial Era and Independence

1524	Council of Indies set up by Spanish Crown to administer empire.
1531	According to much-contested accounts, Juan Diego, an Indian, reports seeing Virgin of Guadalupe near Mexico City. This will become a central myth in fusing Hispanic and indigenous elements into Mexican identity.
1537	Pope decides Indians have souls; hence, they are humans.
1545	Large-scale importation of slaves to plantations in North Brazil begins. Silver boom begins in Bolivia.
1570–1571	Inquisition established in Lima and Mexico City, where Spanish viceroys (stand-ins for king) are based.
1571–1572	Unsuccessful revolt of Tupac Amaru I in Peru.
1588	Spanish Armada defeated by weather and British fleet; beginning of long decline of Spain as world power.
1610	Jesuits establish missions among the Guaraní in Paraguay.
1700	Philip V becomes king of Spain as Bourbon dynasty replaces Hapsburgs, ushering in an era of reform designed to enhance colonial economy for benefit of the mother country.
1780–1781	Revolt of Tupac Amaru II in Peru and Revolt of Comuneros in Colombia demonstrate weakening power of Crown but alarm the *criollo* ruling elite.
1791–1802	Slave revolt in Haiti leads to independence, frightens other slaveholders in hemisphere.
1793–1815	Napoleonic Wars in Europe disturb political order. In 1807, France invades Portugal, and the royal family flees to Brazil. In Spain, Napoleon forces the coronation of his brother, Joseph, in 1807, followed by a French invasion and occupation. Creoles establish ruling councils in several cities, including Caracas; they express loyalty to the Crown but alarm Spanish authorities. The year 1814 sees restoration of the Spanish Crown.
1810–1815	Bloody failed insurrections in Mexico led by Hidalgo and Morelos.
1810–1811	Venezuela and Paraguay declare independence.
1815	Simón Bolívar retreats to Jamaica, after leading war of independence for three years, and writes famous *Carta de Jamaica*, which among other things calls for unity in Latin America.
1817–1821	José de San Martín undertakes military campaigns, marching across Andes from Argentina into Peru, paving way for independence of southern portion of continent.
1821	Mexican independence declared.
1822	King Pedro, living in Brazil after fleeing Napoleonic invasion, declares Brazil independent of Portugal.
1823	Monroe Doctrine, by which the United States warns Europe not to try to establish colonies in the Americas, is issued.
1824	Victory by Bolívar's forces, led by José Antonio Sucre, in Battle of Ayacucho assures independence of South America.
1830	Gran Colombia, created by Bolívar, splits into separate countries of Venezuela, Colombia (including Panama, at the time), Ecuador, Peru, and Bolivia.
1838	Central American republics (Guatemala, Honduras, Nicaragua, El Salvador, Costa Rica) established after breakup of regional federation.

In great measure, the Spanish imperial structures replaced the indigenous tribute systems, which in economic and political (but not religious and cultural) terms resembled one another. Within the Inca system, tribute was rendered in the form of labor or production not by individuals but by clans. In successive waves stretching over several centuries, Europeans and their descendants attempted to replace indigenous customs and economic relationships with systems of individual property and contract. Over centuries, elites introduced a system whereby people exchanged labor, goods, or services on the basis of market relationships and not mutual obligations defined by kinship or sanctioned by tradition and religious authority. This tendency, we shall see, accelerated in the period after 1850, when a period of top-down efforts to modernize took place.

A good example of the legacy of *encomienda* would be the *huasipongo* system in Ecuador. In the late colonial period, elites extracted labor from Indians and poor peasants through a draft system, called *mita* or *quinta*, which required them to provide a certain number of days of labor per year to municipal authorities, who in turn were controlled by landlords. By 1850, this system was replaced by one called *concertaje*, whereby poor peasants would exchange labor for loans and for the right to live on and work a small plot of land, called a *huasipongo*. Supposedly, this was an improvement over the *mita* because workers were not required by law to work for landlords; now they simply agreed to work by entering into a contract. But this is not to say that now peasants were free to work or not work. Usually, the landowner paid in advance or made loans to his "employee." Peasants needed access to land and were not in a position to achieve a good deal. Inevitably, the peasant would fall behind on payments, run deeper into debt, and be forced to keep on working—or give up and allow the landlord to repossess his land. We refer to this system as **peonage** and those caught in its web as "peons." It persisted deep into the twentieth century, not only in parts of Ecuador but also throughout much of Latin America.

In general, indigenous societies were more sedentary and densely populated in the areas of the Aztec and Inca empires and the Mayan region, and this allowed them to be more readily assimilated into Iberian imperial structures. Many Caribbean and Amazonian peoples were completely wiped out by European guns, economic exploitation, and germs (more on this shortly). In Chile and Argentina, the wars between Indians and settlers more closely resembled the similar conflicts in North America, both lasting into the late nineteenth century. Even in the present, mining and oil companies have encountered sometimes violent resistance to their expansion into ever more remote parts of the region. Their motivation—exploitation of mineral wealth—is not much different than that of the Iberians. Like earlier conquistadors, they have religious allies who seek converts, but today, they are more often evangelical Protestants, a development that alarms the Catholic hierarchy.

For Review

How did the Spanish conquistadors see the indigenous peoples, and how did they go about putting them to work? Can you describe the difference between the system of *encomienda* (and similar systems that followed) and straightforward slavery?

Why Did the Conquistadors Succeed? Why Does It Matter Today?

Why did the conquest succeed? After all, only a few hundred Spanish, in the cases of Cortés in Mexico and Pizarro in Peru, managed to defeat Indian empires that were highly organized, experienced in war, and densely populated.

Experts dispute the size of the pre-Columbian population of the Americas, both in the north and in the south. Recent research suggests a population of 57.3 million people, divided roughly equally in thirds among central Mexico, the Peruvian region, and other regions combined. One plausible estimate sees a total population of 90–112 million (Keen and Haynes 2000: 9–10). Were the Europeans responsible for the decimation of the Indian population to anywhere from a fifth to a tenth of its pre-Columbian size (and for the extinction of some peoples, especially in the Caribbean)?

These questions are laden with political ramifications. For those who see history as a playing-out of the Darwinian forces of natural selection (survival of the fittest), the conquest could be seen as proof of the superiority of European civilization. Some Latin Americans (such as Andrés Sosa Pietri, the Venezuelan oilman we encountered in chapter 2) prefer to emphasize the heritage of Iberia; they celebrated the 500th anniversary of the Columbus "discovery" in 1992. In the 1800s, British historians tended to emphasize the cruelty of the conquistadors and the generations of colonial masters who followed them. This "Black Legend" theory tended to disparage all things Iberian and justify the deep involvement of British interests in Latin America in the 1800s. This version of history became commonly accepted in the United States as justification for the war of 1898, when the United States expelled Spain from Cuba and its remaining colonies in the Caribbean and elsewhere.

In a best-selling book, Jared Diamond (1997) explained the Iberian conquest of the Americas in terms of "guns, germs, and steel." Diamond meant by this that a few hundred Spaniards could conquer the great Inca and Aztec empires because the Europeans possessed superior military firepower (guns), technology (steel, though navigation also counted for much), and immunity from diseases (germs) that devastated the Indian populations on contact with the Europeans. Indeed, these were factors. For example, smallpox and other diseases may have taken the lives of up to 95 percent of the indigenous population in the early 1500s. Diamond calls these factor the "proximate" (i.e., immediate) causes for the Iberian success.

Diamond traces these proximate causes to long-range, "ultimate" causes that can be traced to the luck of the historical draw. Those parts of the world where geographical conditions encouraged cultural and technological exchange, early domestication of a variety of plants and animals, and large settled and diversified societies had a large advantage, he argues, over those regions where there were obstacles to these processes. Euro-Asia was in the first category, and the Western Hemisphere and Africa were in the second. The indigenous cultures of the Americas had remarkable cultural and technological achievements, but they had limited cultural and technological exchange with one another and limited species of animals available for domestication. Europeans, Diamond explains, built up immunities as a result of, among other reasons, centuries of interaction with each other and with domesticated animals. Native Americans might have suffered fewer devastating plagues in their history, but this made them more vulnerable to the diseases carried by

Iberians. They had calendars, remarkable architecture, and medical technology (such as brain surgery, in the case of the Incas). Their scientific accomplishments rivaled those of the Europeans but were of limited use in resisting the particular advantages held by the invaders.

Diamond's stress on long-run historical factors as the explanation for the enormous gap between poor and rich countries is controversial. If the conquest of Latin America was merely the result of biological and geographical tendencies dating back millennia, then the cries for justice for descendants of those conquered seem less compelling. After all, if the luck of the historical draw accounts for poverty and vulnerability to foreign domination in Latin America and other parts of the Third World, then there is little use in arguing about moral responsibility in rectifying global inequality. In fact, it could be argued that survival of indigenous peoples would have benefited the conquerors, who were in need of labor to work their mines, plantations, and haciendas.

Mann (2005) agrees with Diamond that geographic factors limited cultural and biological exchange in the Americas, but he takes issue with Diamond's conclusion that European military technology was a deciding factor. Recent evidence suggests that Indian peoples did have adequate technologies to defeat the tiny coteries of invaders led by adventurers such as Cortés and Pizarro. For example, their arrows flew farther and struck targets with more force and more accuracy than did European bullets shot from primitive firearms.

We are also learning that pre-Columbian civilizations had technological and scientific knowledge long before the Eurasian cultures came to dominate globally. For example, the Olmec people of central Mexico had zero in their mathematics at least 550 years before the (Asian) Indians developed it and almost 1,200 years before Europeans managed to figure it out. Mann explains that corn, the most important crop in the world, seems not to have been simply developed from nature, as is the case for other grains; we cannot find a primitive, wild ancestor that yielded something edible and comparable with what we know as corn. In effect, indigenous people (accidentally or purposefully, we do not know) were genetic engineers. He points out that the Spanish soldiers in Mexico quickly discarded their wool clothing for lighter cotton garments obtained from Indians. Mann argues that, far from living harmoniously and lightly in relationship to nature, indigenous Americans shaped the environment, and not always for the better.

Alfred Crosby Jr. (1991), a historian who did much to bring the impact of disease on Indians to our attention, points out that the introduction of European plants and animals undermined the stability of the environment in the New World, reduced the genetic pool, and "caused such vast erosion that it amounts to a crime against posterity." Columbus and those who followed him were interested mainly in gold and silver. Later, when the mines gave out, the Europeans found natural conditions in different regions of the hemisphere suitable for production of coffee, cacao (for chocolate), sugar, and many other products in demand overseas. Even small Caribbean islands, mere microstates today, yielded enormous wealth when their fertile soils were tilled by slave labor. For example, in 1773, the value of sugar exports from the small Caribbean island of Grenada, a British colony, exceeded the total value of exports of all Britain's New England colonies, New York, and Pennsylvania combined (Williams 1970: 151).

Diamond's book is an extended response to a question posed to him by Yali, a local politician from the Pacific tropical island of New Guinea. Yali asked, "Why is it that you white people developed so much cargo and brought it to New Guinea, but we black people had little cargo of our own?" That is, why were you rich and we poor? Are we to believe that the answer is merely, "Well, you had the bad luck to be born in the wrong part of the world"? Would all cultures have been as aggressive and ruthless as were the Europeans? Do long-term technological and biological factors adequately explain, for example, why the Europeans organized the holocaust (to African peoples) known as the transatlantic slave trade?

Accidents and nature played a role in the European conquest of the Americas, but colonialism was neither natural nor accidental. As Mann proposes, we might do well to concentrate less on moral culpability in history and more on our own responsibility to address inequalities and prejudices inherited from the past.

In colonial times, the Spanish and Portuguese Crowns regarded the Indians as little more than children to be civilized through conversion to Christianity. As such, Church authorities, often backed by the Crown, defended indigenous people from some of the harshest forms of exploitation on the part of those "entrusted" with responsibility for this task. This paternalistic attitude was not always welcomed by the **criollo** elite—that is, those members of the predominately European elite who made up the colonial ruling class in the Americas. (The word in English is usually translated as "Creole." We will use this term interchangeably with *criollo*, but keep in mind that in the United States, "Creole" refers more to mixed-race people, and not necessarily those of the upper class.) They had little use as well for indigenous culture and knowledge.

Rather than bring more freedom for Indians and slaves, the disappearance of the Crown after independence freed the *criollos* from some restrictions on their ability to exploit indigenous labor. But the *criollo* elite faced a new question: what made them nations with a right to claim sovereignty—that is, the right to claim independence? Over time, the *criollos*, few of whom could trace their ancestry solely to Iberia, began to include indigenous culture as part of their identity as Colombians, Mexicans, Venezuelans, and so on, without necessarily respecting Indians as equals. For example, in Mexico after expulsion of a French occupation in 1867, indigenous culture was elevated in a way useful to defining a sense of national identity. Mexicans discovered a past that preceded and perhaps even exceeded what it had inherited from Spain. However, this was expressed more in museums, artistic movements, folklore, cuisine, and tourism and not in respect for the rights of indigenous people to govern themselves or regain control of their land. As Benedict Anderson (1983), a theorist of nationalism, would put it, they were "imagining" themselves as a nation.

One of the places where this happened was in the kitchen, where Mexican women continued to prepare corn-based meals despite the attempts of *criollos* to "Europeanize" the country and replace the traditional indigenous cuisine with wheat (Pilcher 1998). Women not only cooked but also collected and printed recipes. In this way, women helped to keep alive a heritage thousands of years old, keeping it available to be incorporated into Mexican culture officially by the policies of governments that emerged out of the 1910 revolution and promoted ***mestizaje*** as the "real Mexico." But the notion that the real Latin America is ***mestizo*** is something that indigenous peoples have come to challenge recently.

For Review

Why were the indigenous people of the Americas vulnerable to European diseases? What other factors made them vulnerable to conquest by the Iberians?

Afro-Latin America: Roots and Slavery

Not long after Columbus's first voyage, the first "illegal immigrant" took part in organizing the system whereby Africans were forcibly transported to the New World as slaves and thrown into the racial stew. In a few cases, such as the southern Brazilian state of Minas Gerais, they were put to work in mines. For the most part, however, African peoples are found today in great numbers in those countries where the climate and soil were most suitable for plantation agriculture and where the indigenous population was scarce and especially resistant to exploitation through *encomienda* or its successor schemes. Women once again played a decisive if unwilling role in the story. In Brazil, Portuguese planters exercised despotic power over black female slaves. White–Indian and black–Indian sexual unions also occurred. In 1775, colonial authorities legitimated white–Indian marriages and made their offspring eligible for offices previously limited (at least officially) to whites. However, children from mixed unions involving blacks and whites were not extended this favor (Keen and Haynes 2000: 130).

Hard labor was identified with slavery, so whites often resisted work that in their minds only befitted the slave. If their skin was not too dark, **mulatos** (or in English, mulattos), people of partial African ancestry, might be admitted into higher socioeconomic positions. The uneasy relationship between class and race was further complicated by the way some slaves could acquire an education and even become artisans (skilled workers and craftsmen—e.g., furniture makers and blacksmiths) with their own small businesses in the towns. In Cuba, a house slave named Juan Manzano acquired an education and became a writer of some note. He wrote mostly about the conditions afflicting himself and his family. He left us the only direct testimony we have from a slave in this period and region of the psychological burden of being an enslaved man with a free mind. He wrote in a letter, "A slave is a dead soul" (Manzano 1996: 21). One of his poems well describes the evil nature of the slave trade itself:

> The Cuban merchant prosecutes his trade
> Without a qualm, or a reproach being made;
> Sits at his desk, and with composure sends
> A formal order to his gold-coast friends
> For some five hundred "bultos" of effects,
> And bids them ship "the goods" as he directs.
> That human cargo, to its full amount,
> Is duly bought and shipped on his account;
> Stowed to the best advantage in the hold,
> And limb to limb in chains, as you behold;
> On every breast, the well-known brand, J. G.

Slavery was a political powder keg, and the periodic revolts worked both for and against prolongation of colonialism. Slave revolts were more numerous in Latin America than in the northern continent, but there is little agreement among historians about why. You can find a summary of the argument in Holloway (n.d.). Holloway lists 64 significant slave revolts between 1512, when 40 people enslaved by Christopher Columbus revolted (all were captured or killed within months), and 1825, when hundreds of enslaved Afro-Cubans revolted. On the one hand, these revolts frightened the *criollos*. Fear of slave revolts made them reluctant to separate from the imperial state and its armies. On the other hand, revolts constituted one more form of resistance that were precursors to the final break. Enslaved Africans often sought freedom in the vast interior, where they established self-governing communities, *cumbes*.

In 1804, slaves led by Toussaint L'Ouverture revolted against their French colonial masters in Haiti and achieved independence—arguably the first true national liberation movement in the history of anticolonialism. The new Haitian regime carried out a bloody expulsion of white planters (especially after L'Ouverture's assassination), which convinced elites in other regions (including the southern colonies of the United States) to guard against social revolution in the struggle for independence from Europe. Elites in several neighboring Caribbean colonies (Cuba, Dominican Republic, and Puerto Rico) resisted the continent's movement into independence for another 70 years. Many looked hopefully toward the United States to replace faltering Spain as guarantor of their dominance, even after manumission. Fear of emancipation also contributed to the willingness of the Brazilian colonial elite to remain loyal to a Portuguese monarch who fled Napoleon's troops in 1807 and set up shop in Brazil (see later discussion).

As we discussed earlier in regard to *mestizaje*, the interaction among race, class, and gender was a complex one, and in Latin America the practice of miscegenation and rape quickly gave rise to a large population that was racially and culturally mixed. Those of partial African descent came to be called *mulatos*, *pardos*, or some similar name. As we have seen, more so in Latin America than in the United States, there was room for some economic advancement and social mobility for enslaved people. This partial disconnect between race and class stamped Brazil and parts of other countries in the Caribbean region with a particular social structure. Certainly, enslaved people yearned for freedom, but it did not always mean a better life materially. In the towns, where those freed from plantation life gathered, there developed a large, poverty-stricken class of "free" homeless people, beggars, prostitutes, and others whose status in colonial society was higher than slaves, but whose economic condition could be even worse.

For Review

In what regions of Latin America do we find people of African descent? What were the main reasons that Europeans decided to enslave Africans and bring them to the New World? How did the exploitation and subjugation of indigenous peoples and enslaved Africans affect the calculation of European descendants about the desirability of independence?

■ Ethnic Identity, National Identity, and the Legacy of Colonialism

How do the pre-Columbian and colonial eras assert themselves in present-day politics? In the 1990s the political influence of indigenous peoples grew to proportions not seen since the conquest. In other places Afro-descendent peoples emerged to demand not only respect for their cultures but also programs and even reparations for the harm inflicted by slavery.

Colonial Legacy: Indigenous Politics

Mexico has felt the impact of indigenous reawakening. In the southern state of Chiapas, the local indigenous people are the country's poorest. However, Chiapas is blessed with considerable natural resources (Figure 3.2). Its rivers supply power to most of the country, and central planners in Mexico City have designs for expanding the energy grid south into Central America. The growth of cattle ranching has depleted the Lacandon rainforest, driving many peasants onto more marginal lands. Almost invisibly, in the early 1990s, a guerrilla movement of resistance began to form, and it burst into view suddenly on January 1, 1994, when the rebels seized the state capital. The guerrillas adopted the name Zapatista Army of National Liberation (Ejército Zapatista de Liberación Nacional—EZLN); they are usually

FIGURE 3.2 Map of Chiapas in Mexico

known as the "Zapatistas," taking their name from the great peasant leader of Mexico's 1910 revolution, Emiliano Zapata (see chapter 9).

The character of this movement has been stamped deeply by indigenous values. This is evident in its strategy, which rejects the idea of taking power by taking control of the Mexican state. Zapatistas say that they want to rethink the entire idea of the state and power, placing less emphasis on national government and more on values of community solidarity, common ownership, and local participatory government. Also, they take a long-term outlook on revolution. Inspired by their Mayan past, the Zapatistas are prepared to work patiently for decades to accomplish their goals. Their slogan, "Change the world without taking power," has been adopted by many social movements opposed to economic globalization.

The movement cannot simply be labeled "indigenous." Its leader, known as "subco-mandante" Marcos, is not an Indian. However, identity is as much in the mind as in the genes. For example, farther north, the people of Atenco successfully resisted an attempt during the early 2000s to build a new airport for nearby Mexico City. Only a few hundred of that town's people speak an indigenous language, but they justified resistance to expro-priation of their communal lands by referring to their native past. This sense of ancestry contributes to a growing identity of people in the region as "Mesoamerican" (Stolle-McAllister 2005: 27).

A similar resurgence has happened in the countries that lie within the historical Inca Empire. For example, in October 2003, descendants of the Aymara people swept down on La Paz, the Bolivian capital, from the sprawling urban slums of nearby El Alto to force President Gonzalo Sánchez de Losada from the presidential palace. They were protesting his plans to place Bolivian natural gas deposits under foreign control. Up to 500,000 Bolivians partici-pated. The organizers and participants alluded to something that had happened in 1781—a failed revolt against colonial authorities—though this time they met with more success. Mass uprisings had forced dictators out of Bolivia before, but in those cases, the protests were led by the middle class and workers affiliated with the unions; Indian organizations were secondary actors. This time the uprising was being led by the indigenous sector (Hylton and Thomson 2004). The event influenced how many mestizo protestors saw their identity. Although many did not speak an Indian language, many came to see themselves as primarily indigenous. They chose, in a sense, like the people of Atenco, to adopt their Indian ancestry as their identity.

It may be that the residents in El Alto are somewhat selectively remembering their past. An anthropologist sympathetic to their cause, who lived in and researched the city for several years before the uprising, contends that before the Spaniards, the Indian communi-ties (*ayllus*) might not have been as egalitarian as we suppose and that the system of rotating leadership introduced by the Spanish conquerors might have been a more democratic sys-tem. The scholar met strong resistance from students at the Public University of El Alto when he made this suggestion (Lazar 2008: 10–11). This suggests that what matters is not just what really happened in history, but what we *think or prefer to think* happened.

In 1990, indigenous peoples from 120 different tribes and organizations from every part of the Western Hemisphere, north and south, came to Ecuador and issued their Dec-laration of Quito, in which they proclaimed that their struggle for "self-determination" had reached a new level of organization, but not in isolation from struggles for social justice waged by other groups. The declaration speaks of "autonomy," not "sovereignty," and in doing so avoids the notion that the people of indigenous movements are separatists, attempting to establish their own states. The declaration demands that autonomy include "the right to control our lands, including the management of natural resources under and above ground, as well as control over our airspace." It includes a "rejection of the capitalist system" and calls for "the elimination of all forms of sociocultural oppression and economic exploitation. Our struggle is geared toward the construction of a new society, pluralistic, democratic and based on popular power."

Evo Morales, an Aymara Indian, elected in December 2005 as the first indigenous president of a Latin American country, rose to prominence in Bolivian politics as leader of the *cocaleros*—cultivators of coca, the base for cocaine. Aymara and Quechua people cultivated and chewed the leaf of the coca plant for centuries, long before the Spanish arrived, but Andeans produce coca today also to take advantage of the international recreational drug market. Morales advocated closing Bolivia's markets to imports of luxury goods and to other products that Bolivians can produce themselves. He advocated that the Bolivian state nationalize the country's mines, railroads, and utilities. He opposed the U.S.-inspired and financed war on drugs, fought partly in Bolivia, regarding it as imperialism. This anti-imperialist message and economic agenda broadened his appeal across ethnic boundaries. Referring to the post-conquest treatment of his people by European descendants, Morales told *New York Times* correspondent Juan Forero he had little interest in compromise. "For more than 500 years, they have not been tolerant of us; now that we have gotten ahead, they want us to be tolerant with them."

Indigenous demands for autonomy are an attempt to defend their culture from disappearing into a mestizo nation. *Mestizo* (sometimes *Ladino*) here means "mixed race," and the term sometimes is expanded to *mestizaje* when it refers to an ideology, a way of thinking. In the 1800s, having shaken off colonial rule, a growing middle class had to come to grips with the various strains of blood running through its veins. Gradually, the notion of *mestizaje*, somewhat akin to the idea of a new race, emerged, changing national identity. Morales gave voice to the demands and grievances of the indigenous population, and once in office he moved to rewrite the constitution and define Bolivia as a "**plurinational state**." Regional and ethnic autonomy were key principles in the charter and to some degree were implemented in subsequent laws. But as president, Morales found it necessary to compromise as he sought to balance the economic reality of a national economy tied closely to extractive export industries (oil, gas, mining) and demands from both indigenous groups resistant to the presence of foreign companies and local elites seeking to use autonomy to keep profits in their own hands, away from the central government headed by the indigenous leader. (See the Punto de Vista "Can 'Plurinationalism' Work?")

PUNTO DE VISTA: CAN "PLURINATIONALISM" WORK?

Bolivia's new constitution of 2009 begins by describing how in colonial times the country's natural resources were raped and how "this Sacred Earth" was populated by peoples whose diversity was not recognized because of racism. The new constitution, it says, recognizes this legacy and the "plural composition" of its inhabitants. Committed to the "integral development and free determination of its peoples," the constitution asserts it accepts "the historical challenge of constructing a 'plurinational' nation state."

Drawing on indigenous culture, it seeks to create a society in which "living well" (*buen vivir*, or *vivir bién*) takes precedence over accumulation of material things. These goals have inspired many people beyond Bolivia's borders, especially those alarmed by climate change and concerned that material wealth does not equate to happiness.

Many political scientists argue that ethnic divisions pose a threat to democratic stability (Rostow 1960), but others (Selverston-Scher 2001) contend that few nation-states in the contemporary world are truly homogeneous anyway. The solution, they argue, is a "plurinational" state. In a **plurinational state** different ethnic groups find a compromise formula permitting shared **governance** and a richer, more diverse society.

Some Bolivians believe the idea of a plurinational state is both unrealistic and undesirable. In 2009, Bolivian president Evo Morales declared that the Wiphala, a rainbow-colored flag used by indigenous peoples throughout the Andean region, should always be flown alongside the tricolor Bolivian national flag. This prompted protests from some Bolivians that the unity and identity of the nation were being undermined, heightening ethnic tensions. You can see a report on the controversy on the Real News Network here: www.youtube.com/watch?v=RQ4wtKW3kEE.

The plurinational idea also raises thorny issues about who controls access to land and resources. In 2011, export from extractive industries (mostly oil, gas, copper, and mining) constituted one-third of Bolivia's gross domestic product and over three-quarters of its total exports. Morales, a native Aymara speaker, has strived to direct more of the profits from these industries toward the needs of the poor, including indigenous peoples. However, some indigenous leaders complain that he has failed to respect their right to control natural resources within the areas where they have autonomy rights.

Bolivian law requires that government agencies consult with indigenous peoples before drilling, mining activity, or road building takes place. In December 2011, the Morales government claimed that 80 percent of tribal groups in one Amazonian region agreed with the government's plans to build a road through one such territory, but a critic in the region complained that consultations organized by the government were not well attended, did not adequately inform participants, and framed discussions with promises to provide a variety of benefits and services if the road were approved (Achtenberg 2012).

Meanwhile, in Santa Cruz province, which lies on the plains south and west of the Andes, the elite—mostly mestizos in this case, but like Creoles elsewhere, still very European-oriented—sit on top of valuable minerals. They want to use new autonomy laws to keep profits in the province and out of the hands of the central government. Here indigenous people support Morales, arguing that since the Conquest, Creoles have exploited the rich ore veins for their own exclusive benefit.

In November 2012, Bolivia conducted its first census since Morales became president. In the census, Bolivians were first asked whether they considered themselves to belong to "an indigenous nation or people with peasant origins or to be Afro-Bolivian." If they answered "yes," then they chose among 38 different ethnic classifications; "mestizo" was not among them. Only those choosing "other," one of the options available, were counted as "mestizo." Opponents of the policy claimed the omission violated the right of Bolivians to express their ethnic identity freely.

Why does it matter whether a Bolivian can choose "mestizo"? "Mestizo" suggests a melting-pot culture where everyone shares a common sense of nationhood. People might have different skin complexions, but all share a common identity as Bolivians. That is, all Bolivians share the same "mixture" of European, indigenous, and other values. To be able to choose among a number of different indigenous classifications suggests this process has largely been a myth. It creates a basis for people in these classifications to make demands about control over their territories, for example, or what children are taught in school.

The controversy over "mestizo" is clearly rooted in the recent debates over national identity; the category did not appear in the previous census. Geofredo Sandoval, a sociologist involved in administering the census, said that the exclusion of mestizo this time was "an attempt to correct a centuries-old subjugation of the Indian majority by the dominant mestizo classes" (Catholic News Services 2012). The census also asked other questions, including one asking the respondent to identify the main language they speak, that could be used afterward to estimate the mestizo population.

See the Bolivia democracy snapshot on the next page.

Point/Counterpoint

Do you think that plurinationalism makes sense for Bolivia? Would you have included "mestizo" as a choice for respondents in the census?

a. If you answered yes to the first question, what do you say in response to those who think that it could cause the country ultimately to come apart and is unrealistic in a world where sovereignty is linked one-to-one with nationhood?
b. If you answered no to the first question, what would you say to indigenous peoples who feel they never have truly been regarded as Bolivian by others?
c. If you answered yes to the second question, how would you answer Sandoval's point?
d. If you answered no to the second question, what would you say to those who think mestizo ought to be a choice?

For more information

Several documentaries at Journeyman.tv look at Bolivia's indigenous politics. *Bolivian Voices* (2008) looks at the rise of indigenous influence, whereas *Two Bolivias* (2007) features critical reactions to indigenous demands. The short (less than seven-minute) piece *The Struggle for a New Constitution* (2008) shows how complicated indigenous politics can be. Katie Kuhn sees the emergence of indigenous influence as a good thing but questions where plurinationalism is workable in "Identify versus Unity: Solving Problems in a Country with 36 Nations," *Diplomacy and Foreign Affairs* (n.d., http://diplomacyandforeignaffairs.com/identity-versus-unity-solving-common-problems-in-a-country-with-36-nations).

Colonial Legacy: Afro-Descendent Politics

We can also see the legacy of colonialism in ethnic issues involving Afro-descendent people in the Americas. As with the case of indigenous peoples, the questions that arise are not simply ethnic but also touch on social class and other social divisions. In Brazil and Cuba, almost everyone is Afro-descendent, meaning there is some connection to enslaved ancestors in their genetic makeup. So when we say that the Brazilian census for the first time in 2010 revealed

that a majority consider themselves non-white, this could be because of differential birthrates over time, or it could be because people have changed how they think about their ancestry, their identity. In Cuba, the 1959 revolution did not target Afro-Cubans for special treatment, but programs to improve literacy, education, and rural conditions disproportionately affected the darker-skinned population. Conversely, in recent years the (limited) opening movement toward an economy based on market relations, as well as the reduction of state employment, has generally been more beneficial to lighter-skinned Cubans, many of whom have relatives in the United States willing to send help with money and gifts. Not only does this connection improve their standard of living; it also means they have more resources to start small businesses, allowed under the new rules.

Venezuela has a substantial number of *pardos* in its population, with African influence most pronounced on its northeast coast, Barlovento, where cacao plantations were the backbone of the colonial economy. After the victory of Hugo Chávez, a *pardo*, in the 1998 election, darker-skinned Venezuelans began to press for more explicit recognition in the new constitution of their distinct cultural identity and of their needs. Like their Brazilian counterparts, they were protesting against the myth of racial democracy. Even in the favorable context provided by Chávez's victory, they failed to achieve formal recognition in the new (1999) constitution. Indigenous peoples were allocated three seats in the national legislature, and some Afro-descendent people feel they merited similar consideration, some kind of guarantee of representation. But Jesús Chucho García, a leading spokesperson for the Afro-Venezuelan movement and a supporter of Chávez, complained,

> We, the African-Venezuelan organizations, made a formal proposal for the constitutional assembly . . . There was someone from the left—racism does not respect ideologies—who said, 'the articles for the indigenous already caused so many problems, are we now going to put something in for the blacks? No, we can't do that.' Still, in the original constitutional proposal that Chavez had made there was a reference to those of African descent, but it and our proposal were completely taken out by the left. By the left! Because they did not understand the problem.
>
> (quoted in Wilpert 2004)

He went on to say that afterward, as key new laws were passed, such as those dealing with land reform and education, once again problems specific to Afro-Venezuelans were not addressed.

> And since we don't appear in the organic [semi-constitutional] laws, we don't appear in the programs of government institutions. For example, in the ministry of social development, there is a program to support ethnic diversity. If you look at the program, the only type of ethnic diversity it refers to are the indigenous peoples, but African ethnicity does not appear . . . So, as you can see, there is a racial exclusion, discrimination, from a juridical perspective and in the area of public policy. This is one of the great challenges that this revolution has to deal with. There is no real, profound, sincere revolution without the incorporation of the issue of African descent.
>
> (quoted in Wilpert 2004)

García was not opposing recognition of indigenous autonomy but claiming that descendants of enslaved peoples deserve recognition of their particular identity and the impact of enslavement and subsequent discrimination.

The issue of racial equality can go to the heart of what it means to be a citizen, as illustrated by the terribly complicated issue of land ownership throughout Latin America. In the colonial era, the Crown and Church often set aside and defended land rights for indigenous peoples. Rebellions and financial calamity could result in land changing hands. Those deposed often would later try to reclaim legal title. Over centuries land was often bought and sold in irregular ways; multiple deeds for the same parcel came into existence. This laid the basis for land conflict not only in rural areas, but also in urban areas. As relatively sleepy towns grew into major cities, poor people were often expelled from city centers to the outskirts, where they built their own housing on parcels of land that were never registered as theirs or, even worse, were registered to someone else in the form of a deed in some dusty Church or municipal archive, laying the basis later for a real estate speculator. This process was often repeated as the small cities became metropolitan areas with millions of people, with half or more living in homes without verifiable legal documents to back them up.

The link to race here is that those living on such parcels, expelled from the city centers and later from other urban areas that became valuable real estate with economic and population growth, are disproportionately non-white. The Brazilian case is instructive. James Holston (2008) notes that Brazilian definitions of citizenship, unlike in North America, allowed for different kinds of citizens, with differences closely related to race. In the colonial era, the government allowed land to be deeded only to residents with sufficient economic means to work it, virtually excluding not only Afro-Brazilians but many freed blacks and *pardos* as well. With a huge landmass and small population, "free" but unequal citizens could usually migrate to vacant land or land owned but not used; in other words, once such land became valuable for agriculture or commercial development, the settlers could have their right to live there challenged. Whites, generally with more resources and lawyers at their disposal, could win out (though they also battled with one another).

Examination of one land-dispute case involving attempts to displace poor residents of a neighborhood of São Paolo (Holston 2008) found that the conflict had multiple sides, with divisions among the neighbors themselves and multiple parties seeking to evict residents from their homes, to establish a dubious ownership over the land to collect rent, or to come to a negotiated settlement. The situation was made even more complicated by swindlers who were expert at using courts and records to establish supposed "ownership" over neighborhoods. Holston (2008:205) says, "I soon discovered that no one could make much sense of the dispute in question without following it back in time. Litigants, lawyers, judges, residents, and swindlers themselves study its genealogies to base their present-day arguments on the authority of history, which dates back to 1580." São Paolo grew from a small city of 30,000 around 1870 to a megalopolis of over 11 million today, and along the way, poor people, mostly black and *pardo*, were successively expelled from the communities they had built to the periphery, building the urban slums that are today called *favelas*.

However, the result here was not, as so often seems to be the case, defeat for the poor. Holston's somewhat surprising conclusion is that the illegality and uncertainty in which people in São Paolo live today has ignited a demand for full equality and inclusion as citizens. That is, after Brazil transitioned from a military dictatorship to an elected democracy,

PUNTO DE VISTA: DOES BRAZIL NEED AFFIRMATIVE ACTION?

Affirmative action refers to governmental policies that attempt to redress the historical legacy of slavery and discrimination on the basis of race, ethnicity, or gender by favoring individuals who are descendants of victims. Courts in the United States have placed obstacles in the way of affirmative action by finding most such policies discriminatory against others, most notably whites and males. But in Brazil, recent governments have implemented the most controversial of such measures—quotas.

On October 12, 2012, President Dilma Rousseff approved a new Law of Quotas, which requires the country's 59 universities to reach the goal of having half of their students come from public schools, whose own students come mostly from poor neighborhoods. The universities must also ensure that half of the admitted students are representative of the local population's racial mix, a measure that heavily favors those of African descent. Universities have been assigned quotas that they must achieve. The law capped off 20 years of gradual implementation of various affirmative action measures. In April 2013, Brazil's Supreme Court approved the constitutionality of the law.

Early signs indicate that despite fears of diluted education, students admitted under the quota are doing fine. However, that may in part reflect the low percentage of Brazilians who make it to college overall—only 19 percent, compared to 45 percent of U.S. residents and 69 percent in South Korea. University education is free, but students must pass qualifying exams to enter.

A slight majority of Brazil's 200 million people identify as Afro-descendent, at least partially. For 300 years in the colonial era, Brazil's export economy depended on enslaved Africans whose labor produced gold, silver, sugar, and other products that enriched an upper class. Brazil imported seven times as many slaves as did the United States, and it was the last country, in 1888, to make slavery illegal. As in Cuba and other

regions with a plantation economy, African descendants—including most of the mulatto population—have not relinquished their sense of connection to mother Africa, which is reflected in religion and culture.

Until recently, Brazil shared the myth of racial democracy with the rest of Latin America. However, during a gradual move from democracy to dictatorship in the 1980s, that began to change. Landless workers, people in the *favelas* without legally verified ownership of their homes, women in poor communities, and many others formed social movements, and this surge of democracy was led by a mulatto union leader, Luiz Inácio Lula da Silva (Lula), who became president in 2002, and Benedita Silva, a devout radical religious woman who became the first black (and black woman) elected to the Brazilian Senate.

One important feature of quotas in Brazil, we should note, is that they are based on social class, not just race. Also, Brazil has very liberal criteria for qualification as black—often described as the "one drop" of blood rule. Given these provisions, it is no surprise that a large part of the population benefits, giving the policy a broad base of support politically. Polls in 2008 showed that 44 percent of the population "strongly agreed" with the quota system, and another 18 percent "agreed." Most of the opposition came from the middle class, and the major media all opposed the idea.

The opposition's argument, that historical discrimination no longer exists, should be familiar to most North Americans, though with a difference. Whereas in the United States the typical claim of whites is that the present generation is not guilty of the injustices of ancestors and many are not even descended from slave owners or others of the past era, in Brazil, the argument is more along the lines that because of miscegenation (births resulting from sexual intercourse among people of different races), the country already is a racial democracy, a claim that lost steam as the social movements of the 1980s began to ask why so few dark-skinned people could be found in prestigious and well-paying professions.

It is too soon to know what positive or negative effects the quota law will have on Brazilian society. Affirmative action may exist in some form in the United States, but it is difficult in a country with such a strong liberal (see chapter 1) ideology to imagine that a quota system will ever be accepted. Clearly, something about Brazil's history and culture is different and—even allowing for the fact that many Brazilians do oppose the law—would permit such a system to be found desirable by most citizens and legal by the courts.

Point/Counterpoint

Is affirmative action in Brazil consistent with the democratic principle of equality?

a. If you answered yes, how would you answer those who say that it penalizes those Brazilians who weren't responsible for the original injustices? Also, are you saying yes because in general you also support affirmative action in the United States and other societies or because Brazil's history with slavery and race is different in some way?

b. If you answered no, how would you answer those who say the legacy of slavery means that Afro-Brazilians and *pardos* do not have the same opportunities as lighter-skinned Brazilians? Would you do nothing?

For more information

See Juliana Barbassa, "Race to the Top," *New York Times*, May 17, 2013 (http://latitude.blogs.nytimes.com/2013/05/17/brazil-has-aggressive-affirmative-action-programs-for-university/?_php=true&_type=blogs&_r=0); Ibram H. Rogers, "Brazil's Affirmative Action Quotas: Progress?," *Chronicle of Higher Education*, November 5, 2012; Edward Telles, "Brazil in Black and White," *Wide Angle* (PBS, June 1, 2009, www.pbs.org/wnet/wideangle/lessons/brazil-in-black-and-white/discrimination-and-affirmative-action-in-brazil/4323).

the social movements led by Lula, Benedita da Silva, and others began to practice what the author calls "insurgent citizenship," challenging an exclusion built on the foundations of colonialism, slavery, and a system of law designed to ensure that political equality would not shake the social order—racial and class-based—inherited from the past. That has led Brazilians to be much more open than are North Americans, for example, to affirmative action programs that use quotas to increase the numbers of Afro-Brazilians in universities (see the Punto de Vista "Does Brazil Need Affirmative Action?").

Before we move away from the topic of race and class, I think it important not to leave you with the impression that there is a strict correlation between race and social class in Latin America. One can find lighter-skinned people in poor urban neighborhoods or eking out a living on small plots of land in northeast Brazil. Similarly, few members of the upper class are without indigenous or African ancestry. The myths of racial democracy and of *mestizaje* persist in part because there is truth in the idea that Latin Americas are, and have been, more comfortable with social and biological racial mixing than we are in the United States. But at the same time we should be wary when this positive aspect of social relations leads to denial that race matters in Latin America.

For Review

Why might a Latin American person's sense of his or her own ethnic identify change, even if the person's skin color and other biological features have not? What are some ways that people turn to history in arguing about issues today in Latin America?

Persistence of Colonial Economic Dependency

Of course, the original impulse for Europeans to conquer the Americas rested in economics. Although religious motives were present as well, the Spanish and Portuguese Crowns were seeking wealth to consolidate control over the Iberian Peninsula and to finance wars with other European powers. Clearly, we would be failing to understand the legacy of colonialism if we did not make reference to the way that Europeans sought to put their colonies at the service of the "mother country."

In the United States, most schoolchildren learn that one of the causes of the American Revolution was the colonists' resistance to attempts by the English Crown to restrict trade with other countries and limit which ships could carry goods in and out of North American harbors. These restrictive policies were even more rigid and harshly enforced in colonial Latin America, especially in the case of the Spanish. For example, the Spanish Crown would not even let its colonies produce olive oil, requiring instead that they import it from Spain. Economic and political forces combined to create a system of **monoculture** whereby distinct regions in Latin America specialized in production of a single particular product—cacao, sugar, hemp, and so on.

Thus, the imperial powers limited the ability of their colonies to produce and trade with one another or to import products from rival European powers. This pattern of monoculture, export of raw materials, and import of finished goods from abroad set a pattern of economic **dependency**, which many Latin Americans believe is the most significant cause of underdevelopment. Latin America's economic fortunes remain highly dependent on the exports.

The reorganization of indigenous social systems to extract and export raw materials and agricultural products contributed to the devastation of the population and set a pattern for the centuries that followed. As Elizabeth Dore (1991) put it,

> Because pre-Columbian societies deified nature and were organized to provide food security, their material and ideological structures generated a profound respect for the environment. Despite their significant differences, Maya, Aztec, Inca, and less numerous native peoples each shared key attributes: ruling classes appropriated surplus labor in the form of food (later distributed in times of scarcity), their cosmology was explicitly linked to the material order, and survival was precarious and highly dependent on preserving the eco-system.

During the colonial era, Latin America was integrated into an emerging world system as an exploited area of what theorists such as Immanuel Wallerstein (1974) call the "**periphery**." This integration meant that Latin America became one of several regions where for centuries a highly exploited labor force produced raw materials (agricultural goods and minerals) for export, exchanging them in the world trading system for more costly manufactured goods. The roots of Latin America's underdevelopment lay here, say dependency and **world systems** theorists.

The Europeans and the European-oriented ruling class (*criollos*) that succeeded the original Iberian masters viewed the New World as a source of wealth. They viewed nature as a woman to be conquered, another reason some call the conquest the "rape" of a continent. Consider the famous boast of Simón Bolívar, the great liberator of South America, who said in 1812 after an earthquake devastated Caracas, "If nature opposes us, we will struggle against her and make her obey."

Earlier, I cited Mann's observation that sometimes we romanticize indigenous culture and fail to recognize that the "first nations," as the Canadians call them, did not always live in harmony with nature. There can be little doubt, however, that indigenous people in the Americas had neither the capacity nor the will to conquer nature, much as Europeans had by 1500. Although environmental consciousness and respect for traditional knowledge has increased in recent years, for many Latin Americans (perhaps for us as well) the bounty of nature still exists mainly to be exploited: if a country wishes to progress, it must open that bounty to investment. If domestic capital and technology is lacking, the goal should be to remove obstacles that prevent foreigners from investing and promoting modernization. Now, in the age of globalization, many economists say that those countries that open their economies will prosper; those that close them will come to grief. To some Latin Americans, this sounds too much like a recipe for environmental disaster and continuing dependency.

The colonial era lasted 300 years; the postcolonial era has barely arrived at two centuries. But two centuries is a significant passage of time—enough for Latin America, much like North America, to have found its own path forward, less encumbered by the negative aspects of colonialism. Indeed, independence has permitted Latin Americans to pursue a forward course and escape some of the severe consequences of colonialism in the nineteenth and twentieth centuries, but at the same time few would argue that the legacy of economic dependency has been overcome.

For Review

How did colonialism introduce a pattern for economic dependency that would persist into the present? How did the attitude of European colonialists toward nature in Latin America differ from that of the indigenous population?

Discussion Questions

1. What does it mean to be a "Latin" American? Do you think it makes any sense to describe as "Latin" people as diverse as an Aymara Indian from Bolivia, a descendant of slaves in Cuba, a white landowner in Chile, and an entrepreneur descended from Asian or Arab immigrants in Venezuela? Are nations nothing more than imagined communities?

2. Find a video (e.g., on YouTube) of the popular singer Shakira, who is partially of Arab descent. Find a biography of her on the web. How would you characterize her place in the racial/class pyramid of Latin America? Do you consider her music to be Latin?

3. Latin American *criollos* came to want independence—that is, territorial sovereignty. What did most of them *not* want to happen with independence?

4. Part of the legacy of colonialism is that indigenous peoples and Afro-descendent peoples still disproportionately populate the ranks of the poor and indigent. Do you think that the persistence of this state of affairs (hardly unknown in the United States, we should acknowledge) is a sign of democratic failure?

Resources for Further Study

Reading: *The Villagers* (*Huasipungo*), by Jorge Icaza, translated by Bernard Dulsey (Edwardsville: Southern Illinois University Press, 1964), is a novel exploring the life of indigenous people in Ecuador under the *latifundia* system. *Women in the Crucible of Conquest*, by Karen Vieira Powers (University of New Mexico, 2005), tells how some women resisted dominance and made a place for themselves in colonial society. *Colonial Legacies: The Problem of Persistence in Latin American History*, edited by Jeremy Adelman (New York: Routledge, 1999), deals with the impacts and influences of colonial life on Latin America today and its likely future relevance. One way to understand the clash between republican values and Creole fears of social upheaval is through the life of Simón Bolívar. A good recent biography is *American Liberator* by Marie Arana (New York: Simon and Schuster, 2013).

Video and Film: *The Mission* (1986), set in colonial Brazil, explores the complex relationship between the Church and exploitation of indigenous people. One of the most important examples of indigenous politics is Bolivia's first indigenous president, Evo Morales. A 2008 Tuttle Films documentary, *Bolivian Voices* (www.journeyman. tv/58726/documentaries/bolivian-voices.html) explores Evo Morales's biography and his rise to the presidency of Bolivia. It also ponders a future under his political guidance and notes mixed feelings of anticipation and hope. The documentary *Cocalero* (2007) looks at the movement that brought him to prominence. *También la lluvia* ("Even the Rain," 2010) links Spanish colonialism to a modern-day conflict over control of water supplies in Bolivia. *A Place Called Chiapas* (1985), about the Zapatista uprising, can now be viewed on YouTube. Controversy about the Wiphala, the indigenous flag, is the subject of this news report from Taiwan TV (TITTV): www.youtube

.com/watch?v=c6MGKbzFG38. *Buried Mirror* (1994), from the PBS *Americas* series, focuses on identity in Latin America.

On the Internet: For women in Latin America, a good portal is http://womenshistory.about. com/od/latinamerica/Central_and_south_america.htm. Perhaps no region is so rich in Afro-Latin history as Bahia, in northeast Brazil (see http://isc.temple.edu/ evanson/brazilhistory/Bahia.htm).

4 Political without Economic Independence

Focus Questions

▶ Why after political independence did most of the social and economic patterns established by colonialism persist?

▶ Why did Portuguese America—that is, Brazil—not break up into smaller nations the way that Spanish America did? How different is Brazilian politics today as a result?

▶ What were the political, social, and economic consequences of the shift of dependency from Iberian Europe to Northern Europe?

▶ Why did countries in the region struggle to establish stable republics, and why did state-building eventually emerge in the final decades of the nineteenth century?

HOW MUCH DIFFERENCE did political independence from Spain and Portugal make in the lives of most Latin Americans? The social class structure stayed largely intact; the majority of Latin Americans remained mired in poverty; and various cultural institutions, including the Catholic Church, remained in place. In much of Spanish America, the disappearance of the colonial power left a vacuum of power that was not filled for many decades. Internal civil war was not unknown in the colonial era, but for most of that time, the Crown provided a degree of political stability. The aftermath of independence saw the rise of **caudilloism**, a tendency that continues to mark Latin American politics today. On the other side of the ledger, independence did result in Latin Americans achieving a sovereign status denied to peoples subject to nineteenth-century European imperialism in Africa, Asia, and the Middle East, and it opened the way for a degree of economic and social development in the later 1800s.

The Path to Independence in Spanish America

The roots of independence were multiple. Part of the story was a growing sense of self-confidence among *criollos*, whose economic interests were diverging in the late 1700s from those of the Iberian homeland. World events, such as the American and French Revolutions and the decline of Spanish power, pushed them further toward that objective. By the eighteenth century, the upper classes of colonial society were 200 years removed from their conquistador ancestors. Within the protective umbrella of Spanish and Portuguese military forces, they had begun to experience a degree of local control over their affairs, especially in *cabildos* (town councils) in Spanish America.

Two rising powers in Northern Europe, France and Britain, knew that control of the Iberian countries brought with it the benefits of its vast American empire. *Criollos* had already seen the French Bourbon dynasty replace the Hapsburgs in 1700, and Spanish forces suffered a humiliating defeat at the hands of the British in the War of the Spanish Succession (1701–1713). The *criollo* ruling class in both Portuguese and Spanish America began to seek more freedom to trade outside the confines of the colonial system. Although gold and silver were still being mined, commodities such as sugar, cacao, coffee, rice, grains, and leather, among others, were increasingly in demand. And when the Industrial Revolution took off, first in Britain (around 1780) and later in other parts of Europe, Latin America's raw materials were in demand.

The Bourbons tried to stanch the decline of the empire by introducing reforms that distressed conservative *criollos*, especially the Catholic hierarchy. They made it easier for colonial exports to enter Spanish ports, but they also cracked down on smuggling and illegal trade, which threatened the *criollos'* access to growing markets in Northern Europe. To improve efficiency and fight corruption, the Bourbons centralized administration in the colonies. Just as *criollos* were seeking new opportunities and markets for their exports, the Crown was reinforcing its monopoly on governance. These policies generated resentment among the colonial elite, who were eager to trade freely and control their own affairs (Table 4.1).

Criollo enthusiasm for independence was held in check by fears of social rebellion by the lower orders. Indigenous resistance to the conquest had never been entirely extinguished. Slavery, **peonage**, and other forms of exploitation required deployments of armies over vast territories to put down revolts. Mass uprisings punctuated the late colonial period. In 1780, a mestizo who took the name Tupac Amaru II, after the last Inca emperor, sparked an uprising that blazed across Peru, resulting in the deaths of many *hacendados* (large landowners) and the burning of their estates. This was followed in 1781 by the Revolt of the Comuneros, as the inhabitants of present-day Colombia and Venezuela were known at the time. This rebellion started as a *criollo*-led tax revolt and evolved into a mass revolt of indigenous peoples. These revolts and others (e.g., see Hidalgo's revolt in Mexico, as described later) are regarded as precursors of independence today, but they inspired fear in Creoles.

The American Revolution in 1776 inspired thoughts of independence and admiration for liberalism among some *criollos*. The French Revolution of 1789 did the same, but its political ramifications in Europe had an even greater impact. By 1800, revolutionary idealism had given way in France to dictatorship and empire. The French ruler and conqueror, Napoleon Bonaparte, threatened to overrun Spain and Portugal altogether and impose liberal ideas by force. In Spain, regional governments proclaimed self-government under *cabildos* (councils) or **juntas**, a word that would later become synonymous with temporary rule after the overthrow of a government. Many Creoles looked to fill the vacuum of legitimacy in Spain. Napoleon's main rival, Great Britain, encouraged them to opt for independence.

In the Viceroyalty of New Granada (modern-day Colombia, Bolivia, Ecuador, Venezuela, and parts of Peru), the leader of the *criollo* revolt was Francisco Miranda, who had fought in the American (U.S.) Revolution of 1776 and participated in the French Revolution of 1787. The French earthquake gave momentum to the ideal of nationalism and the right

TABLE 4.1   Chronology of the Nineteenth Century

1830s	Rise of caudillos, civil wars in most countries.
1823-1855	Santa Anna, a caudillo, presides over chronically unstable Mexican Republic. Loses Texas in war (1833) with the breakaway Republic, later absorbed into U.S. Defeats French forces occupying Veracruz (1838).
1846-48	Mexican American War culminates in Treaty of Guadalupe Hidalgo, ceding half of Mexican territory to U.S. Mayan Rebellion ("Caste War") suppressed in Yucutan region.
1855	U.S. adventurer (known as a filibuster) William Walker invades and occupies Nicaragua, rules as president for two years, undermined by forces backed by Andrew Carnegie and is executed by Hondurans in 1860.
1858-1861	War between Liberals and Conservatives in Mexico.
1862-64	French Army invades Mexico and sets the rule of Austrian archduke Maximilian in alliance with Conservatives
1867	Liberal armies defeat French, Maximilian executed; Benito Juárez becomes president of restored republic.
1864-70	Brazil, Argentina, and Uruguay (Triple Alliance), backed by British, defeat Paraguay in bloodiest international war, resulting in (estimated) deaths of 300,000 of 500,000 Paraguayans.
1868-78	Unsuccessful wars for independence in Cuba and Puerto Rico.
1876	Porfirio Díaz takes power, rules Mexico until 1911
1879-84	Chile, backed by British, defeats Peru and Bolivia in War of the Pacific, seizes nitrate rich northern desert.
1888	Abolition of slavery in Brazil
1889	Pedro II abdicates, Brazil is declared a republic
1895	José Martí leads a war for Cuban independence but is killed in this year.
1897	Brutal repression (15-30,000 killed) in Bahia, Brazil, of Canudos, where thousands of poor peasants had flocked to join movement led by religious mystic and radical.
1898	Spanish American War, United States controls Puerto Rico, Cuba, Guam, and Philippines.

of nations to sovereign independence. Miranda's revolt of 1810 was centered in the Spanish captaincy of Venezuela. It was crushed by the colonial governor, who supplemented Spanish troops with an army he raised by promising freedom and land to slaves and peons. The Spanish quickly forgot these promises to the masses (setting a pattern for the next century) and exacted brutal retribution on the Creoles.

The defeat of Napoleon's army in 1814 brought to the Spanish throne Ferdinand VII, whose father had been deposed by the French. He moved to restore Spanish colonial authority and deployed troops—now freed from the European conflicts—to South America. But the movement for independence could not be stopped. European powers, notably Great Britain, were now actively aiding rebel *criollos* with money and arms. The struggle for independence in Spanish America evolved into a prolonged, violent civil war. Miranda's mantle of leadership was picked up by another *criollo*, Simón Bolívar, a brilliant military tactician who bravely marched his army over the Andes to spread the fight throughout New Granada.

In Argentina the fight was led by José de San Martín, whose tactical military genius and promises of freedom for slaves and peons allowed him to raise a formidable army by 1816. San Martín swept northward and met up with Bolívar's forces in 1822 in Guayaquil, Ecuador. The cause of Pan-Americanism (unity after independence), championed by Bolívar, was dealt a blow when the two leaders failed to agree on a political formula for governing the newly independent lands. San Martín retired into relative obscurity, whereas Bolívar's forces completed the fight against the Spanish, scoring the final decisive victory at the Battle of Ayacucho in Peru, in 1824.

In Mexico, a defrocked priest, Miguel Hidalgo, issued his "Grito de Dolores" ("Cry of Dolores") in 1810 and launched a movement for independence. A huge mass of poor, mostly indigenous Mexican rebels swept down from the north toward the capital of Mexico City, burning all in their path and summarily executing the Spanish *peninsulares*, the name given to officials sent by the Crown to govern the colony. Here was the nightmare that the Creoles had feared! Frightened, they turned to Spain to restore order.

A second mass uprising in Mexico, led by another priest, José María Morelos, followed. Like Hidalgo, Morelos promised to improve the lot of miners and Indian villagers who were losing common lands to renters favored by village leaders. Morelos fought more in the style of a modern guerrilla leader. After he was captured, tried (like Hidalgo, in a Church court), and then shot in 1815, the revolt continued under new leadership, though with less force than before, but then an unexpected group decided to seek independence. Conservative Creoles had become upset when the Spanish government, briefly in the hands of liberals, abolished some of their military and religious privileges. The Conservatives then made an offer of peace to the main guerrilla leader, Vicente Guerrero. In 1821, Mexico became independent under the leadership of General Agustín de Iturbide, who proclaimed himself Emperor Agustín I.

Thus, Mexico's first generation of leaders broke from Spain not because they rejected monarchy but in defense of it! There is no better example of how much fear of the masses could influence the transition from colony to nation. In fact, in some parts of the Americas, the transition was never made for this very reason.

The Haitian Revolution quelled the ardor for independence among Creoles in the Caribbean colonies. The Caribbean seethed with slave revolts and social unrest, but Cuba and Puerto Rico remained Spanish colonies until the United States' defeat of Spain in the war of 1898—although by this time, Cuban rebels had effectively defeated Spanish forces already. Havana, Cuba, was the most important military and economic outpost of Spain's empire in the Americas, which meant that its military power was most concentrated and effective there. As Spain proved increasingly impotent to maintain order, many elites saw the independent United States, which maintained slavery in its southern states, as a substitute. Indeed, politics in most of Mesoamerica and the Caribbean have been influenced by a high degree of U.S. intervention. One island, Puerto Rico, never gained sovereignty.

For Review

What are some ways that events in Europe affected the Americas? How did internal and external factors in Latin America ultimately reinforce the emergence of an independence movement?

Brazil's Divergent Path to Independence

Brazil took a different route to independence, one that was less abrupt and violent and that did not result in the breakup of the colonial territory. However, as in Spanish America, political sovereignty for the Portuguese colony did not produce a decisive break with patterns of economic dependence, and the chasm separating the masses from the elite remained. In the colonial era, Brazil's vast territory was populated by a mere 4 million people; almost all lived not far from the coast, and half of them were slaves. Escaped slaves fled to the interior, where they often intermarried with Indians. But there were also slave rebellions. One of these in Salvador, Bahia, in 1835 was organized by free and enslaved Afro-Brazilians inspired both by Muslim thought, which they had brought with them from their homeland in what is now Nigeria, and by the independence struggle in Haiti earlier in the century. They wore amulets with the image of Haitian president Dessalines, who had declared that country's independence in 1804.

The Portuguese colonial administration operated more on its own authority than did Spain's, but authorities in Brazil had to be constantly on guard against encroachment by the Spanish in the south and by the British, Dutch, and French in the north. The Northern European powers took advantage of Portuguese weakness to establish three colonial enclaves along the north coast of South America (British, French, and Dutch Guyana), complementing European control over several Caribbean islands (Curacao, Haiti, Grenada, Jamaica, Martinique, etc.). These colonies on the continent and in the Caribbean were lucrative sugar export economies, populated mostly by African slaves and their descendants. They would not achieve political independence until after World War II.

In the late colonial era, Portugal, like Spain, attempted to tighten control over its American colony in the face of the challenge from the Northern European powers. This fueled the desire of some Brazilian elites for independence, but as in other parts of the Americas, there was the matter of slavery and social rebellion to consider. Brazilian elites had their problem solved temporarily when the Portuguese monarchy came to them. Napoleon invaded Portugal in 1807, and the Lisbon court fled to Rio de Janeiro. Now the capital of a European empire was located in the Americas! The Portuguese prince regent, João, opened trade, permitted local industries, and founded a national bank. In 1815, he declared Brazil to be equal in status to Portugal. A revolution in Portugal in 1820 paved the way for João to return to the motherland, but he left his son and heir, Dom Pedro, behind to rule Brazil. In 1822, Dom Pedro refused an order from Portugal to return home, and thus the new nation of Brazil was born—as a monarchy.

A superficial examination of Brazilian history suggests the country evolved toward independence without civil war and enjoyed more stability than most Latin American countries. The country seems to have marched progressively toward democracy: from colony to a constitutional monarchy with an elected parliament sharing power and then to a full republic in 1889. However, as in Spanish America, Brazil's nineteenth century was punctuated by slave revolts and movements for land by the poor free population. The collapse of the monarchy and establishment of a republic was due in part to social strife caused by the question of slavery, which was abolished only in 1888, a year before the monarchy came to an end.

From 1889 to 1930, Brazil was formally a republic, with legislatures, civil courts, elected executives, and so on—but not a very democratic one. Of a population of 22 million people, only 360,000 voted in the 1910 presidential election. In 1890, the leaders of the new Brazilian republic established a literacy test as a prerequisite for voting—similar to the way whites did in the U.S. South after the Civil War. Even after slavery was abolished, land remained concentrated in a few hands. In comparison with the United States, race was less of a barrier to social acceptance and ascent in Brazil, but life expectancy was extremely low, and schooling beyond second grade was almost nonexistent for non-elites. How could citizenship flourish where staying alive was a day-to-day struggle?

In the hinterland, the social structure was semifeudal. An oligarchy made up of former slave owners monopolized the land. For the "right" to work small plots of land, their tenants had to provide personal or military service to the landowners. They were kept in line by Brazil's version of the *caudillo*, called the *coronel*, a warlord with his own private army of full-time private soldiers. *Coroneles* often fought one another, and sometimes with or against bands of bandits who became popular Robin Hood figures. Quasi-religious movements of the landless poor periodically broke out and were brutally suppressed. Brazil's social structure had a "medieval atmosphere of constant insecurity and social disintegration" (Keen and Haynes 2000: 241).

The best-known episode of resistance and suppression took place in the state of Bahia, an arid, desperately poor region populated by ex-slaves, mulattos, and indigenous peoples. A marginal geography—far from populated centers with established government, with few economic resources to attract any interest or attention—and the desperate living conditions of the inhabitants seemed to encourage the inhabitants to look toward mystical figures, saviors, or messiahs who could lead them to a better life on earth or afterward.

Antônio Vicente Mendes Maciel, also known as "the Counselor," was such a man, presenting himself as a prophet predicting the return of a mythological Portuguese king. He and some followers founded a town, Canudos, and based on his promises of an imminent better world: thousands flocked to the new settlement. Suddenly, the Church and provincial authorities took notice and began to fear sedition. Their fear increased, and the Counselor's legend grew, when two initial attempts to disband the settlers were met with devastating defeats and massacres of police and troops sent by the Republic (as Brazil's government was known)— with the rebel forces shouting praise for monarchy. By now, Canudos's population exceeded 30,000, and another unsuccessful attempt was made to quash the town, at great loss of life on both sides. In September 1897, the government launched a full-scale military campaign, with well-trained troops, modern arms, and professional planning. On October 2, 1897, after additional fierce fighting, Canudos was destroyed, with only 150 survivors (Levine 1995). Estimates of total casualties range from 15,000 to 30,000.

Like the Revolt of the Comuneros in El Alto, the uprisings in Canudos established a historical precedent well remembered on both sides. In the 1920s, for example, after an abortive rebellion, young army lieutenants led by Luis Carlos Prestes marched through the countryside, attracting tens of thousands of poor peasants, evoking again the hopes and fears that had been crushed at Canudos a quarter century before. More recently, landless peasants have organized themselves into the Landless Workers' Movement (Movimento dos Trabalhadores Sem Terra, or MST), evoking memories of earlier popular movements of resistance.

Popular culture often bestows heroic characteristics on figures who were little more than bandits, as was the case in Brazil with the renegades known as "Lampião" (Virgulino Ferreira da Silva) and "María Bonita" (María Dea), who were killed by Brazilian troops in 1938 after they had spent 19 years terrorizing local power brokers and landowners. There is little evidence that the two robbers and their band were politically motivated, but they were popularized as avengers of the common person against the arbitrary authority and greed of the wealthy. Lampião and María Bonita are kept alive in ballads and puppet plays in the Sertão (desert of the northeast) and the city of Recife. Bands that play the traditional and popular music, *folha*, in the northeast often wear clothing and symbols evocative of the marauders.

For Review

In what ways was Brazil's path to independence different from or similar to that of Spanish America? In what ways were relationships between ruling elites and the masses similar?

Failed States, New Nations

Enlightened Latin American leaders were aware that a new colossus was rising on the North American continent, but for the 1800s, the power that mattered most in making and breaking Latin American governments was Great Britain. The British had the most powerful navy and were the first and only country to have industrialized at the time of Latin America's independence. This gave Britain a decided military and economic advantage in world affairs, which it used to build an enormous empire that spanned Africa, the Middle East, India, and parts of Asia. In the Americas, the British were satisfied with a few Caribbean possessions, one of the Guyanas (to which they brought thousands of indentured South Asians), and Belize (then known as "British Honduras"). Other European states, notably France, Holland, and Prussia (part of what would become Germany), competed with the British and at times financed or armed factions favorable to their interests. When nationalist regimes in Latin America threatened to break from the system that favored European interests in general, the European powers usually united to protect the system. Loans, trade treaties, arms sales, and gunboats were tools by which Latin American economic dependency shifted from Iberia to the new, dynamic economies of Northern Europe after political independence.

Bolívar had called for unity and **Pan-Americanism** (i.e., awareness of a common identity among all peoples in the region), but the Spanish empire in the Americas broke up. The scale of the empire had something to do with this, since it stretched from California (part of Mexico) in North America to the Antarctic Circle. The Spanish Crown by necessity had divided this vast territory into geographic units for governance, but even these were large relative to the state of transportation, especially given formidable geographic obstacles. Local and regional power centers grew up, and some territories that had united briefly after independence dissolved quickly into smaller sovereign units. The Southern Cone republics broke away from the dominance of the colonial viceroyalty based far away and over the Andes in Lima, Peru, and then they split into the two large countries of Argentina and Chile, with Uruguay and Paraguay emerging as buffer states between Brazil and Argentina. By 1830, the northern region of the continent had broken apart into five countries—Venezuela, Colombia (including the province of Panama), Ecuador, Bolivia, and Peru (see Figure 4.1).

FIGURE 4.1   Map—from Colonialism to Independence

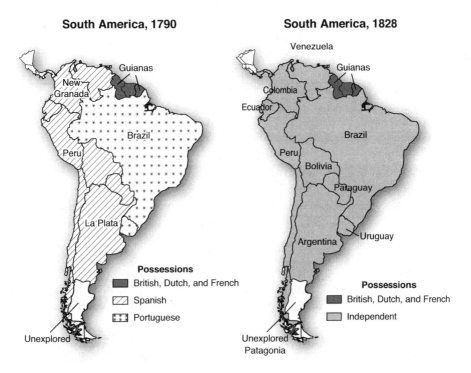

Farther north, southern regions of the greater Mexican empire broke away to form the Central American confederation, which itself splintered rapidly into five (six counting Belize, then part of Guatemala) smaller republics—Guatemala, Honduras, El Salvador, Nicaragua, and Costa Rica. Panama would form another Central American republic when it broke away from Colombia in 1903 (with considerable help from the United States, eager to build a canal there with cooperation from a pliant government).

Even these reduced territories were not well integrated and were afflicted by regional revolts against central authority. In some countries, particular regions were better linked to foreign export markets than to the capital. Transportation routes were built to connect the hinterlands with ports and not to enhance economic exchange of one region with another or to facilitate effective governance from the political capital. In Argentina, the Spanish had routed all trade to the north and west, over the Andes, to Peru. After independence, tensions between the province of Buenos Aires, with its fine Atlantic port, and the northwestern provinces helped fuel a bitter civil war that ended in dictatorship.

Social and economic conflicts further undermined stability. Landowners often found themselves in conflict with merchant houses in the ports and with banks. Together the merchant houses and the banks controlled two matters vital to the landowners' prosperity: finance and prices for their exported commodities. When overseas demand for exports fell and prices plummeted, landowners faced foreclosure on their property by creditors.

Landowners, merchant houses, and banks all turned to the central government for help, leading to grabs for property, bitter political factionalism, and often civil war.

Most Creoles interpreted citizen rights as meant exclusively for themselves and perhaps other literate members of their society, certainly not for the "ignorant" Indians, slaves, and peons. The economic base was land ownership, and their most profitable markets were overseas. Although they were the leading class of an independent nation, they showed little interest in building a strong central state or incorporating the lower classes into political life. Regional economies were linked to overseas markets through ports, but rarely very much to one another. The national market was of little importance. The political capital city was often far away, well beyond the horizon geographically and politically. Local and regional caudillos (*coroneles* in Brazil) were the immediate rulers. Often, regional power brokers turned on one another or on central authority, raising armies by making promises to the exploited masses. However, central authority was not meaningless. The capital city was the most important political link to the international system, an important center of power with military and economic resources that could make or break the fortunes of factions of the elite.

Though caudillos seized power by fighting, they inevitably needed support from some factions among the educated and economically powerful Creoles. Some caudillos could not read or write—an example being Rafael Carrera, dictator of Guatemala from 1844 to 1848 and again from 1851 to 1865. Some caudillos (e.g., Juan Manuel de Rosas, strongman of Argentina from approximately 1830 until 1852) were landowners, but others started out as trusted overseers for owners or as vigilantes hired to keep the peace. They sometimes turned on their employers. More successful caudillos, usually building on their reputation as skilled and fearless fighters, attracted large followings of peasants, slaves, or indentured **peons**, hopeful of gaining land or freedom. With this backing, caudillos could sometimes fight their way into power, but running a government was another matter. As a result, groups of educated elites in the capital never fully lost influence to military strongmen.

Today, in many countries, regional power brokers still resist the sovereign power of the central government. Brazil is especially notable even today in this respect, a tradition reinforced by federalism. Take the case of Blairo Maggi, first elected in 2002 to be governor of Mato Grosso, Brazil's largest state, located in the heart of the Amazonian basin. He is also known as the "king of soy" because he is the state's biggest landowner and has benefited handsomely from the boom in soybeans, produced in the region for export. As governor, Maggi simply refused to implement the central government's mandates to reduce destruction of the rainforest by curbing logging and clearing for more farms. In Maggi's first year (2003) as governor, the rate of deforestation nearly doubled. The combination of Maggi's economic wealth and Brazil's federalism made Maggi virtually untouchable in his own region, perhaps not a military *coronel*, but virtually sovereign in his own backyard.

In 2009, a Brazilian newspaper columnist (complaining about the use of patronage by President Luiz Inácio Lula da Silva—Lula) described how a traditional *coronel* in the state of Pernambuco once gathered his peasants together on election day and one by one handed out ballots, each conveniently filled out with the *coronel*'s choice of candidates, each placed in a sealed envelope ready to be deposited in the ballot box. "Could the Senhor tell me at least for whom we are voting?" asked one of the peasants. "Don't you know that the vote is secret?" the *coronel* responded (Soares 2009).

For Review

How did the phenomena of *caudillos* and *coroneles* first arise? How would you explain the importance of such figures in nineteenth-century Latin America? How did they set back the cause of unity and Pan-Americanism that Bolívar wanted? Why would a weak state, rather than a strong one, produce these kinds of leaders?

◼ Rebuilding Nations and States, Modernization

The new Latin American countries were ill-adapted to republican political ideals and, with a few exceptions (e.g., Chile), not very stable politically. Here, by *republican*, we mean the idea that the authority of the state, the right to govern, comes from the people and not directly from god. The authority is therefore vested in the citizenry and not in a monarchy, emperor, or aristocracy. Men and women like Bolívar were not necessarily representative of Latin America's upper class at the time. Most of the Creoles were unprepared to accept traditional liberal ideals, such as separation of church and state, freedom for slaves, mass education, and so on. Of course, the United States failed to implement fully many of these same ideals, notably freedom for slaves, but Latin Americans faced a much more difficult task in constructing a new identity and social order for a diverse people, living in a geographically daunting territory and inheriting a hyper-exploitative social structure. Was there one Latin American nation—an ideal expressed by Bolívar as "Pan-Americanism"—or several, as suggested by the proliferation of new republics in the wake of independence?

We are accustomed to thinking of nations as bound together by a common language, culture, race, or ethnicity, but few nation-states of the world have populations in which virtually everyone shares any one of these traits, much less all of them. Perhaps the key is economic interdependence or being knit together in a market, but few economies have ever been self-sufficient. In fact, long-distance trade rather than expansion of internal markets gave Europe's monarchies the financial wherewithal to consolidate control—through buildings, the arts, military forces, roads, and so on—over large territories that would become nations on a map. Spain's Latin American empire was governed from several centers of control—Mexico City, Havana, Lima, and Rio de la Plata (in modern Argentina). This was logical given the vastness of the region, but it posed huge obstacles to unification, the goal of Spanish America's independence hero, Simón Bolívar.

Many of the nation-states that formed after independence were also internally fragmented. In border regions, people often communicated and traded across national frontiers more than inside their own country. Anderson (1983: 47–66) tells us that the desire to justify independence from Spain led the colonial elite, the Creoles, of South America to confront what their identity would be afterward. A common pattern, especially in larger countries, saw regional export economies develop rather than one national economy. In Venezuela, for example, cacao was grown and exported from the coastal center; both coffee and cacao were produced and exported in the west near Colombia; dried beef and hides were produced in the plains and floated down the Orinoco River in the east. It took days or weeks to travel from any one of these regions to the capital in Caracas, and the contact among peoples in each region with another was limited. Brazil was an even vaster state, with a thriving sugar export economy in the northeast, mining in parts of the south, and later coffee production. Mexico had sisal (a strong white fiber used for rope, rugs, and so forth) plantations in the Yucatán, but mining predominated in the central and northern regions. Each of these local economies was tied to export markets, with produce flowing from the interior lands to trading houses in the ports. The interaction of one region of the country with others was limited.

Conservatives, Liberals, and Modernization

The century between independence and the **Great Depression** that struck the world economy in 1929 constitutes for Latin America a long, evolutionary period marked by chronic political instability and violent civil war, but ultimately, around 1850, the central state began to assert its sovereignty over the entire territory within its boundaries. We should say "more or less asserted" its sovereignty, because some Latin American states even today remain vulnerable to foreign intervention or unable to enforce national laws and policies over regional power brokers, as we have seen in the case of Brazil.

This period saw a process of economic and social modernization to some degree. Transportation (ports, roads), communication, and other forms of infrastructure were improved with investments designed to boost imports and take advantage of growing demands for raw materials on the world market. New schools were built, and universities were expanded. Government bureaucracies grew. Slavery was abolished, to be replaced with new labor systems. But it is crucial to understand that at the same time the region's elites remained highly prejudiced against the lower classes, composed mostly of people of indigenous and African descent. More liberal factions of the elite studied the social doctrines emanating from European intellectual circles, but debt peonage and semifeudal social relationships remained deeply entrenched, especially in the countryside. Among these doctrines was a distortion of the ideas of Charles Darwin about evolution and natural selection. In short, many Latin American elites argued that the indigenous and African genes had created an inferior racial stock and that it was necessary to "whiten" the population. These ideas were popular elsewhere (including the United States) and were known as Social Darwinism. A closely related theory attributed "inferiority" to the tropical climate in some countries. Changing the region's racial stock through European immigration was the (racist) formula adopted by many.

The issues that divided Creoles over independence continued to shape politics in the new states of the early independence era. In most states, one faction came to define itself as the "Conservative" party, though the name of the political club or party did not always include that term explicitly. Its members tended to support centralized government, to resist policies designed to open the economy to more trade, to defend the Church and its control over education, and to see themselves as bearers of Iberian traditions. Many Conservative landowners saw themselves more as aristocrats than as entrepreneurs. In times of depressed prices for exports, they resented attempts by banks and merchant houses to seize their land through bankruptcy, which explains their reluctance to embrace free trade. Members of the opposing party tended to see themselves as modernizers and to view the land as a source of profit rather than prestige. Again, they usually, but not always, called themselves "Liberals." They tended to favor policies that allowed them to take advantage of new opportunities on the global market—for example, opportunities to grow coffee for the new markets that

PUNTO DE VISTA: PARAGUAY'S UNSUCCESSFUL BREAK WITH THE PATTERN

Latin American history is filled with controversial strongmen who have inspired debate in the present. The debate is not merely confined to academic historians. In popular culture, intellectual salons, and speeches by politicians, these powerful rulers are variously portrayed on the one hand as saints, heroes, or martyrs and on the other hand as devils, cowards, or pathological tyrants.

Paraguay

Perhaps no historical personality has been so shrouded by negatives or positives than José Gaspar Rodríguez de Francia, a leader of Paraguay's struggle for independence (1811) from Spain, who afterward became dictator of that country from 1814 to his death in 1840.

Francia was a complete autocrat who became known as "El Supremo." Most historians describe the dictator as a mentally unbalanced political caricature, but others suspect his idiosyncrasies were exaggerated by his enemies. Francia was austere in dress and customs and determined to make over his country's social and economic structures. He removed Creoles from their positions of power, redistributed land, and stimulated

economic development without foreign credits. One hundred years before the Russian Revolution, Francia expropriated large estates, converted them into state property, and rented land cheaply to those willing to till it. He used his power to create an economy in which common people lived better than in most other Latin American countries. He placed emphasis on production of crops consumed at home by Indians and mestizos. Almost unique in Latin America, Paraguay became self-sufficient in food.

Francia was a child of the French Revolution and made an enemy of the Catholic Church by abolishing its privileges. He confiscated its property and abolished tithes paid to the clergy. His government established iron, textile, and livestock industries, employing thousands. Blockaded by Argentina from exporting their production, Paraguayans traded overland with other Latin American countries. This trade was carefully regulated through licenses. Neither large-scale foreign investments nor debts were accumulated.

However, the country was far from a political democracy. Francia repressed all dissent; his dungeons were notorious.

Francia's experiment was replicated somewhat in a region, disputed by Argentina and Brazil, that would become Uruguay. A caudillo named José Artigas sought to distribute land belonging to supporters of the Spanish Crown to blacks, Indians, poor whites, and mixed-race peoples. Brazil invaded in 1817 and put an end to the experiment. Brazil occupied the region until 1828, when it was forced by Great Britain, who wanted neither Argentina nor Brazil to control the territory, to give it sovereignty as Uruguay.

Francia's successors kept his experiment going until 1870. Neighboring countries, ruled by traditional elites, were hostile to the experiment. Great Britain, the dominant world power, also looked at Paraguay with alarm.

What if other countries broke away from an international economic system so advantageous for the wealthier nations? Brazil, Argentina, and Uruguay, financed by Great Britain, crushed the experiment in the War of the Triple Alliance (1864–1870), a holocaust that nearly exterminated Paraguay's entire male population, including nearly all adults of the native Guaraní population. The victors occupied Paraguay for five years and completely reversed the system that had generated a higher standard of living and more productive economy than any of its neighbors.

Countries that embark on revolutionary experiments at odds with the prevailing economic models and interests of wealthy nations can expect to be targets of subversion from domestic opponents allied with foreign powers. Fidel Castro attempted to escape the fate of Francia's successors by allying himself with a great power, the former Soviet Union, which was eager to compete with the world's dominant power, the United States. An economic embargo imposed by the United States, including pressure on other countries to do the same, forced Cuba to develop alternative trading networks and look at alternative, state-controlled economic institutions. Although much of the anti-Castro rhetoric in the United States is aimed at Cuba's lack of Western-style democracy, it is arguably Cuba's attempt to experiment with a more autonomous economic development model at odds with most of the region that attracts such hostility from the United States.

Georges Fournial, a twentieth-century Paraguayan intellectual, was especially critical of Francia, calling him "a despicable, bloody tyrant that submitted his people for 26 years to the most ferocious terror, and also isolated his people from the outside world, condemning Paraguay to its miserable fate" (quoted in Burns 1996). But other commentators praised his economic plans. One Scottish observer who lived in the country for four years said that Francia "never would defend an unjust cause; while he was ever ready to take the part of the poor and weak against the rich and the strong" (quoted in Burns 1996: 76–77).

Point/Counterpoint

How should we view Francia today—as a visionary leader or another brutal autocrat?

a. If you say "visionary leader," how do you respond to those who say that he was unrealistic, in regard to both his own people and the international situation, and thereby led the country to disaster?

b. If you say "brutal autocrat," how do you respond to the way he tried to rely on his own people to lift the country, rather than foreign interests, as in so many other countries? Given how his powerful neighbors and the British wanted him to fail, could he have afforded to be tolerant in his own country?

Do you think Castro will be seen in a similar way in the future? Do you think that under some circumstances rule by a strong leader, even a dictator, can be justified?

For more information

See "Quién era José Gaspar Francia?" (2012), www.ceibal.edu.uy/contenidos/areas_conocimiento/cs_sociales/090616_donjose/quin_era_jos_gaspar_francia.html. A novel based on this era in Paraguay is *I, the Supreme* (New York: Knopf, 1986) by Augusto Roa Bastos.

opened after 1800. In countries with significant Indian populations, Liberals were eager to break up communal lands collectively owned by villages or the Church. They were more likely to favor **federalism** and decentralized government—at least until they took power for themselves. Many sought to wrest control of education from the Catholic Church. More important to many was stripping the Church of its land.

It is important not to exaggerate the differences between Conservatives and Liberals. Wealthy landowners and elites could be found in both parties, and principle meant little when power and land were at stake in conflicts. Two of the main characters in the novel *House of the Spirits* by Isabel Allende (a relative of the martyred Chilean president Salvador Allende) are a married couple—the husband a Conservative and the wife a Liberal. Gabriel García Márquez, the Colombian novelist, once famously sized up the difference as nothing more than what hour each faction attended church.

Commodity Booms and Busts—New Exports, New Elites

Changing patterns of consumption and production in the wealthy countries (mainly North America, Europe, and Japan) created new opportunities for those controlling land and natural resources in Latin America, generating periodic economic booms—which inevitably turned into busts. In hard times, when **commodity** prices fell on the world markets, elites looked for help from the government against the predatory practices of foreign and domestic competitors eager to seize their lands. Economic crises inevitably caused further misery for the masses. Nitrate miners in Chile, cowboys in Argentina, peons on cacao plantations in Venezuela and sisal plantations in the Yucatán (Mexico), enslaved workers on sugar estates in Cuba, tin miners in Bolivia, and rubber-tappers in Brazil (just to name a few examples) never lived a secure or prosperous existence. The collapse of their markets or the exhaustion of their land or mines could cause a precarious existence to become hopeless, especially for women who could less easily migrate and who sacrificed the most to save the family. In such circumstances, economic grievances have always generated popular unrest, alarming established elites and opening political opportunities for new leaders.

Booms (skyrocketing prices) can also be disruptive, as the experience with coffee shows. In many parts of Central America and Mexico, indigenous peoples escaped total destruction of their way of life in the colonial era. The highland areas were ill-suited for plantation agriculture. If their labor was needed for mining, the Indian peoples were forced to work, but Indians could often continue to live in communal relationships to each other and the land. In Mexico, land was often collectively owned by the local municipality (village) in the form of *ejidos*. Indigenous people have often struggled to maintain this form of communal property, sometimes supported by the Church. When these lands became attractive to elites eager to take advantage of a developing overseas market for coffee, conflict ensued.

One of the more famous commodity booms in the 1800s took place in Chile. That country's northern Atacama Desert is the driest in the world and hardly seemed blessed by natural wealth. What it had in vast quantity were bird droppings accumulated over thousands of years. Suddenly, with the expansion of agriculture and demand for food, this guano became valuable as fertilizer and for making gunpowder because of its high nitrate content. This was Chile's main motive, with British help, for seizing the region as a prize of war from Bolivia in 1879. An immense flow of wealth benefited Chilean elites—until World War I, when the Germans, blocked from access to the Chilean treasure, developed a synthetic fertilizer to replace natural nitrates.

Booms not only affect elites; they also can disrupt ordinary people's lives. In the 1840s, for example, in the lowland areas of the Yucatán Peninsula of southern Mexico, indigenous peoples continued to live on land collectively owned through municipalities. What until then had been neglected territory suddenly became valuable as demand for sisal, an important ingredient for rope and twine, rose in the industrialized world. With the help of new laws and backed by force, a new landowning class converted the land into privately held estates. In the twenty-first century, rope is made largely of synthetic fibers, and tourists today can visit the ruins of what were once palatial estates of hemp plantations, set amid severe, generalized poverty.

Liberals threatened indigenous communities more than Conservatives. Their desire to reduce the power of the Church was motivated not just by the secular ideals of the French and American revolutions but also by their desire to eliminate the control of the Church over the land and people who lived on it. The coffee boom, from roughly 1840 to 1870, brought out this conflict in Mexico and Central America. In El Salvador a new oligarchy arose based on the seizure of land to meet the growing consumer demand for the aromatic bean in North America and Europe. Robert Williams (1994: 124) describes it this way:

> When coffee growers came to power in the 1870s and 1880s, they began to solve both their land and labor problems. National legislation in the early 1880s abolished *ejidal* and communal rights to land, reinforcing a process of encroachment that was well under way. Coffee growers acquired private titles to lands traditionally cultivated by peasants, and with funds from a coffee tax, militias were created with the power to evict previous tenants from the land.

The process was more complicated; many Indians and Latinos took advantage of the same laws to become small, commercial growers themselves. The consolidation of an oligarchy came later—in the 1920s. However, the more general point made by Williams is still valid. Booms, not just busts, can cause political change because they generate winners and losers. For example, in Colombia and Venezuela coffee exports enriched newly prosperous elites who challenged traditional elites for power toward the close of the nineteenth century.

Even Chile and Brazil, the most stable of the new nation-states, saw regional uprisings, rigged elections, strongmen, and irregular transitions of power. But the latter were noticeably less frequent and devastating than civil wars elsewhere. In Venezuela, for example, independence was achieved in 1821 after one-third of the population perished in war. Over the following seven decades—from 1821 to 1888—730 battles and 26 major insurrections occurred. The federal war of 1858 to 1863 took between 60,000 and 100,000 lives, and the population fell from 1.9 million to 1.6 million people. The survivors faced a ruined economy, and the cattle herds were decimated, falling from 12 million to 1.8 million in only five years (Ugalde 1978: 29).

Mexico: From Failed State to Modernizing Dictatorship

New opportunities in world markets, we see, often changed the life-fortunes of people in different parts of the social class structure, sometimes for better, sometimes for worse. External factors played an important role, given that foreign loans paid for the infrastructure (roads, railroad, ports, etc.) needed to link regions to overseas markets. Northern Europeans often established trading houses, and they often became important new players in elite politics. The new exports gave both Latin American elites and foreign interests reason to seek stronger states capable of defending property rights, taming unrest, and collecting taxes to pay for government services and, of course, to repay loans. Mexico is a prime example of what ensued.

Mexico's internal conflicts not only decimated the population and its economy but also left the country vulnerable to foreign invasion and the seizure of two-thirds of its territory by the United States after the war of 1846–1848. The U.S. victory was greatly facilitated by mistrust among Mexican generals, each a caudillo with his own regional base of power. They were mutually suspicious of each other and of the conservative president, General Antonio López de Santa Anna, of Alamo infamy.

Fourteen years later, in 1862, hopeful of restoring order and beating back the challenge of liberals, Mexican Conservatives welcomed a French invasion of 45,000 troops. Napoleon III (nephew of Bonaparte) managed to briefly install Austrian prince Maximilian as ruler of the country in 1864. In 1867, after the Liberals, led by Benito Juárez, defeated the French and executed the unfortunate Maximilian, the Liberals cloaked themselves in the mantle of nationalism and implemented "reforms" similar to ones underway in El Salvador. One of the liberal generals, Porfirio Díaz, seized power in 1876 and kept it until 1911. This hero of the struggle against the French had led revolts twice in the name of constitutional government and elections, but he ruled as a virtual dictator for nearly 35 years. His dictatorship came to be resented and eventually generated a revolution in 1910, but he gave Mexico a measure of stability and economic growth in the Porfiriato—his period of rule.

The exact timing varied, but sometime in the second half of the 1800s, the majority of Latin American countries emerged from a period of intense civil violence and entered a period of relative stability and economic modernization. This usually was engineered by one of a series of skillful caudillos or by local political chiefs, known as *caciques* (e.g., Díaz in Mexico), who seized power in countries exhausted by decades of brutal civil war. These new caudillos borrowed ideas, training, and money from European powers eager to see political stability restored and their own influence enhanced. These "modernizers" brought in Prussian, French, and other European advisors to train professional militaries. They constructed statues and built myths of national unity around independence leaders, many of whom, as in the case of Bolívar, were too controversial among elites to merit such attention earlier in the century. They built new capitols, plazas, theaters, jails, and other public buildings to show the power of the state and to help their citizens imagine themselves as a nation. They built roads and railroads not only to link regions but also to ensure their ability to rapidly deploy troops against other, regional caudillos. They often ruled at the head of an alliance of regional *caudillos, coroneles,* or *caciques,* permitting lesser figures and local landowners to dominate state and local governments in exchange for support. In case of revolts, the modernizing caudillo had at his disposal an army that might be outnumbered but could defeat the foe through superior arms, training, unity of command, and mobility.

In sum, in this era (the late nineteenth and early twentieth centuries), **caudilloism** did not disappear, but the young states began to develop some capacity to exert control over the national population and territory. More roads and railroads and new communications technologies increased the ability of central governments to exert control beyond the capital region. They were able to form better-trained and equipped armies that could be deployed against regional caudillos. What did not change was the economic and social gap between the masses and the elites, even when dominance was masked by republican constitutions. Mexico was the place where these conditions would lead to social revolution in 1910, which we examine in chapter 9, but unrest would appear throughout Latin America as modernization for the few unfolded in the late 1880s and early twentieth century.

For Review

We have seen that Creoles seemed to have a common interest in protecting their wealth and power against the masses. What were, on the other hand, some sources of political division among this group after independence? Explain what García Márquez was saying about Liberals and Conservatives in his famous reference to their churchgoing habits. In economic terms, what did modernizers want to accomplish? How did they attempt to build a stronger state? What obstacles did they have to overcome?

Independence or Neocolonialism—or Both?

Much ink has been spilled over the question of why North America and Latin America followed such different paths after independence. Some argue that the prevalence of liberal values in the north, inherited from England, explains much. Culture indeed might have made a difference, but the way the two regions were integrated differently into the world capitalist system is just as important, if not more so. To understand this better, consider the different ways that the South and North developed in the United States before the Civil War.

Just as North America developed differently than Latin America, the U.S. North developed differently than did the U.S. South. In the southern part of the United States, slaves were crucial to production of raw materials and crops (tobacco, rice, sugar, and cotton) for export to the world market, just as hyper-exploited Indians and slaves were in Latin America. In both cases, wealth became concentrated in the hands of a few landowners, and the pattern persisted after independence from colonial rule. Traveling down the Ohio River between the slave state of Kentucky and the free state of Ohio, Alexis de Tocqueville (1835: chapter 10), the famed French thinker, noticed how much more economically prosperous and energetic the north bank of the river was compared with the southern side. The victory of the North in the Civil War ensured that the United States remained on the path to become part of the center of the world system. Industrialization and agricultural development complemented one another, and a prosperous export sector complemented a growing domestic economy. Latin America had changed from colonial days, but the region was still dominated by oligarchies tied to exporting raw materials using hyper-exploited labor.

These features of its history and economic development give Latin America much in common with most of Africa, the Middle East, and Asia, what came to be known as the 1960s as the Third World—that is, countries that were neither wealthy capitalist nor communist states, most of which were once European colonies. However, Latin America differs from most of the rest of the Third World in the timing of its independence from colonial rule. It was not until the period between 1948 and 1990 that most of Africa and large parts of the Middle East and Asia achieved independence. Leaders in these regions fought not just for independence after World War II but for something called **national liberation**—that is, elimination of **neocolonial** relationships of economic dependence—though it has rarely been achieved.

Simón Rodríguez, Bolívar's teacher, advocated the creation of national education systems that would not only lift the formal education levels of the population but also draw upon the cultural and technological knowledge of the non-European peoples. The failure of Latin American leaders to pursue such a path meant that the region's separation from Spain and Portugal produced independence in the form of territorial sovereignty but not independence from underdevelopment and neocolonialism. This fact became clear as the nineteenth century unfolded.

We should disabuse ourselves of the notion that all Latin America's problems are inherited from Iberian colonialism. Most of Latin America was sovereign throughout the nineteenth century. It was neither the Spanish nor the Portuguese who introduced banana plantations in Colombia, Ecuador, and Central America, nor were the Portuguese in charge when coffee and rubber production on a large scale was introduced into Brazil. The landed oligarchies that came to dominate Central America's coffee-export economies were native to the region in the 1800s. British loans, not Spanish viceroys, tied Argentina's beef exports to European markets. Northern European nations financed the wars that shifted desert lands rich in nitrates from southern Peru and Bolivia to the more friendly sovereign control of Chile. U.S. invaders cost Mexico half its territory in 1848, and French forces laid the country prostrate later in the century. After 1900, European and U.S. capital developed oil fields in Mexico and Venezuela, as well as massive new tin and copper mines in the Andes. In Cuba, Puerto Rico, and the Dominican Republic, it was the United States that came to control the vital sugar estates and mills.

Hence, Spain and Portugal set the pattern, but it was the rising industrial powers of North America and Northern Europe that came to dominate the commodity-export economies after independence. The Latin American elites whose fortunes were made in association with this trade were not necessarily descended from the conquistadors or from the old Creole class. Many indigenous peoples who were left relatively undisturbed by Spanish colonial rulers found themselves dispossessed and forced into the ranks of poor workers once their lands were discovered to be useful for new agricultural exports or mines.

By 1900, Latin American society was becoming more complex, more urban. Ports, railroads, electric utilities, urban streetcars, slaughterhouses, mines, and so on required workers. The period of liberal modernization in Latin America gave impetus to the emergence of new social sectors. Schools, universities, government offices, stores, courts, postal and telegraph offices, newspapers, and other institutions required employees too. Professional associations for lawyers, doctors, professors, and so on grew in size and number. Workers, often faced with terrible conditions and low wages, organized themselves either into unions (especially in mining areas) or into benevolent organizations.

With the growth of a working and middle class and the emergence of a more complex economy, Latin America witnessed the development of a more complex **civil society**. Latin American society was becoming less hospitable to exclusive domination by a narrow land-based oligarchy. Unions advanced demands through strikes. Students organized protests. Associations of street vendors and neighbors began to make demands on municipal

This image is of a banana train in Guatemala around 1915. The United Fruit Company owned the train. Where are the bananas going? Do you think that United Fruit's activities were helping develop the economy by providing employment and building a railroad?

authorities. The middle class pressed for political rights monopolized by the oligarchs. Unions, the military, professional associations, and universities were all social spaces where Latin Americans encountered the influence of foreign ideas. Immigrants from Europe brought the ideas of **anarchists,** socialists, and communists from their homelands. Their ideas were often embraced by university and high school students, and young people in Latin America have tended to feel a developed sense of belonging to a political generation since this time.

Although history tends to record the importance of the men who led these organizations and movements, it is hard to see how they could have achieved anything without the involvement of women. Sometimes women themselves organized, as was the case, for example, among laundry workers who worked in camps near mines and military installations. In other cases, women organized the solidarity networks that helped strikers survive weeks without pay, to buy food, clothing, and other essentials of life. Even within a fiercely patriarchal social structure, women remained protagonists of history, not just victims or accessories.

With the increased social complexity and the influence of European ideologies, new parties began to emerge, and some older ones changed. New ones included parties that characterized themselves as "radical" or "democratic." Especially prominent in Chile, Argentina, and Uruguay, they tended to attract middle-class supporters, especially teachers dissatisfied with the old conservative or liberal options. Sometimes they attracted labor support as well. In some places, older parties, often the Liberals, tended to broaden their views and deepen their penetration in society beyond elites. Meanwhile, and usually a little later, leftist parties began to appear, usually tied to workers, sometimes attracting students. As in other parts of the world, the Russian Revolution of 1917 provoked increased interest in revolutionary Marxism but also a split in socialist movements and parties, with some aligning with more moderate social democratic parties in Western Europe and others aligning with the world communist movement headquartered in Moscow.

Because of the strong presence of foreign investment and the history of external intervention, the entire Latin American left identified itself as "anti-imperialist." In the twentieth century, to be a leftist, one had to espouse nationalism and decry the role of foreign investors. This rarely convinced the military establishment that leftists were loyal to the nation. There are notable exceptions, which we will review later in this text, but on the whole, entering the twentieth century, the military excluded leftists from those embraced by the concept of *la patria* (described in the next section).

For Review

List two or three important ways that the Latin American society of 1900 was different from that of Latin America around 1800. What political implications did this have?

Stirrings of Change at the Dawn of a New Century

As the twentieth century dawned in Latin America, there were stirrings of change. The further development of export-oriented economies meant that many former backwaters of the old Spanish colonial system were being drawn into national webs of communication, transportation, and governance. The institutions of the nation-state—police forces, courts, bureaucracies, public services, and of course, the military—were establishing their presence more forcefully throughout the national territory. Also, the population continued to be affected by immigration. The Southern Cone experienced significant immigration from Europe. Asians began to impact some other countries, with Peru and Brazil standing out. Arab and Jewish names began to appear among others in the economic elite. The industrialization of Europe, North America, and (less directly) Japan created new markets and hence incentives for new foreign investment in Latin America's export sector. Both local and foreign capitalists required infrastructure (roads, railroads, ports, etc.) and needed political stability to succeed.

Political stability served an economic purpose. Investors needed states capable of protecting property, settling contract disputes, and keeping workers in line. However, one person's political "stability" is another person's system of oppression. On the antidemocratic side of the ledger, stronger states generally meant better-trained militaries that, in turn, became political actors themselves. These professional militaries affected politics in several ways. First, military officers retained many privileges inherited from the colonial era. Besides their own court system, these privileges often included special licenses for their own businesses. Second, the military defended what historian Brian Loveman (1999) calls *la patria*, meaning "country" or "fatherland." But what was *la patria*? Latin America's ruling class defined national identity by its Iberian heritage, including Catholicism and European values. The military interpreted uprisings by Indians, slaves, and peons as threats to civil order and to the essence of the nation's Hispanic identity.

The traditional task of providing security from external threat often became linked in the military mind with defense of its own interests as a corporate body. The military, as it usually does today, began to present itself as defender of the nation and often, as a result, above politics. As Latin American militaries became more professional, conflicts developed within the ranks. Generals-on-horseback, whose rank owed more to their family's **oligarchic** status, often treated lower-ranking officers and soldiers as little more than peons, putting them to work building roads or doing projects that made the general's family's land more valuable. Officers trained at foreign academies or by visiting instructors were often blocked from promotions and grew resentful at the abuse by superiors. Gradually, in many of the larger and more complex countries, the military came to identify more with the middle class and less with the traditional oligarchy. The military would come to play an important role in the next century's politics of change.

For Review

What kinds of new forces were emerging at both the social level and the political level in Latin America around 1900? Why did the military become stronger and more influential in the period of modernization?

Independence—Did It Make a Difference?

Most of this chapter argues that political independence did not do much to change the legacy of colonialism, especially the legacy of economic dependence. It is worth noting, however, that Latin America's achievement of political sovereignty did allow it to escape the worst ravages of direct European colonial rule, which have played out in disastrous ways in contemporary Africa. The United States played a small role in discouraging a European "scramble for Latin America" when President James Monroe declared in 1823, in the Monroe Doctrine, that the United States would not tolerate any reestablishment of European colonies. In reality, the United States had little military ability to prevent such efforts, but at least Europeans were put on notice that there might be a diplomatic cost to such ventures. Latin America's problems pale in some ways compared with the acute poverty and violence afflicting most of postcolonial Africa. The political systems of the Middle East for the most part evoke little favorable comparison with the Latin American situation, especially in regard to the status of women. Some Asian countries seem to be advancing more rapidly in terms of economic development, but overall conditions of poverty remain dire in large parts of Asia—even China. If nothing else, after a century of rebuilding state institutions in Latin America—and some export-led economic development in the second half of the century—the stage was set for some new political developments, including the political enfranchisement of urban sectors, and an initial attempt to break away from dependency. It is difficult to see how that would have happened without political independence.

The nineteenth century was an era of state-building that would leave its mark on this process. In most of the region, the collapse of imperial authority left a vacuum of power that was conducive to civil war, chaos, and foreign intervention. In a few cases, such as in Chile, elites managed to build a fairly stable state, one that developed some of the trappings of parliamentary democracy. However, even here, democracy was not on the agenda of the ruling classes. Elsewhere, "republics" existed largely on paper. National legislatures, where they functioned with any degree of real power, were largely arenas in which elite interests played themselves out with little popular influence.

Democratic politics in Latin America is largely a product of the twentieth century, although it too was marked by revolution, populism, and repression. It has also been deeply influenced by the rise of the United States to world hegemony and by the great ideological battle between capitalism and communism. As this Cold War drew to a close, Latin America swung first to a new ("neo") era of liberal reform, which has yet to fully play itself out—or to fully reveal its relationship to democracy. Then, at the dawn of a new century, much of the region began to swing back toward the left.

Discussion Questions

1. Just before he died, Bolívar bitterly and famously remarked that in trying to make a revolution, he had "plowed the sea." What did he mean? Can you identify two or three important features of Latin America's political, economic, or social landscape today that can be traced back to the colonial era?
2. Sometimes we use "counterfactuals" to spur discussion. Here are two for you to consider.
    a. If Bolívar and other liberators had failed to achieve independence, would Latin American history have been different? (You might take the history of Brazil into account in thinking about this question.)
    b. If Latin America had been colonized by the British instead of by the Iberians, what difference, if any, might that have made?
3. It is said that "modernization" took place in the period between 1850 and 1920. What did this mean in political, economic, and military terms?

Resources for Further Study

Reading: John Lynch's *Simón Bolívar: A Life* (New Haven: Yale University Press, 2006) is a new biography that sheds light not only on the liberator but also on his times and conflicts within the Creole ruling class. Of the many surveys of Latin American history, a relatively brief and lively written account is E. Bradford Burns and Julie A. Charlip, *Latin America: An Interpretive History*, 5th ed. (Upper Saddle River, NJ: Prentice Hall, 2007). Gabriel García Márquez's *One Hundred Years of Solitude* is perhaps the best-known novel to come out of the region, and much of the novel explores how the mythical town of Macondo experienced modernization with the arrival of the banana export business.

Video and Film: *The Battle of Canudos* tells the story of a poor family's fate in the bloody conflict in northeast Brazil. Searching for "Canudos" on YouTube will provide access to the film in Portuguese. It is not hard to follow even without knowledge of the language. *Camila* (1984) is the story of star-crossed lovers, a priest and the daughter of wealthy landowners in post-independence Argentina, the era of the dictator Juan Manuel de Rosas.

On the Internet: Paul Hall's Internet Modern History Sourcebook provides thousands of relevant sources, including many on Latin America. His briefing on world systems theory is extremely useful. Consult the left-hand column at the following URL: www .fordham.edu/halsall/mod/modsbook.asp. The world systems summary is located at www.fordham.edu/Halsall/mod/Wallerstein.asp. You can find an 11-minute segment on Canudos on the BBC website, at www.bbc.co.uk/programmes/p0205w53.

5 Populism, Development, and Democracy in the Twentieth Century

Focus Questions

▶ What is populism, and why does it often revolve around charismatic figures, such as Juan Perón in Argentina and Getúlio Vargas in Brazil?

▶ How were populism and the goal of economic development often tied together by policies called "import substitution industrialization"?

▶ How do more recent populist leaders, such as Venezuela's Hugo Chávez, Brazil's Lula, and Peru's Alberto Fujimori, compare as a return to past populists, their base of support, and their policies?

▶ Why did some parts of Latin America begin to industrialize but others did not in the twentieth century?

THE HISTORY OF twentieth-century Latin America, told in full, involves many more facets than we can discuss in this chapter. Our approach here will be to weave together two key interrelated themes: (1) the quest for development, which for most of the century was equated with industrialization, and (2) the entry of the masses into political life, which produced **populism** and ended tragically in military authoritarianism.

In the middle decades of the twentieth century, before manufacturing jobs began to move away from "developed" countries to cheaper labor markets in the Global South, economic development and industrialization were regarded as practically the same thing. Populist governments in the larger nations of Latin America pursued industrialization through **import substitution**, which included protecting new industries from foreign competition with tariffs and import restrictions, tapping export earnings for state-initiated development projects and for subsidies to new factories, and enlarging the domestic market through income redistribution and public spending. The state sought to harmonize relationships between business and labor and dampen conflict in an effort to unite the nation in pursuit of development. Populists were **corporatists** in this respect, but they also did not hesitate in many cases to brand opponents, on the left and the right, as enemies of the nation. Most populists have been men, but women like Eva Perón of Argentina are certainly part of the story of populism as well.

What Is Populism?

Populism is like a suit of clothes. Politicians take it off the rack when they need to rally public support in pursuit of a goal. Carlos Vilas (1987: 31), an Argentine sociologist, once remarked that there is "a populism for every taste—urban populism and agrarian populism, progressive populism and conservative populism, mass populism and elite populism, native populism and Westernized populism, socialist populism and fascist populism, populism 'from below' and populism 'from above.'" The nineteenth century saw "populist" **caudillos** rally peons and slaves to their cause. The twentieth-century version of populism was more urban-oriented. The rise of mass media, especially radio and movies, allowed strong leaders to make appeals directly to the people. The content of this appeal usually has something to do with rhetoric calling upon "the people," a deliberately imprecise term, to confront social groups that are putting their own wealth and privileges ahead of the national interest. Unlike **Marxists**, most populists do not attempt to rally the "working class" against the "capitalists"; populists want to rally the people against the "elite."

Rodolfo Stavenhagen (1974: 138) argues that one of populism's main features seems to be mobilization of "the available working masses . . . in order to build a broader base and provide more maneuvering room for unstable coalitions between certain competing factions of ruling classes." In nineteenth-century Latin America, populist caudillos tended to arise when one faction of landowners launched rebellions against another faction, often disputing control over the capital city. In the twentieth century, such rivalries involved new political and economic sectors emerging in urban areas. However, we should bear in mind that populism may have a progressive, democratic side as well. For the populist to build a mass movement, his or her appeals must be rooted in genuine mass grievances.

Often—but not always—populism forms around a charismatic individual, the most famous case being Juan Perón in Argentina in the 1940s and 1950s. Here populism seems to be associated more with a *style* characterized by inflammatory rhetoric and exaggerated **nationalism**. Populist leaders are usually charismatic, in that they have forceful personalities and are effective at rallying support through rhetoric. However, charisma comes not just from personality or style of the leader, the German sociologist Max Weber (1947: 328–349) pointed out in 1922. Charismatic authority is also something that an eager population projects on the leader. In other words, this kind of leadership is generated as much from below as from above. The populist often presents himself as a kind of political savior or messiah whom the people will follow and obey without question.

Weber pointed out that charisma is not lasting. To consolidate a regime that lasts beyond his career or life, the charismatic leader must somehow institutionalize the changes made. That has often proven more difficult than winning power. Consider, for example, the uncertainty surrounding whether Cuba will remain socialist with the departure of Fidel Castro. The death of Hugo Chávez in 2013 brought great uncertainty to Venezuela. Chávez's chosen successor, Nicolás Maduro, barely held the presidency in the election of April 2013. The opposition, sensing weakness, was emboldened to try to force his resignation through peaceful protest and also some violent protests; in addition, without the personal authority of Chávez, it was not clear that the Chavista political coalition, without the need to repel the opposition protest, would be able to remain united and implement needed economic reforms. Post-Chávez Venezuela became highly volatile politically.

The topic of populism is not just of historical interest. With the **"Pink Tide"** rise of leftist governments, beginning with Chávez in December 1998, populism has become associated with politicians and movements that oppose free trade and neoliberal economic policies. Critics often contend that these new "neopopulists"—promoting new versions of populism—are unrealistically turning back the clock to strategies that not only will deepen underdevelopment but also will put democracy at risk. Not all neopopulists have been leftists, however. Several Latin American countries in the 1990s were led by neopopulists, such as Peru's Alberto Fujimori (1990–2000) and Argentina's Carlos Menem (1989–1999), who governed *in the style* of the populists of the earlier era but implemented market-friendly policies—**neoliberalism**. Hence, although populism in the earlier period was mostly associated with making the state stronger, neopopulism has been sometimes associated with rolling back the influence of the state over the economy.

In sum, we treat two different conceptions of populism together in this chapter: (1) as the political practice of appealing for mass support by championing the cause of ordinary people against powerful elites and (2) as a "style" of politics characterized by a charismatic leader who evokes strong emotional loyalty from a mass following by employing rhetoric that appeals to widespread anger against elite privilege and power—and the alleged betrayal of national welfare to foreign interests. However, a specific episode of populism can be understood only in the context of the time and place in which it occurs. Populism does not belong to any particular place on the left–right spectrum of politics. In fact, populist leaders sometimes are difficult to place on this scale, as in the cases of Argentina's Perón and Brazil's Getúlio Vargas.

For Review

If you were told that some politician—regardless of what country we consider— was a "populist," what would that mean in terms of (1) style and (2) the kind of appeal he or she would make?

Latin America's Masses Enter Politics

What populists have in common is a political style and program that appeals across social classes and an anti-elitist rhetoric that identifies an oligarchy as the enemy of a vaguely defined sector called the "people." The United States experienced it late in the 1800s when farmers and workers, mostly in the South and West, organized themselves into local groups and then into a mass Populist Party to oppose the bankers, railroad companies, and industrial magnates of the East, whom they blamed for their deteriorating economic conditions. During the Great Depression, Louisiana governor Huey Long promised "a chicken in every pot" and to defend the common person against power brokers and businessmen—even as he made deals with these same "enemies of the people." Latin American populists are often cut from the same cloth.

In Latin America, despite inflammatory rhetoric about imperialism, most populists were not hostile to foreign investment. Most preached corporatism—harmony between the interests of capital and labor. Getúlio Vargas of Brazil captured the spirit of populism in a speech given in 1944.

> The possessing classes that genuinely contribute to national grandeur and prosperity, honest merchants, working and fair industrialists, farmers who increase the fertility of the land, have no reason to fear the power of the people. What the law does not protect or tolerate is abuses, unbridled speculation, crime, unfairness, profits by all the castes of favorites, and all sorts of traffickers who feed on the poverty of others, trade in the hunger of their fellow human beings, and sell even their souls to the devil to accumulate wealth off the sweat, the anxiety, and the sacrifice of the majority of the population.
>
> (quoted in Lowy 1987: 34)

The ability of populists to attract support from business sectors was based on their providing state subsidies, investments in infrastructure, lucrative contracts, and tariffs to protect local industries from foreign competition. Businessmen did not like dealing with unions, but charismatic leaders and disciplined populist parties provided some measure of labor stability in their factories, keeping more radical union movements at bay. We will see that populists lost support from business elites and the middle class when movements of workers, peasants, and poor people threatened to spill outside their leadership's control in the 1960s.

The Political Logic of Import Substitution Industrialization (ISI)

From 1930 to 1964, populist leaders and parties in the larger countries of Latin America appealed to workers, businessmen, and the middle class to unite behind import substitution and in opposition to conservative forces and foreign investors blocking change. When commodity prices rose with the onset of World War II, government agencies had funds to make many investments in roads, energy production, and even steel plants. After World War II, Raúl Prebisch (discussed in chapter 6) and other economists at the United Nations Economic Commission for Latin America (ECLA) promoted import substitution through the training of thousands of government bureaucrats. Many countries began to nationalize ownership of the ports, electric and communication utilities, railroads, and other sectors that were vital to national economic development but owned by foreigners. Although considered socialism by some, this mix of private and state capital was more commonly labeled "state capitalism." After 1980, privatization of these assets became a major rallying cry for neoliberals who sought to undo import substitution.

The idea behind **import substitution industrialization (ISI)** was to promote industrialization in stages, beginning with common items previously imported and with products made from raw materials readily at hand. Why export cacao, for example, only to import chocolate? Why not introduce factories at home to produce confections—and the paper to wrap them in? Could not the same thing be done ultimately with thousands of products, keeping more wealth within the country and generating jobs? Once these industries were established, they would form a market for a new phase of industrialization, investment in factories to produce durable consumer goods (e.g., refrigerators and automobiles), basic inputs (e.g., petrochemicals and steel), and capital goods (e.g., machinery, mining equipment, and ships). At least that was the goal.

Under ISI, new industries were protected initially from foreign competition by tariffs, which were already quite high because most of the government's revenues came from customs houses. (Recall that in the chaotic nineteenth century, governments did not have the administrative capability to tax citizens.) The early decades of import substitution were years in which factories still tended to produce a single product on assembly lines, drawing on nearby mines for raw materials and other factories for some of the parts. The ECLA economists warned that protection should not be extended indefinitely, lest it limit competitive incentives to modernize. New technologies, such as transistors and (later) computers, were making industries overseas more productive after World War II, but many industries in Latin America preferred not to adapt. They benefited from cheaper labor, tariffs against foreign competition, and government subsidies, but eventually those advantages would expire.

ISI did not happen everywhere. The poorer and smaller countries, such as Bolivia, Paraguay, and the nations of Central America and the Caribbean, would not experience nearly the degree of industrialization of larger countries. When manufacturing industries finally began to spring up in the 1960s in the Caribbean Basin, they were usually labor-intensive, low-technology installations, *maquilas*, oriented to export to the United States, a tendency that accelerated after 1980.

ISI was closely connected to expanded participation and incorporation of new actors into politics. The entrepreneurs who welcomed state support for new industry were often new immigrants from the Middle East (e.g., the Yarur family textile group in Chile), Asia, and parts of Europe. In return for subsidies, labor peace, and protection from competition, they provided money and votes (of workers and their families) for populist politicians. Jobs, subsidies, protection from foreign competition, licenses, official recognition of unions, and so on were all new resources controlled by politicians to build political machines—**clientelism** at work. Workers and the middle class supported the new parties and politicians, sometimes with support from nationalist sectors of the military. Against these populist forces were conservatives and members of the oligarchies forged in colonial times or in the modernization period of the nineteenth century (see chapter 4).

Nelson Werneck Sodré was one of many Brazilian intellectuals who saw ISI as the only way forward for the nation. Sodré argued that formerly colonized countries such as Brazil inherited an economic structure dominated by foreign interests. Overcoming this legacy was in his eyes a task comparable with the struggle of European countries to overcome feudalism—that is, to take political and economic power away from the old landed aristocracy and put it in the hands of a capitalist **bourgeoisie** that would lead the industrialization of the region. "What for them were feudal relations, restrictions on development, are for us all that still remain of the colonial past. Nationalism thus presents itself as liberation" (quoted in Burns 1993: 177–179). Those favoring industrialization were also striving for democracy, Sodré argued, because only the people could overcome resistance by foreigners and the local oligarchy.

Populists were relying, he continued, on "a new scheme of coordinating class interests, or reducing them to a minimum common denominator, for the struggle in defense of what is national in us." Despite their differences, said Sodré, the national bourgeoisie and working classes should put aside conflict to show the foreigners—who thought that development could not happen without outside aid and capital—that Brazil could do the job itself. Sodré, like many of his generation, argued that this alliance between social classes would promote growth of a *national* bourgeoisie—that is, capitalists interested not just in profit but in developing the country. Workers would benefit from more jobs and a higher standard of living, and they could be mobilized to support industrialization by an emotional appeal to help build the nation. "New are the people," said Sodré. "Nothing more will occur without their participation" (quoted in Burns 1993).

After 1970, ISI was in widespread disrepute, but its failures were far from obvious in the 1960s. Real per capita income in Latin America nearly doubled between 1950 and 1970. **Developmentalists** on both the left and the right thought that Latin America was poised around 1960 to leap forward. Walt Rostow (1960), an influential comparative political scientist and advisor to Presidents Kennedy and Johnson, took the optimistic view that Mexico and Argentina were already in the initial stages of an economic "takeoff" that would move them from the developing into the developed world. Few understood that the capacity of ISI to generate the economic growth sufficient to meet the rising demands of the population was being reached already.

For Review

What were the essential elements of import substitution? How did import substitution policies strengthen the political power of populists? How could ISI be considered a corporatist approach to development?

Case Studies of Populism and ISI

As we review several countries' experiences with populism and ISI, we can see some commonalities. In all these cases, society became more complex as a result of the export-based economic development of the late nineteenth and early twentieth centuries. Working-class and middle-class sectors grew and demanded access to the political system, and the military began to change from an oligarchic to a middle-class institution. These new pressures were building when the Great Depression shook Latin America's economies after 1929. Populist politicians and parties appeared on the scene, promoting ISI and gaining support from workers and the middle class. Populism represented reform and modernization, often cloaked in the rhetoric of "anti-imperialism" but rarely challenging capitalism itself. Most populists supported **state capitalism**—development of a market society with guidance and even ownership of some key industries by the state. With the Cuban Revolution of 1959 as a backdrop, populism took on a more radical dimension in the 1960s. In most cases, the military intervened to defend *la patria* (the "fatherland") and impose an authoritarian "solution" to the crisis.

Although workers and the middle class gained political weight, in Brazil, Argentina, and Chile, democracy was stunted by the incomplete inclusion of peasants and the poor. Elites either advocated or tolerated the entrance of workers and professionals into political life over the objection of the traditional oligarchy, but they were not willing to permit these other groups to participate—especially the peasants, whose inclusion threatened the fundamental economic interests and political power of landowners. There were exceptions. In Mexico populism grew out of revolution, and peasants could not be entirely ignored. In Venezuela, middle-class political leaders organized the countryside as part of an effort to take on the powerful foreign companies that transformed the country into a petrostate—that is, a country whose economy and society was awash with oil-export revenues. Even in these cases, which we will compare in a separate chapter in our analysis of the rise, fall, and rise again of democracy, the peasants and urban poor benefited much less from ISI. These two important countries, Mexico and Venezuela, escaped the wave of military rule that followed the populist era.

Brazil: Getúlio Vargas and the Estado Nôvo

Brazil is too large and complex a society to have its economy dominated by one export alone. However, the economies of each of the country's highly autonomous regions and states were highly dependent on a particular commodity produced for the world market. Along the northeast coast, the poorest region, sugar and cotton were the most important crops. Rubber ruled in the interior plantations. Farther south, gold and diamond mining, coffee, and ranching predominated. The rise and fall of prices for these commodities greatly influenced which region and which elites controlled the most power.

The most important export in Brazil during the Republic (1888–1930) was coffee. Do not mistake "republic" here for democracy. As we saw in chapter 4 in the case of Canudos, where desperately poor, landless peasants seized control of a small town and surrounding land behind the leadership of a religious zealot, the state was capable of ferocious repression. From 1891 until 1930, the central government was controlled largely by oligarchs from two of the most prosperous states, São Paolo and Minas Gerais. State governments in Brazil's federal republic were controlled by *coroneles*, patriarchal heads of ruling families in rural areas (see chapter 4).

Although coffee made some Brazilians very rich, increased production (much of it in Brazil itself) flooded the world market from the 1890s onward—something that happened with many agricultural exports introduced throughout Latin America in the period of liberal modernization (the late 1800s). Already the agricultural economy was in trouble when prices fell by two-thirds between 1893 and 1896. Unable to sell their crop for a profit, but still politically powerful, the coffee growers convinced the government to bail them out by buying much of it. However, by bringing government into their business, the growers could not avoid other wealthy groups from country taking an interest in their affairs.

Everyone was affected because the government financed the coffee subsidies by borrowing abroad and printing money. The growing urban population was taxed to service the debt, and printing additional money led to inflation. To pay the growers, the government devalued the Brazilian currency. In other words, the government converted each dollar or pound sterling (British currency) earned from exports to larger amounts of local money.

FIGURE 5.1   Political map, states and major cities in Brazil. More than any other Latin American country, Brazil's federal constitution vests a high degree of authority in its governors.

The government's simple solution to gain more revenue was costly to some groups. **Devaluation** meant that merchants wanting to import manufactured goods had to charge their customers more *cruzeiros* (Brazil's money at the time) for these products, so that they could pay their suppliers overseas with dollars and sterling. Prices soared, creating widespread political discontent.

But what hurts some can reward others. Devaluation, by making imports *more* expensive, was a form of protection for domestic producers; that is, because importers had to raise prices, goods produced locally became more attractive. For example, as prices of imported shoes went up, customers became more willing to buy shoes made at home, even if they were not of the highest quality or the latest fashion. After the collapse of coffee prices from 22.5 cents per pound in 1929 to 8 cents in 1931, the goal of industrialization became more pressing, with even fewer dollars available to meet demand through imports. With government already helping the export sector, Brazilians began to ask why government did not take some of the profits to help create new industries and jobs. When prices of Brazil's coffee, rubber, beef, and other exports recovered in the 1940s, **import substitution** got underway in earnest. First, however, the people in the cities had to reduce the power of the landed elites, banks, and merchant houses that dominated the old republic through their control over state governments and the power of local *coroneles*; the influence of the middle and working classes would have to increase.

In 1930, two forces united to reduce the power of state governors and *coroneles*. On one side, the oligarchy from states that did not export coffee turned against the coffee magnates from São Paolo, who dominated the old regime; on the other, the middle class revolted, led by a movement of army lieutenants, the *tenentes*. Then a key *tenente* leader broadened the revolt. Luis Carlos Prestes, who would join the Brazilian Communist Party in 1934, threatened to broaden the revolt to include the masses of rural and urban poor. Most of the military was not as revolutionary as Prestes, but it also was not disposed to defend the old system. It was Lieutenant Prestes's victory in elections marred by fraud in 1930 that led his main opponent, Getúlio Vargas, to cooperate with the military plot to overthrow and put an end to the First Brazilian Republic (1889–1930). The junta installed Vargas as president.

In a pattern that was common to populism, Vargas astutely took advantage of the crisis and implemented a program that reinforced his own power. In the shadow of Prestes, he sought reform to *prevent*, not to make, revolution. In 1934, he engineered a new constitution and, under pressure from workers' and women's organizations, included in it a minimum wage, support for worker cooperatives, and the right to vote for women. In 1937, the Brazilian president took advantage of conflict between communist and fascist sympathizers (this was the age of Stalin, Mussolini, and Hitler) to declare himself head of Brazil's Estado Nôvo (New State). He was a semi-dictator, and a popular one.

The period between 1937 and 1964 was dominated by Vargas. He centralized economic policy-making, implemented ISI, and in the vacuum left by the collapse of the old Republic, built not one but two parties to bolster his support. He did this in corporatist style—top-down. One party, the Brazilian Social Democratic Party (PSDB), was for the middle class. The other, the Brazilian Workers' Party (PTB), incorporated workers through unions controlled by the party with the support of the Ministry of Labor. In 1943, Vargas rammed through his Consolidation of Labor Laws, which in corporatist style directly linked the labor unions to the state. For example, the government collected a "trade union tax" imposed on all workers, whether or not they belonged to unions. In keeping with clientelism, the Ministry of Labor then distributed these funds to unions that supported Vargas through the PTB.

Similar systems linking parties and unions were adopted throughout Latin America. In Chile and Venezuela, the government used money earned from copper and oil exports, respectively, to subsidize unions heavily. The result was the same as in Brazil. Unions and their leaders were co-opted and made dependent on government. Workers lost leverage over their own unions and came to depend on a paternalistic state to defend their interests. However, it must be remembered that before populism, workers were repressed and had little political influence at all. Now at least they gained better wages, some benefits (e.g., retirement and unemployment pay), and protection under labor laws. Employers often complained about having to deal with unions, but as long as the unions were part of Vargas's political machine, businesses knew there were limits on the kinds of demands they would face. In exchange for working with unions subservient to Vargas and the PTB, business owners received subsidies and favors from government.

Although neither fully embraced the Axis cause in World War II, both Getúlio Vargas and Juan Perón in Argentina admired aspects of fascism in Germany, Spain, and especially Mussolini's Italy. In Brazil, these tendencies made Vargas a target of opposition by democrats and communists. These forces failed to win the election of 1946, but they did deny Vargas victory. Five years later, in 1951, he recaptured the presidency by veering in a more radical, nationalist direction. His presidency, marked by accusations of growing corruption but significant industrial growth, ended with his suicide in 1954. His suicide note itself was a classic populist statement: he accused foreign interests and the local elite of conducting a campaign of calumny against his government, which he portrayed as a servant of the people and the nation.

During Vargas's first period in power (1930–1945), called the Estado Nôvo (New State), strikes were illegal, but regular wage and benefit increases were granted—a corporatist approach modeled in part on the rule of Antonio Salazar, the dictator in Portugal. In a country where governors have almost always enjoyed great autonomy, he developed patronage networks to undermine governors and to subordinate states to his rule from the capital. Vargas often used a federal "intervener" to take over a state where his programs were being resisted. His programs delivered real benefits to his poor supporters in the cities. His welfare programs earned him the title "Father of the Poor," but his development programs left a huge gap between the industrializing south (Rio de Janeiro and São Paulo) and the impoverished, rural northeast. His import substitution programs were welcomed by businessmen—but when he moved toward more radical policies after returning to the presidency (1951–1954), the capitalist classes and foreign investors, now fearing strong central government more than social unrest, turned on him.

Juscelino Kubitschek was elected president in 1956 and tried to ride the tiger Vargas had created, but it was becoming harder to serve both the rich and the poor simultaneously. Leftist movements, inspired both by Prestes and by the Cuban Revolution of 1959, challenged the Estado Nôvo by mobilizing groups— peasants and the urban poor—left out of the populist system. Kubitschek also urged workers to take radical actions beyond the control of labor leaders tied to the parties created by Vargas. This increase in mass activity occurred just as the economy and the policies of ISI were faltering. In 1960, the system veered further left when João ("Jango") Goulart, who had been elected vice president, assumed the presidency on the resignation of the sitting president. Jango had been a popular minister of labor under Vargas but had been fired for advocating doubling the minimum wage. (Vargas turned around and implemented the raise anyway.) Goulart seemed to be moving in a radical direction, even countenancing the formation of worker militias. This was too much for the military to stomach. As these developments came at the height of the Cold War, and only a few years after the Cuban Revolution of 1959, the United States began to think Brazil might veer toward revolution and communism. In 1964, with U.S. warships offshore, Brazil's armed forces carried out a coup and inaugurated a harsh 24-year dictatorship.

For Review

What were Vargas's political and economic goals, and why did the oligarchy oppose him? How did he manage to gain so much power in a country notorious, even today, for decentralized politics and powerful governors? Why do you think he remains admired by some and despised by others even today?

Argentina: Juan and Eva Perón

The quintessential populist in Latin America was Juan Perón. Before Perón, Argentine politics was dominated by competition between the Conservatives, the traditional party of the landed elites, and the Radical Party, which represented the aspirations of the growing middle class (Corradi 1985; Hodges 1976; Page 1983). Neither of the two parties effectively reached out to workers on the railroads and in the ports and slaughterhouses, all crucial to the main export sectors—beef, grain, and leather. As the Argentine economy grew, immigrants from Italy, Germany, Spain, and other European countries swelled the ranks of the "popular sector"—a term that is used sometimes to refer to a block of peasants, workers, urban poor, and sometimes

Argentina

parts of the middle class. They brought with them socialist and anarchist ideas. The Argentine upper class was, on the other hand, thoroughly British in orientation, both culturally and economically. Economically, Argentine elites were cemented to the British by loans and by their reliance on access to the British market to sell its grain and meat exports. Industrialization would have meant replacing imports from Britain with locally produced products, letting the working class and its unions into the political game, and accepting taxation on exports. The Conservatives had no intention of doing so.

The growth of Argentina's beef- and grain-export economy made the country look incredibly successful in the early twentieth century, with a gross national product (GNP) that rivaled European countries. However, the social gap in the country remained huge, and the prosperity was built on a highly dependent export economy. Things began to change when other nations began to compete with Argentina. The economy suffered between 1913 and 1917 during a depression and World War I. The Conservative Party resisted efforts by the

Radicals, who had won the presidency in 1916, to incorporate workers into the system. But the Radicals were not really on the workers' side either. When workers—including women, who made up 22 percent of the labor force—revolted against the system in a general strike, the Radical president, Hipólito Yrigoyen, fearing a military coup, crushed the workers with heavy loss of life. As we shall see, the Radicals in Chile followed a different path between 1938 and 1952, ruling in alliance with the left.

The Radicals held onto power until 1930. They made some reforms under pressure from women's groups and workers, but they failed to address the burgeoning public debt and deteriorating prices of Argentina's exports. The export economy completely collapsed in the aftermath of the Great Depression, and in 1930 the military staged a coup, ultimately bringing the Conservative Party back to power. Until 1943, the Conservatives presided over a devastated economy, with soaring unemployment and the largest companies in bankruptcy. Immigrants stopped arriving, and workers now had to be recruited from those fleeing the devastated rural areas. Women were especially important in this migration. The Argentine Association for Women's Suffrage not only pursued the vote (won in 1947) but also demanded welfare, maternity leave, health care, and child care. One of the migrants, Eva Duarte, emerged from this milieu to become the key ally of her husband, Colonel Juan Domingo Perón.

Perón recognized the political potency of forging an alliance between Argentina's fledgling industrialists, who were frustrated with the Conservative oligarchy, and the popular sectors, including women and the small but militant working class. The colonel was a member of a secretive military lodge that staged a coup against the Conservatives in 1943. These military officers were nationalistic and angered by the corruption in both major parties. Many, like Perón, saw in Mussolini's fascism an example of how national unity could replace strife and public thievery. The early years of the military government, before Perón took charge, were characterized by repression of the women's movement and workers' organizations.

As the minister of labor, Perón, along with his ambitious wife Eva, recognized that ISI was a program that could cement hyper-nationalism to the aspirations of women and workers. He supported the organization of unions and favored them in collective bargaining. He implemented pension and health care systems. Eva built a formidable charitable organization and urged women to organize on their own behalf. Her charitable work and use of glamour played into gender stereotypes, but she was also a shrewd politician. The *descamisados*, the "shirtless ones" who formed the backbone of Perón's movement, adored her. When the nervous military officers arrested Juan Perón, still the minister of labor in 1945, the *descamisados*, encouraged by Eva, mobilized to save him (Fraser and Navarro 1980). In 1946, they supplied the votes that carried his new political party to victory and him to the presidency.

Perón was the most personalistic of the populist presidents. He expounded an idiosyncratic ideology called *justicialismo*, combining nationalism and **corporatism**, meant to be a "third way" between communism and capitalism, but pleasing neither the left nor the right. His party controlled the labor movement completely, and he did not hesitate to repress communists and other leftists, even those who were Peronists. The Peróns saw a threat in any movement to represent worker interests independently of their party. However, their real basis of power was the carrot, not the stick; Juan and Eva Perón delivered real benefits and incorporated the working class into politics.

They did not do much for the rural workers. Perón had promised to carry out land reform, but he delivered only a few laws improving the condition of peasants renting land from big owners. The land barons hated Perón, but he never decisively moved against them. After all, he needed to tax their exports to finance his industrialization and welfare programs. As in Brazil (and, we shall see, in Chile), the rural sector was left out of the populist equation. This failure to address conditions in the countryside had economic consequences. In the process of industrialization in Europe, Japan, and North America, the rural sector provided affordable food and raw materials for the cities and a market for factories. Land reform was not only a matter of social justice but also crucial to long-term development and modernization of the economy.

Eva's death from cancer in 1952 was a political blow to Juan Perón. Industrialists resented worker militancy and union power; they wanted state help but not restrictions. Military officers, always suspicious of their ambitious colleague, grew increasingly restive. In 1955, they overthrew Perón, and Argentina entered a 19-year period of instability. Perón died in 1974 after a brief, unsuccessful return to power in 1971. Without his charismatic personality, right- and left-wing factions in Peronism began to clash, sometimes violently. Communist groups and left-wing Peronist youth, inspired by the Cuban Revolution, began to pressure the old guard for revolutionary change. As in Brazil, this surge in militancy happened just as the economy was slowing down as import substitution reached its limits. As street violence intensified, a military government led by General Jorge Rafael Videla inaugurated a vicious "Dirty War" against the left between 1976 and 1978, leaving perhaps 30,000 people murdered or disappeared (see chapter 7).

Why do you think Eva's death prompted such an outpouring of emotion in Argentina?

PUNTO DE VISTA: WHAT KIND OF IDEOLOGY WAS PERÓN'S *JUSTICIALISMO*?

No Latin American leader has personified populism more than Juan Perón, and there are a number of historians who think that Eva Perón was even more astute in promoting a close personal identification between Perón and the people. Even if you do not speak Spanish, you may want to go online and watch the many available videos of Juan and Eva addressing masses of Argentines, often in the Plaza del Maya in Buenos Aires, to get a better idea of the emotional connection between these leaders and the people.

Following are excerpts from translations of two speeches, one by Juan Perón to the general assembly of his party, the other by Eva Perón to working-class women. Read through both of these before considering the questions that follow.

From Juan Perón's speech to the general assembly "Qué Es el Peronismo?" ("What Is Peronism?"), August 20, 1948:

A few days ago some legislators of the Congress asked me, "What is Peronism?" Peronism is humanism in action; Peronism is a new conception of politics that does away with the evils of politics of the past. Regarding social questions, it confers a little more equality—more equal opportunities—and assures that in the future no one in this land will lack the basic necessities of life, even should it be necessary, to benefit those with nothing at all, that those whose hands overflow lose their right to waste [wealth]. In the realm of the economy, it seeks to ensure that everything Argentine should work for Argentina, and it replaces an economic policy that was a permanent and perfect school for capitalist exploitation with a social-economic model for distribution of the wealth that we take from the land and produce ourselves; one that distributes wealth proportionately among all those who are involved in creating it with their effort. This is Peronism.

And don't say that Peronism is learned; it is something felt, or not felt. Peronism is a question of the heart more than of the head. Fortunately, I am not one of those presidents that isolates himself but one who lives with the people, as I have always lived. I share with working people all their ups and downs, all their successes and failures. I feel intimate satisfaction when I see today a well-dressed worker, or a worker attending the theater with his family. I then feel such satisfaction; I actually feel like a worker. This is Peronism.

Just as I have never conceived of the possibility that in this world there would be groups of men against other groups, nations against nations, even less I can conceive men of different beliefs being enemies . . . In Argentina there ought not to be more than one class of men alone: men that work for the national good without distinctions. Good Argentines . . . work for the greatness of the Nation; and bad Argentines . . . [are those who] do not everyday lift a stone to construct our nation as an edifice of happiness and grandeur.

(Translated from the original Spanish, www .elhistoriador.com.ar/ documentos/ascenso_y_ auge_del_peronismo/ doctrina_peronista.php)

In 1949, Eva Perón gave a speech to the Women's Auxiliary of the General Confederation of Labor. After urging women to cooperate with the census and lauding them for their role in defending Perón, in this excerpt, she spoke of Peronist doctrine (translated here from the original Spanish):

> To build a great country it is necessary to do justice by the people; to have a happy country it is necessary to do justice by the people; to speak of peace it is necessary to do justice with the people . . .
>
> For this reason we have an eminently social doctrine; for this reason Perón governs with the people and for the people; for this reason every day he delivers blows against the tight circle of traitorous oligarchs.
>
> Already the Argentine people have tired of a small group of so-called "leaders" who constitute a very crude oligarchy and want to govern. The very same ones who are selling out the country to foreigners! The same ones who keep the people down in the worst ignominy and take from them the last thing that a citizen should lose: hope! The same ones who strip the people of their personality! General Perón has restored to each Argentine their feeling of pride, and the greatest thing about Perón is that he stands for men dignifying other men.
>
> I passionately unite with my people, because the more that I interact with them, the more I understand them, the more I love them . . .

Point/Counterpoint

Having read the preceding speeches, and considering the brief history of Peronism, do you think Juan Perón, the populist, was just playing to the masses or was serious about change? What about Eva? Do you think she was sincere in her desire to be one with her *descamisados* (that is, the "shirtless" workers in the slaughterhouses, ports, and railroads)? Why or why not? What alternative motives might she have had?

a. If you generally answered that the Peróns were serious and well-motivated, how do you account for Juan's later turn to the right and attempts to control the unions?
b. If you generally see the Peróns as insincere or opportunistic, how do you account for the enthusiasm of the crowds, especially their evident love of Eva?

For more information

A repository of Peronism can be found at www.pjmoreno.org.ar/documentos/discursoseva3.aspx.

For Review

In what ways was the Peronist era in Argentina similar to that of Vargas in Brazil? What role did Eva Perón play in Argentina's populist experience? Why are the Peróns, even today, either hated or loved in Argentina?

Chile: From the Radical Party to Salvador Allende

Brazil's and Argentina's experiences with populism were stamped by the highly charismatic figures of Vargas and the Peróns. Chile did produce a singular leader, Salvador Allende Gossens, president for three tumultuous years (1970–1973), but not everyone would say Allende was a populist. As a Marxist and Socialist, Allende drew upon an ideology that defined the central conflict in society as one between social classes—between the bourgeoisie and the proletariat and not the people and an elite. Rather than see the Communist Party (Partido Comunista in Spanish, or PC) as a competitor, he was eager to work with the PC to achieve this goal. On the other hand, Allende's political coalition called itself the "Popular Unity" and claimed that the middle class and small businesses had nothing to fear from its policies. Allende resembled a typical populist leader of this period in his attempt to build a broad political base.

Although he called for revolution, Allende did not intend to replicate the Cuban model. He promised to respect the Chilean constitution and the property of the middle class, and he claimed local capitalists willing to invest and help the economy grow had nothing to fear from his government. Allende was an experienced politician, a doctor turned professional politician and the product of a competitive party system. He had no substantial base in the military establishment—in contrast to Vargas and Perón, who both first came to power with military support. Allende might be considered more a revolutionary than a populist leader. It is a matter of judgment. Here, we describe how the Chilean populist system worked, leaving the details of Allende's demise to chapter 7.

Chile entered the twentieth century with Latin America's strongest tradition of parliamentary government, but elections were tightly controlled processes. Local governments were responsible for administering restricted laws of suffrage, and it was easy for landowners to dominate the process. One trick was to distribute a shoe to local peasants with the promise that the second half of the pair would be delivered *if* victory went to the landlords' preferred party and candidates. Fraud, repression, and clientelism made it difficult for new parties and social groups to gain a share of power, even for the middle class and its parties. As in Brazil and Argentina, sympathetic military officers, themselves a part of the growing middle class, intervened to open the system to new forces. This happened in Chile in 1924.

Social change was in part fostered by the late-nineteenth-century boom in the export of nitrates mined from guano in the northern desert (see chapter 4). Toward the end of the nitrate era, foreign capital began to pour into Chile to exploit another of its natural resources, copper. Chile had long been an important copper exporter, but a major boom began in 1912 with large investments from the U.S., made by the Guggenheim family.

Landowners benefited from mining exports, but they had little interest in relinquishing their monopoly on political control or dividing up their estates (*latifundia*), where peasants (*inquilinos*) lived like serfs. Landlords had little incentive, and peasants had few resources, to make the investments (irrigation, fertilizers, machinery, new seeds, etc.) needed to modernize agriculture. European and Chilean merchant families, often linked to families that owned the mines and big-landed estates, controlled import-export houses and had little incentive to support state-initiated development plans.

Thus, resistance to political reform went hand in hand with the failure of elites to modernize the economy or to permit other social sectors to pursue this goal. However, the landowners could not profit from mining exports and still expect nothing to change. Teachers, railroad workers, stevedores, lawyers, laundry workers, construction workers, and a host of other new actors joined miners as a new social force. They formed new organizations and movements. Newly formed labor unions demanded recognition, along with better pay and working conditions. Middle-class groups rarely engaged in violent or extreme protest behavior, but they began to infiltrate the ranks of the Conservative and Liberal parties. Then, similar to developments in Argentina in the late 1800s, they created new parties, including the Radical Party, which would rise in the 1930s to become Chile's most important party. (It continues as a small party today.)

Workers and their unions were combative. Some split from the center parties to form first socialist and later communist parties. Students often supported the workers. Some politicians in the Liberal Party—the most prominent being Arturo Alessandri, who came to be known as the "Lion of Tarapacá" (part of the northern desert and an area populated by many miners)—saw an opportunity to gain an advantage over their Conservative rivals by making populist appeals. Liberals from the northern part of the country and from other mining areas began to appeal to these new actors in politics.

The political pressure cooker heated up when an economic crisis befell Chile after the collapse of the international market for nitrates, a consequence of the German invention of a synthetic substitute during World War I. Alessandri, the Liberal Party caudillo from the north, seized on the discontent to win the presidential election of 1920. Many working-class and poor Chileans put more faith in his personal leadership than in their own organizations, whose leaders were skeptical about the Lion's true intentions. Some of Chile's elite and the middle class supported Alessandri because they thought that only his leadership could head off a revolution. Once in office, Alessandri found that both Conservatives and his own Liberal Party refused to support reform legislation in the Chilean parliament (Drake 1978).

The political situation deteriorated as the Chilean parliament and president reached a stalemate. Factions among the civilian elite began to court the military. The army had become more professional and socially complex, not simply an extension of the landed oligarchy. A coup came in 1924. Middle-class officers rammed through social reform legislation. Over the next 15 years, organized workers and the middle class were incorporated into the political system. However, peasants and the urban poor, whose numbers would grow spectacularly, were left out, denied the right to vote. Beginning with the 1934 election, Chile returned to a stability that was the envy of the continent—and much of Europe too. However, because peasants and poor people in the cities were left out, as in other populist systems an underlying source of instability remained dormant but would eventually come to life.

Chile in the populist years was not governed by a charismatic strongman. There was no equivalent of Vargas or Perón. Populism in Chile was more about parties than about personalities (something true of Venezuela in these years too, as we shall see in chapter 9). However, as in these other cases, populist politics was linked to the strategy of industrialization through import substitution.

The Chilean Corporación de Fomento (Corfo) is a good example of the kind of institutions created to encourage ISI. After a period of turmoil following the collapse of the military government in 1932, a coalition of center and leftist parties, headed by the Radical Party, came to power determined to diversify the economy and escape the confines of export-based development. For three decades, the country pursued industrialization, enjoying relatively stable politics and limited social discontent. The Radicals were joined in the center of the political spectrum by a new party, the Christian Democratic Party (PDC), inspired by Catholic social doctrines (see chapter 2) advocating reforms. By 1958, the PDC had eclipsed the Radicals, but the center began to show signs of strain.

Chile's 1932 constitution served as a framework for the Radical Party to lead the process of import substitution. However, Chilean democracy was extremely limited. Literacy tests, property requirements, and poll taxes kept peasants and poor people away from the ballot box. Women got the vote only in 1949, because of a strong suffrage movement but also because conservatives thought that women would balance leftist tendencies among working-class men. Although the country experienced massive urbanization between 1932 and 1970, representation in Congress was never reapportioned, greatly exaggerating rural areas and thus conservative power. The inability to adapt the 1932 system to social change is a good example of failure of what comparativist Samuel Huntington (1968: 8–31) rightly saw as a crucial feature of healthy institutions—their ability to adapt to new circumstances. The system remained stagnant while portents of change were becoming more obvious.

In 1957, reforms to the electoral system eliminated barriers to voting, and between 1958 and 1970, the size of the electorate tripled. The distribution of votes among leftist, centrist, and rightist parties did not much change, but the politicians now had many more voters to please. The economic limits of ISI were being reached at the same time that this rise in political participation occurred. The tensions played out within the parties and in the political system. In the 1960s, young leftist and Catholic youth began to organize peasants and demand land reform. Allende's Socialist Party also felt the tensions within its ranks. Always unruly and prone to splits, the Socialists were deeply divided between a revolutionary wing and a more moderate faction that tended to align with the communists during the late populist era and during the Allende years (1970–1973).

When Salvador Allende, with his plan to lead a revolution within constitutional and democratic bounds, won a narrow plurality of the vote in 1970, it was not at all clear at first that the Chilean Congress would ratify him as president (which was its function in the event no one got a majority). Only a bungled kidnapping of Chile's head of the armed forces by right-wing groups funded by the United States assured him of the presidency, as the centrist Christian Democratic Party, responding to public anger at the murder, decided not to block his ascent. He would not survive even three years into his presidency. In 1973, he died in a coup encouraged by the United States; General Augusto Pinochet assumed power for 16 years, ending Chile's crisis of populism and replacing it with a brutal military dictatorship.

For Review

What similarities and differences mark Allende's career compared to those of Perón and Vargas? What are some similarities and differences between populism in Chile's case and populism in the other two countries?

Mexico: Populism after Revolution

The period of populism and ISI did not end always in military rule. In Venezuela, the oil boom of the 1970s allowed populism to endure much longer than in most other South American countries. In Colombia, the army never fully seized power, although its political influence grew as the two major parties, Liberals and Conservatives, fought one another for political control, and as an insurgency took root in the countryside after 1952. But the most important country to escape military rule was Mexico, a consequence of that country having experienced the first major social revolution of the twentieth century. We will look more closely at the Mexican Revolution and its consequences in chapter 9. Here, we want only to note that as Mexican politics began to settle down after the revolutionary era (1910–1917), the country's ruling party adopted ISI and populism.

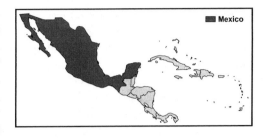

Mexico's liberal modernization lasted for 30 years under the dictator Porfirio Díaz (see chapter 4). In this time of relative political stability, the export sectors of mining and export agriculture expanded. As usual, the benefits flowed to a small upper class. Small landholdings in the north and the communal-owned lands (*ejidos*) in the south were being taken over by big growers and ranchers eager to export to the growing U.S. market. Miners, railroad workers, and a growing population of urban poor were waiting for some of the new wealth to trickle down to them. The middle class chafed under Díaz's refusal to reform the political system. In 1910, Díaz broke a promise to allow free elections and once again engineered his own victory. Francisco Madero, a Liberal opposition candidate, was jailed for protesting the outcome. After his release, he called for towns all over the country to rise up in defense of democracy. Madero got more than he bargained for. He got the Mexican Revolution.

Between 1910 and 1917, Mexico was convulsed by civil war. For 11 more years (1917–1928), the country was racked by sporadic uprisings and assassinations. Nearly all the major leaders of the 1910 revolution were dead by 1928. A formula to end the violence was engineered by Plutarco Calles, who founded a political party that embraced almost all the military strongmen and *caciques* of the country. Calles himself might have become a political patriarch in the style of Díaz, but his chosen successor, Lázaro Cárdenas, elected in 1934, had no intention of serving merely as a puppet for Calles, the caudillo. Cárdenas built his own popular base of support by implementing a program that included land reform (hence, Mexican populism did not entirely exclude the peasantry) and state-supported industrialization—ISI.

Mexican populism, unlike that of the Southern Cone and Brazil, had to incorporate the masses because they had already mobilized to fight the Revolution. They could not be easily sent back to their villages to live in isolation from each other and as peons for big landowners. The result was the Cárdenas presidency, a vibrant era of union organizing, land reform, cultural innovation, and nationalism, culminating in 1938 with the nationalization of the foreign oil companies, a precedent for the region. Cárdenas built a political coalition similar to that found in other episodes of populism we have reviewed. Once again, a coalition of the working and middle classes supported reform and ISI, but the rural sector could not be politically ignored. Mexico underwent land reform in the 1930s, unlike the cases of Argentina and Brazil. The old landlord class had been decisively defeated. However, change stopped short of the kind of rural modernization needed to support industrialization.

For all of his reforms, which made Cárdenas a much-revered statesman throughout the hemisphere, the president opted to moderate his redistributive policies later in his term. This led to divisions within the ruling party of the Mexican Revolution, which had been founded by Calles as a vehicle to resolve disputes within the revolutionary leadership and would soon be renamed the Institutional Revolutionary Party (PRI). The president's chosen successor, Manuel Avila Camacho, prevailed in the 1940 election, but only with the benefit of considerable fraud, repression, and help from the incumbent government.

After 1940, President Camacho greatly slowed land redistribution and reduced aid for agriculture, even though he maintained policies to promote ISI, and for three decades the Mexican economy grew. But when ISI began to falter in the 1960s, political instability began to grow. Once again, ISI development policies and populism were fatefully linked to one another. The Mexican economic crisis of 1982, when the country defaulted on its international debt, was one of the landmark events that spelled the end of ISI and populism and that swung Latin American economic policy toward a more **laissez-faire**, **neoliberal** model.

Mexico's revolution resulted in some exceptional features in its politics (e.g., civil control of the military, an independent foreign policy, strong political institutions for several decades, and orderly political succession). The PRI held onto power for 18 more years after 1982, but it came to rely much more on fraud and repression than in earlier decades, when people had supported it because it was *the party* forged in the fires of Mexico's great revolution. The military never took power, as in Argentina, Brazil, and Chile, but the political system definitely became more authoritarian, based less and less on popular consent over time.

For Review

Mexico underwent ISI in much the same way that Argentina, Brazil, and Chile did. Why, then, did Mexico develop a more stable and institutionalized political system? Why was the rural sector more incorporated into the populist system than in these other cases?

Assessing Populism and ISI—Lessons for Today

The economic development policies associated with populism included creation of investment funds, nationalization of key economic sectors (sometimes), mediated labor policies, investment in infrastructure (dams, roads, ports, etc.), and taxes on imports and exports to fund these activities. These same development policies also provided the patronage (jobs, protection from competition, and subsidies) needed to build parties and networks of support. Populists often sounded leftist, especially when they invoked nationalist and anti-imperialist rhetoric. But they were not Communists. Some even saw their task as heading off communism through reform; some (e.g., Perón and Rómulo Betancourt of Venezuela) turned strongly anticommunist during the Cold War (1945–1991).

When the strategy of industrializing through import substitution reached its limits (in the 1960s, in most cases), and the economic pie began to shrink, populist democracy also entered into crisis. We will examine the causes more closely in chapters 7 and 8, but here we can summarize some of the problems as the failure of business owners, protected by the state from competition from imports, to modernize; the failure to modernize agriculture; strains placed on the export sector, the main source of capital for industrialization; clientelism and corruption, which inhibited more efficient use of resources; unwillingness to redistribute wealth and income to bring more people into the consumer market; and lack of social capacity to innovate technologically.

Corporatist relationships are based on the notion of political reciprocity. An interest group offers support to the state, a leader, or a political party in return for tangible benefits (jobs, subsidies, contracts, services, etc.) that can be doled out to the group's members (clients). Leaders of groups and of parties can use these benefits to reward other members. In a sense, the populist parties and politicians updated traditional patterns of **clientelism**. Jobs and bags of cement could be just as effective as **compadrazgo**, and in fact, *compadrazgo* did not entirely disappear in the cities. If rivals cannot be bought off, repression is almost always lurking—the iron fist inside the velvet glove. At an extreme, this dual system of co-option and coercion resembles fascism, where the state asserts almost complete control over social groups. We saw an example of this kind of power in chapter 2 in the story about Venezuelan workers striking to improve their conditions in a metallurgical plant.

During the populist era, the government became a major economic actor, often owning large industries and expanding its treasury with taxes on export enclaves. The political game revolved around competition among groups and parties seeking to share in these resources, a phenomenon called "**rent-seeking**." In countries such as Chile, which depended heavily on copper exports, and Venezuela, where oil was king, this behavior was pronounced. Terry Karl (1994), a student of oil-exporting states, argues that the presence of great natural wealth in a country can be something of a disadvantage because it fosters rent-seeking capitalists reluctant to take risks or make investments. Why modernize an old textile plant, for example, if the government will subsidize your purchases of cloth and energy, keep the prices of foreign competitors high, and maybe even subsidize the consumers' purchase of your costly products?

The populist era ended tragically. Populism became synonymous with bad **macroeconomic** policy and demagoguery. However, it was in this period that the masses entered national politics. Furthermore, economic growth rates were higher, even in the 1960s. From 1950 until 1980, Latin America's economic output increased on average 5.5 percent per year; GDP per capita increased by 2.2 percent. The movements of peasants, workers, and women who either initiated populist movements or took advantage of opportunities opened by political leaders greatly expanded the scope of democracy. Whatever its flaws, ISI, populism's development strategy, was the only sustained effort to develop Latin America's economy by looking mainly inward, not outward, in nearly 500 years of history.

> ## For Review
>
> Clientelism and corporatism were common in Latin America before the populist era. And they did not disappear with populism. Did anything fundamental change about Latin American politics between 1900 and the end of the populist era?

Peasant Politics and the Crisis of Populism

We sometimes think of peasant societies as simple, perhaps varying little from one to another. However, peasant societies are far from homogeneous, which makes it difficult to unite them into broad national movements. Many rural populations are ethnically and culturally diverse. For example, in south and central Mexico, one finds many indigenous peasants with strong communal traditions. In the northern region one finds individualist, mestizo smallholders. Gender relationships can vary greatly too. Women have different roles and responsibilities, depending on whether their men live at home or must migrate for work on plantations or ranches for months when labor is needed—for example, at harvest time.

Peasants with regular access to land are generally less responsive to political mobilizations. However, when threatened with being uprooted from their land, they become prime subjects to join political movements. Peasants hired to work on plantations, much like workers in the city, generally enjoyed wages and working conditions superior to their rural brethren, or even to poor workers in the cities. However, political activists found that employees on these plantations, strategic enclaves producing crops such as sugar, cacao, palm oil, tobacco, bananas, and so on for the world market, were easier to organize into unions and movements than peasants tied to the land through traditional relationships with landlords. Wage-earning workers in the countryside lived closer together, were often less culturally conservative, and had some education. Although paid better, they had few rights versus management, and it was easier for organizers to reach them with pamphlets and group meetings off company property.

Struggles to organize workers in strategic economic sectors often converged with demands for democracy and lent support to nationalists and reformers (Bergquist 1986). However, with a few exceptions, populists did not aim to reform the traditional countryside. Labor laws usually made it much more difficult to organize peasants than urban workers, and the local political power (including repression) that landlords had at their disposal could make organizing dangerous. In Chile and Brazil, the question of land reform remained explosive and contributed to the coups that ended the radicalization process. Rather than fight the landowners, populist leaders often avoided the difficult task of land reform and modernization of agriculture. Land redistribution required interfering with property rights, worrying middle-class and private capitalists, perhaps inviting a coup by conservative military officers. As a result, the countryside neither produced food efficiently for the growing cities nor provided a market for new industries.

To raise money for ISI and other government expenditures, populist governments taxed exports. In some cases they forced landlords or miners to export through state trading houses that set prices and limited profits. This not only alienated owners of mines, ranches, and plantations; it also induced them—deliberately for political reasons, or simply because of inadequate profits—to produce and export less. For example, Perón forced ranchers to sell their beef to the state, which set the internal price and attempted to market exported meat at a profit. Not only did this alienate the ranchers; it angered foreign traders.

The land question did not go away. In the 1960s, agrarian reform would reemerge as an issue in many countries. Rural conflict added pressure to democracies already facing declining economies and increased demands in the cities. In their gestation, the unions and social organizations formed by workers and women's groups had great vitality and democratic promise. Even when they were subordinated to populist parties and leaders, their incorporation made it impossible to ignore their interests. This is one reason populism usually was ended by fiercely repressive military governments.

For Review

Why was land reform not on the agenda of most populists? To what extent was Mexico an exception, and why? Populist governments needed the export sector to promote development. Why?

Did ISI Reduce Dependency?

The compatibility of populism with ISI was based on an expanding economic pie. As long as the economy was growing, the middle and working classes had jobs, and the urban poor had the hope of a better future. Economic growth continued throughout the ISI period in the four countries considered in this chapter all the way through 1979, although Argentina lagged behind, presaging troubles over the horizon. But the growth rates do not tell the entire story. Millions of people were leaving the countryside for the city during the ISI period, attracted by jobs, schools, hospitals, and so on. Strong as growth rates were, they did not approach the 10 percent annual rates that characterized industrialization in the earlier stages of capitalism in the wealthy countries, as they were transformed into mature, market societies. How could all of these urban migrants, much less those left behind in the rural areas, be integrated—that is, find jobs, contribute their labor, and have sufficient income to expand the market for national industries?

So Latin America's economies continued to grow, but the limits to growth by ISI were reached in the 1960s. Industries protected by tariffs, subsidized by governments, and able to draw upon a supply of cheap labor failed to modernize and fell behind competitors overseas. Without income redistribution and land reform, there was not enough demand for many industrial products. Few countries had a large enough class of consumers who could afford cars, refrigerators, and other durable consumer goods. And when export prices fell, so did revenues to subsidize industries and maintain social programs.

Most factories had to import their capital goods (e.g., power looms for textile factories) and other inputs needed to produce final consumer goods. The traditional export sectors

TABLE 5.1   Latin America's Cities, Population Growth 1900–1990

City	1900	1950	1960	1970	1980	1990
Bogotá	125,429	647,429	1,682,668	2,892,668	4,122,978	4,851,000
Buenos Aires	1,251,000	4,622,959	6,739,045	8,314,341	9,723,966	10,886,163
Caracas	90,000	683,659	1,346,708	2,174,759	2,641,844	2,989,601
Lima	140,000	645,172	1,845,910	3,302,523	4,608,010	6,422,875
Mexico City	349,721	3,145,351	5,173,549	8,900,513	13,811,946	15,047,685
Rio de Janeiro	926,585	2,885,165	4,392,067	6,685,703	8,619,559	9,600,528[a]
Santiago	269,886	1,509,169	2,133,252	2,871,060	3,937,277	4,676,174[a]
São Paolo	2,333,346	2,333,346	4,005,631	7,866,659	12,183,634	15,183,612[a]

Source: For 1900, figures are from *The 1911 Edition Encyclopedia* (of Britannica), accessed July 9, 2002, at www.1911.encyclopedia.org. For other years, national census figures are cited by Alan Gilbert, *The Mega-City in Latin America* (New York: United Nations University Press, 1996), accessed July 9, 2002 at www.unu.edu/unu-press/unupbooks/uu23me/uu23me00.htm#Contents.
[a]Preliminary figures

remained vital to the economy because the subsidies and patronage that greased the system had to be generated by earnings from abroad. Because the prices of Latin America's primary commodities did not keep pace with manufactured goods in most instances, the export sector could not generate the kind of economic surpluses needed to sustain investments. Although some of the new industries, such as petrochemicals and steel, produced inputs for factories producing consumer goods (e.g., clothing, paper, processed foods), Latin American countries could not "deepen" industrialization by producing capital goods (machinery, technology, etc.) and intermediate goods (automobile transmissions, wire, etc.). Instead of classic dependency being overcome, a new form of economic dependence had emerged.

The middle class wanted access to affordable refrigerators, televisions, washing machines, and so on. Foreign enterprises could meet this demand more cheaply if freed from the constraints of quotas, tariffs, and other measures associated with ISI. Some of the most important new enterprises—for example, automobiles—were the result of investments by foreign companies seeking to get under tariff and quota barriers to keep their markets in the larger countries. The purpose of ISI was to jump-start a process of national development and not increase dependency on imports, but import bills were going up, not down. Prebisch and other economists who supported ISI warned that protection was becoming counterproductive.

The most dynamic capitalists in Latin America were coming to identify progress in their country with attracting foreign investment, not ISI. Fernando Henrique Cardoso, the Brazilian political sociologist who later became president, called this unanticipated result "associated-dependent development." Cardoso and his Chilean colleague Enzo Faletto agreed that foreign capital exploited labor (Cardoso and Faletto 1979; first published in Portuguese in 1971). Indeed, suppressing labor to attract foreign capital was a central function of government in dependent countries. Like other **dependency theorists**, however, Cardoso and Faletto rejected the idea that foreign investment *caused* underdevelopment. They argued that foreign capital brought developmental technology and promoted growth of a native capitalist class in the country—one with an internationalist rather than nationalist outlook.

In their view, this new capitalist class was "associated" in a dependent way with foreign capitalists; hence, they coined the term "associated-dependent development." For example, the Brazilian owner of a factory producing industrial paint might have a foreign automobile manufacturer as his principal customer. His economic interest, then, would become linked to the continued presence and prosperity of the foreign manufacturer, who probably has attracted Brazilian partners as co-owners. In a way, Cardoso and Faletto anticipated **globalization** because they saw the development of a different kind of **bourgeoisie**, one that critics of globalization today call a "transnational capitalist class."

Not only was this theory controversial, but also one of its authors, Cardoso, became increasingly controversial himself. He entered politics and became a minister of finance and then president (1995–2003) of Brazil. Cardoso maintained that he was pursuing a pragmatic agenda that neither embraced nor rejected neoliberalism. To many on the left, he had moved from critic to advocate of associated-dependent development.

For Review

From an economic standpoint, what were some of the reasons that ISI faltered? How did ISI on the one hand seem to reinforce economic dependency? What does "associated-dependent development" mean?

Did Populism Advance or Retard Democracy?

Populism in this era was for the most part a top-down rather than bottom-up phenomenon. Although mass participation increased, political leaders and parties used corporatist strategies and clientelism to achieve their own political ends and to limit the horizons of the working class, the peasantry, and the urban poor. In this respect, populism at its apogee most benefited the middle class. The middle class inhabited the ranks of the political parties and the public bureaucracy that thrived off populism. Some political scientists argued that the middle class itself had become the vanguard of democratic development (Johnson 1958). Others (Nun 1976) warned that the middle class had deserted populism upon perceiving that the workers, the peasants, and the poor threatened revolution.

Because populism often ended in a coup that inaugurated a long and brutal period of military rule in most of the region, it is easy to forget that populist regimes rarely came to power without the support of the military. Indeed, populists sometimes came from military ranks, as was the case with Perón and Vargas. As president (1951–1954), Jacobo Arbenz, a Guatemalan colonel, attempted to nationalize unused land from the United Fruit Company. Lázaro Cárdenas was a revolutionary general before he became a state governor and then president. A Peruvian general, Juan Velasco Alvarado, came to power in 1968 and embarked on a program of land reform and income distribution. Even today, populist leaders may rise out of military ranks—and later be threatened by their more conservative military colleagues. Hugo Chávez, who came to power in 1998 with a radical leftist agenda for Venezuela, was a colonel in 1992 when he burst upon the scene after leading an unsuccessful coup against an elected but unpopular government. The lesson is that not only is the military involved in politics, but politics also takes place inside the military.

Today neoliberals see little good about the populist past, but in reality most populists were more interested in promoting capitalism than transforming it. Arbenz sought to nationalize United Fruit's land to promote a social class of small farmers, not collectivize agriculture along the model of the Soviet Union. Arbenz welcomed communist support for his program; the Guatemalan communists were more interested in organizing unions on the fruit plantations than in creating Soviet-style collective farms. However, Perón's anticommunist attitude was more typical of populists in this era. In a speech in 1950 he warned,

> It is beyond doubt that the communist system has its greatest chances of prevailing in the Western World in so far as the capitalist system offers no other doctrine than failed, liberal individualism, while leaving vulnerable its flanks, which are, outside of the United States, people exhausted by poverty and hunger, allied out of desperation with whatever other system is offered them.

Perón promoted his program not as revolutionary socialism but as a third way, an attempt to humanize capitalism and a necessary measure "to battle the communist economic system successfully" (Perón 1950).

Communist parties had become prominent in many Latin American countries, including Argentina. Generally, the Communists concentrated on organizing workers, both on plantations (e.g., sugar estates in Cuba, fruit plantations in Guatemala) and in the factories and mines (e.g., among copper workers in Chile and oil workers in Venezuela and in slaughterhouses in Argentina). But the Communists were not nearly as revolutionary as Perón's words or the rhetoric of the U.S. government suggested. They often took the position that Latin America first had to overcome its "feudal" past and experience capitalism before it could move on to communism. Loyal to Moscow's leadership position, they sometimes decried liberal democracy as "bourgeois," but in times (e.g., during World War II or the détente era of 1968–1976) of relatively good relationships between the United States and the Soviet Union, they promoted alliances with reformist parties.

For Review

Why were most populists sometimes in conflict with communists? Why were populists and communists sometimes able to get along?

Recent Populism in Venezuela, Peru, and Ecuador

When we speak of the "populist era" in Latin America, we are usually referring to the middle decades of the twentieth century, but some say populism has made a comeback in the last decade. Chávez was often compared, usually unfavorably, to Perón, Vargas, and others. Chávez peppered his speeches with denunciations of the wealthy elite, whom he labeled "squalid ones" (*escualidos*), and he rallied support from the poor by referring to them as *el soberano* ("the sovereign ones"). After 2001, he used revenues from an upsurge in the price of oil, Venezuela's main export, to finance widespread social programs. For some, Chávez represented a return to discredited programs and styles of the past; for others, Chávez represented a positive new leadership offering an alternative to policies promoted by the United States, the World Bank, the International Monetary Fund, and other global institutions.

Not all populists come from the left. Peru's Alberto Fujimori won election in 1990 by campaigning as a critic of neoliberalism and challenger to the country's oligarchy. However, once in office he moved to the right, closed the Peruvian Congress in 1992, and ruled in alliance with the military, which under his presidency was given a free hand to crush Sendero Luminoso (Shining Path), a guerrilla movement with a reputation for human rights atrocities that rivaled the military's record. Even conservative businessmen can pose as populists. Alvaro Noboa, who ran second in the race for Ecuador's presidency in 2002, was owner of the country's largest banana plantations. He was accused of crushing independent unions and utilizing child labor on his estates, yet Noboa's "New Humanity Crusade People's Joint Action Foundation" spent lavishly to promote his image as a benevolent hero of the poor. Directly or indirectly, he could claim responsibility for the employment of more than 1 million of Ecuador's 12 million people. He promoted himself as a humanitarian provider of a system of free clinics throughout the country. In 2006, Noboa tried again to gain the presidency, but this time another populist, Rafael Correa, defeated him.

As we have seen, to understand the classic populism of Latin America in the middle decades of the twentieth century, we have to see how strategies of economic development, the emergence of new social actors seeking access to the political game, and political ambitions came together. To understand neopopulism and the more recent surge of populism in the form of the **Pink Tide**, we need to take a similar approach, which we shall do in later chapters that examine the causes and consequences of Latin America's shift away from ISI and toward more laissez-faire, neoliberal-oriented economic policies in the last part of the century.

History and Politics: Some Final Thoughts

As we turn our attention in the following chapters to politics in the present day, we might reflect for a moment on how we can use the historical background presented in chapters 3–5 to better understand contemporary politics. For one thing, we can see broad patterns that recur across different countries and time periods. Political leaders, as well as ordinary people, do not make choices in a vacuum; they are influenced by elective affinities—that is, general tendencies that seem embedded in culture, with culture itself being understood in part as the product of historical experience. For example, Russia has long experience with strong, centralized rule because the country was created and unified by powerful rulers, the czars. Western Europeans are more accepting than Americans of higher tax rates in part because they expect the government to provide many services (mass transportation, day care, and health care for all). Americans (of the United States) have a highly individualistic culture shaped by the frontier experience, lack of an aristocracy, and inheritance of liberal British political ideas.

This book has identified a number of affinities in Latin America—for example, caudilloism and corporatism. However, you need to remember that such affinities are subject to change. Certainly, the twentieth century included important episodes in which Latin Americans tried to redirect the course of their history through revolution, dictatorship, and reform. Leaders constantly have to choose between either working within the boundaries of political culture shaped by history or seeking to change these affinities. Therefore, we will find that presidentialism, personalism, clientelism, corporatism, caudilloism, and so on seem to be recurring themes in Latin American politics, but habits of mind also have roots in the reality of present-day economic and social life. Just as crude economic determinism leads us to forget the importance of culture, cultural determinism may lead us to forget how much economic dependency and Latin America's class structure reinforce its political culture.

Discussion Questions

1.   What social groups in Latin America gained the most from import substitution policies, and which ones gained the least or lost? How did ISI as a development strategy also help populists build a base of political support? Do you think that overall ISI was a success or a failure?
2.   List some of the key factors that brought about the crisis of populism. Do you think the roots of the crisis were predominantly economic or political?
3.   Given the experience with populism in Latin America, would you say that calling a politician a populist was a compliment or an insult? Why?

Resources for Further Study

Reading: On the great mythological woman, see Nicholas Fraser and Marysa Navarro, *Evita: The Real Life of Evita Perón* (New York: Norton, 1996). Paul Drake's *Socialism and Populism in Chile, 1932–52* (Urbana: University of Illinois Press, 1978) is a good case study of midcentury populism. My own *Venezuela: Tarnished Democracy* (Boulder, CO: Westview Press, 1991) reviews the populist experience in that country.

Video and Film: Three episodes of the *Americas* (1992) series—on Brazil ("Capital Sins"), Argentina ("Garden of Forking Paths"), and Chile ("In Women's Hands")— review the twentieth-century rise and fall of populism, military rule, and transitions to democracy. *Hour of the Furnaces* (1968) documents the rise of guerrilla violence and military response in 1968 in Argentina.

On the Internet: You have to be careful with Wikipedia, but the page on Juan Perón is well referenced (see http://en.wikipedia.org/wiki/Juan_Peron).

6

Development and Dependency: Theory and Practice in Latin America

Focus Questions

▶   What do we mean by "economic development" and "dependency"? What are the main debates about the causes and proper way to overcome underdevelopment in Latin America?

▶   What is the relative importance of culture versus the legacy of colonialism in accounting for economic underdevelopment in Latin America?

▶   How has the relationship between the state and the economy varied in the post–World War II era in Latin America?

▶   As Latin Americans look back on the successes and failures of two different eras when the role of the state varied, how do they and experts on the area differ in evaluating import substitution and neoliberalism?

ONE OF THE key contemporary issues regards the proper role of the state in leading development. In the middle decades of the twentieth century, a state-led approach to fomenting industrialization, "import substitution," dominated much of the region. Then, in the closing decades, the pendulum swung away from the state-led approach toward reliance on a free-market strategy, rolling back the influence of the state. Popular discontent with this strategy, called "neoliberalism," has led the pendulum to swing back toward the state, but not necessarily back to import substitution.

In this chapter, we limit ourselves to theories of underdevelopment and development as they directly relate to the state's relationship to economic growth. By doing so, we put aside for the moment two central issues: whether economic growth translates into human development, in particular better living conditions; and whether economic growth is sustainable, especially in environmental terms, a theme that social movements have put on the agenda in Latin America (see chapter 15).

Debates about the best policies that states should implement usually reflect ideological and theoretical positions not only about how to grow the economy but also about the diagnosis of the causes of underdevelopment. The very words (modernization, dependence, and underdevelopment) we use to discuss these issues are laden with implications. How much responsibility for poverty and inequality in the Third World rests with the exploitation of these countries by the Global North? How much of the explanation is rooted internally in the culture, politics, and social class structures of the Global South? We will find that Latin American political leaders and intellectuals have not been absent from this debate.

Contending Approaches to Development

Many **modernization theorists** see the cause of poverty and underdevelopment mainly in social values. More often than not, this perspective starts with the idea that Europe's transition from feudalism to capitalism is the norm, the model. Feudal society was mainly rural. Its traditional values emphasized the importance of people accepting their place in society, with the aristocracy (lords) naturally ruling over peasants (serfs). The latter owed service to the lords, who in turn provided them protection. The bargain was supposedly blessed by God, and the Catholic Church was itself a major landholder. In this system, serfs were not allowed to leave the estates and work elsewhere; they were not free in this sense. However, neither were their overlords "free" to displace them from the land. Unlike today, when land is property (which is why we have deeds), the land and people on it were regarded as one. A small merchant class existed, so there was some exchange, but market relations were not very significant to people's lives; most of what sustained them was produced and consumed on the manor.

This description is nothing more than a broad sketch of a system that varied a lot from place to place, but because Europe evolved from the 1300s to the 1800s from feudalism to **capitalism**—a system where land and other things used to produce are owned, bought, and sold and where people are not guaranteed a high status by birth—it must suffice for us to understand how it has influenced modernization theory and its application to Latin America (and other parts of the **Third World**). Again at risk of oversimplification, modernization theorists generally see what happened in Europe in these centuries as a great transition in which cultural change was at the root. This transition happened later in Spain and Portugal than it did in Northern Europe, so the theory is that Latin America inherited a culture and cultural factors resembling those of feudalism in Europe before capitalism. We encountered a version of this theory in chapter 1, where we noted that some political scientists stress the incompatibility between "traditional" culture and democracy. To some extent, as we saw in chapter 4, some Latin American elites, the liberal modernizers, also believed that economic development required emulating Europe.

To some extent, communists and capitalists could agree upon this interpretation of development. Had not Marx himself said in the *Communist Manifesto* (Marx and Engels 1848) that capitalism was a necessary stage of history before socialism or communism? The big difference, however, was that Marxists have stressed economic change as the generator of social and culture change, not the other way around. From the Marxist root has come dependency theory and other related approaches that stress imperialism and colonialism as the fundamental causes of underdevelopment. In the case of modernization theorists, much of their interpretation builds off the ideas of the great German sociologist Max Weber, whose *Protestant Ethic and the Spirit of Capitalism* argued that the advancement of capitalism was driven by cultural changes associated with the Reformation.

Around 1960, the American social scientist Walt Rostow (1960) wrote his influential treatise *The Stages of Growth*, confidently subtitled "A Non-Communist Manifesto." He too predicted the passing of "feudalistic" social structures into modern capitalist ones, but his goal was to prevent a more radical revolution. He put this objective into action as national security advisor to presidents John F. Kennedy and Lyndon B. Johnson in the 1960s. Rostow recommended providing military aid to fight leftist insurgencies until countries in Latin America and elsewhere in the Third World (notably, Vietnam) were economically developed and politically stable. Rostow is regarded by his critics as responsible for massive bloodshed resulting from U.S. prosecution of the war in Vietnam.

In the 1960s, Latin American social scientists began to raise doubts about Rostow's scenario, but also about the orthodox Marxist view that Latin America needed to repeat Europe's experience and pass through a stage of capitalism. Brazil's Andre Gunder Frank (1967), perhaps the most influential of these thinkers, pointed out that the feudal social structure of medieval Europe differed from that of Latin America. European feudalism was based on a manorial economy that was largely self-contained. In contrast, Latin America's economies produced raw materials for the world market. In Europe, the Christian religion was shared by lord and peasant, cementing the social structure. In Latin America, Christianity was imposed on native peoples and on slaves brought to work mostly in export-oriented economies.

Both schools of thought could agree, however, on a simple formula for most of the twentieth century, one less in fashion today: economic development = industrialization. Today, with many factories migrating from the wealthier countries to poorer ones, few development experts would equate the two terms. Nonetheless, the terminology, concepts, and theories associated with these two broad schools of thought continue to heavily influence analysis of Latin American politics today.

Modernization Theory

Modernization theory interprets the Latin culture forged out of Iberian, African, and Indian social values as the major obstacle to development. In this theory, tradition is something to be overcome and not utilized. Latin Americans need to stop thinking in terms of inherited status, natural inequalities, and the sacredness of old ways of doing things. They have to separate their loyalty to their families and close friends from their responsibility to each other as citizens, customers, employers, and so on. Once this occurs, Latin Americans will progress out of the early stages of capitalism, which are always characterized by great inequalities and poverty for workers, and find the path to sustained economic growth and development beneficial to all.

From this perspective, **underdevelopment** is a condition that has characterized all countries at one time or another and not something imposed by imperialism or colonization. Modernization—and development—theories commonly assume that Latin America has been left behind and will eventually "catch up" and join the ranks of developed nations. For modernization theorists, the most significant political challenge facing political systems in Latin America after World War II was dealing with an "over-all process of change, which happens to substantial parts of the population in countries which are moving from traditional to modern ways of life" (Deutsch 1961: 394). Governments in Africa, the Middle East, Asia, and Latin America, despite the tremendous diversity in cultures, were all dealing with urbanization, industrialization, mass communications, and other changes that undermined the traditional authority typical of the rural village. As Karl Deutsch (1961:493) put it, "These processes tend to go together in certain historical situations and stages of economic development; [they] are identifiable and recurrent, in their essentials from one country to another; and they are relevant for politics."

The classic literature in the field of development is too vast for us to review in all of its complexity; however, two key ideas from the foregoing discussion are worth highlighting—the idea of stages and the idea of social mobilization. Like Weber, Rostow (1960) saw the stages beginning with a period of cultural change that prepared Northern Europe, the United States, and other countries that are today wealthy and developed for a subsequent period of "takeoff" into high economic growth rates. He claimed that traditional culture limited individual initiative, risk taking, and other forms of individual behavior needed to make capitalism thrive. People in rural society accepted their place in life, tended to mix religious and political authority with one another, valued personal relationships and blood ties more than citizenship, and possessed other attitudes that were not conducive to market society. Modernization theorists also usually argue that such traditional values are incompatible with democracy.

According to Rostow, at some point economies reach "takeoff," a period of economic hypergrowth (about 10 percent per year), for about a 40-year period. The arrows in Figure 6.1, taken from his book, show when this occurred for nations that had achieved development at the time (1960) he was writing. By his theory, growth rates level off at "maturity," a stage when nations become mass consumer societies, emulating social and economic patterns found in countries that industrialized early. Note that Rostow thought that Argentina and Mexico, then actively pursuing **import substitution industrialization**, were at the takeoff point.

This transition is difficult and likely to produce political instability as traditional elements in society resist those seeking to modernize. Rostow (as noted previously, an advisor to the Kennedy and Johnson administrations between 1961 and 1968) and others (e.g., Lipset 1960; Huntington 1968) believed that Communists were taking advantage of the turmoil. The solution? Most of these intellectuals, often advisors in government, advocated providing military aid to hold off the communists and economic aid to speed the developmental transition. In Latin America, that task took on special urgency after the Cuban Revolution of 1959.

Samuel Huntington, author of the very influential *Political Order in Changing Societies* (1968), defined "social mobilization" as a process associated with the shift (sometimes called the "demographic transition") from the countryside to the city. Here the word "mobilization" has a dual meaning: (1) movement (migration) from the countryside to town and (2) the movement from traditional relationships of inequality and subjection to the rule of landlords and religious authority to the world of the city, with its markets, mass communications, schools, employment for pay, and other "modern" experiences. Rural areas are not left untouched. Urbanization puts pressure on the countryside to modernize agricultural production. Eventually, reform-minded groups will mobilize the peasantry in hopes of changing the rural economy, resulting in a "green uprising" that is aimed against "imperial power" and the ruling oligarchy (Huntington 1968: 76–77). In several ways this interpretation and template seemed to apply to Latin America in the twentieth century (see chapters 5 and 7),

FIGURE 6.1 Walt Rostow's Stages of Development.

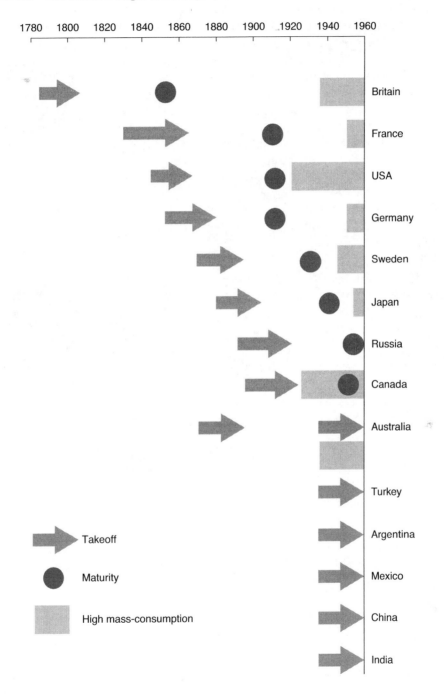

as cities grew and eventually pressures for change (e.g., agrarian reform) in the countryside threatened the power of traditional oligarchies.

For Huntington, economic development must keep pace with rising demands; otherwise, people will grow frustrated. This can lead to more participation than the system can handle; that is, participation comes to overwhelm the capacity of institutions to handle it. A stagnant economy and resistance to reform by traditional elites may limit the opportunities of the working class and middle class to move up the social ladder (mobility). As we saw in chapter 5, **import substitution industrialization** (ISI) seemed to encourage economic growth, but eventually this did not keep pace with social changes, and the expectations of people came to exceed the rate of economic growth. Keep this in mind as we look more closely at democratic breakdown in the next chapter.

For Review

How does Rostow's framework reflect the idea of stages of development? Why does Huntington think that high rates of social and political change require high economic growth if political istability is to be maintained? Why might modernization engender not political stability but unrest?

Dependency Theory and Latin America's Structuralists

A radical school of Latin American intellectuals responded to modernization thought with a revised theory of imperialism, "dependency theory," which later gained traction outside the region. In reality, there were several different versions of dependency theory, some very much in the Marxist tradition, others not. But in moving from Latin America north, the most common version was the one formulated by the Brazilian theorist Andre Gunder Frank. Frank (1969) conceived of underdevelopment as what happened to Latin America and other Third World countries as a result of the development in Europe and North America. Underdevelopment is not a condition in which all societies found themselves before progress; rather, some societies *underdeveloped* others. He wrote,

> Our ignorance of the underdeveloped countries' history leads us to assume that their past and indeed their present resemble earlier stages of the history of the now developed countries. This ignorance and this assumption lead us into serious misconceptions about contemporary underdevelopment and development. Further, most studies of development and underdevelopment fail to take account of the economic and other relations between the metropolis and its economic colonies throughout the history of the worldwide expansion and development of the mercantilist and capitalist system.

Other economists from the Third World, such as the Egyptian Samir Amin (1977), were attracted to the dependency thesis. Amin argued that exporting raw materials and importing finished goods caused a systematic export of wealth from poor nations to rich ones. This idea was popularized throughout the hemisphere in *The Open Veins of Latin America*, published in 1971 by the Uruguayan journalist Eduardo Galeano (new edition, 1997), which helped popularize dependency theory. "Veins" here had a double meaning: the region's mineral wealth (ore veins) was flowing out and depleting the region's natural capital, and its workers were giving up the blood in their veins to produce materials for the wealthy countries.

Modernization theorists see foreign investment and trade as fostering development, not only by providing investment funds, technology, and overseas markets, but also by bringing developed-world social values to "traditional" (sometimes the more pejorative term "backward" is used) societies. Frank and the dependency theorists argued that Latin America's commodity exports were undervalued in the world economy. Therefore, foreign investment in the region's mines and fertile soil really had the effect of decapitalizing the economy, draining its wealth.

Critics of dependency theory point out that the poorest countries in Latin America, the ones with the lowest rates of economic growth, usually are the ones that attract the least foreign investment. Dependency advocates do not deny this but respond that their theory was not meant to be tested in this way. Instead, they argue that dependency should be considered a general approach, one that should include attention to cultural and political—not just economic—dependency (Cardoso 1977).

Dependency theory also attracted followers because some predictions based on modernization did not pan out. Latin American countries were supposedly poised on the brink of takeoff—but growth rates (with the exception of a short period in Brazil in the 1970s) were never reached. In many ways, their economies were getting worse, experiencing high levels of inflation. At the same time, the Cuban Revolution of 1959 generated more interest in dependency theory among leftist intellectuals. Traditional Marxism suggested that Latin American society first had to go through capitalism before a socialist revolution could take place, but here suddenly was Cuba proclaiming its revolution "communist."

Frank's dependency theory largely focused on trade—unequal exchange among nations. Other *dependistas* felt Frank did not place enough emphasis on the way the exported raw materials and agricultural goods were produced. It was not just that Latin America's exports were sold for much less than the manufactured goods imported from abroad; dependency influenced the social class structures and conflicts inside Latin America, said these theorists (Dos Santos 1974; Petras 1980). Other theorists thought Frank's theory fatalistic: it implied that Latin Americans themselves could have no control over their futures (Cueva 2003: 69), subject as they were to global economic powers.

The in-house conflict of ideas among radicals was of less interest to mainstream political scientists, some of whom attempted to test dependency theory using economic data and statistical methods. For example, one study (Kaufman et al. 1975) collected data on foreign investment and correlated it with various measures of economic development. The authors concluded that the higher the levels of foreign investment, the higher the levels of development, a finding that contradicted Frank's thesis that foreign investment was a cause of underdevelopment. As we saw in chapter 5, F. H. Cardoso (1977), later president of Brazil but then a leading exponent of dependency, complained that more complex and subtle ideas about dependency had escaped notice in the north. In his view, many American and European scholars were "consumers" of an intellectual idea fermented in Latin America and not fully understood in the north. Cardoso and Enzo Faletto became known for developing a version of dependency that viewed Latin American political and economic processes as having a dynamic of their own (Cardoso and Faletto 1979).

Among those who try to relate internal and external causes of underdevelopment to one another is a school of economics called "structuralism." Structuralists were inspired by the work of Raúl Prebisch, an Argentine economist and first secretary general of the United Nations Economic Commission for Latin America (**ECLA**; the Spanish equivalent is CEPAL), created after World War II. Prebisch's research on historical patterns of trade supported the *dependista* claim that the terms of trade were stacked against Latin America. However, the structuralists also saw limitations to development in domestic economic structures. In particular, they took aim at "bottlenecks" in the domestic economy. For example, the inefficient countryside could neither provide cheap food for workers in the city nor generate a demand for what urban factories produced. Similarly, the financial system provided little credit to get start-up industries off the ground.

To structuralists, rectifying such bottlenecks required strong government action, something that market-oriented neoliberals, whom we encountered in chapter 1, would later criticize. Structuralists generally supported ISI, but they also recognized the need to change the approach over time.

Import Substitution

Prebisch was head of Argentina's Central Bank during the Depression. Between 1929 and 1932, the prices for food and raw materials dropped about 50 percent (often more), devastating the export-based economies of Latin America, which had never been models of stability in the first place. With unemployment afflicting a quarter to half of workers in North America and Europe, the factories that used copper, tin, rubber, and other Latin American exports were closing. With their wages plummeting, workers and consumers in the wealthy countries reduced their purchases of beef, sugar, and other commodities intended for their tables. The industrialized countries also raised tariffs (import taxes), making it harder for Latin Americans to access their markets.

As the prices for its exports plummeted, Latin America's capacity to import fell 30 percent between 1930 and 1934 (Furtado 1971: 73). As a consequence, even people with money found fewer goods to buy on the domestic market. Chile was hit the worst; in 1932, its copper and nitrates earned only 12 cents for each dollar they had earned in 1929. As a result, the country managed to import only 20 percent of what it had bought before the Depression (Drake 1978: 60–63). In 1920, in Cuba, sugar prices had already fallen from 22.5 cents to 3.625 cents per pound in one year, but they would fall even further, to 1.47 cents in 1929 (Hanson 1951: 107). In El Salvador, the price of coffee fell from US$15.75 per hundred kilograms in 1928 to US$7.50 in 1932 (Armstrong and Shenk 1982). Three-quarters of Cuba's exports consisted of sugar, and 90 percent of Salvadoran exports came from coffee. These crops took up nearly all the best land in each case. These countries, blessed with fertile soil and favorable climate, had little capacity to feed their own people.

World War II (1939–1945) brought a different problem—high prices for exports but not much to buy. Although most Latin American countries capped prices as a contribution to the Allied cause, increased demand for the war caused a surge in prices, especially for vital goods such as copper, oil, and rubber. The industrial countries were pouring all their industrial resources into the war. Instead of manufacturing clothing, they were producing uniforms; instead of cars, they manufactured tanks. Suddenly, Latin American countries had foreign exchange, but there was a shortage on the world market of the goods they wanted to buy.

Latin Americans thought that the situation would change after the war, but they were to be disappointed. The United States by far did the most in shaping the new international rules of the game after 1945. It led the effort after World War II to stabilize the world economy, creating the World Bank, the International Monetary Fund (IMF), and the General Agreement on Tariffs and Trade (predecessor of today's World Trade Organization—WTO) to regulate global financial markets and liberalize trade. Another global organization had been proposed to stabilize the prices of global commodities—that is, the agricultural, oil, and mining products that were the core export industries in Latin America—but that initiative was ultimately blocked by the United States, which argued instead for prices to be set freely on the world market. The gigantic Marshall Plan was geared to Europe. Japan also received generous assistance. Even though Latin Americans had kept prices reasonable during the war, postwar planning did little to help their economies.

Latin Americans had vivid memories of how a freefall in commodity prices could affect their lives. The situation during the Depression had been desperate and, as might be expected, had led to political instability. Sixty thousand of 70,000 miners were unemployed in Chile. In 1932, the country's military government came crashing down amid calls for social revolution. In El Salvador, a peasant revolt was crushed by the military in "La Matanza," which cost anywhere from 10,000 to 30,000 lives in the tiny country, affectionately called "the flea" by its poets. A revolt by a coalition of civilian reformers and military sergeants in Cuba in 1934 nearly produced a revolution. Instead, it led eventually to the dictatorship of one of the sergeants, Fulgencio Batista, whose despotism was overthrown by Fidel Castro in 1959.

Latin America had also noticed that the Depression experience had altered the attitude of the liberal democracies, even in the United States, about government's proper role in regulating the market. Franklin Roosevelt's "New Deal" began to use the government to stimulate demand and restart the economy. He also introduced reforms, such as social security, major infrastructure projects (e.g., dams and electrification), and progressive legislation to help unions. Latin Americans noticed that, in the rising hegemon of the north, an era of laissez-faire capitalism was giving way to a period of active government involvement.

After World War II, Prebisch assembled a team of economists at the United Nations from Latin America, and in the late 1940s and 1950s they worked on demonstrating the importance of structural problems. ECLA researchers believed that inequality limited demand; so they advocated measures to redistribute wealth and thus eliminate this bottleneck to industrialization. To address what they saw as a chronic imbalance of trade between Latin America's raw materials and the developed countries' manufactured goods, they urged governments to take measures to develop industries whose production would *substitute* for imports, adding support for policies already underway as a result of the Depression and World War II. Tapping into export revenues, Chile, Brazil, Argentina, Mexico, and other governments created special financial institutes to fund industry, creating state-owned enterprises and making low-interest loans to private entrepreneurs.

Import substitution and structuralism stand in contradiction to economic theories based on **laissez-faire** and **comparative advantage**. Comparative advantage is the notion that free trade is in the interest of all peoples because each country has natural advantages that make it rational for each to specialize. Ecuador, for example, by this theory should continue to produce and trade oil and bananas for gasoline, processed baby food, automobiles, refrigerators, computers, and so on from more industrialized nations. Its people will be better off if they stick to production of products found in abundance or easily grown in

Look at this photo of a factory built in the era of import substitution in Mexico to produce textile products. Why did Marxists, structuralists, and modernization theorists alike, though they disagree on some things, think that a factory was a sign of development in the country?

their own climate. Government should not try to alter this pattern by "interfering" with the market. Today's modernizers, like the liberal modernizers of the late 1800s, tend to be **laissez-faire**. However, in the era of import substitution, many modernization theorists agreed with the structuralists that state leadership could and should pursue developmental objectives, both economic and political. Modernization theorists and structuralists both were called *developmentalists* because they advocated an active state to overcome underdevelopment.

Institutionalism—Putting Politics into Economic Development Theory

Whichever approach to development a nation adapts, an efficient and effective government is required to implement policy. No school of thought about development has devoted more attention to this issue than **institutionalism**. Though institutionalism might have much to offer socialist as well as capitalist economies, institutionalism is usually associated with market economies. Institutionalists believe that to work effectively, markets need effective public services, efficient bureaucracies, an impartial legal system, and so on. Institutionalism has attracted additional admirers because of the relative success of Asian economies, which have achieved significant rates of economic growth and development with capitalist economies guided by government.

The World Bank and the Inter-American Development Bank mount programs to strengthen institutions, such as cleansing courts and the bureaucracy of corruption and helping regulatory agencies operate more efficiently. Development theorists at these and other institutions have given impetus to the importance of **institutional design**. They argue that countries with stable institutions are more likely to attract foreign investment and encourage domestic entrepreneurship than those with overbearing, corrupt state institutions. Institutionalism has also been rising as a branch of study in comparative politics. These institutionalists argue that we have for too long focused our attention exclusively on social, cultural, and economic factors to explain Latin American politics. We will look more closely at this argument in chapter 13.

Table 6.1 summarizes the way that each of the four theories of development discussed in this book looks at four key issues—the cause of underdevelopment; import substitution and the state; the cause of political instability; and democracy's relationship to social class.

For Review

How and why do dependency theorists and structuralists disagree with laissez-faire approach? How do comparative advantage and ISI differ in regard to the role of trade in development? Why might the design of institutions be a factor influencing possibilities for development?

TABLE 6.1 Theories of Development

	Modernization	Dependency	Marxism	Institutionalism
Root cause of underdevelopment, role of imperialism and foreign investment	Traditional values discourage risk, reward for hard work, social mobility. Foreign investment helps overcome this problem.	Centuries of exploitation siphoned capital away; unequal exchange (low prices for exports relative to imports). Imperialism responsible for underdevelopment.	Exploitation of working classes by landlords and capitalists, reinforced by imperialism, but imperialism accelerates capitalism, setting stage for socialism.	Uncertainty, lack of security, poor performance of government discourages investors, both domestic and foreign. Tends to look favorably on foreign investment.
View of state, import substitution	Before 1970, state provides security against communist subversion and helps with investments in some areas, encourage ISI; since 1970, state's role is to encourage free market, e.g., by privatizing holdings, opening economy to trade and foreign investment.	Structuralists back ISI, some see need to support capitalism to pave way eventually for socialism; more radical dependency theorists advocate break with capitalism.	Serves the interest of capitalists, foreign and domestic. ISI favored some workers but benefited capitalists more. When capitalism matures ("develops fully"), socialist revolution will follow.	Important role for state, as Asian model shows; education and judicial reform are key; state services may be helpful, but fighting corruption and establishing rule of law are priorities.
Political instability	Instability comes from disruption of tradition before economy has fully developed.	Caused by foreign intervention to prevent revolution or back business-friendly dictatorships.	Results from class conflict generated by capitalism and from the weakness of the bourgeoisie in Latin America.	Encouraged by corruption and patronage; seen more as a cause than as a consequence of underdevelopment.
Democracy and social classes	Economic development causes expansion of middle class, strengthening prospects for democracy. Political development ends in democracy; others stress institutions, not necessarily democratic.	Middle class is at best a swing group, sometimes pressing to open up system to more participation but fearful of more radical change. Liberal democracy needs to be replaced by a more popular model.	Only possible once the working class (proletariat) overthrows capitalism and class society. Classical Marxism envisions a "stateless" society (communism) in which democracy is part of everyday life.	Most important quality of democracy is rule of law, respect for contracts. Corruption is best curbed through rule of law, effective judiciary, competitive elections.

PUNTO DE VISTA: CAN CAPITALISM BE FIXED BY MORE CAPITALISM?

The work of Hernando de Soto, a Peruvian economist, has brought about an intense debate about the potential for poor people to lift themselves out of poverty and spur economic development. In *The Other Path* (1989), de Soto contends that in the poor *barrios* of Latin American cities, which have grown largely as a result of occupation of land and self-construction of homes and businesses, residents lack property rights guaranteeing them ownership of their houses, land, and small businesses.

In one of his books, *The Mystery of Capital* (2000), he estimates that the value of the unsecured assets of the poor in the Third World amounts to 40 times the total foreign aid provided these countries since 1945. With guaranteed property rights, he argues, entrepreneurs among the poor will raise investments, and these start-up enterprises will employ others and have a ripple effect throughout the economy.

De Soto's ideas were warmly embraced by the World Bank, the U.S. Agency for International Development (AID), and other agencies. Former president Bill Clinton once called him "the greatest living economist." Many development economists, on the other hand, cast doubt on de Soto's approach.

De Soto's critics say that small businesses would have little chance without protection and help from the state. How can the corner bodega compete with Walmart? How can the local carpenter compete with IKEA? How can a local mechanic repair and service modern automobiles without computerized diagnostic tools? Many poor urban areas feature little more than tin-roofed shacks. Is it really worthwhile for banks or buyers to provide the credit that budding capitalists living in these neighborhoods

need? Is it really shaky property rights that is the obstacle?

Paul Van der Molen (2012), though critical of de Soto, thinks that his ideas highlight one factor that has worked against the poor—their need to have the same secure citizen rights that other citizens enjoy. However, he says, when poor people are bought-out by developers of new middle-class commercial residential projects, the original residents end up living in poor neighborhoods farther from the center of the city. The new residents are not likely to patronize the businesses that served the original inhabitants.

Most Latin American governments have poor records when it comes to the buying and selling of property going back to the conquest, when landed property rights were awarded to conquistadors or set aside for indigenous peoples by far-away monarchs and then subject to multiple claims as a result of civil wars in the independence era and nineteenth century. Brazil in particular is notorious for professional con artists who have sold fraudulently registered land and homes, a practice continued into recent decades. The same property may have multiple owners who bought title to buildings and land in good faith.

A socialist version of de Soto's ideas was implemented by Hugo Chávez in Venezuela. In 2002, Chávez launched an "urban land reform." Rather than the government deciding and handing out titles, residents of *barrios* must organize themselves, write a history of their community from its founding to the present, and collectively recommend how homes, businesses, public spaces, and so on should be titled—some as private property, some as state- or community-owned facilities and land.

Point/Counterpoint

Most analysts agree that if the poor were given more secure property rights, as de Soto advocates, this would spur entrepreneurship and development. Should the law stipulate that ownership of unoccupied or unused land or buildings can be transferred to ownership of someone who would use it?

a. If you answered yes, how would you respond to those who would complain that property rights are basic and should pertain even to unused buildings and land? If exceptions to property rights are made, could people with wealth keep it in their own countries? Would you take the same position about ownership of vacant land and buildings in the United States, or would you say this only for Latin America?

b. If you answered no, how would you answer those who say that property over buildings and land was often acquired through corrupt or unethical ways? How would you respond to those who would say that the need to give the poor a stake in the society is more important than absolute property rights?

For more information

Hernando de Soto has disseminated his ideas throughout the web. A good short introduction can be found at www.youtube.com/watch?v=06Fd76fV3Pl. Two of his most important books are *The Other Path: The Invisible Revolution in the Third World* (New York: HarperCollins, 1999) and *The Mystery of Capital* (New York: Basic Books, 2000). On Venezuela's urban land reform, see Alex Holland, "Venezuela's Urban Land Committees and Participatory Democracy," Venezuelanalysis .com (February 11, 2006), accessible at http://venezuelanalysis.com/analysis/1611. Paul Van der Molen's critique of de Soto is "After 10 Years of Criticism: What Is Left of DeSoto's Ideas?," *Cadastral and Land Administrative Perspectives* (2000), accessible at www.fig.net/pub/fig2012/papers/ts07b/ TS07B_vandermolen_5503.pdf.

▇ Marxism and Development Theory

Critics of dependency theory often see it as a branch of Marxism, but many Marxists think that *dependistas*, such as Frank, did not give adequate attention to internal struggles between the social classes. The theory seemed to let the region's own capitalists off the hook by blaming foreigners. Agustín Cueva (2003: 66–67), an Ecuadorian thinker, remarked in 1976, "Dependency theory has in fact sought to become a 'neo-Marxism' without Marx."

The Communist Manifesto, written by Karl Marx and Friedrich Engels (1848), like modernization theory, offers a theory of development, complete with stages. The *Manifesto* asserts that all human societies pass through five stages—from primitive communism (no real social classes, but life is precarious at best) to slave societies (characteristic of the ancient world), to feudalism (Europe in the Middle Ages), to capitalism (developing first in Europe around 1800 with industrialization), and finally to communism (a classless, stateless society). Because workers, mostly city dwellers, must sell their labor to capitalists (i.e., find employment; get a job) to survive, the "proletariat" (wage earners) can come into existence only once capitalism emerges. The logic, then, was: without capitalism, no proletariat; without a proletariat, no socialist or communist revolution. Hence, communists should support capitalism, and with it "bourgeois democracy" (that is, liberal democracy), until conditions were ripe for revolution.

The *Manifesto* suggests that neither socialism nor communism is possible before capitalism finishes its historical job of making the economy highly productive. Misguided or prophetic, we have here a theory of development: socialism or communism cannot happen until countries pass through other stages, especially capitalism. Although Marxists are known for their opposition to imperialism, Marx and Engels thought that imperialism, though morally wrong, was playing a positive role because it was accelerating the pace by which countries such as China, Brazil, India, and so on were becoming capitalist. In this sense, some Marxists might agree with the modernization theorists—foreign investment is developing, and not underdeveloping, colonial and dependent nations.

This perspective was not just for academic discussion and debate. The Communist Party (PC) emerged as a major actor in several Latin American countries after the Russian Revolution in 1917. For much of that period, PCs adopted the view that revolution in Latin America had to be postponed until the day that capitalism fully matured. When the Cuban Revolution (1959) occurred, and Fidel Castro later declared the country a "Marxist-Leninist" state, old-line communists had a problem. Young leftists all over the hemisphere were ready to embrace the ideas of Castro and his charismatic minister of economic planning, Che Guevara. Guevara believed that the Cuban people could work together in an ethical way to develop the economy. Economic development was not necessary to create a "New Man"; a New Man would create a developed socialist economy. To many Marxists this was heresy, putting cultural change first.

Not all Marxists rushed to refute Guevara. There have always been Marxists who have criticized determinism, and some cite writings by Marx early in his career to support their view. Some Catholics, especially those living and working with poor people, have sought to reconcile Marxism with their religious beliefs, questioning the view that Marxists must be atheists. Thinkers such as Enrique Dussel (1980: 117), an Argentine based in Mexico, have called for a new "theory of religion" among socialists, one that "would allow all the people to be impelled with a profound religious consciousness into the liberating process." For some religious Latin Americas, their faith was a motive for revolution.

For Review

What do both Marx and Rostow, despite their differences, seem to have in common regarding the idea of development? Why do some Marxists criticize dependency theory or at least Frank's version? Why did the Cuban Revolution challenge some key ideas in Marxism?

Peripheral Vision: Latin America in the World System

Although Marxism and dependency theory remain important schools of thought in Latin American studies, another approach, one that draws heavily on these frameworks, is probably today the most widely utilized. That approach is world systems theory, first elaborated by Immanuel Wallerstein (summarized in Wallerstein 2004). Wallerstein sees the world system as having come into existence around 1500 with the European conquest of the Americas. At this point, there emerged a global capitalist system in which nation-states emerged. At the core of the system are wealthy industrialized states. Also, within the core, one state tends to emerge as the strongest—the hegemon, currently a position occupied by the United States. In the periphery are those that were integrated, usually by force of imperialism, into the world system as producers of raw materials (largely agricultural and mining economies). Latin America's poorest states—for example, Bolivia, Haiti, and Nicaragua—are in the periphery. Some states occupy an intermediate condition in the "semiperiphery." These countries have undergone some industrialization and are better off than the poorest countries in the system or have a vital natural resource (e.g., oil) that gives them special weight. In Latin America, this would include Argentina, Brazil, Mexico, and Chile, among others. Venezuela would qualify in part because of its status as an oil-exporting country.

Dependency and world systems theories (in contrast to modernization theory) agree on a diagnosis of underdevelopment as springing from three common elements that Latin America shares with other parts of the Third World, all of which can be traced back to colonialism:

1.   As a result of colonialism, *Latin America was integrated into the world economy as a provider of cheap primary goods*—agricultural products (monoculture), minerals, and other raw materials—and an importer of more expensive manufactured goods. Latin Americans traded their precious metals, minerals, and agricultural goods at disadvantageous terms of trade. They imported all kinds of finished goods, from the peasants' machetes to furniture, carriages, and clothes consumed by elites. This arrangement bled Latin America of wealth that could have been the basis for development and, eventually, industrialization. Industrialization was delayed in part because those who controlled the economy and benefited from exports had little incentive to invest and develop in production of manufactured goods.

2.   *Since the colonial period, elites in Latin America have looked outward, not inward,* for models and inspiration. Despite promoting *mestizaje,* the upper classes tended to look abroad for solutions to problems. Because the economy was oriented to production for foreign markets, it is not surprising that the Latin American elite looked abroad for cultural and political inspiration as well. They tended to send their children to Europe for higher education. After independence, they looked to the United States and France for appropriate models for constitutions. They promoted immigration as a way to improve the "racial stock," deemed by many to be "savage" or not inclined to work hard because of the climate. Their ideal of feminine beauty became the light-skinned blonde.

3.   *The export-oriented economy relied heavily on cheap labor,* accentuating the maldistribution of wealth and creating a difficult political climate for liberal and democratic political arrangements to take root. Exploitation began with slavery and the *encomienda* (see chapter 3). Although abuses led to the abolition of this system, forms of coerced labor continued in Latin America throughout the colonial period and well into the independence era. For example, instead of being paid wages, workers often were allowed access to land in exchange for their labor on the big farms and ranches.

Unlike Frank, Wallerstein sees the possibility of states changing their place in the world pecking order as a result of technological development and interstate rivalries. After all, Spain, once hegemonic, slipped after 1700 into the semiperiphery because it failed to use its colonial wealth to build a competitive economy at home. After 1970, Spain seemed to have rejoined the core as a dynamic economy within the European Union (even allowing for setbacks associated with the global financial crisis of 2008). Some newly industrialized countries in East Asia today may be migrating from peripheral to semiperipheral status or even may be, as in the case of China, becoming part of the core as their economies become more dynamic. Brazil, in particular, has recently been seen as approaching a category reserved for larger, developing countries that have experienced rapid economic growth over the past 10 to 15 years. It is the "b" country in what journalists are calling the "BRICS" countries—Brazil, Russia, India, China, and South Africa.

Dependency theory and world systems theory (compared in Table 6.2) have in common that they challenge the notion, common to some versions of Marxism and modernization theory, that all countries will pass through similar stages on the path to fully developed capitalist economies. Those who promote free trade and capitalist globalization share with modernization theory the assumption that low wages, poor working conditions, and poverty in Latin America are merely symptoms of underdevelopment, likely to be left behind as further stages of development are reached.

TABLE 6.2 World Systems Theory, Dependency, and Modernization

	World Systems Theory	Dependency Theory	Modernization
Relationship between Latin America and Wealthy Countries	Exploitative. Latin America is part of the periphery, but poorest countries are the ones most isolated from global system of markets and investments. Others, e.g., Brazil, Mexico, are part of "semi-periphery"	Exploitative. Foreign investors benefit from cheap labor and rape of region's natural resources, leaving region poorer than it would be without such investment	Developmental. Foreign aid and investment from wealthy countries bring needed technologies and capital to underdeveloped countries
Role of U.S. in the world	Became the dominant, "hegemonic" power of 20th century and acts to maintain its dominance, but also to protect interests of other wealthy nations in core	U.S. is a classic imperial power, acting to protect its own capitalists and preventing Latin America from developing stronger ties with competitor nations	The U.S. is model nation whose culture and economy would be emulated by others. Some theorists take broader view, worry that U.S. may be in decline
Can Latin America develop?	Yes; nations such as South Korea and Japan have shown movement out of periphery, while former members of core have sometimes slipped back to semi-periphery – e.g., Portugal today	Little hope of development as long as capitalism and imperialism exist	Yes. Road is long and difficult, but the problems and obstacles, such as poverty in cities, are not so different as those once found in the "developed" countries today

> ## For Review
>
> What patterns, according to world systems theorists, did colonialism put in place that remained influential in shaping Latin America (a) in its development, (b) in its underdevelopment, and (c) after independence?

State and Market in Latin America Today

Import substitution and structuralism were approaches to economic development closely associated in the twentieth century with populism of the sort we highlighted in chapter 5 (e.g., Peronism in Argentina). The populist era ended in crisis and, in most of Latin America, in harsh military rule. The dismantling of unions, populist parties, and other mass organizations paved the way for a shift away from protectionism and structuralism and toward market-friendly, export-oriented economic policies in most of the hemisphere.

The swing away from import substitution, which emphasized inwardly focused development, and back toward *desarrollo hacia afuera* (outwardly focused development) and laissez-faire economic policies came to be called "neoliberalism" because it philosophically resembled the approach taken by Latin American rulers in the nineteenth century. Although the shift owed something to military rule, broader trends were at work in the international environment that encouraged almost all Latin American governments to implement neoliberalism to some degree. Mexico, Costa Rica, Colombia, and Venezuela—four exceptions that escaped military regimes in this period, the 1980s—saw a shift away from the ISI policies associated with the populist era. Even Cuba, faced with the loss of support from the Soviet bloc, introduced some market reforms and policies friendly to foreign investment. Although the domestic politics behind neoliberal measures varied across the region, the new policies everywhere were implemented in the context of crushing national debts that later limited the capacity of elected governments to break with neoliberalism, which was backed by global international institutions such as the World Bank and IMF and by the United States.

New Economic Policies after ISI

The exhaustion of ISI as a developmental strategy brought great instability into the lives of the middle class and salaried workers in the form of hyperinflation. Deficit spending, trade deficits, debt, and dwindling confidence in local currencies converged at times into astounding monetary instability. In Bolivia, the inflation rate reached 1,300 percent in 1984 and 11,805 percent in 1985. In 1989, Argentina's rate of inflation reached 3,000 percent. In 1991, Brazil's inflation rate was a ridiculous 2,489 percent over one year. To put this in perspective, the same rate applied to the United States would have meant that US$2,489 would have turned into US$1. In comparison with Argentina and Brazil, Mexico's rate of 110 percent in 1988 seems tame, but someone with a bank account in pesos would have seen their savings halved in a matter of months. In many Latin American countries, then, people's life savings were effectively wiped out.

Latin Americans sometimes saw prices double or triple before they could spend their paychecks. Only those who were able to convert their savings into dollars before the crash were spared, and this group, of course, was almost exclusively made up of the wealthiest portions of the population. Therefore, the poor, working class, and middle class bore the highest cost of the economic crisis—and women sacrificed and suffered the consequences more than men. In 1995, the United Nations *Development Report* calculated that women devote two-thirds of their time to unpaid work (e.g., in the home and in collective efforts to maintain poor communities), men only one-fourth. Women tend to be employed in social service sectors (teaching, nursing, etc.) where falling government spending most affected wages and employment. When inflation is high, women face the challenge of providing for families with declining incomes; when inflation is low, they benefit less because so much of their work is unpaid. We should not be surprised to learn that in the struggle for a transition to democracy, women played leading roles.

To maintain political stability, governments often seek corporatist-style pacts in which businesses are asked to hold the line on prices, labor is asked to hold down wage increases, and governments cushion the impact on the poor. However, governments are also expected to implement fiscal austerity. The solution for many governments seemed to be to create more efficient welfare programs designed to bypass politicians and more directly reach poor communities—that is, by eliminating clientelism. In practice, these programs also had political aims and were selectively administered. In most cases, they were a welfare Band-Aid on open wounds caused by economic shock treatments. For example, in Mexico, President Carlos Salinas de Gortari launched his "Pronasol" program under which a fund was created to match community projects. Total spending was impressive, over $2 billion by 1993, but still less than programs it replaced. The idea was that community participation would cut out clientelism and increase efficiency. Nonetheless, total spending did little to reduce poverty, which increased significantly in 1994 when the government devalued the peso against the dollar (lowering the value of real wages) and opened up the economy to competition with the United States under the North American Free Trade Agreement (NAFTA). Just as bad, the program failed to eliminate clientelism, as became evident in the 1994 presidential election (Moguel 1994; Gardy 1994).

An inflation crisis struck most countries *after* the collapse of populist democracy and usually *after* ISI had been abandoned as the overall development strategy; that is, some of the worst episodes of inflation occurred under military rule and not populist governments. Nonetheless, inflation was often attributed to "past failures" that could not be corrected without pain.

For Review

What were some of the outward economic signs of deep problems associated with the end of import substitution?

The "Lost Decade" of the 1980s and the Debt Crisis

The decade of the 1980s, often called the "lost decade," was nothing less than an economic disaster. A major cause of the economic distress was the **debt crisis**, which afflicted—and continues to afflict—not only Latin America but also the entire Third World. The crisis became visible in the international media in August 1982, when Mexico announced to the world banking community that it could no longer service its debt. "Service," as used here, refers to making scheduled payments. As with a personal loan or mortgage to an individual, the earliest repayments on loans to countries consist of interest and service (administrative) fees, with very little, if any, going toward reduction of the principal on the loan. This is what Latin American governments were struggling to pay—not the loan itself, but interest and service fees.

How the Debt Crisis Started

If we consider export earnings to be the income available to Latin American countries to pay their debt, the crisis was truly alarming. As we have already seen, even in those countries that implemented import substitution, the export sector has been the motor force of the formal economy. Whereas exports typically constitute about 10 percent of the economy of developed countries, in Latin America and the Caribbean they constitute approximately 30 percent (Potter 2000: 80). In 1970, the total debt for Latin America and the Caribbean was US$26 billion; by 1980, it had risen to US$191 billion, with US$69 billion slated to fall due within just a few years (Potter 2000; World Bank 1996; see Table 6.3 and Figure 6.2). The total debt in Latin America was more than twice its total export earnings in 1980; and by 1983, only three years later, it was nearly 300 times that amount. Interest payments alone were nearly 20 percent of total export earnings in 1980, rising to 30 percent by 1983; total service payments rose from nearly 37 times the value of export earnings to nearly 48 times (Franko 1999: 90).

The squeeze on Latin America was double. On one side, the prices of its exports fell, reducing its income; on the other side, more debt payments, contracted mostly in the 1970s, were falling due. To put this another way, in 1983, had Latin American governments met their international loan payments, US$1 out of every US$2 earned from exports (total earnings and not just profits) would have gone to the world's bankers.

What caused the debt crisis? Part of the cause can be located in the international system. In 1973, the Arab oil-exporting countries declared an embargo against the United States and other industrialized countries that supported Israel during the October war of that year.

TABLE 6.3 Total Debt and Total Payments in Latin America, 1980–2000

	1980	1990	2000
Total debt, Latin America and Caribbean combined	$191 billion	$480 billion	$750 billion
Total Debt Serviced Paid		$350 billion 1980-1990	$815 billion 1990-2000

Source: Potter (2000: 67)

FIGURE 6.2   Growth of Foreign Debt

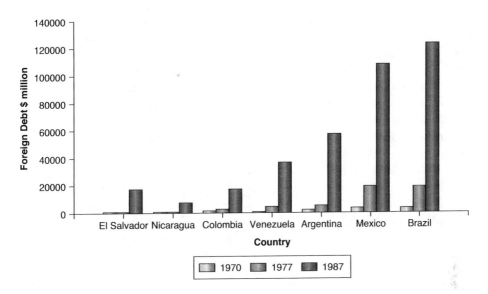

The Iranian Revolution and subsequent war between Iran and Iraq caused prices to rise again in 1980–1981. All oil importers suffered economically, but Third World oil importers were hit the hardest. Not only were their economies afflicted by higher energy costs, but demand and prices for their exports also fell because the rise in oil price contributed to a deep economic recession in Europe, Japan, and North America.

The small Central American countries saw their debt escalate with the fall in the price of coffee, bananas, cotton, sugar, and other agricultural exports. El Salvador, Nicaragua, and other Central American countries had modernized and somewhat diversified their agricultural export sectors after World War II, often with the help of development loans and foreign aid. Their growing sugar, cotton, and beef export sectors were energy-intensive, more so than traditional exports, such as coffee and fruit. Pesticides, fertilizers, trucks, and tractors all increased these countries' thirst for oil. To make matters worse, peasants had often been forced off the land to develop the new export plantations. The expansion of plantation agriculture to take advantage of export markets was a major factor behind the revolutions and wars that wracked Central America in the 1980s, especially in Nicaragua, El Salvador, and Guatemala. Leftist rebels, including the Sandinistas who came to power through revolution in 1979 and governed until 1990, garnered support through promises of land reform.

Elsewhere in Latin America, the global economic situation and the local political situation discouraged foreign investors from making the large-scale investments that the generals and politicians hoped to attract. Memories of political unrest and nationalization were fresh in the minds of foreign investors. The prospects for turning a profit with new investments in Latin America's export sector were bleak. Economic recessions in the wealthy countries in the late 1970s and the 1980s meant low demand for raw materials and other goods produced in Latin America. Foreign investors who might put their money into real projects (not just financial instruments—e.g., bonds and investment funds) thought that it was better to wait for renewed growth in the developed countries.

The international banks were much less cautious than direct investors. Many of them were finding dollars piling up in their accounts in the 1970s. In the years after World War II, the European and Japanese economies had been built with both the real and the symbolic support of dollars, which circulated in great quantity outside the United States. In 1974 alone, the Organization of Petroleum Exporting Countries (OPEC) earned US$74 billion more than the value of their imports. Most put their funds in their Western banks (Wachtel 1977). Most oil purchases were (and are) made with dollars, and OPEC had to dispose of the "petrodollars" flowing into their treasuries during the 1970s oil boom. Why was this a problem? The essence of banking as an industry is to make more money on interest from loans than is paid out in the form of interest on deposits. Banks had to find a way to make new loans, or they would lose money.

With the world industrial economy in recession, where could banks lend the money? One answer was world governments. In theory, a government cannot go bankrupt, so the banks paid little attention to the creditworthiness of the borrowing countries or to the degree of corruption in their politics. By the mid-1970s, Bank of America and First National City Bank were so exposed abroad that 108.2 percent and 126.8 percent, respectively, of their overall income was from foreign sources. How can the percentage be over 100 percent? Simple. They were losing money at home and making it overseas. On average, the 12 largest U.S. banks derived 63 percent of their income from foreign sources (Wachtel 1977). In other words, *their* debt crisis in the Third World was also becoming *ours* in the "First World." The magnitude of the problems did not become clear until Mexico's threat to default on its loan payments in 1982.

The debt burden was made worse in the 1980s by the policies of the U.S. Federal Reserve Bank (the central bank for the United States). The Fed maintained a high-prime interest rate as the administration of Ronald Reagan borrowed heavily to fund deep deficits and increased military spending. Fearing inflation at home, and attracted by high interest in the United States, wealthy Latin Americans converted their own nations' money into dollars and sent them abroad. From the point of view of the rich, why invest in the shaky economies of Latin America if attractive profits could be gained from interest on deposits in the United States? This aggravated the problem of capital (money for investment) flight from the region, and it discouraged foreign investors from putting money into Latin America in the 1980s. Economic reactivation became all the more difficult.

We should not attribute the growing debt to external causes alone. Corruption and inefficiencies, the failure to modernize industries, and lack of investment in education and technological development were all contributory factors. Latin Americans found themselves paying exorbitant interest rates for short-term loans, but desperate governments kept borrowing to keep ambitious, large development projects (roads, airports, public buildings, etc.) afloat. This, in turn, kept some workers employed and generated profits for businesses with close ties to the military regimes. Some of these problems in some places can be attributed to populist politics, but it is also the case that a myth has grown, attributing economic/financial crisis mainly to populist parties and politicians. In fact, military regimes also borrowed heavily. For example, the military regime that overthrew democracy in Brazil in 1964 and tightened its grip on power in 1968 never entirely abandoned state capitalism and sought money to develop the vast Amazonian interior of the country.

After a while, new loans were no longer going into the nations' own economies; instead Latin American governments were merely refinancing loan payments as they fell due. This arrangement was something like loan-sharking: a heavily indebted customer desperate for additional money keeps digging a deeper hole for himself or herself. Without loans to pay back existing debts, Third World countries would find themselves blacklisted from loans needed to sustain government services, finance new investment, or purchase needed imports. It was not a matter of choice. Without finance, it is virtually impossible to do normal business in the world today. Given this context, who is most at fault—the client or the creditor?

Even in the 1990s, when Latin America's economies began to grow again, the debt burden continued to rise. The total debt in Latin America and the Caribbean expanded at the same rate in the 1990s as it did in the "lost decade" of the 1980s. Between 1990 and 2000, countries in the region paid US$815 billion to service the debt, but the amount owed actually increased from US$480 billion to US$750 billion.

If oil prices were high, why did Mexico and Venezuela, two oil-exporting countries, also fall so far into debt? Venezuela borrowed heavily against future oil earnings in an attempt to industrialize overnight (Hellinger 1991; Karl 1994). In the case of Mexico, its oil company (Petróleos de Mexico—PEMEX) had confined itself to producing mainly for the domestic market, partly because the global oil companies had tried to isolate it after they were nationalized in 1938. In an attempt to break the power of OPEC on the world market, the consuming countries and their banks suddenly became eager to make loans to the government of President José López Portillo (1976–1982) to increase oil production in Mexico, which was not a member of the cartel. For Portillo, increased oil exports seemed a solution to economic stagnation.

What neither Mexico nor Venezuela counted on was the fall of oil prices that began in 1982. Economic recessions in developed countries, conservation efforts, and increases in alternative energy production combined to dampen demand for oil on the world market. Increased production outside OPEC created a glut of supply. Something similar happened to Latin America's other major commodities—copper, coffee, rubber, and so on. Prices recovered only near the end of the century, when India and China's rapidly expanding economies generated new demand and as OPEC recovered some influence—partly due to Venezuela's leadership in the organization. The trend upward lasted until oil prices passed US$147 in 2008, only to tumble with the economic recession that began with the financial crisis in the United States in September 2008.

For Review

Why are the 1980s considered the "lost decade" in Latin America? Why did Latin American governments borrow from the international banks? Why did the banks keep lending, even when it seemed that governments might not be creditworthy?

Sovereignty, Democracy, and Structural Adjustment

Latin American governments, democratic or not, became vulnerable to pressure to conform to economic blueprints, called "**structural adjustment**," promoted mainly by the

IMF, the World Bank, and the **United Nations Commission on Trade and Development (UNCTAD)**. Loans made by the IMF to governments are significant in that they signal to other lenders that a country is creditworthy. Often, conditions set by the IMF set the pattern for subsequent deals between debtors and two big consortiums of lenders, one (the London Club) for private institutions that lend money and the other (the Paris Club) for governments that do the same, either directly or through institutions like the World Bank.

Latin American leaders such as Fidel Castro and Aláin García (president of Peru from 1985 to 1990) proposed that Latin Americans band together to seek a moratorium on paying the debt or at least to negotiate better terms. Today, even leftist governments in the region are cautious about policies that might isolate them economically. Venezuelan president Hugo Chávez, regarded as a leading critic of neoliberalism, used earnings from the oil bonanza of the post-2000 period to pay down the country's debt rather than renege on it. On the other hand, in 2001 Argentina did simply declare it would not pay creditors who failed to make concessions. In other words, creditors do not hold all the cards in debt negotiation; if they push too hard, debtors may tip over the game table.

Typically, structural adjustment agreements require governments to implement the following set of policies in exchange for new loans:

- *Free-trade policies.* Governments are expected to reduce protection for domestic enterprises, whether in manufacturing, services, or agriculture.
- *Tax reform designed to increase government revenues.* Because Latin American bureaucracies are notoriously inefficient and because taxes on domestic industries might deter investors, governments frequently resort to imposing a value-added tax, which functions something like a sales tax imposed at each stage of production of a consumer good. Although this tax falls on businesses, it is passed along and embodied in final prices. Generally, it is a less progressive tax than an income or property tax, falling most heavily on consumers and the poor.
- *Reduction of the public sector.* Governments are expected to cut the payroll and reduce spending on welfare. The goal seems laudable: put the budget back in the black and reduce the need to borrow. However, because debt service absorbs typically 30 to 50 percent of government spending, the net result is a transfer of resources from government employees, pensioners, and others (students, the poor, women with families, the sick) to foreign banks. Also, because government employees are a large part of the workforce and typically unionized in Latin America, the effect is to reduce the leverage of organized labor in the private sector as well. Economists often claim this will make the workforce more "flexible" and attractive to investors.
- *Privatization of state-owned enterprises.* The goal here is often to reduce a drain on government resources and to provide an injection of money that can be used to service the debt. The IMF and World Bank often urge privatization as a kind of "modernization" that will supposedly increase efficiency and reduce the influence of the government over the economy.
- *Encouragement of growth in the export sector.* More exports mean more foreign currency, especially dollars, entering the economy. More dollars mean greater resources to pay the debt.
- *Conservative monetary policy.* Here, the banks are less consistent with free-market principles. They have applauded experiments, such as when Argentina in the 1990s pegged

the local currency to the dollar, one peso for one dollar. This was an effective way of boosting investors' confidence and reducing inflation. Ecuador went so far as to eliminate its local money and adopt the dollar as its official currency (joining Panama, which has had the dollar as its official currency since it broke away from Colombia with the help of U.S. intervention in 1904). On the other hand, sometimes banks have insisted on devaluation of a country's money. Devaluation helps exports but makes imports more expensive. Venezuela, for example, was told to devalue in the 1980s and 1990s if it wanted new loans. The problem here is that Venezuela, an oil-exporting country, imports most of what it consumes. Its importers were forced to pay *bolivars* for dollars needed to buy goods abroad, increasing the cost of living for the population.

Taken all together, these measures not only add up to an economic agenda favorable to foreign capital (banks and investors) but also create opportunities for well-connected Latin American elites to take advantage of the weak state. Particularly scandalous was the way privatization of public assets was handled. Wealthy foreigners and domestic elites were able to buy state assets very cheaply, and their purchases were made more profitable by tax relief, mass layoffs of workers, and lax public regulation.

In 1987, there were six billionaires throughout Latin America. By 1994, there were 41, more than in Europe (36) and Japan and the rest of Asia together (40), and not far behind the United States (49) (Potter 2000: 96). However, alongside this development, Latin America's governments faced restive populations demanding payment of the **social debt**—that is, money obligated to them by law, sometimes (as with pensions) accrued through work and savings. Repression and structural adjustment had negative economic consequences for Latin America's workers, peasants, and middle class. The gap between the richest and poorest 1 percent of the population increased from 273:1 to 417:1 between 1970 and 1995 (Franko 1999: 228). Between 1985 and 2000, Latin America experienced several cases of urban protest, including rioting (e.g., Caracas, Buenos Aires); organized blockades of roads protesting attempts to privatize utilities (Peru, Bolivia); peasant marches on local and national capitals (Mexico, Bolivia); and general strikes (Brazil, Venezuela). This reaction is something to keep in mind when we look at politics in the current era, when the left has made something of a comeback because of popular resentment of economic inequality and persistent poverty.

The economic hardships associated with structural adjustment put strains on democracy, but the United States and many free-market proponents believe that ultimately neoliberal economic policies will strengthen democracy. Their theory is that markets disperse power more evenly in society. They argue that reducing government's role in the economy creates greater opportunity for citizens to assert themselves through independent group activity—as **pluralist** theory suggests is desirable (see chapter 1). In other words, a freer market will reduce socialistic and corporatist tendencies—which are seen as antidemocratic—and encourage a more vibrant civil society (see the classic text on this theory, Schumpeter 1947).

Despite all the indications of profound discontent with structural adjustment, candidates and parties associated with these plans often won elections. The most notorious cases were Carlos Menem (1989–1999) in Argentina, Alberto Fujimori (1990–2000) in Peru, and Carlos Andrés Pérez (1989–1993) for his second term in Venezuela. As candidates, they espoused a populist position against neoliberalism, but once in power, they implemented market-oriented policies. For this reason, they were sometimes called "neopopulists." However, since 1998, the pendulum seems to have swung toward leftist candidates critical of neoliberalism, most emphatically in Venezuela with the election in 1998 of Chávez and continuing with Evo Morales in Bolivia and Ricardo Correa in Ecuador in 2006. As different as these politicians are from Menem and Fujimori, they are often called "neopopulists".

For Review

Neoliberalism refers to an overall economic philosophy, whereas structural adjustment refers to specific policies. How do the policies reflect the philosophy, and how did the debt crisis encourage structural adjustment?

The Decline of Economic Nationalism

The shift from populism and ISI to neoliberalism both reflected and influenced events in the international economy. The fall of the Berlin Wall and the collapse of the Soviet superpower between 1989 and 1990 meant that any country wanting to pursue a populist or nationalist, much less socialist, agenda lacked a superpower that might deter efforts by the remaining superpower, the United States, to punish it for challenging the rules of the "new world order."

The period between 1960 and the 1980s had seen the decolonization of Africa, the Middle East, and Asia; the radicalization of the Cuban Revolution; setbacks for the United States in Vietnam; the emergence of Japan and the European Economic Community (today, the European Union) as economic competitors with the United States; and the emergence of OPEC. OPEC's success in the 1970s showed that Third World nations could flex their political and economic muscle through strategic cooperation with one another to regulate supplies of commodities (food and raw materials) in the world marketplace. In this favorable international context, Third World nations began lobbying in the United Nations for a New International Economic Order (NIEO), one that would narrow the gap between the rich nations of the north and the poor nations of the south, the latter highly dependent on export of primary commodities.

Those who promoted the NIEO often cited the instability of world commodity prices as an obstacle to development. They shared the diagnosis of economists like Prebisch that there existed a chronic gap between the prices of raw materials and those of manufactured goods. In a series of meetings sponsored by the United Nations, nonaligned nations (i.e., a group of mostly Third World countries who sought independence from the two superpowers engaged in the Cold War) declared that territorial sovereignty had to include the right of governments to control their natural resources. This assertion was made in defense of nationalization of key industries, especially mining and oil companies. In addition, the UN Commission on Trade and Development (UNCTAD) was authorized to work for the creation of a system of buffer stocks for 22 mineral and agricultural commodities. In times of high commodity prices, UNCTAD would release stocks onto the market; in times of low prices, UNCTAD would buy surplus production.

These measures struck against two fundamental principles underlying a liberal world order and free trade: (1) defense of private property against government expropriation and (2) reliance on free interplay of market forces to set prices. Through collective action at the international level, national sovereignty would be strengthened versus the power of private capital. Some Latin American nations provided crucial support for this initiative. Cuban diplomats emerged as forceful spokespersons for the initiatives. Venezuela was the initiator of the Organization of Petroleum Exporting Countries; its oil minister, Juan Pablo Pérez Alfonzo (1958–1963), is often called the "father of OPEC." In the late 1960s and 1970s, Chile and Peru, two major copper producers, had populist leaders who initiated nationalization (with compensation) of mining industries and sought to coordinate their policies with other countries. Many thought that the next step in implementing an NIEO would come in the form of an international copper cartel, envisioned to be the first step in implementing the UNCTAD plan.

Some leaders in developed countries embraced the idea. In 1980, a commission headed by former West German chancellor Willy Brandt issued a report (the **Brandt Report**) favorable to the UNCTAD initiative and called for efforts to narrow the economic gap between north (core) and south (periphery). However, by this time, the NIEO was already in trouble, in part due to changes in Latin America. The leftist governments in Chile and Peru had been replaced by right-wing military regimes that retreated from nationalist economic philosophy. To get the buffer stock system going, UNCTAD was going to need initial financing from the wealthy countries and OPEC. Although Europe and Japan initially signaled support, the United States opposed the scheme from the start. When oil prices collapsed in the 1980s, any possibility of help from OPEC disappeared. OPEC itself failed to maintain prices through regulation of supply.

The final blow to the NIEO came from the debt crisis. To comply with structural adjustment, governments had to privatize state assets. The result was the reversal of many of the sovereign nationalizations of airlines, mines, railroads, and so on, accomplished in the populist era, and the shifting of many other assets created by state investment (roads, steel companies, and communications industries) to private ownership.

If the world had followed the Brandt Commission lead, we might today be talking about a very different kind of globalization, one regulated by international organizations, instead of by relatively unbridled market forces. Instead, globalization took place under a set of liberal economic and political doctrines that President George H. W. Bush in 1991, following the victory of the United States over Iraq in the first Gulf War (after Iraq's invasion of Kuwait), proclaimed the "New World Order" (NWO) in his victory speech. The NWO elevated security of the property rights of investors over sovereign control of natural resources. New mining and hydrocarbon (gas and oil) legislation followed advice and models provided by the World Bank and guaranteed investors against nationalization or future tax increases. UNCTAD'S role shifted to provide technical advice on how nations could best compete for foreign capital by creating a favorable environment for investors.

A series of financial calamities (in Southeast Asia in 1998 and in Argentina in 2001), the resurgence of oil and other commodity prices since 2002, and rapid economic growth in Brazil, Russia, India, and China seem to have shifted power back somewhat toward the Global South. As national leaders began to meet to confront the world financial crisis of 2008, these countries demanded a seat at the table normally occupied by the "G7" group of Western countries and Japan. Luiz Inácio Lula da Silva (Lula), the Brazilian president, was particularly outspoken and successful in this respect. With a quite uncomfortable visiting British prime minister (Gordon Brown) at Lula's side in a 2009 press conference, the Brazilian said, "This crisis was caused by the irrational behavior of white people with blue eyes, who before the crisis appeared to know everything and now demonstrate that they know nothing" (*Financial Times*, March 17, 2009).

For Review

Describe the underlying ideas of the NIEO and how the NWO that actually emerged was different. What role has Latin America played in the shifts of power between the Global North and South?

Adjusting to the Global Market: Three Variations

In this section, we look at three different experiences, not because they are representative but because they illustrate the diversity of experiences and experiments with economic policy in Latin America. In all three cases, countries have had some macroeconomic success, but uncertainty about the future lingers.

The Chilean Neoliberal "Success Story"

Chile is often held up as a success story of adaptation to the NWO. General Augusto Pinochet's government (1973–1989) decreed new laws guaranteeing investors low tax rates that would never be raised. Pinochet did not privatize the state copper company because the military was receiving 10 percent of its sales (not profits, *sales*) off the top. However, he offered new concessions (leases to exploit natural resources) to foreign companies at low tax rates and under a new mining law that practically guaranteed the companies would never be nationalized. Mining companies were given leases virtually in perpetuity. Meanwhile, the government starved the state copper company (CODELCO) of investment capital to start new mines and modernize old ones.

Even the generous terms of the 1980s were not enough to bring the mining companies back to Chile right away. Copper prices were low, and foreign investors feared that Pinochet's harsh rule might lead to renewed revolution. These factors deterred large investment until the transition to democracy in 1989. When the centrist and leftist politicians came back, they left the new rules in place, partly because of limits on democracy built into the constitution (see chapters 8 and 13) and partly because they were reluctant to disturb an economy in recovery. Rolling back the power of the state, then, was accomplished by dictatorship, but liberal democracy seemed more capable of providing the political security that investors wanted.

New mines were started by foreign investors who were guaranteed low taxes and were relieved of any obligation to pay royalties (compensation to the country for using up its mineral wealth). Today, the big private mines produce and export a majority of the country's copper. In some ways, they have a better deal today than they had before nationalization. When copper prices, driven by demand from China, finally began to climb again in 2003, Chile's earnings from copper exports climbed. CODELCO was still the largest single copper company in the world, so the government did gain some benefit from the boost. However, the big private companies paid very little to the state despite a bonanza in profits. Suddenly, Chileans began to realize they were nearly giving away their copper for nothing. Under mounting public pressure, enough conservative legislators voted with the Concertación majority to impose a very modest 5 percent levy on export profits of the big mines.

Many countries, such as Chile, Peru, and Mexico, became statistically less dependent on export of raw materials, but this does not necessarily mean that they export fewer raw materials. For example, measured by the ton rather than in dollars, Chile actually doubled copper exports in the 1990s, largely on the basis of new large, private mines put in operation. Meanwhile, Chile's percentage of export earnings from copper actually fell from roughly 80 percent to 45 percent between 1970 and 2000. This was not only because Chile diversified its exports in agriculture, forestry, and manufacturing (e.g., armaments) but also because low prices for copper meant that the country was earning less for its mining exports.

A deep recession struck in the aftermath of the 1973 coup, which destroyed much of the economy built up in the populist era. A recovery occurred between 1977 and 1980, but a second deep recession followed in the period between 1981 and 1986, when the economy actually shrank by 0.1 percent. Ten years of growth by between 6 and 9 percent followed, a period that seemed to suggest that Pinochet's neoliberal restructuring, combined with a return to democracy, would pay big dividends. From 1996 until 2000, the rate of growth leveled off at a still healthy 4.1 percent. How was this achieved? The Pinochet regime took advantage of the political weakness of the landed elites to replace the traditional *latifundia* with modern export agriculture. Similarly, it opened the country's rich forests and coastal waters to timber and industrial fishing. Workers who managed to find employment were forced to pay into private pension funds managed by private investors, which provided capital for new investment. The leading growth sectors were fruits, forestry, and other natural resource industries other than copper. In other words, Chile relied on diversification of raw material and food exports more than manufacturing, took advantage of repression to lower wages, created new pools of capital for forced savings, and opened the country's bountiful natural resources to exploitation at bargain prices (and with little regard for the environment). Although the terms were somewhat moderated and made more fair by the democratically elected governments after 1990, Chile remains more firmly neoliberal than any other country in the region.

The biggest problem in Chile is inequality. Overall, poverty declined by some measures from 40 to 18 percent between 1998 and 2005, but 15 percent of the population earned less than the minimum wage, about US$204 per month in 2007. Chile's richest citizens earned 55 percent of total national income; its poorest earned only 4 percent. Education has become an especially sensitive topic; graduates of private schools, greatly expanded in the populist years, tend to make much more money than those from the public system. As a result, although Chile's economic model seems to have produced growth, as the years of democracy have worn on, a kind of resignation has come over what was once one of the most vibrant of Latin American democracies.

Brazil: The Business-Friendly State

Brazil's military government (1964–1985) never fully embraced neoliberalism. In part, this reflects a feature of Brazilian political culture—the nation's sense of *grandeza*, a feeling that so large a country, possessed of so many natural resources, must be destined for economic greatness. During the years of military government, the unions and parties of the populist era were crushed, and the government took measures to open the country to foreign investment. Key policies included government support for developing competitive manufacturing in computers, aviation, small arms, and conventional weapons (for sale to Third World countries) and increased exploitation of the Amazon for timber, soybeans, and ranching.

From 1968 to 1974, Brazil experienced the highest rate of economic growth in the world, and in this period manufacturing exports for the first time surpassed those from mining and agriculture. This experience stands very much in contrast with the process of deindustrialization that characterized Chile and neighboring Argentina. Brazil's military rulers sought to "deepen industrialization" by increasing production of steel, petrochemicals, and durable consumer goods (cars, refrigerators, etc.). The oil price hikes of late 1973 put an end to the miracle, even as the military borrowed money feverishly to maintain it. The debt quadrupled between 1970 and 1980, surpassing US$100 billion and giving Brazil the largest foreign debt in the world. Hyperinflation also became a serious problem.

Brazil, the world's sixth largest economy, was facing an economic crisis that threatened to have a hemispheric, if not global, impact. The "*Real* Plan" (the *real* is Brazil's currency) was adopted in Brazil in 1993 by the finance minister, Fernando Henrique Cardoso, the former socialist intellectual turned politician. In 1994, Cardoso won election as president, promising market-oriented reforms cushioned with an effective safety net. He followed the IMF prescription of privatization, trade liberalization, fiscal restraint, and incentives to foreign investment. Results were mixed. From 2,500 percent in 1993, Brazil's inflation fell to 3 percent by 1998, a remarkable achievement. However, the Asian financial crisis and other world economic traumas threatened Cardoso's plans. Financial speculators and capitalists pulled dollars out of Brazil, forcing the government to borrow dollars heavily to maintain the value of the *real* and economic growth, which was an impressive 4 percent in 2000. Investment started coming back, but a downturn in the United States, an economic collapse next door in Argentina, and the difficulty of continuing to defend the *real* set back Cardoso's plans again. By August 2002, Cardoso's preferred candidate for the presidency in the November elections had lost ground to leftist candidates, leading to the election of a former labor leader, Luiz Inácio Lula da Silva (Lula) and contributing to the rising **Pink Tide** in the region.

Lula had been defeated three times earlier in his quest for the presidency. Many businessmen feared that he and his Workers' Party would enact radical, populist policies that would in turn induce a flight of capital. Lula proved much less radical than his opponents feared. Rather than change fundamental social and economic structures, which his colleague Chávez attempted in Venezuela, Lula attempted to alleviate poverty using the benefits of rapid economic growth. Cardoso had paid a political cost for his macroeconomic policies, but they laid the basis for Lula's popularity; in fact, Lula's popular and successful program to reduce hunger had been pioneered by his predecessor. The leading growth sector has been soybeans, which in turn has raised concerns about the environment and future of the rainforest. Brazil's growth rate over Lula's administration, ending in 2010, hit 5 percent per year, much less than that of China or India, but well ahead of Europe, Japan, and the United States. By some estimates, Brazil could move from the seventh-largest economy in 2005 to the fourth-largest (trailing China, India, and the United States) by 2050.

Has economic growth expanded the middle class? One study by a Brazilian sociologist (reported in Osava 2004) indicates that the middle class, defined in terms of a family's ability to own durable consumer goods (television, car, computer, etc.), shrank from 42.5 percent of the population in 1981 to 36 percent by 2000, and the ranks of the poor increased from 30.5 percent to 39.5 percent. However, the economic boom after 2002 saw 23 million of Brazil's 150 million people enter the lower middle class. One concern is that much of this mobility is built on debt; the number of credit cards issued in Brazil has almost doubled since 2001 (da Costa 2008). Another reason to temper optimism is the fact that the upturn is being led by agricultural exports, much of it to fast-growing China and India, and whether the Brazilian economy could weather an economic slowdown in Asia has yet to be tested. A collaborative study (Pérez et al. 2008: 11) of the soybean sector by the Washington Office on Latin America and Tufts University concluded that South American soybean industries are

> undeniably winners from global trade liberalization, but few of the benefits go to rural communities. Based on high-input, industrialized monoculture, farming, employment and wages have both declined despite rising production. Ecological harm from agricultural expansion onto sensitive lands leaves lasting destruction.

The authors believe that government support for smallholder agriculture would yield long-term developmental benefits to rural communities and better supply the domestic demand for food.

Still, Brazil, like many other Latin American countries, has diversified its export markets, sending more of its production to Europe and Asia than in the past. The latest "miracle" occurred in an era of high oil prices, the variable that burst the last expansion of the early 1970s. In 2007 and 2008, important new reserves of oil were found off the country's coast, raising the prospect of energy self-sufficiency.

For Review

Both Chile and Brazil are regarded by many as economic success stories. Why is Chile, more than Brazil, regarded as a country that has been more fully committed to the neoliberal model of economic development?

Cuba: Escaping the Debt Crisis and Not Escaping Debt or Crisis

Because it is a socialist regime, one might very well question whether Cuba's development model can be compared with that of Chile or Brazil. However, that Cuba has chosen such a different path and that for decades many Latin Americans saw it as an alternative success story makes it intriguing. Today, it is widely assumed that Cuba's economic model is failing. Raúl Castro, since taking over from his brother in 2008, has argued that the basic model is sound but that some pragmatic reforms, including some concessions to the market, can restore the economy's vitality.

In 1986, Cuba's external debt to the noncommunist world stood at US$2.6 billion, a relatively small amount. However, it also carried other obligations to the Soviet Union and Eastern Europe, many in the form of agreements to supply sugar and other agricultural products. These are difficult to quantify in dollars. One study group critical of the Castro regime claimed the external debt was valued at US$9 billion in 1996 (Martínez-Piedra and Pérez 1996: 33–34). However, Russia's own economic woes were Cuba's gain. The *ruble* collapsed in the 1990s, making Cuba's debt technically worth only about US$475 million in 2002 dollars. Cuba's bigger problem was that the Eastern European bloc was no longer available as a trade partner, and the giant U.S. economy 90 miles to Cuba's north was waiting to see the system collapse.

With the collapse of the Eastern Bloc in 1989 and the Soviet Union in 1991, the Cubans decided to open their economy further to foreign investment and to compromise on some of the programs of social welfare and equality for which it had earned admiration. The government asked Cubans to accept a harsh deterioration in their standard of living during the "special period in times of peace." The key difference from structural adjustment is that the government made sure that the burden of sacrifice was relatively evenly shared. Still, Cubans who receive dollars from relatives in the United States or who work for foreign investors (e.g., in tourism) live better than those who enjoy neither privilege.

More recently, the combination of favorable deals with Venezuela for oil and investments from other parts of the world has lifted the economy, but any visitor to Cuba will attest that life remains hard on the island. The Cuban socialist economy has not yet proved that it can generate the economic growth needed to make people believe that the relatively good economy of the 1980s will return, and of course, the country has yet to define what politics will be like in the post-Castro era. President Raúl Castro has implemented measures to expand small private businesses, loosen restrictions on selling private property, and shift employment from the state to the private sector, along with other measures. A visitor to Cuba since 2010 cannot help but notice the increase in commerce on the streets but also can hear the complaints of people, such as workers in the health sector, whose incomes do not allow them to participate as consumers or entrepreneurs in the economic opening.

In the chapter on revolution, we will discuss the Cuban situation in more depth, but it is worth noting that the nation's survival of the economic crisis of the early 1990s owed much to the sense of all Cubans that the burdens of adjustment were being equally borne. Although state authorities clamped down quickly on dissent, Cuba's defiance of constant predictions of imminent political collapse owes much to the legitimacy of the revolutionary government. Now the expansion of markets, competition, private employment, and so on has inspired optimism in some parts, but worry and discontent in others as Raúl and his contemporaries face the inevitable passing of the generation that has led Cuba since the 1959 revolution.

For Review

How did the fall of communism in Eastern Europe affect Cuba? How did the country adjust? What seems similar to and what is different from the adjustment elsewhere?

Did Latin Americans Democratically Choose Neoliberalism?

Though in some cases, such as Chile, neoliberal policies were put in place by military governments, they were maintained subsequently by democratic regimes. In other cases, such as Brazil under Cardoso and even in Argentina under President Carlos Menem (1989–1999), elected presidents implemented neoliberalism. Given the accentuation of poverty and inequality in this period, how can we reconcile implementation of market-oriented reforms with democratic politics (Armijo and Faucher 2000: 2; Remmer 1998)? Leslie Armijo and Phillippe Faucher think that despite increasing inequality in most of the hemisphere, the majority of poor Latin Americans benefited from the shift away from ISI and toward neoliberalism. Large portions of the population were excluded from the benefits of the inward-oriented ISI policies, so they had little to gain from abandoning them. Hyperinflation at the end of the populist era struck hardest at the poor. On the basis of an examination of politics in Argentina, Brazil, Chile, and Mexico, Armijo and Faucher say that the taming of inflation accounts for why politicians favoring neoliberalism won elections.

One has to wonder how much collective memory of the horrors of military rule weighed in the popular mind of the 1990s against the disappointment and frustration with a model of democracy that was not delivering substantial improvement in most people's lives. Some experts on Latin America also argue that Latin American policy makers became increasingly isolated from mass influence, despite elections, in the 1990s. This disagreement is important for democratic theory. Those who define democracy as polyarchy presume that fairly conducted elections allow the public to communicate their demands, ensure the equal distribution of political power, and make public officials responsive to mass preferences. Even if Armijo and

Faucher are right about the preferences of Latin American voters for neoliberal reforms in the 1980s and 1990s, the trend in the subsequent decade suggests that politicians with an anti-neoliberal agenda have been gaining ground.

We have noted the surge in leftist electoral victories since 1998, but that does not mean that the entire region is rebelling against neoliberalism at the ballot box. Mexico and Colombia have retained conservative presidents, and in Chile, the electoral pendulum actually swung back toward the right in the election of 2010 when the left-center Concertación parties lost its first election in 20 years to a right-wing candidate closely associated with neoliberalism.

Toward the end of the first presidency (2006–2010) of the Concertación's Michelle Bachelet, students began to take to the streets to protest the privatization of education in Chile, which they put in the broader context of inequality and persistent poverty. Energized workers, environmentalists, and indigenous peoples quickly joined them in the streets. They both influenced and were influenced by the Occupy movement that burst forth in 2011 in the United States, Europe, and elsewhere. Hence, although neoliberal economics and polyarchy seem to have coexisted if not reinforced one another, the events in Chile should give pause to anyone who would assume liberal economics and democracy have established themselves once and for all as the dominant form of government in Latin America.

Discussion Questions

1. How and why did countries in Latin America adjust to international pressure to abandon import substitution and adopt market-friendly policies? Why were many of the new policies called "neoliberal"?
2. Does the fact that several leaders who implemented neoliberalism were elected mean that Latin American voters supported neoliberalism? What arguments can be made for and against the proposition that strengthening market forces has strengthened democracy in Latin America?
3. What are the key ways that modernization and dependency theory differ? Why do you think dependency first emerged in Latin America rather than in other parts of the Global South?
4. List ways that you think neoliberal economic policies might strengthen or weaken democracy in Latin America. Overall, what do you think is their impact on the democratic condition in the region?

Resources for Further Study

Reading: David Harvey's *A Brief History of Neoliberalism* (New York: Oxford University Press, 2007) brings a critical perspective to the subject. Pedro-Palo Kuczynski and John Williamson defend market-oriented economic policy in their edited volume *After the Washington Consensus: Restarting Growth and Reform in Latin America* (Washington, DC: Peterson Institute, 2003). Before he became a vice minister and a key shaper of Venezuela's oil policies under Chávez, Bernard Mommer wrote *Global*

Oil and the Nation State (New York: Oxford University Press, 2002). Both Rostow's *Stages of Growth* (1960) and Frank's *Latin America: Underdevelopment or Revolution* (1969) are reader-friendly. Frank's "The Development of Underdevelopment" appeared in *Monthly Review* (June 1989). Editor Ronald Chilcote's *Development in Theory and Practice: Latin American Perspectives* (Lanham, MD: Rowman and Littlefield, 2003) provides a good selection of Latin American views on development.

Video and Film: Search "Hernando de Soto" and "economist" on YouTube for various speeches and videos elaborating his pro-market views on urban development. "Capital Sins," the second program in the PBS *Americas* (1992) series, focuses on development issues in Brazil.

On the Internet: One good reference on different theories can be found at www.uia.be/sites/uia.be/db/db/x.php?dbcode=pr&go=e&id=11202060, the website for the Australian Union of International Associations. Salón Chingón (www.salonchingon.com) has several video documentaries about economic struggles in Latin America.

PART III

Regime Transitions in Latin America

Los Presidentes in 1982

Argentina	Chile	Brazil
Galtieri	Pinochet	Figuerido

Las Presidentes in 2014

Argentina	Chile	Brazil
Fernandez	Bachelet	Rousseff

7

Democratic Breakdown and Military Rule

Focus Questions

▶ What economic, international, and social factors contributed to the breakdown of democracy in many countries of Latin America between 1960 and 1985?

▶ What are the signs that the military may stage a coup? What are common factors and motivations behind military coups?

▶ What overall motivations and goals are typical of military regimes? What distinguishes the kinds of military regimes that followed from earlier episodes of military dictatorship in Latin America?

SEPTEMBER 11 (9/11) is one of those days that "live in infamy," but it has a different meaning for Chileans than for most other people in the world. On September 11, 1973, the Chilean Air Force bombed La Moneda, the presidential palace, putting an end to four decades of democracy in Chile. Salvador Allende, Chile's elected socialist president, died in the bombing. It was only the most dramatic of the breakdowns of populist democracy that began with a coup in Brazil in 1964 and soon convulsed most other countries in the region.

In identifying the reasons that the governments of the era were unable to cope with the economic and political crises of the late populist era, political scientists drew upon cases from other parts of the world and other periods of time; these included the rise of fascism in Europe in the 1920s and 1930s and the "colonels' coup" in Greece in 1967. If the precise causes of democratic breakdown could not be determined, at least the research sought to identify some of the outward signs of impending crisis.

Political Instability and Decay

One of the most influential books in comparative politics, *Political Order in Changing Societies* by Samuel Huntington, published in 1968 in the middle of the **Cold War**, boldly opened:

> The most important political distinction among countries concerns not their form of government but their degree of government. The differences between democracies and dictatorship are less than the differences between those countries whose politics embodies consensus, community, legitimacy, organization, effectiveness, stability, and those countries whose politics is deficient in these qualities.
>
> (1968: 1)

Like other modernization theorists, Huntington viewed communism as a threat because it could take advantage of the weak political institutions. "In Latin America," he argued,

> the wealthiest countries are at the middle levels of modernization. Consequently, it is not surprising that they should be more unstable than the more backward Latin American countries . . . Communist and other radical movements have been strong in Cuba, Argentina, Chile, and Venezuela: four of the five wealthier Latin American countries suffered from insurgency.
>
> (1968: 44)

Huntington's use of the term "backward" is significant, implying again (as with economic development) the notion of "stages" and his disdain for "tradition." His conservative, **Cold War** attitude is evident. As an advisor to the State Department, he advocated the widely condemned policy of forcibly concentrating the rural population in South Vietnam during the American war there. (Guatemala's military would repeat the tactic in the 1980s, with disastrous consequences for the Maya.) Regardless of his role as a policy advisor, his theories about how social mobilization (e.g., rural to urban migration, disturbance of social structures in the countryside) challenges political stability are relevant to understanding how populist democracy came under stress. Even those who stress class conflict and imperialism in explaining the collapse of democracy at the end of the populist era recognize that social mobilization contributed to the political crisis and challenged both the economic model and the stability of electoral democracy.

Huntington's argument was summed up (1968: 55) in three equations:

$$\frac{Social\ mobilization}{Economic\ development} = Social\ frustration$$

$$\frac{Social\ frustration}{Mobility\ opportunity} = Political\ participation$$

$$\frac{Political\ participation}{Political\ institutionalization} = Political\ instability$$

Working in reverse, we start with the third equation. An institution is "an arrangement for maintaining order, resolving disputes, selecting leaders, and thus promoting community among two or more social forces," says Huntington (1968: 9). Strong institutions are not unchanging; they show capacity to adapt to new situations—such as strains caused by economic change. The relationship is delicate. "In the total absence of social conflict, political institutions are unnecessary; in the total absence of social harmony, they are impossible" (9).

What Caused Democracy in the Populist Era to Decay?

Without agreeing on the order of importance, political scientists have stressed some combination of the following processes as indications of democracy under stress:

- *A breakdown of consensus among political elites.* Not all the rules of the political game are spelled out in constitutions. The functioning of any democratic system depends on the willingness of leaders of different factions and parties to seek compromises with one another. Opportunism, mistrust, vengeance, deep philosophical differences, and pressure from powerful social and economic groups can erode the willingness of political leaders to "muddle through" and seek an exit from a crisis. One sure sign of trouble is when political elites begin to speculate openly about the possibility of a military coup or call upon the military to defend the nation from the "threat" posed by their opponents (Stepan 1971).

- *Abuse of authority by incumbent governments.* When people asking for change encounter violence or fraud, they are more likely to resort to street protests, strikes, seizure of public buildings, or (eventually) violence. Violence may take the form of organized guerrilla insurgency, terrorism (beginning with bombs in empty buildings and escalating to more murderous actions), or support for a military coup. Sometimes it is difficult to know whether an opposition is protesting because the system is rigged or simply because it is too weak to win. If one player knocks over the chessboard, is it because the other side is cheating or because the other player has achieved a superior position in the game?

- *Abuse of democratic processes by an immoderate, disloyal opposition.* One hallmark of democracy is the right of an opposition to use constitutional means to replace the government of the day. When opponents limit themselves to constitutional means, we call them a "loyal opposition." However, not all opposition to democratic government is loyal, nor is it always the government that abuses power. In the 1960s, several elected governments (in Venezuela, Bolivia, and elsewhere) were challenged by guerrilla movements inspired by the Cuban Revolution. These movements failed in part because the elected governments, even if disappointing to the voters, enjoyed more legitimacy than dictatorships. Examples of leftist, elected governments that have been overthrown by disloyal and violent opposition include Guatemala in 1954, the Dominican Republic in 1965, and Chile in 1973. Venezuela's president Hugo Chávez nearly suffered the same fate in April 2002. Nicaragua's Sandinistas lost an election in 1990 but only after 10 years of civil war waged between the government and the *contras*. These cases have in common that the displaced ruling elite, supported by the United States, engaged in an extralegal, violent attempt to overthrow a revolution legitimized by a free election.

- *Polarization of social classes.* Slower growth and lower profits at the end of the import substitution era put pressure on wages and reduced jobs in the swelling cities. Social activists—including Marxists and leftist Christians—supported peasants demanding land reform and slum dwellers demanding housing and better conditions. Strikes became bitter, and in many cases the labor movement split between leftists and leaders tied to the old system. Leftist calls for revolution, rural land invasions, urban unrest, and inflation all frightened the middle class, whose fears were then exploited by the most conservative groups in society (Nun 1976; Sartori and Sani 1983).

- *Frustration with the pace of change through constitutional procedures.* Elected leftist governments often find themselves caught between groups seeking to accelerate revolution and an opposition that has enough power to forestall change. Caught between the two sides, either the government must speed up and radicalize its policies and thereby risk alienating the loyal opposition and moderates in its own ranks, or it must use force against workers, peasants, and poor people protesting the slow pace of change. For example, governments in Chile between 1964 and 1973 attempted to implement an agrarian reform. The reform law included many opportunities for landowners to use bureaucratic procedures and the courts to delay its implementation. Before the government could take land away for redistribution, it had to show that the land was underproducing. If successful, it next had to determine how much land could be kept by the owner and which peasants were eligible to receive it, then settle on compensation to the owner, and so on. Peasants, frustrated by years of delay—and often organized by radicals—took matters into their own hands in the form of land occupations. The leftist government of Salvador Allende (1970–1973) found itself in a dilemma. No matter which way it acted, large parts of the population would feel disenfranchised.

- *Economic crisis.* One famous definition of politics is that it is about "who gets what, when, and how" (Lasswell 1936). Logically, it is harder to divide a shrinking pie, or at least one not growing as fast as before. This is what happened to the economies of Latin America with the exhaustion of development through **import substitution** industrialization (ISI) in the 1960s.

- *An unfavorable international context.* The populist crisis developed in the decade after the Cuban Revolution (1959), the first successful communist revolution in the hemisphere. The United States, the most powerful nation in the world, seemed to be on the defensive as it fought leftist movements in a variety of places, most notably Vietnam. In the 1960s, the Cuban government morally and sometimes materially supported revolutionary movements in Latin America. Young leftists (Fidelistas) and many intellectuals admired Cuban resistance to U.S. intervention and the revolution's early success in addressing inequality and raising standards of health, education, and literacy. During the Cold War era (1948–1991), the Soviet Union existed as a rival superpower to the United States, and it was essential to the survival of the Cuban regime after the 1959 revolution. At the same time, the existence of a communist superpower reduced the tolerance of the United States for political experiments and any form of radical nationalism.

Most analysts agree that the exhaustion of the import substitution model of development, the radical alternative posed by the Cuban Revolution, and U.S. intervention in the name of anticommunism all contributed to the breakdown of democracy. The agreement ends there. Pluralists (e.g., Linz and Stepan 1978) tend to stress the breakdown of elite consensus as the critical element. **Dependency theorists** and Marxian analysts place more stress on the polarization of social classes and the threat of revolution (e.g., Nun 1976; Zenteño 1977).

In this chapter, we shall focus mostly on the collapse of democracy during the populist crisis of the 1960s and 1970s. We will look more closely at Cuba and the Central American crises of the 1980s in subsequent chapters—although we will bring these countries into this chapter where events there had a bearing on the international context.

Social and Political Polarization

Social class polarization is the process by which the wealthy and businesspeople (the **bourgeoisie**) on one side and the working class (the **proletariat**) and the poor on the other not only are pulled apart by economic crises but also begin to see each other as enemies. Typically, such polarization manifests itself first in street actions and then escalates to illegal and sometimes violent protest. The middle class typically fears such instability and allies itself with more conservative sectors (Nun 1967).

Political polarization is a related process by which politicians, parties, and groups lose the capacity to settle disputes, especially those about constitutional issues. Political polarization can happen even when there is little class polarization. Political factions and parties may simply fight one another over the spoils of government, or ethnic and religious differences may make consensus difficult to achieve. However, class polarization almost always makes political polarization worse. Simply put, when society is torn apart by fundamental issues, the political center cannot hold.

The late populist era (post-1960) in Latin America witnessed the emergence of strong leftist movements that gained strength within labor unions and began to find success organizing the urban poor and peasantry. Many leftists questioned the notion that a revolution required many years of patient organizing to succeed. The Cuban Revolution of 1959 seemed to bring about, in the phrase of Regis Debray, a French philosopher and interpreter of the thought of Che Guevara, a "revolution in the revolution." The rapid collapse of the Batista regime (see chapter 10) in 1959 suggested that the Latin American state rested upon a weak social base and a poorly trained, even if well-armed, military. This proved to be something of an illusion. As leftist movements gained influence and as some populist leaders moved closer to revolutionary politics, the United States and the local capitalist class in Latin America turned to the military to repress the rising tide of revolution.

Theotonio Dos Santos, a leading *dependista*, succinctly described the unfolding of this process in Brazil, where a military coup against President João Goulart in 1964 ushered in the long period of military rule throughout most of the region:

> Ideological tendencies polarized. Bourgeois ideology moved further to the right as evidenced by its conciliatory position towards imperialism, in its rejection of reformist slogans, its anti-Communist attitude, and above all its support for political authoritarianism. In contrast, nationalist thought became more anti-imperialist, radical reformist, and pro-socialist. These increasingly radical tendencies led to the awareness of the need . . . [on the left] for armed confrontation.
>
> (Dos Santos 1974: 457)

Business groups, says Dos Santos, began to encourage military intervention and adopt "intensive fascist mobilization . . . culminating in the organization of a massive march for 'God, Liberty and the Family.'" When João Goulart, the populist president, settled a revolt by rebellious sailors in a way unacceptable to the high command, the military decided to act (Stepan 1971). Dos Santos sees the 1964 coup as a logical response of capitalists (foreign imperialists and domestic ones alike) to the threat of a democratic revolution made by workers, peasants, and the poor. José Nun (1976) puts stress on the way that the middle class abetted the coups by shifting its sympathies over time from the lower classes, increasingly seeing them as a threat. He thus takes issue with the common assumption that growth of the middle class, a product of economic development, was a democratizing force. He argues that the middle class in dependent societies is fundamentally conservative, with enough property at stake to fear the consequences of a social revolution. As mainly middle-class institutions, the armed forces tend to defend that class's interest, argues Nun.

Although Huntington shares little in common politically with the leftist Nun, he takes a similar view of the armed forces. The Latin American military had evolved early in the 1900s from its ragged condition of the nineteenth century, when generals and colonels were mostly landowners, to a more professional body that included middle-class officers trained in academies. As the military evolved, the professional officers chafed at the limitations imposed by superior officers in high ranks populated by the sons and cronies of oligarchs. They were the "doorkeepers to the expansion of political participation in a praetorian society; their historic role is to open the door to the middle class and to close it to the lower class" (Huntington 1991: 222). Military officers (e.g., Perón) were often at the forefront of opening up the closed systems inherited from the era of **liberal modernization** and state-building, abetting the rise of **populism**. But decades later, when populist governments began to radicalize and threaten revolution, the military took on a quite different, reactionary role.

Table 7.1 provides a summary of political transitions that took place in five important Latin American countries, beginning with the establishment of populism, its crisis, and the political changes that ensued. You may find this table to be a useful reference as we discuss timing and consequences of events in these countries in this and the next two chapters.

For Review

Military officers are mostly members of the middle class. Why might this incline them toward intervening in politics when tensions rise between social classes? What is the difference between social and political polarization?

Population Explosion of the Cities

Latin America was a much more urbanized place at the end of the twentieth century than it was at the beginning. Urban dwellers live in a very different environment than rural people. Off land, one cannot produce basic goods so easily. Unemployment hits even harder. The density of cities facilitates social and political mobilization of the sort that political scientists such as Huntington saw as threatening.

The failure to improve conditions in the countryside, while the cities were being industrialized, contributed to a massive demographic revolution throughout Latin America. Major cities all over Latin America were where the jobs, health facilities, and schools were concentrated, and the cities were overwhelmed with migrants from rural areas during the populist era (see Table 5.1 in chapter 5 for the growth of cities). The result was **hyperurbanization**—growth of the population of the cities well out of proportion to their infrastructure (sewers, electricity, telephones, etc.). In other words, although many Latin American countries experienced economic growth and industrialization in the populist era, the opportunities and benefits generated (jobs, education, health care, housing, etc.) did not keep pace with the growth of cities.

TABLE 7.1 A Reference Chart for Understanding Transitions in the Southern Cone, Brazil, Venezuela, and Mexico

	Argentina	Chile	Brazil	Mexico	Venezuela
Populism and its origins	1945-68 Juan Perón (1945-55)	1932-70 Popular Front of parties, 1932-52	1946-64 Vargas + successors	1934-1982 Lázaro Cárdenas (1934-40)	1945-1989 Rómulo Betan-court, Pact of Punto Fijo (1958-98)
Crisis	1968-76 *Cordobazo* (1968)	1970-73 Allende and Popular Unity	1964-68 João Goulart, coup in 1964, resistance	1968 Massacre of student protestors; 1982 debt crisis	1989 Caracazo revolt; 1992-93 failed coup and resignation of Carlos Andrés Pérez
Peak of repression	1976-82 Dirty War	1973-1976 Pinochet's "Caravan of Death"	1968-1973 "Economic Miracle" and silencing of critics	1968-1988 Continual, less visible re-pression; never military rule	1989 Hundreds die in repression of Caracazo; never military rule
Crisis leading to transition	1982-83 Inflation, defeat in Malvinas War, military retreats	1982 Reces-sion; 1986 protests; 1989 plebiscite leads to transition	1984-85 End of "Economic Miracle," pressure in streets, gradual transition	1988 Election fraud; 1994 Zapatista Revolt in Chiapas	1989-1998 Frustration with failure to reform closed nature of party politics
Civilian Neoliberalism	Menem 1989-1999	Concertación 1990-to present	Collor and Cardoso post-1990	Salinas and Zedillo, 1988-2000; NAFTA, 1994	C.A. Pérez, 1989-1993
New parties or electoral movements	New Left Alliance; later left-Peronists	PDC on left, UDI on right	PT	PRD	Causa R, MVR, later PSUV (chavismo)
Post BA military status	Conflict over amnesty – *Carapintadas* revolt of 1990, Menem reduces size, restores amnesty.	Amnesty in 1983; Strong influence, Pinochet still heads until 1998; declin-ing influence since.	Gradual transition and amnesty for both sides, military still influential but little threat of coup	Civilian control but rising repression after 1968 raises spectre of mil-itarized politics, especially in Chiapas	Radical, nationalist sector, led by Chávez grows after repression of Caracazo 1989; coup attempts in 1992
Status around 2010	Amnesty revoked, some trials under Kirchner	No repeal of amnesty, but criminal prosecutions	Recent signs of prosecution for human rights abuses	Pres. Fox fails to keep promise to open files, but pressure remains	As president, Chávez uses military for civilian pro-fects. Dissident sectors purged after failed coup in 2002

Note: NAFTA, North American Free Trade Agreement; MVR, Fifth Republic Movement; PRD, Party of the Demo-cratic Revolution; UDI, Unión Democrata Independiente; PPD, Partido Para Democracia; PSUV, United Socialist Party of Venezuela PT, Partido do Trabahaldores.

The Southern Cone countries already had two large cities (Rio de Janeiro and Buenos Aires) approaching more than 1 million people in 1900, but they nonetheless experienced explosive growth. Countries farther north saw the emergence of "megacities" for the first time after 1900. Mexico City had from 350,000 to 3.1 million people between 1900 and 1950; by 1990, it held 15.2 million people. Caracas was a sleepy capital of 90,000 at the turn of the century. By 1950, Caracas had grown to 684,000, and then it exploded to near 3 million (6.4 million if the whole metropolitan area is counted) over the next 40 years. São Paulo doubled in size in the first 50 years of the century and then exploded from 2.3 to 15 million people in the next 40 years.

The new factories fostered by import substitution industrialization could not absorb the entire flood of migrants. Latin America's factories relied on imported machinery that was often obsolete in the countries of origin, putting them at a competitive disadvantage that could be offset only by the use of cheaper labor. More jobs were generated than might have been created using the most up-to-date technology, but at the same time ISI required less labor than that generated in the early stages of industrialization in Europe and the United States. ISI generated fewer jobs than were needed to absorb the migration from rural to urban areas.

This raises an important issue in development theory. Is the urban poverty experienced in Latin America merely a phase through which all industrializing countries passed at an earlier time? Or have late industrialization and continued dependence on exports and foreign capital made hyperurbanization chronic in Latin America? We have seen cases, such as Korea and Japan, where countries industrialized using imported, older technologies, but at some point, they showed a capacity to innovate on their own. In general, that did not happen in Latin America.

There had always been urban poor in Latin America, but the new urban tide was different. Side by side with the middle class and workers, there were now millions of people living in makeshift houses perched perilously on hillsides. Sociologists often refer to these residents as the "**marginal**" because they typically live outside the networks of services (sanitation, electricity, water, etc.) necessary to live a dignified life in the city. They typically work in the **informal sector** of the economy—that is, they are not employed in wage-paying jobs that are covered by labor laws (e.g., occupational safety, minimum wage standards) or that come with benefits, such as health care and social security. More recently, the term "excluded" has come into use to signify that the deprivation these people experience is not chosen and to indicate that the goal of economic development ought to be *inclusion*—political, social, and economic inclusion—of the poor.

In the worst cases, the **excluded sectors** scratch out a living as petty vendors or temporary employees. The poorest scavenge garbage dumps to survive. Some eventually find jobs in small enterprises, but because of their size, these companies are usually exempted from complying with labor laws and are exempt from unionization. In the countryside, economic well-being depended on a personal connection with a landowner; in the city, the poor depended on a similar connection but with a different kind of *patron* (boss). Knowing a relative or a friend or developing a personal relationship with a well-connected person could be the key to making it in the new environment. The personalistic, clientelistic culture of the countryside was transplanted into the city to some degree.

The overcrowded districts where the migrants arrived took on various names: *favelas* in Brazil and *barrios* in many parts of Spanish America. The term *callampas*, meaning "mushrooms," used in Chile, is an especially apt description of how these poor neighborhoods sprung up on vacant land. In most of Latin America, persons occupying unused lands for 10 years have established a right to ownership of the property. This leads to conflict when squatters seize abandoned or unused parcels of land. Municipal authorities usually evict the newcomers, but many times they return, determined to begin their new life with little more than cardboard, wooden slats, and corrugated tin or zinc roofs. Next come bricks, electricity tapped from a nearby power line, and maybe a bus or jitney route to carry residents into the city center and, they hope, a job.

The political crisis of populism came about in part when political leaders and grassroots activists mobilized the urban poor and peasants and began to demand greater inclusion in social and economic life. This occurred just as growth rates were slowing, and as workers who had jobs began to use strikes and protests to defend their own standard of living.

For Review

What is "hyperurbanization"? How did it increase pressures on the political system in the populist era?

The Breakdown of Populist Democracy

Perhaps the most influential analysis of democratic breakdown was a four-volume series, edited by Juan J. Linz and Alfred Stepan (1978), that examined not only Latin American cases but also others drawn from Mediterranean Europe. The authors placed primary blame on the inability of political elites, particularly party leaders, to negotiate a compromised solution to the crisis of populism. In this view, moderate leaders of leftist, populist parties were pressured by leftist extremists to accelerate revolutionary processes, whereas moderates on the right felt pressure from extremists on the right who resisted any reform or compromise with the "communist threat." The moderates on both sides had an interest in saving democracy, but neither side trusted the will or ability of the other to keep the extremist wings in check.

For example, Salvador Allende, the elected socialist president of Chile, and Eduardo Frei, the most important leader of the centrist Christian Democrats (then in opposition), were unable to negotiate an exit to Chile's crisis in 1973. Arturo Valenzuela (1978: 109), a Chilean political scientist (who later became a U.S. citizen and Assistant Secretary of State for Hemispheric Affairs in the Obama administration), in his contribution to the book on democratic breakdown, blamed leftists, many of whom thought Allende was not sufficiently committed to revolution. "By its actions, the revolutionary Left, which had always ridiculed the possibility of a socialist transformation through peaceful means, was engaged in a self-fulfilling prophecy."

Alfred Stepan (1971), author of the Brazil chapter in the study of "breakdowns," also found the cause of decay in the breakdown of elite compromise under the pressure of social polarization. The Brazilian system was simply overloaded by the mobilization of new sectors at a time of "decreasing extractive capability" for the Brazilian state. By this, Stepan means that economic and political demands were increasing at a time of slow economic growth. The inability of the government to respond to these demands resulted in actors on all sides withdrawing support from the regime. The political party system fragmented under the load, but collapse was not inevitable. Stepan thinks that President Goulart might have staved off a military coup had populist politicians and leaders of movements (e.g., the peasant leagues) not pulled politicians away from a negotiated solution to the conflict (Stepan 1971).

In Argentina the military had already intervened several times after the overthrow of Juan Perón in 1955. So we might argue that Argentina never had a populist, institutionalized democracy to start with. But in these coups the military was acting out what some call the "moderator" role. In this role, the military typically comes to power announcing its intention to act as a caretaker or to rule in the name of honesty or patriotism (Stepan 1971: 61–66). This was typically the case with military coups in Bolivia, which had averaged about one per year since independence. Brazil's General Castelo Branco seems to have had this goal in mind in 1964, but by 1968 the military had shifted to much more ambitious goals of

We generally think that the main responsibility of the military is to defend the nation from aggressors. Do you think the Argentine military, and for that matter other militaries in Latin America in the post-populist era, saw themselves as defending the nation at that time? Why do you think the repression was so violent in this period?

political and economic engineering. Guillermo O'Donnell (1978), in his analysis of Argentina, finds a similar process at work in Argentina between 1956 and 1966 as the Argentine military governments that came and went in this period tried to marginalize the Peronists. But by 1966, as Peronism itself became split between a more radical, revolutionary wing and its more conservative, corporatist wing, a process of social polarization became more evident, eventually producing the coup of 1976. Democracy was never in good shape in Argentina, but the definitive end of the populist era was hastened by a process of acute social and political polarization that led to a breakdown of consensual politics at both the elite and mass levels.

Cuba and Cold War Politics—An External Element in Breakdown

The **Cold War,** and especially the reaction of the U.S. and Latin American right to the 1959 Cuban Revolution, contributed significantly to democratic breakdown. Like all revolutionaries (including the American patriots who attempted to "free" Canada from England's rule in 1812), the Cubans thought their revolution was part of an international wave that they were duty-bound to help along. Cuba offered moral support, some training, and—at least until 1965—arms to revolutionary movements. At the same time, the United States exaggerated the influence of Cuba and the Soviet Union—at times even inventing it—to justify intervention and repression of leftist political movements, democratic or not (see chapter 16).

Cuba's ability to pursue an independent foreign policy and radical revolution at home was facilitated by economic and military support provided by the Soviet Union. The Kennedy administration came to power in January 1961 determined to commit Americans to a crusade against communism. "Bear any burden, pay any price," the new president said in his famous inaugural address. Kennedy, advised by academics such as Huntington and Rostow, also called for reform in Latin America, especially agrarian reform (land distribution, unionization of rural workers, etc.), to quiet the restive peasantry. This program was called the "Alliance for Progress." Concretely, this meant foreign aid packages and advisors (including volunteers in the new Peace Corps) to help centrist parties, such as Chile's Christian Democrats, Venezuela's Democratic Action party, and Brazil's Social Democrats. At the same time, however, Kennedy and his successor, Lyndon Johnson, actively deployed strategies that encouraged reactionary forces in the region.

The CIA is estimated to have spent US$40 million (US$20 million in each case) to influence the outcome of state and congressional elections in Brazil in 1962 and Chile in 1964 (Cockroft 1996: 541, 639), funds greatly in excess of what parties and candidates could themselves muster in these countries. When such tactics failed to quell the threat of revolution, the United States turned to measures, overt and covert, to destabilize the political system and encourage military intervention. Kennedy opened the spigot of military aid; he upgraded the firepower and training of Latin American militaries, which were schooled, like their contemporaries in Vietnam, in counterinsurgency tactics and anticommunist doctrines.

Much as Rostow (the modernization theorist summarized in chapter 6) and Huntington advised, Kennedy strengthened Latin American militaries to fight the "communists" while promoting reforms. The latter included breaking up large landed estates, supporting health and education programs, and promoting "nonpolitical" unions to replace those closely linked to parties. Aid was especially targeted at centrist parties, in an attempt to strengthen them against leftist challenges. But what if the newly strengthened military and the intransigent right saw American-promoted reforms—which after all sought to redistribute property and promote (U.S.-style) unions—as playing into the hands of the communists? Were strong militaries and reformist politicians really compatible with each other? Although the military accepted aid, it frequently resisted implementation of the "strings" attached to this aid, especially land reform and respect for human rights. In the Cold War, Latin American generals correctly calculated that for the United States, defeating the left (elected or not) was a higher priority than reform or rights.

The post–World War II model for destabilization was set by the CIA's successful operation to overthrow the elected government of Jacobo Arbenz in Guatemala in 1954, an operation that had its own precedent in operations elsewhere in Europe (Greece and Italy) and the Middle East (Iran in 1953) (see chapter 16). In Central America and the Caribbean, American military intervention played a direct role in bringing despotic governments to power, keeping them there, or bringing down regimes deemed too radical for comfort.

In the era of gunboat diplomacy (1890–1930; so named because naval forces were deployed), U.S. military invasions and occupations in Central America and the Caribbean were common. They have been less frequent since World War II, but nonetheless have remained an option "on the table," as Washington policy makers like to put it. A U.S. military invasion ousted a democratically elected government in the Dominican Republic in 1965, and an invasion of the tiny island of Grenada in 1982 made sure that no new revolution would emerge from the ashes of a collapsed revolutionary regime. U.S. forces have not invaded any country on the South American continent, but other forms of forceful intervention have been used. The Nixon administration (1968–1975) employed the CIA to engage in economic sabotage, kidnapping, psychological propaganda, and other tactics designed to bring down elected governments that were unacceptable to U.S. interests in the Third World, including Chile (discussed later in this chapter) and the Caribbean.

▪ Case Studies of Democratic Breakdown

Was U.S. intervention the main reason for the collapse of these systems, or were actions of domestic actors of greater weight? In what ways might U.S. officials be morally or legally accountable for the hundreds of thousands of cases of disappearances, torture, and extrajudicial execution that followed military coups in which, to greater or lesser degree in different cases, the United States had a hand? We will take these issues up in detail in chapter 16. Here, we intend only to show that the international situation, especially the policies of the United States during the Cold War, contributed to the breakdown of democracy.

For Review

How did the Cuban Revolution affect politics in other countries in Latin America? How did the response of the United States to the Cuban Revolution affect its response to the crisis of populism that arose in other countries?

Breakdown in Brazil: Setting the Trend

After World War II, Brazilian presidents attempted to maintain the same import substitution policies championed first under Getúlio Vargas, who committed suicide in 1954. After Vargas, Brazil seemed to be jumping forward under President Juscelino Kubitschek, who in three years built a new, gleaming capital, Brasilia, in the interior, where he and many other Brazilians had always believed the future lay. But by 1960, the economy was beginning to slow. When Jânio Quadros became president after winning election in 1960, he vacillated between a more conservative, corporatist version of Vargas's Estado Nôvo and the more radical, leftist brand of populism represented by his vice president, João Goulart, who assumed the presidency on the resignation of Quadros in 1961. Quadros resigned under pressure from the military and conservatives opposed to his friendliness toward the Cuban Revolution, his pro-labor policies, and his attempts to tax the wealthy, including landowners, to keep import substitution going. But Goulart proved even more radical that Quadros.

Goulart faced a hostile parliament that stripped away some of the presidential powers built by Vargas. In 1963, Goulart won back much of his authority in a **plebiscite**. He then moved to carry out nationalization of several industries, land reform, large concessions to labor unions, and so on. Goulart hoped to keep the support of Brazil's businessmen, who had benefited from years of state support under import substitution. However, Goulart's turn to the left alarmed the capitalist class in general. They feared the growing radicalism in the labor movement, and this outweighed the subsidies and other incentives Goulart offered to get the economy moving forward again. It is important to remember that fresh in the minds of both the left and the capitalists was the 1959 Cuban Revolution.

Inflation was an especially thorny issue, and attempts to control prices and wages made no one happy. Small farmers and the poorest urban workers were seeing their living conditions deteriorate. Skilled and organized workers defended their pay more successfully, but this further antagonized business. The highly unequal distribution of income in Brazil limited the possibility of renewed growth through ISI, but internal redistribution of wealth and income was blocked politically. The option of new industrialization through exports to markets abroad would require major adjustments in the economic model to make factories more competitive with manufacturing in other countries. The growing strength of popular movements not only posed a political obstacle to such a change but also deterred foreign investment.

As the Brazilian military—already deeply drawn into the complex web of negotiation among Brazil's political parties—mobilized for a coup in 1964, the United States signaled the go-ahead. President Lyndon Johnson's instructions to his foreign policy advisors in a telephone call were captured by tape recorder (National Security Archives, www.gwu.edu/~nsarchiv, accessed August 8, 2007). Johnson is heard to instruct Undersecretary of State George Ball that revolution in Brazil would be unacceptable. "We just can't take this one," he says. "I'd get right on top of it and stick my neck out a little."

The catalyst for the coup that ended Brazil's first experiment with democracy was concessions that Goulart made to rebellious naval officers, which the high command saw as intrusion on their domain. Politicians welcomed the coup, believing it would, like so many other Latin American coups of the past, simply break the political impasse and open the way for a new election. In his inaugural address of April 15, 1964, General Humberto Castelo Branco promised to "observe and maintain the laws of the country" and said he would call upon the participation of "all the citizens" in his endeavor to continue "striving for progress and advancement." He promised, "My behavior will be that of a head of state who will permit no delay in the process of electing the Brazilian to whom I shall transfer my office on January 31, 1966." The general also promised that his government would work not only to benefit private enterprise but also to extend well-being for "those who toil and suffer in the less-developed regions of the country" (quoted in Sigmund 1970: 132–134).

In 1964, the military junta might very well have had these goals in mind, but it first tried to bring inflation under control at the sole expense of the workers. The political situation grew even more polarized. The violence spilled over into the kidnapping of several foreign diplomats. In 1968, the hard-liners in the military consolidated their rule with Institutional Act #5. The act "legitimized" serious abuses, including torture, disappearances, and limits on political rights. The act's preamble specified that "subversive acts on the part of different political and cultural sectors prove" that the relatively liberal system established in 1964 was "being used as a means to combat and destroy it." As a consequence, the act authorized the military president to close down national and state legislatures indefinitely, to rule by decree, to "suspend the political rights of any citizen for a period of ten years," to declare at will states of siege and suspend habeas corpus, and to confiscate the property of anyone it finds (without a trial) guilty of corruption (Sigmund 1970: 142–145).

The regime was less brutal in many respects than its counterparts in Chile and Argentina, but the legacy of repression remains a controversial factor in present-day Brazilian politics. Hundreds were killed, many thousands more tortured or imprisoned. The military would retain power until 1985. The events in Brazil, the largest and most influential country in the region, proved a harbinger of what would follow in almost every other country in Latin America.

For Review

Review some of the factors that have contributed to military coups (mentioned at the beginning of this chapter). Which ones seem to have been at work in Brazil?

Breakdown in Argentina: The Dirty War

The 1964 coup in Brazil was only the first act in a series of setbacks for democratic rule. In Argentina, the final turn toward tyranny came in 1976. Twenty years before, in 1955, Juan Perón had been overthrown by the military. Perón was anticommunist, but like other populists, he angered foreign investors and local capitalists alike with pro-labor policies and nationalization of some foreign assets, most importantly the oil company, ports, and railroads. The United States welcomed his overthrow. At the time (1955), the Argentine military intended not to govern but only to "restore order" and then hold elections to be contested between two other parties, the Conservatives and Radicals, without the Peronists.

The problem for the military was that the political party built by Perón was the best organized, most popular in the country, and the old parties had no solution to Argentina's severe economic problems, which were growing worse (O'Donnell 1978: 149–155). Inflation soared to 113 percent in 1959 and ranged between 20 and 32 percent for most of the next decade. In the late 1960s, workers' wages fell to levels below where they had been (in real terms) in 1947.

Argentina

Negative growth rates of -3.7, -5.5, and -2.2 percent were recorded for 1962, 1963, and 1966, respectively. ISI had reached its limit, and Argentine meat and grain exports were incapable of sustaining the new urban economy.

As in Brazil, the economic crisis contributed to a radicalization of populism. The Peronist party was deeply divided between a revolutionary leftist wing and a conservative wing. The Peronist Youth, influenced by Cuban events (Che Guevara was an Argentine) and by the emergence of a Marxist-influenced movement (**liberation theology**) for social justice in the Catholic Church, grew more discontented with the party's labor oligarchy. What kept the dysfunctional Peronist party together was the desire to win elections, defense of the labor movement (the leadership's main electoral base) from military repression, and the personality cult around the deceased Eva and the exiled Juan.

The military would not find it easy to expunge Peronism from Argentine politics. Some politicians in the middle-class Radical Party, notably president Arturo Frondizi (1958–1962), tried to strike a deal with the Peronists, but the military moved to block prospects of Perón returning to power. Meanwhile, the intractable economic situation undermined the chances of compromise. A cycle developed: elections were held, but the winners found they could not govern. Strikes and student demonstrations then would escalate until the military would intervene again to prevent the resurgence of Peronism. Coups occurred in 1962, 1966, and 1976. The military would tire of dealing with economic problems and unrest and call elections in which the Peronists would show their power. Then the cycle would start again.

Meanwhile, conservative Peronists (remember, Perón was anticommunist) became alarmed as worker groups began to move beyond traditional demands for better wages and benefits to challenge ownership and management for control. Inspired by the Cuban Revolution, but also frustrated by repression at the hands of Peronist party leaders, some on the left concluded that only armed struggle could bring change, so they formed a guerrilla movement. The most important were the Montoneros, who adopted the theory that in the cities, where most Argentines lived, the people could serve as a refuge for guerrillas, substituting for the mountains, where guerrillas elsewhere typically install themselves. A key moment came in 1969 in the city of Córdoba. Workers and students seized control of the automobile factory and other factories in the city and called for a revolution. The Cordobazo uprising was brutally repressed, but it was evident that populist forces were growing more radical and stronger.

The military now began to think of how to interrupt the cycle of elections and coups, and some thought working with the Peronists might be a solution. General Alejandro Lanusse became president in 1971 and decided to lift the five-year-old ban on political parties, hoping to head off the radicalization process by strengthening moderate and right-wing Peronists. In 1972, he allowed Juan Perón himself to return from exile. After his victory in the July 1973 presidential election, Perón launched a "purification" campaign against the leftists in his ranks. A year later, he died at the age of 78 years. His third wife, Isabel, who had run with her husband for the vice presidency, was no Eva. She took office and continued the purge, with support from the military. As the situation deteriorated toward civil war, the economy was jolted when the price of imported oil tripled in 1973–1974. The popularity of the government plunged. In 1976, the military seized power with substantial support from the middle class, which saw the government as inept and recoiled at the prospect of a leftist revolution (Nun 1976).

Many Argentines thought that the 1976 coup was just one more coup in the cycle. This time, however, the generals had other intentions. Already, Brazil's generals had decided to stay in power and ratchet up repression in 1968; violent military regimes had seized power in Uruguay and Chile in 1973. The Argentine generals decided to launch a "Dirty War" against urban guerrillas and anyone else deemed subversive. From 1976 to 1982, the military killed or "disappeared" as many as 30,000 people. There were only a few thousand guerrillas, but the military targeted anyone (clergy, students, professors, union leaders—anyone) they viewed as possibly connected to "subversion." Merely having your name in the address book of someone detained was enough to find yourself arrested, tortured, disappeared, or murdered.

For Review

Once again review the factors that contribute to coups and identify which ones were at work in the Argentine case. List one or two ways that Argentina's experience seems different from Brazil's and one or two ways it is similar.

Breakdown in Chile: The Allende Tragedy and Pinochet

Although Chile's history includes episodes of military rule and civil war, more than in most other Latin American countries, Chile's elite have governed the country through parliamentary institutions. Saying the country had an elected parliament is not the same as saying it was democratic. When Salvador Allende, a Marxist, was elected president in 1970, Chile was being governed under a constitution written in 1932. As we saw in chapter 5, the 1932 constitution was based on a pact that admitted the middle class and parts of the working class into the political game, but it also limited democracy by restricting voting rights. Until 1949, the right to vote was limited by property and literacy requirements that kept most peasants entirely outside the system and limited participation among the urban population as well. In the countryside, control over registration and the voting process was in the hands of conservative local authorities. Women finally won the vote in 1949, partly because conservatives thought their votes would offset the influence of the newly enfranchised males.

Still, Chile's record of unbroken constitutional government was longer than most European governments by the time the populist crisis struck. Political conflict intensified when Allende achieved the highest vote total (but not a majority) among three major candidates in the 1970 presidential election. Even though the country experienced **hyperurbanization**, congressional representation was never reapportioned after 1932, leaving representation grossly skewed toward the rural areas dominated by the conservative parties. Furthermore, there were additional obstacles to implementing socialism within the existing framework.

When Allende won the presidency, he inherited judges and a bureaucracy from the previous governments. These institutions were biased in most cases against his goals and obstructed his programs, such as land reform. In fact, these same institutions had obstructed the much less radical reforms that Allende's predecessor, Christian Democratic president Eduardo Frei, had attempted (Kaufman 1972).

The history of populism in Chile during this period revolves much more around political parties than around a single charismatic leader, as in the cases of Brazil and Argentina. For most of the populist era, the country was governed by a coalition of urban-based parties, led by the Radicals. The coalition, called the Popular Front, included the Socialist Party and, until 1945, the Communists. It gained control over the government in 1938 and implemented a program of import substitution (Drake 1978), providing cheap loans and subsidies through a special government development agency funded by taxes on the exports of the foreign copper companies—Kennecott and Anaconda.

Just as the parties founded by Perón and Vargas provided labor stability for new industries, the parties in the Popular Front did the same—in exchange, of course, for political support. The union contracts did improve conditions for the growing working class, but at the cost of subordinating the welfare and goals of the workers to those of the parties. The Front never attempted to redistribute Chile's wealth or redistribute land. It never challenged conservative control over the rural areas, which were largely in the hands of the right-wing Liberal and Conservative parties.

The coalition began to falter after World War II. First, President González Videla of the Radical Party outlawed the Communist Party in 1948, after the outbreak of the Cold War. The Socialist Party split into a moderate faction that favored an electoral strategy for change and a faction that favored revolutionary action. The Radicals were a middle-class party of reform whose days were passing. A new political party, the Christian Democrats, formed in the center and by 1958 had displaced the Radicals, who would never recover their old role as the country's largest political party. In the 1952 election, a retired general won the presidency, an indication that the old party system was in trouble. In the 1958 election, a Liberal Party candidate, supported also by the Conservative Party, barely defeated Allende and the candidate of the Christian Democrats. A small splinter vote for a radical, defrocked priest was all that prevented the Socialists from achieving the highest vote. A year later, the Cuban Revolution intensified the right's fear of an Allende victory in 1964. The United States now entered the picture, putting heavy financial backing behind the Christian Democratic candidate, Eduardo Frei, who won the 1964 election with 56 percent of the votes, in part because the right-wing parties, under pressure from the United States, chose not to run a candidate.

Six years of mild reforms under Frei satisfied nobody. Landlords hated his agrarian reform program, but peasants were also resentful because Frei delivered land to only one-fifth the families who had been promised a parcel of their own. Land was also an issue in the cities, where poor workers pressed the government to give them titles to unused land they had occupied. The Christian Democrats suffered from internal divisions over these issues, with a conservative, business-oriented wing providing the financial muscle and a youthful reform-oriented wing providing a political ground army. The latter became increasingly discontented with the careful and moderate course pursued by President Frei. Radical Christians and Marxists organized and exhorted disaffected workers, the urban poor, and heretofore-unorganized peasants. Reforms to electoral laws caused the electorate to triple between 1958 and 1970. At the same time, peasant unionization surged. Both of these developments represented a threat to the landed oligarchy's power in a system that weighted representation heavily in favor of rural areas.

The Kennedy administration (1961–1963) made Chile a major target for foreign aid, but with ISI faltering, this was not enough to keep the economy growing. Plans to increase national control over copper exports also faltered. Frei bought a majority of shares in the two big foreign mining companies, but copper prices began to fall, a disaster for an economy that depended on copper exports for 80 percent of its foreign exchange earnings. Businessmen and workers faced declining profits and wages; the middle class faced mounting inflation. Under the Alliance for Progress, the Kennedy and Johnson administrations promoted and provided aid for land reform. Although President Frei welcomed the help, the Chilean right was outraged. In fact, despite their fear of Allende's revolutionary plans, in 1971 the right voted for Allende's nationalization of the two large American copper companies. They reasoned that there was no reason to protect the property rights of Americans, who seemed eager to support land reform.

The stage was set for a dramatic election in 1970. Could Chile's institutions stand the strain? Despite the polarization and underlying tension, there was some reason to think the answer might be yes. Chile's political party system seemed adaptable. The Christian Democrats had replaced the Radicals in the center, and on both the left and right, parties had shown an ability to form coalitions and compromise. Chile had strong labor unions, but the politicians exercised considerable restraint over unions, which were generally affiliated with parties. The percentage distribution of the vote for the left, right, and center candidates in 1970 was similar to that of 1958, when the politicians worked through the crisis. Compared with most of Latin America, and in fact compared with most of Europe, Chile's military had largely refrained from intervening in politics. From 1892 until 1973, except for 1928 to 1932, Chile was governed as a parliamentary republic.

The center virtually collapsed. In the 1970 election campaign, the Christian Democratic candidate, Radomiro Tomic, in some ways sounded a more populist and radical note than did Allende. What was left of the Radicals had mostly shifted left into Allende's Popular Unity (Unidad Popular—UP) coalition. The process of polarization would accelerate over the next three years, but already it was acute enough to put into doubt whether the Chilean Congress, which was constitutionally charged with choosing the president in the event no candidate achieved a majority (50 percent, plus one) of votes, would follow well-established tradition in the event of a victory by Allende.

Allende won 36 percent of the vote, more (barely) than any other candidate, but not a majority. Congress convened to choose a president. The United States not only pressured it to elect someone other than Allende but also sought to short-circuit the process and provoke a military coup by financing a group that tried to kidnap the commander of the armed forces, intending afterward to blame the left. The plot was exposed after the general involved died resisting the kidnappers. Now the Christian Democrats agreed to vote for Allende in Congress in exchange for his promise to leave the public administration, judiciary, and armed forces independent. Allende controlled the presidency, but Congress, the judiciary, the bureaucracy, and the military were beyond his control.

Allende's plan was to nationalize key sectors of the economy, beginning with the vital copper industry. He would accelerate land reform and create programs to help the poor in the *barrios*. He hoped to stimulate the economy with populist programs (health, education, welfare, price controls, etc.) designed to win broad support for an overhaul of Chile's constitution. The immediate objective was *not* to do away with elections, opposition parties, rights, and so on, but to make it easier for a majority to pass laws socializing a larger portion of the economy. Meanwhile, Allende hoped to keep the allegiance of the middle class and sectors of business by targeting his reforms only at landowners, foreign capital, and the largest private capitalists, especially those resisting his revolution.

It did not work. At the grassroots level, workers and peasants, impatient for real change and improvement in their lives, began to take over factories and form neighborhood organizations. Some began even to arm themselves, to the consternation of the police and military. Most of the popular organizing was profoundly democratic, as anthropologist Peter Winn (1989) showed in his pathbreaking study of a textile factory taken over by workers. But land and factory takeovers forced the hand of the government, which had to choose between tolerating these actions or enforcing laws protecting the property rights of owners, which would require using the police and military to evict the workers and peasants. Allende was pursuing a relatively moderate strategy, but Carlos Altamirano, the leader of his own Socialist Party, was pushing for a more radical approach.

In a highly polarized political situation, each side tends to take on the attitude "If you're not with us, you're against us." Rhetoric escalates, and neighbors choose sides. Politics becomes intensely personal. At the grassroots level, local leaders (often called "cadres" or "militants") of leftist parties often discriminated against people who did not take a clear position in favor of revolution. When local organizers denied milk or other benefits of redistributive programs to eligible people because of their politics, the effect was to drive them further into opposition. Meanwhile, on the right, with the aid and support of the United States, an extraconstitutional, disloyal opposition emerged. It engaged in sabotage and other provocative activities, including propaganda that alarmed Chile's devout Catholic population by raising the specter of atheistic communism.

The Popular Unity coalition was now divided between (1) a "consolidation" faction, headed by Allende himself and including moderate Socialists and the Communist Party, and (2) an "advance without compromise faction," favored by more radical Socialists, a majority of the president's own party. The mass media, the Church, and the Christian Democratic Party moved deeper into opposition and began to raise the specter of a military coup. As the economy worsened in 1971, more women were drawn into the struggle, many into opposition. In December 1971, wealthy and middle-class women staged the "march of the empty pots," a protest tactic that came to be known as the *cacerolazo*. The march drew attention to shortages and led to considerable street violence. Although the participants were predominantly middle-class, greater numbers of poor and working-class women participated than the government would have hoped. Meanwhile, in 1972, the United States doubled military aid, a clear sign of Washington's preferred outcome (Roxborough et al. 1977).

Allende was losing his grip. Leftists called on him to arm the workers, which probably would have brought an immediate coup. Strikes became more common, but the economic situation did not allow the government to offer workers a better deal. In March 1973, congressional elections were held, but they settled nothing. Allende's coalition increased its share of the vote but was far from the majority needed to enact sweeping changes. The opposition won a majority but nowhere near what it needed to remove Allende from office before the next scheduled election in 1976. In fact, the UP percentage had increased over 1970, increasing the opposition's unease. Allende brought generals into his cabinet to try to assuage the opposition, but this was taken as a sign of weakness by the right. A coup was barely averted in June 1973. In August, several naval officers tried to warn the president of an impending coup; they were arrested by their superiors and tortured into implicating some important leftist leaders in planning an alleged uprising. Allende apparently could not even defend his supporters in the armed forces.

On September 11, 1973, American and Chilean naval maneuvers were underway off Chile's coast. Tanks rolled through the streets. Allende rushed to La Moneda, the presidential palace, after hearing news that a coup was underway. He armed himself and broadcast a final message (Allende 2000) to the Chilean people.

> My words are not spoken in bitterness, but in disappointment. There will be a moral judgment on those who have betrayed the oath they took as soldiers of Chile . . . They have the might and they can enslave us, but they cannot halt the world's social processes, not with crimes, nor with guns . . . May you go forward in the knowledge that, sooner rather than later, the great avenues will open once again, along which free citizens will march in order to build a better society. Long live Chile! Long live the people! Long live the workers! These are my last words, and I am sure that this sacrifice will constitute a moral lesson which will punish cowardice, perfidy and treason.

The Chilean Air Force bombed the palace in Santiago. Allende's body was later recovered from the ruins of the palace. Most likely, he committed suicide, feeling he had let down the Chilean people. Either way, he was among only the first of many victims of the military. General Augusto Pinochet emerged soon afterward as the strongman of the new regime. He would rule Chile for 17 years. Officially, 3,129 people were killed, most in the first four years. As in Argentina, the military's goal was to purge the left entirely from political life. Tens of thousands of Chile's 14 million people suffered imprisonment, torture, and exile. Even after Pinochet turned power over to an elected civilian in 1990, he retained considerable power for another decade as a senator-for-life and, most importantly, as commander of the armed forces.

In 2013—40 years after the coup—Chileans were still trying to draw lessons from the breakdown of democracy in 1973, and so were political scientists. Can a revolution, especially a socialist revolution, be accomplished within a pluralist, constitutional framework? Or are revolutions by necessity violent? Was the collapse a failure of elite negotiation, or were deeper social and economic factors responsible? To what degree can the collapse be attributed to the destabilization plan launched by the United States, or would a coup have taken place regardless of U.S. actions?

For Review

Once again, review the factors outlined at the beginning of the chapter and identify which apply to Chile. What kind of difficult choices did Allende face in power?

Shall We Coup? Why and When Does the Military Intervene?

Every Latin American country except Mexico has experienced at least one military coup since 1945. Why do coups happen? Huntington's theory of praetorianism (taken from the Roman Praetorian Guard) focuses on the weakness of political institutions; that is, weak civilian institutions encourage the tendency toward military rule. The transitions literature focuses more on political polarization and a breakdown of elite consensus. Marxist theory emphasizes the military's role as watchman over the interests of capitalists. These approaches and theories find the causes of coups in the nature of political systems. There is also comparative politics literature focused on politics in the military, an attempt to examine the "proximate" causes of coups. What induces officers to take the bold and risky step of attempting an armed uprising?

Internal Factors

The recurrence of coups might lead us to believe that they are easy to organize. Consider, however, the personal risks involved. Some person or small group must initiate a conspiracy and feel out potential collaborators. If even one participant decides to reveal the plot to superiors, the coup may fail, and its organizers may be punished or purged. Where social discontent is widespread, and high-ranking officers are alienated from civilian authorities, the risk may be diminished somewhat. When political uncertainty prevails, even soldiers who oppose a coup may opt for neutrality, lest they find themselves suddenly answering to a new government led by officers they betrayed. Although soldiers take an oath to defend the constitution, the nature of military life makes insubordination dangerous. Military training and corporate identity also work to create networks of personal loyalty within the military organization. In addition, the legacy of military involvement in politics involves a certain degree of tolerance in the ranks for dissenters. Today's rebel may be tomorrow's commander, or even president.

Within the military, the would-be coup maker must of necessity be a conspirator willing to risk his career. (No coups have been led by women—yet.) The military itself may be rife with factions. Not infrequently, it is divided into pro-regime, anti-regime, and constitutionalist (neutral) wings. If one faction moves, will the others resist? Would soldiers fire upon one another in that case, or is loyalty to the military caste likely to restrain the potential for violence? Externally, there may be civilians encouraging or even entering into the conspiracy. Are they to be trusted? Will they be dependable allies in a post-coup government?

Then there is the attitude of the rank and file to be considered. Ordinary soldiers are recruited (sometimes forcibly in the countryside) or drafted, and their ethnic and class (but not gender) characteristics reflect to some degree those of the entire society. The recruit is often poorly educated, subjected to harsh living conditions inferior to those of high-ranking officers, and lacking even the most elemental rights within the military hierarchy. He (most often "he," sometimes "she") is put through a harsh physical regimen designed to instill patriotic values and unquestioned obedience to superior officers. More often than not, the "enemy" against whom the Latin American soldier is deployed is his fellow citizen. Most of the time, soldiers follow the orders of their commanders unquestioningly, even if they are asked to move against their own government. However, discontent deep within the ranks is not unknown. Occasionally, noncommissioned officers (e.g., sergeants) and field officers have led revolts.

Contextual Factors

We have been examining the *internal* military politics of coup making, but these must be put in the context of the political environment at any particular moment. We have already listed some of the contextual factors that make democracies vulnerable to collapse, which usually leads to military rule in some form. What are the more immediate circumstances that prompt military intervention? Not all these factors are present in every case, but we can identify some signs of a civilian government in trouble before a coup actually occurs.

- *Civilian politicians and other elites begin to speculate about the possibility of a coup, often in a manner that seems to invite intervention.* Typically, military officers are "reminded" of their duty to put allegiance to the nation or the constitution above their loyalty to the president and commanding officers. For example, in March 1964, the Brazilian newspaper *Diário de Noticias* editorialized that extremists had "co-opted the president [Goulart] himself" and led him to subvert the rule of law, so that the president had lost "the right to be obeyed . . . because this right emanates from the constitution. The armed forces, by article 177 of the constitution, are obliged to 'defend the country, and to guarantee the constitutional power, law and order.'"
- *Civilian groups take up arms, threatening the military's monopoly of force.* The military has a strong interest in maintaining its status as the sole repository of legalized violence. In 1959, upon seizing power, Cuba's revolutionary government abolished the regular armed forces in favor of a militia, sending shivers down the spines of the hemisphere's military elite. (Today, Cuba has a regular army again.) However, the military rarely views threats from the right with the same alarm as ones from the left. The military has been known to assume a direct leadership role in right-wing death squad activities in Central America and in Colombia. Landowners have hired retired—and sometimes even active—members of the armed forces to attack peasant movements or defend themselves against guerrillas.
- *The military sometimes resents being deployed against the population by the incumbent government.* Although Latin American militaries have a well-earned reputation for repression, they sometimes blame the corruption or inadequacies of politicians for putting them in the position of killing citizens who are often from the same social strata as the rank and file.
- *Political struggles among civilians spill over into military affairs and become factors in promotions and other matters that the military would reserve for itself.* As the executive branch becomes more concerned with the possibility of a coup, the president seeks to ensure that key positions in the command structure are held by his supporters or at least by those opposed to a coup. Sometimes officers with more time in grade or impressive records are passed over for promotion by more junior or less qualified colleagues; this, of course, only exacerbates existing dissension in the ranks.
- *The United States expresses alarm about the policies of the existing government and signals its approval of military intervention.* In some cases, the United States is directly

involved in encouraging a coup. Since the 1980s, Washington has, at least in public diplomacy, condemned military intervention, but its actions (e.g., Venezuela in the failed coup of 2002; the coup in Honduras in 2009) are often inconsistent with its words.

- *Certain political factions gaining political power are deemed threats to the nation.* Under the influence of North American "national security doctrines," Latin American militaries were enlisted by Washington in the fight against communism during the Cold War. In this era, almost any leftist political movement was regarded as communist by domestic elites.

The Spanish term for *coup d'etat* is *golpe* (literally, "blow"). One stereotype we have of these *golpes* is that they are executed by generals or colonels from traditional, landed families or that they lead to dictatorships by superstitious or pathological men, such as El Salvador's General Maximiliano Hernández Martínez, the model for novelist Gabriel García Márquez's *Autumn of the Patriarch*. Martínez once proclaimed, "It is a greater crime to kill an ant than to kill a man." However, as we have already seen in examining Latin American history, military officers have sometimes been agents of modernization, at times even staging coups in alliance with civilians who want to implement democracy.

Sometimes the United States has tried to promote political stability by championing the creation and training of a well-equipped, effective fighting force commanded by officers who stand above partisan political fights. The result is often something quite different. Instead of a neutral military, the training produces a more powerful army that becomes the dominant political force in its own right. The classic example for Central America was the creation of the Nicaraguan National Guard in the early 1930s. The United States had equipped and trained the Guard to take over the fight against the patriotic guerrilla forces of José Augusto Sandino. After the United States withdrew its forces, Sandino agreed to negotiate an end to his resistance with the Guard's commander, Anastasio Somoza. Instead, in 1934, Somoza had Sandino assassinated. He used control of the Guard to establish a family dynasty and amassed a huge fortune (Millet 1977), ruling the country until overthrown by the Sandinistas (FSLN) in 1979.

Politics in the Ranks

Perhaps more than in any other bureaucracy in government, in the military, promotions are supposed to be based on rational criteria—for example, education, performance, and leadership qualities (Janowitz 1964). Hence, on one hand, the nature of its mission—defense of the nation from external threats—creates an internal ethos and *espirit d'corps* that is unique to a military environment. As Eric Nordlinger (1970) put it in a classic study, the penchant of the military for political stability is an outgrowth of its "attachments to order, dignity and hierarchy." On the other hand, as a department of government, the military competes with other departments for a share of state spending. Also, the way the military defines a *threat* is a highly political matter. Finally, the military is an organization with its own corporate political interests and biases, and it is an organization with its own internal politics. Who gets promoted? What branch gets more money for procurement? Who gets an overseas posting? Who gets command over elite units? These questions rarely are decided on purely rational criteria. Hence, not only is the military often involved in politics, but politics also penetrates military life.

The line between a civilian government and a military government is not always clear. President Alberto Fujimori of Peru won election in 1990 promising to resist neoliberalism and effectively combat an extremely violent guerrilla force, Sendero Luminoso (Shining Path). In office, Fujimori completely reversed his stand on economic policy, but he kept his promise on crushing Sendero. To accomplish this, in 1992 he closed the Congress, which at the time was highly unpopular with voters, and turned to the military for support. In exchange, the military was given a free hand (meaning gross violations of human rights) in fighting the internal war. What's more, the top circle of generals, headed by the president's intelligence secretary, Vladimiro Montesinos, made millions of dollars from drug trafficking, arms smuggling, and other questionable businesses. Fujimori's closing of Congress became known as the *auto-golpe*, and some fear that he may have set a pattern for the future: an elected president who allies with the military to exert dominance over the other branches of government.

Marxists have almost always seen the military as the "night watchman" of capitalism, ready to defend the interests of the capitalist ruling class against the threat of revolution. Other analysts (Pye 1962) have seen the military as a transformative force, seeking to modernize society, perhaps even to advance the interests of social forces being blocked by conservatives. As the economies grew more complex and urban, Latin America's militaries became more staunchly middle-class institutions, not least because much of the officer corps came from the ranks of this group—and not, as in the past, exclusively from the ranks of the landed gentry. Amos Perlmutter (1977: 187–190) calls military governments with an agenda "ruler oriented," distinguishing them from the moderator role (discussed earlier in this chapter) of other military juntas (councils). There is little doubt that the military governments that took power after the crisis of populism were ruler oriented, but not on behalf of justice or democracy.

For Review

From the point of view of a military officer, under what conditions might he (occasionally she) be most likely to join a plot to make a coup? Can you break these conditions down into three categories: (1) inside the military, (2) in the broader political and social system, and (3) internationally?

Bureaucratic Authoritarianism

The more radical the threat, the more determined was the military to remake social, economic, and political structures—that is, the more likely the military would act not as a moderator but more in the style of Marx's "night watchman" that intervenes when capitalism is in danger. Guillermo O'Donnell (1973), an Argentine political scientist, coined the term **"bureaucratic authoritarianism"** (BA) for the harsh dictatorships that followed the populist crisis. By qualifying the term "authoritarianism," O'Donnell implies, rightly, that not all authoritarian regimes are the same. Traditional dictatorships were often concentrated in the hands of a single, powerful individual, or *caudillo*, who might be nearly illiterate (e.g., Juan Vicente Gómez of Venezuela, 1908–1935), an economic predator (e.g., Gómez and Nicaragua's Anastasio Somoza and his sons, 1934–1979), or an eccentric megalomaniac determined to force-march a nation to modernity (e.g., Paraguay's José Francia, 1816–1839).

The leaders of the BA regimes came to power convinced that they could not simply restore the status quo. Influenced by the national security doctrines of U.S. training missions, they came to see their mission as that of defeating the threat of another Cuban-style revolution. The prospect of turning government back over to professional politicians seemed unappealing. In addition to the corruption evident in much of the civilian political class, they could see the degree of mobilization of the population and to some extent the growing divisions within their own ranks—for example, the growth of radical tendencies within the ranks of the Brazilian military, or the existence of a small group of officers supportive of Allende.

The military did not necessarily seize government with a preconceived plan of how to implement an alternative to import substitution and purge politics of corruption and polarization, but they did understand that the threat of revolution required more profound change than a mere "moderating" role would imply. The coup makers were convinced that they had to radically restructure the economy, even if that meant bulldozing over anything associated with populism and ISI, but also over the interests of inefficient landlords and businessmen who had urged them to take power. Economic matters were turned over to economists who were often trained in North American universities or locally by professors steeped in the doctrines of laissez-faire capitalism. These "bureaucrats" made policy while the military silenced all political opposition with terror. Frightened by the specter of revolution, the politicians, landlords, and business community offered little resistance as the true nature of the new military regimes revealed itself.

Each of the BAs brutalized the population not only to crush insurrections but also to destroy the power of unions, peasant movements, and leftist parties. Then they turned to economists and other experts to construct a new economic policy. This marked the entrance of the so-called technocrats into power, completing the bureaucratic-authoritarian alliance. The advice of these technocrats could vary. Chile perhaps represents the case where the threat of revolution was most pronounced, and the swing toward neoliberalism was most decisive. Brazil, on the other hand, opted to retain some state control over the economy.

General Jorge Rafael Videla justified the Argentine coup of 1976 as necessary because "the country [was] on the verge of national disintegration." Events associated with the coup represented

> more than the mere overthrow of a government. On the contrary, they signified the final closing of an historic cycle and the opening of a new one whose fundamental characteristics will be manifested by the reorganization of the nation, a task undertaken with a true spirit of service by the armed forces.
>
> (Loveman and Davies 1997: 160)

On its way out of power in 1983, the military argued that the violence of late populist Argentina had justified the "use of classified procedures," a euphemism for the Dirty War.

Even the generals and admirals had to admit, however, that "within this almost apocalyptic framework, errors were committed" (Loveman and Davies 1997: 166).

In 1967, General Castelo Branco was still describing the goals of the 1964 coup in Brazil in terms suggesting a moderator role. The most "urgent task," he said,

> was to contain the extraordinary rise of the general level of prices, to recover the minimum necessary order for the functioning of the national economy, to overcome the crisis of confidence, and to return to entrepreneurs and to the workers the tranquility necessary for productive activities.
>
> (Loveman and Davies 1997: 174)

However, the military found its policy role deepening and its bases of popular support shrinking. Many civilians who had supported the 1964 coup encouraged Castelo Branco's opponents to act against him in 1968. The Brazilian military moved decisively toward the BA model in December 1968. A national state of siege was prolonged, which meant among other things that citizens could be stripped of all their rights for 10 years. Congress and all other legislatures were closed. On September 4, 1969, the U.S. ambassador was kidnapped and later executed by urban guerrillas. Now Brazil's own version of the Dirty War began in earnest, although the amount of political violence was not as great as in Chile and Argentina.

Even in the case of Chile, the full consequences of the Pinochet coup of 1973 were not immediately visible. The initial proclamation of the coup makers on September 11 claimed that the Allende government had forfeited its legitimacy, and the coup makers proclaimed their intention to "reestablish normal economic and social conditions." However, like his colleagues in other countries, Pinochet had no intention of returning power to the politicians, even the ones who had urged him to act. In 1983, he explained, "Our historical experience confirms that political parties, as they were called under the old constitutional framework, tended to transform themselves into monopolistic sources for the generation of power; they made social conflict more acute." The military intended to make sure that the political parties would assume again "their true role as currents of opinion framed within a juridical [legal] order which will save the country from excesses, as parties whose bases are those consecrated by the people of Chile in their new [1981] constitution" (Loveman and Davies 1997: 183–184).

By destroying the institutions of populist democracy and putting an end to ISI, the military in the Southern Cone and Brazil prepared the way for the rise of pro-business policies (see chapter 8). Chile was where neoliberalism struck deepest roots. The "nonpolitical" experts recruited by Pinochet, known as the "Chicago Boys" (because many of them were taught by free-market, antigovernment professors from the University of Chicago), were schooled in the laissez-faire doctrines of Milton Friedman and Friedrich Hayek. These doctrines emphasized minimizing the role of the state in all economic affairs, allowing businesses dependent on subsidies to go bankrupt, eliminating protective trade barriers and forcing native producers to compete with imports and foreign investors, and reducing taxes and regulations. The regime destroyed unions and permitted unemployment to soar, driving down labor costs. Almost all industries nationalized by Allende were privatized again. The Pinochet regime did not privatize the state copper company, but it opened the country's rich copper ore veins on very lucrative terms to new investors.

The fate of land reform perhaps best illustrates how the Pinochet regime went far beyond the expectations of those who supported a coup in 1973. Agrarian reform was indeed reversed, but the land was not simply turned back to its former owners. The land reform and peasant organizing of the Frei and Allende years had fundamentally altered the relationship between peasant and landlord. The social and cultural structures of the past could not simply be restored. Therefore, many landowners tended to accept compensation offered by the government instead of the return of their land. The government then turned around and sold the properties to more efficient, large-scale capitalist farmers who started producing fruit, wine, and other products for export.

Some landowners did opt to reclaim their properties, and some of the peasants were allowed to keep land gained under the Frei and Allende reforms, though in the form of small individual plots, not under collective ownership. However, traditional landlords and small peasants were largely ruined by the economic collapse that ensued in the first two years after Pinochet took power. The large-scale capitalist landowners were able to buy these properties cheaply through bankruptcy and foreclosure. Overall, then, the combination of land reform between 1964 and 1973 and the reactionary policies of the Pinochet regime fundamentally restructured the Chilean countryside, paving the way for the appearance of Chilean fruits and wines in the supermarkets of North America, Europe, and Asia.

Brazil's generals took a somewhat different approach. Their solution to the problem of a stalled import substitution model was more nationalist and **corporatist**. If Brazil was not producing enough steel, then it was up to the government to make a partnership with Brazilian capitalists to create a steel industry. If Brazil was to escape technological dependence, the generals decided it would have to create its own computer industry. If other Third World militaries wanted to buy arms on the international market, why should Brazil not become an exporter of such goods? In other words, although Brazil's technocrats shared a desire with Chile's economists to diversify exports and attract foreign capital, the Brazilians did not abandon the idea that the state should play a key role in the economy. Argentina occupied a somewhat middle ground between these two orientations. All three countries, however, shared a strong pro-business and antiworker posture.

As for political engineering, all these military regimes undertook a "tutelary" role in regard to democracy. Having purged the left and limited the voice of centrist and even conservative politicians, the regimes aimed to prepare a transition to democracy in which the parties would basically accept the new economic model. Brazil went the furthest in this regard. In 1964, the military created a party entirely controlled by the military, the National Renovation Alliance (ARENA), and an official opposition party, the Brazilian Democratic movement (MDB)—what one critic called the "Yes" party and the "Yes, sir" party. This failed experiment sought to artificially produce a two-party system similar to that in the United States. In fact, by abolishing Brazil's old populist parties, this strategy helped clear the way in the 1980s for a new type of labor party, the Workers' Party (PT), which became a major player in the system after the return to democracy.

In Chile and Argentina, the military plan was somewhat different than in Brazil. In these cases, the generals sought to purge the old left from the system and gradually allow the remaining parties to reassume their role in the system—but under terms similar to those spelled out by Pinochet, quoted previously. The mainline leftist parties survived, but as we will see in the next chapter, their left wings had been sharply clipped.

The political strategy of the BAs was only partly successful; their economic strategies were even less so, at least in the short run. The political violence and disruptions to the economies in Argentina and Chile discouraged investment by foreign capital. The Southern Cone and Brazil suffered an additional shock from the sudden rise in international oil prices—by a factor of 4 in 1974 and by a factor of 10 over the entire decade. The rise struck an especially harsh blow to Brazil, which had little oil of its own and which had greatly increased consumption of energy in modernizing industry and agriculture. In addition, almost all export commodities important to these countries (copper, coffee, beef, wheat, rubber, etc.) saw dramatic drops in prices. Countries needed more dollars to buy oil and other crucial imports but were earning less from exports. The "solution" was to borrow, which ultimately led to the debt crisis of the 1980s. Even Brazil, whose economy boomed from 1968 to 1974 in what was called a "miracle" (see chapter 9), entered a new period of crisis. Brazil and Argentina saw rampant inflation. Suddenly in the 1980s, the BA seemed no more capable of promoting economic development than its populist predecessor.

For Review

What were the main political and economic goals of the bureaucratic authoritarian military governments that took power in South America after populism?

Populism in Uniform

The overthrow of democracy and the harsh era of military rule that followed suggest that the military is always anti-populist, but that is not the case. In fact, generals and colonels, such as Carlos Ibañez of Chile (1924–1932), Juan Perón of Argentina (1946–1956), Juan Velasco Alvarado of Peru (1968–1973), and more recently Hugo Chávez (1998–2013) in Venezuela, have practiced populist politics. These military populists were not just lone mavericks in uniform. All were part of organized factions within the ranks. The most famous of these was Perón's Grupo de Oficiales Unidos (GOU—Group of United Officers), founded in 1943 to promote national unity, modernization, and order. Once in power, however, military governments usually experience factionalism. The GOU, for example, divided internally around the question of support for labor. Perón's faction, which sought a coalition with labor, won, but the divisions remained and contributed in 1956 to an anti-Peronist coup. Peru's Velasco met a similar fate at the hands of a more conservative military faction in 1974.

Venezuelan president Chávez, who came to power through an election in 1998, followed a somewhat similar path, 50 years after Perón. Chávez had founded an organization of officers, the Movimiento Bolivariano Revolucionario (MBR), in 1982. It grew stronger as younger officers became distressed with corruption and the failure of elected politicians to turn Venezuela's oil wealth into a viable project of economic development. By 1992, they were organized enough to try a coup; the attempt failed, but Chávez emerged as a popular hero. Chávez set out from the earliest days to redefine the mission of the armed forces. Once in power, the MBR would unite the military and a civilian movement to work on projects of national development and improved living conditions.

As with the GOU and Perón, some members of the MBR split from their leader, and factions in the armed forces conspired to overthrow Chávez in 2002. Eventually, Chávez gained control of the officer corps after his supporters in the streets and in the ranks reversed the coup, which had ousted him for 48 hours in April 2002. However, retired and cashiered officers continued to articulate fierce opposition to Chávez and his plans for the military. The prominence of active and retired military officers in key positions of government led some analysts to compare his elected government to a typical one installed via a coup— "democracy in uniform" (Norden 2003). We should take note that Hugo Chávez was elected with resounding majorities five times (1998, 2000, 2004, 2006, and 2012).

For Review

Most military governments that we have studied in this chapter tried to do away with populism. How were the Velasco government in Peru and the later Chávez regime in Venezuela different?

What Is the Role of Latin America's Military Today?

Since the end of the Cold War, the Latin American military has been forced to rethink its mission. The enemy has become far less clear. Economic globalization has complicated the question of defining national security in the minds of some military officers. The free movement of foreign capital into strategic sectors of Latin America poses a new kind of threat to the integrity of the homeland, *la patria*, as Brian Loveman (1999) calls it. Nationalist resentment is fueled as well by the fact that the United States, Europe, and Japan—while preaching free trade—protect key sectors of their economies (especially in agriculture—e.g., citrus, fruit, soybeans, and sugar) from Latin American exports. Although vital interests of the wealthy nations are secure, the international debt often leaves *la patria* vulnerable to the imposition of neoliberal, **structural adjustment** policies (see chapter 6) that elicit popular anger and resistance. Militaries in turn are deployed to keep protest in check. Are Latin American militaries no more than guardians of the interests of foreign banks and investors?

Geopolitical concerns are also causing concern within Latin America's military. On one hand, U.S. military aid and training missions tie the Latin American military establishment closer to their colleagues to the north. On the other hand, the specter of an unchecked superpower and unilateral use of its power (most Latin American countries opposed, for example, the war in Iraq in 2003) has elicited a nationalistic response from some quarters.

In the 1990s and early 2000s, Latin American civilian presidents were loath to accept any government installed by military coup, and their solidarity against attempted takeovers helped prevent any country from falling back under military rule. However, the military clearly remains an important political factor. Some say that it acts like a political party, except with

PUNTO DE VISTA: COSTA RICA—THE EXCEPTION THAT PROVES THE RULE?

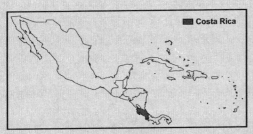

There is one often-cited exceptional case in the history of military rule in Latin America, and that would be Costa Rica. In 1948, after a brief civil war touched off by allegations of a fraudulent election, the winning side, led by Pepe Figueres of the Social Democratic Party, actually abolished the military. In the end, the forces of Figueres defeated an unusual coalition of convenience between Conservatives and Communists. The Conservative Party president from 1945 to 1948, Rafael Angel Calderón García, was something of a populist who had conceded to workers an eight-hour day, created a social security system, instituted an income tax, and built a social welfare program. The Communists, bitter rivals of the Social Democrats, were at the time the largest force in the labor unions that were prominent on the fruit plantations, the key export sector.

The U.S. government and President Harry Truman supported Figueres's revolt against the Conservative candidate, handpicked by Calderón, who had won the 1948 election with support from the Communists. Fighting broke out. Washington and its ally, General Anastasio Somoza in neighboring Nicaragua, provided Figueres with aid to defeat the country's armed forces, which had stood by Calderón. Figueres disbanded Communist unions and the Communist Party, but the Social Democrat also took Calderón's reforms even further—expanding labor rights and the welfare system. At the same time, he boldly abolished the army, replacing it with a "Civil Guard," whose mission was to serve as a national police force. Money saved by disbanding the army helped fund the expansion of social programs.

Since 1986, Costa Rica has celebrated abolition of its army, now also part of its constitution, on December 1. The absence of an army goes a long way toward explaining why Costa Rica escaped the Cold War wave of military rule and brutal dictatorships in Central America, but this has to be set against the economic reforms that reduced social inequalities and lessened political polarization in the country.

Costa Rica has had continuous democratic rule since 1948, for the most part with power alternating between Figueres's Social Democrats and the Conservatives. But there are reasons to wonder about the future. Costa Rica did not escape the social polarization and economic crisis that enveloped Central America in the 1980s (see chapter 10). The United States provided military aid (US$18 million in 1984–1985) to train and modernize Costa Rica's Civil Guard, which began to look more and more like a military establishment. Under weight of debt, the country began to retreat from the welfare programs enacted after 1945 and, as elsewhere, began to open up to market forces and free trade. Inequality, historically low in Costa Rica, increased. In 1980, the Civil Guard opened fire on striking banana workers, and in 1982, the government allowed the United States to train the Guard in "counterinsurgency." Today the Guard has 4,500 members that supplement a police force of 10,000, for a country with only 4.5 million people.

More recently, Costa Rica has found itself dealing with drug trafficking and the infiltration of Mexican crime organizations. It has a dispute with Nicaragua over its river border with that country. In 2011 it created a special border unit to deploy along its borders (Sánchez 2011). It would be an exaggeration to say that Costa Rica now has a military establishment typical of the region, but the increased social

FIGURE 7.1 Support for Democracy in Costa Rica, 1995–2013

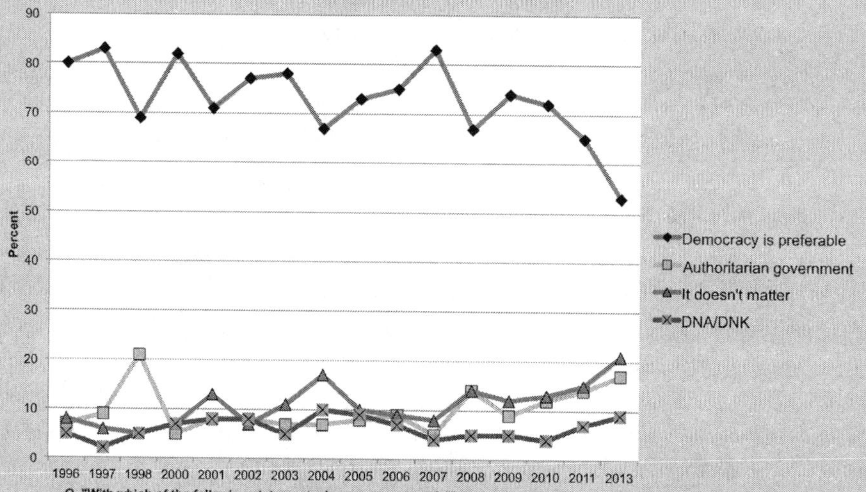

Q. "With which of the following statements do you agree most? "Democracy is preferable to any other kind of government"; "Under some circumstances, and authoritarian government can be preferable to a democratic one"; "For people like me, it doesn't matter whether we have a democratic or non-democratic regime" (Latinobarómetro 2013)

class polarization, the continued economic struggles, and the size and mission of the Guard at least raise the question of whether Latin America's great "democratic exception" is immune from democratic breakdown.

In the post–World War II period, Latin American militaries have been deployed more often against internal "threats," real or manufactured, often at a great cost in lives, than against external enemies. Costa Rica too has had to respond with military-like solutions to modern security problems, such as globalized crime syndicates.

Latinobarómetro's 2013 report shows Costa Rica to have experienced a significant erosion in public support for democracy (see Figure 7.1). The percentage of respondents who agreed that democracy is the best form of government—versus those who said that authoritarian government might sometimes be better or that it doesn't matter—fell from 80 percent in 1996 to only 53 percent in 2013.

In April 2014, an independent leftist candidate, Luis Guillermo Solis, defeated the candidates of the two parties in a landslide. Solis had been in fourth place before the first round of voting in February. Corruption, growing poverty, and inequality were the factors behind his ascent. The new president campaigned on a platform of higher taxes on the wealthy.

Point/Counterpoint: Is Costa Rica Really So Different?

If you say yes, how would you answer those who see rising inequality and poverty occurring despite the country's unusual democratic stability and lack of a military? Has the loyalty of Costa Rica's Civil Guard really been tested?

a. If you say no, then how would you respond to the argument that the lack of a standing military may allow the new president to address some of these problems before they get worse?

b. Whichever way you answered, based on this chapter's review of military intervention, what should we look for to see whether or not Costa Rica might move toward democratic breakdown?

For more information

See Steven Palmer and Iván Molina, eds., *The Costa Rica Reader* (Durham, NC: Duke University Press, 1998); John Booth and Christine Wade, *Understanding Central America* (Boulder CO: Westview Press, 2008).

guns. As we have seen already, the military does not have to actually hold power or take power through a coup to influence politics. This observation pertains to politics throughout the world, but given the long history of *golpes* in Latin America, the continued influence of the military in a variety of ways short of directly governing is worthy of special attention. The loss of prestige of the military after the particularly brutal episodes following the populist crisis and in the Central American crises could give way to less resistance to military rule. A quick sampling of the military's role in various countries shows that it is still potent in the region.

Democratic breakdowns and coup attempts have not entirely disappeared since the **third wave** of democracy washed over Latin America. Honduras experienced an outright coup against an elected president in 2009. Although the incident is somewhat murky, it appears that Ecuador's police may have attempted to oust President Rafael Correa in 2010. In Haiti, President Jean-Bertrand Aristide was ousted via coup in 2004. President Hugo Chávez was briefly removed by coup in 2002, only to be restored 48 hours later.

In several countries, the military has grown into a significant economic actor. As late as 2009, the Chilean military directly received 10 percent of the copper export sales earnings (not only the profits) generated by the state copper company, CODELCO, the largest single copper mining company in the world. Recent changes somewhat restrict military control over the funds, but the principle of tying a portion of the natural wealth of the country to the armed forces remains. In Cuba, the military has been entrusted with running the domestic tourism industry. Retired military officers own or control key economic assets in a number of countries, including Brazil.

In Venezuela, former military associates of the late President Hugo Chávez (who died in 2013) control important posts in government, with one of them, Diosdado Cabello, president of the National Assembly, seen as the second-most powerful person in the country, waiting in the wings to succeed President Nicolás Maduro. No one knows for sure whether the army's loyalty to Chávez extends to Maduro, who has faced an increasingly polarized political atmosphere (with some violence). Mexico's military has been drawn more deeply into the regime's war on drug lords, and in Colombia, talks between the government and guerrilla leaders have stirred discontent among right-wing civilians with allies in the military. In Peru, Ollanta Humala, a former officer with a questionable record during Fujimori's war on the Shining Path guerrillas, won Peru's presidential election of 2011. In Honduras, elections took place in 2013, but the impact of the coup of 2009 still is felt. Honduran security forces today act with impunity reminiscent of the worst years of the civil wars in Central America. Banks under control of the military in Guatemala and Honduras are highly influential throughout the region.

We could go on with other examples, but the main point should be clear enough. Democratic breakdown seems less threatening overall today in Latin America, but it has happened, and there are countries, such as Venezuela, where we can see social and political polarization reminiscent of the crisis years at the end of populism. Latin American militaries may be less likely today to carry out coups for a number of reasons, but they cannot be ruled out.

It is not surprising that predictions about the future vary. On one hand, Jorge Dominguez and Abraham Lowenthal (1996), two of the most prominent political scientists specializing in the region, envisioned an end to coups and a shift toward democracy. On the other hand, Argentine Rut Diamint (2002: 15), a specialist in civilian–military relationships in the region, points out,

> We have also witnessed new forms of military involvement in guises that preserve the semblance of democracy: military control of vast quantities of economic resources, intelligence services with close links to governments, military putschists following populist policies, paramilitary intervention in political disputes and control of society through militarization of domestic law enforcement.

It would seem safe to conclude that military coups enjoy less international legitimacy and seem less likely today to lead to long, sustained personal dictatorships. However, military influence in Latin American politics remains deeply embedded in most political systems in the region.

Discussion Questions

1. Why were the military regimes that took power at the close of the populist era determined to keep power instead of playing a "moderator role"?
2. What seems more important to you, and why, in explaining democratic breakdowns—the role of underlying economic and social forces or the actions of elites?
3. Are military governments and military rulers intrinsically conservative? Whose interest does the military represent when it seizes power?
4. Does the Chilean case prove that socialism cannot be achieved through democracy?

Resources for Further Study

Reading: *The Breakdown of Democracy Regimes*, edited by Juan J. Linz and Alfred Stepan (Baltimore: Johns Hopkins, 1978), remains the best comparative mainstream analysis. In the copious literature on the Chilean road to socialism, I recommend Ian Roxborough, Phil O'Brien, and Jackie Roddick's *Chile: The State and Revolution* (London: Macmillan Press, 1977), which is sympathetic to the Chilean left but not uncritical. *Weavers of Revolution: The Yarur Workers and Chile's Road to Socialism*, by Peter

Winn (New York: Oxford University Press, 1989), an anthropologist, looks at how the Allende years were lived in one textile factory. Brian Loveman's *For La Patria: Politics and the Armed Forces in Latin America* surveys the state of military politics as BA was coming to an end.

Video and Film: The three-part documentary *The Battle of Chile—The Insurrection of the Bourgeoisie* (1975), *The Coup D'état* (1976), and *Popular Power* (1979)—tells the story of the rise and fall of Salvador Allende. The same director made *Salvador Allende* (2002). *The Revolution Will Not Be Televised* (2003) is the remarkable story of the 48-hour coup against Chávez in 2002.

On the Internet: Steve Volk's sources and general resources on Latin America, at www.oberlin .edu/faculty/svolk/latinam.htm, are especially rich on modern history and politics.

8 Transitions and "Pacted" Democracies in Brazil and the Southern Cone

Focus Questions

▶ What do we mean by the terms "democratic transition," "pacts," and "democratization"? How do political scientists see the relationship between elites and the masses in such transitions?

▶ How did the "transition to democracy" play out in Brazil, Chile, and Argentina? What factors induced the military's return to the barracks? What did these transitions have in common, and how did they differ from one another?

▶ What kind of economic policies were implemented by the military **juntas** in each country? How did the economic policies of the new democracies change, if at all?

▶ How were issues regarding the accountability of the military regime for human rights violations handled in the transition?

THE 1960S AND 1970s were decades of the "breakdown of democracy" in Brazil and the Southern Cone, and the subsequent period was one of harsh **bureaucratic authoritarianism** and military rule. The following period saw transitions to democracy—more specifically, **polyarchy**—as part of a **third wave** of democratization around the world (see chapter 1, Figure 1.2). In most cases, the transitions were facilitated by **pacts**—that is, agreements among key actors about rules of the game and policies to be followed in the new democratic era. Although these pacts facilitated the return of control of government to civilians and restored elections, they also limited the ability of the new democracies to hold bureaucratic authoritarian rulers accountable for human rights violations and to make significant changes to the economic model (with significant variation in each respect).

Types of Transition, Democracy, and "Regime Change"

A political transition is usually not a revolution, but a regime change. A "regime" refers mainly to the relationship between society and the state, specifically the rules of the political game that determine who governs (what parties are competitive, what groups have the most influence, and what elites are most powerful) and the overall philosophy regarding the degree and kind of political control exercised over the economy (e.g., a free-market system, a regulated economy with a welfare state, a highly planned economy). Revolutions might be regarded as the most extreme of regime changes because they involve not only changes in the political game and the state's role in the economy but also the radical redistribution of wealth and power among social classes. Revolutions are often violent and involve mass insurgencies; transitions are tumultuous but involve negotiations that seek to change the regime without radically changing the economic system and redistributing social and economic power.

How "democratic" the recent transitions in Latin America and other parts of the world were is subject to debate, but almost all comparativists agree that some kind of global wave reinforced the transition to more liberal states. A number of factors associated with **globalization**—a concept that came increasingly to the forefront in the late twentieth century—seemed to have been at work. Besides economic liberalization, we can point to the global human rights movement, the emergence of international organizations devoted to promoting and monitoring fair elections, and the "demonstration" effect of democratization in various regions of the world. The global **hegemon**, the United States, made promotion of democracy and human rights, at least on the level of official policy, a part of its international diplomacy. As with the breakdown of democracy, the transitions to democracy were not entirely endogenous—that is, generated from within. During the bureaucratic authoritarian era, Latin American governments faced a debt crisis and had to cope with creditors' pressure to enact unpopular economic policies known as structural adjustment. These issues persisted during the transition and have complicated the process of "consolidating" or "deepening" democracy.

The founding of a democracy is forged by processes that include large-scale movements of people demanding more influence over government and, on the other side, ruling elites ready for change but reluctant to concede too much power to "the people." Sometimes, the popular pressure to open the political system emerges after a defeat in war or an economic crisis, either of which undermines the prestige and air of invincibility of the ruling elites. Hard as it is to imagine, democracy has been instituted sometimes at the point of a gun. On a few occasions, occupying powers have successfully insisted that defeated nations formerly under authoritarian rule accept representative democracy. This happened in Germany, Italy, and Japan after World War II.

It is one thing to implant democracy, another to nourish and stabilize it. Just as a young plant needs the right kind of soil to take root, so democracy is more likely to succeed where certain kinds of social conditions exist. Huntington (1991) was relatively optimistic about the prospects for consolidating democracy in Latin America in *The Third Wave*. He saw the best prospects for countries where levels of economic development are relatively high, where military rule is most discredited, and where there have been previous attempts at democracy. By all three of these criteria, some countries of Latin America, such as El Salvador (as Huntington himself acknowledged), face greater challenges than do others.

The popular struggle for democracy is often linked with promises that democracy will deliver greater social justice, redistribution of wealth and income, and greater opportunities for indigenous groups, women, and others traditionally excluded. Some political scientists pay relatively little attention to the shortcomings in these areas, emphasizing instead the importance of building consensus among elites. In the transitions literature of comparative politics, a democratic system is founded on a pact in which various political elites representing these different interests compromise in the midst of uncertainty about the future. This is the approach that dominates the **pluralist** literature (see especially O'Donnell and Schmitter 1986; O'Donnell et al. 1986a, 1986b, 1986c).

The Pluralist Approach to Democratic Transitions

The pluralist view was laid out in a four-volume series published as a kind of sequel to the democratic breakdowns volumes discussed in chapter 7. *Transitions from Authoritarian Rule* viewed the transition to democracy as a kind of complex game of negotiations about rules for the new regime. Guillermo O'Donnell and Philippe Schmitter (1986: 65), who edited the volumes, wrote that popular pressure "may be an efficacious instrument for bringing down a dictatorship but may make subsequent democratic consolidation difficult, and under some circumstances may provide an important motive for regression to an even more brutal form of authoritarian rule." This danger exists, they say, because the negotiating process is not orderly but "tumultuous" and "impulsive."

The main players in the transition game are elites negotiating in the midst of

> people challenging the rules on every move, pushing and shoving to get to the board, shouting out advice and threats from the sidelines, trying to cheat whenever they can—but, nevertheless, becoming progressively mesmerized by the drama they are participating in or watching, and gradually becoming committed to playing more decorously and loyal to the rules they themselves have elaborated.
>
> (O'Donnell and Schmitter 1986:66)

What is all the tumult about? In the case of Latin America, there were several issues to resolve in transitions. The military wants amnesty for alleged human rights crimes; victims and their families want to hold them accountable. Businessmen and foreign capitalists want to guarantee respect for their property rights, even if the property was attained through questionable or corrupt processes. They also want a guarantee that labor and other leftist movements will not try to change the economic model by raising taxes, increasing regulation, or doing anything that will jeopardize profits. On the other side, many leaders of people in the streets call for social justice and redistribution in favor of the poor. Labor unions look to recapture the power lost during the era of repression.

Social issues may also be at stake. The Catholic hierarchy (cardinals, bishops, etc.) typically support human rights demands but seek to defend its role in education and limit changes in family laws, such as those on abortion and divorce. Educational modernizers may want to broaden access to education, whereas women's movements seek to broaden reproductive freedom for women. Having participated in movements to restore democracy, women have often grown audacious in challenging male privilege, both in the public arena and in the home. High-level religious clergy, usually male, resist such change. O'Donnell, Schmitter, and contributors to the series seem to be saying that transition *is and ought to be* a spectator sport. The people are portrayed as an unruly mass whose behavior must be tamed.

The image of elites tensely negotiating while the unruly people press them on the sideline presents us with a rather conservative theory of the process. The people, the *demos*, are more the chorus than the protagonists in the drama. More recently, specialists on democratization, including some from the pluralist school, have tended to give more recognition to the importance of popular pressure (see Welzel 2009), but the studies focused on elite pact-making remain the better-known and more influential approach to democratization.

We will review approaches that put the people more at the center, but first let us review the pluralist theory in detail. As an aid in tracking the changes, you may wish to refer to

Table 7.1 (A Reference Chart for Understanding Transitions in the Southern Cone, Brazil, Venezuela, and Mexico) in chapter 7, which provides a general comparative guide and chronology to the breakdown and transition in the three countries described in this chapter (Brazil, Chile, and Argentina). Venezuela and Mexico also underwent significant regime change, but the process was different in these two countries, which never slipped into military rule in the late populist era. We examine those transitions in chapter 9.

For Review

How does a transition involving regime change differ from one that simply changes control of government through an election? How is it different from a revolution?

Negotiating Democratic Transitions: Compromise and Risk

Adam Przeworski's (1986: 47–63) contribution to *Transitions* lays out the nature of the "game" of transition played by elite actors. He argues that the threat of force underlies their search for agreement on new rules of the game. The success of their negotiations depends not only on public pressure for an end to military rule but also on a fear of return to repression. That is, in societies not far removed from the trauma of state terrorism (especially relevant to Argentina and Chile), a significant part of the population might favor democracy but also want to avoid a return to the crisis years at the end of the populist era. For others, the issue is the specter of more years of military rule. For still others, it is both.

Transitions begin, Przeworski says, when certain conservative sectors among business elites and politicians begin to protest the dominance of a small clique of military officers and civilian allies in control of government. Business elites are dissatisfied with persistent economic problems, such as inflation, slow economic growth, and the cronyism and corruption that favor some of their number over others. Politicians who once favored military rule begin to leave government and express criticism in the press. Inside the military, officers become uncomfortable with the politicization of their services and their loss of prestige with the general population. These *blandos* (soft ones) begin to urge a quicker transition to democracy; they provide political cover for other elites to express dissent openly. Once conservative sectors pry the lid off dissent, other sectors become bolder, and the fear needed to keep critics in line begins to dissipate. Criticism spreads to other sectors, and the populace becomes emboldened to challenge the regime more openly in the streets.

The concept of a politics as a game, borrowing from the study of economics, is known as "rational choice theory." You may have encountered rational choice theory in a popular book called *Freakonomics* (Levitt and Dubner 2005), whose authors used the assumption that individuals act to maximize gains and minimize losses (rationality) to explain such phenomena as why and when students or sumo wrestlers cheat or what kinds of information real estate agents hide or reveal. Critics often ask whether humans actually make decisions this way—that is, rationally. Also, in the case of transitions, we are looking not only at the behavior of individuals (elites) but also at the behavior of groups (labor leaders, social movements, the military, etc.); that is, we are assuming that groups make choices on the same basis that individuals do. Still, the technique has provided insights into conflict resolution and negotiation, which includes the study of how political transitions take place.

Przeworski groups players in the transition game into four categories: *duros* (hard-liners) and *blandos* (soft-liners) on the government side and a similar alignment on the opposition side. *Blandos* and moderate civilians bargain over the institutions that will govern the decision-making in the post-military era. Think of the range of issues to be discussed. Are the military and police to face criminal prosecution for allegations of torture, disappearances, and murder, or are these matters to be put aside in the interest of reconciliation and hastening their willingness to return to the barracks? Will neoliberal economic policies (see chapter 6) be subject to repeal by a legislative majority, or will these policies be made irreversible by limiting majority power? Will conservative judges and bureaucrats appointed by the military hold onto their jobs-for-life, or can they be replaced by the elected government?

According to Przeworski, moderates (*blandos*) on the government side want to negotiate a transition that prevents a return to populism and preserves what they like about the pro-capitalist policies of the military era. However, they have to worry that the longer the dictatorship lingers, the greater the threat of revolution, as opposition grows impatient and street protests become more intense. Moderates on the opposition side want to make the rules of the game more democratic, but they have to worry that the conservative *blandos* will decide to stick with the devil they know, dictatorship, rather than risk the outcome of a democratic game. Pushed too hard, the military *duros* (hardliners) will crack down and delay a return to democracy for many years, at the cost of many lives.

The centrists in both camps keep a wary eye on the protestors in the streets. Culturally, perhaps even politically, civilian elites at the negotiating table probably have more in common with one another than with the people in the streets or the hard-liners in the military. Some of them were colleagues in cabinets or legislatures in the era before military rule.

This game can be significantly influenced by international events. Two important Third World revolutions, in Iran (1978) and Nicaragua (1979), heightened the sense that delay could lead to radical outcomes. On the other hand, in the Philippines, a dictator, Ferdinand Marcos, was driven from power in 1986 by a popular movement before the armed forces completely collapsed, leading to a moderate, elected government. Preferring the Philippine outcome, Washington began to back the idea of a "democratic transition" in Latin America. Even the administration of U.S. president Ronald Reagan, which blamed Reagan's predecessor (President Jimmy Carter) for allegedly abandoning pro-U.S. regimes in Iran and Nicaragua, took this view.

In the mid-1980s, another international factor in favor of liberal democracy emerged as president and Communist Party Secretary Mikhail Gorbachev sought to reduce conflict between the United States and the Soviet Union. The collapse of the Berlin Wall in 1989 and then of the Soviet regime itself in 1991 removed communism as an excuse for repression. Cuba remained communist, but it had long ago shifted its policies away from support for insurgencies, seeking normal trade and diplomatic relationships with other Latin American countries. The European Community (today the European Union) asserted important influence in brokering settlements of civil wars in Guatemala, El Salvador, and Nicaragua. Spain's turn toward polyarchy between 1978 and 1984, after nearly four decades of rule by the dictator Francisco Franco, was not lost on Latin Americans.

Cuba's economic problems and uncertain future diminished leftist enthusiasm to adopt its system as a model. One prominent Mexican intellectual, Jorge Castañeda (1993), claimed in a widely read book, *Utopia Unarmed*, that not only the Cuban model but also the entire notion of revolution through guerrilla warfare had been discredited and abandoned by the left. The ink was barely dry in 1994 when the Zapatista uprising in the southern Mexican state of Chiapas proved him partly wrong. Still, Castañeda identified an important trend within much of the "old left"—a movement away from viewing Cuba as a model for their own society and a shift toward contesting power through elections.

For Review

How can a transition from an authoritarian regime to a military regime be considered a game? Who are some of the key actors, and what do they want? Specifically, how do *blandos* and *duros* differ from one another in the "game" of transition? What role do pluralists see for the people in this game?

Cases of Transition in the Southern Cone and Brazil

The breakdown and transitions back to democracy in Brazil, Chile, and Argentina received the most attention among comparativists. All three countries—and we can add Uruguay as well—seem to have social and economic resemblance to Mediterranean countries that were undergoing similar political experiences. The literature on transitions, like that about breakdown, was more influenced by these countries' experiences than by those of others in the region.

Chile's Controlled Transition

Chile is the South American case where the threat of revolution had been most pronounced. However, by 1976, three years after the coup that brought General Augusto Pinochet to power, fierce repression had completely erased the prospect of socialism. An official truth commission (Rettig 2000) documented over 2,279 killed for political reasons, over 90 percent by forces linked to the military. Nearly 1,000 were "disappeared," an especially fear-inspiring tactic. Later estimates put the dead at over 3,000. Beyond this, hundreds of thousands of people were exiled, tortured, and imprisoned (some in prison camps in the remote parts of the country). Officially, in 2011 the government recognized over 40,000 people eligible for compensation as a result of acts com-

mitted by Pinochet's **junta**. The vast majority of these acts took place in the first three years (1973–1976), which effectively snuffed out all political activity in the aftermath of the intensely polarized atmosphere of the Allende years.

The regime at first was unsure of its policy direction, but it soon settled on a new economic model, one that was to make Chile the free-market poster boy of Latin America. The land reform of 1964–1973 was to be undone, but General Augusto Pinochet's economic team had no intention of restoring the old, traditional system. Landowners were compensated for holdings taken during the years of Frei (Christian Democrat president, 1964–1970) and Allende, but as we noted in chapter 7, Pinochet's technocrats made sure that the land itself ended up in the hands of big capitalist farmers who would reorganize the rural economy and increase exports of fruit, wine, and so on.

Although the factories taken over by workers were returned to owners, the capitalists who benefited from import substitution faced the choice of adaptation or ruination. Tight money supplies and cuts in spending (except for the military) tamed inflation but threw the economy into deep recessions in 1974–1976 and the early 1980s. Many businesses would not survive the elimination of protection for industry and the regime's commitment to free trade, spurring a process of deindustrialization. Closed factories meant unemployment and plunging wages for workers, which provided a ready pool of cheap labor for new and surviving businesses. A new social security law forced workers to put some of their earnings in accounts that were then used to finance new projects launched by capitalists. President George W. Bush (2001–2008) admired the system so much that he proposed using Chile as a model to privatize the American social security system.

CODELCO, the state copper company, was never privatized, but the regime squeezed it for higher profits by reducing miners' pay and safety and by increasing production. Chile is to copper exports what Saudi Arabia is to oil; increased production helped to create a glut of the red ore on the world market and made the price fall even further. Instead of new investments in the state company, the regime decreed new laws granting generous tax breaks for new mines owned by foreign companies. Fearful that a radical government might return, the big international companies did not take advantage of these incentives at first; most waited until the return to civilian rule (1989). In the 1990s, some big, profitable mines paid no taxes or royalties at all to the new government, thanks to the generous system put in place by the Pinochet regime. Other natural resources were treated similarly. For example, the bountiful virgin forests in the southern region were opened for clear-cutting timber operations.

As different as they were ideologically from Pinochet, the Frei and Allende administrations were in some ways indispensable to Pinochet and his economists, the **Chicago Boys**. The peasant movements in the countryside and the land reform that came in the last decade of the populist years broke the back of the old agricultural system that had been holding back economic development. Although Pinochet is sometimes given credit for "modernizing" the Chilean economy, it is doubtful that he could have done so without the sense of threat of revolution that induced Chile's elite to give his regime a blank check to "save" capitalism.

By 1977, some supporters of the government were questioning the desirability of indefinite military rule; General Pinochet responded by tightening his personal grip on power. In 1980, several high-profile political murders took place, and now some Pinochet supporters began to yearn for more lawful rule. In response, Pinochet proposed a new constitution that opened the possibility that he would leave the presidency eight years later, but only if he lost a plebiscite on his rule. Even then, he would remain the supreme commander of the armed forces. In September 1980, with his grip on power firm and no public opposition permitted, Pinochet won a referendum ratifying his new constitution, promulgated in 1981 (see Garretón 1986).

The early 1980s were difficult years. Pinochet had tamed inflation, reducing it from more than 500 percent to 10 percent, but a recession devastated the business community. Living standards declined, while foreign investment was reluctant to come back to a country whose stability seemed questionable. Much of the world believed that the dictator's days were numbered. However, by 1986, the plunge in world oil prices was helping the Chilean economy to recover. In September of that year, a failed assassination attempt on the dictator strengthened Pinochet's hand and that of the military *duros*.

Still, Pinochet had to make concessions and gestures toward "normalization" of politics. By the Przeworski model, the game of transition probably began in 1983 when a group of centrist politicians approached the Minister of the Interior, Sergio Onofre Jarpa, a conservative politician, and asked for the resignation of Pinochet and modifications in the constitution. Jarpa rejected both demands, but he agreed to open a dialogue. Then a prominent Christian Democrat, Patricio Aylwin, who in 1990 would become the first elected president after Pinochet, made a crucial concession on behalf of the opposition politicians: the transition back to civilian rule could take place under the guise of the 1981 constitution. This decision severely limited the prospect for any new government changing economic policies or holding the generals responsible for human rights violations. The concession deeply divided the opposition. Moderate Socialists and members of the Christian Democratic Party were eager to strike a deal, but more radical Socialists and the Communists, who were more connected to rising protests in poor neighborhoods, rejected the deal. The assassination attempt on Pinochet in 1986 (which raised fears of instability in the mind of the population) and the visit of Pope John Paul II later that year boosted Pinochet's stature. The pope was critical of neoliberal economic policies, but he expressed approval of Chile's conservative laws making divorce and birth control illegal. Still, there remained general fatigue with military rule and street protests.

Socialists who had advocated a go-slow approach or moved toward the center in the Allende years were brought more easily into the moderate alliance, whose largest component was the Christian Democratic Party (PDC). A few of the leftist Socialists also accepted the pact, eager to end the dictatorship; others disagreed. In this way, Aylwin's PDC and moderate Socialists (divided into two parties) began to forge a relationship, which later became an alliance known as the Concertación. As the moderates negotiated with conservative politicians interested in engineering a controlled transition, the two sides developed confidence that each would respect the pact in the future. Although the Communist Party (PC) was playing an important role in organizing popular resistance to the dictatorship, the center alliance had no interest in bringing that party into the transition process. A transition was also encouraged by the United States. Pinochet had friends in American conservative circles, but he was wearing out his welcome with pragmatists in the administration of Ronald Reagan.

The PC had suffered the purge and exile of its moderate leaders; its young and remaining cadre threw themselves into the dangerous work of organizing the poor in shanties. One legacy of this trial by fire is that the PC of Chile today, though it mobilizes fewer votes than before 1973, survives and continues to play a role as a critic of the system that emerged after 1988. In the 2006 election, the party's presidential candidate garnered about 5 percent of the national vote, enough to prevent the Concertación candidate, Socialist Michelle Bachelet, from winning on the first round. In 2013, the highly visible leader of the student protest movement, Camila Vallejo, joined the party.

One sign of changing times in Chile was that Bachelet sought and got young Vallejo's endorsement in her victorious campaign for a second term. Vallejo, running on the Communist Party ballot, won election to the country's House of Deputies. However, this rapprochement has at least as much to do with the popular fatigue with the Concertación after 20 years of dominance by the PDC and Socialists. After defeat in the 2010 presidential election, and recognizing the force of the new protest movement in the streets, Bachelet was elected in 2014 as leader of a "New Majority" coalition, made up most of the old Concertación and the Communist Party.

For "transitionologists," such as Przeworski, the story of the return to democracy in Chile is the story of how moderates forged an agreement despite the pressure from the extreme left, which organized in the streets. But did the transition succeed *despite* or *because of* popular pressure? Another view holds that the transition was really the story of how the mobilization of the *barrios*, and not negotiations among elites, forced the military from power. Lois Hecht Oppenheim (1993: 138) says of the period 1983–1986,

> The popular mobilization of this period was characterized by its grassroots nature. Civil society led the way, with political parties, especially at first, following their lead. The mobilization period demonstrated how civil society could organize itself autonomously from political parties. It also highlighted the divisions between parties (especially party elites) and grassroots groups. What happened in Chile was similar to what took place in many Latin American countries as they threw off the yoke of military rule.

In fact, the politicians' meeting with Jarpa (the interior minister for Pinochet) took place only *after* the first signs of popular resistance to the dictatorship. The process began on May Day (May 1) in 1983, when the copper miners called for a day of protest, and the public responded with several days of street demonstrations. Some of the politicians who met with Jarpa urged the grassroots leaders to ease up, but the Communists and others, with women especially prominent, organized more protests.

When repression strikes, it is women who have the most visibly organized protests in public plazas. They sometimes pay a severe price for their political courage. Torture, all too common in the hemisphere, often includes sexual humiliation reflecting the ugliest side of human nature. Rape and sexual torture are ways that men can punish women for stepping "out of their roles" and assuming political leadership. They are brutal statements of power as patriarchy, but more and more, they are having the effect of bringing women into politics, not keeping them out.

The events of 1986 (the assassination attempt on Pinochet; the Pope's visit) overall weakened those who wanted an uncompromised transition, and the opposition politicians seeking a negotiated transition decided to go along with the 1989 plebiscite. Within the opposition camp, much of the left felt betrayed. Acceptance of the plebiscite legitimated the very undemocratic constitution of 1981, limiting prospects for changing policies or holding human rights violators accountable. However, after years of repression, most of the population was ready to join the centrist politicians in a campaign of "no" to Pinochet's desire to rule for another 10 years. Pinochet threw the resources of government behind a campaign based on fear, but the opposition won 56 percent of the vote behind the slogan *"Vuelve la alegría"*—"happiness is coming back." In 1990, Aylwin was elected president as the candidate of, the Concertación, an alliance based on the willingness of the left and center parties to coordinate both their electoral strategy and their platform for government. The alliance was early dominated by the PDC and then after 2000 by the Socialist Party.

Although the opposition celebrated his exit from the presidency, Pinochet remained commander of the armed forces for another decade, periodically rattling the sabers when he felt the government threatened to modify the economic model put in place by his regime or to investigate military officers for human rights abuses or corruption. The 1981 constitution inherited by President Aylwin (1990–1994) included a Senate with enough nonelected, life-long members to block any legislation unacceptable to the general's supporters. If that were not enough, each state elected its two senators by a system that made it almost impossible for the Concertación to win enough seats to counteract these so-called bionic senators. Under the election rules, the Concertación could win 60 percent or more of the votes nationally but still win only half the seats in the Senate, where changing the most important laws ("**organic laws**") left behind by the dictatorship requires a two-thirds majority in both houses of the Chilean Congress. Those laws decreed (not legislated) by the military junta that deal with basic economic policy and military affairs are all organic.

If that was not enough, the military's legacy was defended by local officials, judges, and bureaucrats, who were left in place from the dictatorship and by law could not be replaced. Furthermore, Pinochet, as commander of the armed forces, held the biggest trump card. Whenever it seemed that the new government might undertake some unacceptable action (such as threatening to prosecute human rights offenders), he could, as noted previously, rattle the sabers—usually in the form of noisy military maneuvers in the streets.

That the Concertación held together at all is something of a phenomenon. The three largest parties in the coalition were the PDC and two socialist parties, the Socialist Party (PS) and the smaller Popular Socialist Party (PPS), whose ideological differences are not enough to detain us here. On the PDC side, many politicians had to explain their support for the coup of 1973, but more amazing was the transformation of many of the Socialists. The painful experience of repression under Pinochet chastised the mainstream politicians of these parties. Rather than demand accountability for the overthrow of the elected government, most of the politicians in the PS and PPS seemed more eager to offer apologies for their actions during the Allende years.

The ministers of the Concertación governments found themselves in charge of implementing the very economic policies that they had fiercely criticized during the dictatorship, but they had the good fortune to come to office just as the global economy improved. So too, as a result of the transition, did the confidence of foreign investors in Chile's political stability and friendly business environment improve. Foreign and domestic capitalists began to take advantage of the extraordinarily generous tax breaks and incentives for foreign and domestic capitalists enacted by the Pinochet regime. The **neoliberal** economic policies achieved impressive macroeconomic results; the gross domestic product (GDP) per capita grew by an average of 8 percent from 1991 to 1997. The share of the population below the official poverty line was cut in half. However, the gap between rich and poor grew larger than ever. Chilean workers are forced to pay 10 percent of their wages into accounts managed by private banks. These forced savings provided capital for new investment, but around 2005, as workers started reaching the age of retirement, suddenly it was discovered that the accounts were underfunded.

Concertación politicians sometimes point to constitutional limitations as the reason that they did not change course, but they also seem comfortable with the system. For example, in August 2003, Chile's national union confederation launched its first general strike since the dictatorship in protest against the neoliberal model. Rather than recognize and address the grievances, President Ricardo Lagos (2000–March 2006), a Socialist, criticized the unions for putting Chile's international credibility and reputation for stability in doubt and threatening its economic future.

The Concertación faced opposition mainly from two conservative parties. One is the Renovación Nacional (National Renovation—RN), which to some degree groups together the forces that constituted the right before Pinochet. It has a reputation for more pragmatic politics than the other right-wing party, the Unión Democrata Independiente (UDI), a party that openly defends the historical legacy of the dictatorship and promotes extremely traditional Catholic views on divorce, birth control, and other "family issues." The UDI, then, is more a party of populism—that is, conservative populism. Like their center-left rival bloc, the two conservative parties bitterly contest one another but usually come together in the interest of defeating the opposing coalition. Under the banner of the Alliance, it ran a common candidate, Evilyn Matthei, and in 2013 Chile became the first Latin American country to feature two women as the main candidates for president.

This milestone was reached even though political pacts more often seem to reduce the political influence of women rather than enhance it. Women found themselves on the outside looking in during the years after the transition, even if there was no explicit pact among the parties to exclude them. They had been prominent in the mobilizations against the dictatorship, but no women were included in the first cabinet. This time, though, women would not remain excluded from government indefinitely. They continued to be politically active and began to win electoral posts. Although they remain far from having achieved equality with men, their progress became apparent when Bachelet won election in 2006.

In the Allende years, women were often treated as though they were little more than the ladies' auxiliary on the left. The Allende government failed to tap full support from women who would most benefit from populist programs to help families. Women in the opposition who helped to topple Allende, such as the middle-class women in the noisy marches (*cacerolazos*; clanging of empty pots), were treated in a similar way by the generals. Some political scientists argue that the transitions to democracy were, therefore, "gendered" (see Friedman 2000). With the return of democracy, women went, *or were sent*, out of the public space, back into the home—hence, the importance of Bachelet's victory. A socialist woman from a military family, who had been tortured by Pinochet but served under Lagos as minister of defense, would become president. However, Bachelet, though personally popular, failed to stem a general decline in the fortunes of the Concertación, who lost the January 2010 presidential election.

In 2009, the major right-wing parties formed the "Coalition for Change," a name emphasizing their sense that Chileans, though favorably inclined toward President Bachelet (who was constitutionally ineligible for reelection), were fatigued and disappointed with the Concertación's 20 years in office. The Coalition's candidate, billionaire tycoon Sebastian Piñera, who had campaigned against Pinochet (that is, he favored ending the dictatorship) in the 1988 plebiscite, ran as a moderate and defeated former president Frei (the younger) in January 2010, ending the Concertación's grip on the presidency but not the underlying systemic pact.

Because of coalition politics, Chile, though it has a multiparty system, has politics more like those associated with a two-party system; that is, politicians and candidates move toward the center. The party coalitions, if not the parties themselves, tend to be catch-all types (see chapter 12); they are less

DEMOCRACY IN CHILE

MEAN SUPPORT	55%
SUPPORT 2013	63%
SATISFACTION 2013	38%

ideological. Although this may contribute to political stability, many citizens feel their interests are not represented and are discouraged from participating (Moulian 2002).

The Chilean transition looks like a classic example of what Przeworski described as a game. Moderates in opposition and in the government cooperated to make the 1989 plebiscite possible. The dictatorship's *blandos* had to worry that street protests led by the left might eventually trigger a revolution that would jeopardize the neoliberal model put in place by Pinochet. They also wanted to moderate the arbitrary excesses of the military regime. Center and center-left politicians feared the specter of indefinite military rule and crackdowns. Both sides had reason to help the other control more extreme factions, but both had to wonder whether their negotiating partners across the table could deliver the promised moderation. Defenders of the outcome say Chile has compiled an enviable macroeconomic record and degree of political stability. Many others feel that the limited democracy has made "*Vuelve la alegría*" ring very hollow.

In a book widely read and discussed in his country, sociologist Tomás Moulian (2002) argued that Chilean society has experienced not only a widening gap between rich and poor but also an impoverishment of its national soul. Moulian says that Chileans have become market-oriented, individualistic, and consumer-oriented at the cost of social solidarity. Moulian has little nostalgia for the polarized ideological battles of the Allende era, but he lamented the lack of dialogue and debate about how to create the "good society" of the era before the dictatorship. The crisis of Chile now, he wrote, "arises in reality from utopian neoliberalism, which tends to make politics a technical matter, killing off other ideologies" (62).

It came as a surprise, then, when there suddenly emerged a student movement protesting inequalities and privatization of education, a movement that was rapidly enlarged by the unions, indigenous peoples, human rights organizations, women's groups, and others. In her 2013 campaign Bachelet promised to work to call for a constituent assembly to rewrite the constitution. It would seem that neither those who think Chile was put on the right track by Pinochet nor those, like Moulian, who despaired for its political soul were entirely right.

For Review

Who were the major players in the game of transition in Chile? Why did the more centrist actors "win" the game against those who wanted a more radical transition or wanted to keep Pinochet in power? How did the pact among the centrists affect politics in the first years after Pinochet? How have Chilean politics changed since 2009?

Argentina's Transition and National Humiliation

The Argentine case somewhat replicates the Chilean model, but with a major difference: the military's departure from power was hastened by a disastrous defeat in a war launched ostensibly to reassert Argentine sovereignty over the Malvinas Islands, known to the British as the Falklands. After a devastating defeat, the generals decided to retreat to the barracks. They rapidly threw up as many barriers as possible to avoid being held accountable for massive human rights abuses of the Dirty War. In part, the officers were successful because many Argentines feared a relapse into violence (a factor in Chile too) and because of divisions within the most important party, the Peronists.

Argentina's military saw its Dirty War of the mid-1970s as part of an international struggle against communism. There were indeed Marxist guerrillas, the Montoneros, operating in the cities. Argentine governments, military and civilian alike, had increased repression between 1966 and 1976, which convinced many on the left that only violent revolution could succeed in changing the system. The overthrow of Allende in 1973 reinforced this judgment. Between 1974 and 1976, Juan Perón's third wife, Isabel, who had taken over the presidency after the *caudillo*'s death in office in 1974, cracked down on the Peronist leftists in the unions and youth movement. Lacking the kind of mountains (*montañas*, hence "Montoneros") that provided sanctuary for Fidel Castro's guerrillas in the early stages of the Cuban Revolution, the youthful Montoneros sought to find sanctuary in the cities, which would be their "mountains."

Isabel Perón veered wildly in policy, crushing strikes and rejecting large wage increases, only to reinstate them in the face of huge, militant protests and new strikes. Inflation reached 335 percent in 1975. Meanwhile, falling prices for Argentina's staple export products (beef and wheat) coincided with skyrocketing oil prices (following the Middle East war of October 1973). Perón accepted stringent restrictions on government spending and wage increases to get a desperately needed loan from the **International Monetary Fund (IMF)**. The Montoneros appeared to be gaining strength. Right-wing death squads began to appear as the political situation and economic conditions deteriorated. Fear ruled the streets as the violence escalated. Montonero tactics, which they justified as a response to repression leveled against the left by the military and right-wing Peronists, included kidnapping and violence against civilians. In 1974, the guerrillas obtained US$14 million in exchange for a captive executive of Exxon Corporation. Their targets included rival unionists within the Peronist Party. In March 1976, a military junta seized power, and General Jorge Rafael Videla launched the **Dirty War**.

Despite the kidnappings and violence attributable to the Montoneros, analysts (e.g., Andersen 1993) agree that the military campaign of terror went far beyond what could be justified. The junta disappeared as many as 30,000 people. With the encouragement of Argentina's wealthy oligarchy, support from a fearful middle class, and tolerance from Washington, one of the most murderous military regimes ever to rule a Latin American country won its war to the death with the Montoneros—by eliminating anyone remotely connected to them. The military officers banned unions and took control over social institutions, even soccer clubs. The middle class, although gripped by fear in the final days of Isabel Perón's government, found that it had traded one form of insecurity, a violent form of anarchy, for another: state terrorism, unleashed with little moral or political restraint.

Like the Pinochet government next door, the junta favored more laissez-faire policies and privatization of many state-owned companies. Many considered it a victory that inflation had been brought down to 88 percent in 1980. But Argentina's economic problems went deeper. Workers suffered the most, but businessmen also had to struggle against a worldwide recession and lack of access to foreign credit. Although the junta implemented business-friendly policies, many foreign investors preferred to avoid visible collaboration with a pariah state.

The Argentine transition began, one might argue, on April 30, 1977, barely a year after the coup, when a small group of mothers of the disappeared, frustrated at authorities' lack of response to their entreaties about their sons and daughters, decided to go to Plaza de Mayo, in front of the presidential palace to silently bear witness to the atrocities under-way. The military, accustomed to fighting guerrillas, had little notion of how to cope with a protest by a group of middle-aged and elderly women. After all, what threat could such a group pose to these men? The junta failed to anticipate how much international attention and solidarity the women would engender and the way their ranks would steadily grow. They became a powerful international symbol of resistance to repression—Las Madres de la Plaza de Mayo.

The **junta** stood firm for five more years, but by 1982, the economy was in free fall. On April 2, 1982, the largest antigovernment demonstration since 1976 took place. The junta, now led by General Leopoldo Galtieri, needed a distraction. Confident of support from the conservative, anticommunist administration of Ronald Reagan, the generals decided to launch an invasion of the desolate Malvinas (Falkland) Islands (population of 1,800) in the Atlantic Ocean. It is important to note that many, if not most, Argentines believe the Malvinas were stolen from them by British imperialism in the 1800s, and this remain true today. It is easy to see why the military thought it would be a good, patriotic unity today. Argentines have been contesting British control of the Malvinas for a long, long time. The junta hoped that the British colonial government would simply abandon the islands. After all, in London, a bill was pending in Parliament that would have stripped the Falklands residents of their equal status as British citizens. As Galtieri hoped, the Argentine public enthusiastically supported him. However, the government of Prime Minister Margaret Thatcher, fiercely conservative itself, was not prepared to be defeated by a Third World country. After 257 British deaths and 649 deaths on the Argentine side, the British forced the surrender of Argentina's 7,500 troops. Government propaganda had led the public to believe that Argentina was winning handily. Public euphoria in Argentina swiftly changed to anger, made worse when inflation shot up to 200 percent in 1982.

Galtieri resigned in favor of a retired general, Reynaldo Bignone, who promised an election and return to civilian rule by 1984. In July 1983, the junta decreed an "amnesty" for itself. A demonstration of 50,000 people dissuaded the parties from endorsing the move. Raúl Alfonsín, of the Radical Civic Union, won the election and took office in 1983, partly on his reputation as a defender of human rights and his promise to prosecute those responsible for the Dirty War.

With a Radical Party majority in the newly elected Chamber of Deputies and the military thoroughly discredited, Alfonsín seemed poised to take the initiative to consolidate democracy without a limiting pact. Indeed, defying the military's self-pardon, Alfonsín's government indicted nine generals and admirals, five of whom were convicted and sent to jail. The high command—it seemed—would be held accountable. That was not to be. A barracks revolt in 1987 induced the fearful Congress to grant an amnesty to all officers below the highest rank and to end further prosecutions. The Peronists presented themselves as a nationalist alternative to the more moderate Radicals, but in the end they were no more willing to punish those responsible for the Dirty War. This became obvious when they came to control the presidency in 1989.

President Alfonsín's hand was limited by several factors. The international economy was stagnant when he took office, so Argentina's export earnings remained dismal. Inflation had not been tamed (soaring to 400 percent in 1983), and—with the military's demolition of **import substitution**—factories were closing. Unemployment and poverty were on the rise. Overall, per capita income fell by 25 percent in the 1980s as Argentines experienced their particular version of Latin America's "lost decade." The Peronist unions, motivated both by politics and by the severe erosion of their members' living standards, resisted wage controls, which fell apart, unleashing inflation again. Food riots broke out in 1989. In that year's election, the Peronist candidate for president, Carlos Saúl Menem, won a clear-cut victory (47 percent) running under the slogan *Argentina a vuelve tener peso.* The double meaning was "Argentina will have weight again" in the world after its humiliations in war and debt negotiations, and "Argentina will again have a peso"—that is, a viable currency. Alfonsín surrendered the presidency right after the election, even before his term ran out.

President Menem forged an unholy alliance between his wing of the Peronists and the military, two sectors that had been mortal enemies since the fall of Juan Perón in 1955. In December 1990, a group of nationalist officers (*carapintados*, or "painted faces") revolted. Menem defeated the revolt but then pardoned the convicted officers. He was now in a position of strength to deal with the military. But his intentions were not to return to the old populism. Against expectations, Menem, the Peronist, proved to be an enthusiastic neoliberal reformer. He privatized major industries (railroads, communications, energy, airlines, etc.), fought the unions at the bargaining tables and in the streets, and replaced all savings accounts with 10-year bonds—essentially confiscating the savings of the middle class for a period of time. However, in return, the middle class got protection from inflation. In a successful bid to halt the free fall of the currency, Menem pegged the new Argentine peso directly to the dollar—one to one.

President Menem tamed his fellow Peronists with divide-and-conquer tactics. He favored careerist politicians loyal to him over nationalists and leftists. The labor ministry helped the union leaders willing to endorse his overall policies to obtain relatively favorable labor contracts; those critical of the president's technocratic policies and deals with the IMF were isolated. Pegging the peso did, at least temporarily, restore monetary stability, which made Menem popular until his last years in office. He rewrote the constitution and won a second four-year term in 1995. But opposition was gathering. In 1994, human rights advocates and disaffected Radicals and Peronists formed a new, leftist alliance, offering voters a third alternative to the Radicals and Menem's Peronists. In the election of October 1999,

Fernando de la Rúa, joint candidate of the new coalition and the Radicals, won the election to succeed Menem.

To understand how Argentina's economy fell on hard times, we have to digress to consider the politics of monetary supply and exchange rates. Menem had tamed inflation by abolishing the old currency and guaranteeing that the new peso would always be exchangeable at one to the dollar. For a while, the strategy worked, but when the economic growth rate began to decline, the guarantee suddenly turned into a huge liability. Holders of the peso fled to the dollar at the guaranteed rate of one to one. These dollars, concentrated in the hands of the wealthy, flowed abroad out of Argentina into foreign banks. Now the government had to find more dollars to meet the guarantee, which meant more borrowing—and also a more drastic devaluation once dollars ran out. The one-to-one peso guarantee became unsustainable—and a political albatross.

Devaluation is a policy whereby a government reduces the value of the national currency against foreign currencies—that is, one dollar, for example, buys more money (e.g., more pesos) than before; conversely, it takes more money (e.g., more pesos) to buy one dollar than before. Even the *possibility* of devaluation can disturb an economy. Anticipating devaluation, those with savings take their money out of the economy to seek shelter in, for example, dollars safely deposited in overseas bank accounts and investments. Matters are made worse when those with connections to the government know in advance that devaluation is coming. Corrupt public officials and speculators can make a tidy profit simply by buying dollars in advance and then selling them later. As tawdry tales of corruption and speculation fill the headlines, they take a toll on the legitimacy of government.

Devaluation does allow a government to convert the dollars it has in its reserves to much more of its own currency, so it has more money to meet promises in its budget. Devaluation also encourages exports—every dollar or Euro earned abroad buys that much more of the local currency at home. However, this also means that everything imported will cost more to businesses and consumers. Devaluation causes the real value of salaries and wages to fall, at least in the short run. At the same time, rising costs for imports raise prices. Not surprisingly, governments are reluctant to risk the unpopularity that comes with devaluation, and they are especially keen to postpone or avoid it in election years.

It was the misfortune of Fernando de la Rúa to assume the presidency of Argentina as years of economic stagnation reached crisis levels. Although elected in response to Menem's plunging popularity, de la Rúa did not attempt to overhaul Menem's neoliberal policies. Debt payments bled the economy. In the year 2000, the growth rate was actually negative (-0.8 percent), and things got worse in 2001. De la Rúa's response to the crisis was to try to (1) eliminate the government pension system, (2) reform the tax system to fall more heavily on businesses, (3) privatize some government operations (including parts of the tax collection system), and (4) freeze federal spending. He asked governors of the provinces to do the same. Not surprisingly, labor unions, people dependent on welfare, and small businesses rebelled. The Peronist opposition, despite Menem's role in creating the economic mess, was content to let the president stew in it.

De la Rúa now confronted rising popular anger about the **social debt**. In Argentina, and throughout Latin America, the majority of poor people felt that they had seen little or no benefit from the rash of government borrowing that had begun in the 1970s. They felt no obligation to pay these bills, especially when the funds to service the debt would come out of their pensions, wages, and already inadequate government services. Nonetheless, de la Rúa continued to pursue unpopular policies because the IMF, Washington, and private banks insisted on fiscal austerity as a condition ("conditionality," or **structural adjustment**) for renegotiating overdue foreign debts. Without such an agreement, Argentina could not hope to obtain the injection of new dollars that it so desperately needed to keep the peso stable. We will shortly encounter a similar situation—Venezuela in the 1990s—with somewhat similar political results.

In December 2001, violent street protests in Buenos Aires left 27 people dead. De la Rúa resigned, and his vice president declared a state of siege. The real value of the peso would have plummeted were it not pegged, but no one trusted the government to keep it that way. Wealthy people and speculators kept changing the peso into dollars, sending much of this money abroad, forcing the government to borrow more to meet the demand. As capital fled and investment fell, unemployment and poverty increased. In January, the government finally abandoned the one-to-one peg. The exchange rate plunged, and inflation skyrocketed. Savings were wiped out; factories were closed. Provincial governments lacked money to provide basic services (schools, police, sanitation, and health care) and took to issuing promissory notes (*bonos*) that, of course, had even less value than the peso itself.

Things finally bottomed out in late 2002 but not before a political crisis that saw a succession of presidential resignations and changes. Finally, investment began to return to the country, which for all its problems has a relatively educated workforce and rich farm and grazing lands. The peso began to make a comeback in 2003, and overall the economy grew, largely on the strength of exports (beef, grain, and soybeans), much of it to China. A new president, Nestor Kirchner, a leftist Peronist and opponent of Menem within the Peronist Party, defeated the former president's bid for a comeback and took office in May 2003. Kirchner faced on one side pressures from the IMF (the debt remained at US$60 billion) to implement austerity and, on the other side, an aroused populace. He turned toward **populism** in an international context much more favorable to resistance to neoliberalism than his predecessors had experienced.

Kirchner reached out to other leftist presidents in Chile, Brazil, Venezuela, and Cuba and made clear his dissent from the **Washington Consensus**. He also won popular approval at home for meeting with the Madres de la Plaza, which resulted in Congress repealing Menem's amnesty for the military. The president moved decisively to replace the high command with officials less tainted by the Dirty War. Kirchner was also fortunate that Venezuela's president, Hugo Chávez, flush with petrodollars from a new oil boom, came to his aid with oil shipments and a willingness to buy up some of Argentina's debt, much to the dismay of the United States and the IMF.

One result of the unrest during the depths of the economic crisis was the formation of neighborhood and factory committees all over the country. *Piqueteros*, a movement of poor and unemployed workers, blockaded roads and supported popular actions to create an alternative economy. Neighborhood groups sought to pool resources to survive the economic collapse; the worker committees reopened factories abandoned by their owners and ran them themselves—what some leftists say is the essence of socialism, worker democracy.

With economic recovery, the hard work of the former employees was paying off, but the owners in many cases wanted their factories back (Trigona 2006). This posed a challenge to Kirchner and to the country's judicial system. Should property rights be respected and factories returned to the owners who had abandoned them, or did workers deserve to keep control over enterprises they had rescued through risk, sacrifice, and hard work? In the end, new bankruptcy laws opened the way for 600 factories to remain "recovered" and run by cooperatives of workers under self-management schemes. The recovery of the economy in the 2000s, fueled by exports to growing economies in Brazil and Asia, has slowed the growth of the alternative economy in Argentina, but *piqueteros* remain as a social movement that stands as an obstacle to the return of neoliberal economic policies.

Overall, Argentina has had less stable economic and political conditions than has Chile. At the same time, Argentina's transition to democracy closed off fewer options for the future than did Chile's transition. Both economic and human rights issues have remained contested. As it hastily retreated to the barracks in 1983, the Argentine officer corps had called for a *concertación*, or agreement, under which the major parties (Radicals and Peronists) would agree to continue basic economic and social policies and not prosecute officers. However, the military's prestige and power had been undermined by defeat in warfare.

In Argentina, it was not the constitution that restricted democracy in the subsequent period, but the realities of power, both economic and political. The Menem government was outspoken in support of U.S. foreign policy, committed to free trade and privatization, and willing to service the international debt at a high cost to Argentina's people, but Menem also seemed to have restored stability and economic growth. Saber rattling by *duros* reminded the public of the military's power, awakening fears of a relapse into the violent era between 1966 and 1982, but support from Washington and Menem's acceptance of the military's self-proclaimed amnesty allowed the Peronist to reduce the size of the armed forces. With the onset of a new economic crisis, however, human rights issues and popular protest burst out anew, well beyond anything that has happened in Chile. Argentine democracy is pacted, but less so than Chile's.

Argentina was the only state to prosecute any officers for political murders during the bureaucratic authoritarian era, but as in the other cases, the military retained enough power to prevent a full accounting for its crimes. The Madres de la Plaza have maintained their protests demanding justice. Argentina's most influential political party, the Peronists (Partido Justicialista), survived the repression, but it has become much more of a "catch-all" than a solely labor-based party. Kirchner, who died in 2010, was succeeded in 2008 by his wife, María Cristina Fernández de Kirchner, a career politician and senator herself. The Radical Civic Union remains the largest opposition party, but competition for power in Argentina takes place as much within the ranks of Peronism as between Peronism and the opposition. In other words, the post-military regime in Argentina shows a more fluid, changeable relationship between state and society, a mixed economic system that has partially but not completely rolled back neoliberalism, and a fluid party system less institutionalized than in the case of Chile.

For Review

How did the Malvinas (Falklands) War hasten transition in Argentina? The military failed to destroy Peronism, but Peronism after military rule was different when it returned, under Menem. How and why? How did the Peronist presidencies of Menem, on one hand, and the two Kirchners, on the other, differ from each other?

Brazil's Gradual Transition

As in Chile and Argentina, mass movements in Brazil lent political weight to the entreaties of politicians and moderates inside the regime for a transition back to civilian rule. The military junta had used torture, imprisonment, restrictions of civil liberties, and disappearances. The repression took its toll in lives and constituted state terrorism, but it was more selective than in Argentina and Chile, where victims numbered in the tens of thousands. Brazil experienced 240 killed and 150 disappeared in 21 years of military rule. One Brazilian political scientist suggests that today the country experiences higher rates of violence in the form of crime, police abuse in urban *favelas*, and violence used by ranchers and landholders against peasants (Avritzer 2002: 112–117). The unflattering thought is that Brazilians are more tolerant of political violence because the society itself is more violent.

Brazil

The Brazilian military did not pardon itself. In the late 1970s, human rights organizations, the Church, and exiled or disenfranchised politicians proposed reconciliation as part of a process to resume democratic political life. In 2004, a group called Torture Never Again (GTNM)—formed by relatives of 150 Brazilians killed, tortured, or disappeared—successfully pressured the new president, Lula, to open secret archives dating back to military rule. When a newspaper published photos of a prominent journalist who died after undergoing torture, the military insisted that its actions were "a legitimate response to the violence waged by those who refused to engage in dialogue and opted for radicalism and illegal actions" (Osava 2004). When the president and his party protested the army position, the military refused to retract the statement, issuing instead a weak statement of regret for the journalist's death. Human rights issues thus remain, as in Chile and Argentina, as a residue of the transition process, even if they are less potent in Brazil.

Although empowered to act without limits by an infamous decree known as Institutional Act #5, issued by a military government that replaced a more moderate junta in 1968, the Brazilian military closed Congress for only a few months and did not seek to prohibit all political activity. Its goal was to channel political participation within narrow limits. The military created two officially recognized political parties, one pro-regime and one opposition, in an attempt to engineer a two-party, centrist system to replace the populist system overthrown in the first coup of 1964. The military silenced left-wing politicians by exiling them or by taking away their citizenship rights. There were enough disappearances and murders to maintain an atmosphere of fear, but the political class of the old regime was never totally excluded from politics. As the economic situation worsened in the late 1970s, talk of a transition began. The pro-regime party (called ARENA) began to experience defections, and the official opposition party (the MDB, later PMDB) began to assert more independence. At the same time, the presidents (Generals Ernesto Geisel and João Figueiredo) responded to deteriorating economic conditions, growing social protest, and bolder opposition from the MDB with more international borrowing and with political reforms. Among the latter was an electoral law that permitted new parties to form, a tactical effort to split the opposition that produced unexpected results for the generals. Instead of dividing, the opposition broadened.

In the period of 1968–1974, the Brazilian government adopted many pro-business policies typical of the **bureaucratic authoritarian** states. It repressed unions and held down wages. It stressed exports rather than production for internal consumption. It used financial policies to stabilize the currency. The military welcomed foreign investments on favorable terms. The military also opened the Amazon to economic penetration, touching off a huge ecological disaster with the burning of thousands of square kilometers of Amazonian rainforest. But government was not fully committed to the neoliberal model. Rather than abandon all industries to their fate in a competitive world market, as did Pinochet and (after the transition) Menem, Brazil's generals and **technocrats** favored big infrastructure projects (dams, roads, etc.) and subsidies to heavy industries. The regime fostered partnerships between Brazilian industrialists and foreign corporations. Their hope was that industrialization would move past the import substitution stage and deepen—that is, factories would produce durable consumer goods (refrigerators, cars, etc.) and basic industrial goods (e.g., steel and chemicals). The military fostered a new arms industry that could both supply Brazil's own forces and find markets in other Third World countries. The result was a fourfold increase in exports and an astounding average growth rate of 10 percent per year, the "Brazilian miracle." But the "miracle" proved unsustainable. Rising prices for imported oil, corruption, limited domestic demand, and the mounting debt crisis took their toll after 1974.

The military had always planned to engineer a lengthy, guided transition back to civilian rule, but divisions arose in its ranks. The *blandos* favored a faster return; the *duros* thought that it was important to complete the remake of the economy and political system before returning to the barracks. However, the pace of change was ultimately not of the military's own making. Led by the vigorous new democratic labor movement, the Brazilian people would have much to say about the timetable. Here, it may be worth noting that the Roman Catholic Church, influenced greatly by the doctrines of Vatican II and the philosophy of a "**preferential option for the poor**," provided significant political cover for the opposition. This was true in other cases as well, most notably in Chile, where the Vicariate of Solidarity of the Archdiocese of Santiago was for many years the only voice capable of speaking up against human rights abuses. Brazil's bishops went even further, the majority endorsing **liberation theology**.

By destroying the old unions and breaking their **clientelist** ties to populist parties and leaders, the military had removed some considerable obstacles to new actors in politics. The new union movement started in the metallurgical sector in the belt of heavy industries in the suburbs of São Paolo in the 1970s. Its leader was Luiz Inácio Lula da Silva, "Lula." Lula would be elected president in October 2002. He was the leader of a new political party, the PT (Partido do Trabahaldores), launched in 1980.

Organizing itself openly but illegally and hoping to avoid the negative experience of political parties during the populist era, the PT emphasized political participation at the base. It developed a set of democratic norms that attracted new social movements forming among blacks, landless peasants, environmentalists, human rights organizations, neighborhood movements, women's organizations, the Catholic and religious left, and others (Keck 1992). This solidarity proved crucial when the military attempted to control the pace of the transition by arresting Lula in 1981. Massive demonstrations posed the question of whether the military was prepared—17 years after initially seizing power and with the economy uncertain—to direct firepower against the people. The *duros* had to recognize that taking this option would exhaust the regime's remaining prestige at home, invite international condemnation, and risk a more revolutionary upsurge. The military retreated and freed Lula.

Next, the Brazilian opposition sought to accelerate democratization under the banner of "*Diretas Já!*" ("Direct elections now!"). The gradual transition began to accelerate as a new party system was emerging. Lula and the workers' movement had created the PT; ARENA morphed into the pro-military, conservative Party of Social Democracy (PDS); the Brazilian Democratic Movement added "party" to its name to become the PMDB; and Leonel Brizola, a protégé of the populist president João Goulart (overthrown in 1964; see chapter 7) and governor of the state of Rio de Janeiro, founded the Party of Democratic Workers (PDT). The politicians, much to the dismay of the military, managed to cooperate with one another in demanding direct elections. Failing to achieve this concession, they united in 1984 around one slate for president and vice president and won the indirect elections. The winner, Tancredo Neves of the PMDB, underwent surgery just before his scheduled inauguration in March 1985 and died shortly afterward. His vice president, José Sarney, assumed the presidency.

The new president confronted a grave economic crisis, including spiraling inflation. In February 1986, he implemented a new economic program, the Cruzado Plan. The plan created a new currency (the *cruzado*), increased the wages of the poorest workers, and froze prices and other wages. Sarney appealed to Brazilian citizens to enforce price restraints by directly confronting retailers who tried to raise prices. Rising consumer demand gave the economy a temporary shot in the arm. The initial popularity of the president allowed his supporters to win the congressional election of 1986, which had added importance because the Congress was to write a new constitution (of 1988). In the long term, the Cruzado Plan did not work. Consumer demand increased, but productivity did not. The economy lapsed into crisis in the late 1980s. Sarney limped to the completion of his term. The new direct elections of 1990 were won by a governor, Fernando Collor de Mello, completing the formal transition from military to elected civilian regime.

Collor defeated Lula, who had entered the election as the favorite to win. The new constitution (still in effect today) provided for a runoff election if no candidate achieved a majority in the first round. Lula emerged from round one with the most votes but not enough to win outright. Facing the prospect of victory by the socialist-oriented PT, the Brazilian oligarchy put aside its internal divisions to unite behind the candidacy of Collor de

Mello. Especially important was the Brazilian media, which constantly warned of chaos and the dangers of a relapse into instability if Lula were elected.

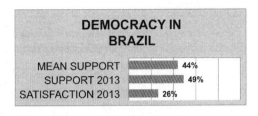

Lula's formal education was limited, and his presence on TV was much less impressive than Collor's. The more professional, polished politician impressed the public on TV. The business community and big landowners, fearing a union leader as president, lavishly financed the Collor campaign, and the country's media barons made sure that coverage was heavily slanted toward their candidate. Lula was also swimming against an international tide running against leftist governments. The Berlin Wall was falling, and the United States was trumpeting the Washington Consensus, which painted **pluralist** democracy and a free-market economy as the only alternatives to the failed experiment with communism.

Collor proved corrupt even by Latin American standards, and Brazil's Congress impeached him in 1992. In doing so, the Brazilian legislature showed an unprecedented degree of institutional power in the region. Collor's vice president, Itamar Franco, succeeded him and put Brazil's economic policies in the hands of the brilliant political sociologist Fernando Henrique Cardoso. Cardoso, author of an influential neo-Marxist analysis of **dependency theory**, was appointed minister of finance and implemented the *Real* Plan, named after the country's new currency. Leftist critics assailed Cardoso for implementing a conservative monetary plan that reduced inflation but did little to compensate workers for two decades of falling real wages. Nor did Cardoso take direct aim at redistributing income and land, a serious problem in Brazil. However, the economy rebounded; Cardoso got much of the credit.

Cardoso and Lula faced off in the 1994 elections. Lula again was the early favorite, but again he lost, as the opposition, media, and international forces coalesced to prevent the "radical" PT candidate from taking office. Brazil's economy continued to grow, and Cardoso, at the peak of his popularity in 1997, resorted to a frequent political tactic in Latin America. He amended the constitution to make himself eligible for another term; he defeated Lula again. However, his second term was less successful as economic stagnation returned after an international financial crisis, which had originated in far-off Thailand in 1998 and had thrown the world economy into a recession. Economic conditions worsened in Brazil. The center and right had no respected figure of the caliber of Cardoso to contest Lula, who finally won the presidency in 2002.

In Lula's eight years in office, it was clear that even a president elected directly out of the ranks of Brazil's working class was not going to abruptly change the direction of Brazil's gradual transition. Lula proved much less radical than Washington and the business community had feared. Many high PT officials were enveloped in corruption scandals, some of which involved bribes to members of other parties whose support was needed to ensure control of the Congress. In short, Brazil's transition had opened the possibility of the establishment of a more radical democracy than normally associated with pluralism, but the prospects of an innovative democratic experiment faded as the PT failed to purge itself of the corrupt practices of the past. According to Latinobarómetro (2013), satisfaction with democracy in Brazil is among the lowest in Latin America.

Luiz Inácio Lula da Silva ("Lula"), a union leader with only a second-grade education, led the struggle to end military rule in Brazil and eventually, in 2002, was elected president of his country. (In this photo, he is the man being carried.)

Still, one cannot say that the country simply returned to politics as usual before the military regime. Lula expanded education and anti-hunger policies, which led many of his opponents to accuse him of communism or (heaven forbid!) vote buying. Lula's origins were an indication of change, given his racial and class origins. More indication of change can be found in the example of Benedita da Silva (no relation to Lula), who broke down barriers linked to class, race, and gender. Da Silva emerged out of the *favelas* of Rio de Janeiro through her involvement in an evangelical Protestant movement (linked to **liberation theology**) and several local struggles to improve living conditions. Besides her leadership on issues of concern to women, da Silva became an important leader of the movement to recognize and redress racial discrimination, a fact of life long denied in Brazilian culture. She was elected as a PT candidate to the Brazilian Senate in 1994 and headed the reelection campaign of President Luiz Inácio Lula da Silva in 2006.

In 2010, Lula was succeeded in the presidency by another PT leader, Dilma Rousseff, a former guerrilla who had been captured and tortured between 1970 and 1972. After the 2013 election in Chile, all three of the countries considered in this chapter had women as presidents.

A Uruguayan woman carries a photo of a disappeared person at a 2010 protest against amnesty for human rights abuses during the military regime.

For Review

In what way was Brazil's transition gradual compared with the other two we have examined? The only really new party to come out of the transition in these three cases was the PT. What was its original base? What did it stand for? Who is Lula, and how and why has his presidency surprised many people?

Forbidden to Forget

Although the transitions to democracy occurred 20 to 30 years ago, the experience of military government remains as a specter hanging over politics. In Argentina and Uruguay, the issues of human rights remain especially acute. In Chile, in addition to human rights issues, there remain many critics who say that the country's enviable

DEMOCRACY IN URUGUAY

MEAN SUPPORT	78%
SUPPORT 2013	71%
SATISFACTION 2013	82%

record of economic growth is compromised by inequalities that can be attributed to deals made to secure the transition to democracy. Still, one issue does seem settled. As Rubén Blades, the salsa star, put it in one of his songs, "*Prohibido olvidar*"—"It is forbidden to forget."

PUNTO DE VISTA: HUMAN RIGHTS AND AMNESTY

The case of Uruguay shows how difficult it has been for Latin Americans to deal with the issue of accountability for human rights violations committed during the era of military rule. Like Brazil, Chile, and Argentina, Uruguay, a country known for having one of Latin America's most developed welfare systems and strongest middle classes, fell under bureaucratic authoritarian rule between 1973 and 1985. The populist crisis began in 1968, when an elected conservative government signed an agreement with the IMF that rolled back many economic rights won in prior decades by unions. Protests followed, and the government ratcheted up the use of military force to keep order. This spurred an urban guerrilla movement, known as the Tupamaros, comparable to the Montoneros in Argentina.

In early 1973, the military proclaimed that the Tupamaros had been wiped out, but in the face of a severe economic recession, the junta nonetheless closed Congress and undertook to reengineer the economy and political system. Half a million books were burned; universities and cultural institutions were purged of their intellectuals; one in every 50 citizens was detained; nearly one-fifth of the population was forced into exile. The country became infamous for ingenuous new types of torture, much of it directed toward women and children in front of men,

a blatant attempt to demonstrate total power through humiliation.

Economic failure and popular anger at human rights abuses in the 1980s led to negotiations between the military and the Colorados, the largest political party. However, the transition and exit was initiated by the generals and negotiated "with political elites in a secretive, top-down process, which enabled them [the generals] . . . to maintain a political role after the elections" (Mallinder 2009: 2). The generals, who had always governed behind a civilian facade, permitted elections won by the Colorados in 1986.

One of the first acts of the new government was to proclaim an amnesty for all military personnel. Before the vote, then President Julio Maria Sanguinetti explained why he favored amnesty and was refusing to prosecute gross violators of human rights:

> First . . . there wasn't enough evidence [to prosecute cases]. It was going to disturb society, and there would be a lot of confrontation. Second . . . it was a question of moral equivalency . . . A lot of those involved in left-wing groups had never been to jail at all. To begin the arithmetic of judging levels of responsibility, we would have been faced with complications of such magnitude that we thought it best to amnesty everybody—the left and the military. Third . . . it was necessary to have a climate of stability to consolidate democracy . . . Finally, for historical reasons. Traditionally after all great conflicts in a country there is an amnesty.
>
> (quoted in Mallinder 2009: 41–42)

Outraged citizens responded with a massive petition drive that placed the question of repeal of the amnesty on the ballot for a referendum. More than 600,000 citizens signed the petition, more than one-fourth of all voters. However, in April 1989, the electorate voted by a 58 percent majority to uphold the amnesty. Human rights advocates were demoralized, but some continued to fight for accountability. They took their battle to the Inter-American Commission on Human Rights, which in 1994 said that the military's amnesty law was incompatible with the country's treaty obligations and added that it

> notes with deep concern that the adoption of this law effectively excludes in a number of cases the possibility of investigation into past human rights abuses and thereby prevents the State party from discharging its responsibility to provide effective remedies to the victims of those abuses. Moreover, the Committee is concerned that, in adopting this law, the State party has contributed to an atmosphere of impunity which may undermine the democratic order and give rise to further grave human rights violations.
>
> (quoted in Mallinder 2009: 60)

A moderate leftist president, Tabaré Vázquez, elected in 2005, reopened a number of cases, with focus on the military's transporting of prisoners to Argentina, where the prisoners were killed or disappeared. Popular pressure resulted in the second referendum in 2009. Once again, the vote went against repeal of amnesty, but the issue was not closed. In July 2011 a presidential decree permitted prosecutions of the military for certain types of crimes, and in October 2011, the Uruguayan Congress, pressured to comply with its treaty obligations, finally voted to repeal the law—by only one vote (16 to 15) in the Senate. Then in February 2013, the country's Supreme Court threw out two key provisions of the 2011 decree permitting prosecutions, effectively nullifying it.

These arguments about amnesty and prosecution for perpetrators of gross human rights violations are found in many countries. In sum, those who oppose reopening the cases against the military argue that it risks renewing conflicts and weakening democracy. To this we can add the argument, in the case of Uruguay, that a popular vote was taken on the question. On the other side are the moral arguments of victims and their supporters and the concern that impunity for past crimes will someday lead to new ones.

Point/Counterpoint

Should Uruguay's government continue attempts to prosecute former government and former military officials for the human rights atrocities committed?

a. If you say yes, how do you respond to the arguments that it is wrong to go back on the amnesty, especially because it was submitted to a plebiscite, and that the country needs to move on?

b. If you say no, what do you say to the hundreds of thousands of relatives of the victims? What about the argument that failure to hold former officials responsible makes it more likely that the past will be repeated?

For more information

See Francisa Lessa and Leigh Payne, *Amnesty in the Age of Human Rights* (Cambridge University Press, 2012). Long before WikiLeaks, the National Security Archive, a private repository at George Washington University, was legally collecting declassified U.S. documents, including candid descriptions of the military regime's actions in Uruguay. It is online at www2.gwu.edu/~nsarchiv. *State of Siege* (1972) shows events leading to military rule.

Discussion Questions

1. Do you think that the Chilean Concertación made the right choice in not going back on its agreement not to change Pinochet's constitution?
2. What do you think most influenced the transition from dictatorship in the Southern Cone and Brazil? Which do you regard as more important in inducing change—the international context or domestic politics? Would you weight domestic versus international factors differently for each case, or the same?
3. The new rules of the game that followed transitions from military rule in the four countries considered in this chapter were negotiated among elites in the context of popular pressure in the streets. Did the elites on the opposition side give away too much to achieve the transition?
4. Can it be coincidence that three countries analyzed here have seen women advance to the presidency since the transitions? If not coincidental, what might account for their success?

Resources for Further Study

Reading: The sequel to *The Breakdown of Democratic Regimes* was *Transitions from Authoritarian Rule*, four volumes edited by Guillermo O'Donnell and Laurence Whitehead (Baltimore: Johns Hopkins Press, 1986). Manuel Puig, *Kiss of the Spider Woman* (New York: Vintage, reissued in 1991), deliberately tangles the themes of political and sexual repression. It was adapted to film in 1985.

Video and Film: Search for Rubén Blades and "Prohibido olvidar" (prohibited to forget) on YouTube to find the Panamanian's salsa warning. *La Historia Oficial* (1985) tells the story of a schoolteacher who must come to grips with her story and her country's story when she suspects her adopted children may have been birthed by a victim of the Dirty War. *Johnny 100 Pesos* (1994) is set in Chile right after the transition (1994) and poses a test for the new democracy about how much violence it should use in a hostage situation. *No* (2012) tells the story of a young advertising executive who donates his skills to design TV ads for the winning 1989 campaign to force Pinochet to leave the presidency. *Capital Sins* (1991), in the *Americas* series, looks at the "Brazilian miracle" and the transition to democracy. *Operation Condor* (2003) details U.S. covert support for state terrorism in the three countries examined in this chapter.

On the Internet: *Inside Pinochet's Prisons* is a Euro TV film with real footage and interviews from within the prisons that gives an interesting look at the cruelty of the government and at the different political views of Chile's people. It can be found at www.journeyman.tv/8946/documentaries/inside-pinochets-prisons.html. The comparative democratization section of the American Political Science Association, which is associated with the U.S. government's National Endowment for Democracy, can be found at www.ned.org/apsa-cd/home.html.

9 Transitions from Party-Dominant Regimes: Mexico and Venezuela

Focus Questions

▶ Why did these two countries avoid the wave of military rule that engulfed so much of Latin America after the populist period?

▶ What was the relationship between the political parties and social forces in these two countries? What was different, and what was the same in the two cases?

▶ What was the nature of the political pact that established the Mexican political system after the revolution? In what way did the 2000 election signal significant change in the regime created by the pact?

▶ What was the nature of the political pact that established the Venezuelan political system in the transition from military dictatorship to polyarchy in 1958? In what way did the election of Hugo Chávez in 1998 signal significant change in the regime created by the pact?

▶ What conclusions should we draw about "regime change" from consideration of the six cases examined in this chapter and the previous one?

THE TRANSITIONS EXAMINED in chapters 7 and 8 were drawn from the Southern Cone (Argentina, Chile, and Uruguay) and Brazil. In these four cases, the trajectory of political change took these countries from the breakdown of populism and import substitution through an era of bureaucratic authoritarianism, and finally through a transition back to an elected civilian government—a "transition to democracy," pluralists would say. Mexico and Venezuela both avoided military rule, though each also experienced tensions and problems toward the end of the populist era. Both countries did, however, experience a significant change of regime, mainly in regard to the political party system and relationship between the state and the market.

The Venezuelan case puts to the test the question of whether elite pacts, the kind that result from the transition negotiation game we examined in chapter 8, lay the basis for stable democracy. In 1958, after a 10-year dictatorship, Venezuela's non-Communist political leaders negotiated among themselves a power-sharing agreement that became known as the Pact of Punto Fijo (named for the house in Caracas where it was negotiated). The two-party system seemed extraordinarily stable and came to be regarded by many political scientists as the key to understanding stability in Venezuela (e.g., Levine 1978). However, the party system came crashing down in the early years of the presidency of President Hugo Chávez Frías, a former army colonel cashiered for attempting a coup in 1992. Contributing to the illusion of stability was the seemingly inexhaustible resources at the disposal of the Venezuelan state, derived from exports of oil, the bounty of the country's subsoil.

The pact underlying Mexican stability went back further in history, traceable first to the decision in 1928 by Mexican leaders of its great social revolution of 1910 to put aside their violent conflicts with one another. They did this by creating a single party, eventually known as the Institutional Revolutionary Party (PRI). Second, in the 1930s, led by their great president, Lázaro Cárdenas, the party formally incorporated the middle class, the working class, and much of the peasantry into its organizational structure, delivering significant benefits to members of unions, peasant associations, and professional groups from these sectors. To some, the seven-decade rule by the PRI was a "perfect dictatorship"—what today we might call a "**hybrid**" or "**illiberal**" regime. To other political scientists, the regime was, despite significant defects, a form of democracy appropriate to Mexico's own history (Middlebrook 1986).

As in Brazil and the Southern Cone, **import substitution industrialization** (ISI) was the economic engine for this combination of **populism** and **corporatism**. The exhaustion of ISI contributed, as in those cases, to the erosion of the political regime created by the pact. However, the ultimate outcome was not outright military rule but a shift under the PRI to a more **neoliberal** economic model, consolidated by joining the United States and Canada in the North American Free Trade Agreement (NAFTA) of 1994 and, in related fashion, opening the political system to competitive party politics—in other words, moving toward **polyarchy**. The victory of Vicente Fox, a former Coca-Cola executive and candidate of the National Action Party (PAN), in the 2000 presidential election ended the 72-year monopoly of the PRI over national politics. (See photos below.)

Venezuela and Mexico have in common that between 1968 and 1989, citizens increasingly saw the political party systems as unrepresentative and unresponsive to groups and

Cuauhtémoc Cárdenas (left) campaigns for the Mexican presidency in 1988; Vicente Fox (right) does the same with more success in 2000. Which of the two played the important role in ending the PRI monopoly on national power?

movements demanding change. In both cases, Mexico in 1968 and Venezuela in 1989, the military was called out to quell protest and unrest and acted with an excess of force and loss of life that contributed ultimately to a transition to a new regime. This transition included popular pressures to make democracy more genuine through political decentralization, reform of political parties, and participation of social movements in public life. Large segments of the ruling elite agreed to restructure the economy, to implement policies typical of **neoliberalism**. These reforms tended to impose the greatest sacrifice on the poor, and in both countries, the traditional parties paid a heavy economic price for adopting them. However, the new regimes were quite different from one another. In Mexico, conservative candidates were declared winners (though with considerable and plausible complaints of fraud) of competitive multiparty elections in 2000 and 2006; in 2012, the PRI candidate won, but two other candidates were competitive. In Venezuela, Hugo Chávez proclaimed himself dedicated to making a "Bolivarian revolution," but whether a new regime had been consolidated was open to doubt as 2013 opened with Chávez dying from cancer and with his chosen successor, Nicolás Maduro, surviving a special election (in April) by a bare majority—less than 2 percent of the voters.

Regime change can be considered something more than a simple change of government, but less than a full-scale revolution. It involves a change in the relationship between state and society—for example, a significant shift away from or toward a market-directed economy, but not a total transformation of economic relations. It also usually involves significant changes in the rules of the political game, changes that shift the social origins of the political elite (e.g., from the military to civilians or from the upper class to the middle class) without, however, radically redistributing wealth or totally destroying the influence of those who held power before. The paths followed by these two countries in the end represent two very different philosophies about the best way to move into the world economy in the twenty-first century. One of them, Mexico, has sought integration with the U.S. economy through the free-trade model established by NAFTA; the other rejected this model and has used its petrodollars in the hemisphere to promote an alternative socialist form of economic integration through the Bolivarian Alliance for the Americas (ALBA). We look more closely at these alternatives in chapters 15 and 16 and conclude that neither is likely to be fully embraced in the rest of Latin America. Understanding why requires understanding the virtues and shortcomings of the regimes now in power in the two countries.

The Mexican Revolution

The 70-year dominance of PRI arose directly out of the most radical type of transition—revolution (which we examine in chapter 10). The great Mexican Revolution of 1910 put an end to a 40-year dictatorship but gave birth to a 20-year period of violence, including assassinations that claimed the lives of most of its leaders. It was a pact among the remaining leaders that formally gave rise to a political party that enabled them to compete for power within a framework of political rules. The new regime was consolidated after Latin

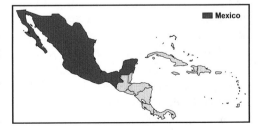

America's most revered leader, Lázaro Cárdenas, implemented reforms that delivered on at least some of the key social demands of the revolution (land reform, labor rights, educational opportunities, etc.). Cárdenas also put Mexico on the path of import substitution. Like the countries examined in chapter 8, Mexico experienced exhaustion of ISI and a populist crisis of its own, leading first to a change in the state's relationship to the society and economy and later to a change in the political rules of the power game.

Origins: Modernization for the Few

The Mexican Revolution began with a cry for political rights, but the subsequent uprising went far beyond this limited objective. In the 1800s, Mexico suffered invasion and defeat by both the United States and France and the loss (to the United States) of almost half its national territory—clear indications of the weakness of its central state. Behind this weakness lay fractious elites and warring *caudillos* who were unable to organize a defense of the country. Mexico was hardly unusual in this regard, but this liability proved especially disastrous because of its proximity to the United States. "Poor Mexico, so far from God and so close to the United States," said Porfirio Díaz, the strongman who finally put an end to the political chaos. However, his policies also sowed the seeds of revolution.

General Díaz, a liberal caudillo and hero of the war to expel French troops, presided over decades of significant economic growth in Mexico after 1876, even as he ruled behind a facade of liberal constitutional government. Díaz's successful formula for economic growth involved opening the country to foreign investment, while allowing conditions for the workers and rural masses, especially Indians, to deteriorate. In designing policies, Díaz relied on a group of lawyers, businessmen, landowners, bankers, and intellectuals called *científicos*, who besides lending their expertise accumulated great fortunes during the dictatorship. The concentration of landownership, as more of the country's natural resources were opened to foreign investment and export production, was an especially incendiary situation, and demand for land by impoverished peasants was the crucial component of the discontent.

In 1910, Francisco Madero, a liberal landowner who had rallied popular support for a transition to genuine constitutional government, was jailed by Díaz and then expelled from the country. From exile, Madero called for Mexican villages to revolt against the old caudillo's attempt to perpetrate another electoral fraud and extend his rule. Madero did not know he would ignite a much broader social conflict that would not settle down again until after 1928, when Plutarco Calles, Cárdenas, and others created a political party, eventually to be called the PRI (Partido Revolucionario Institucional), to resolve conflicts among revolutionary forces.

In Mexico, after years of growth under Díaz, fewer than 200 families owned one-quarter of the land, and much of the best land (perhaps one-fifth of all acres) was foreign-owned. Some rural estates were larger than 10 million acres, keeping land beyond the reach of Mexico's rural poor, many of whom were Indians whose common lands had been lost to big landowners during the liberal era. The small but growing middle class faced limited opportunities to rise in a social system dominated by Creoles. Rigged elections ensured that only reliable allies of Díaz could win political office. To some degree, these frustrations were kept in check by economic growth, but this slowed in the final decade of the Porfiriato. Rural peons earned much less than a dollar a day. Meanwhile, prices for basic goods, such as corn and chili peppers, doubled; the price of beans rose six times. Mestizo workers in the newly built railroads, mines, ports, and (few) factories were poorly paid and blocked from organizing unions.

Under pressure, Díaz first announced he would not run for an eighth term as president, but then he changed his mind and won reelection by fraud in 1910, prompting Madero to call for "effective suffrage and no reelection"—that is, political democracy (Burns and Charlip 2002: 200–211). Popular resistance worked. Díaz fled to Paris but warned Madero that he would now have to "ride the tiger." Madero indeed found that Mexico's people wanted more than fair elections and freedom of speech. Like many leaders of a revolution, he learned that the hardest part of revolution is not necessarily overthrowing the old regime.

All revolutions are complex, but it is especially difficult to tell the story of the Mexican Revolution because there was no one central leader, movement, or party responsible for leading the insurrection. A generation of regional leaders, some little more than ambitious caudillos, others remarkable idealists with charismatic appeal, raised armies by recruiting peasants displaced from land that big owners had seized to produce crops and beef for export—not so different from the forces that unleashed revolution in Central America 60 years later (see chapter 10). In the north of Mexico, General Pancho Villa raised an army based on peasants who worked their own small plots of land. With not-well-documented property rights, they were threatened by big new mines and ranches—some owned by Americans such as William Randolph Hearst (the newspaper tycoon)—producing for the growing U.S. market. In the southern state of Morelos, Emiliano Zapata rallied peasants squeezed off land being converted into large sugar plantations (see Womack 1968: 3–9). Zapata was perhaps most emblematic of the democratic and social justice goals of a revolution that would, unfortunately, slide later into more chaotic and internecine violence.

Madero's cry for fair elections certainly lent a democratic quality to the struggle, but the call for elections was quickly overtaken by social convulsions around land and labor rights. For a while, after 1914, the most radical leaders, Zapata and Villa, seemed to have the upper hand, bringing their forces together in Mexico City in December 1914. However, the "bandit" from the ranching north, with its highly individualistic small landholders, and the communal peasant leader of the agricultural south failed to unite, leaving both vulnerable to their common enemies. Still, their defeat did not mean the reversal of the revolution. Carranza and Obregón carried out important land and labor reforms, in part to undercut support for Zapata and Villa.

As Burns and Charlip (2002: 203–204) put it, "the Revolution swept all before it. The destruction was as total as the chaos. It cost more than a million lives. It ruined much of the agrarian, ranching and mining economy. No major bank or newspaper that predated the Revolution survived."

In the pitched battles of the revolution, Mexico's masses were uprooted from village life to fight with and against other Mexicans from all over the country. In the 1920s, many of these illiterate fighters were—just like the illiterate commoners of the Middle Ages in Europe— "shown" what to believe in the great murals and paintings promoted by a new set of rulers. The revolutionary message was one of social justice wrapped in the mantle of nationalism.

Zapata took up arms reluctantly, after extended and widespread consultation with villagers throughout Morelos. His land reform program, the Plan de Ayala of 1911, was proclaimed in support of Madero's call to arms, but Madero was more interested in political reform than redistribution of the wealth. "*Tierra, justicia y ley*" (land, justice, and law) was the rallying cry of the plan, which linked social justice to political change. Madero remains today a historical hero for his courage in challenging Díaz in Mexico, but he showed little interest in or understanding of peasant demands. Zapata remains alive in spirit, in particular in the poor southern state of Chiapas, where a "Zapatista" rebellion made in his name broke out in 1994.

The Revolutionary Civil War

Madero was deposed in February 1913 (and assassinated four days later) by an opportunistic ally of Díaz, General Victoriano Huerta. The U.S. ambassador supported the conspiracy, thereby stoking the flames of Mexican nationalism. Huerta raised an army of Federales to fight the insurgents organized in armies raised by Zapata, Villa, and other revolutionary generals. Among the latter, Calles, Venustiano Carranza, Cárdenas, and Álvaro Obregón all eventually became presidents of Mexico. After defeating and killing Huerta in 1914, the revolutionary armies fell into battling one another. The United States settled on Venustiano Carranza as the most acceptable alternative among the rebels and helped to arm and to finance his fight against Zapata and Villa. Carranza offered the best deal to American oil companies, who hoped to get leases and displace the British as Mexico's main producer of the newly valuable resource. Villa was furious and in 1916 staged a retaliatory raid on Columbus, New Mexico, earning a reputation in the United States not unlike that of Osama bin Laden after the attacks of September 11, 2001. President Woodrow Wilson sent General John J. ("Blackjack") Pershing with an expeditionary force to punish Villa, but in rugged northern Mexico, the army had little success. Villa assumed legendary status in his homeland.

In 1917, various leaders and their followers came together at the town of Aguascalientes and framed a new constitution that embodied Madero's initial demands for democracy but added land reform, labor rights, **secularism** (stripping the Church of its privileges), and sovereign control over natural resources as founding principles of a new Mexico. However, it would be another two decades before the new political order was firmly established. Only when President Cárdenas (1934–1940) delivered on some of these promises did Mexicans successfully reconstitute the state on the foundations of the constitution of 1917.

Emiliano Zapata and Pancho Villa were allies, but they fought separately, and they failed to promote a common national agenda. Zapata was ambushed and killed in 1919, on the orders of Carranza. Although the United States provided money and arms to Carranza, the general could not restore order. Some of the staunchest resistance came from Obregón. Villa was bought off and eventually assassinated. Carranza emerged victorious, but he too was assassinated, and in 1920 General Obregón took power. Obregón was sympathetic to demands for labor and agrarian reform. He also patronized the generation of great Mexican muralists, including Diego Rivera, whose art glorified a radical new vision of what it meant to be Mexican, drawing upon the country's indigenous past, glorifying *mestizaje*, and linking this new identity to demands for social justice. Rivera and the Mexican cultural giants were influenced by the Russian Revolution of 1917 and other currents of radical thought.

The Mexican Revolution appeared to be settling down; indeed, its most violent episodes were now in the past. But the shape of the new political regime remained unclear. Obregón survived his term and passed the presidency to one of his cabinet ministers, Plutarco Calles. In 1928 Obregón was elected to a new term, but then he was cut down by an assassin's bullet.

Fear of death can be a motivator. Mexico's fractious revolutionary generals, led by Calles, now settled on a pact to compete for power within the structure of a new political party, later called the Institutional Revolutionary Party—the PRI.

The *criollos* were replaced by a new elite that exalted *mestizaje*, in part by promoting the indigenous past through the fabulous images of Diego Rivera and the other muralists. These imposing murals were painted in chapels, convents, and churches that had been seized from the Catholic hierarchy. In countless kitchens, national identity was being created in a popular way. Women began to replace European cuisines with tamales and other foods that you have probably tried in Mexican restaurants but that were denigrated in prerevolutionary Mexico because of their association with Indian culture (Pilcher 1998).

Revolutionaries often find that building a new state out of the ashes of the old is more difficult than overthrowing the old order. One vexing problem is often the place of organized religion in the new order. The Mexican Church had inherited many political privileges from the colonial past. It controlled much of the education system, resisted changes in women's status, and was itself a major property owner. The leaders of revolutions mistrusted the Church hierarchy, and they were influenced by social philosophies that saw religion as a drag on progress. At the grass roots, many of the clergy were not so conservative, especially priests and nuns working with the poor, but the new constitution reflected the leaders' resentment of the Church's conservative social philosophy and its accumulated wealth.

Tensions between Catholicism and the revolution burst open in the Cristero Revolt of 1926–1929. In Mexico's central heartland, conservative Catholics were preaching a kind of mystical religious ideology that attracted peasants, whose lives had been disrupted by political violence and wild swings of the economy. Their way of life had been turned upside down, but the revolution had delivered neither land nor stability. The Mexican president, Calles (1924–1928), who continued to hold power behind the scenes until 1934, moved to limit the number of Catholic priests and took other measures to enforce anticlerical provisions in the 1917 constitution. As priests fled the countryside, baptisms, masses, local feast days of saints, and a variety of other customs and practices central to rural life were suddenly absent. And we should not reduce this conflict to religious issues. The Vatican had finally begun to respond to socialist and communist appeals to the working class and poor with doctrines calling for social justice. This was unwelcome competition and suspicious to the revolutionaries. All these forces culminated in a three-year, bloody revolt in Jalisco and several other states, with terrorism used as a tactic on both sides. As so often happens with revolutionary regimes, the quest to hold onto power was becoming a higher priority than pursuing social justice.

From Revolution to ISI and Populism

Madero had called for political democracy in the form of competitive, fair elections. Out of revolution came a system in which no one strongman could dominate as Díaz had done; instead, a single political party amassed power to nearly monopolize Mexican politics for the rest of the twentieth century. Many peasants got access to land in the form of the *ejidos* (municipally owned lands). But after 1940, the program was virtually halted (briefly revived in the 1970s), and support for those peasants who got land (credits, irrigation, roads, etc.) was reduced. Peasant organizations and unions that formed between 1910 and 1940 came to be dominated by the party, whose very name, the PRI or Institutional Revolutionary Party, seems a contradiction in terms.

Can a revolution be "institutionalized"? Although Calles engineered the pact that put an end to the violence, it was Lázaro Cárdenas who, beginning with the election of 1934, rooted the new political system in the populace. Although he had already virtually won the election, Cárdenas used the campaign to build national support for his own administration. When Calles challenged the president after 1934, the old caudillo was packed off into exile in the United States. Cárdenas then implemented a series of policies that became associated in the popular mind with the social questions raised by the Mexican Revolution. Though these promises were never fully achieved, millions of Mexican peasants benefited from land reform, millions of workers benefited from unions, millions of children benefited from new schools and educational reform, and millions of Mexicans found new opportunities in working-class and professional jobs as the economy grew under **ISI**. Also, Cárdenas appealed to a growing sense of national identity, one that had been consciously fostered by state patronage of intellectuals and artists such as Rivera.

The land reform in particular was of enormous symbolic—not just economic—importance. Most of the land in the central and southern parts of the country was distributed in the form of municipally owned, communal parcels, called *ejidos*, a form of property linked to the indigenous past, glorified by the muralists. Enshrined in the constitution, *ejidos* could not be bought and sold. Fifty years later, to create appropriate conditions to implement NAFTA—which allows foreign investment in agriculture and favors the development of large, export-oriented farms relying on high-tech cultivation—the government of President Salinas (1988–1994) amended the constitution to eliminate protection of *ejidos*.

Cárdenas rallied Mexican nationalism through his confrontation with U.S. oil companies. Land and control of natural resources had been a major rallying cry of the revolution. In 1938, Cárdenas nationalized foreign oil companies, a move aided by the refusal of the companies to obey Mexico's labor laws. The U.S. administration of President Franklin Delano Roosevelt (1932–1945) refused to help the companies survive a crisis of their own making. Cárdenas even capitalized on compensation to the companies. He mobilized Mexicans, including children who broke open their piggy banks, to make contributions toward the fund used to pay for nationalization. After 1938, the Mexican state oil company (PEMEX) was not merely another state-owned industry; it enjoyed mythological status as a symbol of national independence (Levy and Székely 1983: 213–242). This is one reason that U.S. negotiators failed to get Mexico to agree under NAFTA to privatization of PEMEX or to allow direct exploitation of Mexican oil by U.S. companies (Orme 1996: 139–145).

Cárdenas was not attempting to create a socialist or communist state in Mexico. His land reform benefited 800,000 families but did not reach all Mexicans in need of land. The *ejidos* were communal organizations, but they had to operate as enterprises in the marketplace. PEMEX was state-owned, and its profits were a major source of patronage for the PRI. Cheap energy subsidized both industry and consumers, encouraging import substitution.

More radical sectors of the PRI wanted to build further on the reforms of Cárdenas, but the president slowed the momentum of revolution by agreeing to nominate Manuel Ávila Camacho, a moderate conservative, to succeed him. Camacho won, but the election of 1940 was rife with fraud. In the same election, a pro-Church party, the National Action Party (PAN), emerged. The PAN drew strength in traditionally Catholic regions and also had a regional base in the north, where the spirit of individualism was strong among small farmers and ranchers. Over time, the PAN would become less religious and more business-oriented; it was its candidate, Vicente Fox, who scored the breakthrough against the PRI in the 2000 election (Shirk 2005).

Cárdenas, by stepping aside in 1940, reinforced the most fundamental rule of the game in Mexican politics, a product of the pact engineered by Calles and not found in the country's constitution. From 1928, every sixth year (the length of the presidential term), the outgoing president of the country selected his successor from fellow party officials. Technically, he was only choosing the candidate of the PRI, but no other party could seriously compete in the general election. By tradition, the president then stepped aside, allowing the new leader of the country a free hand to rule without interference. Mexicans called this process the *dedazo* ("fingering"; Langston 2006).

The revolution made Mexican politics distinct from the rest of Latin America in several respects. (For a general history, see Meyer and Beezley 2000; also Handelman 1997: 1–46.) Mexico under the PRI did not suffer a military coup or full military rule, as did almost every other country in the region at some time in the twentieth century. Mexico's foreign policy, although not hostile toward the United States, has been marked (until recently, anyway) by insistence on its independence. For example, Mexico maintained diplomatic relationships with Cuba after the communist revolution of 1959 and offered a degree of sympathy and refuge for revolutionary movements in Central America in the 1980s. *Mestizaje* may not have truly addressed the plight of the indigenous population, but it did legitimate indigenous culture and make it difficult to ignore entirely demands from that sector.

Mexico's politics in the PRI era was highly **corporatist**, and in this respect typical of the relationship between parties and social groups in Latin America. The PRI exercised control over unions, professional organizations, peasant groups, and so on through an immense patronage network, symbiotically linked to the import substitution strategy. From 1940 to 1970, Mexican economic growth averaged 6 percent per year. The PRI incorporated peasants politically, but this does not mean that its development strategy adequately addressed the need for rural sector development.

Some (e.g., Padgett 1966) regarded Mexico's political system as a good example of an alternative Third World path to modernization and democracy. Although Mexico lacked a competitive party system, significant debate and conflict over policy and allocation of resources occurred within the ranks of the PRI itself. However, Mario Vargas Llosa, the Peruvian novelist-turned-politician, called it the "perfect dictatorship" in a 1990 debate with Octavio Paz, a Mexican intellectual, and the phrase stuck.

A U.S. Library of Congress study (Merrill and Miró 1996) neatly describes the major features of the system:

> The PRI has been widely described as a coalition of networks of aspiring politicians seeking not only positions of power and prestige but also the concomitant opportunity for personal enrichment. At the highest levels of the political system, the major vehicles for corruption have been illegal landholdings and the manipulation of public-sector enterprises. In the lower reaches of the party and governmental hierarchies, the preferred methods of corruption have been bribery, charging the public for legally free public services, charging members of unions for positions, nepotism, and outright theft of public money. This corruption, although condemned by Mexican and foreign observers alike, historically served an important function in the political

system by providing a means of upward mobility within the system and ensuring that those who were forced to retire from politics by the principle of no reelection would have little incentive to seek alternatives outside the PRI structure.

The government dispensed subsidies, jobs, land, welfare, and myriad other benefits. Its structures of clientelism reached deeply into almost every corner of Mexican society, even the most remote villages. Dissenters had a hard time mobilizing opposition against a party that enjoyed stature as a symbol of revolutionary nationalism and used the resources of the state to co-opt challengers. The PRI allowed the PAN and a few small leftist parties to hold some local offices in regional pockets, thus burnishing its democratic image without having to deal with any significant opposition on a national level (Camp 1999).

If we were to look for a comparable political institution in the Third World, we might look at the Congress Party of India, founded by Mahatma Gandhi and Jawaharlal Nehru after India's revolt against British colonial rule after World War II. Both the PRI and the Congress Party nearly monopolized power in constitutional systems that were formally, at least, pluralistic; that is, neither Mexico nor India was officially a single-party state, but one political party ruled for a long period after a revolution. Both pursued industrialization through a strategy of import substitution. The power of both parties came from (1) their standing as the embodiment of national independence, (2) their very popular commitment to using the state to foster industrial development in partnership with private capital (i.e., state capitalism), and (3) their use of patronage resources to maintain control. Perhaps it is not surprising that with the passing of generations, the fading of the dream of state-led development, and international pressures to reduce state control over the economy, both India and Mexico have, in the last two decades, seen the emergence of party competition, without the complete collapse of the former ruling parties.

Beginning in 1982, the state's relationship with society and the economy began to change. Neoliberal policies were carried out by a series of technocratic presidents. Many of the socially advanced policies of the Cárdenas era have been rolled back but remain hot-button issues in Mexican politics today (see Collier 1999). As with the military dictatorships elsewhere, popular pressure built against the authoritarian and corrupt practices. A combination of elites seeking to dismantle old corporatist structures and populist movements invoking the original values of the revolution brought about a political transition to a pluralist party system, complementing the shift to neoliberal economic development strategy.

For Review

In what ways did the Mexican Revolution (1) help to shape Mexican identity and nationalism, (2) produce some important social reforms, and (3) help make the PRI the dominant party in Mexico for the next 70 years? Describe the pact underlying Mexican politics in two aspects: the relationship among competing political leaders and the relationship between the political class and the rest of society.

Mexico's Drift toward Authoritarianism, Transition to Multiparty Politics

In 1968, about the same time that bureaucratic authoritarian governments began to emerge in South America, the violent side of PRI hegemony became visible, and by the 1990s, the party was fully in crisis. It was not hard to imagine Mexico relapsing into the kind of bloody civil war that had marked the period between 1910 and 1917. Instead, in 2000 Mexico marked a watershed in its politics when the PAN's Vicente Fox defeated the candidates of, respectively, the PRI and the leftist Party of the Democratic Revolution (PRD) that had emerged in 1988.

By 1988, Mexicans were disillusioned with the corrupt and increasingly repressive PRI regime. Clean elections would reduce the power of precisely those elements in the PRI most opposed to rolling back policies associated with the revolution, which provided the material resources needed for **clientelist** politics. However, the party was already relying less on material incentives and resorting to fraud and more frequently resorting to repression.

Some sectors in the PRI were ready for a change and a closer economic relationship to the United States. To convince the country's northern neighbor that it was ready for integration, the PRI "reformers" had to reduce the power of **populists** in their own party (NACLA 1994). The populists in the PRI stood opposed, for both ideological reasons (nationalism) and practical ones (the need to protect local jobs, state enterprises, subsidies, and welfare programs, all of which provided patronage). Just as Menem changed the stripes of the Peronist Party in Argentina, Presidents Miguel de la Madrid (1982–1988), Carlos Salinas de Gortari (1988–1994), and Ernesto Zedillo (1994–2000) sought to change the PRI. The last of them, Zedillo, whose 1994 victory came after a particularly violent and bitter internal contest in the PRI, did the most to open up the system to more competition.

Despite the experience of revolution, Mexico's socioeconomic profile does not differ drastically from the other larger countries that underwent import substitution and populism. The country escaped military rule, but after 1968, security forces assumed a more prominent role in curbing protest. Since 1982, Mexico has struggled with a debt crisis and adopted many neoliberal policies that seem contradictory to the ideals of the revolution. Although Mexico had asserted control over its land, oil, and mineral wealth, in the 1990s the PRI began to open the economy and allow important basic sectors to be foreign-owned.

Through this period, Mexico's civilian rulers remained firmly in control of the government, but with increasing reliance on repression. The first crack in PRI hegemony became visible in 1968 when the PRI rulers used the security forces to repress a student movement demanding reforms. The students were generally sympathetic to Cuba, where Fidelismo seemed to be producing more social justice than they saw in Mexico. Their movement was attracting support from other sectors. Despite the promises of the Mexican Revolution and three decades of economic growth, illiteracy and poverty were growing in the countryside, and economic development could not keep up with a swelling urban population (Levy and Székely 1983).

Things came to a head as the 1968 Summer Olympics approached. Students protested expenditures on the games and attempted to diminish the accomplishments of the PRI since 1940, angering the government, which wanted to use the games to show the world Mexico's strides toward modernity. On October 2, 1968, paramilitary troops and police, including deadly snipers on rooftops, opened fire on student protestors in the Plaza of Tlatelolco in the capital. Hundreds were slain, and hundreds more were wounded, in front of a shocked national television audience. The government said that demonstrators opened fire first, but the claim was never really convincing. Decades later, after the Fox government permitted some long-closed files to be reopened, we learned that hundreds of Mexicans, including students, poor peasants, labor activists, and others, were brutally murdered or tortured by the military and police in the subsequent period. Mexico, in other words, had its own **Dirty War**, but with civilians running the government instead of military men.

Mexico's government remained committed to **ISI** at this time. In fact, President Luis Echeverria, the minister who had deployed the security forces against the students, even briefly resuscitated land reform during his presidency (1970–1976). However, the country was beginning to feel economic stagnation (inflation with low economic growth rates) and political strains associated with the end of populism and ISI. Still, Mexico had an asset that might have pulled it through: oil.

The United States, drawing for many decades on its own oil production, had shown little interest in buying oil from Mexico, where a state company monopolized the business. That attitude began to change after Arab countries cut off oil exports to the West for a few months in late 1973, and after OPEC (Mexico was not part of the cartel) began to flex its economic muscle. Now the United States became eager to build up Mexico's productive capacity, so the Mexican government borrowed huge amounts of dollars to finance an expansion of the oil industry—and also to stabilize the peso against inflation and keep the patronage machine humming. Private international banks were eager to lend to governments as the market for loans dried up and dollars began piling up in their vaults. Most Latin American countries borrowed heavily from the willing lenders, but few so freely as Mexico. Under the PRI, the government accumulated US$57 billion in debt by 1981 and US$80 billion by 1982.

By the early 1980s, Mexico's oil industry was ready to enter the world market, but the market was not ready for it anymore (Mommer 2002: 82–83). Deep in recession, and wary of dependence on foreign suppliers, the United States, Europe, and Japan were now importing less oil, not more. Prices, sustained for a while by OPEC's cuts in production and the Iranian Revolution of 1978, began to fall. Mexico was out of dollars to make payments on the interest and service of its debt. The debt crisis had arrived in Latin America and the world, showing its face first in Mexico in 1982.

Dissatisfaction would produce a new left party formed out of the populist candidacy of Cuauhtémoc Cárdenas, the son of Lázaro, who bolted from the PRI to seek the presidency in 1988. He put together a coalition of dissident members of the PRI and small leftist parties. Afterward, this coalition would form itself into the Party of the Democratic Revolution (PRD), which remains one of the three major parties in Mexico today. Cárdenas appealed to Mexicans unhappy with the PRI's embrace of neoliberalism, which had become obvious with the administration of President Miguel De la Madrid (1982–1988), a **technocrat** trained at Harvard. De la Madrid had been chosen via the *dedazo* of José López Portillo (1976–1982), whose speech leaving office was a tearful apology for having led the country deep into debt and economic crisis. The new president had never won an election—something that would be true of the next two PRI presidents. In effect, Portillo felt it more important to please the IMF than the Mexican public, and it hardly surprises that De la Madrid implement a **structural adjustment** program while in office.

In addition to the economic shock treatment, Mexico experienced another one, literally. At 7:19 a.m. on September 19, 1985, a devastating earthquake struck Mexico City. International observers estimated that 10,000–30,000 people died, and 100,000 homes were destroyed. The government mustered a completely inadequate response to the tragedy. This brought two interrelated consequences. First, it raised more questions about the legitimacy of the government. Second, Mexicans began to organize self-help groups outside the corporatist, **clientelist** structures that linked groups to the PRI (Foweracker and Craig 1990). It spurred a movement of neighborhood associations, women's groups, and human rights organizations. Civic action groups began to press for fair elections, a tendency that would ultimately help guarantee respect for Fox's victory in the 2000 presidential election.

De la Madrid's *dedazo* in 1988 fell on another U.S.-trained economist, Carlos Salinas de Gortari, his minister for planning the budget. This choice indicated that the neoliberal approach was to be continued, but now the political scene had become more complicated. There were deep rifts in the PRI, fomented by anger at technocrats from parts of the PRI that saw neoliberal reforms as a betrayal of the revolution and also from PRI politicians loath to give up the patronage and corruption that flowed through the party's arteries and veins. A combination of social movement resistance to **neoliberalism** and PRI defectors laid the basis for the Cárdenas candidacy of 1988 (La Botz 1995).

The election was a three-way race between Salinas, Cárdenas, and a PAN candidate. Between them, the PAN candidate and the coalition behind Cárdenas won nearly half the seats in the lower house of Congress. Cárdenas ran strongly in urban areas, especially in Mexico City where neighborhood movements were strongest. The PRI kept its grip on rural areas where patronage politics and manipulation of the voting process were easiest to carry out. PAN carried record-high votes in the northern region, its stronghold; it took control of the governorship of Baja California. But the presidency was where the stakes were highest. The presidency was the big prize, and on election evening, Cárdenas was ahead in early returns when suddenly and conveniently a "computer glitch" suspended reports until the next morning. Remarkably, when the count resumed, Salinas de Gortari was pronounced to have captured more than 50 percent of the vote, with Cárdenas garnering about 30 percent. Cárdenas reasonably cried "fraud." No one knows for sure who won. Clearly, however, PRI hegemony was in serious trouble, and Washington took notice.

In the United States, many conservatives, riding high with Ronald Reagan in office, were alarmed by the rise of Cárdenas. The ideological extreme in Reagan's circle had little love for the PRI, whose rule and penchant for state influence over the economy they saw as communism next door. More moderate Republicans realized—along with Democrats—that a storm was gathering in Mexico, one that could launch a new Mexican revolution. Nearby in Central America, Nicaragua had already experienced revolution in 1979, and Guatemala and El Salvador were seething with unrest. Instability threatened a refugee crisis right on the border of the United States. Hence, when Salinas approached George Bush (the elder, president from 1989 to 1993), who had just won the election in 1988, with the idea of linking Mexico's economy up to the United States, he was well received. There were economic and political motives on both sides to pursue the initiative that led to NAFTA (Orme 1996).

The PRI technocrats were less interested in preserving the party's monopoly on political power than in making the transition to a more market-oriented democracy. A more pluralist political system might weaken the grip of the old party guard—the "dinosaurs," the party's **caciques** and **caudillos**. The dinosaurs were resisting privatization of state assets vital to the patronage machine. The old guard also was not eager to introduce more transparency (to foster foreign investment) in economic and political affairs. With the populist wing of the PRI restive and a new left party, the PRD, now challenging the PRI, NAFTA was important to both the United States and Mexico's reformers in preventing any future Mexican president from deviating from the neoliberal model.

Salinas, whose family was itself mired in corruption, initially pointed the *dedazo* at a politician—party president Luis Donaldo Coliseo. Coliseo was assassinated under still-unexplained circumstances in March 1994. Salinas turned next to a technocrat, Ernesto Zedillo, who won the 1994 election, which was once again marred by fraud, though there is little doubt this time that the PRI candidate obtained the most votes. The new economic model was now in place, and now Zedillo sought to complete the regime transition in Mexico, implementing political pluralism. He fostered the transition from the PRI political monopoly to a competitive, three-plus party political system.

Zedillo had to deal with a new peso crisis (the first having happened during the 1982 debt crisis). To keep the Mexican economy looking stable, the government had pegged its currency to the dollar, much as Menem did in Argentina. The government continued to borrow dollars and keep the exchange rate level. It was easy (as Argentina would later discover) for speculators to make a lot of money by getting their hands on pesos (using other countries' currencies or borrowing) and then trading them in for dollars and repeating the cycle. The "easy money" for speculators got even better when it became clear that devaluation was inevitable. Still, the PRI government was not going to take action before the elections that year. In December 1994, a few months after NAFTA was irreversibly implemented, and with Zedillo safely elected, the government abandoned the effort and allowed the peso to rise. Rather than just rise, it skyrocketed, doubling overnight, effectively cutting the value of savings and wages in half.

All these factors converged in 2000 to produce the electoral victory of Vicente Fox. But why had Cárdenas failed to dislodge the PRI in 1994? After all, it was Cárdenas who had cracked open the PRI in the first place. NAFTA was unpopular, and most Mexicans suspected he had been robbed of victory in 1988. Cárdenas has never been a particularly dynamic campaigner. His party had nowhere near the financial resources of either the PAN or PRI to contest the 1994 and 2000 elections, in which news coverage and political commercials reached an unprecedented level of importance. The devaluation of the currency and fall in wages did not occur until after the December 1994 election had taken place. The growing climate of political uncertainty hurt the PRD. The election of 1994 was marked by the guerrilla revolt in Chiapas, two political assassinations, and economic uncertainty. Certainly, Mexicans could not be blamed for looking for some stability.

By 2000, Cárdenas showed signs of becoming something of a new caudillo himself. He won election as mayor of the capital in 1997, which seemed to position him well for 2000. However, his administration as mayor of Mexico City, a city with overwhelming problems that would have frustrated any reformist, left much to be desired. The luster of the PRD as a reformist alternative had dimmed, and the country's impressive social movements were not simply going to hand the party its votes because it was leftist and talked a good game. Many PRD politicians were former *pristas* (members of the PRI). Some PRD members decided to support the PAN, at least for the 2000 election. Like much of the electorate, they saw that party as having the best chance of defeating the PRI.

In Fox, the former Coca-Cola executive, PAN offered a candidate who was well financed, articulate, and able to extend the party's appeal beyond its original base in the north and among more religious Mexicans. In 2006, the PAN rejected the Fox-preferred nominee for Felipe Calderón, more conservative in both social and economic policy. Calderón was declared victorious over the PRD's Andrés Manuel López Obrador, the populist former mayor of Mexico City, in another highly disputed election. Although the PRI had declined, it did not disappear, finishing ahead of the PRD and PAN overall in local and congressional elections in 2009. The results of those elections show a Mexico with a highly competitive party system. (See Figure 9.1.) In fact, the PRI would recapture the presidency in 2012, when it once again captured the most congressional seats as well. However, grave economic and security questions continue to confront Mexico. Although its transition to pluralism seems unlikely to be undone soon, the issues that produced the great revolution of 1910 are in many ways dormant, not resolved.

Was the Mexican transition merely the result of a game played by elites—in particular the reformist, modernizing faction of the PRI and the business-oriented PAN? As in Brazil and the Southern Cone, democratizing forces were bubbling at the grass roots. An important new movement resulted from outrage at the fraud of 1988. Seven different human rights organizations united in 1993 to form the Alianza Cívica (Civic Alliance, AC) to monitor the 1994 elections. More than 18,000 Mexican citizens monitored the election in more than 10,000 voting stations (Avritzer 2002: 97). The AC went on to champion electoral reforms and undertook to monitor public officials, sponsoring an "adopt an official" program to root out corruption. Zedillo, in a sense, completed Mexico's transition to democracy by refusing to use the *dedazo*, which resulted in a bruising but more democratic internal fight within the PRI for its nomination. However, Zedillo and NAFTA could not restore the living standards of most Mexicans. The aura of invincibility of the PRI had been broken by the Cárdenas challenge and Zapatista revolt in Chiapas.

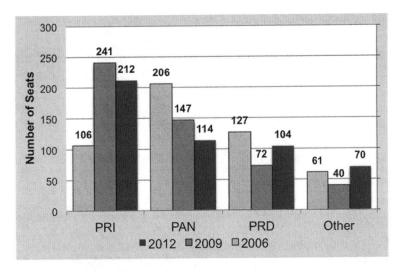

FIGURE 9.1   Seats in Mexican chamber of deputies, 2006, 2009 and 2012

In electing Fox, the Mexican electorate was not much different from voters in Brazil, Chile, and Argentina. In all these cases, centrist politicians who promised a degree of stability after decades of political repression and turmoil won the first elections after military rule. In fact, it can be argued that the real regime change in Mexico occurred dur-

ing the three PRI presidencies before Fox, because in those years the relationship between the state and the economy shifted significantly from the developmentalist role of government during the era of ISI to the **laissez-faire** approach that culminated in NAFTA. NAFTA required substantially reducing the role of the state in the economy—privatization, economic deregulation, elimination of protection, and so on. These neoliberal economic policies looked suspiciously like those implemented by Díaz, with similar results—enriching a handful of wealthy elites and increasing the influence of the United States in all things Mexican (Ruiz 2000).

Then, in 2012, the PRI came back to the presidency when its candidate, Enrique Peña Nieto, defeated the PAN candidate and, once again, López Obrador, who again claimed that the election had been stolen. Regardless of whether this is true or not (we look more closely at Mexico's recent elections in chapter 13), the first 16 months of Peña Nieto's presidency did not suggest that he intends to roll back either the economic or the political reforms of the last 30 years. Perhaps most emblematic of his administration in this time is his proposed legislation to privatize many of the operations of PEMEX, the state oil company, which has been both a symbol and an institutional bulwark of Mexican nationalism.

For Review

Mexico did not undergo military rule, nor was a new constitution written. If we refer back to the idea of "regime change" at the beginning of this chapter, can we call the changes that took place in Mexico's politics, culminating in the election of 2000, a regime change?

Venezuela's Transition from Pacted Democracy to Radical Populism

In February 1992, Lieutenant Colonel Hugo Chávez led a coup attempt against the elected government of President Carlos Andrés Pérez. The uprising stalled, and Chávez himself was captured. Defeat was turned into political victory, however, as a result of the electrifying moments in which Chávez appealed on national television for the revolting troops to surrender. He accepted sole responsibility for the defeat, something that impressed Venezuelans

accustomed to politicians dodging responsibility. His claim that the objectives had not been met "for now" (*por ahora*) stirred popular hope that the struggle had only begun. On the streets, civilian supporters, especially younger parts of the population, began appearing in red berets similar to those worn by the paratroop commander and his followers.

Why were Venezuelans so ready to support this military coup? After all, the country had enjoyed 34 years of political stability and regular elections between 1958, when the last dictatorship fell, and the February coup attempt of 1992 (a second failed coup occurred in November). Polls at the time showed no great enthusiasm for military rule, even though the economy had been rocked by nine years of low oil prices. Why then did Chávez's popularity soar after 1992?

The short answer is that Venezuelans' faith in democracy had been shaken because their dream of rapid development into a modern society had evaporated after decades of economic growth generated by oil exports (Hellinger 1991). The widespread perception was that the oil money had been stolen by corrupt politicians associated with two political parties that dominated the electoral process: Democratic Action (AD), Pérez's party, and the Political Electoral Independent Organizing Committee—a Christian Democratic party better known by its Spanish acronym, COPEI.

Like Mexico, Venezuela had escaped the wave of military rule that swept Latin America in the 1970s and 1980s, so the fear of a military coup was not nearly so strong. In fact, historically Venezuela's military had portrayed itself as the defender of the people against rapacious elites. Military populism had become especially potent as a counterweight to the designs of Venezuelan elites who, under Pérez's leadership, were attempting to implement reforms not unlike the ones championed by Mexico's technocrats (McCoy and Myers 2006).

Venezuela's "pacted democracy" was founded after General Marcos Pérez Jiménez fled the country in January 1958, leading to the election of Rómulo Betancourt, founder and leader of AD, in December of that year. Betancourt turned power over to a successor from AD after elections in 1963, but democracy really seemed to be consolidated after Rafael Caldera, founder and leader of COPEI, was elected president in December 1968. Six more presidential elections, every five years, brought either an *adeco* (member of AD) or *copeyano* (member of COPEI) to the presidency—but in a sign of problems for the two-party system, Caldera broke from COPEI to run and win a new term in 1993. Even so, the two large parties continued after that election to control both houses of Congress. They knew that accepting popular demands for a constituent assembly to rewrite or change the 1961 constitution would put that control in jeopardy.

If Mexico's single-party system was a perfect dictatorship hidden in democratic trappings, in many ways Venezuela had an even better disguise for a system in which parties did more to smother civil society than to represent it (Hellinger 1991; Karl 1986). AD and COPEI competed to control not only government but also unions, professional organizations, peasant leagues, student associations, and neighborhood groups—just about every civic association. Two fundamental reasons existed for this unfriendly collaboration.

First, after the fall of General Pérez Jiménez in 1958, the major forces in Venezuelan society met and negotiated limits on the transition to democracy—that is, a pact. The military was determined that there would be no retribution directed toward the officer corps as individuals or as a group. The Church sought to ensure that it would continue to have influence, especially in education, which the secular-oriented AD had long wished to modernize by asserting state control over the curriculum. Business groups had become disenchanted with the dictatorship because it had reneged on paying debts, but they wanted a government that would continue subsidies and protection, and one that would eschew socialism. Communists and leftist youth in AD had led resistance to the dictatorship, and conservative business and social organizations were worried that the transition might turn in a radical direction. The centrists put aside their differences in the interest of political stability—heading off revolution—and agreed to support an elected government. The Venezuelan Communist Party, which had played an important role in overthrowing the dictatorship, was excluded from the agreement to share power.

Second, Venezuela is either cursed or blessed, depending on your point of view, with oil, which generates one-third of its GDP, 80 to 90 percent of export earnings, and more than half the government's revenues. The state therefore has tremendous fiscal revenues, and this provides the wherewithal for a huge patronage system. Democracy became linked in the Venezuelan mind with sovereign ownership of the oil and just distribution of the super-profits derived from it.

Betancourt was the most important of leftists and had begun organizing Venezuelans after the 1935 death of General Juan Vicente Gómez brought his harsh dictatorship to an end. At the time, the majority of the population was rural and poor, with low life expectancy. Betancourt's platform was that only a directly elected government could be counted on to "sow the oil" in projects of economic development and improvement of health, education, and other aspects of human welfare. For 10 years he and his followers organized a movement for direct, free elections. They were blocked by factions in the military associated with Gómez and other parts of the agrarian oligarchy, but oil earnings streaming into the country were changing both society and the military. A faction of officers, frustrated with a high command dominated by unprofessional cronies of Gómez, was also ready for change. In 1945, they staged a coup and put Betancourt and AD into power. The party then organized and won three elections by huge majorities between 1945 and 1948.

Betancourt had dallied with communism and Marxism in his youth, making him suspect to Venezuela's elites, but by 1945 he had moved to the center. Many other *adecos* were more radical and militant, but the Venezuelan Communist Party (PCV) and AD had become bitter rivals as they battled each other for control of the unions in the oil fields, where workers had already struck (in 1936) to advance not only their own interests but also those of the nation. There were other unions, but the country had hardly begun to industrialize. With oil revenues available to import goods, import substitution was not as high on the agenda. Venezuela's business leaders had little experience with—or use for—unions, the backbone of AD's support.

COPEI (founded in 1946 in reaction to the secular PCV and AD), the Communists, and other civilian politicians could not compete with the immensely popular *adecos*. Neither the *adecos* nor their opponents had much experience with liberal democracy. Venezuela had never had a transition of government by election from one party to another. In 1948, ambitious officers, led by Pérez Jiménez, responded affirmatively to thinly veiled opposition calls for a coup. By 1958, after 10 years of corrupt and brutal military rule backed by the United States in the name of fighting communism, Venezuela's business, religious, military, and political elites were ready to make pacts with one another to prevent another unsuccessful transition. The most important agreement was signed at the villa Punto Fijo in Caracas; the subsequent system became identified with the "Pact of Punto Fijo."

The left felt cheated. Inspired by the Cuban Revolution of 1959, young members of the PCV and AD launched a guerrilla war to overthrow the new system. It proved a disaster. Whatever shortcomings the new regime had in terms of respecting civil liberties and delivering social justice, it enjoyed the legitimacy bestowed by fair elections. After 1968, most of the guerrillas returned to party politics, many in the mainstream parties. They accepted an amnesty extended by President Rafael Caldera, the founder of COPEI (a Christian Democratic party), who had evolved from archenemy of Betancourt to cofounder of the Punto Fijo system.

The Venezuelan political scientist Juan Carlos Rey (1972) described the new system, based on the Pact of Punto Fijo and the constitution of 1961, as a "populist system of reconciliation." What he meant was that the pact allowed Venezuela's elites to compete with one another through elections for access to the country's oil-export earnings. Probably no country in Latin America was so dependent on a single export product, but this product had an unusual ability to generate profits.

Unlike Mexico, Venezuela's regime had competition between incumbents and opposition in elections. But this disguises an important similarity in the way the *party system* functioned in each case. Although the competition between COPEI and AD was fierce, they would unite with one another in the face of any challenge from a breakaway group. In many ways, the two parties dominated groups in Venezuela in the same way that the PRI did in Mexico: through the promise of economic development, nationalism in defending sovereign control of the country's natural wealth, use of patronage to ward off challenges, and in the end—if necessary—fraud and repression. More colorfully than Rey put it, another political scientist referred to this system of cooperation with limited competition as a "cartel" (Cyr 2013).

As in Mexico, nationalist populism and neoliberal globalization came into conflict. From 1935 onward, Venezuelan democrats had linked the country's underdevelopment and poverty to "oil imperialism" and military rule. Betancourt and his followers said that democratically elected governments would challenge the companies, capture a fair share of the profits, and use them to develop the country. The political elites who dominated the post-1958 era repeatedly associated military rulers of the past with the unpatriotic giveaway of the country's wealth.

Actually, some generals had often been as nationalist as civilian rulers. For example, in 1943, President (and General) Medina Angarita significantly raised royalties and taxes, forcing the companies to acknowledge the Venezuelan state's right to set tax rates. From 1935 until the nationalization of oil companies in 1976, this meant continually raising taxes and the royalties (fixed payments levied as compensation for the exploitation of a natural, exhaustible resource) that foreign companies had to pay to extract oil from the subsoil. On the other hand, it was an AD oil minister in Betancourt's first government who traveled to the Middle East and convinced Iran, Saudi Arabia, and other oil producers to form the Organization of Petroleum Exporting Countries (OPEC), which began to coordinate efforts to boost export earnings by regulating global production and setting "reference prices" for taxation.

By the 1970s, in part because of the growing power of OPEC and in part because their 40-year concessions were running out, the companies were ready for change. In 1973, a Middle East war and Arab oil boycott (Venezuela kept producing) sent crude oil prices soaring, and they stayed there. In 1976, the companies accepted nationalization with compensation. President Carlos Andrés Pérez (1974–1978) proclaimed that Venezuela was now master of its own fate for the first time because "*el petroleo es nuestro*" ("the oil is ours"; see Hellinger 2003). He decided to invest the flood of petrodollars in a crash program to industrialize the country overnight. In fact, he tried to accelerate the program by borrowing heavily against future petrodollars. As Fernando Coronil (1997) put it, the petrodollars allowed the "magical state" to conjure up factories, schools, roads, and so on.

This strategy proved disastrous; the economy was not able to absorb the flow of dollars even without borrowing. Venezuelans became accustomed to what economists call "rent-seeking"; that is, political competition came to revolve around gaining access to the financial resources of the state. The way to get rich was not to invent something or build an industry but to obtain contracts or subsidies from government. Not surprisingly, corruption, graft, and inefficiency became widespread. For a while, when things went wrong, the government could fix them simply by spending more petrodollars; losses were easily absorbed for most of the decade. The day of reckoning came in 1983, 10 years after Pérez had promised to use the great OPEC oil bonanza of those years to turn Venezuela overnight into the "Ruhr" (the industrial heartland of Germany) of Latin America. Until 1976 Venezuelan politicians could always blame oil imperialism for economic failures. Now, facing failure in 1983, they would have to account for themselves.

Collapse of the Punto Fijo System

In the 1980s the dream of overnight progress through oil exports collapsed. Oil prices fell from well more than US$40 in the early 1980s to US$9 in 1986. Corruption became more visible and less tolerable during this period. In May 1988, the military announced it had killed 16 Colombian guerrillas in a firefight along Apure River on the border. However, two of the so-called guerrillas survived and set the record straight. The military had killed 16 Venezuelan fishermen and tried to cover it up. A subsequent investigation suggested that the military was mixed up in a protection scheme involving extortion of money from ranchers. Several other human rights scandals began to raise questions about impunity in supposedly democratic Venezuela, and some officers (we learned only later) began to worry about the military's role and how it conflicted with the military's historical self-image as defender of the people, a heritage dating to the struggle of Simón Bolívar (a Venezuelan) in the independence era (Jones 2007).

In December 1988, Pérez won a new term as president. He promised in his populist campaign to bring back the good old days of the 1970s boom. Instead, he signed a structural adjustment agreement with the IMF that included raising gasoline prices. This was a harsh economic medicine and clashed with the fundamental connection that Venezuelan politicians had made between democracy and sovereign control over oil: ownership of oil guaranteed development to be shared by everyone.

The popular response, beginning on February 27, 1989, the day transportation fares were due to rise with the price of gasoline, was an astounding, spontaneous revolt—the Caracazo, which engulfed 22 major cities. Caracas was rocked by looting for nearly a week. Pérez sent in the army, but only after the riots had pretty much subsided. Human rights organizations estimated that the death toll was well more than 1,000. U.S. training and the successful counterinsurgency of the 1960s had led academic experts on Venezuela (including me) to assume that the military was firmly linked to the status quo. But the Venezuelan military was not the Chilean or Argentine military. It turned out that Chávez and others had been meeting for many years with former guerrilla leaders, who had not altogether given up hope that they could win the army itself to their cause (Jones 2007).

The 1989 riots were a turning point. The old political class and the political parties associated with the pact of 1958 were in complete disrepute. An explosion of popular organizing and protest characterized the early 1990s, and it continued, albeit at a lower level of intensity, through the Caldera presidency (1994–1998). Chávez tapped into this surge of participation and protest. Released from prison in 1994 in a gesture of reconciliation, he entered the political stage as a candidate promising to overhaul the system radically, to sweep the old parties from power, and put the oil money back in the hands of the people. The old parties lay in ruin after his victory of December 1998. The new president convened (after a referendum) a constituent assembly that wrote a new constitution and renamed the country the "**Bolivarian** republic of Venezuela." The expressed goal of the new charter was to institute participatory democracy—though whether the objective was to replace or to strengthen representative democracy was less clear. In any case, on paper at least, the reforms promised more direct power for people through social movements and popular organization in governance (see chapter 11 for more on social movements).

For Review

Why did oil become so closely linked to democracy in the Venezuelan mind? Who was Rómulo Betancourt, and what was his program? What was the Pact of Punto Fijo? Why did it lend stability to Venezuelan politics, and what happened to undermine that stability over time?

The Chávez Era

In the first four years of his term, President Chávez survived an attempted military coup (April 11, 2002) and a partially successful general strike, both orchestrated by a coalition of his enemies—the big private media, executives of the state oil company opposed to his nationalist oil policies, labor bosses associated with the old parties, and the business community. The United States welcomed these attempts to overthrow Chávez; it may have actively aided the conspirators. Having failed to remove Chávez through these methods, the opposition finally decided to try a constitutional route and remove him from office via a recall vote

PUNTO DE VISTA: A COUP FOR OR AGAINST DEMOCRACY?

On February 4, 1992, Lieutenant Colonel Hugo Chávez and his Bolivarian Revolutionary Movement (MBR 200, referring to its founding on the 200th anniversary of Bolívar's birth) attempted a coup against the elected president of Venezuela, Carlos Andrés Pérez. At the time of the coup, more than 80 percent of Venezuelans expressed no confidence at all in the country's political parties. In the aftermath, Venezuelan politicians called on the people to defend democracy, but to their surprise, many Venezuelans came out to demonstrate against the existing system—though not necessarily in support of a coup.

Chávez, who died in March 2013, became president in 1999. Ever since, government supporters have annually commemorated the February 4 date. The opposition instead celebrates January 23, the anniversary of the overthrow of the last military dictatorship in 1958. Chavistas accuse the opposition of being "golpistas" because the opposition tried to oust Chávez in a short-lived 48-hour coup in April 2002. The opposition questions the late president's own democratic credentials because of his leadership of the 1992 coup.

In 2002, two months after the opposition coup, Chilean journalist Marta Harnecker interviewed Chávez and asked him to explain the motives behind his 1992 uprising.

> Chávez: When the people of Caracas came out into the streets en masse [the "Caracazo"] on February 27, 1989 to reject the economic package that had been approved by the then-president Carlos Andrés Pérez, and we saw the massacres that took place in response, it made a huge impact on my generation . . . When [Pérez] sent the Armed Forces into the streets to repress that social uprising and there was

a massacre, the members of the MBR 200 realized we had passed the point of no return and we had to take up arms. We could not continue to defend a murderous regime . . .

> We discussed how to break free from the past, how to move beyond the kind of democracy that only responded to the interests of the oligarchy, how to stop the corruption. We always rejected the idea of a traditional military coup, of a military dictatorship, or a military junta . . . We agreed to issue decrees to convene a constitutional assembly . . . We began to prepare for the rebellion.

Chávez went on to describe the preparation, including planning with leftist groups to encourage civilians to come into the streets in support of the coup, hopes that fell short of expectations that day. "There was no popular mobilization. So it was just us rebelling," Chávez told Harnecker. However, afterward, he claimed, people began to see the military as allies.

> Chávez: The popular protest movement was really unleashed when the people realized that a group of the military was with them . . . After the February 4 rebellion, the MBR 200 changed substantially, because until then we were a small, clandestine military movement, a group of young officers, a few civilians, a few leftist movements that were incorporated into the MBR 200 . . . [When we got out of prison] we went from being a clandestine military organization to a popular movement; though there was always a military presence, it was a civilian-military movement.

Later in the interview, Chávez said,

> I am very much aware of what Bolívar once said: 'I am but a light feather dragged along by the revolutionary hurricane.' Leaders find themselves in front of an avalanche that drags us forward. It would be very unfortunate, sad, if a revolutionary process of change were to depend on a caudillo.

Point/Counterpoint

Do you think that Chávez persuasively defended the coup attempt of 1992?

    a. If you say yes, how do you respond to the criticism that whatever his policies were, Carlos Andrés Pérez was an elected leader? Can a coup against an elected president ever be justified?

    b. If you say no, how do you respond to the argument that there was a crisis of representation in Venezuela—that elections were not doing the job of keeping government responsive to the people?

For more information

See Marta Harnecker, *Understanding the Venezuelan Revolution: Hugo Chávez Talks to Marta Harnecker* (New York: Monthly Review Press, 2005). See also Bart Jones, *Hugo!* (Hanover, NH: Steerforth Press, 2007). More critical of Chávez is Cristina Marcano and Alberto Barrera Tryszka, *Hugo Chávez: The Definitive Biography of Venezuela's Controversial President* (Random House, 2007).

in August 2004. Chávez, already directly elected twice (1998 and 2000) with solid majorities, won the recall with nearly 60 percent of the vote. He won reelection in December 2006 with 63 percent of the vote. He could not be dismissed as an autocrat out of step with "democratic" trends (on the Chávez era, see Ellner and Hellinger 2003).

As one of the top 10 producers of crude oil in the world—the third-largest exporter of petroleum to the United States—and with proven oil reserves of more than 300 billion barrels, the largest in the world, Venezuela rates high on the diplomatic radar screen in Washington. Depending on the rate of increase of oil consumption globally in the future, the country may become even more important. If technology and economics develop favorably, Venezuela's vast reserves of heavy oil (a tar-like substance, difficult to get out of the ground and transport) will become viable to produce. Venezuela could be the new Saudi Arabia at some future date.

Besides providing economic power at home, oil provided Chávez some diplomatic cover. Any other Latin American leader bold enough to question the conduct of the war in Afghanistan, to visit Saddam Hussein in Iraq, to refuse to cooperate with the U.S. drug war in Colombia, and to question the wisdom of free-market economics probably would have felt the wrath of economic sanctions, or worse, from Washington. For the United States, the political survival of Chávez, who not only criticized U.S. proposals for a Free Trade Area of the Americas (FTAA) but advanced his own alternative for Latin American economic integration independent of the United States, was a setback to its plans to meld all Latin America into a hemispheric version of **NAFTA**. Not surprisingly, the right-wing factions in the United States called Chávez, along with Lula of Brazil, Rafael Correa of Ecuador, Daniel

Ortega in Nicaragua, Evo Morales in Bolivia, and the Castro brothers in Cuba, an "axis of evil" in Latin America.

The Venezuelan transition, as in the case of Mexico, involved not a struggle against military authoritarianism but the struggle of a nation to adapt after the political class lost legitimacy. The elite had failed to use the country's great economic advantage, oil, as leverage to develop the economy. They were perceived, accurately enough, as thoroughly corrupt. A large part of the officer corps identified with popular frustration. Venezuelans seemed to welcome military rebellion but not, if polls are to be believed, military rule. A new political class organized around the figure of Chávez began to deploy new models of democracy and economic development, but we have yet to see whether they can succeed.

What we can say is that the period between the Caracazo of 1989 and what persisted through the Chávez presidency, to his death in March 2013, was not just an explosion of popular anger but a mass mobilization by poor Venezuelans demanding access to the benefits provided by the state. This produced a new constitution in 1999, one that envisioned a participatory democracy with a "protagonistic" role for civil society. That is, political movements and organ-ization were vested with the right to participate in making policy and filling important judicial and watchdog offices (to combat corruption and protect human rights). The most controversial and debated part of this plan was advanced in 2007, when Chávez decreed a law (under author-ity given to him by the National Assembly) to create community councils directly funded by the petrostate. To his Bolivarian grassroots supporters, this was the democratization of the benefits of oil. To the opposition, these councils are little more than an attempt to circumvent representative democracy and construct a new, stronger system of patronage controlled by the executive branch of government. The most extreme parts of the opposition charge Chávez and his successor, Nicolás Maduro, with attempting to import the Cuban model.

Even before 2007, however, Venezuela politics and society had begun to polarize. In the first 20 months of his presidency, Chávez had concentrated on dismantling the Punto Fijo regime, which was something that many people who had not voted for him in 1998 supported. But in November 2001, Chávez decreed (as with the later laws about communal councils, under authority granted by the National Assembly) a series of laws promoting land reform and and changing the system of property rights (though still recognizing private property). What really stirred the political pot was the new oil law, which reversed the **neoliberal** oil opening of the 1990s by raising royalties and taxes and insisting on enforcement of the provisions in the oil nationalization law of 1975 requiring that all basic operations be majority-owned. In taking this action, Chávez took on the most powerful group in the country, the high executives run-ning Petróleos de Venezuela, the state oil company. They were the ones who had designed and promoted the oil opening. During the crisis years of the 1980s and 1990s, they had convinced the government to allow foreign capital back into Venezuela's oil fields on terms that were very generous to the investors. The country's oil production did increase, but when prices col-lapsed again in 1998–1999, the prestige of the executives plummeted with them. The executives became deeply involved in the efforts to overthrow Chávez, but they and their allies failed to appreciate how popular he was among the majority of Venezuelans.

Venezuelans rallied behind Chávez to force his return after he was deposed for 48 hours in the 2002 coup. They stayed by him through an oil-export shutdown, and they voted to keep him in a recall election in 2004. Chávez's government rewarded the people with social programs, called "missions," that have eradicated illiteracy, put high school and college edu-cation in reach of most people, and spread health clinics and state-run subsidized markets throughout the country. He was able to do this because oil prices and earnings rose substantially in the decade following 2000, partly because of demand in industrializing Asia, but also because Chávez took the lead to reinvigorate OPEC and because, with the oil reform law, the government regained control over fields that had been leased by the oil company to foreign companies at lucrative terms in the 1990s.

However, the Venezuelan transition cannot be said to be complete. The Bolivarian constitution of 1999 established many innovative new institutions and ways for people to influence the state, but it has not yet been shown that these can be used by the people independently of the leadership of Chávez, who died in March 2013. Chávez established a party, the United Socialist Party of Venezuela (PSUV), in 2006. His opposition, though divided into several parties, united to form a coalition, the Democratic United Roundtable (MUD). The MUD never came close to defeating Chávez in a presidential election, but it saw its vote total rise between 2010 and 2013, and in the April 2013 election to replace the deceased Chávez, it came within a whisker of defeating Maduro, the popular president's anointed successor.

Its candidate against Chávez in December 2012, and then Maduro a few months later, was a governor, Enrique Capriles. Capriles says he would adhere to the 1999 constitution. Some question his sincerity. Even if sincere, Capriles would face tremendous pressure from his constituents to end some popular programs. Chávez negotiated a deal with Cuba that included that country sending 10,000 medical personnel to work in the poor *barrios* and rural areas; in exchange, Cuba gets oil. Capriles is committed to ending oil exports to Cuba, but then how would he replace the doctors?

It is not clear that the PSUV can hold together without Chávez. Grassroots Chavistas want more resources and power transferred to the communal councils, but professional politicians, including many mayors and governors in the PSUV, are not keen to lose their control over local funding. Chávez held the reins of power closely to his own chest. He had the support of the military, which he had once led. He had the ability to make final decisions when members of his cabinet quarreled over economic policy. Maduro, by contrast, was a bus driver by trade and leader of the unions. His performance in the April 2013 election to replace Chávez raised many doubts about his political capacity; Maduro defeated Enrique Capriles by less than two percentage points—in comparison to Chávez's victory over Capriles by almost 11 percentage points in October 2012.

What may save Maduro is the opposition. So far, even Capriles has not laid out a program that assures poor Venezuelans that they will be included in the benefits of the oil bounty in the way that Chavismo does. Much of opposition is still tainted in the public mind with the Punto Fijo past. Capriles himself reinforced this perception when he failed to curb demonstrations, some of which turned violent, claiming fraud in the aftermath of the April election. Then, in February 2014, rivals to Capriles seized on the emergence of an opposition student movement protesting high rates of violent crime and economic shortages. The movement had some legitimate grievances to protest, but Leopoldo López, a former mayor in the Caracas metropolitan area, put himself at the head of the movement and called for the "exit" (i.e., resignation) of Maduro and his government. By April, some of the demonstrators had turned violent, and dozens of security personnel, demonstrators, and bystanders were killed in confrontation.

Almost all the protests took place in middle-class parts of large cities. The poorer parts of the cities were noticeably quiet by comparison. However, this does not mean that the *barrios* are as enthusiastically behind the Bolivarian government today as they were when they saved Chávez from the 2002 coup.

There are reasons to question whether the ideals and mechanisms for popular influence over policy were ever fully realized under Chávez himself. In particular, it is not clear whether the participatory democracy envisioned in the constitution has been realized, despite the establishment of grassroots communal councils that are directly funded to carry out programs set by their own priorities. The jury is out regarding whether these councils will prove to be new participatory mechanisms of democracy or whether they will be converted simply into new clientelist networks, controlled by politicians administering programs funded directly by the executive branch and an oil company–controlled fund—something that could occur with either the MUD or PSUV in power in the future.

What we can say is that the old Punto Fijo regime has been swept away and that Venezuelans have regained a sense that they have democratic rights to demand influence over government. There has been regime change, but how democratic it will be is still an open question. Although Maduro seemed to have weathered the demands for his ouster in 2014, it is not at all clear that the political system envisioned under the 1999 constitution is truly institutionalized.

For Review

The "old regime" in Venezuela featured two parties competing in elections on a regular basis. What undermined the stability of this system? Was it just the drop in oil prices in the 1980s, or were there other political factors? As in Mexico, regime change came in an election, that of 1998. Describe what happened and what followed.

Conclusions Drawn from Six Cases of Transition

The notion that a pact is the underlying basis for democratic government is deeply rooted in pluralist theory and the conception of democracy as a polyarchy. Many political scientists have argued that there must be an underlying consensus about the largest social issues (national identity, the place of religion in society, whether a capitalist or socialist economic system is best, etc.) and about the best way to resolve disputes. The idea is that democracy cannot itself ensure consensus and acceptance of fundamental principles. Consensus is what makes democracy possible. It would seem, then, that the foundation of democracy is something like Rey's populist system of reconciliation—that is, a system whereby elites contest their differences with one another but a system that also allows some degree of participation.

Political pacts are attempts by elites to construct institutional arrangements, either through constitutional structures (clearest in the case of Chile) or through agreements by political parties, to ensure victory by centrist and moderate leftists and to exclude political forces that might pursue alternative economic and political models. In the case of Venezuela, such a pact (1958) broke down and was replaced by a regime that claimed to want to break away from neoliberalism and fashion a radical alternative. In Mexico, the PRI was created through an elite pact that eventually quieted revolutionary unrest by incorporating new social actors, a variation on the populist experience discussed in chapters 6 and 7. In this case, the desire of elites to install neoliberal economic policies coincided with political reforms designed to open the system to more competition. In the cases of Brazil and the Southern Cone, the pacts also coincided with a move toward more neoliberal economic policies. Therefore, in these cases and in the case of Mexico, the transitions involved introducing liberal economic policies to coincide with political liberalization. In the sixth case, Venezuela, the new regime was dedicated, at least in its rhetoric, to more radical change that flew in the face of the global hegemon, and the new system had not by the time of Chávez's death in 2013 proven itself institutionalized.

As Brazilian social scientist Leonardo Avritzer (2002) points out, Huntington's famous analysis of political stability tends to see political participation as a threat to democracy. Huntington (1968; see chapter 7) proposed that we see institutions as mechanisms to control and channel participation. Therefore, one of his equations, we saw, was

$$\frac{Political\ participation}{Political\ institutionalization} = Political\ instability$$

That is, as participation increases, it eventually can overtake **institutionalization** and increase instability. This was made quite explicit by Huntington and like-minded colleagues who developed a theory (popularized by the Trilateral Commission in Crozier et al. 1975) that the world was in the throes of a governability crisis caused by the upsurge of mass movements demanding democracy. Similarly, Avritzer points out, the framework of the "transitionologists," especially Przeworski (1986), tends to emphasize the importance of elite pacts. Popular participation and protest are largely seen as part of the environment in which the elites negotiate. The people (*demos* in Greek) are seen not as protagonists constructing democracy but as the unruly mob that makes elites put aside deep-seated animosities and conflicts. The unruly chorus encourages them to negotiate a solution before the protests take on revolutionary dimensions or before the military once again takes over.

Avritzer, drawing mostly on the Brazilian and Mexican cases, argues that the people themselves ought to get more credit for what has been achieved in the transitions to democracy. He claims that popular participation as it emerged in Brazil through the innovative practices of the PT (Partido do Trabahaldores)—for example, organizing people to directly participate in making municipal budgets—and the Alianza Cívica in Mexico offers the best prospects for deepening and consolidating democracy. He argues that social movements in Latin America are creating a new kind of "public space." We will look more closely at this argument about democracy's future in Latin America in chapter 13.

Although the Latin American transitions treated here differ from one another in several important respects, there are some important ways that the Southern Cone countries, Brazil, Mexico, and Venezuela resembled each other.

- In all of these cases, the combination of the exhaustion of import substitution and falling prices for key commodity exports contributed to an economic crisis that resulted in slowing rates of growth and eventually a debt crisis.
- At the very time when economic growth slowed, sectors that had only marginally benefited, if at all, from ISI (notably, much of the peasantry and urban poor) were being mobilized by radical sectors, especially young leftists inspired by the Cuban Revolution and Christians associated with the doctrine of a "preferential option" for the poor.
- Political polarization became more pronounced at both elite levels and social levels.

- The polarization was accentuated by the policies of the United States, which encouraged militaries in the region to interpret the crisis as a threat to *la patria*, or the homeland. (Mexico is a partial exception here, since the United States became more preoccupied with instability than with the immediate threat of the left.)

- In all cases the populist regimes gave way to increased authoritarianism, though the degree of repression varied, from increased abuses of human rights by militaries still subordinate to civilian authority to the intense violence of "dirty wars."

- Neoliberal economic policies began to be implemented as the perceived only possible response to the exhaustion of state-led developmentalism under ISI.

- A combination of frustration with the corruption and **clientelism** of the populist era, the disruption of the corporatist relations of that era, and the openings encouraged by the global human rights movement increased the leverage of mass movements for democratic transitions or democratic reforms (the latter in the cases of Mexico and Venezuela).

- The post-2000 era saw in all of these cases the resurgence of the left, what has become called the "Pink Tide." However, within this overall tendency is tremendous diversity across countries and time in the fortunes of the left.

From 1998 to the present, **Pink Tide** presidents proclaiming their resistance to the Washington Consensus have won elections in Argentina, Bolivia, Brazil, the Dominican Republic, Ecuador, Nicaragua, Panama, Paraguay, El Salvador, Uruguay, and Venezuela. Lula, Chávez, and Bolivia's Morales were part of a social, if not a political, vanguard in the region, as the faces of power quite literally began to resemble Latin America's ethnic mix more faithfully. The election of Chile's Michelle Bachelet in 2006 also represented a modest move leftward and certainly an important symbolic step forward for women. Major leftist challenges emerged in other countries as well, including Peru and Mexico, although the left-ists did not gain the presidency. In 2013, the presidencies of Mexico and Colombia remained in conservative hands, and in Chile's 2010 election the Concertación suffered its first defeat. Although Bachelet returned to the presidency in 2014, it should be understood that the Pink Tide—pink because it leans socialist but is not "red"—will not inevitably rise higher or even maintain its present level.

But 90 miles from the United States, there remains a regime that insists on the need for revolution beyond the limits set by pacts and polyarchy. Will Communist Cuba undergo transition? Thirty years ago, much of Central America was engulfed in revolution and counterinsurgency. Have the underlying conditions that gave rise to insurgencies in Central America changed? What about the Zapatistas? In short, has the "fire in the mind," as Nicaragua's Omar Cabezas once put it, been extinguished in the cool waters of the Pink Tide?

Discussion Questions

1. What do you regard as the key similarities and the key differences between the experiences of Mexico and Venezuela? Were the forces of change similar or different from the ones that caused breakdowns of and later transitions to democracy in the Southern Cone and Brazil?

2. Would it be fair to say that neoliberalism undermined democracy in Venezuela but strengthened it in Mexico? Why or why not?

3. Some political scientists credited the Pact of Punto Fijo with preventing Venezuela from experiencing the military rule that swept much of the rest of the continent in the 1970s and 1980s. Would you agree? What lessons should Latin America's relatively new democracies take from the Venezuelan case?

4. Do you think that in either case true "regime change" took place, and if so, when do you think it took place?

Resources for Further Study

Reading: Bart Jones's *Hugo! The Hugo Chávez Story from Mud Hut to Perpetual Revolution* (Hanover, NH: Steerforth Press, 2007) is a sympathetic biography but very accessible and a good window into many different aspects of Venezuela's transition. Steve Ellner and I edited *Venezuelan Politics in the Chávez Era* (Boulder: Lynne Rienner, 2003). Miguel Tinker Salas's *The Enduring Legacy: Oil, Culture, and Society* (Durham: Duke University Press, 2009) examines the profound influence of U.S. investment and consumer values on Venezuela. Matthew Gutmann's *The Romance of Democracy* (Berkeley: University of California Press, 2002) looks at ordinary people's hopes and disappointments during the Mexican transition. The fifth edition of Roderic Camp's *Politics in Mexico: The Democratic Consolidation* (New York: Oxford University Press, 2007) is an optimistic but critical look at Mexico's political reforms.

Video and Film: *The Revolution Will Not Be Televised* is a remarkable documentary of the attempted 2002 coup against Chávez. *¿Puedo Hablar?* (2007) looks at the 2006 presidential election, crediting Chávez for helping the poor but raising questions about the health of democracy. *A Place Called Chiapas* (1998) is one of the many good documentaries on the Zapatistas.

On the Internet: Venezuela Analysis, www.venezuelanalysis.com, disputes the general U.S. media view of Venezuela but also provides critical analysis and debate. An opposition viewpoint that generally avoids hysterical rhetoric is Caracas Chronicles at www.caracaschronicles.com. You can find good perspectives from different points of view on Mexican politics at www.latinamericanstudies.org/mexico.htm. A good source of alternative news with much analysis of Mexico and which is much less optimistic than the Camp book has the unfortunate name of Narco News Network (www.narconews.com).

10 Democracy in Times of Revolution

Focus Questions

▶ What were the underlying causes that gave rise to the Cuban Revolution?

▶ What challenges face Cuba as a new political generation enters the political stage?

▶ To what degree has the settlement of civil conflicts in Central America addressed underlying social tensions in that region?

▶ What is an insurgency, and what ramifications do insurgencies have for building democracy in the post-conflict era?

THE PHILOSOPHER HANNAH Arendt (1963: 27) argued that revolutions have two things in common: they are characterized by a striving for freedom against repression, and this quest for freedom must be connected to "novelty"—that is, an attempt to create a new social order. Since Marx wrote in the mid-1880s, said Arendt, these themes have been tied to the "social question"; that is, the makers of revolution seek freedom but believe that it cannot be fully achieved without radical changes in social and economic conditions (55–61). Latin America's break from colonialism brought about a political revolution accompanied by violence and social upheaval, but in the end it would not qualify as a revolution in the terms defined by Arendt. Bolívar's frustration and bitterness reflect that fact.

Revolutionary *movements* have been relatively common in Latin America, but revolutionary *regimes* are rare. What distinguishes these few "success stories" from the more numerous failures? Once in power, revolutionary movements rarely carry out their political plans as promised. Why? Do they achieve anything or merely culminate in a new system of repression—old wine in new bottles?

Latin America's revolutionary movements have usually linked the "social question" to breaking economic dependence and asserting national sovereignty. Latin America's mythic revolutionary heroes—for example, Venezuela's Simón Bolívar, Cuba's José Martí, Argentina's (and Cuba's) Ernesto Che Guevara, and Nicaragua's José Augusto Cesar Sandino—all saw the United States as a threat to the region's independence and ability to reform its social order. It is no coincidence that the revolutions in Mexico (1910–1917), Cuba (1959), and Nicaragua (1979) took place in three countries that have suffered direct military occupation by U.S. forces in their history. Mexico lost half its territory to the northern colossus in 1846–1848 and endured several subsequent interventions. The United States invaded Cuba in 1898 as it was on the verge of achieving independence from

Spain and then occupied it for three years. Nicaragua, thought to be a desirable site for a trans-isthmus canal, attracted frequent intervention by the United States and European nations vying for influence and control of such a project. (Ultimately, the United States built the Panama Canal.)

The Mexican and Cuban revolutions gave birth to a long period of rule by a single party that tried to unite the population behind a program of national economic development and resistance to U.S. pressures. Cuba's rebels consolidated their control after 1959 in a state modeled on Marxist–Leninist principles; the one-party system was formally incorporated into a constitution in 1976. Mexico, we saw in chapter 9, finally moved after 72 years to a multiparty system. In both of these cases, however, the catalysts for revolution included rebellion against dictatorship and a demand for fair and competitive elections. The same can be said for Nicaragua. In that case, a much more rapid transition to **polyarchy** took place, but after an initial period of social and economic gains for the poor, the revolution ultimately ceased addressing the social questions that had rallied peasants and the poor to the Sandinista banner. In other words, the Latin American experience raises questions about whether revolutionary regimes can really deliver on both the social question and democracy. Recent years have seen some new thinking about revolution and the usefulness of seeking control of the state, some of it spurred by the Zapatista uprising in Chiapas, Mexico.

The Cuban Revolution

The commitment of Fidel and Raúl Castro and the Cuban Communist Party (PCC) to preserve Cuba's current political system grows out of a long history of resistance to U.S. domination. The Castros believe that maintaining a one-party state is crucial to unity against the threat of Cuba becoming once again a virtual colony of the United States. Given the sad history of U.S. intervention in Guatemala, Chile, and (in the 1980s) revolutionary Nicaragua, we can question but not dismiss his perspective. Critics, including some who are sympathetic to Cuba's revolution, argue that the party is clinging to a type of political system discredited nearly everywhere in the world today and that the aversion to competitive party elections is nothing less than an admission that the government dares not put its legitimacy to test in an election.

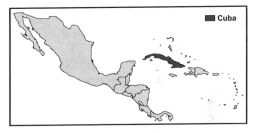

Origins: Nationalism and Neocolonialism

Cuba was among the very last of Spain's colonial possessions to achieve independence. Havana, the capital, was the departure point for Spain's armada of merchant vessels and warships during the colonial era, a military stronghold of the empire. The colonial economy was based on plantations producing sugar and tobacco for export. Slaves were imported into Cuba as late as the 1870s, which gives the island deep historical and cultural connections with Africa. The **criollo** elite chafed under Spanish rule but feared social rebellion and emancipation, lest they suffer the fate of French slaveholders in nearby Haiti. As in several other Caribbean nations, the elite seriously considered exchanging colonial rule for entry into the United States as a slave state. Several promising movements for independence were thwarted when elites, fearful of social revolution, changed sides (Pérez 1988).

The last of these revolts was led by the extraordinary patriot and intellectual José Martí. Visitors to Communist Cuba are often surprised that Martí's busts, statues, and portraits, more than images of Fidel Castro, are found everywhere. Martí mobilized Cuba's Afro-descendant black population by promising to create a race-blind social order of opportunity for all (De la Fuente 2001). Martí was killed in battle in 1895, not before warning his countrymen about American intentions. Still, in 1898 most Cubans welcomed U.S. intervention, believing it would shorten the bloodshed. Cuban elites hoped that U.S. intervention, by ending the independence struggle quickly, would forestall deeper social revolution.

U.S. troops left in 1903, but only after forcing the Cuban government to accept the Platt Amendment, which gave Washington the "right" to intervene in Cuba to maintain stability. Under Platt, the United States established the naval base at Guantánamo Bay, which it still occupies despite Cuban protests and uses as a prison in its "war on terror." In fact, the amendment encouraged rather than discouraged instability. The U.S. embassy became a major player in Cuban domestic politics. Whenever any political faction disliked the outcome of an election, it would organize civil unrest. In both 1905 and 1917, the United States intervened militarily under provisions of the Platt Amendment, and although the amendment was repealed in 1934, American interference in Cuban affairs had become a fact of political life on the island by that time.

The United States had already replaced Spain as the key foreign actor in Cuba's economy. North Americans owned many of the plantations and sugar mills; Cuban planters became their agents or employees. U.S. economic control increased after the Spanish–American War. North American investments went from US$50 million near the end of the 1800s to US$1.3 billion by the 1920s (Pérez 1988: 13). Britain and the United States actually set the price of sugar through an international sugar committee. As a result, Cubans came to link economic distress to this neocolonial status. Something similar happened throughout Central America and much of the Caribbean, including the Dominican Republic, Haiti, and Puerto Rico. U.S. interests owned most of the banks, port facilities, railroads, utilities, and so forth. These investments modernized the infrastructure, but mostly to facilitate an export-based, highly dependent economic system. The dominance of foreign capital in the economy and the buying-out of the planters meant that in this region the domestic **bourgeoisie** was numerically and politically weak, even by Latin American standards. U.S. investment did provide some employment and opportunities for a middle class to develop, but at the top levels of society, there was an economic and political void. The presence of the United States was a magnet for anti-imperialist sentiment and action.

In the Cuban case, Martí's promise of racial egalitarianism posed a direct challenge to the U.S. ruling class, especially to the white southerners who maintained white supremacy in the former Confederate states. Here was a revolution promising racial equality only 90 miles away from Florida. The U.S. armed forces were segregated and would remain so until the end of World War II. Their presence in bases and on shore leave in Cuba reinforced racial segregation, accentuating tensions on the island.

Cuba's politics post-independence became an elite game, full of corruption and fraud. Two Cuban parties, Liberals and Conservatives, competed for power behind a facade of democracy. Corrupt politicians and an inefficient bureaucracy certainly are no strangers to Latin America, but in the Cuban case, they were associated with frustrated revolution, compromised sovereignty, and a government that looked to its patron in the north to solve problems. In 1924, the Liberal Gerardo Machado was elected and changed the constitution to grant himself a new six-year term in 1927. Then the world economy collapsed and sent Cuban sugar prices plummeting. Machado met strikes and protests with harsh repression.

In Latin America, many such crises have spawned a cohort of student activists, many of whom later undertake political careers and assume a generational identity. Some of the key political leaders of the populist era—for example, in Venezuela, Peru, Bolivia, and elsewhere—came out of the student movements. In Cuba, a "Generation of 1930" sprung up to oppose the Machado dictatorship. Fidel Castro was not of the 1930s cohort, but he began his political career at the University of Havana and was influenced by the radical nationalists of 1930; many would join him in revolutionary struggle after World War II.

Despite President Franklin Roosevelt's (1932–1945) "Good Neighbor" policy, the United States intervened to quell radical change through the machinations of Ambassador Sumner Welles. Welles worked to replace the dictator Machado, who was driven from the country by a revolt of army officers. His replacement (Carlos Manuel Céspedes) was too close to Machado to please the opposition. Meanwhile, workers in the sugar cane fields pressed their demands in the midst of a worsening economic crisis. The government moved to freeze military pay, and in response, a group of noncommissioned officers, led by sergeant Fulgencio Batista, staged a coup that ultimately brought a reformist university professor, Ramón Grau San Martín, to power.

Grau instituted some reforms, such as nationalization of the electric utilities and expansion of legal rights for unions, which alarmed both the Cuban ruling class and the United States. Welles began to plot Grau's removal. He found an ally in the ambitious Batista. As the U.S. fleet made an ominous appearance in the harbor, ostensibly to protect American lives and property, Batista staged a *golpe* against Grau. For the next 25 years, Batista ruled Cuba—either in the presidency or as the power behind the throne. Grau managed to win election as president in 1944, but he and his Cuban revolutionary party (Auténticos) had by this time been tamed. He failed to deliver on social justice reforms embodied in a new constitution written in 1940. Grau, his successor (Carlos Prío Socarras), and his (Auténtico) party were drawn into corruption.

Cubans were becoming frustrated with the failure of electoral democracy. The most active opposition came not from the Communist Party, which pragmatically aligned with Batista at times, but from the Cuban People's Party (Orthodoxos). Eduardo Chibas, a member of the Generation of 1930 and a fiery orator, was their leader. The head of the party's youth wing was a law student at the University of Havana, Fidel Castro Ruz.

For Review

What the role did the United States play in the Cuban struggle for independence from Spain? How would this role influence Cuba in the years between 1898 and 1952? How did this legacy come to be taken up by the young Fidel Castro?

The Rise of Fidel Castro and the Revolution of 1959

In 1952, Batista canceled elections and moved from behind the scenes into the presidency. Batista—corrupt, brutal, mafia-connected, and U.S.-supported—would be overthrown in 1959 by a few hundred guerrillas under Castro's leadership in the countryside and by tens of thousands of other Cubans in the cities, especially Havana. A signal event occurred when Castro led an attack by students and workers on the Moncada army base in Santiago, in eastern Cuba, on July 26, 1953. The attack failed. Most of the rebels were eventually killed, but Castro survived. The bold move sparked a 26th of July Movement, formed officially in November 1956. Under its umbrella, opponents of Batista united behind a program calling for both political democracy and deep social change.

Fidel Castro drew a connection between these goals in his famous speech made in 1953 at his trial for leading the Moncada attack. In "History Will Absolve Me," Castro laid out the stark injustices afflicting Cuba's laboring masses, the corruption and brutality of the government, and other problems. He argued,

> The problem of land, the problem of industrialization, the problem of housing, the problem of unemployment, the problem of education and the problem of people's health: these are the six problems we would take immediate steps to solve, along with restoration of civil liberties and political democracy.
>
> (quoted in Brenner et al. 1989: 32)

Castro concluded his speech at the trial with an appeal to Martí's words—"a true man does not seek the path where advantage lies, but rather the path where duty lies"—and with a defiant proclamation: "I know that imprisonment will be harder for me than it has ever been for anyone, filled with cowardly threats and hideous cruelty. But I do not fear prison, as I do not fear the fury of the miserable tyrant who took the lives of 70 of my comrades. Condemn me. It does not matter. History will absolve me" (quoted in Brenner et al. 1989: 35).

Here, two aspects of Hannah Arendt's conception of revolution, the quest for freedom and the desire for social change, were brought together in a revolutionary movement—just as they were in Mexico when Francisco Madero's call for clean elections in 1910 was supplemented by the social justice themes enunciated by Pancho Villa and Emiliano Zapata. Similarly, the Sandinista Front for National Liberation (FSLN) would pair social justice and the fight against dictatorship in the struggle leading to the 1979 revolution in Nicaragua.

Castro served 22 months in prison and then was released after Batista, under popular pressure, declared an amnesty. He left the country for exile in Mexico, where he met the free-thinking Argentine Marxist, Ernesto Che Guevara. As the urban fighters of the 26th of July Movement drew Batista's army into the cities, Fidel, his brother Raúl, Che, and others landed an insurrectionary force in eastern Cuba in November 1956. They were nearly wiped out and fled to the nearby Sierra Maestra mountains. It was there, protected by sympathetic, poor peasants, that the rebels' commitment to revolutionary change and understanding of Cuban society was deepened. It is worth noting that Raúl Castro and Che were already Marxists by this time; neither, however, was a communist.

In 1957, Herbert Matthews, a journalist for the *New York Times*, would report that Castro had "a political mind rather than a military one. He has strong ideas of liberty, democracy, social justice, the need to restore the Constitution, to hold elections. He has strong ideas on economy, too, but an economist would consider them weak." Matthews said Castro expressed no animosity toward the United States and quoted him: "Above all we are fighting for a democratic Cuba and an end to the dictatorship" (Matthews 1957).

From their base in the mountains, the rebel band reorganized and grew into an effective fighting force, often taking weapons and gaining new recruits from captured soldiers, as the 26th of July Movement kept up the pressure in the cities. Batista's heavy-handed response brought death or torture to thousands. Altogether, 20,000 civilians died in the fighting, creating deep popular anger against anyone associated with the regime. Batista's political support crumbled, and the army with it. This same scenario of an isolated, unpopular, repressive dictator vulnerable to revolutionary insurrection would repeat itself in 1979 when the Sandinistas overthrew the Somoza regime in Nicaragua.

In January 1959, Batista fled. Castro and his guerrilla forces moved across the country toward Havana, slowly, gathering support and adulation along the way. They entered Havana in February with wild and enthusiastic crowds. Fidel did not make himself part of the new revolutionary government, but no one could rival his political influence. His guerrilla force rapidly transformed itself into the new national army, stepping into the void left by the total collapse of Batista's forces. This makeover of the military meant that the rebels would have the decisive element of power on their side in shaping the new order. Castro had something going for him that Jacobo Arbenz of Guatemala lacked when overthrown in 1954, and Allende too in Chile in 1973—that is, control over the coercive apparatus of government. However, we should not exaggerate this single factor. The Sandinistas would take power in 1979, and they too controlled the armed forces. Yet they lost control of government only 11 years later.

Batista's collapse surprised everyone. Superficially, it seemed as though Cuba's new leaders had defied the notion that revolutions require patient organizing. Perhaps Latin American governments everywhere were weak and doomed to collapse—if only a dedicated band of rebels would dare to take up armed struggle. A new theory, a "revolution in the revolution," as the French writer Regis Debray (1967) put it, took hold in the form of the theory of the "armed *foco*." Rather than concentrate patiently on developing a social base among workers and peasants, the "armed *foco*" theory stressed insurrection. This view failed to take into account adequately the importance of broad opposition to Batista in the cities organized by the 26th of July Movement. It also assumed wrongly that other Latin American states were as weak as that of semicolonial Cuba, and it failed to recognize that the United States and these states were also analyzing why Batista had fallen, to prevent the same thing from happening elsewhere. But the gospel of revolution spread by Cuba was embraced by a generation of young Latin American leftists. Here at last was a leader, Fidel Castro, ready to make a real social revolution. In the 1960s, Cuba's young rulers saw their revolution as a harbinger of change on a global scale and supported young Fidelistas elsewhere.

Once Washington realized that Fidel Castro was determined to carry out his agenda of social and economic reform, the Eisenhower administration reacted as it had to efforts by Arbenz to make radical change in Guatemala in 1954—that is, with a campaign of propaganda, sabotage, and economic sanctions against the new regime, measures continued by presidents John F. Kennedy (1960–1963) and Lyndon Baines Johnson (1963–1968). Perhaps Castro and his close collaborators would have moved against dissenters to his plans in any case, but the external threats and subversion reinforced an inhospitable climate for tolerance of opposition. Washington did not like the way that the new government dealt with popular rage directed toward the dictator and his circle, who had committed gross atrocities, including assassinations and tortures. Batista had left the country on a mobster's plane, but most of his henchmen were left behind. Many were put on trial, and 550 were executed. These actions prevented mobs from exacting their own revenge, but the firing squads alienated some parts of the anti-Batista coalition.

Fidel Castro and his companions were prioritizing their radical agenda of redistribution and social restructuring, and they were wary of an imperial power with an interventionist history 90 miles away. The United States saw Castro defying its authority in an unprecedented way and feared the establishment of a communist regime in the hemisphere. In some ways, the latter proved a self-fulfilling prophecy.

On a visit to the United Nations in New York in 1960, Castro shocked the U.S. State Department and many in his own entourage by refusing to ask for economic aid, a symbolic demonstration of his determination not to subordinate Cuban sovereignty to Washington's influence. Upon his return, Castro consolidated his popular base of support by implementing a far-reaching land reform, expropriating (with compensation in bonds) all parcels of land of more than 1,000 acres. Other measures quickly followed. Big wage increases and price freezes were proclaimed. Mandatory reduction of rents alone redistributed about 15 percent of national income. In 1960, more than US$1 billion in U.S. property was expropriated, as Cuba seized control of its oil refineries, transportation system, and utilities. In that same year, hundreds of thousands of young students went to the countryside on a campaign to eradicate illiteracy. This far-reaching populist program is crucial to understanding how the rebel leadership was able to fend off U.S. intervention and consolidate a regime distinct from the kind of **pluralist** democracy originally promised. Heavily influenced by his brother Raúl, Fidel Castro looked to the Communist Party, the best-organized force on the left (but slow to have joined the revolution), to provide support, especially in transforming his guerrilla force into a new army. These actions alienated centrist leaders of the 26th of July Movement and even some leaders of Castro's guerrilla army. By moving decisively toward radical change, the Cuban Revolution's young leaders were closing the door to the kind of negotiated pact that results in **polyarchy**.

The United States stepped up its efforts to exploit divisions within the revolutionary forces, raising the specter of a repeat of the Guatemala episode of 1954. Castro forced dissident members of the governing council to resign. Some of them were arrested, charged with collaborating with the enemy, and imprisoned for decades. It is impossible to know how many opponents were jailed for collaborating with CIA subversion versus how many were jailed for merely dissenting from the direction Fidel was taking. Was fear of U.S. intervention driving repression, or was the imperialist threat a convenient excuse?

Many opponents of Castro went into exile in Miami, where they plotted and organized a counterrevolution. At the direction of the Eisenhower administration, the CIA planned and encouraged acts of sabotage and terror, which were implemented during the Kennedy administration. For example, one six-man CIA team blew up a Cuban industrial facility in 1962, killing 400 workers. Among the angriest enemies of the new regime were *mafiosos* who had enjoyed Batista's patronage. They had turned Havana into one of the world's most decadent playgrounds for the rich, and now they had lost their glittery hotels and casinos to a bearded Marxist. We know that some of them eagerly collaborated with the CIA in attempts to assassinate Castro (Hinckle and Turner 1981). In response, the Castro regime cracked down on press freedoms and other civil liberties, hastening the exodus to Miami. Not all those fleeing to exile were collaborators with the old regime; many were angered by the loss of their property or prestige as the revolution leveled the social class system.

On April 17, 1961, the Kennedy administration put into action a plan devised under President Eisenhower. Cuban exiles trained by the CIA in southern Florida and Guatemala invaded Cuba at the Bay of Pigs. Just a few days before the invasion, the exile force had carried out the terrorist bombing of the seven-story El Encanto department store in Havana in an attempt to sow fear. The exile army was routed by Cuban forces at the beach, Playa Girón. Kennedy had temporized by withdrawing promised American air cover for the invasion, but more serious was the miscalculation that the Cuban population would rise against the new government. Castro defeated the invaders. The die was cast. Cuba now moved firmly into the communist bloc of nations. In October 1962, the world would be brought to the brink of Armageddon with the Cuban Missile Crisis. Castro permitted the Soviets to base intermediate-range missiles on the island. Kennedy reacted with a naval blockade that could have led to nuclear war. The Russians, without consulting Castro, agreed to pull their missiles from Cuba in exchange for, among other things, a promise from Kennedy that the United States would not invade Cuba again.

For Review

Why do Cubans celebrate July 26 as the anniversary of their revolution? How did Fidel Castro's goals, as expressed before 1959, reflect a desire for freedom on one hand and raise Arendt's social question on the other? How did the United States respond to revolution in Cuba? What actions by the new government created divisions among the revolutionary coalition? How did U.S. policy reinforce the government's concerns?

Consolidation of the Cuban Revolution

Havana met the U.S. challenge not only by repressing dissidents but also by mobilizing the population to defend the revolution. Most important were a militia and Committees for the Defense of the Revolution (CDRs). The CDRs are composed of local residents who volunteer to participate in revolutionary activities in their neighborhood. They form a nationwide, grassroots network that exercises surveillance over dissidents, but as neighborhood organizations they also carry out a range of other functions, such as intervening against domestic violence and checking on the welfare of children. They form a low-technology alternative for security against infiltration of Cuban exiles intent on carrying out sabotage. They continue to exist today but recently have been scaled back.

Fidel Castro declared himself a Marxist–Leninist in 1961, but even then the Communist Party (called the Popular Socialist Party until 1961) remained but one element in a revolutionary coalition. The ruling group declared itself to be a party in 1962 and formally declared itself the Communist Party of Cuba (PCC) in 1965; still, no party Congress was held until 1975. The decisive move toward the economic and political model of the Soviet Union came after a series of economic setbacks, most notably a failure to reach the goal of a

10-million-ton sugar harvest in 1970. The objective had been to capture a larger share of the world sugar market and use the profits for an ambitious program of economic development. The country's entire human and physical infrastructure was thrown into an effort that fell 2.4 million tons short, an economic disaster. As a result, Cuba would have to join the Eastern Bloc and synchronize its economy with these nations. The Cuban leadership decided to abandon Guevara's humanist economic theories and embraced the model of centralized planning promoted by the Soviets. Also, by 1970 it was clear that revolutions elsewhere in Latin America were unlikely to be successful, and the Soviets were more interested in détente than confrontation with the United States. Diplomatically, Cuba pursued better relations with Latin American governments.

To this day the PCC remains the only legal party in Cuba, but its relationship to Cuban civil society has been more complicated than in other communist nations—for example, in Eastern Europe. Before the PCC became the official party of the revolution, several mass organizations (including the CDRs) linking the society to the state had been created. In addition, the Communist Party in Batista's time was less interested in revolution and more oriented to reforms and keeping influence in the labor movement. By 1970 the Fidelistas had displaced many older Communist leaders from leadership of the party. The PCC does not nominate or campaign for candidates, but that does not prevent it from exerting strong influence over the state bureaucracy and major social institutions. There is no disputing the fact that the PCC is the most powerful institution in Cuba. You can rise to significant positions of authority and not be a member of the party, but you cannot rise or keep those positions if the party decides you unfit.

Was Fidel Castro a closet Communist before 1960? Was he sincere about restoring political democracy? More important for us is the question of whether pluralist democracy in Cuba was compatible with the radical social and economic agenda expressed by Castro and the revolutionary movement. Could the social and economic promises of the 26th of July Movement have been implemented by a government constituted as a liberal democracy— that is, as a polyarchy? The Cuban leaders might remind us that they had tried electoral democracy, and it had failed to produce reforms—for example, after the 1933 revolt. Given the record of U.S. intervention in the region, especially in Cuba, the revolutionary leadership had many reasons to place unity above the value of pluralism. If forced to choose between his promise of elections and his promises of socioeconomic change and real independence from the United States, which should Castro have honored?

It was Machiavelli (1947: 48) who noted 450 years earlier that for new rulers "above all it is impossible not to earn a reputation for cruelty since new states are full of dangers." The Italian thinker also warned that only "armed prophets" succeed in founding new states; "unarmed prophets" fail. Cuba's new rulers acted accordingly. Fidel Castro and his comrades relied on swift and effective suppression of opposition to consolidate their power; to this day, a kind of siege mentality has been used to justify repression of dissent deemed outside the boundaries of the revolution.

Machiavelli also warned against excessive reliance on cruelty and fear, counseling new rulers to commit necessary cruelties early. That lesson also seems to pertain to Cuba. Those who think that force is the only factor holding the regime together are overlooking the significant accomplishments of the Cuban Revolution and the political spaces it opened for significant public participation in shaping policies (explored in our next chapter). Besides the CDRs, Cubans are integrated into government and politics through other "mass organizations" that are formed by artists, women, labor unions, and so on. Even among Cubans who have become disaffected with the regime, many share a spirit of common sacrifice, pride in Cuba's place on the world stage, and a deep commitment to defense of its sovereignty. Many Cubans are proud of the performance of their army in Africa in the 1970s and 1980s, especially in Angola and Namibia, where the army backed new governments against force backed by the apartheid regime of South Africa. In fact, the army actually fought impressively against a white South African military force in battle in 1988. The army today no longer has the capability to fight so far abroad, but it has been entrusted with managing much of the tourism sector, the most important generator of foreign exchange.

Since 2000, Cubans have benefited from highly discounted oil provided by Venezuela. That could disappear should the party (the United Socialist Party of Venezuela—PSUV) of Chávez, who died in March 2013, lose control of government. On the other hand, sugar prices have recovered, and the country is benefiting from a large investment made in a pharmaceutical industry whose patents and exports of medicine are now the second-largest source of export earnings, after tourism. If the reforms introduced by Castro can induce higher productivity in agriculture, and with Asian, European, and Latin American capital and markets playing an increasing role, the future could be brighter—especially if the search for offshore oil, fruitless so far, is successful.

In February 2013, Raúl Castro (at age 81) was reelected to a five-year term, but he promised not to seek another one, and some Cubans on the island think he will leave even sooner. The first leaders not to fight in the 1959 revolution will soon hold the reins of power. Without the prestige of that struggle to their credit, can a new generation hold the allegiance of Cubans fatigued by decades of sacrifice? Do Cubans still see socialism as the way to develop their economy and keep their independence from the colossus 90 miles away? Have limited reforms whetted their appetite for more capitalism?

For Review

By 1970, how was Cuba's political system different from the one led by the coalition of anti-Batista forces that formed the government in 1959? What, in your mind, were the main factors that produced this result? What are CDRs, and why were they created?

Taking Stock of Cuba's Revolution

Cuba's social accomplishments are what have always attracted admiration in Latin America, accomplishments that have been put in doubt since the Eastern Bloc communist states collapsed between 1989 and 1991. Suddenly, Cuba lost almost 87 percent of its trade, including imports of vital machinery, fertilizer, and energy. Between 1989 and 1993, oil imports were more than halved, leading to planned, rolling blackouts. In these four years, the size of the economy was cut in half. It is difficult to find any comparable case among the world's nations where such contraction occurred; however, the system survived, and after 1994 the economy began to recover.

By 2014, the economic situation had much improved but not yet recovered to pre-1990 standards. It is worth reviewing where Cuba stood before the Soviet demise, because to some extent the survival of the regime certainly was due to its past accomplishments and because these statistics represent a standard of living that in some sense represents "normality" for Cubans of adult age.

By the early 1980s, Cuba had dramatically reduced infant mortality from 60 per 1,000 to 19 per 1,000 (the U.S. rate was 14 at the time), largely by eliminating gastrointestinal inflammation and respiratory infection. The number of medical practitioners was doubled, despite the fact that most of Cuba's existing doctors had fled the island in the early 1960s. Malaria, diphtheria, and polio were eliminated. Advances in tuberculosis were recorded. In 1959, there were 18 refrigerators per 100 homes; in 1985, there were 63. There were 49 radios per 100 homes in 1959; by 1985, there were 135. There were only 6 televisions per 100 homes in 1959; in 1985, there were 79. Before the revolution there were 1.3 million housing units, of which only half had access to electricity; by 1982, of 2.4 million housing units, 79 percent had access to electricity. The literacy rate was 32 percent before the revolution; by the 1980s, it was 98 percent. In the days before the Internet, the United Nations said that every country should have 100 newspaper copies, 50 radio receivers, and 20 cinema seats for every 1,000 people. Cuba was the only Third World country to meet all of these criteria.

Although the other economies of Latin America contracted by 8 percent in the 1980s, Cuba's grew by 33 percent. The real material conditions of Cubans improved in the 1980s. A good comparison can be made to the second-largest Spanish-speaking Caribbean country, the Dominican Republic. Cubans lived 12 years longer, on average, than Dominicans. Infant mortality was four times higher in Santo Domingo than in Cuba. Illiteracy had been eradicated in Cuba; the literacy rate was only 77 percent in the Dominican Republic. Cuba had twice as many doctors per capita and 8.5 times as many nurses. Unemployment in Cuba was 5 percent; the informal sector and unemployed rate were more than 60 percent in the Dominican Republic. Cuba's most important source of foreign earnings was sugar exports; the Dominican Republic relied more on remittances (money sent home) from emigrants.

Despite recovery since 1994, Cubans were still coping with shortages 20 years later in 2014. By this time, tourism, exports of nickel (used to make steel), and remittances from Cubans living abroad had replaced the sugar industry as the most important source of foreign exchange. In 2002, the government closed down half of the sugar mills. Discounted Venezuelan oil eased the energy shortage. In 2008, Raúl Castro, having taken over leadership after the retirement of his brother, began to lift some regulations and open some space for markets. A combination of urban gardens and increased production of fruit and vegetables in the countryside had improved diets. Minimum nutritional standards were being met, but meat, eggs, and other common goods were in short supply. More seriously, the government faced the problem that although the limited opening for the market was lifting overall production, for the first time in 50 years, slums and social exclusion were beginning to reappear in urban areas.

Ironically, Cuba's success in education may be breeding frustration. A highly educated workforce lacks sufficient job opportunities in Cuba and can earn much more abroad. Many have looked to immigrate legally or illegally to the United States. Women and Afro-Cubans, who benefited the most from postrevolutionary advances, suffered the most from

PUNTO DE VISTA: THE STRUGGLE FOR THE LEGACY OF JOSÉ MARTÍ

Fidel and Raúl Castro, Che Guevara, and the other "bearded ones" created the first and only self-proclaimed Marxist state in the hemisphere. However, the social thought of José Martí resonates more deeply with the Cuban people than Marxism. Both the government and the exile community in Miami have sought to tie themselves to Martí, the former by linking his thought to socialism, the latter by linking it to **liberalism**. Both have an argument to make.

Martí never embraced socialism or **Marxism**, but he also feared that no significant change could come to Cuba unless deep social reform accompanied independence. Martí and his collaborators kept their ultimate plans hidden from view of the colony's elites. He feared that they would trade colonial status with Spain for a neocolonial dependency on the United States to protect their wealth and status. And though he admired much about the United States, where he lived and traveled, organizing Cubans abroad to support the fight for independence, he feared U.S. imperialism would overrun not only Cuba but all of Latin America. In an unfinished letter, written on the day he died, May 18, 1895, Martí told a friend,

> Now I can write, now I can tell you how tenderly and gratefully and respectfully I love you and that home which I consider my pride and responsibility. I am in daily danger of giving my life for my country and duty, for I understand that duty and have the courage to carry it out—the duty of preventing the United States from spreading through the Antilles as Cuba gains its independence, and from overpowering with that additional strength our American lands. All I have done thus far, and all I will do, is for this purpose. I have had to work quietly and somewhat indirectly, because to achieve certain objectives, they must be kept undercover; to say what they are would raise such difficulties that the objectives could not be achieved.
> (Martí 1999: 234)

Martí went on to use an analogy drawn from the biblical story of David and Goliath. "I have lived in the monster and I know its entrails; my sling is David's."

Cuban exiles believe that by consolidating his personal power, Fidel Castro has contradicted Martí's spirit, that Martí never would have made Cuba so dependent on the Soviet Union, as it was before 1990. A Texas-based exile found this quotation from Martí to post on her website (xld.com/public/Cuba/marti.htm, accessed on February 13, 2004):

> Socialist ideology, like so many others, has two main dangers. One stems from confused and incomplete readings of foreign texts, and the other from the arrogance and hidden rage of those who, in order to climb up in the world, pretend to be frantic defenders of the helpless so as to have shoulders on which to stand.

Another dissident website (Cuban-junky.com, accessed February 13, 2004) in the Netherlands argued,

> All of Martí's teachings . . . condemn all despotic regimes and the abridgment of human rights. Furthermore, he goes on to denounce the lack of spirituality and type of arrogance that we find in the current dictatorship. For this reason, the publication of Martí's thoughts, in all its force, is of the greatest importance today. His beliefs, which can guide democracies and if heeded, offer them greater security, speak more eloquently against the Cuban apostasy than all the accusations that others might make.

Fidel sees himself as following in Martí's footsteps. Consider his remarks (Castro Ruz 1991) to a party congress called to deal with the harsh economic conditions threatening the revolution in the wake of the collapse of the Soviet Union in 1991:

> The world is looking at Cuba today with great hope. The world wants us to resist and win because it will be their victory. The world admires this small country. The world admires this island of freedom and dignity that defies all and is capable of defying all. The world admires the Cuba of today and will admire it more and more, to the extent that we are capable of courage, that we are capable of fighting, and that we are capable of winning.

Martí without a doubt saw himself as a liberal republican. After all, Marxism in his lifetime was largely a European intellectual and working-class movement. The Russian Revolution was two decades away. But he also, like Bolívar, believed true independence required deep social and economic change. Cuba had to become a "country for all," he said, cognizant that slavery had left a racial hierarchy that had to be overturned by revolutionary means.

Point/Counterpoint

So who has the better claim to Martí's legacy—exiles or Havana?

a. If you say "the exiles," how do you respond to the argument that the more moderate parts of the coalition that fought Batista would have ultimately subordinated the Cuban Revolution to Washington's hegemony and failed to achieve the social gains (health care, education, more equality for Afro-Cubans and women) made by the Fidelistas?
b. If you say "Havana," how do you respond to the fact that Martí never embraced Marxism and, like Fidel in his Moncada speech, envisioned Cuba as a republic after independence from Spain?

For more information

See Esther Allen and Roberto Gonzalez Echevarria, *José Martí: Selected Writings* (New York: Penguin Classics, 2002). The PBS program *Latino Americans* has an episode on José Martí at http://video .pbs.org/video/2365053101.

the economic contraction of the 1990s. Women had to absorb more of the stress that difficult economic conditions placed on the family. Despite enormous progress in reducing racism in Cuban society, Afro-Cubans were still disproportionately in occupations most affected by cuts, and some discriminatory practices reappeared.

Human Rights, One-Party Rule, and Cuba's Uncertain Future

Cuban politics is more complex than the simple image of dictatorship so often portrayed in the U.S. media. How the Cuban political system actually functions, and what exactly the balance is between consent and repression, is hard to answer.

Visitors to Cuba are often struck by the lack of heavily armed police and military, a common sight in other Latin American countries. Assassinations, disappearances, and states of siege, common throughout much of "democratic" Latin America, have not occurred at all in Cuba. Cuban elections are contested by multiple candidates, open to all, not just party members. Elections are held for local, provincial, and national assemblies. Candidates present themselves in well-attended meetings at the local level. Incumbents often lose (Roman 2003). Mass organizations can influence the outcome and pressure officials in office. Many economic policies are debated and discussed at grassroots meetings and in these organizations. The leaders of these organizations are in large majority members of the PCC, but there does not appear to be as much party control over these organizations or government agencies as there was in Eastern Europe under communism.

Still, opposition parties are not free to organize and compete in elections. Dissident voices continue to be repressed in Cuba, and political prisoners (how many is debated) suffer harsh conditions in jails. Usually, the general direction of policy, especially economic policy, has been set by the PCC, and often only after Fidel—or now Raúl—has pronounced the matter open for debate. For example, the decision to allow private business to operate is a matter of policy set from above; how large those businesses may be or how they are taxed is subject to discussion and debate.

Clearly, Fidel Castro has played a crucial role in Cuban politics for nearly 50 years. During Fidel's illness in 2006–2007, Raúl took center stage; he formally became president of the Council of State in 2008, and contrary to what Miami and Washington hoped, Cubans seemed to react more with concern than with elation at the prospect of life without Fidel. In that year, Raúl made several cautious but significant moves. For the first time, Cubans were allowed to own cell phones and personal computers. Farmers were told that they could produce and sell crops grown on up to 100 acres of land, an attempt to rectify a situation in which Cuba imports 80 percent of its food. Castro has opened the media to facilitate criticism of the government, and millions of suggestions for change have been generated from thousands of grassroots meetings.

In August 2010, Raúl Castro announced that as many as 1.3 million state employees would be discharged and expected to find work in the private sectors. To absorb these workers (one-quarter of the workforce), the government has been allowing small private businesses to form. Some observers think Cuba might be headed for the Chinese model—a one-party state that retains control over the most important economic sectors (finance and key industries) but otherwise aims to produce economic growth through capitalism and the market. In January 2013, the government lifted the requirement for Cubans to secure an exit visa to travel abroad.

Castro sees this as modernizing socialism, not compromising it. However, greater political space for the market and private property potentially threatens the sense of common sacrifice and egalitarianism that allowed the regime to survive the devastating economic consequences of the collapse of the Soviet Union. The right to own cell phones and computers and to travel is indeed liberalization—but along with the good (more freedom to communicate and criticize) comes the bad. Only those who can afford consumer goods and tickets abroad will enjoy the new freedom. A Cuban who receives US$100 per month from relatives in Florida can live a comfortable life because he or she does not pay for health, education, or housing and can buy basic foodstuffs at subsidized prices. Cubans without relatives abroad continue to struggle. And to start up a small business requires capital—which has to be accumulated or provided by relatives abroad. In either case, that favors some Cubans more than others, and it favors white males more than blacks and women.

International pressure has continued to grow on the United States to lift the economic embargo (which Cuba calls a blockade) that it imposed on Cuba in 1962, by which the United States seeks to prohibit not only its own citizens and companies from doing business in Cuba, but also those of other countries (see chapter 16). Pressure increased after the release of many Cuban political dissidents from jail in the summer of 2010. A majority of the Miami Cuban community favors ending the blockade, but its powerful anti-Castro lobby remains firmly opposed. The Obama administration did lift some restrictions on travel and on the ability of Miami Cubans to send remittances to relatives. Under people-to-people travel agencies in the United States, most Americans can now travel easily to Cuba. The interesting question is whether the end of economic sanctions by the United States would boost the regime by giving the economy a lift, or whether the sudden influx of U.S. tourists and consumer culture would ultimately further undermine the egalitarian values inherited from Martí and the revolution.

As noted previously, in February 2013, Raúl Castro was elected to a new five-year term at age 81 and announced that he would retire at that end of that time. At the same time, the National Assembly chose Miguel Díaz-Canel, 52, a former education minister, as first vice president. Given his age, and perhaps depending on how things are going, nothing ensures that Raúl will not retire even sooner. All indications are that Díaz-Canel would continue the economic and (more limited) political openings championed by Castro. However, the Castros and those of their comrades from the Sierra Maestra who are still living enjoy a prestige that no successor can match because of the heroic mythology surrounding the 1959 revolution.

One can imagine scenarios where the Cuban regime collapses and undergoes a transition more like that which occurred in Eastern Europe; similarly, one can imagine the regime shifting to a more authoritarian and bureaucratic mode, perhaps a Cuban version of China's hybrid state that mixes one-party rule with a market economy. However, one can also see the imperatives of protecting sovereignty against U.S. power and defending the social gains of the revolution as trumping these alternatives. Without the Castros to guide the revolution, the PCC might become more pluralist. Although a "transition to democracy" of the sort that happened in Eastern Europe, Brazil, or the Southern Cone might happen, so too may the Cuban future bring some alternative unforeseen by the Castros or the Miami exile community.

For Review

What gains were made in social conditions in Cuba after the revolution? How did the Cuban regime survive the devastating economic impact of the Soviet collapse? How has economic policy changed with the ascent of Raúl? What positives and negatives have resulted? Anticipating the departure of the revolutionary generation from power in a very few years, what are some alternative scenarios for Cuba's political system?

Insurgencies: The Social Question and Revolution in Central America

We could have a lively debate about whether revolutions can happen without insurgencies—that is, armed revolutionary movements that attempt to overturn an existing regime. Here, we concentrate on the way revolutionary insurgencies may leave a significant mark on politics even without succeeding. In fact, the Zapatista uprising in Chiapas, Mexico, has questioned the very idea that revolutionary movements should even aim to take over the state. Insurgencies by their nature require violence and a paramilitary organization. If successful in taking power or gaining a share of power (as a result of a negotiated end of civil conflict), they bring this experience and culture into the state or politics.

The Central American nations experienced insurgencies in the 1980s. In the case of Nicaragua, an insurgency led by the Sandinista Front for National Liberation (FSLN) succeeded (1979) in taking power through a mass revolution. In two other cases, El Salvador and Guatemala, left-wing insurgencies failed to overthrow existing regimes but did achieve some significant democratic political reforms. However, by the end of a decade of acute civil violence, the region as a whole was left with a more troubling set of social questions than it had at the beginning.

As in the cases of Mexico and Cuba, one can see the two underlying factors identified by Arendt at work generating revolution in Central America. Repressive regimes unwilling to open political structures to new forces made the cry for democracy salient. At the same time, changes in the economic export economy disrupted the social structures and helped to make people responsive to calls for social justice by both religious and **secular** revolutionary organizers.

Revolutionaries seek support by offering answers to deep-rooted problems of poverty and injustice. These issues become more pressing, say some political scientists (Goldstone et al. 1991), when rising expectations are frustrated. This often happens when a period of economic growth feeds expectations in the population that life will continue to get better, at least for their children, but instead things suddenly get worse. If the benefits of growth fail to reach most people, or if a downturn in the economy causes living standards to fall after a period of steady improvement, the population may experience relative deprivation. These factors seem to have been at work in the case of Mexico during the Porfiriato era (1876–1910; see chapter 9), and they may have been at work in Central America in the post–World War II era, when the region saw high rates of economic growth generated by export booms. And just as in Porfiriato Mexico, this boom disrupted rural economic and social life.

In the period between 1850 and 1920, traditional life in much of the Central American countryside was disturbed by liberal modernization (see chapter 4). The process was complex, and peasants were not simply passive victims in this process (see Lauria-Santiago 1999), but by the early twentieth century, oligarchies had formed, and many peasants were driven from the land to make room for export agriculture, mostly coffee and fruit. Coffee *fincas* (plots of land) were generally owned by local elites, with the most famous example being El Salvador's Fourteen Families. Fruit plantations were developed originally by foreign companies, such as Castle and Cook and the United Fruit Company. Neither economy generated the kind of export wealth that provided capital for industrialization in Mexico and most of South America. Nonetheless, the Central American nations did undergo a form of "economic modernization" in the era after World War II.

Allowing for some variation, we can say that El Salvador, Nicaragua, Honduras, and Guatemala all evolved into oligarchies—in which a small clique of wealthy elites ran the country with no regard for the broader interests of the people. A family clique came to dominate Nicaragua and ruled it like a private hacienda. In El Salvador, a proud, nationalist, landed oligarchy liked to run things themselves with the help of the military. In Guatemala, dominance of the foreign fruit companies suffocated the development of a local bourgeoisie. After the 1954 overthrow of Arbenz, the fruit companies sold much of their land to wealthy or politically connected Guatemalans, including retired military officers who had little experience or commitment to democracy and who were heavily prejudiced against the nation's large indigenous population.

The grip of oligarchy was shaken by the stirrings of change after World War II, as U.S. investors began to see the region as a place for investments in new forms of export agriculture and light, labor-intensive industry. The World Bank encouraged Central American governments to embrace a strategy of development that involved borrowing money for infrastructure (roads, ports, etc.) and to take other measures to encourage investment in new exports. The region recorded great increases in the export of nontraditional products, such as cotton, sugar, and meat, but also labor-intensive manufacturing products, such as blouses, jeans, and pajamas (Barry and Preusch 1986).

The new export model brought several consequences, including the emergence of some new elites and expansion of the middle class and working class. At the other end of the social pyramid, thousands of peasant families were displaced from the land to make way for new pastures and plantations. They had to live on the margins and seek work in these agricultural enterprises, migrate to the cities, or seek work in the new export factories. Neither the new agricultural business nor manufacturing jobs (making bras and pajamas; assembling transistor radios and TVs) could absorb the displaced poor. In the 1960s these forces of socioeconomic change converged with an organizing cadre drawn from leftist students and clergy, the former inspired by the Cuban Revolution, the latter by social justice messages promoted after the Second Vatican Council blew winds of change through the Catholic Church.

Central America's economic signs looked great between World War II and 1975. The economy was booming and diversifying. But lurking below the surface was an accelerating process of social displacement.

The new economic model was slammed by the energy crisis that hit in 1974. The new export-agriculture economy depended heavily on oil for crop dusters, transport, fertilizer, irrigation, and other inputs that had been much less important in the labor-intensive, pre-war exports economy. At the same time, consumers abroad were feeling the pinch of energy prices; demand for the region's exports slackened, and prices fell. By the end of the 1970s, the economies had stopped growing; debt was at record levels. The oligarchy showed little concern for the impact on the masses. Hundreds of thousands of additional landless and unemployed workers were available to answer the call for revolutionary change or to take jobs in the only growing sector, the military. The United States blamed Cuba for the unrest, and the oligarchy saw communism behind every call for reform.

For Review

Why was access to land a major issue in the Central American revolutionary wars of the 1980s? How did changes in the export economy contribute to the outbreak of insurgency in this period?

The Nicaraguan Revolution

Nicaragua until 1979 was ruled by the Somoza family, a regime inaugurated in 1934 with the help of the United States. Anastasio Somoza was the U.S.-appointed commander of the country's National Guard. The Guard was a constabulary trained by the Americans to fight the nationalist patriot José Augusto Cesar Sandino. Sandino had worked in Mexico and had the support and sympathy of its

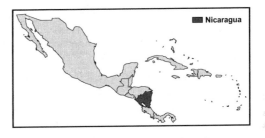

revolutionary government when he took up arms against the U.S. Marines, who had occupied the country periodically since 1910. Sandino drew his support from Nicaragua's poor peasantry. In what was a forerunner of U.S. policy in Vietnam 35 years later, the United States decided to retreat from Nicaragua because the casualties inflicted by Sandino's forces were increasingly costly in political terms at home. The U.S. idea was to train a professional army that would carry on the fight against Sandino but stay neutral in the political battles between rival Liberal and Conservative *caudillos*, allowing the country to settle conflicts through elections.

This early experiment in "democratization" imposed from abroad proved disastrous for the Nicaraguan people. Instead of a professional, apolitical military that would allow political disputes to be settled through elections, the U.S.-trained and armed Guard served as an instrument for Anastasio Somoza to rise from the status of a modestly wealthy liberal landlord to patriarch of a family that amassed a huge fortune and repressed all opponents (Millet 1977).

The elder Somoza was assassinated in 1956. His sons were just as ruthless as Batista in Cuba and even greedier. They used their power to extort other elites and move in on their wealth. After an earthquake devastated Managua in 1972, Anastasio Somoza Debayle used foreign aid to rebuild family businesses while withholding help from competitors. This induced many middle- and upper-class Nicaraguans to take their chances with the Sandinistas. Fearing a repeat of the 1959 episode in Cuba, the Carter administration (1976–1980) tried to induce the dictator to leave before his entire regime collapsed. Somoza stubbornly refused to leave. After the popular uprising showed how willing Nicaragua's people were to make the ultimate sacrifice for change, the Sandinista National Liberation Front (Frente Sandinista de Liberación Nacional, or FSLN) began to gain momentum. Somoza desperately clung to power with air assaults and brutal repression. At the last moment, as the FSLN was closing in on Managua, in 1979 the American government reluctantly abandoned the dictator. Somoza fled on July 19, 1979. The collective leadership (nine *comandantes*) entered Managua to the same kind of cheering reception that had greeted Fidel Castro in Havana in 1959.

The FSLN took power with an agenda of radical land redistribution, union organizing, political reform at home, and friendly relationships with Cuba. As in Cuba, there was euphoria and a spirit of national unity in the beginning. One significant difference, however, is that there was a shared collective leadership of nine *comandantes*, not one outstanding personality, like Fidel Castro. The Sandinista leadership and their supporters included an important component of grassroots Catholic clergy. Priests occupied three of the most important ministries in the new government—culture, education, and foreign relations. A significant gap opened between the hierarchy of the Church and many grassroots clergy over the role of religion in revolution.

There were ways that the Cuban Revolution addressed the social question that in turn served as an inspiration for Sandinista programs in Nicaragua. The Sandinistas organized mass literacy brigades, carried out a land reform, and implemented many other measures that resembled the mobilization campaigns of the early years of the Cuban Revolution. As in Cuba, mass organizations of peasants, indigenous people, *barrio*-dwelling workers, and so on came into existence. Although the government kept an official distance from events in nearby El Salvador, sympathetic FSLN commanders and government officials lent support to the guerrillas fighting that country's military regime. Friendly relationships were established with Havana, further irritating the United States. The Carter administration kept the door open and induced the Sandinistas to limit support to their Salvadoran brethren, but the election of hard-line, anticommunist President Ronald Reagan in 1980 led to a change in policy.

The Reagan administration organized and armed a counterrevolutionary army (the *contras*, a name derived from the Spanish word *contrarrevolución*) and touched off a bloody civil war that wracked the country, setting back further progress on social development after 1984. Reagan could do this in part because the Sandinistas had not carried out a bloody purge of Somoza allies, most of whom had escaped the retribution experienced by Batista's henchmen. Somoza's Guardsmen had been allowed to flee to Miami; no mass public trials or executions were held. As a result, forces from the old regime in Nicaragua were available to wage a counterrevolution with Washington's support. This raises an interesting question: should we praise the Sandinistas for a generous and procedurally just policy toward their former enemies, or should we condemn them for naïveté in allowing their enemies to remain a threat?

The FSLN held power 10 years before losing the 1990 elections. Besides impressive policies addressing the social question—literacy and health campaigns, land reform, and so on—they experimented with a form of participatory democracy, setting up a Council of State in which mass organizations (unions, women's groups, entrepreneurs, students, peasants, students, etc.) were directly represented. In 1982, under pressure from European and other governments, the FSLN sought international legitimacy by writing a constitution erecting a more familiar set of institutions resembling **polyarchy**, replacing the Council of State with a national assembly in which representatives would be chosen by vote of the people for candidates nominated by political parties.

In the first elections in 1984 under the new constitution, the Sandinistas did well. They hoped the election would show the world that they were democratic and would put diplomatic pressure on the United States to end the *contra* war. However, intransigent sectors of the opposition, under direction of and with financing from the United States, decided to continue the war. It is difficult to sort out how much of the subsequent suffering in Nicaragua was due directly to the war versus how much can be attributed to the actions of the Sandinistas. The U.S. government is estimated to have spent altogether nearly US$1 billion in the 10-year campaign to oust the Sandinistas through military and political means, including a harsh campaign of terror that included burning down new schools and health clinics, killing teachers and doctors, mining the country's harbors, and causing as much havoc as possible. When new elections came around in 1990, Washington spent US$30 million (US$20 per voter) to influence the outcome (Robinson 1992: 60–65).

Daniel Ortega, one of the nine *comandantes*, was elected president in 1984. Already having emerged as first among equals after the 1979 triumph, Ortega gradually asserted control over the FSLN as it was transformed from an insurgency to a governing political party. Ortega had to respond to a difficult economic situation. The 1980s were Latin America's lost decade, which itself dictated austerity (Prevost and Vanden 1996), but he also faced the burden of fighting the *contras*, proxies for the United States. He may have had little choice but to bleed the economy to fight the war, but that was exactly what the Reagan administration had hoped would happen. At the same time, however, with the shift to polyarchy in 1984, the FSLN began to act more like a party of politicians eager to preserve power than a revolutionary party carrying out social transformation.

Nicaraguan voters punished the Sandinistas for losing their connection to the masses when a majority voted in 1990 for Violeta Chamorro, whose husband was a crusading newspaper editor assassinated by Somoza's forces. The brutal economic and military war waged by the United States helped make her promises of peace and reconciliation appealing. Voted out, the Sandinistas further tarnished their revolutionary credentials by transferring ownership of many assets taken from the Somoza dictatorship to the party or government officials, a practice known as the *piñata*. In opposition, the Sandinistas sometimes rallied labor and other social sectors to oppose neoliberal austerity measures, but the party just as often supported these measures in deals to protect themselves from prosecution for the *piñata* and to protect Daniel Ortega from being prosecuted for alleged sexual abuse of his niece.

Chamorro inherited an impossible economic situation, but neither did she show much leadership in addressing the issues. The period between her leaving office in 1996 and Ortega's return in 2006 was largely a period of unseemly bargaining between the FSLN, now completely controlled by Ortega, and the Liberal Party, which itself was deeply divided and corrupt. At one point, the Liberal president, Enrique Bolaños, was about to be impeached by a coalition of the dissident, disaffected Liberals and the Sandinistas, which was prevented only when other Central American presidents warned they would not accept a "slow-motion" coup. In effect, the Liberal Party (the party of Somoza) seemed to have learned nothing from the fall of the Somoza dynasty; the Sandinistas seemed mostly to have forgotten why they had won the revolution.

Still, the FSLN remained the most coherent single party in Nicaragua, on the right or left. In 2006 Ortega won election once again to the presidency, and he was reelected in 2011. By this time, both he and the FSLN had evolved into something quite different from what they had been when the Sandinistas, however briefly, inspired the world and alarmed the United States. The FSLN had become a more personalist party, and it cut some unsavory deals with the opposition to keep control of government. One clear sign of its evolution was Ortega's acceptance of a severely restric-

DEMOCRACY IN NICARAGUA

MEAN SUPPORT	53%
SUPPORT 2013	50%
SATISFACTION 2013	52%

tive ban on abortion, legislated in November 2012, making Nicaragua one of only a handful of countries that ban abortions without any exceptions whatsoever. On the other hand, there were ways that Nicaragua under Ortega remained aligned with more radical governments of the **Pink Tide**. The FSLN became staunch allies of Hugo Chávez and joined the Bolivarian Alliance for the Americas (ALBA), an economic integration scheme promoted by Chávez as an alternative to the **neoliberal** NAFTA (see chapter 15). Along with Chávez, Evo Morales of Bolivia, and Eduardo Correa of Ecuador, Ortega became a vocal critic of neoliberalism. But at home, Ortega's deal making and cautious economic record made clear that his return to power did not mean the return of revolutionary politics.

For Review

Who was Sandino, and what does he mean to leftist revolutionaries in Nicaragua? Who were the *contras*, and why were they supported by the United States? What factors led Nicaraguans to vote the Sandinistas out in 1990? How are Daniel Ortega and the FSLN different in power today from what they were in the early 1980s?

El Salvador's Near Revolution

In El Salvador, military dictators and right-wing oligarchs, known as the "Fourteen Families," had dominated politics in partnership ever since the military crushed an uprising led by Agustín Farabundo Martí, a communist union organizer whose followers were protesting the canceling of elections they were expected to win in 1934. The

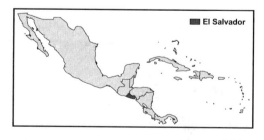

slaughter of 10,000–30,000 of the country's Indian population that year is simply known as *La Matanza* (Anderson 1971). In the 1960s, Christian and secular leftists began again to organize El Salvador's poor. As in the liberal modernization era (see chapter 4), social and economic changes were shaking lives. New cotton and sugar plantations, as well as large ranches, had displaced many peasants from land that already provided only a meager living. Some fled for the cities, seeking jobs in labor-intensive factories producing pajamas, bras, electronic goods, toys, and so on for export north.

In this environment, religious and social justice activists made progress organizing unions, peasant leagues, and other organizations. They joined professional groups and reformist parties to challenge the Salvadoran oligarchy's monopoly of power. By the late 1970s, they had made significant progress, but they were blocked by the oligarchy and the army. Briefly, in 1979, in the aftermath of the FSLN victory in Nicaragua, a reformist military-civilian junta seized power and attempted to implement economic reforms and political reforms that were to lead to democracy, but the right-wing oligarchy struck back, brutally, determined to repeat 1934. As in Nicaragua, the insurgency took on the name of the popular hero of the earlier uprising and formed the Farabundo Martí National Liberation Front (FMLN), a coalition of five different guerrilla movements. A revolutionary civil war loomed (Armstrong and Shenk 1982).

The United States feared the oligarchy's resistance to change would lead to revolution, as in neighboring Nicaragua. The oligarchy had already instigated a coup against a reform-minded government in 1980. The ranks of the guerrilla forces and their supporters swelled. In response, but much to the consternation of the oligarchy, Washington invested heavily on organizing the election of a Christian Democrat, José Napoleón Duarte, in 1982. The Reagan administration sent civilian advisors to shore up the Christian Democratic government of Duarte; at the same time, military aid was sent to keep the fledgling insurgency at bay.

The United States promoted new unions to rival ones that had connections with the left. The United States also promoted a land reform program aimed at creating a small capitalist peasant class, an effort to take the land reform issue away from the insurgents. The oligarchy, on the other hand, was accustomed to responding to "communist" threats in the way it had in 1934. It formed a political party (ARENA) that would eventually defeat the Christian Democrats in the 1989 elections. The founder of ARENA was Robert D'Aubuisson, a former army death-squad leader, notorious torturer (known as "Blow Torch Bob"), and author of the assassination of Monsignor Oscar Arnulfo Romero, the archbishop of San Salvador. Romero had become a spokesperson for the poor and an outspoken critic of the army's human rights atrocities. Archbishop Romero had pleaded to U.S. president Jimmy Carter, "You say that you are Christian. If you are really Christian, please stop sending military aid to the military here, because they use it only to kill my people." Carter had refused to cut off the military aid. In an interview two weeks before he was killed, Romero said, "Christians do not fear combat; they know how to fight . . . The Church speaks of the legitimate right of insurrectional violence" (www.infed.org/thinkers/oscar_romero.htm, accessed July 28, 2009).

On March 30, 1980, some 250,000 people attended Romero's funeral. Twenty to thirty were killed when military snipers opened fire on people gathered on the cathedral steps. Two days later, the U.S. Congress approved another round of military aid. El Salvador's progressive politicians and social leaders, moderates and radicals alike, coalesced into a Democratic Revolutionary Front, which offered a political alternative, while the FMLN fought an increasingly aggressive war. The guerrillas tried to repeat the Nicaraguan experience by touching off a mass insurrection in early 1981. They gained ground but not power. Meanwhile, in the United States, the Reagan administration succeeded Carter, determined to prevent an FMLN victory at any cost. The stage was set for a decade of civil war, which ended only after an internationally brokered agreement among all parties in 1990. An estimated 75,000 people

died in the 10-year conflict, the vast majority killed by government forces.

Duarte had become highly unpopular as the 1989 election approached. Under pressure from Washington, and with Salvadoran business elites feeling the economic consequences of the war, ARENA put forth as its candidate Alfredo Christiani, a businessman without the baggage of the internationally reviled D'Aubuisson. Christiani won. Under prodding from the new administration of George Bush (senior) and, more importantly, diplomatic pressure from the European Union and a number of Latin American countries, Christiani negotiated with the FMLN to end the Salvadoran civil war, much to the displeasure of his party.

At the end of the bitter war, the FMLN had achieved some of the democratic reforms it sought in 1980, but El Salvador had made little progress toward resolving its social question, which in many ways had been worsened by war. The FMLN became the single largest political party in the country, and in 2009, its candidate Mauricio Funes won the presidential election. Funes said that his election was a mandate to reduce poverty and make good on some of the unrealized promises in the pact that had ended the civil war. However, the FMLN's commitment and ability to bring about social change has been tested by the global recession and the continued presence of the right in the courts and public bureaucracy. Funes acted cautiously, being careful not to offend the military and the United States. He assumed office the same month as Honduras suffered a coup, in part a retaliation against a president who had allied himself too closely, in the view of the military, with Chávez and had challenged the economic model.

El Salvador, then, has emerged from brutal civil war with a polyarchy strong enough to survive the election of a candidate from the FMLN. But one year after the election, many of Funes's supporters were wondering what they had truly won. Funes officially apologized for the state violence of the 1980s and opened the country's institutions to ensure more transparency and less corruption. But no trials of those responsible for truly horrible mass atrocities of the 1980s were in the offing. A nearly bankrupt economy limited the president's economic options, but he advanced no long-term plan for addressing the social questions that had sparked revolution.

In 2014, the FMLN candidate Salvador Sánchez Cerén, a former guerrilla, defeated the ARENA candidate. It was a narrow victory, but the leftist victory suggested more reform might be forthcoming. The FMLN benefited from the positive impact that Venezuelan aid programs were having, including among small businesses and farmers. Sánchez Cerén was expected to move cautiously, but the FMLN will at least have to make progress on two key issues: reduction of corruption and continued progress, even if slow, on raising living standards. ARENA, meanwhile, has suffered two defeats, and if nothing else the FMLN has a chance to dispel the fear among many Salvadorans, including the poor, that a leftist government will plunge the country back into crisis.

View from the steps of the National Cathedral (above) as Salvadoran troops open fire on mourners at the funeral of slain Archbishop Oscar Arnulfo Romero (portrayed in the painting on the left) with weapons supplied by the United States. How could this happen in a Catholic country? Should the United States apologize for its role in these events?

For Review

What is the FMLN, and how did it evolve from the civil war to the present time? What are the origins of the FMLN's major opposition, ARENA? What challenges faced the FMLN after its victories in the presidential elections of 2009 and 2014?

Genocide and Revolution in Guatemala

One reason that pluralist democracy is suspect to many revolutionaries is the apparent vulnerability of pluralist systems to outside intervention. Perhaps no experience has reinforced that concern more than the overthrow of Jacobo Arbenz, Guatemala's reformist president, in 1954, a case in which the CIA acted with cold calculation to abet the overthrow of a democracy.

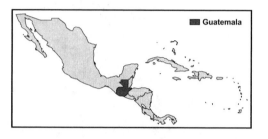

In 1944, a military coup in Guatemala brought a reformist, democratically oriented government to power. After several years of reforms, most supported by the country's small middle class, the outgoing president, Juan Arévalo, handed power to Colonel Arbenz, who was committed to deepening the reforms. Arbenz had won an internal battle in the reform movement against a more conservative candidate. In 1950, he won the election with 65 percent of the vote and the support of Guatemala's small but influential Communist Party (PC). The party was not really a threat to the United States, but it was no phantasm either. Although small in numbers, the Communists were the single best-organized party and the only one with a truly mass base; it was especially strong among workers that it organized into unions in the foreign-owned fruit plantations, railroad, and utility companies.

In 1952, Arbenz took the radical step of expropriating unused lands, including those of his own family and of the country's biggest landowner, the United Fruit Company of Boston (UFC). He also expropriated (all with compensation) utilities, roads, and other parts of the country's infrastructure controlled by UFC, which because of its tentacles everywhere in the economy was known as "the Octopus." The PC, rather than urge Arbenz on, warned Arbenz that he had made a powerful enemy. The company's allies in Washington included Secretary of State John Foster Dulles and his brother Allen, director of the CIA. They convinced the Eisenhower administration that Guatemala was being drawn into the orbit of Moscow.

The U.S. Central Intelligence Agency found ready allies when it launched an operation to destabilize and overthrow the Arbenz regime. The agency's disdain for Arbenz was reflected in an internal memorandum where it summarized his program as "an intensely nationalistic program of progress colored by the touchy, anti-foreign inferiority complex of the 'Banana Republic'" (Doyle and Kornbluth 1997). Some of the same CIA operatives that helped to organize a coup against a nationalist government in Iran in 1953 went into action in Guatemala, boosted by the US$2.7 million authorized by President Dwight Eisenhower. It was not difficult to alarm anticommunist sectors in the military. Local elites were recruited to form a "liberation army" and invade the country from Honduras. Inept and ill-armed, the counterrevolutionary forces had little chance of succeeding, but conservative army officers showed no inclination to defeat the rebel offensive, which quickly stalled once it crossed the border. Meanwhile, the United States launched a diplomatic and propaganda war, openly encouraging the army to overthrow the government.

In 1954, the conservative factions of Guatemala's military overthrew Arbenz, leading to an era of almost three decades of fierce repression by the military, most of it directed against the Mayan Indian population. An American University report summarizes what happened:

> The civil war took a turn for the worse in the early 1980's, when the Guatemalan army, backed by the CIA, began a campaign of genocide against the Maya peoples. Several hundred Indian villages were obliterated and their inhabitants, presumed to be guerrilla sympathizers, were either killed or forced into exile in Mexico.
> (www.American.edu/TED/ice/peten.htm, accessed August 2008)

The 1954 events in Guatemala left a deep impression on the Latin American left. Arbenz had said his objective was to redistribute land and use the country's infrastructure to breed capitalists who would develop the country. However, in Cold War Washington, under the grip of right-wing hysteria (McCarthyism), the only thing visible was communism. Che Guevara was an eyewitness to the events in Guatemala. In Mexico, a young Fidel Castro took note of Washington's actions and had to wonder whether democracies could defend themselves adequately against outside intervention. The prospect of revolution reappeared in Guatemala in the 1970s. The military officers who had carried out the coup against Arbenz had used power to elbow their way into the ranks of the economic elite (Jonas 1991). For the next 35 years, the country lived a nightmare of repression. Various guerrilla movements struggled with mixed success to resist the army.

By 1977, army repression had reached levels that caused the Catholic Church to speak out and the Carter administration to cut off military aid, but the Israeli government, which was eager for arms sales and diplomatic support in its conflict with the Palestinians, and Argentina, which was then engaged in its Dirty War, stepped into the breach. In 1981, the Reagan administration restored aid. In 1982, these foreign governments wholeheartedly backed a scorched-earth campaign waged by the newly elected president, General Efraín Ríos Montt, a born-again Christian with ties to the right wing of the U.S. Republican Party, including televangelist Pat Robertson and Attorney General Edwin Meese. Ríos Montt unleashed a wave of terror to flush out the guerrillas. Between 1981 and 1983 alone, more than 100,000 Indians were killed, and 440 of their villages were destroyed. The army, with U.S. backing, engaged in **ethnic cleansing**, forcibly relocated the population into government-controlled towns, and obliged Indians to join "civil patrols" to hunt down guerrillas. The violence continued until the United Nations fostered successful negotiations to end the war, at least for the time being, in 1992.

In 2007, a leftist candidate, Álvaro Colom, won election as president. In 2009, Colom began to open security files on the civil war. He managed to stabilize the economy in a difficult global environment, but as elsewhere, he has made little progress addressing the social question. In 2011, former general Otto Pérez Molina defeated a centrist candidate. Unlike the case in El Salvador, the guerrilla movement in Guatemala never approached the levels of support needed to gain significant political concessions in the negotiations that ended the civil war. Its supporters were scattered in the highlands, mostly among the indigenous peoples, many of whom were forced into ref-

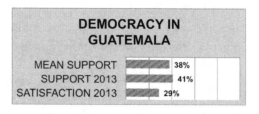

DEMOCRACY IN GUATEMALA

MEAN SUPPORT	38%
SUPPORT 2013	41%
SATISFACTION 2013	29%

ugee camps in neighboring Mexico. An indication of this weakness is the fate of Ríos Montt. In 2013 he was tried and found guilty of genocide against the Ixil Mayas, only to have the country's Supreme Court—heavily lobbied by the Guatemalan business community—annul the verdict against the dictator.

For Review

Why was the United States intervention against Arbenz a turning point for Guatemala? What role did ethnic cleansing play in the civil war? Against whom was it practiced? Why does the Guatemalan left have less influence today than its counterparts in El Salvador and Nicaragua?

Violence, Civil Society, and Revolution

One problem with revolutionary organizations is that by their nature they require tough internal discipline. The extreme consequences of someone being captured and facing torture to disclose the identity and location of colleagues partly explain this fact, so secrecy and discipline must be maintained. These habits, essential to insurrection, may be unhealthy for democracy. Another factor is the revolutionary fighter's understanding of his or her role in organizing a popular insurrection and effecting social change. Those who take up arms or engage in risky nonviolent actions in support of revolution are usually trying to raise the consciousness of ordinary people. This requires an educational process by which those already "enlightened" (in the forefront or vanguard) try to convince others that a new society is possible.

Leninist political thought envisions a revolutionary process by which leaders of the new social order form a political party to help the oppressed "pull themselves up by their own bootstraps." C.B. MacPherson, whom we met in chapter 1, pointed out that this way of thinking is not unlike that of conservative thinkers who have often yearned for something like Plato's "philosopher king" to rule. The French thinker Rousseau seemed to long for a leader "whose greatness of soul," says MacPherson, "would create a general will capable of sustaining an equal, free and democratic society." Lenin's formula for revolution, he goes on, argued for a vanguard to take control of the state and "forcibly transform the basic relations of society in such a way that the people would become undebased and capable of a fully human existence, at which point compulsive government would no longer be needed." That approach has yielded tyranny in many parts of the world, notes Canadian philosopher MacPherson.

This pessimistic assessment of revolution has to be balanced against the fact that guerrilla armies must rely on the support of the population to survive. To a certain extent, this support can be won by fear of reprisal. Ultimately, however, the willingness of people to provide food, hide the rebels' location from more powerful government forces, care for the wounded, and perhaps even rise up themselves at the right moment depends on their sense of identity and sympathy for the revolutionary fighters. This is one reason that revolutionary wars are among the most brutal: both sides are asserting their right to be the state, to exercise legitimate violence against those opposed to their ends. Revolutionary terror, counterrevolutionary terror, and state terror are all used in the battle for hearts and minds. It is hardly an environment friendly to democracy.

Recent insurgencies in the Andean region illustrate the way that insurgencies that begin with a high degree of sympathy from the civil society can over time lose their political compass and come to rely almost exclusively on military or even terrorist tactics. This turn has been futile and costly in lives to the very people in whose names these insurgents fought.

Sendero Luminoso in Peru

A case of an insurgency resorting to extreme violence and alienating most of civil society is the Shining Path (Sendero Luminoso—SL) guerrillas in Peru. SL adopted a Maoist strategy of prioritizing a takeover of the countryside over urban organizing, and the group had considerable success in the 1980s appealing to indigenous peasants, long excluded and subject to racist discrimination by the more prosperous populations of Lima and the Pacific Coast and, of course, by regional landowners. SL also protected coca growers from abuse by traffickers and the Peruvian military, which was carrying out drug-eradication operations with aid from the United States, netting the guerrillas support from the peasant-cultivators and "taxes" from the traffickers. Sendero also spoke to the peasants' long-standing grievances and hunger for land in the Quechua language of the indigenous people.

Under President Alberto Fujimori (1990–2000), the Peruvian military began to respond, which only intensified the violence as Peruvians found themselves caught between state terror and revolutionary terror. SL ruthlessly carried out massacres in uncooperative villages and assassinations of dissenters. Not only did SL target the military forces and the right, but it also took aim at human rights workers, leaders of neighborhood organizations, religious base communities, and any other individuals or groups who did not fit its vision of a society cleansed of European colonialism. Peasants and progressive groups found themselves caught between SL and Peru's well-trained, 70,000-man army. The army employed classic counterinsurgency tactics (learned from U.S., Israeli, and Argentine instructors)

that included massive relocation of villagers, much like the scorched-earth policy employed by Montt in Guatemala. Police units massacred suspected sympathizers, in one case by the thousands.

Subduing SL came at a high cost to democracy. To carry out the counterinsurgency, Fujimori made an alliance with the military and shut down the elected but highly unpopular and corruption-ridden Congress—something that came to be called the *autogolpe* (self-coup). The capture of Sendero's leader, university professor Abimael Gúzman, in 1992 severely weakened the organization, as did the arrest of other leaders in 1995. Since 2000, small cells of Sendero have carried out some small, spectacular actions, but the movement has also suffered defeats and arrests of other leaders. The movement has never been fully extinguished.

Insurgency in Colombia

Colombia has experienced guerrilla warfare almost constantly for 50 years. The roots of the conflict can be traced to 1946, when the Conservative Party launched a war against peasants who had supported its Liberal Party rivals. This gave birth to the 10-year period known as La Violencia. The violence intensified as a Liberal and leftist firebrand, Jorge Eliécer Gaitán, seemed poised to win the presidency in the 1950 elections. He was assassinated in 1948, touching off rioting all over the country. In the next 10 years, La Violencia would claim the lives of one of every 40 Colombians (in a population of 10 million at this time). This era came to a close in 1957, when leaders of the two parties met and agreed to share power in government after the 1958 elections. Another "pacted democracy" was born. Since that time, Colombia's two parties have controlled the government.

Given La Violencia, it hardly surprises that guerrilla movements have sprung up in various regions of Colombia since 1957. One movement, M-19, arose after claiming, with good reason, fraud in the defeat of its candidates in the 1970 elections. In 1985, M-19 seized the Supreme Court building and the justices, demanding that the government publish a report showing violations of a cease-fire agreement. Instead, the military attacked and burned the building to the ground, killing more than 100 people, including the chief justice and 11 of his colleagues. M-19, though divided, eventually did return to civil politics, but it suffered the murder of hundreds of its candidates and of allied leaders of unions, peasant associations, and other civilians. Another smaller guerrilla organization, the Popular Liberation Army (EPL), suffered a similar fate after agreeing to a truce in 1991.

Two large guerrilla movements, the National Liberation Army (ELN) and the Revolutionary Armed Forces of Colombia (FARC), formed by communists in 1966, have remained active in Colombia. The two groups are divided from each other ideologically (the former Maoist, the latter more inclined toward the Cuban model) and geographically (the ELN in the eastern areas closer to Venezuela and the FARC in the central regions and also with some presence near the border). They are opposed by the Colombian armed forces and by death squads that are well connected to the military and right-wing landlords. The leftists finance their rebellion mainly from two sources, both of which are controversial. One is through taxing the drug trade, much like Sendero. The other is through kidnappings. The ELN also

Columbia

extorts funds from oil companies operating in its zones of control.

Government forces are also highly dependent on drug money. Coca products became the country's most important export, and the traffickers, like all wealthy interest groups, make heavy donations to politicians. Even the U.S. State Department, though committed to fighting the "terrorist" guerrillas, in 1997 labeled Colombia a "narco-democracy." A major problem was that big companies and ranchers had privately funded a paramilitary group, the United Self-Defense Forces of Colombia (AUC), composed of many former and active soldiers. A major source of AUC funds was derived from drug trafficking. Even the United States considered the AUC a terrorist organization, but by 2001, the United States decided that the Colombian government had made enough "progress" in distancing itself from the drug lords to justify President Bill Clinton's signing a US$1.3 billion package of mostly military aid, over the objections of human rights organizations and civilian organizations caught in the crossfire in Colombia. In 2005–2006, Colombian president Álvaro Uribe declared an amnesty for AUC members who turned in their weapons. Human rights organizations condemned the action, which absolved the AUC for thousands of serious human rights atrocities.

Although neither is as sectarian and ruthless as Sendero, both Colombian guerrilla organizations have been criticized for significant abuses of human rights. On the other side, drug lords and ranchers in Colombia supported death squads, many organized by active and retired army officers, to fight the guerrillas. In 1983, 59 members of the armed forces were found to be members of one of the death squad organizations. In the mid-1980s, the FARC set up a political wing, the Patriotic Union, to test the possibilities of abandoning armed struggle for an electoral strategy. An estimated 2,000–4,000 of the Patriotic Union's members were murdered. In 1987, the minister of the interior listed 137 rightist death squads. In 1987, there were more than 1,500 political assassinations; in that year, dozens of leaders of a banana workers' union were assassinated. In 1988, 40 banana workers were mass-murdered in front of their families. M-19 claimed that 3,000 of its members were assassinated in 1990, and the EPL said that more than 100 of its members were killed in 1991.

Despite the violence, in 1991 M-19 and the EPL won more than one-third of the delegates to a Constituent Assembly that wrote a remarkably progressive constitution, promising land reform and social justice. The Colombian Human Rights Network (CHRN)(2001) details the aftermath:

> People assumed that the political landscape would be transformed by the Constitution but, in reality, it had no impact on the level of violence and the search for peace. One reason was that the FARC and ELN, the two largest guerrilla groups, did not participate in the process because, rather than a few representatives in Congress, they wanted

social and land reform and restructuring of the army. The M-19 collapsed from political ineptness. The dirty war resumed and violence tripled. The guerrilla movement grew stronger, with activity in two-thirds of the municipalities, but was politically weak and no longer commanded the support of students and the middle class.

All sides in the conflict have committed atrocities. The CHRN states, "Over 25,000 homicides took place in Colombia during 1995. The paramilitaries are believed responsible for 60 percent of political killings, the guerrillas for 25 percent, and the military for 10 percent." President Uribe, before leaving office in 2010, achieved significant success against the guerrillas, especially the FARC. Over time the FARC has progressively lost its ideological character and appeal to the general population. Still, applying the label "terrorist" to the ELN and FARC, as the United States has done, vastly oversimplifies their character, masking the deep roots of the unrest but simplifying the ability of the United States to justify military aid to the Colombian government, as well as to establish seven military bases in the country. On the other hand, the conduct of the guerrilla forces has alienated those elements of Colombian society who most want to address the social question in their country.

Juan Manuel Santos, Uribe's minister of defense, succeeded Uribe to the presidency in August 2010. Against expectations, Santos initiated negotiations with the guerrillas. In contrast to Uribe, Santos looked to Raúl Castro and Hugo Chávez to urge the FARC to negotiate, and talks began in Havana in 2011 under Cuban mediation. Santos by no means can be considered part of the **Pink Tide**; his government remained Washington's closest ally in the region. And though severely weakened by the killing or capture of several leaders and by the success of the U.S.-aided counterinsurgency, the FARC remained a strong presence, with an estimated 8,000 men and women under arms and present in 25 of 32 provinces. Some progress has been made on issues such as land reform and reintegration of the guerrilla into political life, but many other points remained unresolved.

The case of Sendero Luminoso and, to a lesser degree, the FARC stands in contrast to the Central American leftist insurgencies of the 1980s. The FSLN in Nicaragua and the FMLN in El Salvador, though guilty of some serious human rights violations, put a high premium on gaining support from civil society. Still, what all these insurgencies have in common is the aim of taking power, seizing control of the state. In this regard, Mexico's Zapatista movement in Chiapas is different.

DEMOCRACY IN COLOMBIA

MEAN SUPPORT	48%
SUPPORT 2013	52%
SATISFACTION 2013	28%

For Review

What were the goals and tactics of Sendero Luminoso and those of the Central American insurgencies? Who is the FARC, and how has the illegal drug trade and U.S.-aided drug war influenced the long civil war in Colombia? Why do some consider FARC to be a terrorist organization?

▓ Revolution's Uneasy Relationship to Democracy

Are democracy and revolution compatible with one another? All three of Latin America's major social revolutions (Mexico in 1910, Cuba in 1959, and Nicaragua in 1979) resulted in a period of single-party dominance. In Mexico, it would be 90 years before a peaceful transfer of power to an opposition party would take place after an election. Cuba remains today a single-party state. In Nicaragua, the Sandinistas gambled on elections and were rudely displaced from power.

History suggests, however, that revolutionaries are not without grounds for being suspicious of the pluralist brand of democracy. Counterrevolutionaries often claim they want to restore democracy, but they often show even less commitment to democracy. Both in Guatemala (1954) and Chile (1973), the United States, as the hegemonic power in the region, worked diligently and with success to destabilize elected governments it did not like. It supported opposition groups that resorted to economic sabotage and terror to achieve their objectives. Although it won the 1984 elections, the Nicaraguan FSLN was punished by a more intensely violent counterrevolution that significantly contributed to defeat at the polls in 1990.

We could argue that revolutionary movements have contributed to democracy even when they have not fully achieved their goals. Compared to El Salvador in the era of the Fourteen Families or Nicaragua in the age of Somoza, the current regimes seem more open to popular influence through elections and other forms of political action. Against this accomplishment, however, must be weighed the failure of peace accords to deliver progress toward social justice. In fact, conditions have worsened in many respects. For example, the Pan American Health Organization reported that in 2001, in Central America, between 60 and 80 percent of all communicable diseases could be traced to deficient drinkable water and sanitation, which are unavailable to at least one-fourth of the population. However much Cuba's revolution may lack in pluralist democracy, its health, education, housing, and nutritional resources are more evenly and democratically distributed than in any other country in Latin America.

Revolutionaries find it necessary to appeal to democracy to build broad popular support, but social and economic transformations of a profound nature conjure up enemies within and abroad. Revolutionaries tend to come to see themselves as saviors and prophets with a special mandate to rule without submitting themselves to democracy. When counterrevolutionaries are financed from abroad, antidemocratic tendencies are reinforced. Would-be democrats seem to put aside their principles when the poor majority uses the processes of democracy to challenge their wealth and privileges.

Revolutionaries seek profound social and economic change that would make people freer to exercise democratic rights. Illness, hunger, and homelessness are surely enemies of democracy as well because freedom means little in such circumstances. Hannah Arendt rightly understood that revolutions are about both freedom and addressing the social question. Neither liberal democracy nor the one-party state satisfactorily addresses both imperatives.

Discussion Questions

1. The outbreaks of revolution in Cuba and Mexico took place nearly 50 years apart. None-theless, do you see any common factors that led to both? Why do you think both cases veered away from the pluralist model (polyarchy) after defeating the old regime?
2. Why do you think that Cuba came to identify its revolution with communism rather than with some nationalist label?
3. Would Cuba's socialist system crumble if its leaders abandoned the single-party system? What do you think would be the impact on Cuban politics if the United States ended its economic embargo?
4. El Salvador, Guatemala, and Nicaragua are poorer and more violent today than before the insurgencies of the 1980s, but for all their flaws, they now have 25 years of experience with elected democracy. When all is said and done, can we say that the insurgencies in Central America accomplished anything?
5. What brought Colombia and the FARC to the negotiating table? Does it help or hurt the peace process to list the FARC as a terrorist organization?
6. Based on the Latin American experience, can revolutions succeed in addressing both of the issues cited by Arendt: freedom *and* the social question? If revolutionaries must choose, which should take priority?

Resources for Further Study

Reading: Two excellent biographies capture the essence of revolution in Cuba and Mexico, respectively: Sebastian Balfour's *Castro*, 2nd ed. (New York: Longman, 1995) is an evenhanded look at the Cuban leader, and John Womack's *Zapata and the Mexican Revolution* (New York: Vintage Books, 1968) is an accessible classic. *A Nation for All: Race, Inequality, and Politics in Twentieth-Century Cuba* by Alejandro De la Fuente (Chapel Hill: University of North Carolina Press, 2001) puts the shortcomings and accomplishments of the Cuban Revolution into perspective. See also Walter LaFeber's *Inevitable Revolutions: The United States in Central America*, 2nd ed. (Norton, 1993).

Video and Film: *Strawberry and Chocolate* (1995) is remarkable for its commentary on gay life and frustrated idealism, all the more so for having been made in Cuba. *Continent on the Move* (1992) in the *Americas* series looks at the economic factors behind migration within Mexico and out of Mexico to the United States. *The Uncompromising Revolution* (1992) looks at Fidel's leadership style on the eve of momentous change. *Yo Soy Cuba* (1964) is a Russian-made documentary with a surprisingly objective point of view. *El Norte* (1983) tells the story of a young Guatemalan boy caught in the counterinsurgency. *When the Mountains Tremble* (1983) is about the Guatemalan army's assault on the Mayan people, narrated by Nobel Prize winner Rigoberta Menchú.

On the Internet: The Center for Cuban Studies at www.cubaupdate.org offers a sympathetic view of the revolution. The Cuba Transition Project site at http://ctp.iccas.miami .edu/main.htm at the University of Miami promotes pluralist democratization of the island. The section on the Mexican Muralists at http://smarthistory.khanacademy.org/ los-tres-grandes.html provides a highly visual portrait of the changes wrought and ideology of the Mexican revolution. On the Colombia and the FARC, the process is described and analyzed by the Washington Office on Latin America at http://colombiapeace.org.

PART IV

Civil Society, Institutions, Human Rights, and Rule of Law

11 Social Class and Social Movements in Latin America

Focus Questions

▶ What are the major features of the social class structures of Latin America?

▶ How do economic inequalities interact with other social cleavages in the region?

▶ How do social movements in Latin America relate to the market on the one hand and the state on the other? How are they shaping civil society?

POLITICS, THE ARENA of our lives where we compete and cooperate to defend our interests but also to build a good society, takes place not only through the formal institutions of the state but also at the level of group life, what is often called "**civil society**." Like so many other key concepts in political science, the meaning of this term is contested. Pluralists conceive of civil society as group activity and as the associations occupying social space between the individual and family on one hand and the government and state on the other. From the pluralists' perspective, the marketplace is a part of civil society, or at least markets promote stronger civil societies. A strong civil society, in turn, is a check on tyranny. In fact, the idea of "totalitarianism" is often conceived as a policy where the state has obliterated the boundary between state and society, including the market. As some critics (e.g., Barber 1969) have noted, this way of thinking about "totalitarianism" is closely wedded to the liberal tradition of thinking about freedom as something we enjoy as individuals who freely choose to organize groups and make choices in the marketplace. However, it is also possible to think of the state as something that enhances freedom by protecting us from predators more powerful than we are and by empowering us to achieve our aspirations in harmony with others in society.

In recent decades, social movements in Latin America seem to have taken a view that synthesizes these two different ways of thinking about the state and civil society. **Social movements** are loosely associated individuals or organizations that take action in response to common problems, in defense of common interests, or in the quest to force the government or other social actors to respond to widely supported demands. They are wary of attempts at subordination by populist parties and politicians, but they also mistrust the market. Whereas **neoliberals** see the market as enhancing freedom in civil society, many social movements fear that the competitive nature of the market, left unchecked, will corrode the social solidarity needed for a strong civil society, imposing the greatest costs of economic change on those least able to bear it. They want a strong, democratic state that works in and with civil society, not standing apart from it. Whether they can achieve this without **clientelism** and **corporatism** is a significant issue.

In this chapter we focus on movements, groups, and social classes, three types of associational life that make up civil society. We already looked at some aspects of social class in Latin America in chapter 2, which focuses on inequality. We return to that subject but flesh it out more by relating it to occupational structures and ownership of the **means of production**.

The Social Class System

Few social scientists would argue anymore, as some Marxists have, that all other divisions, such as race and gender, would simply disappear if social classes were abolished, but some would argue that not enough attention is given to social class. Two distinguished students of Latin America's class structures have argued that the international organizations that study poverty and inequality generally do not describe the distribution of wealth and income in terms of class "because of its Marxist origin and consequent evocation of notions of conflict, privilege and exploitation. Yet its omission obscures significant aspects of contemporary social dynamics and deprives us of a valuable analytic tool" (Portes and Hoffman 2003: 42).

We can define "class" as it is being used by Portes and Hoffman as people's relationship to the **means of production**—land, machinery, buildings, and so on used to produce other goods and services. Put another way, the way people are organized to produce out of nature the necessities and good things of life pervades all other areas of human endeavor, including culture and politics. This means more than just "occupation." In narrowest terms, Marxists define the **bourgeoisie** as owners of the means of production; the **proletariat** are those who must sell their labor (for wages) to gain access to the means of production. However, Marx himself recognized that social class structures are more complex, made up of peasants, middle-class sectors, different types of capitalists (bankers, manufacturers, merchants, small versus large businesspeople, etc.), and poor people (*lumpen*). Also, how people think about themselves (the "subjective" factor) must be taken into account in describing class structures (Thompson 1966). Just as is the case with racial and ethnic identity, how people self-classify themselves helps to define the politics of social class.

The most in-depth study of the social class structure that approximates the way Marx conceptualized class in Latin America was published by Portes and Hoffman in 2003. Their results are summarized in Tables 11.1 and 11.2. Many studies have suggested that Latin America has experienced a growth of its middle class and a significant decline in poverty since 2000. Table 11.3 provides a gauge of the modest but important reduction in poverty and inequality in the region since 2000. I hasten to add that the global slowdown since the financial crisis began to be felt in Latin America after 2010.

Portes and Hoffman estimated that around 2000 between 1 and 2 percent of the economically active population in Latin America owned medium or large companies. If we include managers with high incomes, we can expand the size of the upper class (*bourgeoisie*) to about 5 percent. To them we can add the professional classes (engineers, doctors, lawyers, etc.), who make up 5 to 10 percent of the workforce. Taken as a group, then, with the exception of Cuba, the bourgeoisie constitutes 5 to 15 percent of the population. They interact personally with counterparts in other parts of the world through conferences and travel; they often work for transnational corporations or in sectors linked to the global economy; they are "plugged into" the Internet, satellite radio and television, and other information

TABLE 11.1   Typical Urban Social Class Structure in Latin America around 2000

Social class	Characteristics	% labor force
Capitalists	Owners and high-salaried managers of large and medium companies	1.8
Executives	Managers and administrators of large and medium companies	1.6
Well-off middle class	University-trained, salaried professionals in public service, large and medium companies (e.g., engineers, accountants)	2.8
Petty bourgeoisie (small capitalists)	Small-scale entrepreneurs who have employees and/ or provide a professional/technical service (e.g., doctor, owner of auto-repair shop, computer technician)	8.5
White-collar wage workers	Skilled or professionally educated employees typically found in offices (e.g., bank clerks)	12.4
Workers, classic proletariat	Manual workers, formally employed for wages, often unionized or protected by labor laws; workers on modern farms	23.4
Marginalized, informal workforce	Day laborers, street vendors, family workers; undercounted because temporary contract workers in large companies are not included	45.9

Source: Portes and Hoffman 2003: 46–49.

TABLE 11.2   Variations in Urban Class Structure in Latin America around Year 2000[1]

	Brazil %	Chile %	Colombia %	Costa Rica %	El Salvador %	Mexico %	Panama %	Venezuela %
Upper class[2]	3.8	2.6	3.0	4.1	2.7	2.9	6.0	3.9
Middle sectors[3]	8.8	16.9	17.0	14.0	14.8	12.2	13.5	21.2
Working class[4]	33.4	45.2	35.0	42.3	33.0	39.1	37.2	36.4
Informal sector[5]	48.1	34.9	44.9	38.9	50.0	45.7	43.0	38.0

[1]Percentages do not add up to 100 because different sources were used to estimate the categories; figures most likely underestimate percentages at bottom of class structure.
[2]Owners of large companies and highly paid executives.
[3]Professionals, small-scale capitalists, skilled or professional employees.
[4]Formally employed wage workers.
[5]Urban poor, marginalized.

Source: Adapted from Portes and Hoffman 2003: 52.

TABLE 11.3   Latin America (10 Countries): Households in the Middle Social Strata, around 1990 and 2007

Country	Year	With middle incomes[a]	Middle stratum with low incomes[b]	Middle social strata	Total Households
		(percentages[c])			(thousands)
Argentina[d]	1990	25	42	67	2 181
	2006	54	20	74	3 134
Brazil	1990	24	22	46	15 825
	2007	26	27	53	33 454
Chile	1990	31	23	54	1 702
	2006	54	16	70	3 645
Colombia	1991	23	20	43	3 012
	2005	23	16	39	4 674
Costa Rica	1990	45	13	58	320
	2007	50	12	62	834
Honduras	1990	9	12	21	170
	2007	11	17	28	544
Mexico	1989	23	21	44	6 940
		26	22	48	14 160
Panama	1991	39	12	51	260
	2007	47	12	59	610
Peru	1997	16	16	32	1 665
	2003	14	18	32	2 248
Dominican Republic	1997	28	11	39	633
	2007	20	18	38	1 081

[a]Households where the income of the MHIR (Spanish acronym for Media Real Household Income) is greater than four times the per capita urban poverty line and less than the 95 percentile value
[b]Households in the middle occupational stratum where the income of the MHIR is four times the per capita urban poverty line or less
[c]Percentages of all households in the country
[d]Greater Buenos Aires

Source: Economic Commission for Latin America and the Caribbean (ECLAC), on the basis of special tabulations of household surveys from the countries concerned. Adapted from *CEPAL Review 103* (April 2011).

systems. Through such networks this social class has considerable capacity to meet, plan, and exchange views, nationally and internationally. Its members usually belong to some kind of professional association or to a chamber of commerce or industry federation. They form a class of people able to make their own political opportunities and not just take advantage of the ones that present themselves.

Small capitalists (the *petit bourgeoisie*) in Latin America are middle-class professionals— for example, teachers and technicians—and micro-entrepreneurs (shopkeepers) who employ a handful of workers, often drawn from the ranks of family. They specialize in providing low-cost services for consumers (e.g., shoe repair and plumbing) or for businesses (jan-itorial services, message services, etc.). This sector grew in the late twentieth century as a result of neoliberal economic policies. Employees of downsized public bureaucracies and closed factories suddenly had to fend for themselves. A teacher now becomes a personal tutor. An architect becomes a cab driver. Perhaps the metalworker in an alumi-num fabrication plant hires himself (or herself) out for construction jobs or roof repair. Under better circumstances, this individual might start a small business that fabricates parts for auto shops. In the worst cases, these individuals fall into the ranks of the infor-mal sector.

Hernando de Soto (1989), a Peruvian entrepreneur who founded the neoliberal think tank the Institute for Liberty and Democracy (Instituto Libertad y Democracia), has pro-moted the idea that this sector could lay the basis for a prosperous capitalist economy—if only the burden of government regulation were lifted (see page 167). However, small entrepreneurs sometimes find the market a threat, and the government their ally. Many small entrepreneurs have been cast out of more secure employment and face competition from bigger companies, so they may not be so hospitable to laissez-faire capitalism. For example, El Barzón (The Yoke), a movement of small business owners and farmers, has criticized neoliberalism and called for reform of campaign financing in Mexican elections. Affiliated groups included the national credit card holders' association, the Mexican bank debtors' association, the National Confederation of Small and Micro Businesses, and the National Union of Agricultural Producers. They began to undertake blockades of streets and banks to press their demands. Most demands went unfulfilled, but the group forced the government to respond with some relief, including a moratorium on paying their debts (Senzek 1997).

However, more often, small-scale entrepreneurs oppose radical change, especially when they feel that their property is threatened by a leftist government. Such was the case with Patria y Libertad (Homeland and Liberty), a right-wing group that used violence and sabotage to help to destabilize the Allende government in Chile between 1970 and 1973 (see chapter 7). Truck and bus drivers, both self-employed and those working for small busi-nesses, participated in strikes with the same goal in mind. Abetted by intervention of one faction of the United States (see U.S. Senate 1975), they heightened the polarization that brought about the breakdown of Chilean democracy.

According to Portes and Hoffman (2003), a slightly larger sector is made up of white-collar employees and technicians with vocational training—teachers, accountants, clerks, computer programmers, and so on. Adding this group to the small business sector and adjusting for evidence of growth in the middle class since 2000, we can estimate that the middle class constitutes 30 to 40 percent of the population, perhaps more in some countries, such as Brazil. The quality of their lives, however, remains precarious. Inflation and unem-ployment can strike quickly and devastate this class. For example, in 2005–2007, Argentina, a relatively wealthy country, experienced a wave of education strikes as teachers protested that their salaries had fallen below the poverty line—equivalent to about US$270 per month. An increase brought them to about US$330, but inflation of the peso virtually wiped out their gains in the next year.

The blue-collar working class (the classic proletariat)—that is, manual workers who are paid wages—made up about a quarter of the Latin American workforce at the height of import substitution, but their number is shrinking. These workers are the backbone of organized labor. They are formally covered by social security, some form of pension plan, or welfare rights. Though usually far from adequate, these benefits help to get them through illness, unemployment, or old age. They are a varied lot: ranging from relatively well-paid skilled workers in automobile or small arms industries to highly vulnerable women working in *maquilas*—labor-intensive factories located in "free-trade zones," often located near ports or (in Mexico) near international borders.

At the bottom of the urban social class pyramid is the informal sector of unpaid family workers, sex workers, street vendors, and day workers who made up almost half (45.9 percent) of the workforce around 2000, but this sector may have shrunk in the last decade. Besides "informal," this sector is sometimes called "marginalized" or "excluded" because its members are not integrated into the nation's social networks—schools, welfare systems, health care systems, and so on. This sector is even larger if we take into account the rural sector, where peasants and small farmers live a precarious existence. The informal sectors' children are least likely to be in school; their neighborhoods suffer the highest crime rates and are scenes of vigilante justice; their jobs are day-to-day, with few rights versus those who employ them. This is especially true for women, especially those who work in domestic service and as maids and caretakers of children.

As we can see from Table 11.2, the class structure in Latin America varies from country to country. According to Portes and Hoffman's data, the poorest sector constituted at the time half of all Salvadorans, but "only" 35 percent of Chileans fell into this category. Costa Rica's informal sector was closer in size to the Chilean figure. Is it coincidence that Chile (despite the Pinochet dictatorship) and Costa Rica are regarded as the most stable polyarchies in the region, and El Salvador among the least stable? Between 1981 and 1998, Chile's informal sector shrank from 37 to 30.8 percent. Marginality in nearby Paraguay, on the other hand, registered more than 20 percentage points higher, at 52 percent. Nearly 60 percent of Bolivians were counted in the informal sector. Since 2006 the Morales government has redirected benefits toward this group, many of them indigenous people, through a program of conditional cash transfers (e.g., recipients must keep their children in school to receive support payments). The program produced a significant reduction in poverty.

Overall, most analysts conclude that neoliberal economic policies made inequality worse in Latin America. Portes and Hoffman (2003: 77), referring to the consequence of President Menem's policies in Argentina (See Chapter 8), summarized what we might expect politically from this tendency:

> Neoliberalism has proven more successful as a political than as an economic project, as the transformations that it has wrought in society have weakened the basis for organized class struggle and the channels for the effective mobilization of popular discontent. Nevertheless, the dislocations wrought by economic orthodoxy on Latin American societies—rising inequality, rising crime and insecurity, forced entrepreneurship, and emigration—lead to the expectation that the present situation will be unsustainable and that new forms of popular and political organizations will emerge. In that sense, the massive Argentine revolts [of 2001] that brought down one of the governments that most carefully sought to adhere to neoliberal ideology may well represent not an isolated incident, but a harbinger of things to come.

Portes and Hoffman proved prescient in this regard—though there already were signs of discontent in several urban uprisings against austerity and then of a political realignment in the election of Hugo Chávez in Venezuela in December 1998.

For Review

Starting at either end of the social pyramid in Latin America, describe the major social classes. What do we mean by the "informal sector," and why has it become more important politically in recent years? How are informal workers different from the rest of the working class in, for example, factory jobs?

Business Interests: Merchants, Bankers, Landowners, and Industrialists

At one time, the image of a Latin American businessperson was that of a male descendant of a landowning family, unwilling to take risks and mainly interested in accumulating enough wealth to become a landowner. Latin America's oligarchs were thought to want to keep their fingernails clean. They tended to favor social conservatism and corporatism and were not especially friendly to the idea of a competitive market society. They ran their companies much like landowners ran their estates and the people on them. Employees with proper deference and the right family connections (e.g., **compadrazgo**) might receive extra benefits and promotions. Latin American businessmen showed little interest in paying their workers well and regarded all efforts at unionization as little more than communist subversion. However, in the populist era, businessmen favored by **ISI** policies looked to government, using their personal connections to obtain commissions, contracts, subsidies, and protection from competition.

Although the business environment has modernized, business interests in Latin America are still often organized into groups under the dominance of a single family. This limits the ability of competitors to bid for contracts or create business associations because these families prefer to associate only with one another. Similarly, they would rather use personal ties to exert influence and patronage over politicians than associate into effective interest groups.

The degree to which these business organizations are coherent and can influence policy varies considerably from country to country. One study (Schneider 2004) found that businesses were better and more effectively able to coordinate their influence in Mexico, Chile, and Colombia than in Argentina and Brazil. In the first three countries, at crucial moments in the import substitution era, governments explicitly granted certain business confederations exclusive access to government. Businesses that refused to join the associations were thereby frozen out of subsidies and protection from foreign competition. In Argentina and Brazil, however, the populist governments dealt individually with enterprises and business interests, reducing the power of big business confederations. Still, in the face of a radical threat, business interests tend to unite regardless of their earlier relationship with the government.

PUNTO DE VISTA: DOES ECONOMIC INEQUALITY WEAKEN SUPPORT FOR DEMOCRACY?

We might think that inequality does not much impact support for a political system (democracy or otherwise) as long as there is economic growth and people are experiencing material improvement in their lives. Poverty reduction may be more important than redistribution. In Brazil, the goals of poverty and inequality reduction seem to have benefited from both economic growth and redistribution, but not without raising some questions about the growth model.

Measures to redistribute income might include using taxation and "targeted benefit programs." In Brazil, former president Luis Inácio Lula da Silva (Lula) made the Bolsa Família (family package) program a central focus of his efforts to reduce poverty. Under this program, poor families are subsidized if and only if their children are attending school and have been vaccinated. This has the dual benefit of promoting income redistribution and promoting longer-term improvements in poor health and schooling, two conditions highly associated with poverty. However, the fiscal resources that make this spending possible have not been generated so much by increased taxes as by Brazil's high rate of economic growth since 2000. Much of this growth has been based on exports from agriculture (soybeans, sugar), mining, and ranching.

So we see here an example of a government program that has aimed at reducing exclusion, but it is tied to success in expanding exports of commodities, some of which are produced in environmentally questionable ways.

Although not all of Latin America has experienced the economic success of Brazil, we can see that in the region overall, there is a positive record of poverty reduction. In 2012, the United Nations Economic Development Commission showed that significant reduction in poverty had occurred in Latin America, with the number of people living in poverty falling from 225 million to 167 million people since 2002. Yet at the same time, when we look at the commission's findings on growth and wages in Latin America, it is clear that working people in the region have actually lost ground. (See Figure 2.2 and Table 2.2 on page 55.) Their wages have not kept pace with economic growth; in real terms their wages have not returned to what they were in 1980.

In its 2011 report, Latinobarómetro argued,

> [Latin America's] elites have to move faster to keep up with the population's demands. It is no longer acceptable to offer the solutions that were acceptable a decade ago. Economic growth and the increase in the size of the "pie," combined with ever better education, mean that there are large majorities in Latin American countries no longer prepared to tolerate inequality. This is the effect of prosperity and the "Chilean syndrome," which will be repeated in all those spheres where inequalities are not tolerable for the modern world of which we want to be part.

Point/Counterpoint

Do you think that the **polyarchy** model of democracy has adequately addressed inequality? Review the Figures 0.1 and 0.2 in the introduction, and look at the figures and tables in this chapter.

a. If you answered no, how would you answer the objection that overall poverty rates have fallen?

b. If you answered yes, how would you answer the objection that the data indicate that inequality grew in the 1990s, after electoral democracy and economic growth had been restored in the region?

For more information

You may want to go online and look at other graphs provided by Latinobarómetro, at latinobarometro .org. Gapminder.org is a great resource on changes in living conditions and inequality in countries of the world.

Drug Lords—A New Business Sector

Latin America's most dynamic "business" sector may be the one that Washington and many other countries would prefer disappear: narcotics production and trafficking. Because the drug trade is illegal, it is conducted underground and is often linked to political violence.

As with any commodity, the peasant cultivators (*cocaleros*) who provide the raw material make the least amount; the largest profits come from processing and moving the product itself. *Cocaleros* are often at the mercy of the traffickers, who use paramilitary forces to force them to sell cheap. They are also most vulnerable to U.S. and domestic military operations to eradicate their fields. Guerrilla organizations in Peru and Colombia (see chapter 10) built local support by defending cultivators from military and paramilitary forces and forcing traffickers to pay higher prices, at the same time that they provided security for both by fighting antidrug units sent by the government and the United States.

For a while in Colombia, production of cocaine became perhaps the largest business in the country—whether measured by employment, export income, or profit. Under the neoliberal economic policies of the government in the 1990s, Colombia's average annual growth rate from 1980 to 1997 was 3.2 percent, much lower than the 5.5 percent in the previous 30 years. Unemployment rose from a low of 7.5 percent in 1994 to 20 percent in 2000. In this period, between 1995 and 2000, production of coca increased 22 percent. Coffee, Colombia's main legal export, employed 12.5 percent of the population, whereas the cocaine industry is estimated to employ about 12 percent. As coffee prices fell, small farmers were being ruined (Holmes and Gutiérrez de Piñeres 2006). One need only ponder these data briefly to understand why one sector was shrinking and the other growing.

Dollars earned from drug trafficking are laundered and passed into the legal economy with substantial impact. Like any other commodity boom, the dollars generated by narcotics exports circulate in the market, making it easier to import consumer goods from abroad but hurting local producers. Why buy locally produced clothing when you can buy the latest Miami fashions and chic brands so cheaply? Dollars from international drug sales can be used to buy land in the country's agricultural heartland. In other words, drug lords gradually may become part of the legitimate landowning class, shaping the elite contour of civil society, controlling perhaps 30 percent of the wealth in the country. Inevitably, these new oligarchs impact politics, financing candidates and determining the outcome of internal competition for nominations within each of the two major parties, the Liberals and the Conservatives (see the next chapter).

The key here is to understand that we are not simply dealing with a question of the morality of engaging in the drug trade or accepting bribes or contributions from the "businessmen" who control this sector. The problem is structural. A global market exists for cocaine and other illegal drugs. Profits from this trade will inevitably find their way through legal and illegal channels into politics—including into the pockets of security forces or insurgencies, as in Peru or Colombia. And of course, Bolivia represents a case where, within limitations, *coca* is regarded as a legitimate crop, and *cocaleros* (cultivators) form the initial base for Evo Morales and his MAS (Movimiento al Socialismo) party. However, cocaine, as opposed to the chewed coca leaf, is consumed domestically throughout the Andes. A United Nations study in 2008 found that 4.1 percent of the population between 18 and 65 in Bolivia had used cocaine. In nearby Argentina and Chile, the figures were, respectively, 8.25 percent and 6.4 percent. For Argentina, of those who had used cocaine, 45.2 percent showed signs of addiction (United Nations 2008: 48–49). In other words, drug production and trafficking today has a domestic, not just foreign, market.

For Review

We often think of drug cartels merely as criminal syndicates. How are they also businesses? How can these cartels impact politics and the economy?

Labor Unions

Before unions, the first worker groups to form were solidarity organizations. Workers would pool a small portion of their poor wages in funereal societies to make sure that they would have a proper burial. These funds, in the absence of insurance or state welfare, provided some small financial support for families left behind. These organizations were incubators for unions that would later emerge. Leadership for the formation of unions was often provided by European immigrants who brought with them experience from home, where labor movements and political parties are typically tightly and formally linked to one another, and where socialist and anarchist movements have historically been influential.

Thus, in contrast to the United States, labor unions in Latin America more often than not associate themselves with political parties and ideological tendencies. Many Latin American parties incorporated workers directly into their ranks through an officially sanctioned "labor bureau." Some parties, such as Brazil's Workers' Party (PT) and Argentina's Peronists, historically grew directly out of labor movements, much like the Labour Party did in Great Britain. Although party affiliation can give workers greater political representation, partisanship also is a source of divisiveness. Recall the conflicts between Communist unions and Peronists in the early 1950s. In Venezuela, since 1999 the political competition for control of unions in heavily industrialized Ciudad Guyana has often turned violent.

Unions are often strongest in strategic export sectors, in state-owned industries, and in government bureaucracies. As a result, even though a relatively small percentage of the total workforce is organized, labor strife is often at the center of Latin American political struggles. For 1999–2001, International Labour Office (ILO) data indicate that nearly one in six formally employed Latin Americans worked in the public sector; the statistic was approximately one in five in Argentina, Ecuador, Mexico, Uruguay, Venezuela, and Costa Rica, ranging to a high of one in three in Panama. Public employment is an important source of patronage for politicians, but many workers employed in the public bureaucracy and state-owned companies are not necessarily docile before the government. Public workers tend to be a relatively well-organized sector positioned to place pressure on the government. They are especially prone to do so when the party associated with their union is in opposition.

Workers in key export enclaves played a crucial role in promoting democracy (Bergquist 1986). By "export enclaves" we mean those sectors of the economy that were crucial to the overall prosperity of the economy. Slaughterhouse workers in Argentina, copper workers in Chile, oil workers in Venezuela, and coffee cultivators and workers in Colombia crucially supported democracy and shaped the political structures of these nations through their strikes, protests, and votes. We could add examples from every Latin American country to this list, including copper miners in Peru, tin miners in Bolivia, fruit plantation workers in Central America, sugar plantation workers in Cuba, and oil workers in Mexico. Joined by railroad workers, port workers, and other employees in sectors vital to exports, these workers were usually in the vanguard of union organizing and of broader democratic and nationalist struggles. They had leverage because labor stoppages entailed high costs for government and ruling elites. The oligarchs often used repression to end strikes but invariably had to seek long-term political solutions to the strife.

On the other hand, corruption and **clientelism** have limited the ability of workers and their unions to defend their interests or advance broader ideological goals. For example, for decades leaders of the oil workers' union in Venezuela—affiliated with the Democratic Action (AD) party—had the right to actually hire a quarter of the employees in the oil fields. Their Mexican counterparts had similar power, and virtually all hiring of teachers was controlled by the national educators' union. Union leaders were often rewarded with bonuses and lucrative compensation for their expenses when negotiating contracts. Unions often used funds provided by government or collected from workers with government sanction to fund enterprises—stores, resorts, and even banks. In theory, these enterprises served workers, but in reality, they were sinecures for union officials who began to act more like managers than defenders of labor.

In the populist era, Latin American labor movements often came to be dominated by a stratum of privileged labor bosses beholden to politicians and vice versa. Union leaders tended to dampen labor strife when their party was in power; conversely, they intensified it when it was politically convenient to embarrass the government. Either decision might open a gap between the interests of workers and those of the union's leadership.

How workers and their unions were incorporated into the political system left a lasting impression on subsequent political structures (Berins Collier and Collier 1991). "Incorporated" refers to how workers won legal recognition of labor rights and how they won admission to the political game. As we have already noted in discussing **populism**, this happened in different ways from country to country. In some cases, such as Chile,

Venezuela, and Mexico, organized labor was just one sector under the broader umbrella of multiclass parties—that is, the parties that sought votes from both workers and the middle class. In other cases, such as in Argentina with Peronism, a working-class party was more narrowly built on a working-class base and often battled with others more rooted in the middle class. This pattern changed in the 1990s under the neoliberal administration of President Carlos Menem (1989–1999), who attracted middle-class support until his policy of stabilizing the peso by pegging it to the dollar (see Chapter 8) collapsed into economic crisis. Since that time, during the administrations of the two Kirchners (Nestor and Cristina; see chapter 8), middle-class support for the Peronist government has shifted back and forth, but it seems safe to say that the Peronist party still depends more on labor than on any other sector of the population.

Although labor has played a key role at crucial junctures in Latin America's quest for democracy, its influence has been limited not only by internal divisions, but also by characteristics of the workforce. Latin America suffers from chronically high rates of unemployment and a large proportion of workers employed in the informal sector—for example, domestic labor, ambulant street vendors, shoe shiners, and construction day laborers—all looking for better jobs. Labor laws usually limit the rights of workers in small and family-run businesses from organizing, often excluding them from benefits legally mandated for others. Peasants usually have even more limited labor rights. This large supply of labor outside the formal economy gives employers the upper hand in wage negotiations. To this source of pressure, we can add economic globalization, which has made capital more mobile and has undercut bargaining strength in many labor-intensive industries (textiles, assembly, electronics, etc.). A high proportion of workers in these sectors are women (*maquiladoras*), and their unorganized situation makes them vulnerable to sexual discrimination, harassment, and too often, rape.

In recent decades, traditional industries have shed jobs (especially in Mexico, Argentina, Venezuela, and Chile), as noncompetitive factories closed their doors or modernized with labor-saving technologies. Privatization reduced public-sector jobs, and new owners often have been keen to implement labor savings. The older populist parties can no longer deliver benefits as they did before. As a result, even leaders of older union organizations, especially the Mexican Workers Confederation (CTM) and the Venezuelan Workers Confederation (CTV), have faced competition from new confederations.

The military dictatorships of the **bureaucratic authoritarian** era struck harsh blows against labor organizations, but by crushing the populist structures inherited from the **ISI** era, the military also weakened or eliminated obstacles to more democratic and broadly organized unions. Even where the military did not seize power outright (e.g., in Mexico and Venezuela), dissatisfaction with ineffective union leadership and liberal reform tendencies (e.g., less international tolerance for repression of labor leaders) opened space either for new union federations or for reformist movements within older ones.

In the cases of Brazil and Argentina, the labor movement took the leading role in the struggle to restore democracy. In both cases, labor unions have been disappointed with the economic policies that have followed. This was especially so in the case of Argentina, where President Carlos Menem (1989–1999) implemented a program of monetary and fiscal stability and privatized many state-owned enterprises. Menem used these policies to his political advantage, using a divide-and-conquer strategy, rewarding union leaders who cooperated with his policies while implementing measures, such as privatization, that resulted in many lost jobs.

In Chile, copper workers' strikes in 1982 and 1983, largely around unsafe working conditions, were the first crack in the iron-fisted policies of the Pinochet dictatorship (see chapters 7 and 8). The neoliberal policies of the Concertación governments after the return of democracy caused labor some disgruntlement, but for a decade, the threat of a return of the military or the prospects of electoral victories by right-wing parties tempered popular resistance. Labor leaders were reluctant to undertake strikes or other actions that might weaken the center-left parties. Still, in August 2004, much to the chagrin of the socialist president, Ricardo Lagos, unions organized the first general work stoppage since the dictatorship, a protest against the "economic model." Union leaders were warning the politicians not to take them for granted, though their strikes had limited impact at the time. However, since 2010, workers have added their voice to student protestors whose demonstrations against inequality in education proved to be a catalyst for expression of wider discontent. It is fair to say, however, that the Chilean unions do not enjoy the kind of clout they did in the populist era.

In Venezuela, the collapse of oil prices and higher unemployment caused real wages to fall in the 1980s, and the labor unions, tied closely to the political parties, did little to check the slide. In the heart of new steel and aluminum industries in the eastern region around Ciudad Guayana, in Bolívar state, workers joined a leftist reform movement called Nuevo Sindicalismo (NS, "new unionism"), breaking the stranglehold of the Democratic Action party (AD) on unions (Hellinger 1996). In 1989, one of its leaders, Andrés Velásquez, successfully ran for governor of Bolívar, and in December 1993 he narrowly lost the presidency—some think that he was denied victory by fraud. This erosion of AD's base in labor was a significant factor in ushering in the regime transition (see chapter 9) from Punto Fijo to the Hugo Chávez era (1998–2013). Although the largest labor federation in Venezuela today is the Chavista National Workers' Union (UNT), the labor movement has been a thorn in the side of the Bolivarian government because workers learned from the Punto Fijo era the cost of subordination to the interests of a party. Chávez's successor, Nicolás Maduro, was a union organizer of Caracas transport workers, but this fact has not meant that worker movements and unions are any more complacent than they were under Chávez.

In Mexico, the CTM (Mexican Confederation of Workers) long dominated the labor movement and formed (along with the peasant association and a bloc of professions and entrepreneurs) one of the three pillars of support for the PRI. As discussed in chapter 5, the PRI shifted to the right after Lázaro Cárdenas left the presidency in 1940. This shift would have been difficult without the collaboration of Fidel Velázquez, who became head of the CTM in 1941. Thanks to government support, Velázquez had won a battle with a leftist (Lombardo Toledano) for control over the CTM. He subsequently led the confederation into a formal relationship with the PRI in 1946. He remained its head until his death in 1997. In this period of time, Velásquez worked closely with the PRI to repress independent or alternative labor organizing, and he acquired an international reputation for corruption. An aide to a Mexican president once told reporter Tina Rosenburg (1987), "The first thing you do when you're elected president is go to the shrine of the Virgin of Guadalupe and pray for the health of Fidel Velázquez for the next six years." In 1987 Velázquez sought the expulsion of Cuauhtémoc Cárdenas, who would later found the PRD, for advocating reform of the PRI. In the early 1990s he kept labor resistance muted during the controversies over NAFTA, even though the latter was to contribute to weakening of the political dinosaurs that had led the PRI throughout his tenure. Like Menem in Argentina, President Carlos Salinas de Gortari (1982–1988) rewarded friends and punished enemies in labor unions to achieve objectives such as privatization of state companies.

Several factors have eroded the hegemony of the traditional CTM leadership of Mexico in recent years. Privatization of key industries (e.g., telecommunications) and pressures to eliminate waste and corruption in the state oil company (PEMEX) eliminated some key patronage resources. The labor side agreement of NAFTA, though it lacked any significant enforcement power, put the spotlight on the undemocratic nature of Mexican unions. North American unions, recognizing that more effective Mexican unions might mitigate the incentives to move jobs from Canada and the United States to the south, began providing support for reform. A new federation, the National Union of Workers, and a movement, the Authentic Labor Front, appeared. These groups have tended to favor the PRD, the leftist party that emerged from the ranks of disgruntled PRI members and leftists after 1988, but like other social movements, they have resisted any formal alignment that might smack of the old relationship between the CTM and the PRI. But the corruption and clientelism in Mexican unions ultimately has taken its toll on labor's influence.

In December 2012, the Mexican Congress passed a labor law reform. To its credit, the law requires greater access for disabled people and women to employment, requires publication of negotiated contracts, and introduces a number of popular, progressive reforms. But the price of these democratic advances was the weakening of unemployment compensation, reduced rights to collect owed back pay, greater ease for companies to subcontract work done now by permanent employees, the enabling of companies to change jobs into temporary or part-time status, and so on. The arrest two months later of the powerful teachers' union leader (though her corruption was undeniable) struck a blow against the entire labor union movement, weakening Mexican unions across the board, including the oil workers' union, easing the way for privatization of many of PEMEX's operations. Smaller independent unions have been pressuring the government to strengthen protections for workers, especially against employers using subcontracting to break unions, but for now the CTM has not vigorously supported their efforts (Alexander and La Botz 2014; Cypher 2014).

Perhaps the most powerful new labor movement in Latin America emerged in the region's most influential country, Brazil. The PT (Workers' Party) was founded in São Paolo in 1980 by a coalition of leftist Christians, Marxists, unionists, environmentalists, and others motivated by the desire to encourage workers and the poor to organize themselves. They were searching for an alternative to the way that many previous leftist parties had sought to lead workers by promoting themselves as a "vanguard" (Keck 1992). They were motivated not only by disillusionment with old-style unions but also by social justice movements in the Catholic Church and by the democratic practices of a new labor movement emerging in the industrial suburbs of São Paolo.

Brazil's dictatorship (1964–1981) demolished the old populist parties and unions but was not nearly as repressive as the **bureaucratic authoritarian** regimes of the Southern Cone. This prepared the way for a new union movement that sought to strengthen the position of workers by seeking support from neighborhoods and from broader emerging movements. Women, environmentalists, and Afro-Brazilians began to coalesce with labor as never before. From the ranks of mulattos came the most important leader, Luiz Inácio Lula da Silva—"Lula"—a steel worker. When the military regime arrested Lula during a general strike in 1980, the agitated population responded with mass protests that forced the military to choose between bloody repression or concessions. The generals chose concessions (see chapter 8).

Latin American unions remain more politicized than their North American counterparts, but today overall they are less beholden to political parties. Certainly, this can be read as a plus for democracy, but on the negative side of the ledger, we must enter the erosion of union membership caused by economic and social change, the legacy of repression and corruption that still marks much of the labor movement, and the internal divisions that diminish the power of labor in national politics.

For Review

Historically, how did unions support democracy in the first half of the twentieth century? What kind of relationship developed between unions and political parties in Latin America? What can be said of the positive and negative implications for workers of a close relationship between parties and unions?

Social Movements

As we have seen already, some of the most important forces for change in Latin America have emerged from social movements. It can be difficult to draw a bright line between an interest (or "advocacy") group and a social movement. The former is usually a well-established player that regularly interacts with government to influence policy and to obtain benefits for its members. The social movements we are examining here vary in degree of formal organization but in general do not have institutionalized relationships with parties and the state. A social movement can be simply a popular cultural movement (e.g., a dance or music craze), but here we are talking about social movements that emerge in civil society with an explicitly political purpose. They are composed of people who work together with a common purpose to challenge authority or demand change, which involves regular interaction with elites, authorities, and opponents (Tarrow 1994: 4). Movements such as the Movimento dos Trabalhadores Rurais Sem Terra (MST, Landless Workers' Movement) have taken on some more formal degree of organization and regular interaction with the state, but the MST's popular nature, resistance to formal incorporation into party or government structures, and challenge to the status quo qualify it as a social movement.

Tarrow's concept of **political opportunity structures** describes how movements arise in civil society and impact politics by taking advantage of changes within the institutional or opportunity structures that allow a movement to emerge or gain strength. The existing political situation may encourage or discourage people from using collective action. Any group that wants to demand something from the state must take into account the environment in which it operates. For example, repression may make it physically risky for opponents to speak out or to demonstrate, which may lead a movement eventually to take up arms. On the other hand, an existing party or politician may open itself to a movement in the quest for votes or influence. Social movements form, says Tarrow, "when ordinary citizens, sometimes encouraged by leaders, respond to changes in opportunities that lower the costs of collective action, reveal potential allies, and show where elites and authorities are vulnerable" (1994: 17–18). When sufficiently organized, they can widen or create new openings thereafter.

The members of Brazil's Landless Workers' Movement have occupied vacant land and are holding a sign that says, "Enough of violence in the countryside and criminalization of social movements." They would later peacefully leave after confrontation with the police. Do you think their protest is justified?

For example, we have already seen that politicians and parties in Latin America often work to co-opt new leaders challenging them for influence. In the era of populism and import substitution, movements of workers often obtained material benefits and a quota of political influence but usually at the expense of their autonomy and internal democracy. This system could be maintained until import substitution no longer generated sufficient growth to satisfy expanding demands from the **popular sectors**, contributing to a crisis. Movements that tried to radicalize populism emerged. We saw this happen in Chile, Argentina, and Brazil in the period leading to bureaucratic authoritarianism. Eventually, in the latter era, democracy movements emerged to foster a transition from one institutional system to another.

In some circumstances social movements may evolve to challenge the structures themselves. This process is often a feature of politics in democracies where institutions have decayed—that is, failed to adapt to new circumstances and drifted away from serving the public interest. This happened in Venezuela to the political parties Acción Democrática (AD, Democratic Action) and COPEI in the waning years of the Punto Fijo regime (see chapter 9). Party leaders resisted demands to change the constitutional game because they feared reform would threaten their joint monopoly of power.

Tarrow places emphasis on how outside factors (e.g., a political entrepreneur's ambitions or an external shock, such as a loss in war or natural calamity) shape movements. It is also the case that movements shape their environments. Charles Tilly (1978), somewhat in contrast to Tarrow, sees opportunity structures as only one of many factors shaping movements and political outcomes. Other factors include the degree to which individuals share a common interest, the capacity they have to mobilize (i.e., the ability of members and scattered groups to create a network and communicate with each other), and the resources at the command of the movement.

Consider the following:

- Employed workers have in common that they labor for a wage; it is difficult to organize strikes, but when workers persist and stick together, they have considerable power to wield against more wealthy employers.
- Middle-class citizens can write letters to newspapers, perhaps as a group buy an advertisement to express their grievances, maybe withhold taxes, or demonstrate. Their incomes provide a power resource that is easier to use because it is less risky, but they do not have enough income to create an electoral or widespread advertising campaign unless they are mobilized into a group or network—something becoming more common with the advent of the Internet. The Zapatistas were perhaps the first insurgency/movement to take full advantage of the Internet to mobilize international solidarity with their cause.
- Poor people in the informal ("marginalized" or "excluded") sector often have little influence over day-to-day politics. They are harder to organize than workers and do not have the threat of withholding their labor. Their main power resource versus the state may be disruption—for example, occupations of the street or public buildings. This is a high-risk activity, but once unleashed, it may have a powerful influence on events. Now that many of the poorest people have access to social media through cell phones, their capacity to organize may have significantly increased, something that first became visible elsewhere in the world, in the Arab Spring (especially in Tunisia and Egypt in late 2013).

Tilly argues that understanding social movements must go beyond the task of analyzing the individuals, leaders, resources, and so on involved. People's objective interests form the basis of their unifying for collective action. Race, gender, ethnicity, and language offer potential bases for movement politics, but Tilly argues that social class is the most profound. In Latin America, the worsening of class inequalities certainly has been a catalyst for many of the most influential social movements.

Earlier in this chapter, we described the class structure and also some of the working class and poor people's movements and organizations that contributed greatly to the struggle for democracy. Class-based organizations and movements remain important in Latin America, but a variety of other types have sprung up in recent years. Some Latin Americanists would challenge the notion that these groups are really new, but there is little doubt that they are leaving a mark on politics in the region today. In the following pages we profile some of the most important of these movements, but this is not an exhaustive list by any means. For example, environmental organizations, LGBT (lesbian, gay, bisexual, and transgender) peoples, youth, and community media are just a few of the other movements that are shaping Latin America's future.

Worker Resistance Movements in Argentina

As we have seen (chapter 6), one major force for economic globalization has been the pressure to adopt neoliberal economic policies, applied on Latin American governments by the **International Monetary Fund (IMF)**, the World Bank (International Bank for Reconstruction and Development), and private financial institutions. The Argentine case is perhaps most indicative of the politics involved. Two great hemispheric forces were joined in the Argentine drama: neoliberal **globalization** came up against Latin America's new social movements.

After a decade of inflation, with a rate that reached 5,000 percent in 1989, in 1991 Peronist President Menem tried to stabilize the situation by issuing a new currency pegged at an exchange rate of one peso to US$1. No more pesos would be printed than there were dollars in the country's foreign exchange account. Inflation did indeed recede, and new foreign investment and loans arrived, but less of the incoming capital was invested in creating new industries than in buying assets being privatized by the state. Corruption was rampant. Rates of poverty and unemployment for the working class showed little improvement even though the economic growth rate averaged 8 percent for four years after 1991.

As long as overall economic growth was robust, the peso scheme worked. Argentina's economy was faltering by 1995, but the peso kept its value against other currencies because it was pegged to the dollar. Exports were choked off because the high peso meant that clients overseas had to spend much more (perhaps twice as much) of their own currencies to buy anything Argentina wanted to sell. For example, Brazil, Argentina's largest trading partner, nearly stopped buying Argentina's large rice crop, which could find no other outlet. Usually, these economic setbacks would cause the value of a country's currency to fall, but at the time the U.S. economy was doing well, and hence the **peso** held its value based on the dollar's strength. By October 2001, the financial speculators were swooping down. They bought pesos cheaply with other currencies and then used the pesos to buy dollars at one-to-one, subsequently sending them out of the country. The only way Argentina could guarantee the value of the peso was to borrow more dollars, but speculators quickly swept up the additional greenbacks (though most of this money was, in fact, electronic rather than paper currency). Pesos began piling up in government accounts; the dollars kept flowing out. To make things worse, pesos were useless in paying the international debt. Soon the state had no money to pay its own employees and keep social programs, schools, and so on going. The economy began to collapse, and so did the government, and so did what was left of the safety net for Argentine workers.

The IMF's solution to the crisis was austerity, including drastic cuts in the budget. The government, headed by President Fernando de la Rua (elected in December 1999 by a coalition of the Radical Party and a smaller party) decided in December 2001 to freeze all bank accounts, though not before well-connected clients had a chance to move their savings safely abroad. Middle-class Argentineans were cut off from their savings and joined the poor in scouring the streets for food. Argentineans began to engage in episodes of rioting and looting, driving de la Rua from office before his term expired. The country had three more presidents within two weeks following de la Rua's resignation. In January 2002, the government abandoned the one-to-one peg and devalued the peso by 30 percent. The IMF insisted that the budget be cut another 10 percent, even in the face of rising anger from public employees who had not been paid in months.

In middle-class and poor neighborhoods, citizens organized popular assemblies and began to experiment with local solutions and to confront national authorities. Some of the assemblies invaded closed factories and resumed production. When owners attempted to take them back, the assemblies defended them. Some of the assemblies organized economic markets where goods and services, from haircuts to airline tickets, could be bartered, creating a parallel market to the realm of the peso. Groups of unemployed people in the provinces, called *piqueteros*, sprung up around 1996. They began to seize highways and buildings, causing serious disruption. Eventually they organized themselves into a national association (Burbach 2002).

In May 2003, a Peronist, Nestor Kirchner, was sworn in as Argentina's new president. Kirchner had done better than most governors in managing the crisis in the small province of Santa Cruz. By the time he came to office, Argentina had defaulted on several payments due on its US$178 billion public debt. Kirchner took advantage of the situation to drive hard bargains with the international financial community. The situation brought to mind John Paul Getty's observation, "If you owe the bank $100 that's your problem. If you owe the bank $100 million, that's the bank's problem." Kirchner offered the country's creditors US$.25 on the dollar, and some began to accept or at least to renegotiate terms. Kirchner was helped when Venezuela agreed to send several oil tankers to eliminate the prospect that Argentineans would have no oil in the approaching winter. The government prevailed, thereby gaining resources to resume spending and kick-start the economy. Kirchner's popularity soared.

By 2005, as the economy recovered, the popular assemblies and the *piquetero* movement had become less visible. The government had negotiated and not renounced its international obligations. With the economy stabilized and prosperity returning to the middle class, it might seem that the social movements had lost influence. However, people had become more conscious of their power. Even hints that the government might turn back in a neoliberal direction can generate protests, reminding international and national elites of the limits of popular tolerance for globalization as it is commonly understood. Similar scenarios are unfolding in many parts of Latin America.

The Urban Poor and Neighborhood Movements

The men and women who make up the informal sector often have a harder time than labor in organizing to exercise political influence. The International Labour Organization breaks this category of workers into three parts: "independent workers," "domestic service," and "microfirms." A handful of highly skilled individuals may fall into the first or third category, but most of this sector is very poor, eking out a living by selling smuggled goods (cosmetics, plastic toys, pirated DVDs, etc.) on the sidewalk; finding temporary work in, for example, construction; or working in other people's homes. This last group, the domestic sector, is mostly composed of women working as maids, nannies, and so on. Almost none are covered by social security, most live in the poorest neighborhoods, and most must rely on pooling the meager income of family members, including children who have little time or inclination for school. Often, workers in the informal sector are caught up in the illicit economies of prostitution and drugs, vulnerable to both police abuse and social predators.

Despite their social exclusion and vulnerability, the urban poor have entered the political arena repeatedly, organizing themselves in their neighborhoods or places of commerce (e.g., sidewalk vendors). When they do so, class tension escalates. In many countries, this sector is disproportionately of African or indigenous heritage. To the middle class and wealthy, the presence of poor people of color in their neighborhoods (other than when they are working) is disconcerting and threatening. They are the *descamisados* (shirtless ones) who followed Perón, the *turbas* (mobs) who turned out in support of Hugo Chávez, the *cholos* (Indians) blocking highways in the Andean countries, or the *piqueteros* occupying streets in Argentina. To many in the middle class, they represent the opposite of civil society; they are the people who need to be modernized and tutored in the ways of democracy. To the "responsible left" favored by intellectuals such as Mexico's Jorge Castañeda, they are an obstacle to democracy; to politicians such as Chávez and Morales, they are *el pueblo*, and democracy cannot come until their voices are heard. To Latin America's new left, they *are* civil society, demanding to be heard and recognized.

Latin America's cities, with few exceptions, have populations well beyond their capacity to sustain a good quality of life. Community organizations sometimes begin at the very moment a *toma* takes place, as invaders of vacant land or buildings struggle to gain a foothold in the municipality. With the onset of the debt crisis and economic policy changes that fell most heavily on the poor, neighbors had to rely on one another to survive. In Chile, *barrio* dwellers came together to form *ollas comunas* ("common pot," i.e., a soup kitchen) during the Pinochet dictatorship. These community kitchens sought more than anything else to maintain minimum nutrition for children. As such, they were not founded with political goals in mind. However, in a society where fierce repression had erased most of the leftist presence, these groups were among the first to raise their voices and demonstrate against the dictatorship, which responded with water cannons and military sweeps through neighborhoods. Given the origins of these kinds of groups, it should not be surprising that women were most frequently in the vanguard of this struggle to restore democracy.

Asociaciones de vecinos (neighborhood associations, AVs) now network with one another and in doing so have become important actors almost everywhere in Latin America. In Mexico City, people found they had to organize themselves to compensate for an entirely inadequate government response to the earthquake of 1985. In Peru, neighborhoods organized not only in response to poverty but also in reaction to violence unleashed by both President Alberto Fujimori's security forces and the ultra-extreme guerrilla group Sendero Luminoso. In Venezuela, AVs first emerged as actors in the 1970s and became a force for political change after riots greeted President Carlos Andrés Pérez's announcement of an agreement with the IMF for structural adjustment (see chapter 9) in 1989.

Argentina has seen one of the strongest efforts by nonunionized workers to organize. The *piquetero* movement emerged in the 1990s when desperate poor people began to block highways and rail lines to protest government cuts. Mayors, governors, and other politicians in the provinces were not always unhappy with this development because it put pressure on the central government to provide states and municipalities with resources needed to carry out government tasks. By 2000, the *piqueteros*, discovering their power, formed national networks. Such action is not limited to poor people's protest. Venezuelan president Hugo Chávez found middle-class opponents adopting *piquetero* tactics in 2003 as part of an unsuccessful effort to drive him from office.

Organizations based on where people reside have assumed more prominence in recent decades. Their struggles often express social class interests, but here the basis for common concern is where people live, not where they work. Now that many city residents are three or four generations removed from the arrival of the first migrants, more of them are accommodating to urban life. Unlike their predecessors, they are not content with the relative improvement that city life offered over life in the countryside. Struggles against dictatorships, personal insecurity, and economic hardships have generated more deeply rooted associations where people live, as opposed to where they work.

Although they share some objectives, neighborhood organizations in poor *barrios* differ somewhat from those in middle-class neighborhoods. Both organize themselves in part to demand more responsive local government, but the middle class often focuses on defending urban parks and pedestrian zones from encroachment by developers and also from the informal sector. Their actions can be motivated by a sincere desire to preserve common urban living space or by baser motives related to racist or class prejudice—or both. Poor residents often first organized themselves in the land takeovers that created new communities, but they also came into existence as an attempt to pool resources in a struggle for economic survival (e.g., the *ollas comunas*—"common pots"—that sprung up in Chilean cities in the Pinochet years).

In Central America, the guerrilla movements that either toppled dictatorships (Nicaragua in 1979) or achieved political concessions (El Salvador and Guatemala) were mostly based in rural areas, but they also depended greatly on civil society in the towns. Guerrilla armies must be fed, armed, and clothed; their dead must be buried, their wounded cared for, their spiritual needs attended to, and their ideas communicated. In other words, actual fighting is only one part of a revolutionary struggle. The civil conflicts did leave as a legacy a variety of women's organizations, peasant groups, human rights organizations, cooperatives, environmental groups, unions, and so on that have become part of the permanent political landscape in the region. In the past, such organizations in Central America were usually stamped out violently by the oligarchy and armed forces (excepting Costa Rica). They continue to face repression today, but they survive.

In Brazil, neighborhood associations in poor areas were critical to the growth of the PT and brought Afro-Brazilians, and their issues, into national politics. Outstanding among the leaders to emerge from the *favelas* is Benedita da Silva, whom we met in chapter 8, who says in *I Was Born a Black Woman*, a documentary film about her life, "I live in a country of 30 million impoverished people, people who can't read or write, people who live in cardboard shacks in the shantytowns, under bridges, on the streets. I know their stories because I have lived it myself."

Sometimes neighborhood organizations have been formed as a result of initiatives from government. In Cuba, the Committees for Defense of the Revolution (CDRs; see chapter 10) can be found every few blocks in every corner of the country, founded originally in part to defend the young revolution from U.S. efforts to overturn the new regime. They also serve to identify and repress dissidents. However, CDRs also play an active role in organizing communities to deal with scarcity and social problems, such as child abuse and violence against women. Every Cuban neighborhood is also organized into an association, called Poder Popular (PP). These serve as vehicles for people to voice complaints and demand responses from local officials and the bureaucracy. The PPs are the base units of government and are responsible for organizing elections at the municipal level in Cuba.

Cuba's CDRs, PPs, and other large mass organizations, including women's organizations, cultural associations, and unions, are officially sanctioned. At the national level, their leaders are usually members of the Communist Party. Because of the limits on forming voluntary organizations, most political scientists see them as instruments of the regime and not as agencies of a civil society. However, this is not a unanimous view. Some analysts believe that these groups exercise significant influence over government policies and act to transmit demands from people to government and the bureaucracy (Azcri 2000; Roman 2003). Perhaps the most unruly (from the government's view) of these mass organizations is the Union of Writers and Artists of Cuba. Movie directors, novelists, painters, dancers, and musicians have produced devastating critiques of social ills. Although direct criticism of Raúl Castro and/or advocacy of multiparty democracy is not tolerated, almost anything else, including censorship, appears in Cuban art and culture.

Although insisting that he was not attempting to import the Cuban model, Venezuela's Chávez (1999–2013), lacking a strong political party and relying greatly on his personal **charisma**, sought in the early 2000s to mobilize supporters into "Bolivarian Circles." More than Chávez's own efforts, it was the opposition's attempted coup against him that mobilized the *barrios*, as residents turned out in massive numbers to demonstrate for his survival. Various kinds of neighborhood organizations formed to collaborate with the armed forces and government agencies to undertake "missions" to improve health and literacy. Cuban aid workers were invited to help and were deployed around the country in the poorest areas. Later, many of the circles were replaced by "urban land committees," formed to take advantage of a new law that gave *barrio* residents the chance to register legal ownership of their *ranchos* (poor homes)—but only after the committees worked to carry out a census and establish property lines. In August 2004, when he faced a crucial referendum on whether to cut short his term of office, Chávez found that his political party at that time, the Fifth Republic Movement (MVR), was inadequate to the task, so he turned to these organizations to mount his successful campaign, organizing them into "electoral battle units."

In 2006 and 2007, Venezuela's Bolivarian government launched an effort to stimulate the formation of communal councils, made up of a minimum of 200 families in urban areas and 20 in rural areas. The councils receive funds directly from the central government and state oil company to deploy in projects determined by their members. Chávez's goal was, on one hand, to organize a more secure basis of power for his government and, on the other hand, to stimulate local initiatives (cooperatives, land redistribution, and civic improvements) to address the country's deteriorating standard of living and to create a "bottom-up" development model, linking it to participatory democracy and "**twenty-first-century socialism**." Thus, members of the *consejos* (councils) are called *voceros* (spokespersons), not *representantes* (representatives). They are subject to recall by the organized community.

This experiment is highly controversial, with critics claiming that Chávez merely built a new patronage structure outside the normal structures of municipal and state government, or worse, in the minds of opponents, was preparing to import the Cuban model, complete with CDRs, into Venezuela. Admirers see a bold experiment in participatory democracy. The most successful application of the program has been in the municipality of Carora, population 90,000, in the west-central region, where the local mayor, Julio Chávez (no relationship to the president), turned over the entire capital budget (50 percent of the city's available revenues) to the local communities to allocate themselves.

Opposition to Chavismo, mostly from the middle-class and wealthy sectors, has a territorial, not just class dimension. Massive marches by hundreds of thousands of Venezuelans characterized tactics on both the pro- and anti-Chávez forces during his presidency. The largest contingents on the Chavista side usually emanated from the western *barrios* of Caracas, whereas opposition demonstrations always departed from the more affluent eastern areas of the metropolitan area. To some extent, the polarization diminished between the defeat of an effort to recall Chávez in a national referendum in 2004 and his death in 2013, but the highly polarized political culture reemerged after the narrow electoral victory of Maduro in April 2013. Caracas and the country remained in 2013 in the wake of Chávez's death intensely polarized and greatly divided about "twenty-first-century socialism," with the opposition convinced it is not really different from the Cuban model, Chavista activists defending the government but pressing for a faster and more radical transition to socialism, and a majority of Venezuelans unhappy with a government performing poorly and an opposition offering little alternative other than bringing down the government.

For Review

Why are neighborhood associations and other kinds of poor people's movements playing a greater role today in urban areas? What kinds of issues do these associations address?

Peasants, Rural Movements, and Landlords

Although most Latin Americans now live in the city, the absolute size of the rural population has remained constant. Peasants and farmers may organize not only around access to land ("usufruct") but also around government support in the form of cheap credit, roads, organized markets, price supports and subsidies, irrigation projects, and so on.

In most of Latin America, peasants were left out of the political alliances that sustained populism. However, struggles around land are as old as Latin America itself, so it hardly surprises that peasant movements have been part of the "new social movements" tendency. They have been especially visible in recent years in Brazil, in Central America, in parts of the Andes where indigenous peoples make up a large percentage of the population, and in Mexico, where many peasants feel the government has abandoned the promises of the 1910 revolution.

It is easy to stereotype rural society as a mass sea of illiterate peasants. However, peasants live in different kinds of social and economic contexts. Some are landless day laborers, and others work for wages on large plantations; some have small plots of their own to subsidize meager earnings, whereas others live on the traditional landed estates in a kind of feudal relationship to the landowner. Gender and racial divisions also give peasants different outlooks and interests. For example, men from the Maya villages in the Guatemala highlands regularly migrate during harvest periods to the coastal plantations to supplement incomes, leaving women behind to hold families and communities together. In the Andean nations of Bolivia, Ecuador, and Peru, peasant unrest is most intense among indigenous peoples who remain acutely aware that their ancestors once ruled these lands. The Movimento dos Trabalhadores Rurais Sem Terra (Rural Landless Workers' Movement—MST) in Brazil, which emerged on the scene in the 1990s, has inspired a new social movement for land redistribution throughout the continent. The MST is the largest single-movement organization in Latin America, perhaps the world.

These peasant movements constitute a part of civil society that challenges the Anglo-American ideal of respect for private property as a democratic bulwark. The MST engages in land seizures to pressure the government to follow through on promises of land redistribution. Peasants are organized in nuclei of 10 and then upward. No major action, such as an occupation, occurs without thorough discussion and a vote by the grassroots base. The same goes for the movement's political decisions, which are also decided only after extensive grassroots consultation. The MST's decision to endorse Lula was vital to his reelection in 2006—even though the movement sharply criticized the Brazilian president for failing to deliver on his promise on land reform in 2002. Thus, the MST sidestepped an often divisive decision for social movements—whether to engage in electoral politics and risk co-optation by the system.

As we've seen already, the relationship of social movements to the state and to leftist political parties is complex in most cases. Unlike many North Americans, Latin Americans look to the state for support, in terms of both material and policies. However, most also are wary of the kinds of clientelism that characterized the relationship among the state, parties, and groups in the populist era. Many are seeking a relationship of autonomy but not necessarily independence from the state.

The Evolving Rural Economy

The traditional *hacienda* has given way in most parts of Latin America to farms, ranches, vineyards, or plantations in which workers are hired and fired ("proletarianized") as they are in the city. This also means ownership and management of land has changed, eroding the base for traditional, conservative politics. Nowhere has this change been more pronounced than in Chile. There, until 1973, political parties on the Chilean right counted it among their basic functions to defend landlords against agrarian reform and to preserve a traditional, almost feudalistic culture. Chile was one of the most socially conservative countries (on issues such as divorce, religious education, etc.) in Latin America, a legacy of this period, but 10 years of land reform (1964–1973), followed by Pinochet's determination to make Chilean agriculture more commercially successful, stripped the countryside of the social basis for traditional conservatism.

Chile has two right-wing parties that form a conservative bloc, and both court the urban middle class and business interests for votes. However, these parties still rely on and exercise additional clout in the political system because they draw votes from the countryside, which is overrepresented in Congress, thanks to Pinochet's 1982 constitution. This is especially true in the Senate, where they need only about one-third of the vote to win one of the two seats allotted each province. However, the Chilean countryside has changed too, with more capitalist-style big farms replacing the old traditional *haciendas*. The decline of traditional conservatism rooted in this old system manifested itself in 2004 when Chile finally made divorce legal (albeit difficult to obtain).

Extreme concentration of private land ownership characterizes virtually all of Latin America except Cuba. However, the relationship between landowners varies as a result of historical experience and the kind of product produced. Argentina shares with Chile a highly unequal pattern of land distribution, but agriculture and ranching were organized somewhat more along capitalist lines from the start. Possessed of extremely fertile black earth, Argentina's pampas, about the size of the state of Texas, provided the basis for a highly successful export sector based on ranching and agriculture. Two-thirds of Argentina's arable land is concentrated in 2.5 percent of large estates, mostly ranches given over to production of cattle and sheep. Production of meat created the fiercely independent cowboys, *gauchos*, on one hand, but processing meat and moving it to market required railroads and slaughterhouses where a proletariat sprang up. The latter was much easier to organize than ranch hands and herders.

Brazil has a similar maldistribution of land, with half of the productive land concentrated in 1 percent of farms. Peasants living on these estates are poor, often illiterate, and highly dependent on the personal largesse of landowners, especially in the poor, chronically drought-stricken northeast, where the MST first arose. Where state-subsidized irrigation projects exist, the benefits go mostly to big landowners, leaving the poor as destitute as ever. The region has seen repeated movements of desperate, poor peasants. In the late 1800s, they were sometimes led by religious mystics and never achieved permanent victory.

The MST has largely shed this mystical dimension and taken on environmentalism as part of its rationale for agrarian reform. On its English-language website (www.mstbrazil.org, accessed June 26, 2006), besides calling for land redistribution, the MST invites visitors to read "a portion of text below, written by Benedictine monk Marcelo Barros for the Fifth conference on agroecology—Developing a Popular and Sovereign Project for Agriculture." This meeting brought 5,000 agriculturalists together in Cascavel, Paraná state, to "exchange experiences and discuss agroecological production and sustainable development." The MST also advocates redistribution of land to dwellers in poor *barrios* who want to return to rural life.

As we saw in chapter 10, the civil wars that wracked El Salvador, Guatemala, and Nicaragua in the 1980s were rooted in land inequality and the displacement of peasants from land taken for production of cattle, cotton, and sugar (Barry and Preusch 1986: 144–161; LaFeber 1993). These conflicts left a minimum of 200,000 people dead or disappeared in the region. The Sandinistas redistributed much land in Nicaragua in the 1980s, but the agrarian reform of those years was undone after their electoral defeat in 1990. Negotiated settlements of civil wars in El Salvador and Guatemala were supposed to have addressed rural inequality, but only modest redistribution took place (see chapter 10).

Urban and rural inequalities feed on one another, and the situation in Central America is perhaps must illustrative of this fact. The region's cities were swollen by refugees from the wars, and the great majority of these people have never been resettled. Urban areas are now populated by legions of unemployed youth; firearms are more obtainable than ever. El Salvador and Honduras (though the latter escaped the worst violence of the 1980s) have seen spectacular growth in gangs organized by young men who returned from inner cities in the United States after the end of the wars. On May 17, 2004, a fire in one Honduran prison killed 103 young inmates, victims of an overcrowded penal system that cannot absorb prisoners, most of whom were arrested merely for wearing the tattoos of gangs. They were swept up in a government crackdown encouraged by a fearful population. Analyzing the tragedy, *The Economist* ("Bring It All Back Home," May 20, 2004), said,

> With no jobs, the deportees set up their own gangs. According to government estimates, 36,000 people are said to belong to gangs in Honduras, 14,000 in Guatemala, 10,500 in El Salvador, 1,100 in Nicaragua and 2,600 in Costa Rica. The true

PUNTO DE VISTA: IS THE MST'S CALL FOR SUSTAINABLE AGRICULTURE ECONOMICALLY REALISTIC?

During the presidency of Lula in Brazil, significant reductions in poverty took place, contributing considerably not only to his popularity but also to that of the Workers' Party (PT). Government funding of programs to reduce poverty was based in part on economic growth through expanded production of and high global prices for mining and agribusiness exports, such as soybeans, beef, and tropical fruits. Lula and the PT have been supported by Latin America's largest social movement, the Landless Workers' Movement (MST). However, the MST's vision of land reform clashes with the existing structure of large landholdings, highly technological agriculture, and production for export. The following extract includes two components of what the MST called in a 2009 proclamation a "People's Agrarian Reform." (For the full document, see www.mstbrazil.org/resource/msts-proposal-peoples-agrarian-reform.)

1. Earth

The land and property of nature is above all a heritage of the peoples that inhabit each area, and must serve the development of humanity. Democratize access to land, to the goods of nature and to the means of production in agriculture to all who want it to live and work. The ownership, possession and use of land and goods of nature must be subordinated to the general interests of the Brazilian people, to meet the needs of the entire population.

Key measures

1.1. Establish a maximum size of the farm, for each farmer, established according to each region . . . and expropriate all farms above this module, regardless of level of production and productivity.

1.2. Ensure access to land for every family that wants to live and work there.

1.3. Expropriate all farms of foreign companies, banks, industries, construction companies and churches, which do not depend on agriculture for their activities.

1.4. Expropriate ALL large estates that do not comply with the social function. That is, they are either below the average productivity of the region, not respecting the environment, have problems of compliance with labor laws with their employees or are involved in smuggling, drug trafficking, slave labor. The compensation paid (compensation for the expropriation) should be equal to that declared for taxes, discounted by all taxes owed, with loans of public banks, and with environmental and social damage. . . .

2. The Organization of Production in Rural Areas

Key measures

2.1. Agricultural production will be directed with priority to produce healthy food for all the Brazilian people, thus ensuring the principle of food sovereignty.

2.2. Production will be organized based on the development of all forms of agricultural cooperation, such as task forces, traditional forms of community organizations, associations, cooperatives, public companies, companies providing services, etc.

2.3. Agribusinesses should be arranged near the location of agricultural production in the form of cooperatives under the control of farmers and workers in agribusiness. Technical training programs should be conducted for workers in management of agro-industrial cooperatives.

2.4. Promote diversified agriculture, breaking the **monoculture**, seeking to promote sustainable agriculture based on agro-ecological principles, without pesticides and GMOs, creating a healthy diet. This new production model also manages a new base and new forms of food consumption, balanced and appropriate to local ecosystems and culturally appropriate.

Point/Counterpoint

Given how much Brazil's economy overall depends on modern, export agriculture, is the MST's vision for the land reform realistic and in the best interest of the country?

   a. If you say no, how would you answer those who say that large-scale export agriculture has not helped most rural Brazilians and is environmentally unsustainable?
   b. If you say yes, how do you respond to those who say that the agricultural exports have provided the basis to lift millions of Brazilians overall out of poverty?

For more information

Friends of the MST is a worldwide solidarity movement with the Brazilian movement, with a web page at www.mstbrazil.org/whatismst. Among many good grassroots documentaries, a series of three videos chronicling a land takeover and confrontation with the government is at www.youtube.com/watch?v=hWjrTKuYsJg.

figure is almost certainly much higher. The most notorious of hundreds of gangs, or *maras*, is the Mara Salvatrucha, named for its Salvadoran founders who claimed to be as wise as a trout (*truchas*). Its initials appear in graffiti across the region.

It is difficult to imagine democracy taking firm root in these "not so civil" societies. To some degree, all Latin American countries face this dilemma. Crime rates in urban areas are soaring, and justice systems—underfunded and often riddled by corruption—cannot bear the load. Frightened citizens are disposed to give government further-reaching powers to crack down, leading to increased militarization of society.

For Review

What do peasants want? What causes peasant movements to arise? What else besides land do peasants need to be productive and contribute to economic development?

The Human Rights Movement

Although in North America we tend to think of human rights associations primarily as organizations formed to preserve *civil* rights, most Latin American groups are committed to a broader agenda. The human rights movement emerged as a result of the confluence of international events and regional responses to repressive regimes and persistent social injustices.

The administration of U.S. president Jimmy Carter (1977–1981) can be credited with raising worldwide concern for human rights, but Carter often failed to act forcefully and consistently (e.g., sending military aid to the Argentine and Salvadoran military juntas) on rights issues. The administration of President Ronald Reagan (1981–1988) discovered that the promotion of human rights was a useful tool to embarrass communist regimes; however, soon some of its own allies were being criticized as among the world's most repressive regimes. U.S. policy had helped create an "opportunity" for the movement for human rights in Latin America to press its agenda.

Human rights organizations in Latin America in most cases were formed in the womb of dictatorships, by people who took enormous risks, in many cases losing their lives. In some cases, the Catholic Church provided a protective social umbrella for the first groups. For example, Chile's Servicio Paz y Justicia (Service for Peace and Justice—SERPAJ), part of the Archdiocese of Santiago, was established in 1977 at the height of the dictatorship. Among its activities was training people in "control of fear" and in nonviolent protest. The Chilean Corporación de Promoción y Defensa de los Derechos de Pueblo (CODEPU; www.codepu.cl) devotes itself to preserving memory of the Pinochet era; it organizes people to demand investigations and prosecutions in individual cases and pressures the judiciary to reopen abuse cases.

Some human rights groups focus narrowly on civil rights, but others extend their work into other areas. Nizkor (Hebrew for "we will remember," an allusion to the Jewish Holocaust) is one of the networks that link these types of groups throughout the hemisphere. SERPAJ, Chile's chapter of Nizkor, has involved itself in indigenous and environmental issues. Its web page (www.derechos.org/nizkor/espana/doc/endesa, accessed August 2010) included a call to support the Mapuche Indians in their conflict with a Spanish corporation that wanted to build hydroelectric dams on the Bio-Bio River in southern Chile.

In El Salvador, the Centro de Documentación en Derechos Humanos, a prominent human rights organization, was founded by father Segundo Montes, a Jesuit murdered by the military in 1989. Based at the Catholic order's Central American University in San Salvador, the organization campaigned for the direct election of the country's attorney general, a position of importance because it has independent authority to prosecute corruption and human rights abuses. Like SERPAJ, the organization does not limit itself to these types of issues. On its website the organization defines its mission to be not only to create a safer atmosphere for participation by reducing repression but also to identify the roots of that repression in poverty, marginalization, and exclusion (www.uca.edu.sv/publica/idhuca, accessed August 23, 2014).

Citizen organizations of a similar nature have arisen everywhere, not just in countries that lived through military rule. In Venezuela, PROVEA (Venezuelan Program of Education and Action on Human Rights) is one of several groups that formed as the economy deteriorated in the 1980s, prompting riots and government repression in 1989. PROVEA certainly takes on civil rights cases, but it defines its mission as defense of "economic, cultural and social rights" as well. In 2006, it was one of several organizations that protested the Supreme Court's decision to void major provisions of a women's rights bill. The sections struck down had authorized government agencies in emergency situations to prevent abusive men from entering the homes and workplaces of threatened women. PROVEA has involved itself in investigating and pressuring the government of President Chávez and his successor, Nicolás Maduro, not just on political rights but also to make good on a variety of social rights, most importantly in housing and health.

Related to the human rights movement are groups that emerged to defend the transparency of electoral processes. These have been particularly significant in the Mexican and Venezuelan transitions, where the probity of elections has been a major battleground. In Venezuela, Ojo Electoral (Electoral Eye) emerged after the opposition to Chávez claimed fraud in the 2004 recall election. Ojo generally rejected these claims, but the organization decided to go beyond merely investigating fraud after the fact. Ojo itself disbanded but has been succeed by a similar organization, Observatorio Electoral, that has worked to ensure a fair count of ballots and to build popular confidence in electoral mechanisms. Mexico's Alianza Cívica (see chapter 9), founded with similar goals to those of Venezuela's Observatorio, has gone even further, broadening its focus after 2000 to include anticorruption efforts.

Women's Movements

As we have seen already, many popular movements overlap one another, sometimes blurring the boundaries between one social sector and another. Perhaps nowhere is this more evident than in the case of women, whose leadership in democratization was highlighted in chapter 8. Often, women in the past participated in battles to overthrow a dictatorship or in revolutions only to be relegated back to the political margins afterward. Certainly this problem has not nearly disappeared, but supported by a global movement for women's rights, there are signs that Latin American women are not accepting this marginalization without a fight in the current era.

Women's movements are pressing for progress on reproductive freedom, family issues, justice in the workplace, environmental defense, and protection from violence. For example, in Tijuana, Mexico, women workers organized themselves to battle large companies that refused to pay them severance pay after closing their doors and moving to even cheaper labor markets (cheaper than the US$11 per day earned by the Mexicans). The *promotadoras*, as they called themselves, won their struggle, one they documented in a film called *Maquilapolis*. The leaders collaborated with North American filmmakers who provided cameras, so that the women could document their work. New media technologies in this way are helping grassroots movements support one another on a transnational level.

Social movements often arise in a molecular way, almost invisibly until an outside observer from the world of academia or media takes notice. In Ciudad Juarez, poor women founded Casa Amiga not as an organization seeking immediate political benefits from government, but as in Chile during the Pinochet era, simply to coordinate and exchange services and survival skills. Joanna Swanger (2007: 112) argues that cooperative efforts to build community (*convivir*) are subversive in a subtler but lasting way, "planting the seeds of a workable culture that will grow up underneath the faceless structural forces of globalization." A student doing an internship in Casa Amiga wrote Swanger,

> So now I feel like part of a community of women who respect each other, and it makes me feel so content and secure. Isn't that funny? A little thing like sharing lunch can bring women together, empower them individually and as a group, and build real commitment between them . . . This atmosphere is very different from the one I'm used to in the U.S.
>
> (Swanger 2007: 117–118)

Racial and Ethnic Movements

As noted in chapter 2, Latin American national identity has been forged around the idea of **mestizaje**, which on the one hand recognized the history of indigenous and African peoples' contribution to the region's culture, but on the other hand created a basis for denying that racism existed or influenced social class patterns. Peruvians and Mexicans learned to glorify the Mayan, Incan, or Aztec past but not necessarily the Indian present. In the twentieth century, the most important movements for social justice often included indigenous peoples in their ranks, but they were almost always led by **mestizos**, such as Haya de la Torre, the Peruvian reformist who founded APRA; Lázaro Cárdenas, the Mexican president who made good on some of the promises of the Mexican Revolution; and Victor Paz Estenssoro, leader of the 1952 revolution in Bolivia and founder of that country's main party of the populist era, the Movimiento Nacionalista Revolucionario (MNR). The Cuban Revolution greatly benefited Afro-Cubans, but here once again the top leaders (Fidel and Raúl Castro, Che Guevara, and others) were in the great majority either *criollo* or white.

Afro-Descendant Movements in Brazil and the Caribbean

New social movements are seeking to bring the persistence of racism and race-based inequalities into the open by challenging the myth of racial democracy in Latin America (Rodríguez 1996). In Brazil, under pressure from the PT and a movement of people of African descent, Brazilians have now set hiring goals for Afro-Brazilians in a number of ministries. The initiative was taken by Fernando Henrique Cardoso during his presidency (1995–2003). Cardoso had attracted criticism for adopting fiscal and monetary policies that hurt the poorer sectors, who are more likely to be black, but he showed leadership on the issue of race, which was the subject of his PhD dissertation. One study showed that in Brazil only 2 percent of black students entered universities in 2000, compared with 10 percent of whites. More than 50 percent of Brazil's blacks were illiterate, compared with 20 percent of the overall population, and the rate of infant mortality was twice as high for blacks as for whites (Ikawa 2009). Below the federal level, three Brazilian states passed laws allocating 40 percent of university slots to Afro-Brazilians. (See the Punto de Vista in chapter 3.) Afro-Brazilian members of the PT organized a black caucus.

In liberal democracies, the idea of using measures (affirmative action) to help groups that have historically felt discrimination regain equality of opportunities often encounters opposition from those who say such policies discriminate against men and whites. The privileged sectors of Latin America respond in much the same way, arguing that they should not in some sense be "penalized" for injustices committed by ancestors. Added to this argument is the notion that racism is not prevalent in Latin America because of the historical mixture of ethnic groups—the "myth of **mestizaje**."

Cardoso's initiatives might not have taken root but for an international black consciousness movement, fed in part by the civil rights movement in the southern United States and the antiapartheid movement in South Africa. Brazilians began to reassess the myth of racial democracy in their country. Like some other social movements we have reviewed, Afro-Brazilian organizations did not begin with avowedly political goals. The movement emerged first in the form of cultural groups, such as Caiana dos Crioulos, a black community of descendants of runaway slaves, and Banda Yle Odara, which practices martial arts, music, and dance. Afro-Brazilian religious groups, including practitioners of Candomble and Umbanda, began to defend their spiritual ways as legitimate. Women's organizations often proved open to views critical of Brazil's prevailing myths of racial equality.

Racism remains a difficult fact of life in Brazil. For example, Kathleen Bond, a Maryknoll missionary working for social justice in Brazil, reports (www.hartford-hwp.com/archives/42/132.html) that when Margarida Pereira da Silva launched her candidacy for mayor of Pombal in the northeastern state of Paraiba, she was offered a bribe to drop out of the contest. When she refused, her posters were defaced with "negra feia" (ugly negress), and many of her supporters were paid to defame her reputation. She lost the election badly. Nevertheless, it is worth noting that black women have won some races, and some now even have seats in the Brazilian Congress. In the same vein, the electoral successes of Lula in Brazil and Chávez in Venezuela (along with indigenous politicians, such as Bolivia's Evo Morales, and female presidents such as Chile's Michelle Bachelet and Argentina's Cristina Fernández Kirchner) have literally changed the "face" of leadership in Latin America.

Racism divides populations in some parts of the Caribbean. For example, Dominicans share both the island of Hispaniola and a common African ancestry with Haitians. As their country was wracked by poverty and political violence, many Haitians migrated to the Dominican (eastern) side of the island. There they suffer mistreatment and often expulsion, not only because Dominicans resent the additional competition for jobs but also because Dominicans choose to describe themselves as "Indian" or *mulato*—implying that it is better to fit into one of these categories than to be considered black (Sagas 1993).

This denial of African ancestry has been reinforced by the influence of the United States in the Caribbean. Before the integration of the U.S. armed forces after World War II, U.S. military bases and local clubs nearby practiced racial discrimination. Before Jackie Robinson broke Major League Baseball's ban on black athletes, skilled baseball players from Cuba and the Dominican Republic could sometimes find jobs with professional clubs, 300 of them (out of 2,600 total players) in the Negro Leagues. If Latin Americans could convince North Americans that they were "Latin," not "black," they could play in the Major Leagues.

Indigenous Movements

Most reformist or revolutionary movements in Latin America since independence have been led by mestizos who looked to indigenous people for support but not for leadership. This

Bolivia

was the case with Mexico's revolution, and the situation was similar in Bolivia in 1952. The emergence today of strong indigenous movements in the Andes must be regarded as epochal because they are putting Indian peoples in the forefront of change.

In 1952, Bolivia's middle and working classes, in particular the country's miners, rose up to install the MNR (National Revolutionary Movement) in power after the party had won the 1951 elections but was prevented from taking power by the army (Cusicanqui 2004; Hylton and Thomson 2003). As the economy deteriorated and mass hunger marches were launched against the capital, the army became demoralized and suffered defections. Miners, mostly mestizos, began to arm themselves in support of the MNR. The party, led by Victor Paz Estenssoro, took power after the miners and dissident army forces fought the military for three days, costing 600 lives. Estenssoro proved less radical than his followers hoped and failed to follow through on abolishing the **latifundia**. He focused instead on schools, but rural education meant preparing the Indians for Western-style modernization, not learning from indigenous ways. The MNR divided into factions, and the military began to recover its power. Beginning in 1964, a series of repressive military governments took power.

By the late 1990s, the situation had begun to change; civil society began to reassert itself against the military and against neoliberal economic policies that did nothing to alleviate conditions in South America's poorest country. This time, however, the upsurge came directly out of indigenous communities. President Gonzalo Sánchez de Lozada ("Goni") was attempting to privatize water services in major cities and to dismantle the state energy company. He planned to grant major leases for oil and gas production on very generous terms to foreign companies, many of which already had obtained lucrative contracts after the energy privatization. On top of that, gas production from new fields was to move through a pipeline to a port in northern Chile, territory that Bolivia had lost in a war in the late 1800s. Goni sent the military out to quell protests, resulting in 67 deaths. In October 2003, 500,000 people, led by indigenous leader Felipe Quispe, marched on La Paz, the capital, under the Aymara flag (the Wiphala) protesting privatization and other economic policies, forcing Goni to flee the country for Miami. In 2008, the Bolivian government asked the United States to extradite Goni, so that he could be tried for his role in the deaths, but Washington did not respond favorably to the request.

Meanwhile, impoverished farmers had turned in large numbers to cultivation of coca, a traditional crop now in great demand (though illegal) on the world market. Goni's government had cooperated with a huge U.S. effort to eradicate the crop, part of a drug war carried out in the Andean region. The repression, ecological destruction (caused by fumigation), and economic hardship had generated a movement among the *cocaleros*, a peasant union, and a party (MAS) led by Evo Morales, who emerged as the most popular politician in the country. These forces came together in the massive march of 2003. It originated in El Alto, a suburb of 900,000, where 82 percent of the population identified themselves as indigenous in the 2001 census. Although this reflected a huge migration from countryside to city, it also reflected changes in the way that people in the lower social classes self-identified—less so as mestizo and more so as indigenous.

The process of organizing indigenous people has itself meant adaptation of traditional ways to the rules of the modern world system. For example, Inca leaders were not known to use flags, so the use of the Wiphala is an adaptation to the rituals and symbols of modern nationalism. Now the Wiphala has been adopted by indigenous movements throughout the region—one flag uniting a very linguistically and culturally diverse people covered by the notion of "indigenous."

In December 2005, not only did Evo Morales become the first indigenous person to win a presidential election in Bolivia, but he also became the first candidate ever to win a majority of votes and avoid having the decision thrown into Congress. Morales pledged to halt the coca eradication program, nationalize the country's copious natural gas reserves, and reject neoliberal economic policies. Morales faced difficult challenges, not the least opposition from the growing Santa Cruz region in the southeast, where the gas fields are located. Like Chávez in Venezuela, he successfully won a referendum to call a constitutional assembly, but his supporters did not gain enough seats in the 2007 election to engineer all the changes sought by the president. On his left, Quispe was demanding that Morales deliver more on promises of land reform, protection for the *cocaleros*, and strict national control over energy. But on the right, there was mounting resistance in Santa Cruz and other states where a majority of people were mestizo. The issue was not just who would control the gas deposits and the land, but whether Bolivia's identity would be redefined in the image of indigenous cultures. To make matters more complicated, the Aymara and Quechua people themselves were not united on what kind of nation-state Bolivia should be. Eventually, Morales won out with his **plurinational** vision articulated in the constitution, but the question of how much control indigenous people will have in regions granted autonomy under the constitution is likely to remain a live issue.

Neighboring Ecuador has also seen political change growing out of indigenous mobilization. In 2000, CONAIE (Confederation of Indigenous Nationalities of Ecuador) carried out a massive mobilization of indigenous peoples to march on the capital, Quito, demanding a "government of national salvation" in the face of an extreme economic crisis. Ecuador's politicians had earned a reputation as the most corrupt elite in the entire hemisphere. This corruption made President Jamil Mahuad's austerity measures—which hit the indigenous populations the hardest—particularly difficult to tolerate. The country's middle class and unions also were fed up with corruption and austerity. Parts of the military officer corps, especially lower-ranking officers whose pay and living conditions were worsening, were growing restless. To the astonishment of the political and social elite, some officers, including Colonel Lucio Gutiérrez, cleared the way for CONAIE protestors to take over Congress, an action that eventually forced the resignation of President Mahuad and establishment of a **junta** that included Gutiérrez and CONAIE.

Subsequently, under pressure from the United States, higher-ranking officers prevailed on the junta

to allow the country's vice president to replace Mahuad, thereby applying a fig leaf of constitutional legitimacy over what in effect was a coup. CONAIE and Gutiérrez felt betrayed. Gutiérrez put together a coalition, including a mostly indigenous political movement called Pachakutik (the Plurinational Unity Movement), and won the presidential election of January 2003. The indigenous movement had representatives in Gutiérrez's cabinet, but when the president accepted a draconian set of economic policies in exchange for IMF loans, the group left his government. In April 2005, Ecuadorian troops violently repressed a huge protest march called against Gutiérrez.

Into the political chaos strode Rafael Correa, an outsider, a *criollo* economist educated in the United States. Correa put together a coalition of indigenous support with the disaffected urban middle class and poor. As Catherine Conaghan put it, "Out on the stump, Correa seemed to channel Ecuador's past and present in his dueling personas. On one hand, he was the fire-breathing, oligarch-denouncing populist of old . . . On the other, he was the unmistakable candidate of modernity: the hip new guy on YouTube and the uber-technocrat with Power Point slides" (2011:262). Correa swept to victory in the presidential election of 2006 and was reelected in a landslide in 2013. His indigenous supporters increasingly distanced themselves, but his success in rewriting the country's constitution and the redistribution of oil-export revenues toward the poor sectors contributed to his consolidation of power. Not unlike the MST, members of Ecuador's indigenous movements apparently found Correa's administration a better alternative than an uncertain future.

What unites indigenous movements in the region is a common history of exploitation and discrimination; in a very broad way, most indigenous movements also posit more environmentally sustainable forms of economic development and challenge capitalist ideas about ownership of land and nature. The Ecuadorian, Mexican (Zapatistas), Guatemalan (Mayan), and Bolivian cases show that demands by the movements are expressed as matters of identity. Movements there, but also in places like Brazil (the MST, for example), mount their own distinctive parties, flags, unions, guerrilla organizations, and so on. However, indigenous movements are not trying to turn back the clock, nor do they seem to want to separate from the rest of civil society. From this point onward, however, they will shape civil society and politics with more power than at any time since the conquest.

For Review

What makes a social movement different from an interest group? As social movements get involved in political struggles, they often must decide whether or not to support particular parties or politicians. What issues does this pose for these movements? What can be said for and against supporting candidates or parties—or even forming a party?

Uncivil and Civil Society

We should not romanticize social movements or think that a majority of the poor have been incorporated into their ranks. Some of them, such as Central America's gangs, Andean para-military forces, drug lords, and some guerrilla movements (e.g., Sendero Luminoso and the FARC), employ violence systematically and criminally and not just as a matter of self-defense or as an occasional abuse. They make up part of Latin America's "uncivil society" and hardly strengthen democracy.

One of the great paradoxes in Latin America is that the cities have grown more violent and uncivil in many ways, but at the same time impressive new movements and associations have sprung up. What is "new" is debatable, but most analysts agree that these movements (which include some that have already been discussed, such as the MST) differ from the past in regard to their determination to avoid co-optation by parties and the state, their resistance to neoliberalism (or at least globalization, neoliberal style), and the greater emphasis they place on "inclusion"—overcoming barriers to participation posed by race, class, and gender. This makes it difficult to decide whether to be pessimistic because of the deterioration of civility and security or to be optimistic because associational life has become more rooted and politically sophisticated.

Because of popular dissatisfaction with economic hardship, corruption, and other issues, the "politics of the street" continues to be a major feature of Latin American civil society. This kind of politics often alarms **pluralists**; they generally believe that democracy functions best when citizens use the vote to hold politicians accountable but do not obstruct governance with too much participation. For pluralists, movements to create or restore democracy are healthy; but movements that pressure governments to intervene in the market or shake the prevailing social order are threats to democracy (Crozier et al. 1975).

In contrast, many social movements believe that the problem with democracy in Latin America is not too much but *too little* participation. Their leaders seem increasingly unwilling to accept the logic that governments have little choice but to live up to the agreements to pay off the debt, limit tax increases on foreign investors, put national resources (e.g., water and mineral resources) in private hands, and so on. An irony of globalization is that in certain ways it has fostered the growth and influence of social movements. The Internet, cheaper and faster transportation, and the growth of international nongovernmental organizations (NGOs) have enabled movements to communicate and meet to support one another and exchange experiences.

Social movements are neither smitten with the virtues of the "free market" nor rushing to embrace state control over the economy. The shortcomings of import substitution and the collapse of the former Soviet Union and its "command economy" have influenced the search for an alternative model of development and democracy. Only in Cuba has centralized economic planning ever been tried in Latin America, and even there the political leadership never fully embraced the Soviet model. Import substitution policies, called "**state capitalism**" by some, not only produced considerable economic growth but also fostered clientelism and corruption, limiting the autonomy of the groups that made up civil society. Unions, business organizations, and public bureaucracies were all colonized by political parties that often delivered benefits to supporters but allowed for little effective initiative and participation by citizens. We saw particularly extreme examples of that tendency in Mexico and Venezuela (see chapter 9). This helps to explain why new social movements became strong not only in countries where they arose to oppose dictatorships but also in other countries where they grew out of dissatisfaction with the rule of traditional political parties.

If liberalization was the dominant *economic* trend in Latin America after 1980, the formation of new grassroots organizations and movements was the most important *social* trend. Some of these social movements arose in struggles to survive economic hardships. Others emerged to defend human rights and to force military regimes back to the barracks—part of the process of democratization that we reviewed in chapter 8. Later, many of these grassroots organizations and movements organized permanently, and today they continue to work on economic justice, cultural identity, and human rights. Older movements have been joined by more recent ones and by a relatively new phenomenon, branches of **nongovernmental organizations**. Some of the latter are branches of relatively politically liberal, privately funded groups, such as wealthy financier George Soros's Open Society Foundation, aimed mostly at supporting democracy and more effective government. Others are think tanks founded by businesses and liberal intellectuals—often with encouragement of international organizations dedicated to the promotion of free-market ideas, and sometimes with financing from the World Bank, the IMF, or governments in the United States or Europe.

Today, then, social movements are not only jealously guarding their autonomy relative to political parties but are also seeking the protection of the state against globalization's most harmful impacts. Civil society in Latin America is developing simultaneously *out of* and *in reaction to* market forces. Civil society is coming into existence as public space between the globalized market and the state.

Discussion Questions

1. Can Latin American countries be considered democracies given the large gaps between rich and poor in the social class system?
2. Labor unions have played a historically important role in struggles for democracy, yet some would say that other types of movements of poor people where they live have become an even more important force in Latin American politics. Why might this be? Do you agree?
3. Land redistribution has been a central demand of peasants for centuries, yet we have few successful cases of success. Why do you think peasants have faced such difficulties achieving reform? Can movements like the MST change the record?
4. How might the emergence of social movements strengthen democracy, and how might they threaten it?
5. To some degree, social movements are wary of both the market and the state. But do they really have an alternative to working with both?

Resources for Further Study

Reading: Finding a comprehensive description of social class structures in Latin America is difficult. I rely mainly on Alejandro Portes and Kelly Hoffman, "Latin American Class Structures: Their Composition and Change during the Neoliberal Era," *Latin*

American Research Review 38, no. 1 (February 2003): 41–77. Rodolfo Stavenhagen is a Mexican sociologist who has extensively studied social classes, urban and rural. His edited *Agrarian Problems and Social Movements in Latin America* (Garden City, NY: Doubleday, 1970) is a good place to start to appreciate the variety of peasant communities and organization. Hernando de Soto's *The Other Path: The Invisible Revolution in the Third World* (New York: Harper and Row, 1989) argues for freeing small-scale capital in cities by reducing the reach of the state. *El Alto, Rebel City: Self and Citizenship in Andean Bolivia* by Sian Lazar (Durham, NC: Duke University Press, 2008) is a good study of how social change, political change, and self-identity are interrelated. Patricia Fernández Kelly and Jon Shefner's *Out of the Shadows: Political Action and the Informal Economy in Latin America* (University Park: Pennsylvania State University Press, 2006) deals with urban protest movements. Editors Arturo Escobar and Sonia E. Alvarez's *The Making of Social Movements in Latin America: Identity Strategy and Democracy* (Boulder: Westview Press, 1992) was among the first publications to recognize the growing importance of movements and still remains relevant.

Video and Film: *Pixote* (1981) is a portrait of a child's life in the *favelas* of Rio. Simon Romero's report on motorcyclists in Caracas *barrios* can be found at the *New York Times* website (www.nytimes.com) and YouTube by searching for "Caracas barrios." *Las Madres de la Plaza de Mayo* (1985) documents the most famous of human rights movements led by women. *Neighboring Sounds* (2012), called the "best Brazilian film since 1976" by John Powers, film critic for National Public Radio, directed and written by Kleber Mendonca Filho, looks at the life of the new middle class in Recife, Brazil.

On the Internet: Hans Rosling's "Gapminder" website (www.gapminder.org) lets you explore inequality across regions and countries. News from the point of view of social movements, in English, can be found at Upside Down World (http://upsidedownworld.org/main). Information on the *maquiladora* movement of Mexican women can be found at www.corpwatch.org/article.php?id=1528. Searching for "MST" on YouTube turns up several documentaries on the Landless Workers' Movement. Particularly good is *MST—Landless Movement in Brazil*, in three parts.

12 Parties, Media, and the Left-Right Dimension in Latin America

Focus Questions

▶ What types of political parties compete in Latin America, and what kinds of ideologies and programs do they present?

▶ Why has the ideological pendulum swung toward the left since 1990 in Latin America, and how has this been expressed in elections?

▶ Why are so many Latin American social movements deeply skeptical about parties? How have think tanks and media somewhat displaced parties from their traditional role in politics?

MAURICE DUVERGER (1972:1–2), one of the most influential thinkers about political parties and party systems, argues that what makes parties different from other organizations is that, in contrast to interest groups, they "draw their support from a broad base," and "they have as their primary goal the conquest of power or a share in its exercise." Most political parties do this primarily through contesting elections, but sometimes they work through other means—for example, propagating a revolution or mobilizing for democratization against a dictatorship. Parties emerging from revolutionary processes (see chapters 9 and 10) are often charged with mobilizing society for carrying out social and economic change. Even in **polyarchies**, parties usually do more than just mobilize voters. They fulfill important functions critical to governance, including organizing the legislative process, recruiting people to serve in government, and informing the public.

Thinking of the kinds of parties that are more focused on programs and ideology, the Italian political theorist Antonio Gramsci (1971:16) once described a political party as an organization in **civil society** that people join for the purpose of promoting an agenda "with a national or international character." A businessperson might join a chamber of commerce to promote a particular industry; a worker might join a union to negotiate better wages. But by supporting or joining a political party, the same individuals join an organization with broader objectives, some of which might require sacrifices on their part. However, the motives for joining a party may be less noble. Where **clientelism** is deep-rooted, having a party membership card might be a prerequisite for getting or keeping a job, obtaining an export license from a government bureaucrat, or getting pension payments started. When parties mainly attract members in this way, they often lose touch with the ideology or programs that motivated their founding.

Some Latin American parties have been top-down creations of **charismatic** leaders; others were created from the bottom up by social movements—though often it is difficult to tell which emerged first. Often, a party that starts as an ideological movement or outgrowth of a social movement evolves toward "catch-all" status; rarely does the opposite happen. By **catch-all**, we mean those that try to win elections by attracting votes across different social classes and other kinds of groups. In this chapter, we will examine some of the major types of parties that influence Latin American politics. We will describe them in part by their ideologies, but we will also pay particular attention to the way they relate to the **social movements**, classes, and groups described in the preceding chapter. How we classify parties as left, right, or center is an indication of their relationship to civil society and goals. Though we risk oversimplifying their ideologies and programs in doing so, there is some value in using this spectrum to trace recent developments in Latin America, including the emergence of a "new left" somewhat connected to the social movements we examined in chapter 11. However, Latin America also can be said to have a "new right" that exerts its interests not only in parties but also in think tanks and media.

Thus, parties not only connect (or fail to connect) civil society to government but also give clues as to how left, center, and right have evolved in recent decades. Their relationship to civil society, however, has been changing in ways that are not limited to Latin America. Social movements have grown so distrustful of parties that one of Latin America's most globally influential movements, Mexico's Zapatistas, has even questioned the usefulness of doing what Duverger holds is central to parties—seeking control over the state. If this is not enough, parties are finding competition for their roles from the media and from think tanks. Parties remain at the heart of **polyarchy**, but they have lost the near monopoly they previously had on organizing the linkages between civil society and government. Lain America is not unique in this respect.

Party Systems

A "**party system**" refers to the way that parties interact with one another and with **civil society**, especially in regard to the way they structure political competition. One-party systems are incompatible with the idea of polyarchy, but these systems vary from one another regarding the degrees of internal participation and possibilities for opposition; that is, there is a degree of **pluralism** even in single-party systems. Competition within a single party may permit some opposition and debate even in the absence of competitive elections. Although not all observers of Mexico would agree, it can be argued that at least until the 1960s, the PRI was not just a **corporatist** machine but did have to respond to popular expectation born out of the country's 1910 revolution. On the opposite end of the scale are multiparty systems. Some such systems are very fluid and unstable, as has been common in Ecuador, for example. Some are highly stable, as in the case of Chile, where parties on each side of the left and right of the spectrum tend to come together in coalitions that make the system function much like the third general kind of party system, the two-party system. A two-party system allows competition but frequently generates the complaint that the parties converge toward the center (as catch-all parties tend to do) and offer voters very limited choices—a criticism often heard in the United States but also echoed in many Latin American countries. In chapter 9, the argument presented was that in many ways Venezuela's two-party system dominated civil society through clientelism and corruption, and toward the end of the Punto Fijo era (1958–1998) through manipulation of elections.

Think of different party systems, then, as alternative ways of bridging civil society and government. The existence of a large number of parties tends to provide citizens with more choice, but sometimes this is at the cost of political stability. It is less likely that someone will have a majority in the legislature, so forging coalitions becomes important. That process in turn depends on the willingness of party leaders to compromise and the degree of social and economic polarization in society. You might think about the way that democracy broke down in Chile (see chapter 7) in this respect. Two-party systems can be more easily managed, but they too are vulnerable to decay (Consider the Venezuelan case in the 1990s). Keep in mind that the traffic on the bridge linking government and society is a two-way street. This is especially important in the aftermath of revolution, when the triumphant party of the rebellion, now in control of government, attempts to mobilize the population and use the resources of the state to transform society.

Parties and party systems are shaped by constitutions and institutions. We look more closely at this theme in the next chapter, but we need to pay some attention to the system of representation to understand why party systems vary. Countries that use **proportional representation** are more likely to have fewer parties—or at least to have less competition in national elections than those that use **uninomial representation**, also known as a single-member district system—that is, one representative chosen from each territorial district. Most countries use a combination of the two systems today, a practice originally implemented in Germany that has spread throughout much of the world.

How presidents are elected matters in a region where strong executive power (and **caudilloism**) is the norm. Most countries use a runoff system (e.g., Brazil, Chile, Argentina, and Mexico), but some (e.g., Venezuela) simply award the presidency to whoever gets the most votes (a plurality) in one election. The systems are further complicated by different ways of selecting local authorities. A small change can make a big difference. When in 1989 Venezuela replaced a system whereby governors were appointed by the president with one whereby they were elected, suddenly ambitious politicians were freed to some degree from having to follow their national leaders slavishly. However, decentralized systems are not necessarily good for **governance**. Brazil is a case where there is so little party discipline that coalitions must be organized bill by bill—and sometimes by unsavory and illegal incentives, such as bribery.

Another example of the importance of institutional factors is Chile, where the five largest parties (two on the moderate left, one in the center, and two on the right) have coalesced into two blocks—center-left and center-right—in part because the system for choosing a president and especially the Senate makes it difficult for small parties to have influence. In assuming the presidency for a second time in 2014, President Michelle Bachelet promised to move decisively to change this system, but whether she would have enough votes from conservative parties to achieve this goal was in question.

For Review

How does a party system differ from a party? What are some functions that parties serve in a political system? More specifically, why have parties been so central to the functioning of polyarchy as a system? How can a change in the system of representation affect a party system? What are the positives, and what are the negatives to strong party discipline?

Types of Parties in Latin America

In Latin America today, we can categorize most parties as one of three types: (1) traditional parties, sometimes called the "dinosaurs," that were born out of competition among the **criollo** elite in the 1800s or in the populist era and that have survived into the present century; (2) personalist parties, often formed originally as electoral movements supporting charismatic personalities; and (3) parties seeking to represent the "new social movements." The boundaries between each type and others are not brightly drawn; some parties that were founded by *caudillos*, such as the Peronist Party in Argentina, are very dinosaur-like today. Some parties born out of ideological or social movements were brought into existence by strong leaders, such as Haya de la Torre in Peru or Rómulo Betancourt of Venezuela.

In this book, we have usually used the translated English names of parties; in this chapter, we will use the Spanish or Portuguese names and translate only when the English equivalent is not obvious from the cognates (words very similar in two different languages). One reason for this is that Latin Americans usually refer to parties by the initials in their native language.

Dinosaurs: Traditional and Populist Parties

The epithet "dinosaur" has been used in Mexico to refer to Partido Revolucionario Institucional (PRI), especially to the older generation of politicians who dominated the organization during its long reign as Mexico's only viable national party. These politicians were challenged internally by **technocrats** (chapter 9) whose base was in the bureaucracy and not electoral politics. Externally, they were challenged by the rise of the leftist Partido de la Revolución Democrática (PRD), created by a coalition of smaller leftist parties with *pristas* (members of the PRI, most prominently, Cuauhtémoc Cárdenas, whom we met in the earlier chapters) unhappy with their leaders' direction, and by the surge of an older party, the conservative Partido Acción Nacional (PAN), which won the 2000 presidential election. The "dinosaur" proved not to be extinct, however, since its candidate, Enrique Peña Nieto, won (at least officially) the 2012 election.

In many ways, the determination and ability of Mexico's dinosaurs to remain relevant in national politics typifies the challenge faced by other Latin American parties that first emerged either as factions of the oligarchy in the nineteenth century or during the populist era. Latin America's first important parties emerged in the 1800s when intellectuals and other elites organized themselves into political clubs to compete for control of national legislatures and regional governments. Two main currents formed: Liberals and Conservatives, with Liberals tending to favor more openness to the world market, greater separation of church and state, federalism, and overall modernization (see chapter 4). Conservatives defended the privileges of the Catholic Church and the traditional *criollo* elite. In fact, neither Liberals nor Conservatives struck very deep roots in mass society, except when caudillos mobilized peasant armies to fight under one banner or against one another in civil wars. Most of these parties eventually disappeared, but if they recognized early enough that they needed to appeal to new groups and classes, they survived

The growth of the middle and working classes in the late 1800s challenged these first parties and laid the basis for new ones, such as the Radicals, who were especially significant in the Southern Cone. This kind of centrist party survives as the Blancos in Uruguay and the Colorados in Paraguay. Today they tend to draw votes from the middle class, having lost their working-class appeal to socialist-oriented and other leftist parties. This period also saw the emergence of socialist parties, which come in several varieties. The biggest and often bitter divide is between socialists who admired the Russian Revolution of 1917 and formed what we know today as communist parties and those socialists who followed the more moderate and reform-minded path of "social democracy". These social democratic parties (which sometimes use that name, sometimes not) no longer seek to overthrow capitalism but to make it more humane. Unionized workers have been their most secure base of support, but over time most have become catch-all parties that attract middle-class, not just working-class, support. Venezuela's Acción Democrática (AD), Costa Rica's Partido Social Democratico (PSD), and the Partido Socialista (PS) of Chile are good examples of these kinds of political parties. Communist parties still claim to seek the replacement of capitalism by communism, but by now you should realize that most of the parties that hark back to the 1917 revolution have often made compromises. Nonetheless, there exists a legacy of bitterness between the two major factions of socialism, born out of not only ideology but also their intense competition for the votes of the working class or control over unions.

There also remains a variety of other radical leftist parties with some impact on politics in Latin America. These include Maoists, anarchists, and a radical branch of socialists founded by Leon Trotsky—who was murdered by Joseph Stalin's agents in Mexico in 1940 after leaving Russia in 1928. These parties run candidates, but winning elections is not their main goal. Trotskyites in particular exert influence through leadership in strikes, factory and farm takeovers, and protests, pressuring leftist governments inclined toward moderation.

Another type of centrist party, **Christian Democracy**, arose in many Latin American countries from changes in the role of the Catholic Church. Under challenge from Marxist parties in Europe, Pope Leo XIII in 1891 issued an encyclical, *Rerum Novarum*, that addressed the need for social justice by asserting, in corporatist fashion, that both labor and capital had rights that must be respected. The pope rejected socialism and defended private property but also said, "Whenever the general interest or any particular class suffers, or is threatened with harm, which can in no other way be met or prevented, the public authority must step in to deal with it" (see Pecci 1891). In corporatist fashion, Leo argued that the state had a legitimate interest to moderate the competition of the marketplace and ensure adequate remuneration, leisure, and safe job conditions for workers. Founded to compete with socialist parties, the programs of Christian Democratic parties in many ways resemble those of the moderate social democrats. Nowhere has this been more evident than in Chile, where two moderate socialist parties joined with the Christian Democrats to create an alliance called Concertación to contest elections after the transition from military rule and the plebiscite of 1989. Both social democrats and Christian Democrats look to European counterparts, especially in Germany, for material support (foundations, think tanks, publishing houses) to aid their political activities at home.

Christian Democratic parties are appearing more dinosaur-like today. Venezuela's COPEI (Comité de Organización Política Electoral Independiente) nearly disappeared in the Chávez landslide of 1998. However, Christian Democracy remains influential in Chile, where the Partido Democrático Cristiano is the single largest party in the country, and somewhat in Central America. In some ways, the region's communist parties have followed a similar trajectory to that of the Christian Democrats. By the 1940s, most had abandoned ambitions to lead a Russian-style revolution, though their enemies (including in the United States) always painted them as subversive (see chapter 10). During World War II (1939–1945), when the

Soviet Union was allied with the United States, Communist parties often used their influence over workers to limit strikes and political agitation. After the Cuban Revolution of 1959, revolutionary and leftist youth challenged these more pragmatic politicians, and other leftist parties have eclipsed them in places such as Venezuela and Chile. Chile is again an exception; the Partido Comunista de Chile, after having been excluded from the Concertación for 25 years, in 2013 joined the coalition, called Nueva Mayoría (New Majority), that elected Bachelet to her second term in 2014. One of the reasons is that the Party actively participated in the surge of protests against inequality led by university students.

Both the communist and the socialist parties have faced competition from smaller leftist parties, though more so in regard to influence in civil society than in elections. For example, in Argentina, the Communist Party's (PC) Institute for the Mobilization of Cooperative Funds has provided funding for community economic projects set up by the independent Movimiento Territorial de Liberación (MTL). The MTL preferred to work with the PC rather than risk co-optation by the Peronists, who have a well-earned reputation for clientelism. Asked by a researcher whether MTL members would vote PC in a coming election, a leader of the party responded, "Of course not; they vote Peronist" (Alcoñiz and Scheier 2007: 169).

Personalist Parties

Political parties are collective actors, but we have seen that personalism is a deeply entrenched tendency in Latin America. Caudillos sometimes seek to rule "above politics," but most find it necessary or useful to create some form of political organization to support their aspirations. If they hope to legitimate their rule through elections, they must have some organizational vehicle for rounding up votes—even if the main strategy is to mobilize voters through distributing patronage.

Many of the parties that emerged in the populist era typically had strong leaders but relied less on **charisma**. Examples include several parties that emerged in the populist era in the Andean region, including Alianza Popular Revolucionaria Americana (APRA) in Peru, led by the dynamic Haya de la Torre; Acción Democrática in Venezuela, led by Rómulo Betancourt; and the Movimiento Nacional Revolucionario (MNR) in Bolivia, led by Victor Paz Estenssoro. University students and intellectuals were in the vanguard of these parties, which throughout the middle decades of the twentieth century maintained close ties. Like Juan Perón in Argentina and Getúlio Vargas in Brazil, these parties and their leaders sought to unite the middle class, the working class, and some capitalists in a coalition behind **import substitution** (see chapter 5). They often issued fiery denunciations of imperialism, but the rhetoric often hid a less revolutionary agenda. In the past few decades, several of these parties edged themselves into extinction by promoting unpopular neoliberal policies of the post-1980 period and failing to adapt their political practices to the demands made by new social movements.

In Brazil, parties formed late relative to some other countries (Mainwaring 1995). Vargas founded the Partido Trabalhista Brasileiro (PTB, Brazilian Workers' Party) in 1945 to mobilize and control workers; he simultaneously created a similar organization for the middle class, named (despite its class orientation) the Partido Social Democrática, or PSD. Vargas created these parties to provide electoral support as he transformed his regime, founded via a *golpe* in 1930, into an electoral democracy after World War II. Perón founded the Partido

Justicialista (Justice Party), which, like its Brazilian counterparts, sought to mobilize supporters behind his political ambitions. In some ways, the Partido Socialista Unido de Venezuela (PSUV), founded by Hugo Chávez, is the latest manifestation of this phenomenon, though Chávez unambiguously identified with revolutionary socialism. The PTB and PSD virtually disappeared beneath the steamroller of dictatorship in 1964, but parties with similar names reemerged in the country's gradual transition to democracy.

Argentine Peronist president Carlos Saúl Menem (1989–1999) angered much of the party's base in the organized working class, but as long as the economy seemed to be recovering, the party easily defeated its rivals. In these years, the Peronists made incursions into the middle class, impressed with government's success in taming inflation. The economic crisis that struck Argentina in 1998 put an end to Menem's political career; a new generation of left-populist leaders rose to fill the void. Peronism has become a kind of catch-all party within which various factions compete. Argentina uses a runoff system to choose a president, and the first round has become virtually a primary to decide which Peronist candidate will go on, almost certain to win the second round. In 2003, a center-leftist governor, Nestor Kirchner, won, and his wife Cristina, herself a prominent politician, kept the presidency in the family in 2007. (Nestor died in 2010.) As discussed later in the chapter, Cristina Kirchner's administration has seen the erosion of middle-class support.

Parties Appealing to Social Movements

As we saw in chapter 11, Latin America's social movements envision a more participatory civil society that goes beyond the role for citizens envisioned in a typical polyarchy. They also tend to reject the **laissez-faire** philosophy of neoliberalism and demand a more activist economic role for the state. However, in seeking more transparent government and resisting co-optation, Latin America's new social movements have some common ground with business-oriented neoliberals suspicious of **clientelism** and corruption. In fact, many newer parties initially presented themselves as "electoral movements" rather than parties with a well-developed platform and disciplined internal structure, a reflection of general frustration and discontent with party politics in the electorate. This terminology has not allayed the suspicions of social movements that the "electoral movements" fail to eschew the clientelist and corrupt practices of the old system.

A number of important new left parties in Latin America either have arisen as political expressions of these movements or at least present themselves as their allies. Among these parties are Causa R (Radical Cause) in Venezuela, the Partido dos Trabalhadores (Workers' Party—PT) in Brazil, the Movimiento al Socialismo (MAS) in Bolivia, and the Partido de la Revolución Democrática (PRD) in Mexico. In some cases, these parties are little more than very loose coalitions—for example, the Frente Amplio in (Broad Front) Uruguay; Pachakutik (Plurinational Unity Movement) in Ecuador; and Frente Grande in Argentina. A third variation on this theme is parties that were created by political leaders, often outsiders, who take advantage of the discontent of social movements with existing parties to found parties that are often highly personalist. Examples include parties founded to support the candidacies of Ollanta Humana in Peru, Rafael Correa in Ecuador, and Hugo Chávez in Venezuela. Each of these latter three parties might easily be discussed in the section immediately preceding this one; but we discuss them here because they have all attempted to appeal to social movements. They originated as electoral movements that attracted support as "antiparty" forces, but they certainly quickly developed into more formally organized parties themselves.

In the following pages, we describe the experience of some leftist parties that have to some degree attracted support from social movements but nonetheless have an uneasy relationship with them.

Mexico's PRD

The interaction between the PRD of Mexico and social movements is typical of the uneasy relationship between leftist reform parties and social movements. The PRD originated in a coalition of small leftist parties and dissenters from the Mexican PRI—organizations that backed the candidacy of Cuauhtémoc Cárdenas (see chapter 9). From the start, then, the PRD has had to grapple with differences of style and substance among politicians who were, respectively, former members of the PRI, leaders of small Marxist parties with regional strength, and leaders of social movements. The PRD has had a rocky relationship since 1994 with the Zapatistas, sharing some of their political aims but unwilling to endorse armed struggle. The Zapatistas, for their part, are suspicious of the motives and constancy of PRD politicians, so much so that they withheld endorsement from Andrés Manuel López Obrador (AMLO), the party's candidate for president in 2006. With their philosophy of making revolution "without taking power," the Zapatistas espoused a strategy of challenging the entire modern concept of the state (discussed later).

By official counts, AMLO narrowly lost the 2006 election and by a wider margin the 2012 elections, and in both cases he charged fraud. Nonetheless, the PRD has established itself as one of the three major parties in the Mexican Congress. Since 1997, the party has controlled the mayoralty of Mexico City, the largest metropolitan urban conglomerate in the world. The party draws support from Mexicans in economic sectors (especially farming) that have been harmed or threatened by NAFTA. Of course, it was not the center-left PRD but the center-right PAN that ended the PRI's 72-year control of the presidency in 2000 with the victory of Vicente Fox. In that same election, the PAN and PRD took enough seats together to deny the PRI control of Congress. In 2012, the PRI's candidate won the presidency. None of the three major parties seems likely to dominate politics in the new century the way the PRI did for most of the twentieth century.

Like many other **Pink Tide** parties, the PRD increasingly finds itself drawn into the "old game" of politics—not entirely surprising given that one wing of the party is made up of refugees from the PRI. Caudillo politics reared its head in the PRD as Obrador battled other aspirants for leadership within the party. In the 2012 election, though the Zapatistas were harshly critical of him, AMLO attracted support from social movements, despite disenchantment with the party's overall direction. Massive marches against electoral fraud took place after the election, but it is fair to say that Mexicans were more motivated by their alarm about the fraud itself than by their enthusiasm for AMLO. The PRD attracted only approximately 18 percent of the vote in Mexico's election for the National Assembly, but AMLO by the official count received 31.6 percent of the vote, and adding votes for leftist parties that tend to align with the PRD, the left in Mexico attracted one-third of the electorate.

For Review

What are the three major political parties that contest presidential elections in Mexico? In what respect has the PRD been successful, and to what extent has it fallen short of expectations? What is the Zapatista view of the PRD? How has the PRI done since losing the presidency in 2000?

Leftist Parties in Central America

Although they were originally founded as coalitions among guerrilla movements, El Salvador's FMLN (Frente Farabundo Martí de Liberación Nacional) and Nicaragua's FSLN (Frente Sandinista de Liberación Nacional; see chapter 10) also can be considered parties that grew out of social movements. Both emerged out of the negotiated process that brought armed hostilities to an end. Upon taking power or reorganizing themselves to contest for power through elections, insurgencies face the challenge not only of maintaining their revolutionary credentials, also but of casting off the habits inherited from clandestine and dangerous armed struggle.

The Nicaraguan revolution gave promise of bold innovations in democracy in its early years, between 1979 and 1984 (Prevost and Vanden 1997: 46–52). In those years, the Sandinistas experimented with a system where mass organizations (peasant groups, members of unions, women's organizations, and others) would directly elect representatives to a Council of State. It mobilized Nicaragua's population in literacy and health campaigns and a variety of other efforts, including land reform, in attempt to raise living conditions; this system probably served the interests of democracy. In 1984, partly to gain international legitimacy, the FSLN implemented a new constitution establishing a pluralist political system—that is, a polyarchy. As we saw in chapter 10, unlike the case of the revolutionary parties that grew out of the Cuban and Mexican revolutions, the FSLN lost control of government only 11 years after taking power.

The FSLN won the 1984 vote but lost six years later to Violeta Chamorro, widow of a crusading newspaper editor who had been assassinated by the Somoza government. What caused the FSLN decline?

- The Sandinistas were for the most part very young leaders in a country lacking any historical experience with democracy. Many Sandinista leaders regarded themselves as a kind of "vanguard" that had earned the right to run the country because of the great sacrifices made in the overthrow of Somoza. There was some communist influence in the FSLN, but more significant was internal discipline and secrecy in the struggle to defeat the Somoza dictatorship, never entirely expunged after victory.
- The United States reinforced the hierarchical tendencies of the FSLN by organizing and financing a brutal counterrevolutionary army, the *contras*. The civil war caused 30,000 deaths and more than US$12 billion in economic losses between 1982 and 1990. This devastating civil war ruined much of the progress made in the revolution's

early years and made it difficult for the government to maintain an environment of tolerance. Some FSLN actions, such as the forcible relocation of Miskito Indians in the northeast part of the country, tarnished their human rights record.

- The Sandinistas were the pioneers, attempting to combine Cuba's successful efforts at lifting social conditions and political mobilization with liberal democratic norms, including checks and balances, defense of civil liberties, and so on. In the context of war, they had little chance of succeeding.

Undoubtedly, the war and economic pressure, as well as heavy U.S. subsidies to the opposition parties, contributed to the Sandinista defeat, but the campaign itself indicated that between 1979 and 1990, the FSLN had changed, and not for the better. President Daniel Ortega, running for reelection, conducted a campaign in 1990 that relied on image advertising, sexy female campaign workers at rallies (a sharp contrast to the early Sandinista efforts to raise the dignity and living conditions of women), and patronage (Harris 1993). Upon exiting power, party leaders allocated much property confiscated from the Somoza family to themselves (the *piñata*). This included Ortega.

Ortega returned to the presidency after winning the 2006 election. He was welcomed to the **Pink Tide** by Venezuelan president Chávez. However, as discussed in chapter 9, over the years since losing the 1990 election, Ortega has proven himself an adept deal maker with various opposition forces, including sectors linked to Somoza's old party, the Liberals. For example, just before the 2006 election, Ortega's faction of the Sandinistas endorsed a law outlawing abortion, angering the FSLN's women's movement. He was reelected in 2011, partly because of the fracturing of the Liberals and the inability of dissident Sandinistas to organize an effective challenge.

The FSLN may have been a party of social movements during the years of revolution, but it finds itself at odds with these movements in Ortega's second presidency. But in most elections these movements are faced with a dilemma: sit out the election and risk a return of a government even more hostile to their goals or vote for the left and hope for better options in the future. In this respect, El Salvador's FMLN has done somewhat better, though it too has its detractors among social movements.

The FMLN and its noncombatant allies became a political party in 1992 under terms of a treaty that ended the 12-year civil war in the country. The party began to grow in influence, becoming the largest party in the national legislature in 2003. In 2009, its candidate, Mauricio Funes (an independent journalist), won the presidency. And it won the 2014 presidential election with its own candidate, Salvador Sánchez Cerén. The party has remained more consistently anti-neoliberal in ideology than the Nicaraguan FSLN. No one current politician or personality dominates the FMLN. Although it has suffered divisions, the FMLN tolerates considerable disagreement and debate within its ranks. This endangers its unity but also prevents it from being dominated by the force of a single personality, as is the FSLN in Nicaragua by Ortega.

An FMLN leader named Rubén Zamora (1997: 176) explained how the party adapted: "A history of exile and clandestine operations had transformed the party into a sect. To correct this, we made a conscious decision to de-professionalize the party." That shift clearly has helped the FMLN avoid being transformed into a personalist vehicle for particular politicians. But the party, though it holds the presidency, does not have a majority in the country's National Assembly. This means it will have to compromise, which many social movements see as unseemly deal-making. The key to the FMLN surmounting this challenge may be its ability to fight corruption and continue to broaden its support among common Salvadorans who fear a lapse again into civil war and conflict with the United States.

For Review

In El Salvador and Nicaragua, how have revolutionary movements of the 1980s evolved? How do the left parties resemble one another? How do they differ from one another?

Brazilian Workers' Party (PT)

As parties rooted in social movements move from the politics of opposition to the politics of government, they usually find themselves facing new and different challenges as a result of success. A good example here is the Partido dos Trabalhadores (PT), Brazil's broadest, national mass-based party. The PT began as a labor union–based party, but rapidly it incorporated Afro-Brazilians, indigenous peoples, women, and other identity-based movements. The PT pioneered the use of "participatory budgeting," by which citizens were able to directly influence spending priorities in municipalities through a series of local meetings.

The PT's leader, José Ignacio Lula da Silva, more widely known as "Lula," lost runs for the presidency in 1989, 1994, and 1998 before winning in 2002 and 2006. Once Lula finally achieved the presidency in November 2002, his supporters expected him to fulfill his promise to abandon neoliberalism and find an alternative economic development strategy. He had promised to make rapid progress toward ending hunger, to reverse the degradation of the Amazonian rainforest, to resettle landless peasants, and to reduce poverty—a daunting agenda.

Although Lula did reach important goals toward eliminating hunger, he fell far short of the expectations of some of the largest social movements. Those expecting a shift from neoliberalism were dismayed that he maintained the conservative fiscal and monetary policies of his predecessor. The Movimento dos Trabalhadores Rurais Sem Terra (Landless Workers' Movement—MST; see chapter 11) was bitterly disappointed that he did not deliver nearly the amount of land reform promised in his campaign. In part, Lula's shift reflected the fear of disturbing the growing agribusiness sector, responsible for generating much of the high economic growth rates of the 2000s, the new Brazilian "miracle." Lula was also cautious about any policy that might reintroduce high rates of inflation. Furthermore, the PT, having gained national power, did not bring along with it the innovative participatory experiments it had undertaken in several cities; worse yet, some of its leading politicians proved equally as susceptible to the old-fashioned patronage and corrupt practices associated with the past.

Lula won reelection in a runoff in 2006, but his path was made more difficult by the eruption in 2005 of a scandal known as *mensalão*. *Mensalão* refers to the thousands of dollars distributed to PT legislators and members of opposition parties in return for their support for government programs. The practice is an old and common form of corruption in Brazil.

It can be traced to the weakness of national parties and the realities of local politics in a federal system in which states have considerable autonomy, and their governors have considerable power (discussed in detail in the next chapter, on institutions). Most legislators, both at the national level and at the state level, have short careers. While in elected office, they are expected to deliver goods and services to constituents in return for a comfortable retirement once their terms are finished. Because party leaders have little leverage to discipline their legislators, they often resort to regular payments, bribes, paid on a monthly basis—the *mensalão*.

One of Lula's closest political advisors, José Dirceu, once famed for his radical opposition to the military regime, emerged as the mastermind of the *mensalão*. Dirceu was an advocate of Lula's reconciliation with the policies associated with Cardoso, including accommodation of the **IMF**, the target of harsh criticism by Lula when he was in opposition. The political party that had promised an alternative to neoliberalism and seemed a paragon of honesty appeared to have sunk into a dunghill of corruption and patronage. Lula and the PT survived, but some of the party's left wing split away. And Brazil's many influential social movements had reason to question whether the political party that had once promised a cleaner, more responsive democracy had become just like the dinosaurs of the populist era.

For Review

Describe how the PT in Brazil was different, at least in its early years, from the populist parties (dinosaurs) that had preceded it. How did it fail to live up to expectations of social movements? What is *mensalão*?

Why Do Movement Parties Often Disappoint Movements?

The scandals that tarnished the PT raise the question of whether reform-minded parties and politicians have the capacity to surmount the powerful forces that draw them into "politics as usual." Even Venezuela's Hugo Chávez, whose administration drew fierce opposition from the middle class and business community, came under criticism by his own grassroots supporters for continuing the flow of patronage from his government to business and commercial elites with personal ties to his regime. His critics, inside and outside his Bolivarian movement, called the beneficiaries derogatorily the "Bolibourgeoisie."

The parties that draw support from social movements often have difficulty in constructing internal governance structures that simultaneously achieve two objectives: (1) encouraging democratic control from below and (2) providing enough internal organization and discipline to permit the party to act with unity and purpose in national politics. In the media age, electoral campaigns can be an expensive proposition, and there is a temptation to stress image over substance. Even the best-organized grassroots campaign may fail in the face of a well-coordinated and well-financed media-based campaign by more conservative parties. After three defeats, Lula turned to public-relations tactics, and his party leaders turned to established traditions of political bribery to achieve their objectives. In

Nicaragua, the Sandinistas similarly turned away from movement politics and toward public-relationships politics in the 1990 elections. Even had their candidate, Daniel Ortega, won those elections, it is quite possible that the revolutionary impulse of the FSLN had already run its course. The party conducted itself in opposition not much differently than its main opponents, the Liberals. The victory by Ortega in Nicaragua's 2006 elections did not, for this reason, mean a return to the revolutionary politics of the early 1980s.

Recently, some parties in Latin America have experimented with primaries, a type of election familiar to many U.S. citizens. The idea of this reform is to substitute voting for highly centralized, indirect methods of candidate selection. However, primaries pose a different set of problems for democracy because they place a greater premium on advertising and other tactics that cost money. This problem is exemplified by the case of Brazil's PT, which was the first political party in that country to choose its candidates through a primary. The cost of campaigning for the nomination added significantly to the need for money to contest for office and helped to create the environment that engrossed party leaders in the *mensalão*.

In Venezuela, Hugo Chávez tried to prohibit expenditures on advertising in the PSUV's primary to choose candidates for the National Assembly election in 2010. The idea was to ensure that candidates had real grassroots support. The professional politicians and wealthier supporters of Chávez dutifully avoided broadcast advertising, but they used donations and patronage to print posters and flyers (and to hire people to hand them out), effectively campaigning under the radar and violating the spirit of the party rules—and with success. The PSUV's main opposition, the Democratic United Roundtable, held primary elections for its presidential candidate for the 2012 election, and the strategy helped it maintain unity and gave a significant boost to its candidate, Enrique Capriles, who ran a credible campaign in losing to Chávez and who nearly defeated the late Venezuelan leader's designated successor, Nicolás Maduro, in April 2013.

Social movements in Latin America are mindful of the powerful influence of the media in their societies. Grassroots community radio and television stations have sprung up. Computer technology does make community production more economically feasible than ever. The Internet allows community activists to communicate with one another and share experiences. This development seems promising, but it will be difficult for these groups to wean populations away from Hollywood movies, soap operas, beauty pageants, low-brow comedy and variety shows, pro-business newscasts, Miami-produced recordings, and so on.

Right and Left Today in Latin America

It should already be clear from our review of parties that what is "right" and "left" in Latin America is very relative. Parties such as AD in Venezuela and the PRI in Mexico were for decades in the last century generally seen as leftist. Today, most new social movements and the political parties that draw strength from them (whether or not these movements consciously lend support) now regard these parties as part of the "right."

The concept of "left-right" comes from the way that representatives to the French National Assembly have been seated since the French Revolution, with those wanting rapid and deep change seated on the left, facing toward the front of the chamber, and those defending tradition and monarchy seated on the right. In this section of the chapter, we will attempt to categorize the major political forces today, recognizing that this exercise is highly subjective.

The Right: Old and New

For many years, students of Latin America tended to ignore conservative parties. Until very recently, these parties were associated mainly with the landed oligarchy. Many industries, economic empires, and businesses were nurtured by the state in the import substitution era, so few entrepreneurs were apostles of **laissez-faire** policies. Business interests were often incorporated under the wing of populist parties, the dinosaurs. Few conservative parties promoting free-market capitalism could be found.

An exception is Mexico's PAN, which was founded in 1939 as a vehicle to serve the interests of powerful industrialists (concentrated in the city of Monterrey) and small land-holders who felt threatened by land reform. The PAN also attracted support from religious voters resentful about the Mexican Revolution's strident policies to strip the Catholic Church of its privileges, which sometimes spilled over into attacks on religion itself. Over time, professionals from the middle class began to enter the party, seeing it as a vehicle for protesting the corruption and fraud practiced by the PRI. In 2000, some members of the PRD also supported the PAN candidate, Vicente Fox, for president as the candidate best positioned to break the PRI's monopoly of power.

Just like the "movement" parties we have examined, the PAN found it easier to be a party of opposition than the party of government. By the end of his term, Fox was very unpopular, and the party's nominee in the 2006 election, Felipe Calderón, trailed badly in the polls for most of the year. Calderón won the official count in the July election but only after a bitter campaign and a contested count on election night, which left his presidency wounded from the start of his term (which concluded in 2012).

Chile is one of the few other Latin American countries—and certainly the most important—where one finds business-oriented parties with a relatively stable mass base. Two conservative parties vie with each other to promote somewhat different visions of capitalism. One, the National Renovation (RN), is a descendant of the rightist (Liberal and Conservative) parties, which in the pre-Pinochet years (1973–1989) merged in an attempt to stop Allende in 1970 (see chapter 7). The RN has a base in domestic mining interests, the older business elites, and social conservatives. The newer Independent Democrat Union (UDI) was founded by young, ardent admirers of General Pinochet, whose regime swung Chile's economy radically in the direction of a more laissez-faire capitalism. The UDI tends to attract support from neoliberal intellectuals and business interests that sprung up in the free-market environment.

Both of these parties compete for business support and for the votes of social conservatives, but like the left, they tend to unite around a common candidate in elections. In effect, Chile's electoral politics have become more and more centrist with two broad alliances, one on the right, the other (the Concertación, consisting of the socialists and Christian Democrats) on the left, competing with one another. However, there is constant tension within each coalition as the major partners vie with one another over nominations. Unity on each side seems constantly in jeopardy, but the goal of winning elections usually prevails over internal divisions. This tendency was interrupted in 2005 when Joaquin Lavin of UDI, who seemed to have won the rightist coalition nomination, was challenged in the general election by the RN's Sebastian Piñera, who finished second and won the right to contest the second round against the Concertación candidate, Bachelet. Bachelet won the runoff in January 2006. Piñera came back as the candidate of the united coalition to win the January 2010 elections—an event that certainly lowered the waterline of the Pink Tide—although Bachelet would return to win a new term in 2014.

Most of Central America's right-wing parties were little more than factions of the oligarchy until the 1980s. In Guatemala, Panama, and El Salvador, the stronger parties had close ties to retired and active military officers. But the civil and revolutionary wars forced right-wing sectors to organize themselves to contest elections more effectively. As reviewed in chapter 10, El Salvador's ARENA party remains staunchly right-wing, though it has largely cast off the negative international reputation lent it by its founder, Roberto D'Aubuisson, the prime mover of the country's notorious death squads in the 1980s. In Nicaragua, after the defeat of the Sandinistas in 1990, the right wing fragmented, but it usually comes together long enough to contest the FSLN in elections. The Partido Independiente Liberal (Independent Liberal Party—PLI) has been most successful in this respect. Ortega's victories in 2006 and 2011 and the Funes victory in El Salvador in 2009 posed major tests for the new "democratic" right in Central America. As of 2013, the right still seemed committed to contesting for power through electoral means.

In the cases where the right was deeply implicated in harsh dictatorships and widespread human rights abuses (e.g., Chile, El Salvador), we have to consider the impact that this traumatic violence may have on voters and on the behavior of the center and left. Although we are 25 years removed from the worst of the violence, these civil societies were deeply scarred. Voters can be forgiven if they think not only about which party or candidate best represents their interests, but also about which is less likely to make their worst fears of a return to that era a reality.

To many on the left in Latin America, being part of the "right" in Latin America is equated with being a **neoliberal**—that is, favoring the economic policies associated with the **Washington Consensus**. So today, Teodoro Petkoff, a guerrilla leader in Venezuela in the 1960s, is seen by Chavistas as part of the right because he served as minister of planning from 1994 to 1998 and backed many of the **structural adjustment** policies that President Rafael Caldera embraced in that era.

Few Latin American presidents have campaigned openly as neoliberals, and when they do, they often claim that their administrations (e.g., Carlos Salinas in Mexico, Carlos Andrés Pérez in Venezuela, and Carlos Menem in Argentina) will soften the impact on the poor. Sometimes they campaign as populists but then govern as neoliberals, as occurred in the 1990 election in Peru. The more conservative candidate in the race was the famous novelist Mario Vargas Llosa, who early on seemed a favorite to win as he drew on public disgust with the corruption and ineffectiveness of Peru's traditional parties and in particular with the president at the time, Alan García Pérez of APRA. García had played the populist card in 1985 by declaring a moratorium on payments of the international debt and by nationalizing Peru's banking system. The

Peru

international banks had punished Peru for his temerity, and García had made things worse by mismanaging the economy and presiding over rampant corruption. Meanwhile, the Shining Path guerrillas stepped up their violent attacks and became more visible and bold (see chapter 10). Voters were desperate for something new, and at first, Vargas Llosa looked like he would be the beneficiary.

But what would Vargas Llosa stand for? Perhaps a professional politician would have hidden his agenda, but the appeal of Vargas Llosa, after all, was precisely that he was *not* a politician. The novelist would not turn to the left; he was disenchanted with the Cuban model and did not see the state-led strategy of import substitution as viable anymore. He turned to the ideas of his countryman Hernando De Soto, who had founded an organization called the Liberty and Democracy Institute to promote laissez-faire capitalism (see chapter 11). As we shall see, such think tanks were important incubators for neoliberal policies and helped shape the right.

Peruvian voters stunned Vargas Llosa and the world in 1990 by electing instead a Peruvian of Japanese descent, Alberto Fujimori, who had put together a coalition of parties, including APRA and the left, opposed to neoliberal economic ideas. Fujimori's candidacy appealed to Peru's highland Indians because his Asian countenance was not the face of a typical Peruvian *criollo*. He characterized Vargas Llosa's supporters as white oligarchs out of touch with the indigenous and mestizo masses. He also appealed to the growing Protestant population, wary of the Catholic hierarchy's endorsement of Vargas Llosa. Once in power, Fujimori turned on his supporters, closing Congress and aligning himself with the military. He turned the military loose to fight the Sendero Luminoso without human rights constraints. In economic matters, he implemented the very policies promoted by Vargas Llosa.

Fujimori's policies did not revive the Peruvian economy. Human rights atrocities soon made the armed forces—despite their success in capturing Sendero's leader—as unpopular as the Congress Fujimori had closed. His closest military advisor, Vladimir Montesinos, was deeply implicated in international narcotics trafficking. Facing defeat, Fujimori attempted to rig the 2000 election, but he was thwarted by international and domestic opposition. His successor, President Alejandro Toledo, a former businessman, won the election, but his popularity very quickly plummeted, reaching single digits in 2005. Although an upstart challenger, Humala Ollanta, a former military officer, launched a strong challenge, the victor in 2006 was the APRA candidate, García. APRA proved to be one dinosaur not quite extinct, but García's turn back toward neoliberalism proved highly unpopular. Not unlike what had happened in Venezuela in 1998, the party system as a bridge between civil society and government collapsed, leaving a cavernous gap between the two. Ollanta won the 2011 election, though he proved considerably more moderate in office than the ferocious propaganda campaign against him in 2006 suggested.

DEMOCRACY IN PERU

MEAN SUPPORT	54%
SUPPORT 2013	56%
SATISFACTION 2013	25%

Technopols and Think Tanks

As we have seen, throughout Latin America parties and candidates have run populist campaigns promising relief from economic policies, but once in power, they often leave economic policy-making to policy intellectuals trained in the United States or in "think tanks" heavily influenced by neoliberal ideas. Jorge Domínguez (1997) calls these intellectual politicians "technopols."

Unlike technocrats who remain aloof from politics, technopols see it as their mission not only to design economic policy but also to build political movements and interest groups dedicated to promote neoliberal ideas. Typical is Argentina's former finance minister, Domingo Felipe Cavallo, who founded a think tank (Fundación Meditarránea) to promote market-oriented policies. Cavallo moved into the Peronist Party in 1991 at the invitation of President Menem. Chile's Alejandro Foxley, in contrast to Cavallo, had a reputation as an academic leftist before moving in the Concertación cabinet as the first post-dictatorship finance minister under President Patricio Aylwin. Foxley had been severely critical of the economists ("Chicago Boys"; see chapters 7 and 8) who designed the neoliberal policies implemented under Pinochet. However, as finance minister he made few changes—partly because of restrictions imposed by the constitution of 1982, partly because market-oriented policies seemed to be the *only* possible ones in a globalized economy. Foxley explained what happened in an interview (PBS 2001):

> Interviewer: Is it fair to say that you came to have a greater faith in the role that the market can play in an economy?
> Alejandro Foxley: We have all learned during these years that it's only a very strong person who, when he sees that the world is changing very fast, doesn't adjust his own views to the changes that he's seeing in the world. Today we appreciate the strength and the power of the market much more as a force that will allow an economy to grow fast.

The technopols use their intellectual credentials, experience with media, and modern public-relationships techniques to propagate their market-oriented policies. Domínguez claims technopols have a "passion" for a set of ideas and a shared responsibility to seek to implement them. He describes them as effectively merging their scholarly experience with political engagement, so they and their teams become "partisans" in pursuit of their ideas. This means they "behave as 'teachers to the nation,' that is, bearers of a more impersonal loyalty to a democratic regime, committed to educate the public about facts that may be inconvenient for their party opinions" (Domínguez 1997: 11). Latin American think tanks have trained hundreds of like-mined technopols who can be imported into key ministries, displacing the politicians from state institutions that have been critical to party cohesion in the past. Out of office, these individuals often assume positions as board members of prestigious North American universities, think tanks, or financial corporations.

Although leftist candidates have proven adept at using media, the ability to communicate directly using the technique of public relations is of even greater importance to technopols. As the Argentine analyst Oscar Landi (1995: 210) puts it, "When I am in a situation of hyperinflation, I am going to turn on the television to guide me in my daily action. I'm not going to visit the local headquarters of a party." Production of television commercials, focus groups, polls, and advertising cost significant amounts of money. A typical poll in Latin America costs US$12,000–US$15,000 (Rial 1995: 503). These resources can be crucial in blunting challenges from leftist movements, at least temporarily. In Brazil, for example, the PT seemed poised to win the presidency behind Lula in 1989, but international and national business sectors rallied behind Fernando Collor de Mello, a relatively inexperienced politician. Collor owned a television station in a rural state and was supported by the country's most important national TV network. With money, media savvy, and the backing of Brazil's worried business community, Collor put together an effective campaign despite the lack of an established, organized party. News organizations in both Brazil and Mexico, closely linked to monopoly business interests and heavily dependent on a friendly state, have magnified poor performances by leftists, replaying heavily biased clips of debates repeatedly and slanting news coverage.

The increased role of media in politics is a worldwide tendency. Radio, film, Internet, and television permit politicians to bypass parties and communicate directly with the masses. In Venezuela, after the collapse of AD and COPEI, the owners of the country's major television networks and newspapers moved into the void. The media not only was biased against the new Chávez government but also undertook to call opponents into the streets in protest. In April 2002, Venezuela's media moguls were among those who collaborated in orchestrating (i.e., more than merely "backing") the military coup that removed the president from power for two days.

Among the most ready sources of money to finance the staggering costs of media-centered campaigns are the lords of the region's most dynamic export commodity, narcotics. Colombia's porous party system is especially vulnerable. Here, "porous" refers to legal provisions that allow several slates of legislative candidates from the same party to run in each state and district. Hence, the parties have a difficult time controlling nominations. The candidate who raises the most money has a huge advantage in pursuing a party's nomination.

The Left: Old and New

We have already reviewed one basic distinction in terms of Latin America's "left"—that between communism and social democracy. Although these two tendencies continue to battle each other as much as cooperate, they both represent the "old left." You undoubtedly have seen or heard leftists called "Reds," a term that dates back to the color used by social democrats in the late nineteenth century and then used as a description of communists after the 1917 revolution. As we have discussed in several chapters, the resurgence of the left in elections throughout Latin America has been called the Pink Tide to signify a group of leaders that share a commitment to change, and hence are left, but present themselves as alternatives to the old social democratic and communist left.

The Old Left and Cuba

There are several reasons that Latin American leftists have attempted in recent decades to redefine themselves. Some have to do with internal developments, including the emergence of new social movements (see chapter 11), the desire to avoid the mistakes that contributed to democratic breakdown, the desire to limit the corrosive influence of clientelism, and so on. But another reason has to do with disillusionment with the Cuban Revolution and

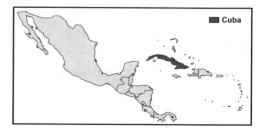

suspicions that the Cuban model is unsustainable. So we need to review briefly the Cuban experience to understand why Latin America has turned "pink," not "red."

Cuba is the only country in the hemisphere and one of the few in the world that enshrines one-party rule in its constitution. The Partido Comunista Cubano (PCC) operates by internal structures patterned on the model called "democratic centralism." This idea was first developed and implemented by Vladimir Lenin. In theory, party members debate policy and by majority vote pass decisions up to higher levels, where debate and voting recur. Once a decision is made at the highest level, all members of the party are supposed to implement it without question. These parties have central organs that have power to discipline members who fail to do so. Although on paper the system should ensure internal democracy, with higher organs merely making sure everyone agrees with the democratic majority, the powers of discipline and control everywhere seem to override democracy, especially when the party is in power. In Communist countries, the Party is usually the only legal party. In general, the party appoints or at least must approve appointments to major positions not only in government but also in civil society.

The PCC debated and rejected a proposal to introduce multiparty politics in 1992, and it has not revisited that decision since then. However, the PCC will certainly face the question again. A number of small NGOs gained permission to operate independently of the party and state in the 1990s, though some have been shut down or subjected to discipline in recent years. In the post-Fidel era (post 2008) Cuba may experience some of the same kind of tensions between movements and its single party that other leftist parties in Latin America must resolve. Fidel Castro exercised personal authority not just through the PCC but also through direct communication with people and through these mass organizations. With his exit from government, and the announced exit of his brother Raúl by 2018, the future for democracy in Cuba will have a lot to do with whether the mass organizations have more ability than typical of communist regimes to articulate the demands of their members and hold the bureaucracy accountable.

Hence, though Cuba defines itself as a revolutionary regime, the ruling party, under leadership of Raúl Castro, faces some questions not unlike those facing parties elsewhere. What should be the party's relationship with social movements and organizations? How can it prevent clientelism and corruption from eroding democratic tendencies and commitments to social justice? To what extent should the regime compromise its socialist ideology to adjust to external pressures and internal demands for a less statist economy with a larger sphere of operation for the market? And though no Cuban leader will say so publically, the issue of a transition to a multiparty regime will at some point surface again for two reasons: (1) the changes in civil society as the economy is reformed to open space for the market; (2) the general rejection on the left of the twentieth-century notions of the vanguard.

Neopopulism on the Left—the Chávez Legacy

The roots of the Pink Tide are in the reaction of Latin American social movements to the experiences of populism and military rule. Indeed, although Latin Americans were no longer looking to Cuba for a political model, they were hardly enthralled with the performance of the old left in Chile or Venezuela, to name only two examples. The breakthrough for hemispheric change came in Venezuela with the ascent of Hugo Chávez.

As we have already noted, Hugo Chávez appealed to Venezuelans as a champion of those disillusioned with what has been called "partyarchy," the dominance of the two main parties, AD and COPEI, over **civil society** (see chapter 9). However, Chávez found it necessary to maintain the MVR (Fifth Republic Movement) as a permanent vehicle to move his legislative agenda and to contest elections. The party was an instrument to gather votes and discipline Chavista members of the National Assembly, but it was much less successful as a vehicle of mobilization for the kind of revolutionary changes Chávez hoped to bring about. Furthermore, it became increasingly obvious that the party had weak roots in the leader's main social base, in the poor *barrios*. The party played no role in mobilizing the population that descended from the *barrios* to rescue Chávez from coup makers who temporarily deposed him in April 2002. It did not dissuade enough citizens from signing petitions to force a recall election in August of 2004. When the MVR faltered in the early stages of the recall campaign, Chávez reorganized his grassroots supporters into an ad hoc system of "electoral battle units" (UBEs). He won handily, but the MVR had proved weak (Hellinger 2005).

Chávez himself was partly to blame. He was a masterful social communicator, using television and radio on a weekly basis to communicate directly with the people. In these programs, carried on state television, Chávez dispensed state resources to solve individual problems, rebutted the often vitriolic criticism of the opposition-controlled media, reviewed history (especially history that seemed to provide lessons favorable to his project), and offered opinions about world economic and political trends. He did this in words and symbols (his "discourse") that resonated with the poor majority, most of whom held him with deep affection. This was the basis of his charismatic appeal.

Charismatic appeal is a great asset for a president, but unless it is used to build institutions, it does not necessarily reinforce democracy, especially if the goal is, as Chavismo and the Bolivarian constitution of 1999 promise, to establish institutions that facilitate bottom-up democracy. The MVR functioned in some ways like the very parties that Chávez had displaced—a vehicle to distribute patronage and discipline members of the governing coalition. In early 2007, Chávez decided to launch the PSUV (Unified Socialist Party of Venezuela), which suffered from the same shortcomings as the MVR but at least was organized in principle to maximize the influence of grassroots activists working in the communities. Even with Chávez alive and in office, the goal of establishing a political party dedicated to fomenting participatory democracy and democratic control over use of the country's oil-export earnings would be difficult. Chávez's death in March 2013 and succession by Vice President Nicolás Maduro makes the enterprise even more problematic.

A party similar to the MVR, the Partido Nacionalista Peruano, formed in Peru around the candidacy of Humala Ollanta, who emerged as a serious presidential candidate (endorsed by Chávez) in 2006. A former military officer accused of involvement in human rights atrocities (denied by Ollanta) during the war against Sendero Luminoso, Ollanta, like Chávez, first emerged as the leader of a military faction disgruntled with corruption and neoliberalism. Although Ollanta lost in the second round against APRA's Alan García, he established his movement as the largest single party in Peruvian politics. García's victory was due in part to ballots from voters who had favored a neoliberal candidate in the first round. They evidently preferred a dinosaur to the leftist caudillo, but the final chapter in the story was not written in this election, as Humala won the presidential election of 2011.

In Ecuador, President Correa, first elected in late 2006, does not fit the profile of a populist caudillo, having attained advanced economic degrees overseas, including a PhD from the University of Illinois. He speaks Aymara, the most important indigenous language, but he dresses like a Creole. Correa was the beneficiary of the frustration of the Ecuadorian people with neoliberalism and the ineffectiveness of their Congress. Like Evo Morales and Chávez, Correa rallied this sentiment not only to win the presidency but also to call a constituent assembly to rewrite the constitution. His election shows that the new-left populism of 2000 cannot be reduced to ethnic appeal alone and should be viewed mainly as a part of the overall regional dissatisfaction with neoliberalism. However, the party he founded, the Alianza PAIS (Proud and Sovereign Fatherland Alliance—*país* means "country" in Spanish), is best compared with the MVR, an "antiparty party" cobbled together by its leaders as his vehicle for election.

In Bolivia, the main vehicle for Morales's successful campaign for president in 2005 was the Movimiento al Socialismo (MAS). The MAS emerged out of indigenous movements, the most important of which was the *cocaleros* (peasant growers of coca, a traditional crop and the basis for the raw material of cocaine). Morales's party is less a personal vehicle than is the PSUV, but it shares many characteristics with its Venezuelan and Peruvian counterparts, especially in regard to natural resource nationalism and opposition to neoliberalism. However, the MAS, more so than the PSUV or PAIS, seems to have sprung from a movement rather than a candidacy.

Some observers welcome forces that have tended to moderate leftist political tendencies. Mexico's Jorge Castañeda (2006) argued in the influential journal *Foreign Affairs* that Bachelet and Chávez are examples of a "responsible left" and a "populist left," respectively. One is modern, open-minded, reformist, and internationalist, and it springs, paradoxically, from the hard-core left of the past. The other, born of the great tradition of Latin American populism, is nationalist, strident, and closed-minded. The first is well aware of its past mistakes (as well as those of its erstwhile role models in Cuba and the Soviet Union) and has changed accordingly. The second, if Castañeda is to be believed, unfortunately, has not. Castañeda argues that neoliberal economic measures are positive and necessary correctives to populist mistakes—in a way appropriate to a country's problems and history. To Castañeda "responsible" means abjuring the populist approaches of the past in favor of polyarchy; to critics (e.g., Quandt 2007), "responsible" means being faithful to promises to implement an alternative to neoliberal economic policy and respecting the autonomy of social movements.

For Review

Despite the emergence of new social movements and the Pink Tide, how do **caudilloism** and personalism continue to manifest themselves in elections in Latin America? How did the **charisma** of Hugo Chávez both enhance and limit his ability to achieve broader goals as president?

The Media versus the Left in Latin America

The print media has been influential in Latin American politics from the earliest days of independence. But literacy rates were low. The emergence of film, television, and radio in the twentieth century changed the political game in the respect that newspapers lost influence to these new media. To some degree, social media and the Internet have changed the game again, but the shift may not be quite so dramatic as the one being introduced by the growth of mega-media corporations that still dominate mass markets and control many of the means of dissemination of information, including access to the Internet and various media platforms (e.g., cable and satellite transmission; large social media outlets, such as Twitter, YouTube, and Facebook, that began as independent start-ups but now are commercial; popular apps for cell phones). In several recent cases, media organizations have not merely acted with bias toward more radical Pink Tide candidates and presidents; they have taken on the role of organizing opposition.

In Argentina, the Kirchners have done battle with the influential conservative newspaper *Clarín* and the vast media empire associated with it. Private media are corporations often owned by families or groups with vested economic interests throughout the country. In Mexico, privatization of communications—TV, telecommunications, and so on—in the 1980s and 1990s laid the basis for the global media empire of Carlos Slim, ranked by *Forbes* magazine as the world's richest man since 2010. Cárdenas and AMLO, the PRD's candidates, have had to battle in an extremely hostile media environment.

Venezuela's President Hugo Chávez used a weekly radio and television program, *Aló, Presidente*, broadcast on the government networks, to rally popular support against his enemies, who control the large private media outlets in the country. Chávez used oil revenues to create a new hemispheric network, Telesur, launched in 2005, in an attempt to provide an alternative news and cultural voice. His Ministry of Telecommunications also provided subsidies and licenses to hundreds of "microbroadcasters," mostly radio and Internet and mostly set up by his grassroots supporters.

However, Chávez came under intense international criticism for several actions against privately owned media. In early 2008, Chávez refused to renew the license of one (RCTV) of four private television networks that had cooperated in bringing about the coup that had ousted him for 48 hours in April 2002. In doing so, the president appealed to a media responsibility law, one that had been revised in earlier years by the National Assembly, under control of his supporters. Critics pointed out that there were deficiencies in the procedures by which the law was invoked, but much of the popular protest against the government's actions could be attributed to the disappearance of highly popular soap operas. Financial pressure drove another opposition station, Globovisión, to sell out in 2013 to new owners whose political orientation is not entirely clear. The two largest, most watched TV stations remain opposed to the government, though both have assumed a more professional and less confrontational style in recent years.

There are few (if any) societies anywhere in the world that have effectively put the power of mass media at the disposal of ordinary citizens—a form of positive freedom. Generally, discussion of press freedoms and media rights reflects the frameworks in liberal capitalist societies and focuses on negative freedom—the right of the press and citizens to express their political views freely without censorship. This reflects a theory of democracy that presumes that civil society in this way achieves a "marketplace of ideas" in which the

Mexico's "Yo Soy 132" ("I am 132") movement emerged after the PRI claimed that a video showing 131 students protesting the influence of money and media in the 2012 presidential campaign was staged by the party's opponents. The video went viral and spurred a movement demanding election reform.

best ones win out in competition, much like elections supposedly function in a **polyarchy**. What if some of the best ideas are those of groups of people who cannot afford to promote them through privately owned mass media? Suppose the wealthiest people, or the owners of the media themselves, are interested only in promoting their own interests? In all of the world's polyarchies, even the ones that provide guaranteed access to media or public funding of campaigns, the ability to amass money is crucial to effective communication. Is the freedom to speak sufficient, or should there also be some kind of a freedom to be heard?

In Latin America there have been several recent initiatives, nationally and internationally, to broaden media access. Venezuela's President Hugo Chávez, we have seen, made encouragement of community-controlled media a goal of his Bolivarian revolution. However, the charismatic Venezuelan president at the same time turned the state broadcasting network into a virtual propaganda arm that (unlike community stations) tolerated little criticism even within his own movement. The state media by law are supposed to be even-handed, but Chávez (and his successor Nicolás Maduro, in the April 2013 election to succeed him) needed control over state broadcasting in part to fight back against the monopoly power of private media, which had gone so far as to help organize the short-lived coup of April 2002.

In the post-2000 period, several other Latin American presidents were virtually at war with media establishments. Ecuador's Rafael Correa took over two private TV networks owned by corrupt bankers and used the outlets. He filed and won a $40 million libel suit against a newspaper columnist and then sent a proposal to Congress to prohibit

PUNTO DE VISTA: ECUADOR'S CONTROVERSIAL PROPOSED MEDIA LAW

In recent years, several leftist governments in Latin America have been accused by some major human rights organizations of attempting to muzzle critics with constitutional provisions and media laws that limit ownership of media by large economic groups, limit the number of media outlets any one owner can control, guarantee the public the right to "truthful reporting" or reporting in context, and support the creation of more state owned media and also of community based media.

Wendy Pérez has been a working journalist and editor in several Latin American countries, a rapporteur and fellow at Gabriel García Máquez's New Iberoamerican Journalism Foundation (FNPI), and a fellow at the University of Michigan. In March, Pérez summarized the controversy about Ecuador's new media law (see http://latam .portada-online.com/2013/03/28/the-most-controversial-points-of-ecuadors-media-law/#ixzz2Q0k3o520).

Pérez says the bill was based on a similar Argentine law and provides that 34% of all frequencies go to community media, 33% to public ones, and 33% to for-profit businesses. Until now, 85.5% of Ecuador's frequencies have been private, 12.9% public, and 1.6% community based. For television, 71% were private and 21% public.

According to Pérez, the new law envisions social communication as a public service that should be high quality and accountable. Community media are defined in the law as those whose "ownership, management and direction resides in districts/communes, communities, countries, nationalities, groups/collectives or non-profit organizations." The law requires government to support them "to promote plurality, diversity, interculturality and plurinationality." Ecuador has a large indigenous population that rarely finds itself represented in popular media. Ecuador's Confederation of Indigenous Nationalities of Ecuador (CONAIE)

claims that a third of the population is indigenous. The law also requires that 40% to 50% of music and programs be nationally produced.

Allocation of frequencies would be placed in the hands of a Regulatory and Communications Development Council, made up of both government representatives and those of the media and human rights organizations. Media are required to carry verified information and correct inaccurate reporting. Working journalists must be certified as professionally prepared, but editorialists, opinion writers (including bloggers), and journalists who speak an indigenous language are exempted.

The Inter-American Press Association (IAPA), a hemispheric organization of owners of large private media, has asked Ecuador's Supreme Court to overturn the law, claiming the legislation establishes "a kidnap of information" on the part of the government. The IAPA criticizes the power of the Council to fine media who refuse to correct misinformation. The Committee to Protect Journalists, a global association that speaks out against violence and intimidation of journalists, says that the law is President Rafael Correa's attempt at "muzzling all critics of his administration."

Supporters of laws like the one in Ecuador charge the media in Latin America of becoming increasingly and directly involved in politics. Not only are many of the largest, most influential outlets critical in their reporting, they collude with opponents of leftist presidents to orchestrate opposition, sometimes cooperating with efforts to oust presidents by various means, even coups.

As noted in chapter 9, for example, in 2002 large media outlets in Venezuela collaborated with organizers of a coup against an elected president (Hugo Chávez), cooperating with opponents to provoke violence and blame it on the government. The tactic has precedents. *El Mercurio,* Chile's most prestigious newspaper, received funds from the CIA to cooperate in the campaign to destabilize the elected government of Salvador Allende (1970–1973).

In Argentina, the owners of the newspaper *Clarín* controlled, according to *The Guardian* (London, August 20, 2013), "60% of the cable market, 25% of the internet market, Argentina's second most popular TV channel, three provincial channels, and 10 radio stations, as well as six other papers, a news agency and a printing works." It initially supported President Cristina Kirchner but turned against her when she moved to prevent the company from gaining majority control over the Internet.

In Ecuador, eight private groups with extensive interests dominate media ownership. In cables leaked by Wikileaks, the U.S. embassy acknowledged that the country's media lords were colluding to undermine Correa. Early after he became president in 2007, 11 main Ecuadorian daily newspapers issued the same front-page editorial attacking him, which a US embassy cable called "an unprecedented example of coordinated press rebuke to a sitting president." Another cable acknowledged that "the Ecuadorian media play a political role, in this case the role of the opposition." The reason? "Many media outlet owners come from the elite business class that feels threatened by Correa's reform agenda, and defend their own economic interests via their outlets."

Point/Counterpoint

Are Ecuador and other Latin American governments justified in passing laws that require media responsibility and a certain amount of national programming, and also limit the number of media outlets one owner can control? Why or why not?

   a. If you say yes, how would you answer those who say that media control by government is worse than control by private owners? Do you oppose all of the measures in these new media laws, or just some of them?
   b. If you say no, how do you respond to the criticism that media has become very concentrated and has in several cases participated in attempts to overthrow elected governments in Latin America by deliberately distorting news? Do you also think it wrong to allocate frequencies and government support go to community media? Would you oppose all of the measures in these new media laws, or just some of them?

For more information

The Committee to Protect Journalists issued some critical reports on conditions in Ecuador at its website, www.cpj.org. The Irish documentary, *The Revolution Will Not be Televised* (2002) illustrates the power of media in Venezuela in the Chávez era. The U.S. embassy cable can be found at https://cablegatesearch.wikileaks.org/cable.php?id=09QUITO225&q=correa%20newspapers.

media from taking partisan positions for or against candidates in elections. On the other hand, as in Venezuela, the private media in Ecuador were engaged in an all-out effort to defeat the leftist populist's programs and rising popularity. (They failed, as Correa achieved easy reelection and 70 percent popularity in 2013.) In Argentina, President Cristina Kirchner and Grupo Clarín, a giant media company that owns the most important newspaper, broadcast, and cable outlets, were engaged in a bitter battle. Clarín, founded by a fascist sympathizer during World War II, secured its dominant place in the Argentine media during the military dictatorship. Tax agents of Kirchner's government raided the Grupo's home offices, and the government introduced a bill into Congress to strip the conglomerate of its lucrative cable outlets.

The actions of these populist presidents and the extreme hostility of the media empires under fire raise difficult questions. On one side, many human rights observers abroad condemned the actions as ones that would suffocate free speech in a country where the president had already gathered significant power around his person. On the other side, one could ask whether any government in the world would permit a television or radio station that had participated in a coup attempt to continue operating.

For Review

What is a technopol? In what way does the increased role of the media pose both challenges and opportunities to democracy?

Zapatistas and the Question of Power

The history of the state of Chiapas in Mexico has been punctuated by rebellion on the part of indigenous people, and the revolution did little to address the underlying causes of the persistent unrest. After 1910, the new mestizo elite acquired 4.5 million acres of Chiapas land during the Díaz era; it avoided the revolutionary land reforms of the 1930s because landowners switched sides early and avoided confrontation with the new regime. Zapata became the namesake of the Chiapas movement not because he fought there but because of his reputation as an almost saintly and humble peasant leader who picked up arms only after being called to leadership by his people (Womack 1968).

The Zapatistas, heavily Mayan, made their entry onto the world stage in dramatic fashion on January 1, 1994, when they seized San Cristóbal de las Casas, the capital of the state. In Mexico City, the new President Salinas and the elite around him were celebrating the New Year and the launch of the North American Free Trade Association (NAFTA), a treaty between Mexico, Canada, and the United States. The peasants in Chiapas were in no mood to celebrate. They were already being pushed off the land by the expansion of ranching and export-oriented crops, such as sugar and cotton. A birth rate spiraling out of control (3.35 per woman) increased pressure on the land. Expansion of export agriculture and the influx of displaced peasants in search of new land had greatly reduced the Lacandon rainforest, located in Chiapas. "Modernization" was destroying the ecology that sustained many of the state's inhabitants. Out of 1,000 live births, 66 infants would not survive their first year because of disease and malnutrition. Over half the population could not read or write. Worst affected were 200,000 descendants of the original Mayan population. All these were in a state that was Mexico's leading source of electric power (Tangeman 1995: 4–7).

The Catholic Church, though it did not endorse the Zapatistas (Ejército Zapatista de Liberación Nacional, EZLN), was sympathetic to the demands of peasants. San Cristóbal de las Casas had once been the diocese governed by Bartolomé de las Casas, the sixteenth-century bishop who had battled the local colonial landholding elite and successfully urged the Spanish crown to abolish the *encomienda* system (see chapter 3). His Dominican order subsequently abandoned these ideals, but 415 years later, another progressive bishop, Samuel Ruiz, assumed office in the diocese (January 1960). Only one year before, Pope John XXIII had launched his important initiative to modernize the Catholic Church and make it more sensitive to the needs of the poor. This would culminate in the Second Vatican Council of 1962–1965, which laid the basis for some theologians to develop the idea of a **preferential option for the poor**. Bishop Ruiz became an outspoken critic of social injustice and defender of human rights, without endorsing or joining the Zapatistas. This distance from the EZLN allowed him to play a role as mediator between the rebels and the national government.

The conflict in Chiapas cannot be reduced to a simple confrontation between humble Christian peasants and the elite. It is complicated by the growth of Protestant evangelical churches. In some parts of Latin America, politically conservative Protestants have sometimes been backed by the U.S. government and the CIA, especially in areas where indigenous people are facing incursions by big mining and oil companies (see Lewis 1989). However, the evangelical movement in Latin America is complex and not easily stereotyped as conservative. The Zapatistas face the challenge of bridging the gap between Protestant poor and Catholic poor if they are to resist the Mexican army's attempts to isolate them from their social base.

One might question whether the Zapatistas really qualify as a revolutionary organization or whether they are more accurately a social movement. The Zapatistas differ from other guerrilla movements because they do not aim to take immediate control of national government. Marcos (actually Rafael Sebastián Guillén Vicente, a university professor) and his followers see their struggle as an extension of centuries of indigenous resistance to a state that has always reflected a form of politics alien to indigenous interests and traditions. The Zapatistas have said that they conceive of their struggle as one that will take generations to achieve.

Marcos has spoken of making change "without taking power." However, the existence of the Mexican state is a fact of life that the EZLN cannot ignore. Hence, the movement has sought to extend its influence with other movements seeking social justice and a more democratic state. A 1914 convention that gathered social movements from the length and breadth of Mexico in the town of Aguascalientes, at which forces of the Mexican Revolution mapped out the future of the country, was among several actions in which the Zapatistas have both supported and inspired grassroots democratization efforts in Mexico. Like these movements, the EZLN has some affinity to the leftist PRD, but it has avoided aligning itself with the party, arguing that the PRD does not represent a fundamental break with the style and substance of the present regime.

The Zapatistas have attracted attention and solidarity worldwide. Still, they remain far from achieving their goals, and the Mexican army remains poised to ratchet up counterinsurgency efforts. Frustrated by the lack of progress in negotiations on autonomy, and accusing president Vicente Fox (2000–2006) of breaking promises to withdraw the army and negotiate seriously on autonomy, the Zapatistas declared certain villages and adjacent

PUNTO DE VISTA: ZAPATISTAS AGAINST REVOLUTIONARY VANGUARDS

Following is an excerpt from a letter by Commander Marcos of the EZLN (Zapatistas) to the Basque (Spain) guerrilla group, ETA, which had criticized the Mexican movement for rejecting the idea that a revolution must have a "vanguard" to lead the oppressed working class in revolution. The full letter is at flag.blackened.net/revolt/mexico/ezln/2003/marcos/etaJAN.html.

We don't grieve when we recognize that our ideas and proposals don't have an eternal horizon, and that there are ideas and proposals better suited than ours. So we have renounced the role of vanguards, and to obligate anyone to accept our thinking over another argument wouldn't be the force of reason.

Our weapons are not used to impose ideas or ways of life, rather to defend a way of thinking and a way of seeing the world and relating to it, something that, even though it can learn a lot from other thoughts and ways of life, also has a lot to teach. . . .

What are you going to teach us? To kill journalists who speak badly about the struggle? To justify the death of children for reason of the "cause"? We don't need or want your support or solidarity. We already have the support and solidarity of many people in Mexico and the world. Our struggle has a code of honor, inherited from our guerilla ancestors and it contains, among other things: respect of civilian lives (even though they may occupy government positions that oppress us); we don't use crime to get resources for ourselves (we don't rob, not even a snack store); we don't respond to words with fire (even though many hurt us or lie to us). One could think that to renounce these traditionally "revolutionary" methods is renouncing the advancement of our struggle. But, in the faint light of our history it seems that we have advanced more than those that resort to such arguments . . . Our enemies (who are not just a few nor just in Mexico) want us to resort to these methods. Nothing would be better for them than the EZLN converting into a Mexican and indigenous version of ETA.

P.S. Before I forget . . . in respect to your final "¡Viva Chiapas Libre!" [Long Live a Free Chiapas!]: . . . We don't want to make ourselves independent from Mexico. We want to be a part of it, but without leaving who we are: indigenous . . . We struggle for . . . all the men and women of Mexico no matter if they are Indian or not . . .

Another P.S. It should already be evident, but I want to remark: I shit on all the revolutionary vanguards of this planet.

Point/Counterpoint

C. B. MacPherson (1965), the Canadian philosopher we met in chapter 1, was not approving of Lenin's notion that a vanguard is a necessary part of a revolutionary movement, but he also pointed out that social injustice and exploitation might make them necessary. So with apologies for the vulgarity, is not Marcos himself part of a vanguard?

a. If you answered yes, how do you respond to the way that Marcos and the Zapatistas have so far avoided betraying their philosophy of trying to make revolution without taking power?

b. If you answered no, how then do you account for Marcos having become the visible spokesperson for the Zapatistas? Could the members of the Zapatistas have organized their insurrection without a leader like Marcos?

For more information

On leadership and revolution, see MacPherson (1965) in the bibliography. On the Zapatistas, there is an extensive literature. For more about the Zapatista movement, see Tom Hayden (ed.), *The Zapatista Reader* (New York: Nation Books, 2002).

areas autonomous liberated zones (*caracoles*, "snails"). Presidents Fox and Felipe Calderón (2006–2012) were restrained by world sympathy for the rebels and the prospect of major bloodletting if the army were to be turned loose in the region. Such an operation might very well touch off violent resistance in other parts of the country.

For Review

The rebels in Chiapas call themselves Zapatistas to invoke the memory of the Mexican Revolution. How might this help them appeal to ordinary Mexicans?

Shall We Party?

Although parties emerged in Europe and North America in the nineteenth century, democratic theorists have seen them as keys to democratic governance. Pluralists have seen them as the crucial intermediaries between civil society and the state. Nationalists have seen them as instruments to forge unity in divided societies facing the challenges of development and foreign intervention. Marxist revolutionaries have seen them as the organizations that can lead exploited classes to power and transform capitalism into socialism. Parties, as organizations dedicated to contesting for control of the state, remain the most important vehicles in contesting for power in a democracy, but the media has increasingly stepped into this role, especially in systems where wealthy and powerful media owners have seen the collapse of parties that defend the status quo. Populist caudillos and revolutionary leaders can now address the masses through the media, but they still today find it necessary to organize a party to carry out organizational tasks, especially to win votes.

Parties may be under suspicion throughout the hemisphere, but no other social or political institution has yet shown a capacity to serve as effectively as an instrument of governance and contestation for power. Even though parties that emerge out of social movements may often disappoint their followers, they may leave a mark on politics by changing the rules of the game or bringing new policy ideas into the political arena.

The pluralist view tends to see strong government as the enemy of a strong civil society. However, some pluralists, such as Benjamin Barber (1984) and Robert Putnam (2002), present a somewhat different formula: a strong civil society reinforces a strong democracy. This version of pluralist thought is less hostile to the state and more skeptical about the democratic benefits of free-market capitalism. It tends to value participation more than the traditional pluralism espoused by Dahl and the "transition to democracy" theorists. In the end, the role of parties should not be to control participation but to institutionalize rule by the people. So far, other institutions—for example, the military and mass media—have not proven more capable than parties in meeting this task.

Discussion Questions

1. Why are Latin Americans in general so skeptical about parties? Do you think it would be possible for democracy to function in Latin America without parties?
2. Do you think that media, think tanks, and short-lived parties supporting particular candidates will someday displace political parties altogether in Latin America?
3. We have discussed several cases of relatively new parties that have sought to represent the views of social movements. One could argue that in every case, once in power—or close to power—these parties seem to fall back into the practices of the older parties. Why? Do you think that this pitfall (at least from the point of view of the movements) can be avoided?

Resources for Further Study

Reading: Julia Buxton analyzes the collapse of the Punto Fijo system in *The Failure of Political Reform in Venezuela* (Aldershot, UK: Ashgate, 2001). Nancy R. Powers looks at the political choices made by poor Argentine voters in *Grassroots Expectations of Democracy and Economy: Argentina in Comparative Perspective* (University of Pittsburg Press, 2001). As for politicians' choices, see Barry Ames, *Political Survival: Politicians and Public Policy in Latin America* (Berkeley: University of California Press, 1987).

Video and Film: Oliver Stone's *South of the Border* (2010) takes a sympathetic view of the rise of leftist politicians and parties in recent years. *Our Brand Is Crisis* (2005) looks at culture clash and democratic values as U.S. campaign advisors try to work with Bolivian elites while indigenous people demonstrate in the streets.

On the Internet: Latin Pulse (www.linktv.org/latin-pulse) carries regular reports on elections and parties in Latin America.

13 Constitutions, Institutions, and the Electoral Arena

Focus Questions

▶ How much weight should institutions have today in a region where in the past they have often been ignored or abused?

▶ By what criteria should the quality of "governance" be judged? To what extent are Latin American democracies capable of providing this public benefit?

▶ With some exceptions, constitutions have not had long life spans in Latin America. Why? What is behind the recent tendency for new charters to be written through constitutional assemblies?

IF THE BREAKDOWN of democracy preoccupied political scientists in the 1970s and "transitions" preoccupied comparativists in the 1980s, then the "consolidation" and "deepening" of democracy became the favored theme of the 1990s. Von Mettenheim and Malloy (1998: 178–179) argued,

> Creative political leadership and spontaneous popular demands ended military rule, empowered citizens and civil society along new lines of gender, race, ethnicity, and identity, and overcame seemingly intractable problems such as high foreign debt, hyperinflation, and economic adjustment. Although not blind to policy failures and facile appeals to authoritarianism, the series of policy successes through open, pluralistic governance by new civilian leaders in Latin America . . . suggests that deepening democracy is possible.

This relatively optimistic perspective has encouraged some Latin Americanists to apply analysis drawn from a school of comparativists called the **new institutionalists**. These political scientists say the time has come to focus more attention "on the process whereby elected leaders, working through the institutions of democracy, make decisions" (Munck 2004: 437). Institutions are political arrangements, rules, or organizations that are valued for themselves as ways to process demands, resolve conflicts, or promote the general welfare of the population. Some are established through constitutions that define the role of different branches of government or lay out the major responsibilities of public entities. In Latin America, there exist so-called organic or semi-constitutional laws that are not formally codified in the constitution, but that have a special status as foundational laws that can be changed only by extraordinary majorities. For example, laws that govern taxation, rules for foreign invest-ment, or electoral processes often have this status.

However, an arrangement, set of rules, or formal organization is not an institution simply because it is found in law; it must acquire that status by virtue of having earned the acceptance of the population, or at least of those whose interests are affected by its functions. One positive sign of an institutionalized process or organization is that those who disagree with its decisions or outcomes continue to respect, or at least accept, the outcomes. For example, if citizens think that the rules and political organizations responsible for conduct-ing elections carry them out fairly and impartially, they are likely to accept the outcomes as legitimate even if their preferred candidate or party loses. That is a sign that electoral pro-cesses are institutionalized.

Promoting Democratic Institutions

Some institutionalists go beyond studying their subject and use their expertise to promote judicial reform (specifically, the creation of more independent and less corrupt and politicized courts) and the rule of law, increase citizen engagement in politics, and foster a cultural com-mitment to democracy as a way of life. International NGOs have been formed to promote human rights, clean elections, anticorruption efforts, and judicial reform. The Open Society Institute (OSI), for example, was founded and is heavily funded by George Soros, the multibil-lionaire who made his money in international finance. OSI states that it "works to build vibrant and tolerant democracies whose governments are accountable to their citizens. To achieve its mission, OSI seeks to shape public policies that assure greater fairness in political, legal, and economic systems and safeguard fundamental rights" (see www.soros.org). OSI operates inde-pendently of any government, but that does not prevent some countries from criticizing it for promotion of democracy in the "American style." Arousing more suspicion is the **National Endowment for Democracy (NED)**, funded directly with U.S. taxpayer money. Both groups employ prominent political scientists to help to achieve their objectives. NED's work is comple-mented by the Office of Transition Assistance in the State Department and by special programs of the Agency for International Development (AID). NED has the advantage in its work of appearing to operate independently, though its government funding and its ties to the Demo-cratic and Republican parties in the United States belie that image abroad.

The early work on democratic transitions brought forth the concept of a "**hybrid regime**," one that combines features of **polyarchy** (most commonly, direct elections of the president) with authoritarian institutions or practices, such as weakness in the system of checks and balances and abuses of power by powerful presidents. The notion of hybrid regimes was influ-enced by the experiences of Eastern Europe, where promising movements for democracy in the late communist era gave way to elected autocrats, of whom Russian president Vladimir Putin is often seen as a prototype. More recently, the term has been used to describe the new regimes in the Middle East that have arisen as hopes for democratic consolidation have faded since the Arab Spring uprisings in Egypt and Tunisia in 2010–2011. In Latin America, the regimes led by leftist populists—in particular, Chávez (now Maduro) in Venezuela, Morales in Bolivia, Ortega in Nicaragua, and Correa in Ecuador—are often seen in this category. Several studies of the Chávez presidency described the Venezuelan regime as being in a "grey zone" or as a "competitive autocracy," a typical case of a "hybrid" democracy (respectively, Carothers 2002; McCoy and Myers 2004; Corrales 2006; see also Hawkins 2010).

In the study of transitions, hybrid regimes were often regarded as temporary stopping points on the journey toward democracy (polyarchy) for regimes being carried along on the "third wave." Increasingly, they are seen as types of regimes themselves (see Brown 2011)—sometimes called simply "non-liberal democracies." This can be taken in different ways. Some (e.g., Plattner 1998) say that a "non-liberal democracy" is a contradiction in terms; you can't have one without the other. However, as we saw in chapter 1, there is a long tradition of other claims on the word "democracy." Fareed Zakaria (1997) has even defined some polyarchies, such as Sweden, as "illiberal"—in Sweden's case because Swedes seem to place community rights ahead of individual property rights. For the most part, however, he regards Latin American countries that have strong elected presidents but weak constitutional restraints on power to be "offenders" of democratic norms. But democratic theorists have also (as we saw in chapter 1) bemoaned the lack of participation in liberal democracies and called for more participatory and "deliberative" democracies. Without discarding all of the positive values of liberalism, we still might think that democracies need not adopt the view that restrictions on individual rights and markets compromise democracy, as the term "illiberal" implies.

Because institutions and constitutions are decision-making mechanisms, the redesign of democratic governance through constituent assemblies is rarely something that happens in times of normalcy. Changing the rules of the game usually influences the distribution of wealth and status. In Bolivia, Ecuador, and Venezuela, newly elected leftist presidents followed through on campaign promises to convene constituent assemblies to design institutions for governance based not only on representation but also on direct and active participation of the people in politics. For many (though not all) **Pink Tide** leaders, institutionalizing democracy also means overcoming the problem of exclusion—that is, ensuring equal access and participation to those sectors of the population that because of discrimination and poverty have historically been denied rights, privileges, and equal treatment under the law. Even from this perspective, however, it is reasonable to ask whether the participatory and inclusionary mechanisms are really working, or whether they have merely served the interests of populist caudillos.

Ultimately, democracy of any sort depends on consolidation of rules that reflect the principle of rule by the people. No one set of democratic institutions is best for all societies at every point in their history, but the design of representation, the balancing of majority and minority rights, the channeling of effective citizen control over government, and the peaceful transfer of power from one generation to the next are all examples of political challenges that can be met only through constitutional and institutional mechanisms. These mechanisms provide stability in political life. It is reasonable, then, to ask, how effectively do institutions *channel* political participation? I suggest we consider as well, how effectively do institutions *enable* political participation?

For Review

What does it mean to say that a political process, agreement, or organization has been "institutionalized"? What is democracy promotion? What is a hybrid regime?

PUNTO DE VISTA: IMPEACHMENT OR COUP? PARAGUAY 2012

In June 2012, President Fernando Lugo of Paraguay, one of the poorest countries in Latin America, was impeached and removed from office. An estimated 60% of Paraguayans were living in poverty, and Lugo was known as the "bishop of the poor" before he left the priesthood and entered politics. In 2008 he won Paraguay's presidential election, promising to end corruption and to carry out a agrarian reform, angering the tiny percentage of citizens who owned 80% of the country's land. Lugo promised to deliver land to 87,000 landless families and refused to take a salary as president.

He was impeached by a 76 to 1 vote in the lower house and then convicted and ousted the very next day by a 39–4 vote in the Senate, both controlled by the two traditional parties, the Liberal Party and the Colorado Party. The Colorados had controlled Paraguay's presidency for 61 years, including the dictatorship of Alfredo Stroessner from 1954 to 1989. Lugo was replaced by his vice-president, Federico Franco, a member of the Liberal Party. The impeachment motion blamed the violence on Lugo's supposedly poor performance.

There were other reasons for the Paraguayan right's discontent with Lugo. Lugo was working to bring Venezuela and its leftist leader, Hugo Chávez, into the Mercosur trade bloc. The only thing standing in the way was the Paraguayan Congress, as other members (Brazil, Argentina, and Uruguay) had already approved Venezuelan ascension. The impeachment may have backfired, as the other countries condemned the hasty removal of Lugo as a coup and suspended Paraguay's membership long enough to admit Venezuela.

In a cable (Wikileaks, March 2009), the U.S. embassy said Lugo's opponents were maneuvering to impeach Lugo in order to "regain their own political relevance" and would do so "even on spurious grounds." Lugo protested that he had no opportunity to prepare a defense before the Senate vote and called his removal "a legislative coup d'etat against the people's will." He said the new government had no legitimacy and had "altered the Republic's institutionalism."

The new president, Federico Franco, a Liberal, rejected Lugo's claim. According to *Al Jazeera English*, he said: "I ratify and reaffirm that there was no coup here, there is no institutional breakdown. This was carried out in accordance with the constitution and the laws. It is a legal situation that the constitution and the laws of my country permit us to do in order to carry out changes when the situation calls for it. What was carried out was a political trial in accordance with the constitution and the laws."

A senator whose party favored impeachment, Miguel Carrizosa Galiano, seemed untroubled by the haste with which Lugo was evicted. His party was willing to wait four days to give Lugo time to defend himself against the charge. However, he said, "We lost. That is democracy."

Al Jazeera English quotes Adrienne Pine, an anthropologist, for a different view: "It is clear that this was modeled after the Honduran coup in 2009; the same kind of rhetoric is being used and the same kind of powerful oligarchic figures are behind it. . . . It's a very shady justification and one that shows that allowing the Honduran coup to stand has paved the way for other similar procedural coups."

Point/Counterpoint

Was what happened in Paraguay a constitutional process consistent with the rule of law, or was it some kind of coup?

a. If you say it was constitutional and consistent with rule of law, how do you respond to those who say the hurried proceedings were unfair and that Lugo was removed from office simply because he sought to make changes unpopular with the elite?

b. If you say it was a coup, how do you respond to Carrizosa Galiano and others who point out that no laws or provisions of the constitution were violated?

For More Information

The June 26, 2008, *Al Jazeera English* report on the constitutional legality of Lugo's ouster can be found here: www.aljazeera.com/programmes/insidestoryamericas/2012/06/20126265451105780.html. The U.S. embassy cable can be found at https://wikileaks.org/cable/2009/03/09ASUNCION189.html. *Upside Down World* carried several background pieces on the "coup." See http://upsidedownworld.org/main/paraguay-archives-44.

▪ Presidentialism and "Impeachment of the Street"

One test of the capacity of political institutions in Latin America is their relevance in curtailing the concentration of power in the hands of the executive, a tendency exacerbated by the tradition of **caudilloism**. Twenty years ago, Guillermo O'Donnell (1994), the distinguished Argentine comparativist, warned in an often-cited essay that old patterns of presidentialism and personalism have asserted themselves within the new "democratic" framework. Rather than participatory democracy or pluralist democracy with institutional checks and balances, O'Donnell sees a much weaker **"delegative democracy,"** one where legislatures concede enormous powers to presidents whose rule is legitimated by elections that are little more than plebiscites. There certainly is a place for plebiscites when questions about the foundations of a state are in question. But simple yes-or-no questions on a ballot do little to make governments responsive to the people. Rather than empowering citizens, plebiscitary elections may allow powerful executives to acquire near dictatorial powers beyond the control of legislatures, states, and bureaucracies.

Since 1990, several Latin American presidents have used their popularity to remove limits on reelection. These include, among others, Fujimori in 2000, Chávez in 2007, Brazil's F. H. Cardoso in 1998, and Argentina's Carlos Menem in 1994. Yet the recent history of Latin America also continues to be punctuated by irregular resignations or removal of presidents across the ideological spectrum. These include the rise of the Peruvian right-wing populist Alberto Fujimori, who shut down the country's Congress in 1992 but fled the country in disgrace in 2000. Venezuela's Chávez initially sought power through a failed *coup d'etat* in 1992; subsequent pressure from the military and street protests forced the resignation of President Carlos Andrés Pérez in 1993. After

DEMOCRACY IN PARAGUAY

MEAN SUPPORT	45%
SUPPORT 2013	50%
SATISFACTION 2013	25%

achieving office through elections in 1998, Chávez himself was temporarily ousted by a coup in 2002. A similar sequence of events forced out Presidents Jamil Mahuad and Lucio Gutiér-rez of Ecuador in 2000 and 2004, respectively; Fernando de la Rúa in Argentina in 2001; Gonzalo Sánchez de Lozada in Bolivia in 2003; and Jean Bertrand Aristide in Haiti in 2004. In Paraguay, President Fernando Lugo was impeached and ousted from office in a matter of 24 hours in 2012. In some of these cases, the constitutional formalities were observed, but what all have in common is that power politics and social unrest were more influential fac-tors than institutionalized procedures.

What is more important to democracy—respect for the constitution or the will of the majority? Polyarchies are constitutionally designed to limit majority power, and we can readily grasp that protection of minority rights from the tyranny of the majority is a good reason for limiting that power. However, what if, as in Honduras, the restrictions go to the point of making it absolutely impossible to change the rules of the game (See the Punto de Vista on the next page.)? What about the other side of the question? In at least several of the cases of presidents who failed to complete terms cited previously, the executives were attempting to carry out policies that were widely and deeply unpopular, or they were with little doubt guilty of gross human rights violations or corruption. Are removals of presi-dents within constitutional rules but under enormous popular pressure—"impeachments of the street"—signs of democratic health or decay?

"Impeachments of the street," whereby masses of people call in the streets for an elected president's resignation or induce the legislature to remove him or her from office, might make countries less governable, but at least in some cases, they also are linked to demands for more popular accountability—that is, demands for *more* democracy. The protests that ousted Pérez, Mahuad, Gutiérrez, Sánchez de Lozada ("Goni"), and de la Rúa were all gen-erated by the failure of these leaders to make good on promises made to the poorer social classes and by highly unpopular programs tied to structural adjustment or privatizations. In Ecuador, Gutiérrez, who as a colonel had played a key role in the ouster of Mahuad, was ousted himself by a military coup provoked by street demonstrations in April 2004 because he broke promises that he had made to get elected—especially promises made to the coun-try's indigenous groups. Sánchez de Lozada and two of his successors in Bolivia were forced to resign under popular pressure between 2003 and 2005 for pursuing highly unpopular policies, including privatizing water supplies, cooperating with the drug war, and opening new territory to foreign oil companies.

Some presidents have survived scandals that temporarily at least threatened their ability to finish their terms. Brazil's Lula, who took office with high opinion ratings and a reputation for probity, came under fire in 2005 as a result of several bribery scandals touching close aides. In Mexico, President Vicente Fox, who enjoyed similar popularity and repute, suffered a similar fate when his interior minister (the most important cabi-net position in most Latin American governments), Santiago Creel, was caught allocating lucrative gambling permits to Televisa, the country's huge media conglomerate, and sev-eral other big corporations.

Two **Pink Tide** presidents have suffered premature removals from office. President Fernando Lugo, a former Catholic bishop elected in 2008, was forced from office by the Paraguayan Congress in a hastily implemented impeachment proceeding after a clash between security forces and peasants who were encouraged by Lugo's plans for land reform. José Manuel Zelaya's removal was even more controversial because the military seized him

PUNTO DE VISTA: HONDURAS'S UNAMENDABLE CONSTITUTION

The most contentious case of the removal of an elected president from office occurred in Honduras in June 2009 when the Honduran military ousted President Manuel Zelaya from office and spirited him out of the country. The Honduran case raises an interesting issue: can a constitution's restrictions on the ability of presidents to amend the rules of the game go too far?

The Honduran elites and the military who removed Zelaya from office alleged that his attempt to hold a nonbinding referendum on allowing presidential reelection violated a constitutional provision that not only limited presidents to one term but also made it unconstitutional to amend the constitution for this purpose! The strange rule was written in 1982, when the country was still ruled by a military junta, and while Honduras was the main base for U.S. training and support for counterinsurgency in El Salvador and Guatemala and for the *contras* in Nicaragua. Honduras borders on all three countries. In this classic "banana republic," fruit represented two-thirds of the country's exports, and foreign companies owned over 1 million acres of the small republic's best land. By the 1950s, though, peasant movements and cooperatives began to fight back, and as in neighboring countries, some labor-intensive manufacturing and a modest middle class began to complicate politics—but not enough to break the stranglehold of the Liberal Party and the slightly more conservative National Party over the country's civilian politics. The military was key to keeping the emerging political tensions in check.

Honduran elites, encouraged by Washington to stabilize politics in the geopolitically strategic country, sought to break a pattern of coups and irregular changes in government. In January 1982, the legislature proclaimed a new constitution that included a provision to prevent presidents from trying to extend their terms in office. Article 373 explicitly rules out the possibility of amending the document to change the presidential term or permit reelection of the president. However, the constitution also explicitly states in Article 2, "The sovereignty of the People may also [be] exercised directly, through the plebiscite and the Referendum." Zelaya saw in this clause a way to get around Article 373.

Zelaya, who took office in January 2006, was viewed as just another Liberal oligarch, but he unexpectedly turned toward the left after his election, angering traditional elites and much of the middle class, but striking a responsive chord with poor Hondurans, whose living conditions had deteriorated. Figure 13.1 shows that approximately three of every five Hondurans live in poverty, two of four in extreme poverty. Figures 13.2 and 13.3 demonstrate that inequality and poverty were growing worse leading up to Zelaya's presidency, but some modest gains in addressing these trends were made in his shortened term. His programs included a free education program for children, an 80 percent increase in the minimum wage, subsidies for small farmers, extension of social security coverage to domestic employees (mostly women), free electricity, and other aid for the poorest Hondurans.

Probably what was most alarming to the military and Honduran elites was Zelaya's intention to have Honduras join the Bolivarian Alliance for the Americas (ALBA), Hugo Chávez's brainchild for economic integration, developed explicitly as an alternative to the neoliberal Central American Free Trade Association (CAFTA), to which Honduras belonged. The switch was especially alarming to the newer Honduran business class whose manufacturing profits are based largely on exports of labor-intensive products (electronic goods, clothing, etc.) to the North American market; and the military wanted no part of anything connected with Hugo Chávez. The military's top legal affairs officer made this clear when he told the Salvadoran newspaper *El Faro* (July 2, 2009) that if Chávez followed through on his plans to visit

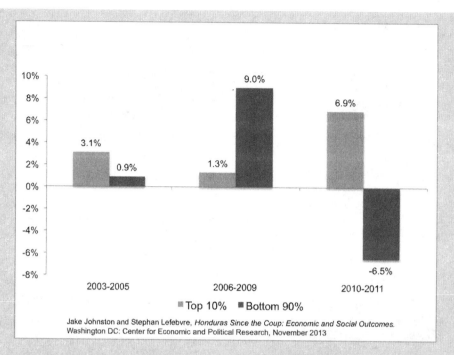

Jake Johnston and Stephan Lefebvre, *Honduras Since the Coup: Economic and Social Outcomes.*
Washington DC: Center for Economic and Political Research, November 2013

FIGURE 13.1   Honduras' Average Annual Per Capita Income Growth, by Decile

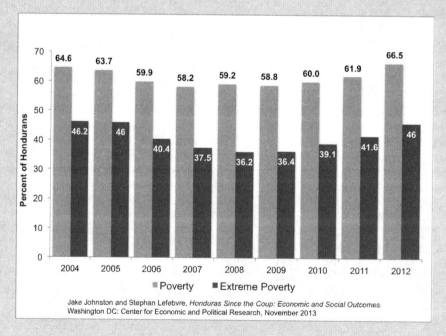

Jake Johnston and Stephan Lefebvre. *Honduras Since the Coup: Economic and Social Outcomes.*
Washington DC: Center for Economic and Political Research, November 2013

FIGURE 13.2   Honduras: Poverty and Extreme Poverty Rates

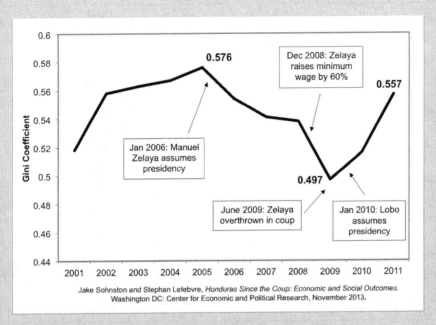

FIGURE 13.3   Honduras: Gini Coefficient

Honduras, he should fear being assassinated by sniper.

The political crisis became acute when Zelaya decided to hold an advisory referendum on amending the constitution to permit reelection. The balloting would have taken place on Election Day, and Zelaya would not have been a candidate, in accord with existing prohibition on reelection. The country's Supreme Court and the Congress both ruled the referendum unconstitutional, but Zelaya ordered the military to deliver the ballots for the referendum around the country. Instead the military seized Zelaya and flew him out of the country, to Costa Rica.

Zelaya was allowed to return to Honduras, but not to run for office. Meanwhile, the country has earned a reputation as the poorest and most violent in the hemisphere. The mass movement stimulated by Zelaya's reforms has grown, less so around Zelaya's political ambitions (though the movement supports him and his new party, LIBRE) than around demands for the country to address the issues that he addressed—whether motivated by a sense of justice, political ambition, or both.

The United States initially condemned the action as a coup, but Washington broke ranks in endorsing the election of a new president in November 2009. Latin American countries eventually decided to accept the *fait accompli*. In December 2013, the nominees of the two traditional parties qualified for the January runoff, won by the Liberal, Juan Orlando Hernández. LIBRE protested fraud and questioned the viability of elections contested in the context of a highly repressive environment. (See Human Rights Watch, www.hrw .org/americas/honduras.)

Point/Counterpoint

Was there a coup in Honduras, and if so, why?

a. If you say yes, how do you answer the claim that Zelaya was seeking to change a part of the constitution that is not subject to amendment? Whatever his motives for introducing social and economic reforms, why could he not have simply organized a party to promote a new pro-reform candidate?

b. If you say no, how do you answer the claim that the referendum was clearly advisory and that it should have been permitted under Article 2? In any event, were not the real motives for the action actually rooted in Zelaya's policies, not legalities?

For more information

You can find an English translation of the Honduran constitution at www.honduras.com/honduras-constitution//#sthash.2RXIGDaZ.dpuf. For good background on Honduras's history up to the 1980s, see Tom Barry and Deb Preusch, *The Central America Fact Book* (New York: Grove Press: 1986). WikiLeaks documents give many details about the removal of Zelaya and include cables showing that the U.S. embassy regarded the action as a coup. See www.wikileaks.org/plusd/cables/09TEGUCI-GALPA645_a.html. The graphs in this section are adapted from articles from the Washington-based Center for Economic and Policy Research (CEPR), which has several follow-up articles on Honduras since the "coup" at www.cepr.net.

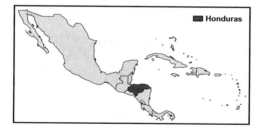

in the middle of night and flew him out of the country in June 2009. The military said it acted because Zelaya had ordered them to cooperate in holding an unconstitutional referendum. Both incidents attracted criticism from most other Latin American nations, while the conservative opposition to both presidents argued that the removals were constitutional, not coups. The argument and causes are laid out in two "Punto de Vista" sections of this chapter.

Political scientists who stress the importance of orderly governance see these events as democracy turned into mob rule; others see in these events an unprecedented awakening of people determined to no longer allow politicians to promise one thing and do another. A third interpretation sees the cases of Lugo and Zelaya as a kind of "constitutional coup" by which conservative elites, without the direct intervention of the military but with its support, remove a democratically elected president with a leftist agenda. After the leader is ousted, the new regime calls elections that "legitimize a successor" but effectively block the predecessor's efforts at social change (Maher 2012).

It is worth noting that the United States decried the forced resignations in Ecuador and Bolivia but expressed approval of the coups against Chávez and Aristide, elected presidents who resisted Washington's agenda for the hemisphere. In the case of Zelaya, the Obama

DEMOCRACY IN
HONDURAS

MEAN SUPPORT	47%
SUPPORT 2013	44%
SATISFACTION 2013	18%

administration objected but not long afterward retreated and ultimately accepted, over Latin American protests, the legitimacy of elections that installed a successor. In the case of Paraguay, Latin American governments expressed concerns about Lugo's removal, orchestrated by the right-wing majority in the country's Senate, but they did not take strong diplomatic action, as they did in the case of Honduras. The Obama administration limited itself publicly to calling for respect for democracy.

What these cases tell us is that institutions may be designed to function in a neutral fashion on paper, but in all countries they are embedded in social and economic systems that affect how well they function. If institutions did not matter at all, power would be exercised nakedly. Although some might welcome the opportunity to show the emperor without clothes, institutions are also what allow social and political life to function with some stability. Although institutions may be used by the powerful to restrict aspirations for change, it is difficult to imagine how any kind of democracy—direct, representative, participatory, and so on—could function without them. Polyarchies require institutions, but so would any other kind of democracy that might replace them. Institutions are critical to the function of **governance**.

For Review

What is impeachment of the street? How does the irregular, even if constitutional removal of presidents from office before their term reflect on the strength of political institutions and when does it reflect their weakness?

Fair Elections and Democratic Legitimacy

Whatever we may think about pluralism's strengths and weaknesses as a form of democracy, there is little doubt that in the post–Cold War world the holding of fair elections is the minimum standard by which democracy is judged. In a democracy, citizens must have the opportunity to turn out incumbents and elect a new government. Elections may not be a *sufficient* condition for democracy in the absence of equality and human rights, but they are a *necessary* condition. Hence, the health of the institution charged with conducting elections is critical to the overall health of democracy.

During the 1980s, Edward S. Herman and Frank Brodhead, dismayed by what they called "demonstration elections" staged by the United States in the Dominican Republic, Vietnam, and El Salvador, suggested six "criteria of election integrity" (Herman and Brodhead 1984: 11–15). They called these contests "demonstration elections" because the main purpose, say the authors, was to convince U.S. citizens that El Salvador was a democracy worth the support provided to wage counterinsurgency warfare against the FMLN. The criteria are listed here, along with the authors' assessment of how well El Salvador's 1982 elections, won by Christian Democrat Duarte, the candidate heavily backed by the United States, met them:

1. *Freedom of speech.* Citizens should be able to raise questions and criticize leaders. In El Salvador, in the early 1980s, a state of siege and rampant violence violated this provision. In 1982 alone, 1,500 citizens died at the hands of security forces.
2. *Freedom of the media.* This means a variety of media organs not under centralized control. In El Salvador, independent stations and newspapers had been subject to shut-downs, violence, and censorship in the years leading up to the 1982 elections.
3. *Freedom of organization of intermediate groups.* In effect, this is the freedom to associate and organize for change. In El Salvador, social movements and organizations had been decimated by violence.
4. *The absence of highly developed and pervasive instruments of state-sponsored terror.* This refers to the use of secret police, the military, and death squads linked to the incumbent regime to intimidate and silence opponents, a well-documented practice in the Salvadoran case.
5. *Freedom of party organization and ability to field candidates.* Organizations and parties must be able to support candidates and make alternatives known to citizens. In El Salvador, leftist and moderate leftist parties and candidates were assassinated and driven underground.
6. *Absence of coercion and fear on the part of the general population.* People have to be confident that their ballot will be secret and not subject them to harm. Salvadoran authorities used clear ballot boxes guarded by military personnel (an attempt in part to reduce fraud but intimidating nonetheless) and required voting by law. Voters were required to dip their thumbs in ink to show they voted and to prevent them from voting more than once. However, this meant that voters who might choose to abstain were readily identifiable to security forces and death squads.

Note that Frank and Brodhead concentrate less on the issue of fraudulent balloting on the day of the election and more on conditions in the period before the campaign. International observers often fly into a country to observe conditions on an election day, or perhaps the last few days before. Fewer are present to observe the atmosphere and conditions of the campaign itself and, therefore, to judge the six criteria we have just reviewed. That does not mean that observation serves no purpose. Obviously, ballots must be counted fairly on election day. Too often, that is in question in Latin America—though in the United States we should be somewhat cautious, given growing irregularities in our own election system. These irregularities were glaring in 2000 when the winning candidate actually received fewer votes than the loser in the Electoral College, and a bitter dispute crawled through the courts over the question of uncounted ballots in Florida. Although many in the United States believed our political institutions worked because the Supreme Court resolved the case, to many Latin Americans an outcome whereby the "winner" lacked a majority of votes, and where nine non-elected judges ruled in this way, took away a lot of moral authority from Washington's criticism of elections in their region.

The Mexican presidential elections of 2006 and 2012 were extremely controversial. In 2006, the Federal Election Institute (FEI) declared the PAN's Felipe Calderón the winner by only half of 1 percent of the total vote (243,000 of 41 million votes). López Obrador (known as AMLO), the PRD candidate, charged that there were irregularities at 50,000 of Mexico's 130,500 voting places. Some voting places reported turnouts of more than 100 percent. More than 1.6 million ballots were disallowed in areas where AMLO ran strongly. AMLO demanded a vote-by-vote recount, but the FEI only agreed to review the tallies from the voting places. In the end, Calderón was sworn in amid street demonstrations and turmoil. The 2012 election, won by the PRI candidate Peña Nieto, was similarly controversial, perhaps even more so, because in contrast to 2006, it generated huge protest marches by a nonpartisan movement, Yo Soy 132. The name, "I am 132," emerged after the PRI claimed that 131 protest videos uploaded to Facebook and YouTube by students had really been planted by Pena's political rivals. The demonstrators took to the streets supporting the students with signs saying they were each "132."

Examining the most recent records on voter turnout (defined as percentage of the voting-age population voting in the most recent legislative election), as of May 2014 only one country in Latin America (Colombia) had a lower turnout rate (see Table 13.1) in legislative elections than did the United States; and if we look only at legislative elections that did not coincide with presidential elections, the U.S. turnout of 38.5 percent is abysmal, even compared to Mexico and Colombia. Ecuador and Uruguay each had an amazing turnout of over 96 percent.

This is certainly a healthy sign for democracy, but it is worth keeping in mind that voting is compulsory in many countries. This practice is not unique to Latin America; several European countries also regard voting not merely as a right but as a duty. Failure to produce proof of voting (usually on a citizen ID) can result in a fine and loss of privileges, such as the right to obtain a passport or to open a bank account. However, we must remember as well that the era of military rule is still relatively fresh in the minds of most Latin Americans. The transitions to electoral democracy, however flawed they may have been, were the result of struggles carried out in the context of severe repression. Having won back the right to vote, Latin Americans may value it more.

Electoral laws and procedures are only as good as the institutions charged with implementing them. The emergence of international and national electoral observation as a fairly routine practice has helped in many cases to increase confidence and legitimacy of elections in politically polarized circumstances. Mexico's elections of 2000, when the PAN's Vicente Fox broke the 70-year hold of the PRI over the presidency, were significantly enhanced not only by international observer teams but also by the formation of Alianza Cívica, the mass movement of thousands of Mexican citizens who were deployed around the country to help ensure that fraud would not occur. But a good election means more than living up to the letter of law; it requires a bona fide commitment to fairness to the spirit. In highly polarized countries, that can be in short supply.

Although foreign observers can reinforce electoral fairness, sometimes they arrive with their own political agenda. Such was the case with a U.S. State Department team that observed the 1984 elections in Nicaragua. In that year the Sandinistas, only five years after seizing power through a popular insurrection against the Somoza dictatorship, decided to implement their first direct popular elections. The country had never before had an honest, contested election. In addition to the State Department, delegations came from a wide

TABLE 13.1 Turnout (% of Eligible Population) in Most Recent National Legislative Election

Country		Year	Last legislative only	Year
Argentina*	78.0%	2013	78.0%	2013
Bolivia*	85.6%	2009		
Brazil*	80.6%	2010		
Canada	53.7%	2011		
Chile*	73.1%	2013		
Colombia	45.9%	2014	45.9%	2014
Costa Rica*	64.3%	2014		
Cuba	88.8%	2013		
Dominican Republic*	58.6%	2010	58.6%	2006
Ecuador*	94.3%	2013		
El Salvador	61.6%	2009	52.7%	2006
Guatemala	70.0%	2011		
Honduras*	69.2%	2013		
Jamaica	46.2%	2011		
Mexico*	63.7%	2012	47.8%	2009
Nicaragua	71.8%	2011		
Panama*	70.5%	2009		
Paraguay*	58.1%	2013		
Peru*	87.4%	2011		
United States	54.6%	2012	38.5%	2010
Uruguay	96.9%	2009		
Venezuela	66.6%	2010	66.6%	2010

*Countries where voting is mandatory. Chile will no longer have mandatory voting in future elections.
Source: International Institute for Democracy and Electoral Assistance (www.idea.int/vt). Data from Center for Economic and Policy Research (CEPR)

variety of organizations and countries, including the Carter Center, Canada, the European Community, the Organization of American States (OAS), and the U.S.-based Latin American Studies Association (LASA).

Turnout in the election was 91 percent. Juan Tamayo, reporter for the *Miami Herald*, quoted a 67-year-old carpenter on the difference between this election and the ones he remembered. "Under Somoza you voted once, and someone else voted two more times in your name. These elections have a different air." Not surprisingly, the U.S. State Department observation team was the only one that denounced the elections, won convincingly by the Sandinistas, as unfair; all the others were positive. The LASA report called the elections the "cleanest held in Nicaragua since 1928, when U.S. marines were organizing and supervising the balloting" (LASA 1984: 26). There was a climate of fear, but the LASA delegation rejected

U.S. charges that the Sandinistas had created it. LASA (1984: 36) instead said the climate of fear was created by the U.S.-backed *contras* (see chapter 16) and the United States, which sent supersonic jets to create daily sonic booms over the country the week before the election. Despite the generally positive assessment of the 1984 election, many political scientists who are not area specialists date Nicaragua's "return to democracy" from the 1990 election of an opposition candidate, Violeta Chamorro.

In contrast to the 1984 Nicaraguan elections, the Salvadoran elections of 1982 studied by Herman and Brodhead were praised by the United States, even though the two main opposition newspapers had been shut down the previous year and between 20,000 and 30,000 people had been killed by security forces in the prior 30 months, including nearly 200 clergy, union and peasant organizers, and centrist and leftist politicians. The elections were marked by poor organization, with few polling places in many poor areas and with citizens having to drop ballots into clear boxes guarded by an army guilty of many abhorrent human rights atrocities. As noted previously in the discussion of Herman and Brodhead's criteria for election integrity, voters had their thumbs dipped in ink to prevent fraud, but this also meant that those not voting would be easily identified and marked as "traitors" by the military and death squads organized by D'Aubuisson (who backed a right-wing candidate in the election). However, this election, won by Washington's preferred candidate, Duarte, was certified "free and fair" by the State Department (Herman and Brodhead 1984: 93–152).

In recent years, controversial elections have taken place in Venezuela. Prior to 2006, the opposition to President Hugo Chávez generally insisted that his victories and those of his party were fraudulent. But the opposition candidate in the 2006 election acknowledged the reality of his landslide loss to Chávez. In 2007 the opposition in fact defeated two Chávez-backed packages of constitutional reforms by narrow margins. The National Electoral Council (CNE) uses computerized voting machines that, in addition to tallying ballots, checks thumbprints against a national registry to prevent duplicate voting and provides each voter with a paper receipt. In October 2012 former U.S. president Jimmy Carter said, "As a matter of fact, of the 92 elections that we've monitored, I would say the election process in Venezuela is the best in the world." In April 2013, Henrique Capriles, the opposition candidate, charged manipulation of the tabulations and called for a recount. The CNE was required by law only to audit a sample, but in an attempt to quell suspicion, it completed a complete audit of tabulations and confirmed the results.

So does this mean that the election was "free and fair"? If we apply Herman and Brodhead's criteria, we can say that the opposition had some grounds to contest the fairness of the broader process, but overall it was not prevented from getting out its message and contesting the election. The strongest case can be made on the charge of *ventajismo*—the illegal use of state resources to promote Maduro's candidacy. This included state vehicles to transport supporters to rallies and to the polls, favoritism on the state-owned television network, and not so thinly veiled messages to public employees that they had to vote for Maduro to keep their jobs. In addition, there was some reason to question whether the media and voters may have felt government intimidation. The government had refused to renew the license of a TV network implicated in fomenting a 48-hour coup against Chávez in 2002, and there were well-founded charges that the government had used a list of those who signed a petition to recall Chávez in 2004 to discriminate against opponents. However, one can debate whether any government would have renewed the license of a broadcaster that had participated in a coup attempt, and there never has been evidence that the secrecy of the ballot box (as opposed to a public petition) was compromised.

On the other side of the ledger, despite some legitimate concerns about suspending some candidates' eligibility for office based on charges of corruption, there were few restraints on the opposition's ability to campaign, and private media overwhelmingly supported the opposition. There is little doubt that Venezuelan voters were well aware of their options at the ballot box. The CNE had taken measures to ensure the anonymity of the vote. Venezuela has a high rate of criminal violence, but there was little real intimidation by the government. And the opposition benefited from going well beyond virtually unenforceable limits on campaign spending.

In short, there were legitimate concerns to be raised regarding Venezuela's electoral institutions' capacity to enforce rules of the campaign game and limit *ventajismo*. But there was little evidence to support the charge of outright fraud or to say that the opposition lacked a chance to get its message across to the people. To some extent, it is in the opposition's interest to attempt to discredit the legitimacy of electoral institutions. In 2014 several key opposition leaders, seizing the initiative in the context of student and middle-class protests against corruption and economic shortages, demanded President Maduro's resignation. Months of violence followed, much of it initiated by the opposition protestors but also including some abuses of authority by security forces. As of this writing, the next elections are for the National Assembly in 2015. It is highly unlikely that the opposition, should it lose, will accept them as legitimate, even if the votes are fairly counted on Election Day.

For Review

If you were sent on an observer team, what kinds of homework would you want to do in advance to do a better job? Why is it important to assess the campaigns and overall context of an election, not just the casting and counting of ballots?

Democratic Governance

Larry Diamond (2005:14), a **comparativist** who serves as a consultant to the NED, sees a "triple crisis of governance" in the world, including Latin America. The elements of this crisis, in his view, are (1) lack of accountability and rule of law as evidenced by criminal activity, human rights abuses, corruption, and so on; (2) "inability to manage regional and ethnic divisions peacefully and inclusively"; and (3) economic challenges resulting from failure to carry out neoliberal economic reforms fully. NED's approach to governance was initially promoted in the 1970s by the Trilateral Commission, an international association founded by David Rockefeller in 1973, a time when American influence in the world seemed to be ebbing and when European and Japanese influence seemed to be rising. The idea was to bring intellectual, political, and economic elites of the developed world together to work on problems of global governance. Many commission members were influential in the presidential administration of Jimmy Carter (1977–1980), when Washington first began to promote democratization as a way to head off revolution in the third world. The NED was created by the administration of Ronald Reagan to promote democracy. The *Journal of Democracy*, edited by Diamond and published by the NED, is a key intellectual forum for this purpose today.

Diamond and other political scientists involved in democracy promotion with the NED assume that neoliberal economic reforms—that is, reduction of the influence of the state over the market—will produce prosperity that will trickle down to everyone. Good government in this framework generally promotes honesty and transparency to reduce corruption and favoritism—whether to build political clientelism or preferences for local citizens in economic policies (such as policies that once promoted **import substitution**). For the World Bank, for example, good governance requires enforcement of contracts and effective enforcement of rules, but also a minimum regulatory burden on business. Good governance, it said in a study published in 1999, means "a well established system of market institutions—clear and transparent rules, fully functioning checks and balances (including strong enforcement mechanisms), and a robust competitive environment—[that] reduces opportunities for rent-seeking and hence incentives for corruption" (Broadman and Recanatini 1999: 2).

"**Rent-seeking**" refers to a tendency for private actors to seek wealth through their connections to government rather than through hard work and investments that involve risk taking. Looking back on the era of import substitution, the World Bank economists were drawing from the lesson that too much government ownership and regulation of economic goods and services leads citizens to such rent-seeking behavior. The market, they claimed, supposedly discourages such behavior. However, in the middle of 2008, that "consensus" came crashing down when deregulated banks and financial corporations faced bankruptcy as a consequence of financial speculation linked to the real estate market. In October of that year, the U.S. government moved to "bail out" these corporations by injecting US$700 billion into the credit market and buying equity (ownership shares) of several of them.

Many Latin American leaders reflected somewhat bitterly on how poorly governance seemed to function in the north. They also took note of how readily Washington seemed prepared to abandon deregulation of the market when faced with its own economic crisis. "There was plenty of advice from supposed specialists, to poor, developing countries," said Lula. "What was lacking was advice for rich countries, about the signs of financial mayhem that had been accumulating over time." Reflecting on his own personal history, and referring to the broad association of 20 large economies (in contrast to the few countries convened for summits of the G8), the Brazilian president went on to say,

> My whole life when I was a metal worker, was for me to buy a TV. I had to work another 40–60 hours per month, nearly killing myself. Today someone can become a billionaire without producing a single piece of paper, a single job, without producing a single salary. For this we need serious regulation coming from the G-20.
>
> (quoted in Astor 2008)

A broader conception of governance, one less tied to a particular economic system, was developed by the British Council, which considers governance as the "interaction between the formal institutions and those in civil society. Governance refers to a process whereby elements in society wield power, authority and influence and enact policies and decisions concerning public life and social upliftment" (Global Development Research Center n.d.). This definition raises the question, who needs to be "uplifted"? Still, in contrast to the Trilateral Commission, NED, and World Bank view, this approach does recognize that governance involves the ability of democracy to produce substantive, positive improvement in people's lives. In this respect, it goes beyond the idea that governance (and by implication, democratic governance) is to be judged in terms of efficient procedures.

Good governance and democracy are not the same. For example, an honest and efficient administration made up of aristocrats may produce less social upheaval than a corrupt, populist administration. This argument is made by some Asian political scientists and political leaders. Pan Wei, an American-educated political scientist at Beijing University, argues that the **rule of law** is more important to good governance than is democracy. The rule of law implies that law rather than the decisions of the rulers is what governs citizens. Democracy does not guarantee rule of law, Wei points out. Without rule of law, those who have won majority votes hold concentrated power, and they might turn a democracy into a tyranny of the majority that abuses the individuals' civil liberties. With the above distinctions, we also understand that "electoral democracy" is easy to build. Distributing ballot boxes is far easier than building checks and balances. That explains the many unstable and "low-quality" democracies in the world (Wei 2006: 9).

Critics of Wei think that only democracy ultimately guarantees rule by law. Without the discipline provided by periodic elections and freedom of the press, it is too easy for ruling sectors to hide their culpability and escape punishment. Wei, citing the ancient Greeks, responds that many other forms of state have relied on rule by law, not by men, to provide fairness and wisdom. Corruption is rife in many electoral democracies—something borne out by the Latin American experience. It seems easier to hold an election than to create fair and honest bureaucracies and judicial systems.

On the other hand, why should Latin Americans, or any people in a democracy for that matter, not expect both good governance and policies aimed at social uplift? Institutionalists such as Crisp (2000) generally advocate that constitutions be designed not only to represent diverse parts of society but also to facilitate decision-making by governing elites. Electoral systems and relationships among branches of government need to fulfill two goals that are somewhat at odds with one another: they should ensure deliberation and prevent passionate majorities from dominating minority rights and interests, but they should not throw the legislative and policy-making process into gridlock. This is closer to what Diamond and most of the transition theorists have in mind.

Effective rule of law requires working and respected judicial institutions. Several NGOs, as well as the World Bank and U.S. Agency for International Development, have put resources since 1980 toward expanding the number of judges, training prosecutors, and expanding budgets. Still, research (see Hammergren 2008, on the judiciaries) suggests that citizens have little confidence overall in these institutions. As we shall see in the next chapter, criminal justice systems in particular have come in for harsh criticism, and the perception of widespread impunity for corrupt officials persists.

Democratic governance can also be imagined to be something like Rousseau's concept of the social contract: one in which citizens are politically informed participants not just oriented toward their interests but concerned about the general will—about what is best for society as a whole. This is closer to good governance as expressed by the British Council and to the approach advocated by the Brazilian political scientist Leonardo Avritzer (2002). Crisp argues that good institutions encourage good governance by ensuring that participation is channeled and influences elite decision-making, whereas Avritzer sees good institutions as those that foster decision-making through popular participation.

For Review

Why do some say that the concepts of "good governance" and "rule of law" should be separated from democracy? What role does a judiciary have in making rule of law a reality? What role do checks and balances play in promoting rule of law? Why might rule of law and good governance be needed to promote economic development?

New Institutionalism and Constitutional Design

The "new institutionalism" departs from the uncontroversial premise that constitutional designs affect the decisions that politicians and citizens make, and in doing so, they may enhance or inhibit effective governance. A few go beyond this assumption to argue that institutions be designed to reflect the assumption that institutions are most wisely structured when they assume that all humans, regardless of culture, act to maximize benefits and minimize costs—that is, they exercise rational choice (Morgenstern and Nacif 2002). This includes assuming, as the writers of the U.S. constitution did, that when it comes to politicians, they are motivated mainly by ambition. Many area studies specialists, including Latin Americanists, believe that such an approach fails to take cultural and social class differences into account adequately. Still, virtually all of the region's constitutions attempt to incorporate the U.S. tradition of checks and balances, especially in regard to relations between the executive branch and the legislative branch. But in their constitutions, Latin American countries differ from the United States and among themselves in regard to how the president is elected, the system of representation used in legislative elections, the rules for passing legislation, and the powers assigned to each branch.

Executive–Legislative Relationships

Institutionalists argue that constitutional design affects, among many things, the ability of leaders to forge coalitions in legislatures, the ability of courts or legislatures to check the programs of presidents, and the ability of people to hold elected officials accountable. When it comes to immediate matters of public policy—for example, the ability of presidents to privatize the banking system, nationalize copper mines, push a treaty through a congress, and so on—the institutions and the rules of the game defined by constitutions can determine success or failure, at least at the moment of decision-making. Of course, social and economic sources of power can be brought to bear upon the institution and its members.

Latin American constitutions have tended to emulate the U.S. system in providing for election of the president and separation of powers, rather than the parliamentary model, more common elsewhere in the world. In a parliamentary model, a prime minister and/ or cabinet is chosen by an elected, representative assembly that can also remove the chief executive by a vote of no confidence. This pattern is found often in the small Caribbean republics that were once colonies of Britain, France, and the Netherlands. Few institutionalists advocate substitution of the parliamentary model for the U.S.-style system (Mainwaring and Shugart 1997). Instead, they tend to emphasize strengthening the capacity of the legislative and judicial branches to check the power of presidents to act in excess of the spirit or letter of the constitution.

In general, Latin American constitutions give significant decree powers to presidents. Usually, these powers are limited to "emergencies," but this condition is interpreted loosely, to say the least, by many presidents. Legislatures also grant decree powers to a president to escape responsibility for unpopular policies, thereby allowing the president to assume credit or blame. This was a factor in Argentina when President Carlos Menem, the Peronist who governed for two terms from 1989 to 1999, issued 166 "decrees of necessity and urgency" in his first eight years. In the prior 140 years, presidents had used this power, bestowed by the constitution of 1853, only 35 times. Most of these decrees were anything but necessary or urgent, and the Argentine courts could have acted to curb the president's abuse of authority. However, Menem had packed the country's Supreme Court with supporters to ensure that they would not be overturned (data cited by Mustapic 2002: 30).

Research on the degree to which presidents can successfully move programs through legislatures rather than around them suggests that in general, legislatures in Latin America do not have the institutional power characteristic of the U.S. Congress, where bills originate before they become law. In one case (Chile), the executive even has the right to have its own representatives participate in the deliberations of legislative committees, quite a departure from the principle of separation of powers (Crisp 2000; Morgenstern and Nacif 2002). Many of the most important measures enacted by President Chávez in Venezuela in 2001 and 2007 were done through decree-making powers granted by the National Assembly, where the government party enjoyed a strong majority.

The success of presidents in advancing agendas varies in some predictable ways. Obviously, it helps when the president's party has a majority or at least a large plurality in the legislature. This tends to be the case when legislative elections occur at the same time or shortly after the presidential election, so constitutional design can matter here. A second variable that matters is the degree of discipline that party leaders exercise over their delegations in legislatures. This can be an advantage when the president has a majority but a disadvantage (making it harder to pry opposition votes away) when he or she faces a Congress controlled by opposition parties.

Legislatures in polyarchies often have investigative and oversight powers as well, usually exercised through committees. Latin American legislatures might have these powers on paper, but they rarely exercise them effectively in routine situations. However, when presidents with radical agendas face legislatures with opposition majorities, the result can be toxic to democracy, as Salvador Allende discovered with tragic consequences in 1973 (see chapter 7).

Cuba would seem to represent one more case of highly centralized power, although it is not clear whether the decisive actor in votes of National Assembly members is the Cuban

Communist Party (PCC) or the personal power of Raúl Castro (who succeeded Fidel in 2006). Although the Cuban legislature often reaches decisions by unanimous vote, there often takes place beforehand a long period of discussion and consultation with people in local meetings before a consensus is reached (Roman 2003). Unlike the former communist states of Eastern Europe and those of contemporary Asia, the PCC does not seem to act strictly as a shadow government behind Cuba's political institutions. However, the PCC is constitutionally defined as the country's only legal party, and Cuba certainly falls into the category of countries with powerful executives and highly disciplined party politics. Raúl says that he will retire from politics when his five-year term as president expires in 2018. New social forces arising from openings to the market and the passing, finally, of the generation that led Cuba's 1959 revolution are likely to put the durability of Cuba's institutions to the test and generate pressures for political liberalization.

Parties, Legislatures, Executives, and Reform

Party systems, election systems, and the rules by which legislatures operate all interact with one another in ways that vary from country to country, not only in Latin America, but everywhere in the world. Many Latin American parties exercise a high degree of discipline over legislators, meaning that the representatives tend to vote as party leaders dictate and defy them only at risk to their careers. Sometimes this can be an advantage for governance because it makes it easier to fashion majorities to pass legislation, but discipline can also be used to block compromise. At an extreme, highly disciplined parties that allow for little independent judgment by members of a congress or assembly may result in a "crisis of representation." That is, citizens may feel they have no real representation because politicians are completely at the mercy of their party authorities.

Perhaps the best example of such a crisis was the utter collapse of Venezuela's party system in the 1998 and 2000 elections. As we reviewed in chapter 9, the two main parties that dominated the Punto Fijo era, AD (Democratic Action) and COPEI (Christian Democrats), suffered ignominious falls, due in part to pent-up civic anger at their resistance to democratic reform and inability to respond to economic woes. Throughout most of this period, Venezuela appeared to be a model **polyarchy** because of its two-party system and accumulated experience with peaceful presidential transitions through elections, standing in contrast to the stark military rule elsewhere in the region. There were multiple reasons that this system unraveled so quickly in the 1990s, not the least of which was tumbling oil prices. A crisis of representation linked closely to party structures impervious to popular discontent was certainly among those reasons too.

The political careers of legislators in both AD and COPEI depended entirely on the good will of national party leaders. These leaders could award or deny aspiring politicians a place on the party's ballot anywhere in the country, regardless of the particular politician's standing at the local level. Both parties had disciplinary committees that could and did expel politicians who might break ranks on important legislative votes or speak out independently on important issues. This discipline was exerted not only on deputies and senators in Caracas but also on state and local politicians, rendering the constitutional system of federalism, which on paper gave some autonomy to state governments, virtually meaningless. Party leaders could also punish maverick party members by denying them resources from the budget, a factor reinforced in this case by the copious financial resources concentrated in the central government as a result of its control over oil-export earnings (see Buxton 2001; Coppedge 1994; Crisp 2000).

In the Venezuelan case, on some occasions (when COPEI held the presidency and AD the legislature), the president faced a disciplined opposition majority in Congress. This made negotiation necessary to break stalemates. This took place among party leaders outside the halls of Congress, not through a process of compromise and adaptation, as bills moved through the Senate or Chamber of Deputies (Crisp 2000). When serious differences over legislation arose, as was the case with attempts to revise the pension system in the 1990s, the president often looked outside the legislative process, asking commissions composed of representatives of labor unions, business, and government to reach an accord. There was little drama in legislative votes themselves as the word of party leaders was law within each congressional delegation. Congressional votes could be recorded simply by noting a nod of the head from the leader of the largest party or coalition of parties. Smaller parties operated under the same rules. Centralization was so complete that central party authorities could impose nominees from one part of the country on another and be confident of winning because of disciplined voting by party members. Venezuelans called these politicos *paracaídos* (parachutists) because they dropped in out of nowhere, anointed by *caciques* far away in Caracas to "represent" local communities where they did not live.

Under pressure, Venezuela's two main parties did initiate some reforms, but partial reform in some ways was worse than none at all. For example, by allowing governors to be elected by direct popular vote for the first time in 1989, the parties allowed the emergence of political leaders with an independent base of support—the direct support of voters in their home state. The parties continued to deny more comprehensive reform, but at the same time, they had created a new class of politicians not subjected to their discipline. Meanwhile, the national leaders continued to absorb the blame for squandering the country's oil wealth. Then came political Armageddon when Chávez was swept into office in 1998 and fulfilled his promise to call a constituent assembly to write a new constitution (see chapter 9).

One thing institutional design does is establish the rules of the political game. That is, it establishes the mechanisms by which decisions are made, and thus, changing them can affect (but not always) the distribution of power, the regime. Chávez used his overwhelming popularity, including considerable support from the middle class (which later turned against him), to change the rules of the political game in Venezuela. He had most of the constituent assembly elected by the uninominal method—that is, one representative per district—which greatly favored the alliance of parties that backed him in his comfortable presidential victory. He also enjoyed power that emanated from his charisma; Chávez mattered more than the organizational strength of the old parties. The new constitution of 1999 created a mixed system (part proportional, part uninominal), but by the time of elections for the new national assembly, the grip of AD and COPEI had already been broken. In the July 2000 contest, COPEI almost disappeared off the political map entirely; AD survived as a moderate-size opposition party, just one part of a coalition of numerous parties opposed to Chávez.

The new "Bolivarian" constitution, not surprisingly, was written with the maladies of the old system in mind. It requires internal primaries (only sometimes respected in practice) to weaken the grip of party secretaries (leaders), and it mandates quotas for representation of women. In keeping with the spirit of fostering participatory government, civil groups are supposed to be consulted about appointments of judges and three key government posts—the attorney general, human rights ombudsman (someone who acts on behalf of the citizenry), and comptroller (auditor). These are significant changes, but as so often happens, they have not been fully implemented. The party founded by Chávez, the United Socialist Party of Venezuela (PSUV), is supposed to serve as a vehicle for social movements and grassroots activists to participate actively in making policies. Party cadres are often inspired to work to make this goal a reality in their communities, but the practices of the past continue to manifest themselves in the present. As oil income is passed from the executive branch to local communal councils, there are great opportunities for graft and patronage.

As long as Chávez was alive, there was little question about who had the final word on nominations or how the party would vote in the assembly. With his death in March 2013, the party rallied behind his designated successor, Nicolás Maduro. Maduro won the election to replace Chávez but by such a narrow margin (less than two points) that it left the Bolivarian movement stunned, as though Maduro had lost. Without the charismatic Bolivarian leader, it was not clear how well both the constitution and the PSUV would function. The national charter lays out impressive mechanisms both to check centralized power and to empower citizens to be protagonists of legislation. However, these principles run up against the reality that the financial resources are necessarily accumulated by the state, which manages how the valuable resource below its soil is exploited. Ultimately, Venezuela needs institutions that channel the financial resources in directions that promote the general welfare. The country has been struggling since 1935 to build such institutions, and today the country is divided into two highly polarized camps. The polarization is in part about who controls the oil revenues and in part about whether the institutions of polyarchy or some form of **twenty-first-century socialism** provides the best way to manage them.

Mexico's political institutions (pre-2000) arguably responded with more agility to that country's crisis of representation, which was increasingly visible between 1968 and 2000. The 1918 Mexican constitution was written in part to prevent another president from accumulating the power achieved by Porfirio Díaz before the 1910 revolution. However, the dominance of the highly disciplined Institutional Revolutionary Party (PRI) and centralized control over spending defeated this goal. The formation of a disciplined revolutionary party between 1924 and 1940 assured that the new system *would not* be characterized by a weak presidency. In fact, the president's command over the party made the Mexican Congress little more than a rubber stamp. Because the PRI held an overwhelming majority of seats, virtually no institutional check over the president's legislative power existed. The system suddenly changed when the PRI lost its majority in 1997, and Mexican presidents since that time, beginning with Fox, have had much more difficulty assembling a stable legislative majority than did their predecessors (see Craig and Cornelius 1995).

The PRI in 1997 finally lost its ability to hold onto a congressional majority through fraud. The new legislative majority, composed of the conservative PAN and leftist PRD, cooperated enough to deny the PRI and the Mexican president (Ernesto Zedillo) a majority in Congress. After Vicente Fox of the PAN won the 2000 election, he faced a similar situation, now with the PRI and the PRD in the majority. Mexico evolved into a three-party system, with little love lost among any of the three for one another. The result, in contrast to the Venezuelan case, for better or worse, was gridlock. President Vicente Fox (2001–2006) of the PAN found an even more difficult situation. A fiscal conservative, Fox found it almost impossible to move his budget through a Congress in which his party was a distinct minority. The populist PRI and the leftist PRD not only had different budget priorities than the business-oriented Fox but also had a political motive to embarrass the president and his party. Fox's successor, Felipe Calderón (2007–2012), was even less successful in gaining legislative support for his agenda.

Until 1997, Mexico's presidents had experienced little trouble getting an annual budget passed, despite constitutional provisions that give the Mexican Congress great discretion to change it. These provisions are quite unusual for Latin America. For example, in Chile the president introduces the budget, and it becomes law in 60 days even if Congress fails to approve it. Mexican president Ernesto Zedillo (1994–2000) was the victim of his own good intentions. Having refused to cooperate with his party's (PRI) attempts to hold onto a congressional majority by electoral fraud, he now had to negotiate with the two opposition parties to pass his budgets. Though they were ideologically opposed, the PAN and PRD cooperated in the new environment to seize a share of some of the patronage previously monopolized by the PRI.

Does this mean Mexican presidents have lost the ability to move legislation as their predecessors did in the era before the neoliberal economic and political reforms of the 1990s? President Enrique Peña Nieto, who recaptured the presidency for the PRI in 2012, was able to forge a pact among the three parties for some important measures, including opening the oil sector to private investment, creating a new regulatory commission, restricting the power of some of the most corrupt unions, and reducing the monopoly power of the media networks privatized in the 1990s. To some observers, these were needed reforms (*Christian Science Monitor*, editorial, March 24, 2013); to others (e.g., La Botz 2012) they are setbacks for Mexican workers. Either way, they show some recovery of an institutional capacity lacking in the first 12 years after the defeat of the PRI by Fox in 2000.

Latin America's party systems impose more discipline on legislators than does the U.S. system, but most are not as tight as in the Cuban, the Venezuelan, and (formerly) the Mexican cases. Probably the least disciplined parties are found in Brazil and Colombia, where legislators have high incentives to think first of their own interest in getting elected and not of the party's interest. They get relatively little help from national parties in elections. In Colombia, primaries within the dominant Liberal and Conservative parties make for intense intraparty competition. As noted in the preceding chapter, this makes Colombian parties porous—quite unlike the Chilean and Venezuelan cases, and more like the Brazilian case. That is, Colombian parties are more like vehicles that different movements, factions, and interests can ride. Argentina's Peronism seems have taken on this porous quality as well.

In Brazil, most representatives serve one term in the Chamber of Deputies or the Senate and then return to their states or cities to continue their careers in elective office or the bureaucracy. Their main objective, then, is to deliver enough benefits to their home areas that local political bosses will provide a job or support their political ambitions on their return to home. "No one who follows Brazilian politics doubts that pork-barrel programs and control over appointive jobs are the mother's milk of legislative majorities," writes Barry Ames (2002:196). The large number of Brazilian parties—six major ones alone—further complicates the situation. A Brazilian president must use great skill and all the patronage resources he can muster to move legislation through Congress. Fernando Collor de Mello (1990–1992) tried to do this with decrees and outright corruption, and he ended up being impeached and removed from office. Fernando Henrique Cardoso (1995–2002) used a different tactic, giving small parties positions in the cabinet. To some degree, then, Brazil's presidential system functions somewhat like parliamentary systems, where minority premiers must cobble together majority coalitions in the same way (Ames 2002; Neto 2002). The result is coalition politics built around patronage, not an agenda for government. This fact of political life in Brazil partly explains the *mensalão* (see chapter 12 and later in this chapter) scandal that engulfed Lula and the Workers' Party (PT) in 2005–2006.

We have already seen that federalism does not always result in decentralized politics, but in the right circumstances, governors and even mayors (e.g., of capital cities such as Caracas, Mexico City, and Santiago de Chile) can play a key role in determining the ability of a president to carry out a program. Brazil is where this has had the greatest relevance. Governors control security forces and have used them to thwart environmental protection of the rainforest and efforts to prosecute landlords who have used violence, including murder, to repress the environmental and the landless peasants' movement in several states.

Decentralization of budget resources, direct election of governors, and relaxed party discipline strengthened the role of state officials, especially governors, in Mexico and Venezuela in the 1990s. Both countries saw presidential candidates of weight emerge from state houses as a result of governors gaining more political independence and resources. In three presidential elections won by Chávez, his main competition came from a governor. Governors are often looking ahead in their careers; presidents are usually at the pinnacle of their political lives. Elected governors have a base to oppose unpopular policies and leaders. Their independent budgetary power may thwart attempts to impose neoliberal policies in the center, as Argentine presidents discovered in the late 1990s. Argentina's Nestor Kirchner, president from 2003 until 2007, was governor of the relatively remote Santa Cruz province from 1991 to 2001. Although his fellow Peronist, Carlos Menem, experienced a dramatic collapse of his popularity in 1999, Kirchner remained popular for having successfully promoted and presided over a high rate of economic growth in Santa Cruz. In 2003, Kirchner got only 22 percent of the vote in the first round of presidential voting; Menem, trying to return to office, got 24 percent, but he sensed correctly that the voters would swing behind Kirchner in the second round, so the former president withdrew. Thus, the obscure governor of a remote province rose to the presidency.

Though technically not a primary, the first round in Argentina now functions that way. In the first round, multiple Peronists run, but the opposition is so weak that there is little doubt that the top two finishers will both be Peronists. Of course, this could change in the future should a new alternative to the Peronists emerge. Nonetheless, we can see in this example that what constitutes a political system is more than just the complex of institutions defined and shaped by its formal constitution; the same formal rules may function differently in reality. In France, for example, the first round features many different parties running candidates, with two going on to the second. In Argentina, it would not be surprising to see two Peronists face each other in the second round. **Institutional design** is done with intentions, but they do not always work as planned.

Inside Political Parties

The foregoing discussion demonstrates the way that (1) party politics, (2) relationships between the executive and legislative branches, and (3) the degree to which political power is centralized are all interrelated. Despite strong traditions of federalism in Venezuela and Mexico, tightly disciplined parties foster a high degree of centralization. Colombia's parties are extremely porous—that is, less tightly disciplined, looser in their organization. Parties in Argentina, Brazil, and Chile fall somewhere in between the extremes of Venezuela and Mexico on one side and Colombia on the other.

Argentina

President Carlos Menem of Argentina (1989–1999) faced considerable opposition to his neoliberal economic program within his own Peronist Party. Although Menem used and abused decree powers to circumvent problems with Peronists in Congress, he sought legislative approval on some matters (e.g., broad tax reform) to make it more difficult to reverse his program in the future. Menem was able to use patronage to exert enough control over the Partido Justicialista (PJ, as the Peronist organization is officially named) to place allies in key positions in Congress.

Four factors facilitated the president's task. First, although unionized workers were the key sector organized by Juan Perón in building his party in the 1940s, the internal structures of the PJ did not give the unions a formal voting power; that is, Perón never *institutionalized* labor's influence in his party, so Menem could ignore the unions in formal party votes. Second, the Peronists returned to power in 1983 after a harsh dictatorship had violently repressed labor, leaving unions significantly weaker than they were before the military government. Peronist politicians now relied less on labor support than on the distribution of patronage in general. They began to think of the party less as a labor-based party and more as a catch-all party seeking broad support to win political office in different provinces. Third, the closing of many factories and the shift to service industries had reduced the weight of organized labor in the workforce. Fourth, the growth of right-wing civilian influence offered Menem some allies to help him prevail over opponents in his own party (Levitsky 2000).

What we see here is an example of how social changes (the shift in workforce patterns, changing attitudes in the electorate) reshaped one of the key institutions in Argentine politics. Menem ruled over and through the Peronist Party, but by the time he left office, the party had become much more of a catch-all party and less of a working-class party. When economic crisis arrived and Menem fell from grace with the public, the party proved incapable of pulling together the needed leadership to emerge from the crisis—until another strong figure, Nestor Kirchner, emerged. Kirchner, with considerable assistance (oil and financing) from Venezuela's President Chávez, was able to resist an IMF structural adjustment plan, and Argentina experienced significant economic growth during his presidency. Like Menem at the height of his popularity, Kirchner ruled over and through the party, but it was not long before events showed how porous Peronism had become.

Kirchner's successor, Maria Cristina Fernández de Kirchner, his wife but also a successful politician in her own right, came to the presidency in 2007. She assumed office in fortuitous circumstances. Argentina's agricultural exports, especially soybeans, were experiencing a boom. Fernández de Kirchner attempted to impose what amounts to a windfall-profits tax on farmers, but they responded with mass protests, including blockades of highways linking the cities to food supplies in the countryside. President Kirchner thought that she would lessen her association with the unpopular measure if she had Congress vote on the tax rather than use executive power to impose it. The lower house approved it by a scant 128–122 margin. Then, to her surprise, she lost the vote in the Senate when her own vice president, a fellow Peronist, broke a tie and defeated the proposal. By 2009, the Kirchner faction of Peronism had lost the dominance it once enjoyed, faring badly in local elections (though it recovered along with the economy afterward). There may have been an element of gender bias at work as well—a desire to put a female president "in her place." For whatever reason, we see that presidentialism does not always win out in power struggles.

Chile

Post-dictatorial Chile is where constitutional design has probably left the strongest imprint on presidential powers. Here, the parties are more defined and disciplined than in Argentina, but the constitutional framework greatly limits legislative powers in key areas dealing with human rights and economic policy.

Before 1973 three blocks of parties—left, center, and right—contested one another for power, but the experience of dictatorship and the retreat of the socialists from revolutionary politics brought about a reconfiguration. The Christian Democratic Party (PDC) joined with two socialist parties to form the Concertación coalition in support of the 1989 plebiscite that forced Pinochet from the presidency. The Concertación had incentives to stay together for the subsequent elections. One is success; Concertación candidates won four presidential elections in succession after 1990. Christian Democrats Ricardo Aylwin and Eduardo Frei Jr. were the successful coalition candidates in the first two elections. They were followed by two socialists, Ricardo Lagos in 2000 and Michelle Bachelet in 2006. In January 2010, Sebastian Piñera, candidate of the conservative bloc opposing the Concertación, broke through to win.

Presidents in Chile need party support to move legislation, and they have some leverage. Chilean legislators, unlike most of their counterparts in Latin America, seem oriented toward political careers, not short stays in the Senate or the Chamber of Deputies. Members need to balance pleasing their party (to get on the ballot) with pleasing their constituents because, with some limited exceptions, voters cast a ballot for parties, each of which decides who will appear on a list of two candidates for each district (or each province for Senate elections). But there is a countervailing influence. Legislators who hope to be reelected also need to deliver benefits at home, and to do this, they must avoid alienating the president, who enjoys very strong control over the budget (Cary 2002).

This system is a legacy of the Pinochet era. The price of ending his dictatorship (1973–1989) was acceptance of his 1981 constitution (see chapter 8), which contains various mechanisms that make it difficult for any profound change in the economic and political model to be put in place. The biggest obstacle is the Senate. The constitution allowed Pinochet to appoint nine senators, while he himself was a senator for life. Although this advantage would diminish over time until it was finally abolished in 2005, it made the Senate a major obstacle to any attempt to change economic policies or move on issues such as human rights.

Also, it takes a three-fifths majority to reform the constitution, and the system of election continues to load the chamber in favor of the conservative parties. In each province or district, two senators or deputies (respectively) are elected simultaneously, and as we have seen, each voter casts only one ballot. Votes are counted, and one seat goes to the party with the most votes, with the other going to the party that finishes second—unless the top vote-getting party doubles the total obtained by the party finishing second. To change the most important ("organic") laws requires a super two-thirds majority, making it almost impossible to change tax laws favorable to foreign investors, reverse privatization, eliminate the automatic reservation of a percentage of copper export earnings (the largest source of Chile's foreign exchange) for the military, or make changes in the constitution. In the December 2006 elections, the Concertación won 52 percent of the Senate vote nationally, with 40 percent for the right-wing coalition (the rest going to smaller parties), but it controlled only 20 of 38 seats, far short of what it would need to change organic laws.

Perhaps there is no better example of how institutions can limit as well as enhance democracy. Many Chileans thought that Pinochet's departure would bring the military to account for killings, torture, or disappearances under the dictatorship. Many thought that the neoliberal economic model, which had been criticized by many Concertación public figures in the Pinochet years, would be modified to narrow the gap between rich and poor. Once in control of the executive, the Concertación did increase social spending in some areas, and toward the end of the 1990s, it finally pressed human rights investigations and indictments for some crimes committed under Pinochet. However, the new government largely honored its commitment—arguably made under duress—to accept the 1981 constitution, which severely limited its ability to change basic laws or prosecute perpetrators of gross human rights violations. Defenders of the limits on majority rule point to the relative degree of macroeconomic success enjoyed by Chile under this system, which they attribute at least in part to the political stability the constitution seems to have brought. In 2009, President Bachelet managed to pass a new law that automatically registers all citizens, making them eligible to vote. However, part of the compromise needed to gain enough votes from the opposition was elimination of the law requiring voting (a common requirement in Latin America, though often unenforced).

It is difficult to assess the degree to which Concertación leaders have used the constitution to avoid making significant changes in an economic model they fiercely criticized in the Pinochet era. Are the institutions driving the policy, or is a conservative impulse not to disturb the economic model the motive for a less aggressive attempt to make the institutions more democratic? In 2010, Bachelet, popular but ineligible to run for reelection, saw the Concertación lose a presidential election for the first time to Piñera. As noted in chapter 8, the election also saw the emergence of a leftist candidacy independent of the Concertación, but at the same time, the election was notable for low turnout and lack of voter enthusiasm. In addition, the end of Bachelet's term saw the sudden emergence of a mass student movement, which quickly grew into a larger civic protest movement encompassing workers, indigenous people, environmentalists, and others.

As elections approached in 2014, the Concertación decided to expand the left-center coalition to take in the Chilean Communist Party, which had gained in prestige for its support of the protests against inequality. Neither the new coalition, New Majority, on the left nor the Alliance coalition on the right generated enthusiasm from voters. Bachelet (eligible again) ultimately secured the nomination to launch a bid for a new presidential term, promising to seek an overhaul of the system by calling a constituent assembly to rewrite the constitution. She won the presidential election in a runoff, but legislative elections did not provide a large enough majority to call an assembly without some votes from the right. Early in 2014 the demonstrations largely focused on supporting the new president's efforts

Supporters listening to Michelle Bachelet give a speech on election night after winning a new term as president. She has promised to narrow the gap between rich and poor. Are Latin Americans expecting too much from their presidents?

to secure the votes she needed. There were some indications that some sectors in the opposition were ready for some reform, but it will be difficult for Bachelet to meet the demands of protestors and make the compromises needed to secure these votes. Chile, which has generally replaced Venezuela as the model "polyarchy," may soon face a test to see whether it can reform its institutions before a crisis of representation overtakes them.

Brazil

Brazil's highly fractured party system, long ridden by clientelism and corruption, raises a question: to what extent is corruption a product of bad people versus bad institutions? The election of Lula in 2002 was greeted as a landmark event. He was one of the 13 children born to Euridice Ferreira de Mello, whose husband left home to work on the docks, carrying coffee sacks onto freighters in the port of Santos. Lula went to work at the age of 12 years and eventually found a good job in São Paolo's metallurgical industry, where he became a union leader. In 1980, he cofounded the Workers' Party (PT) and led it through the strikes and protests that sent the military back to the barracks. Workers with dark skin had little prospects of political success before the PT emerged, but in his fourth try, in November 2002, Lula won the Brazilian presidency with 61 percent of the vote in the runoff.

Lula's own background, the way that the PT had emerged as the bottom-up movement of social movements, and the general swing to the left in Latin American politics around this time suggested that Brazil would become a political and economic laboratory for confronting poverty. Lula did implement an anti-hunger program and an aid plan for alleviation of poverty among the poor. By tying aid to school attendance, he not only had success in reducing hunger but also substantially increased school attendance. It should be noted, however, that Fernando Henrique Cardoso, his predecessor, had initiated the policy.

In international affairs Lula challenged the United States on several issues, but his economic policies did not radically depart from that of Cardoso. In fact, one of the first laws passed during his term was a social security reform that reduced pension rights. Land reform fell well behind promised goals, prompting the Landless Workers' Movement (MST; see chapter 11) to begin seizing properties it deemed eligible for redistribution, resulting in violent confrontations with local authorities and landowners. To gain the confidence of international banks, but much to the dismay of his supporters, Lula appointed a member of the conservative opposition to be president of the Central Bank. He appointed a member of the PT as finance minister, but one who as mayor had privatized a municipal phone company. The "worker president" began to hear criticism from the ranks of the PT; in response, he expelled the party's left wing, which formed a new party, the Party of Socialism and Liberty.

Despite these policies, not all conservatives were mollified. Some remained eager to corral the president, even to topple him, if necessary. In 2005, they were presented with an opportunity when several serious scandals erupted. Two major corruption scandals involving payoffs to politicians of the PT and allied parties by the construction and insurance industries were the first blows, but the hardest came in the form of charges in Congress that the votes of opposition deputies were being bought with payoffs of US$12,000 per month— the *mensalão*. Most seriously, Lula's chief of staff, Minister José Dirceu, was among those indicted for corruption. The scandals severely reduced the president's influence in Congress and left him vulnerable to losing his reelection campaign in 2006.

Lula faced a choice in 2006. One option was to turn left and attempt to mobilize Brazil's poor with a more vigorous popular program, but this would jeopardize the stability of the capitalist economy. The other was to govern within the parameters set by Washington and influential business interests in the hope that Brazilians would prefer a president symbolically from the ranks of the workers but unable to introduce substantial changes in the economic model. The second strategy proved successful. Lula lost the election in the heartland of the PT, the industrial states of the south, but he picked up votes from the middle class and from voters in the impoverished northeast to prevail. His second term did not produce major advances on promises made in 2002, but Lula was more assertive in his diplomacy, challenging Washington on Honduras, Cuba, Iran, economic integration, and a host of other issues.

What do Lula's problems have to do with Brazil's institutions? Legislative elections had already occurred in October, one month before the final presidential runoff in 2003, so Lula's initial victory did little to help his party in Congress. As Lula entered office, the PT held only 14 seats in the 81-seat Senate. Only one-third of the Senate was to be replaced in October 2006, so the party had little prospect of controlling the upper chamber. In the Chamber of Deputies, the PT held only 81 of 513 seats. The entire chamber was scheduled to be renewed in the presidential election year of 2006, but Lula was now damaged goods, mired in scandal, his party divided and demoralized. The party suffered a stinging defeat, falling to just 11 seats in the Senate and gaining only 2 seats in the lower chamber. Lula would have to build coalitions, as in his first term, to govern.

Brazil's Congress is highly fragmented. Six parties are considered major players, but no fewer than 11 parties had 12 or more seats in the lower chamber after the 2002 elections. Brazilian politicians are notorious for changing party identifications, especially if they can enhance career prospects near the end of their terms (few run for reelection). Brazil's voters choose elected representatives by the proportional method that ordinarily strengthens party leaders. However, until the advent of the PT, none of Brazil's parties had deployed an effective organized presence throughout all regions of the country. Parties have tended to form in states and regions around powerful personalities, the *coroneles*. Remember, Brazil is a huge country, a landmass corresponding to the entire Portuguese empire in America, which did not break up after independence. Much power remains on the local and state levels. In the age of populist president Getúlio Vargas (see chapter 5), two large national parties formed around his leadership, but these political organizations were often fractured into suborganizations supporting local leaders. Not unlike the United States, a large landmass and strong tradition of federalism have combined to dampen the coherence of national parties—something the PT itself has experienced in recent years.

The PT, like other left parties, found it hard to shift from being the opposition to becoming the party of government. The party rose to power in part as a result of public disgust with clientelism and corruption, and it had organically grown out of social movements. Here again the structures and institutions have to be considered, not just the personal morality of Lula and other PT leaders. Just like his predecessors, Lula found himself offering cabinet positions, policy concessions, and patronage to members of other parties to pass laws. The resources at his disposal were considerable—as many as 20,000 government jobs. Leaders linked to social movements became politicians, and experience in government changed the perspective of many. The party has become divided between grassroots members who remain linked to social movements and see the PT as a political tool to make profound social change and more pragmatic members who seek to broaden the party's support in the interest of keeping government power.

Brazil's social movements found themselves in a dilemma. In a "Letter to the Brazilian People" (circulated by e-mail on June 23, 2005), the Coordinator of Social Movements (CMS), which unites the largest popular organizations in the country, attributed the *mensalão* scandal to elites who "with the 2006 election in mind initiated a campaign to demoralize the government and President Lula, seeking to weaken him, to overthrow him, or to oblige him to deepen current economic policy and neoliberal reforms, obedient to the interests of international capital." The CMS called for full investigation of corruption accusations and charged that President Cardoso had employed the same tactics to privatize state enterprises and secure a constitutional amendment allowing his reelection.

The CMS also asked Lula to change economic course, "to prioritize the needs of the people and construct a new model of development," but it also called for political reforms—an indication that the social movements recognized that institutions, not just international economic pressures and personal failings, were behind the president's problems. Specifically, the CMS called for rules limiting the ability of elected officials to change parties, instituting public financing of campaigns and outlawing of private contributions, eliminating minimum percentages needed for small parties to achieve representation (which might increase fragmentation but enhance the influence of social movements), and opening heretofore-closed candidate lists ("closed" in the sense that voters choose parties but do not choose among candidates on a party's list). The CMS demanded that half of the slots on the ballot be reserved for women and ethnic groups (indigenous and Afro-descendent). The CMS also called for creation of referendums and plebiscites. Some of these measures were achieved in 2007, but it is too soon to determine whether they will seriously alter the "normal" mode of doing politics in Brazil.

Lula's chosen successor, Dilma Rousseff, won the election to succeed him in 2010, and with Brazil doing relatively well despite the global economic crisis, Rousseff seemed poised to easily reelection in 2014. But Rousseff too had her popularity dented by revelations of corruption during the Lula years; instead she was forced into a second round a won by a bare two percentage points. Lula himself had to face judicial investigation for corruption in 2013, though he was not indicted. The PT ran strongly in the 2012 local elections, but Rousseff and PT leaders seemed just as happy that some of its larger rival parties ran well. Having fewer smaller parties would make the task of forming legislative coalitions easier. This seemed to signal that the PT had fully evolved from a movement party to a party of the status quo.

Rousseff and most of the Brazilian political class hoped that 2014 and 2016 would be years through which they would trumpet to the world the country's economic success and social modernization, with the country set to host soccer's World Cup in 2014 and the Summer Olympic Games in 2016. But 2014 began with protests against extravagant spending on stadiums and infrastructure, wholesale militarization of *favelas* in the name of security for tourists, and scandals arising from shoddy workmanship and graft from lucrative construction projects. Rousseff responded to protests with new populist programs, including one that pays Cuba to deploy 13,000 doctors to work in the poor *favelas*. Whether these measures would buy the government some respite from internal protests and scandals was to be seen at the time of this book's writing.

For Review

Latin America is known for highly concentrated power—**delegative democracy**, say many political scientists. Why, then, have a number of the region's presidents had a difficult time moving their agendas through the legislature? How can the political party system help or hinder their efforts?

Institutions and Innovation

Samuel Huntington's (1968) influential *Political Order in Changing Societies* viewed institutions as necessary to channel participation, to control it. However, rather than viewing institutions and participation as separate spheres of politics, we can also think of institutions as guaranteeing and encouraging participation, often in innovative ways. Latin America has become an interesting laboratory in recent years for attempts to institutionalize not just representative but also participatory democracy.

In some large Brazilian cities, citizens gather in local assemblies to set priorities for spending large portions of the municipal budget, a process called "participatory budgeting." Indigenous traditions of collective decision-making (e.g., over use of land and water) remain strong in many areas populated by indigenous peoples. In Nicaragua, the Sandinista government, between 1979 and 1984, experimented with incorporating representatives of mass organizations directly into the main legislative body, the Council of State. All these experiences differ from the traditional way that representative democracy works in the United States, where citizen participation in and knowledge of local and state government is notoriously low. (Quick, can you name three members of your city council?)

Cuba's government engages citizens in participatory decisions over many activities (police services, education, maintenance of streets, etc.) that immediately touch people's lives. A system of councils (*Poder Popular*, or "People's Power") at the neighborhood, municipal, provincial, and national levels requires representatives to periodically "render accounts" to assemblies of voters at the local level. This system probably helped the regime survive the devastating impact of the collapse of its main economic trade partners in Eastern Europe between 1989 and 1991. For example, in December 1993 the Ministry of Finance put forth a proposal greatly reducing subsidies and increasing prices of many state-provided goods and services. Instead of passing the measure, the assembly sent the proposal for discussion to more than 80,000 local meetings, attended by more than 3 million workers. Some austerity measures were eventually accepted, but others rejected, whereas taxes were increased on rum and cigarettes to help make up the shortfall. Instead of a tax on wages, a general income tax was implemented (Saney 2004: 51–54).

Venezuela's Bolivarian constitution embodies several bold initiatives in an attempt to institutionalize participatory democracy, to make the people "protagonists" in policymaking. Probably no country has gone so far to make possible the recall of elected officials. In 2004, the opposition successfully gathered enough signatures to force a recall election of President Chávez. They lost; at least for another 10 years the recall put to rest the question of whether Chávez was legitimate. But Venezuelans remained deeply divided over an institutional change initiated by Chávez, whereby authority over spending the country's petrodollar earnings has moved from local and state governments to grassroots organizations called "communal councils." Since 2007 the government has encouraged formation of thousands of these councils, composed of 200 to 400 families in urban areas, smaller elsewhere. They are supposed to set priorities for local projects financed by the national government and state oil company. Residents are supposed to participate in carrying out these projects, not just decide what government will do.

The councils are now being drawn into large geographic networks, "communes," that could further erode states and municipalities, alarming many politicians in both the government and opposition. The opposition in Venezuela fears that this is a precursor to replacing the current constitution with a Cuban-style system. More immediately, the question seems to be whether the communal councils can function as autonomous institutions for participatory democracy, or whether the direct financing by the state and oil company will simply create a new network of centrally controlled clientelism. Researchers (e.g., McCarthy 2012) have found it almost impossible to generalize about this issue. In some cases, communal councils have displaced older organizations with a history of effectively expressing community demands. In others, they have been co-opted by local Chavista party leaders. However, in many cases they have served to empower local leaders, especially women. As mentioned previously, after the death of Chávez, political polarization around the future of the country's institutions and control over the oil revenues intensified, leaving the future of Bolivarianism more in doubt than it has been since the short-lived coup against Chávez in 2002.

Peter Roman (2003), who studied Cuba's electoral and representative system for more than 12 years (1986–1998, mostly on the municipal level), provides extensive empirical evidence that elections are very participatory and the debates lively and serious within the assemblies. Roman claims that Cuban representatives act more like "instructed delegates," faithful to their constituents, and less like trustees expected to vote their own sense of what is best for the country. Delegates are required to keep office hours and respond to constituent complaints, and the local councils have considerable discretion over the budget. Even Roman admits that the system is still much too top-down. Haroldo Dilla Alfonso (2006), a Cuban social scientist who lost his position in 1995 at the prestigious Center for the Study of the Americas in Havana and was expelled from the PCC in 1999, thinks the Cuban system needs to be more open and to have government operate more autonomously. However, Dilla acknowledges that the participatory institutions of Cuba do work and did help the regime survive the extraordinary hardships that came with the collapse of communism in Eastern Europe. The system produced some important reforms, including expansion of religious tolerance, administrative decentralization, and direct election of the national and provincial assemblies.

Social movements throughout the region, and especially in Ecuador and Bolivia, are pressing an agenda to require greater direct popular input into the legislative process, including the right to initiate legislation by petition (another provision of the new Venezuelan constitution). They have also called for laws that require the media, which is dominated everywhere by large corporations and wealthy owners, to be more socially responsible. Some of these measures, such as plebiscites, recall elections, initiatives, and referendums, have worked in other areas of the world, including some states in the United States. Others are controversial. For example, can social responsibility laws for media be enforced without state censorship? How would the boards responsible for oversight be formed? As for the right to be consulted or represented directly in making or enforcing laws, how are authorities to verify which organizations most represent relevant sectors of the population? Who decides, for example, which human rights organizations authentically represent groups of citizens and which are merely fronts for wealthy or politically powerful interests, or for the state itself?

Leonardo Avritzer (2002) has argued that Latin American democracies should be credited with creating more open, egalitarian public spaces than typically found in liberal democracies. He thinks that participatory experiments are extending democracy beyond the formal institutions (elections, party systems, etc.) and engaging more citizens in new ways politically. To be successful, he argues, Latin American governments need to cultivate capacity for **deliberative democracy**, which should include greater civil involvement in organizing and protecting the integrity of elections, better civic education, and more widespread and effective use of new information technology. Avritzer sees these new democratic institutions as an extension of the struggles to restore democracy at the end of military rule, but others (see Cameron, Hershberg, and Sharpe 2012) would add that these demands are linked to a more general crisis of representation. Social movements not only want better-quality government under polyarchy; they want better-quality democracy that goes beyond the limits of polyarchy.

Conclusion: Institutions Matter

In the end, even the best-designed institutions cannot save a system characterized by deep social and political polarization around basic issues. Those with power and privilege in a society will not give them up just because a majority has demanded change through democratic institutions. The failed Chilean road to socialism of 1973 was but one demonstration of this political fact. However, institutions matter because they establish the rules of the political game, which need to be in place for people to accept the legitimacy of decisions made by the government. Political institutions, many of which are established in constitutions, are the sites where important social conflicts are played out. Even revolutions eventually require institutions to consolidate change.

In contrast to political scientists who think Latin America needs stronger institutions to tame participation, Latin American social movements are asking for participatory democracies. They will need institutions to make them work. They also need laws that provide real protection from violence and arbitrary treatment, whether the protection originates from the state or from private sources. We turn to those laws in the next chapter.

Discussion Questions

1. Most of this book is consistent with the area studies tradition that puts the focus on historical, socioeconomic, and cultural influences in politics. Should we put more effort into examining institutions and constitutional design? Or should someone who wants to understand Latin America place more emphasis on the distribution of economic and social power?
2. To what extent can and should political scientists be involved in designing constitutions—for example, systems of representation and executive–legislative relationships? Is that our job?
4. Is your view of institutions closer to Huntington's or Avritzer's? Why?

Resources for Further Study

Reading: A good example of the institutionalist approach, enriched by its drawing upon social and economic factors, is Joe Foweraker, Tod Landman, and Neil Harvey, *Governing Latin America* (Cambridge, UK: Polity Press, 2003). Leonardo Avritzer, *Democracy and the Public Space in Latin America* (Princeton, NJ: Princeton University Press, 2002), examines participatory democracy experiments approvingly. Gianpaolo Baiocchi, *Radicals in Power: The Workers' Party (PT) and Experiments in Urban Democracy*, looks at how attaining power affects parties linked to social movements. Álvaro Vargas Llosa examines 500 years of oppression and sees reforming institutions and their underlying culture as the only way to reverse this history in *Liberty for Latin America* (New York: Farrar, Straus & Grioux, 2005). Gabriel L. Negretto, "Replacing and Amending Constitutions: The Logic of Constitutional Change in Latin America," *Law & Society Review* 46, no. 4 (December 2012), reviews recent changes in Latin American constitutions and the causes.

Video and Film: *Beyond Elections* (2009) looks at participatory budgeting and other experiments in deliberative democracy. It can also be found on YouTube. *¿Puedo Hablar?* (2007) documents the Venezuelan electoral campaign and election of 2006, won by Hugo Chávez. *Lula's Brazil* examines the first two years of the presidency of Luiz Inácio Lula da Silva, examining Lula's personal life and critically evaluating his political decisions.

On the Internet: As just mentioned, the documentary *Beyond Elections* can be found on YouTube with a search. LANIC at the University of Texas has a page devoted to government affairs (http://lanic.utexas.edu/subject/government). The World Bank's views on good governance can be found at the "governance and anticorruption" section of www.worldbank.org. The website of the International Institute for Democracy and Electoral Assistance (IDEA, at www.idea.int/index.cfm) provides a wealth of information on voting and election procedures from around the world.

14 Human Rights, Corruption, and the Rule of Law

Focus Questions

▶ What criteria do human rights organizations use to evaluate conditions in Latin America? How do human rights conditions vary in the region?

▶ How have problems with crime and corruption impacted the degree of popular support for democracy in the region?

▶ How well do judicial systems and criminal justice systems function in Latin America?

IT COULD BE argued that democracy—majority rule through elections—is possible without the rule of law. That is, we have plenty of examples of governments that qualify as democracies but are characterized by rampant corruption. Still, the quality of democracy would certainly seem to depend on whether citizens are protected from arbitrary authority and can hold officials accountable for their actions—and whether they think their fellow citizens obey the law. As Figure 14.1 indicates, not even one in three Latin Americans were confident of this last condition in 2011 (the last year that Latinobarómetro asked the question).

Certainly, it is hard to believe that democracy can be stable and effective as long as crime, human rights violations, and corruption go unpunished. If citizens sense that some people—wealthier, politically connected, beyond the control of police—are not subject to law (have "impunity"), whereas others seem particularly vulnerable to repression and violence by the very authorities charged with protecting them, what faith would they have in democracy as a system of government? What progress, if any, has been made in reducing crime and in reducing the sense of impunity that many public officials and powerful private individuals seem to enjoy when they violate human rights or engage in corruption?

What Is "Rule of Law?" Is It Necessary for Democracy?

"**Rule of law**" refers to two interrelated but somewhat distinct ideas: the idea that all citizens should be treated the same under the law and the idea that they can rely on the state to guarantee justice and security for persons and property, especially personal property. The implications for democracy go beyond fairness and equal treatment. Personal security—that is, freedom from violence or fear of violence—is vital to democracy. On the most basic level, citizens cannot vote on Election Day or go to a neighborhood meeting if leaving the house

FIGURE 14.1   Confidence that Citizens are Law Abiding

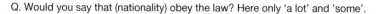

Q. Would you say that (nationality) obey the law? Here only 'a lot' and 'some'.

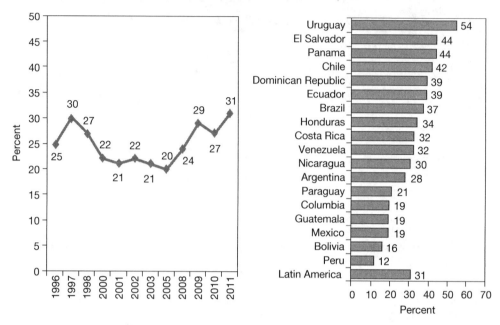

puts them at risk of rape, robbery, or murder. Fear of violent crime also makes people more inclined to accept repression and grant arbitrary powers to the state.

The rule of law can be broken into several components.

- *Concern with human rights and impunity.* "Impunity" exists when security forces violate human rights through torture, disappearances, extrajudicial executions, and so on without fear of sanction. Effective courts and a humane criminal justice system are also crucial to what is called the rule of law.
- *Concern about violent crime.*
- *Concerns about corruption,* which may discourage investment and erode public confidence in the fairness of institutions and independence of the judiciary.
- *Concerns about constitutional processes* (a major focus of chapter 13).
- *Concerns about international treaties* that weaken the authority of local courts and administrative bodies by placing final judgments about disputes in international tribunals, beyond the realm of national sovereignty. Free-trade treaties have removed some issues out of the control of national or local governments. We will leave this concern to the next chapter, where we look at the impact of globalization on Latin America.

A United Nations–sponsored study of anticorruption (UNDP 2012) sees the incapacity of Latin American democracies to improve the quality of **governance** as a major cause of their vulnerability to corruption. This is another way that institutions matter in Latin America (see Figure 14.2). But the study also finds that the growing inequality in wealth

FIGURE 14.2   Corruption and Opinions on What Democracy is Lacking

Q. What do you think is lacking within democracy in your country or is democracy in your country good as is? *Multiple choice questions, totals are higher than 100%*

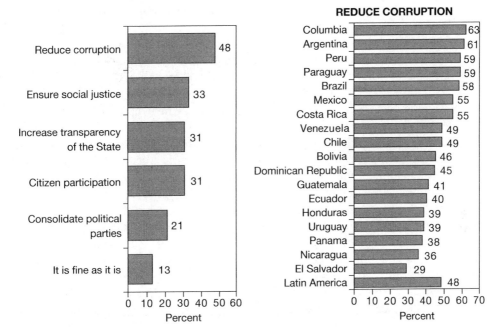

and income is another factor inhibiting anticorruption efforts. In fact, the Latinobarómetro survey finds that the rich are the group Latin Americans most often identify as most likely to break the law—though they are followed closely by politicians.

Wealthy citizens are always more capable of insisting on lawful treatment and respect for rights than are the poor. One important example of this inequality in Latin America is visible in the area of land reform. Land reform laws, even in revolutionary situations, such as once prevailed in Chile (1970–1973) and Nicaragua (1979–1990), usually have provisions defining the size and type of holdings that can be redistributed. Whether a parcel of land can be expropriated depends by law on the size of the parcel, whether the land is cultivated or idle, what kinds of improvements (irrigation, fertilization, etc.) have been made, and so on. Peasants with little income or formal education, and lacking experience in dealing with courts or a bureaucracy, have to organize and petition in a formal way to press a claim against landowners. Landowners use every procedural method available to drag out the process in the bureaucracy and courts (see Kaufman 1972 on the Chilean case), using their political connections to influence an often corrupt judicial system. Frustrated peasants, sometimes encouraged by organizers from the cities or leaders of peasant movements, invade estates to speed up the process. This in turn brings about cries of abuse from landowners and arouses sympathy from other sectors (e.g., the middle class) that fear radical change. Judges and civil servants (bureaucrats) are often holdovers from past governments and do not share enthusiasm for reform.

Sometimes, national and international groups (environmentalists, unions, and human rights groups) help the poor and less powerful to be heard, but more often peasants, workers, and the urban poor feel abandoned by the state, which is often incapable of delivering basic security and protecting them from hired thugs or gunmen. Such is the case in northeast Brazil, where in the 1990s members of the MST, inspired by **liberation theology**, began seizing land and defending themselves from the small private armies created by ranchers. The movement claims that despite the transition to democracy begun in 1985, around 1,600 peasants have been killed in land conflicts (CIP 2006). On April 17, 1996, 19 MST members were killed and 69 wounded by military police in the Eldorado de Carajá massacre in the Amazonas state of Pará. More than 150 police were brought to trial, but only two were ever convicted and sentenced, and in 2001 it remained unclear whether they were ever jailed (Issa 2007: 124–125).

Politicians are skilled at bending the laws and using the courts to tarnish the reputation of opponents or even to prevent them from running for office. For example, in 2005, Andrés López Obrador, mayor of Mexico City and leader in the polls to win Mexico's 2006 national presidential election, was accused of violating a court order against the municipal construction of a road leading from a poor community to a hospital. The Mexican Congress, where his party held only a minority of seats, stripped the mayor of the immunity from prosecution enjoyed by elected officials, and he was subsequently indicted. By Mexican law, citizens under indictment cannot run for office; López Obrador protested that the charges against him were trumped up. He pointedly referred to many contemporary and former Mexican officials investigated for far more serious allegations but never indicted. On April 24, 2005, an estimated 1 million marchers in Mexico City protested the imminent indictment of the presidential candidate. The mayor, known for his populist campaign style, planned to campaign from prison as a martyr, but two members of Congress from the ruling party of President Vicente Fox thwarted the plan by paying his bail. By May, the government had dropped the charges. (As noted in the previous chapter, López Obrador lost a disputed election at the end of the campaign.)

Leopoldo López was one of the founders of an opposition political party in Venezuela. He was active in the coup that deposed President Hugo Chávez for 48 hours in 2002. In 2008, the government barred him from seeking election as mayor of a Caracas-area municipality, but on charges related to the coup. He was one of 80 politicians (including many from Chávez's own party) banned from running because of charges of corruption under investigation by an administrative agency. He appealed in Venezuelan courts but lost and then took his case to the Inter-American Commission on Human Rights, which supported his contention that because he had not been tried and convicted on the charges, the ban violated his right to run for office. He was a candidate for the opposition nomination to run against Chávez in 2010, but he withdrew in favor of the eventual nominee, Henrique Capriles. In spring 2014 López was jailed again on charges that he had incited violent antigovernment protests. In public speeches López called for peaceful demonstrations, but even as protests turned violent he continued to demand the "exit" of President Nicolás Maduro.

The Chavistas think that López and some other opposition leaders were once again, as in 2002, trying to draw the military into a coup. They contend that it is disingenuous to think he was merely encouraging peaceful protest. Opponents of Maduro charge that the judiciary is controlled by the government, so López is unlikely to get a fair trial. After 16 years of government controlled by Chávez and Maduro, the judiciary is staffed by judges sympathetic to

Chavismo. They do not always rule in the government's favor, but as we saw in chapter 13, Venezuelan political institutions are not well established, and this includes the judiciary.

We should not assume that rule of law requires that a country follow the same procedures and customs practiced in the United States and Britain. Latin America has borrowed some legal traditions from these countries, but for the most part, rights and appeals to law are handled by judiciaries modeled on French practices derived from "code law," also known as "Napoleonic law." The Anglo legal tradition includes the presumption of innocence until proven guilty, whereas most Latin American systems presume neither innocence nor guilt. The idea of seeking compensation against a fellow citizen through civil litigation for harm is fairly unusual. A Latin American injured in an auto accident or from falling into a gaping hole in the street will tell you that he or she has little recourse. In the Anglo tradition, an adversarial process decides guilt or innocence in criminal trials and allocates responsibility and damages in civil suits. In both cases, all involved make the best possible argument for their side, trusting that the truth will emerge from the competition. In Latin American systems, an indictment often means that the accused loses certain rights, and prosecutors are supposed to seek out the truth and not simply pursue conviction.

There is, however, a route for Latin Americans to demand their rights in the legal system. In much of Latin America, this means seeking an *amparo*, a court decision stating that a citizen is "covered" or "protected" by some constitutional right from a government action or from failure of government to act—for example, to rectify unlawful dismissal from a job, prosecution for an alleged crime, relocation to make room for a highway or economic project, or a prohibition to publish or speak.

Crime and Justice

If the Latin American and Anglo systems of law differ, one similarity is the difficulty in ensuring that citizens of different economic means have equal access and treatment under the law. Although long incarceration before trial is common in North America, the problem is magnified in Latin America; in many countries, more than half of the prison population consists of inmates who have yet to be given a trial. Panama, Guatemala, Venezuela, Argentina, Bolivia, Uruguay, Peru, Honduras, and the Dominican Republic all fall into this category, a list that includes countries that have some of the best (Uruguay) and the worst (Honduras) overall human rights conditions (see data at prisonstudies.org). Conditions in prisons are degrading, and in recent years inmates have undertaken desperate mass escape attempts and revolts. The problem is especially acute in Central America, where crime rates and problems with youth gangs soared in the aftermath of the civil wars of the 1980s and the deepening economic crises, but prison revolts have also happened in Venezuela, Brazil, and elsewhere.

As economic conditions improved after 2000, concerns about crime began to show a marked increase, according to the 2013 Latinobarómetro report. Crime has surpassed concerns about poverty and economic progress in Brazil, Chile, and Venezuela, among other places. According to Latinobarómetro, in 2011 only 30 percent of Latin Americans agreed that their country guaranteed protection against crime (see Figure 14.3). Meagerly paid municipal police are often untrained and treat poor areas as a no-man's-land, where "shoot to kill" is standard operating procedure. In many poor *barrios*, the police no longer provide any

FIGURE 14.3   Citizen Views on Freedoms and Rights

To what extent do the following freedoms, rights, life chances and guarantees apply in (country)?
* Here only "Fully guaranteed" plus "Fairly-generally guaranteed".

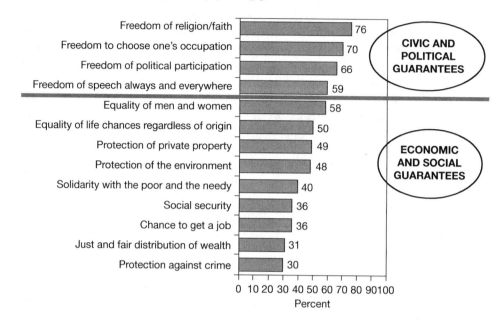

security, which leads often to vigilante justice, including hangings, beatings, and "necklacing," the practice of burning the accused alive by placing a tire around his neck and lighting it. Given this grim picture, some experts on Latin America's judiciary have concluded that "equality of law is a meaningless abstraction since the powerful need not obey the law which is designed primarily to control the behavior of the lower classes" (Schor 2003). Even worse, in many Latin American countries, the police are widely seen as corrupt and as perpetrators of crime, and surveys of Latin American public opinion draw a direct connection between distrust of the police and support for democracy. In 2008, in every Latin American country, no fewer than 20 percent of those surveyed in a Vanderbilt University study said they believed that police were involved in crime; and in Venezuela and Guatemala, this view was held by more than 60 percent (Cruz 2010).

Particularly distressing in the Latin American case is the number of major cities where police and gangs dispute territory in poor *barrios*. In May 2006, in São Paolo, Brazil, the First Capital Command gang staged what might best be described as a military offensive against the police, carrying out more than 70 attacks over a two-day period, killing at least 70 police and many civilians. The attacks were coordinated with dozens of prison uprisings and the torching of banks and buses. The immediate catalyst for the offensive was apparently the government's decision to transfer 600 prisoners, including First Capital members, to other jails as an attempt to break the hold of the inmates over prison society. The police responded over the next few days with a systematic campaign of revenge against presumed gang members in the city's poor *favelas*, killing 93 "suspects" in one day (Phillips 2006).

The homicide rate in Latin America in 2012 was 25.6 per 100,000 residents (UNODC 2014). By comparison, the rate was 8.9 in Europe. Among countries, Honduras had the highest murder rate in 2012 at 90.4 per 100,000 inhabitants. The highest in South America was Venezuela at 53.7. The rate for poor and middle-class youth reached nearly 90 per 100,000. Rates in northern Latin America and Brazil are double the rates in major U.S. cities and seven times the typical rate in Canada, according to the Pan American Health Organization (PAHO 1999). Among large cities, Caracas, Venezuela, had the highest rate, at 122 per 100,000 inhabitants (for 2009, last data available; see UNODC 2014). That country's rising murder rate in the 2000s defies the conventional logic that poverty causes crime since Venezuela recorded the region's best record of poverty reduction in that period. Some attribute the rise to a culture of impunity that the Chávez government failed to address; others point to rising drug consumption brought about by the trafficking originating in the nearby Andean countries. Personal security is often the number one issue mentioned by Venezuelans responding to poll questions asking them to name the most important issue in the country.

Visitors to Latin America are often struck by the sight of sharp pieces of glass protruding from the top of walls and windowsills. In most cities, private guards armed with automatic weapons patrol wealthy neighborhoods and are stationed outside banks and other public buildings. However, murder rates, fueled by poverty, alcohol, and drugs, are highest in poor areas.

The situation is not hopeless. For example, Medellín, Colombia, was regarded as a chronically violent city, wracked by violence inflicted by gangs linked to notorious drug wars and clashes between leftist guerrillas and right-wing death squads (often the squads and gangs are indistinguishable). In 1991, the murder rate per 100,000 was well more than 350; by 2005, it had fallen to 37, lower than many major U.S. cities. Why? Three factors were involved, says the Center for International Policy (CIP 2006). First, right-wing paramilitary forces, which had gained control over criminal activities, were offered amnesty in exchange for good behavior; second, police and military forces began to reestablish a presence in the poorest sectors of the city; and third, the city government decided to invest money in the poorest areas, offering hope to the poor and an opportunity for demobilized fighters involved in the country's civil war (see chapter 10) to reintegrate into society.

Although increased deployment of police and military seemed to have played a positive role in Medellín, just the opposite result was being obtained in Mexico. President Felipe Calderón inherited spiraling, drug trade–related violence from his predecessor after winning the disputed election of July 2006. Oddly, some of his problems may be the result of the liberal democratization process of the 1990s. The mayors and governors of the PRI may have held power through clientelism, corruption, and electoral fraud, but violence was moderated by a corrupt but effective working relationship between PRI politicians and the drug lords. In many cases, especially in the north, local drug lords—whose business prospered with the increase in traffic across the U.S. border after NAFTA—sought to step into the power void left by the well-intentioned reforms of the Zedillo administration in 1994–2000. However, with the PRI political monopoly broken up, political turf wars erupted.

In early 2007, finding that not only local but also federal police authorities had been thoroughly corrupted, Calderón decided to use the military to deal with his security problem; in late 2000s, the news was filled daily with stories of violent clashes among local police, the Mexican military, and drug lords, with a rising civilian toll. Unfortunately, the drug lords beat the Mexican government to the punch in terms of preparing for war (Bremer 2007). The most notorious and violent of the gangs targeted by Calderón were the Zetas, who formed a heavily armed, elite network of well-trained former soldiers. The militarization seemed to produce results at first in Mexico City and Tijuana, but the relative peace was short-lived. By mid-2007 violence was escalating and spreading to cities in the south. Dozens of civilians were killed in one firefight alone in a small mining town. Severed heads of rival gang members were rolled out on dance floors in one incident in Veracruz. Although Mexican citizens initially seemed supportive of using the army to crack down on the traffickers, the rising scale of violence, including grenade attacks that caused indiscriminate casualties among civilians, undermined confidence in a political system already burdened by a disputed election outcome and economic woes. (We should also note that the easy availability of firearms in the United States is a major contributory factor to the violence.)

The escalating violence contributed to the decision of voters to turn back to the PRI in the 2012 election that brought Enrique Peña Nieto to the presidency. Peña Nieto has moved to restrict U.S. involvement in the war and, out of concern for the impact on the country's tourism industry, sought to scale down prominence of the war, if not the war itself. The government scored some noticeable successes in capturing some of the "big fish" narco-traffickers, but it found itself embroiled in a new problem when citizens despairing of the government's ability to protect them from both gangs and corrupt officials began to take matters into their own hands. In the state of Michoacán, villagers organized to take back land and homes seized by a particularly vicious gang, the Knights-Templar. Rather than disband the vigilante groups, in 2014 the government tried to bring them under control through integrating them into "civil patrols," but it was not clear how successful the effort would be.

A particularly disturbing trend in Mexico is the victimization of women in this low-intensity civil war. In Ciudad Juarez, a Mexican city along the border with Texas, Amnesty International reported that almost 400 women and girls had been murdered in the period between 1993 and 2005, most of them employees in the *maquiladora* industries, without charges being brought against anyone. Suspicions fall on powerful local *caudillos* and gangs who have links to or are part of the government in the region. International publicity induced the Mexican federal government to investigate what is now being called "femicide," a term denoting the way victims were being killed as a social class—a consequence of their gender. The Mexican attorney general found that 177 officials of Chihuahua were guilty of negligence or omission in investigating, but none were brought to justice on grounds that the statute of limitations (the maximum time period during which one can be prosecuted after committing a crime) had run out (see Amnesty International 2006).

The Observatory on Gender Equality of the UN Economic Commission for Latin America has found (2012) that the governments in the region have made some progress reducing rates of violent assault, murder, and rape of women, but there are indications that "intimate violence," or violence against women by their sexual partners, may have increased. This is always a difficult thing to measure because the rate may rise or fall according to victims' willingness to report such crime and police sensitivity to the issue. The good news is that this particular problem has come more into the open, but the statistics certainly indicate that women remain highly vulnerable.

Criminal violence spills over into election campaigns in many countries. In the 2007 Guatemalan elections, authorities registered 61 violent attacks on candidates and campaigners, resulting in 26 deaths, including those of seven members of Congress. The legacy of 36 years of civil war (see chapter 10) could be cited as the cause, but the upsurge of violence in

This woman in Honduras is carrying a fake coffin in a demonstration against femicide. Do you think that this kind of protest will bring more attention to the problem?

2007 was also caused by "narcotics traffickers and their allies intent on infiltrating Guatemala's political system" (Lacey 2007). U.S. drug enforcement officials say Guatemala's "dire poverty and lawlessness" create an environment where the traffickers can influence politicians and local government. Police themselves have been implicated in several murders. In this context, citizens showed little sympathy for investigating the deaths of seven inmates killed after being captured when police suppressed a prison revolt.

The degree of coordination among gangs in Brazil and Mexico is particularly disturbing, presenting the possibility of significant social space becoming permanently beyond the reach of state authority. Should this condition become widespread and permanent, it can only lead to further deterioration of the quality of life for poor urban residents, whereas in middle-class neighborhoods there will prevail an atmosphere of insecurity and fear of a racially distinct, class-distinct "other" mass of citizens. This certainly is unhealthy for democracy.

The inability of Latin American states to provide security from crime for citizens is pervasive and deeply rooted. With the exception of Havana, there is probably no Latin American city where citizens can feel safe from violence walking in the evening in all neighborhoods. The *barrios* and *favelas* of Latin America, by contrast, have a reputation as no-man's-land, areas where upper-class and especially white people fear to tread. The poor in these areas, especially when they mobilize to demand social and political inclusion in the broader national community, may be depicted in the mainstream media as *turbas*, mobs, the antithesis of "civil society." In this way, racial and class divides widen and deepen, reinforcing exclusion of the poor from participation in the mainstream of the social, economic, and political life of the city.

It is easy to paint a picture of overwhelming despair when one examines social conditions in most of Latin America's cities. It is easy to develop paranoia when reading statistics or hearing anecdotes about crime. In fact, you need to know that you can visit Latin American countries at very low personal risk, lower than in many U.S. cities. Latin American cities have vibrant cultures, and the countryside can be spectacular. Be street-smart, but do not forgo the pleasure of visiting Latin America out of fear.

For Review

What does "rule of law" have to do with political equality? What are some of the different ways that citizens may feel they are living under rule of law, or not feel that way? Why might it be difficult in a particular case to judge the political motives for prosecution of a particular public official? List some of the ways that street crime and violence might imperil democracy. Where does crime rank in comparison to some other issues of concern to Latin Americans today?

Corruption

Almost anyone who has dealt with Latin American bureaucracies is aware of corruption. The Mexican *mordita*, the "little bite" taken by Mexico City's traffic policemen, is perhaps the best-known example, but the problem is widespread and deeper. Poorly paid civil servants, who often hold their jobs because they have a connection with a local politician or party, make citizens return day after day to secure a passport renewal, replace a lost *cédula* (identity card), or obtain a permit to open a business. To obtain telephone service from the state, clients might need to offer an appropriate "gift" to the dispatcher and crew—though in the age of cellular phones, this nuisance is in decline. These day-to-day irregularities not only are annoying but also sap confidence in government institutions. They feed the perception that having the right connections or being affluent enough to pay a bribe counts more than meeting criteria defined by laws and regulations. In this way, corruption undermines the rule of law and respect for institutions.

The line between **clientelism** and corruption is not always a bright one. Everywhere in the world, successful politicians reward followers with paid positions in public administration. The problem becomes more serious when appointees not only secure positions through connections but also are unqualified or incompetent. In some cases, this may produce risks to public health and safety—for example, failures to enforce codes for high-rise buildings in earthquake zones, lax inspection of food, and poor maintenance of highways. Thefts from hospitals mean that patients not able to afford private clinics have to bring their own sheets and pillows.

Transparency International (TI) is an organization that rates the degree of corruption in national governments. TI's press release accompanying its 2005 report highlighted the costs of bribery in large-scale construction projects, such as the Yacyretá hydropower project.

> The Yacyretá hydropower project on the border of Argentina and Paraguay, built with World Bank support, is flooding the Ibera Marshes [one of the biggest wildlife wetlands in the world]. Due to cost overruns, the power generated by Yacyretá is not economic and needs to be subsidised by the government. According to the head of Paraguay's General Accounting Office, US$1.87 billion in expenditures for the project "lack the legal and administrative support documentation to justify the expenditures."

TI's 2005 report included TI's reported expert perceptions of corruption in 146 countries. It ranked Chile fairly positively (twentieth overall) with a score of 7.3 out of 10, the best reputation for clean government of any Third World nation except for Singapore and Hong Kong (part of China). Chile ranked just behind the United States and ahead of several other developed countries. Only Uruguay joined Chile in scoring better than 5 out of 10. By contrast, Haiti had the lowest score, at 1.5.

TI's report highlighted continuing "evident misuse of state funds at various levels" and criticized the weakness of the judiciary in Bolivia "where parliamentary immunity and a compliant congressional commission responsible for investigating high-profile corruption cases allowed five-year-old allegations of corruption" against a former defense minister to stall. The Brazilian government's anticorruption efforts "continued to be characterized by knee-jerk reactions to scandals rather than a concerted effort to tackle the problem branch and root." Peru, said TI, had failed to put control measures into place in its efforts to decentralize the government, with the result that 8 of 25 regional presidents were under investigation for corruption. In October 2008, the entire Peruvian cabinet submitted its resignation to President García as a result of corruption scandals.

At the same time, TI pointed to progress in some countries. It credited Argentina with having developed new procedures for appointing judges with consultation from the legal community, academics, and citizen groups. TI also praised a new Argentine political finance law—though it lamented that the financial reports filed by the parties "often bear little relation to reality." Colombia's new law requiring local officials to sign "transparency pacts" was praised as a good idea but criticized for the vagueness of the pacts.

The perception of corruption may be worse than the actual practice. Latinobarómetro turned up data that suggest that reputation and actual experience are not necessarily consistent. In its 2005 report, only one in five Latin Americans reported direct knowledge of someone receiving favorable treatment because they were connected with a public official (i.e., clientelism), and likewise only 20 percent of respondents reported that they or a member of their family had direct knowledge of an act of corruption. Venezuela, which ranked near the bottom of Latin American countries in the TI index, ranked considerably higher according to the public opinion data. Brazil and Mexico were in the top tier on TI's list, indicating relatively low rates of corruption by hemispheric standards. But the percentage of people in these countries reporting direct knowledge of corruption far exceeded the Latin American average in the Latinobarómetro reports for 2005. Another poll for TI in 2005 asked respondents whether "anyone in their household" had paid a bribe of any sort in the last year; out of 54 nations, two Latin American countries were among the 10 with the highest percentage responding "yes": Bolivia with 29 percent and Ecuador with 27 percent. However, this also means that in these two worst cases, 70 percent of respondents *did not* report paying bribes (Latinobarómetro 2005: 241). Corruption is a serious problem, but it may be somewhat exaggerated in popular imagination, at least for some countries.

Still, perception matters, not just reality. When civic skepticism becomes civic cynicism, people lose faith in democracy. Military officers often think that they can clean out the stables. Ambitious politicians may close down elected congresses with little protest from citizens, as happened in 1992 when President Alberto Fujimori dissolved Peru's Congress and inaugurated a period of harsh repression. Rather than cleanse the country, Fujimori merely shifted corruption down to other corridors of power. As we noted in chapter 13, even reformist politicians who led the democracy movements, such as Brazil's Lula, are vulnerable. As politicians invoke congressional immunity, manipulate courts, and trade accusations of corruption and mendacity with one another, citizens become even more cynical. As Figure 14.4 shows, the curbing of corruption was the most frequently named condition lacking in democracy overall in the region.

Because of the corruption associated with the populist era and the inefficiency of government, one might think that reducing the size of government by outsourcing public

FIGURE 14.4   Rich Seen as Most Likely to Break Laws

Q. Which of the following groups do you think complies less with the law? *Multiple choice question, totals are higher than 100% **Here only answer with more than 3%

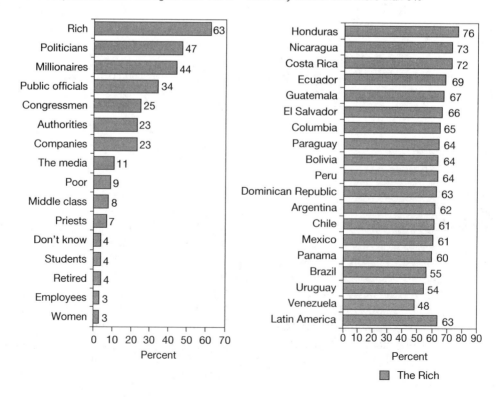

■ The Rich

services to private corporations would be popular. However, corruption has been a factor in eroding public support—which was never strong for privatization. A delegation from the Mennonite Church returned from a fact-finding trip to Nicaragua pessimistic about the capacity of Latin American political institutions to cope with privatization. In their judgment,

> privatization without regulation does not work. Nicaragua is a great example of this. The electric company was privatized five years ago and in its contract agreed to raise the costs for the public [only] once in the next five-year period. In that time the electric prices have been raised at least four times, and the government is unable to control them. It should be pointed out that all the companies that have bought out the government utilities (at very cheap prices) are all foreign transnationals, and it has been proven again and again that the government here does not have the power to contend with them. In Brazil, privatization of certain things such as phones has been successful, but the reality there is different. The Brazilian government has the power to regulate.
>
> (Miller 2003)

Wealth and social status draw special treatment from bureaucracies. Although this rule probably holds true in all political systems, the poor feel the discrimination more acutely in Latin America, where inequality is more glaring. Guillermo O'Donnell (1998) writes,

> Perhaps nothing underlines better the deprivation of rights of the poor and the socially weak than when they interact with the bureaucracies from which they must obtain work, or a working permit, or apply for retirement benefits, or simply (but often tragically) when they have to go to a hospital or a police station. This is, for the privileged, the other face of the moon, one that they mount elaborate strategies and networks of relationships to avoid. For the others, those who cannot avoid this ugly face of the state, it is not only the immense difficulty they confront for obtaining, if at all, what nominally is their right; it is also the indifferent if not disdainful way in which they are treated, and the obvious inequality entailed by the privileged skipping these hardships.

TI's recent reports highlight an increased awareness among Latin America's politicians that corruption is eroding their legitimacy. The solution may lie in more democracy, not more police or military action. Robert Putnam's research (1993) on corruption and good government in Italian cities has emphasized the importance of communities organizing and participating in politics, not just leaving decisions to public officials. Of course, this raises the question of how to develop such a culture of civic virtue and active involvement, but as we saw in the previous chapter, social movements seem on the upsurge throughout Latin America.

Anticorruption civic organizations have sprung up in several countries. Massive civic protest has forced governments to roll back plans to sell public assets in several cases, most notably in 2000 in the Bolivian city of Cochabamba, where citizens mobilized to prevent privatization of water. The question now seems to be, can Latin American nations develop institutions that will make the government responsive and the elected officials accountable to more systematic and peaceful citizen action?

For Review

What are some of the ways that corruption weakens support for democracy? What is impunity, and how does it weaken respect for rule of law?

■ Human Rights and State Violence

More publicized and controversial violations of human rights are those where governments are accused of carrying out, abetting, or tolerating repression of citizens attempting to exercise these rights. Although human rights reports continue to identify serious abuses, most of the region as a whole showed improvement in the civil rights areas of human rights after the collapse of the dictatorships of the Southern Cone and the end of Central America's civil wars. However, the reality is that no country has a perfect human rights record, and we have already seen in earlier chapters plenty of evidence that in some areas state violence continues to be a serious issue.

The Legacy of Military Rule

To appreciate the scale of state violence during military rule, consider that between 1976 and 1982 Argentina's military junta killed or "disappeared" (referring to citizens swept up by security forces, never to reappear) at least 10,000 people. In Chile, which has two-fifths the population of Argentina, 3,129 people died in the first three years after General Augusto Pinochet seized power in 1973. In Brazil, "only" 400 citizens were killed or disappeared by military forces after 1964.

In these and other cases, the numbers do not reflect the multitude of citizens detained, tortured, stripped of the right to speak or act publicly, or deprived of their places of employment or university study. An estimated 40,000 people in Chile were directly victimized in some way. In Central America, the human rights toll was even grimmer, especially given the size of these republics. The cases of El Salvador and Guatemala are especially indicative of the causes and consequences of mass human rights abuses. El Salvador was governed for most of the twentieth century by a ferocious and rapacious oligarchy, the so-called Fourteen Families that owned 80 percent of the country's arable land, having forced small producers, including Indians, off the land and having proceeded to create export-oriented estates (Lauria-Santiago 1999).

Accumulated grievances against the oligarchy led to successful peasant organizing in the 1920s by the Communist Party, led by the nationalist patriot Farabundo Martí. After the annulment of the party's victory in the municipal elections of 1931, the oligarchy found a savior in General Maximiliano Hernández Martínez, who unleashed a massacre, variously estimated to have taken the lives of 10,000–50,000 peasants, with Indians especially targeted. Forty years later, the tragedy repeated itself. Between 1979 and 1981—while some civilians and a handful of sympathetic military officers supported land reform and other measures demanded by labor—35,000 people, including labor leaders, nuns and priests, and peasant leaders, of a total population of 5 million people, were killed, often in the most brutal and public fashion. By the end of the civil war, 75,000 people were dead in the tiny country, sometimes known as the "flea."

What about the human rights situation since the war? The U.S. State Department, which approved the post-war conservative government and endorsed its free-market policies, produced in February 2004 a report (no longer available online) with mild criticism, typical of the approach it takes with regimes seen as allies of Washington.

> The Government generally respected the human rights of its citizens; however, there were significant problems in some areas. Some alleged politically motivated killings were under investigation at year's end. There were no reports of politically motivated disappearances. Some police officers used excessive force and mistreated detainees; at times police arbitrarily arrested and detained persons without adequate cause. Prison conditions remained poor, and overcrowding was a continuing problem. Lengthy pretrial detention remained a problem . . . Violence and discrimination against women remained a serious problem. Discrimination against disabled persons also remained a problem. Abuse of children, child labor, and forced child prostitution were also problems. The Government did not adequately protect workers' rights to organize and bargain collectively. Trafficking in women and children was a problem.
>
> (U.S. Department of State 2004)

In contrast, consider Amnesty International's 2002 report:

> January marked the 10th anniversary of the Peace Accords which brought an end to the armed conflict in El Salvador. Despite improvements in the human rights situation during this period, those responsible for the massive human rights violations committed during the country's 11-year conflict had not yet been brought to justice, an issue central to the peace process. However, local organizations renewed their efforts to ensure accountability for the violations. Economic conditions in some areas of the country deteriorated dramatically as a result of bad weather or low prices for agricultural products in the international market, leading to high levels of child malnutrition, in some cases resulting in deaths.
>
> (Amnesty International 2002)

On September 30, 2013, employees of Tutela Legal, a legal aid organization affiliated with a human rights office founded by Archbishop Oscar Romero (see chapter 10), found themselves locked out of the office in the National Cathedral by the Archbishop José Luis Escobar Alas, who said its work was no longer relevant. Critics said the move was made to separate the Church from a controversial investigation into one of the most notorious massacres (*El Mozote*) carried out by the army (*Los Angeles Times*, October 4, 2013).

For Review

How did the civil wars of the 1980s heighten human rights issues in Central America? What kind of human rights issues have remained thorny since the war? Are they different from those that afflicted the region in the 1980s?

Drug Wars and the "War on Terrorism"

Intervention in Central America was the last major hemispheric conflict of the Cold War. The mission entrusted to U.S. forces in the postwar period is broader today than that of any previous era. Latin America falls under the aegis of Southcom (U.S. Southern Command), one of the five U.S. commands whose areas of responsibility divide up the globe. Southcom has 1,400 staff, making it larger than all other U.S. government agencies in the region (e.g., the embassy and consulate staff) put together. It has an annual budget of US$800 million, and it administers a large military aid program. In 2005, its commander, General Brantz Craddock, told the U.S. Congress that his theater of command was brimming with threats to U.S. national security, listing them as "transnational terrorism, narcoterrorism, illicit trafficking, forgery and money laundering, kidnapping, urban gangs, radical movements, natural disasters, and mass migrations." Craddock attributed the problems to "anti-U.S., anti-globalization, and anti-free trade demagogues, thus effectively linking U.S. security objectives with wider economic goals" (quoted in Barry 2005).

Craddock outlined seven objectives in response to these "challenges." At the top of the list is to make sure that "regional energy supplies will flow freely" to markets and "not be targets of aggression." To achieve this, training will help "partner" nations protect "critical infrastructure"—defined as the second objective. Protecting infrastructure in turn leads to objective number three—training the military of the Andean nations (the "Andean Ridge," in the new jargon of the day) in joint operations to "establish dominion over ungoverned spaces," a clear reference to areas under guerrilla control or in sparsely populated (mostly indigenous) areas. Most of these "spaces" are in the Amazonian region, where mining and oil companies are operating and want to expand. Training would require deployment of more troops on the ground on the continent. Two other objectives are to support stable democracies and to prevent "rogue nations" from supporting terrorism. Cuba was already on the "rogue" state list, and U.S. conservatives pressed to add Chávez's Venezuela. Two other objectives on Craddock's list remained classified.

The U.S. military presence in South America has been expanded mainly under the guise of the drug war. Counterterrorism, in the wake of the attacks on New York and Washington on September 11, 2001 (coincidentally the anniversary date of Pinochet's 1973 coup in Chile), is sometimes cited as an objective, but usually in the context of the drug war.

International trade in narcotics has been a major feature of the global economic system since the Opium Wars. It is worth remembering that in these wars, China was resisting drug trafficking being carried out by Americans and Europeans. And in Latin America in recent decades, the United States has sometimes either backed traffickers or tolerated them. In numerous conflicts, including the Vietnam War and the Islamic Mujahideen's war against the Soviet occupation of Afghanistan in the 1980s, the United States allied itself with opium producers and traffickers. These alliances often have involved covert operations orchestrated by the CIA. In the 1980s, the U.S. Congress, alarmed at human rights violations by the *contras*, prohibited the use of taxpayer dollars to support the insurgency. One way to keep the proxy army funded was to ignore—if not to actively facilitate—their role in trafficking drugs. Central American operatives aligned with the CIA were implicated in the marketing of crack cocaine in the dawning era of the crack epidemic (Webb 1999). Although the United States operated training programs at the School of the Americas both in Panama and in Fort Benning, Georgia, and despite deep involvement in the Central American wars, the United States had not until recently established military bases in the region.

The illegal, global trade in narcotics sustains an enormous slush fund that can be utilized by both states and guerrilla movements. Usually, the armed forces of the group offer protection to growers, processors, or traffickers in exchange for a cut ("tax") on the profits. This is the principal relationship among armed groups, the military, and law enforcement officials in the Andean region. Colombians could be forgiven if they were confused about U.S. intentions. In 2000, the State Department found that two Colombian battalions that had lost U.S. aid because of human rights violations and connections to paramilitary groups were still operating, with new battalion designations created simply to qualify for aid. In 2005, President Uribe's decision to pardon notorious right-wing death squad leaders further shook the U.S. Congress's support for the war. On the other hand, a delegation of conservative U.S. members of Congress in 2000, including future speaker of the House of Representatives Dennis Hastert, encouraged Colombian military commanders to ignore human rights restrictions.

The assassination of a prominent Colombian presidential candidate by a drug lord of the notorious Medellín cartel in 1989 was the occasion for U.S. President George H. W. Bush to announce a significant increase in funds for the drug war in Colombia and for a deployment of U.S. military forces to help in training. These actions were publicly justified as interdiction of the drug trade, the only argument that the U.S. Congress would accept. National security directives and diplomatic correspondence show, however, that fighting guerrillas was just as important (see the National Security Archive's Colombia Project, http://www2.gwu.edu/~nsarchiv/colombia/). Under scrutiny from Congress and public interest groups in North and South America, U.S. officials continue to claim that American aid and training are to professionalize the military, and they stress respect for human rights.

Columbia

Estimating the size of the illegal drug trade is difficult. Some experts think that 90 percent of the street value of drugs in the United States stays in the north. Still, the trade is big enough that exports, especially of coca, exceed the value of any legally exported commodity from the Andean Ridge south of Venezuela (Kawell 2002). The profits are concentrated more in processing and trafficking than in the production of the raw material.

Antidrug efforts measure "success" in terms of reducing supply and land under cultivation, but it is not clear that this does much more than raise prices and open opportunities for new entrepreneurs to fill the gap when older traffickers are detained. But it is the cultivators, mostly poor peasants, who are at the greatest risk. They are the easiest to find, and their lower share of profits deprives them of political influence—something that has begun to change as growers' unions have emerged in the Andes, most notably in Bolivia. Human rights issues almost inevitably arise not only because those at the bottom of the supply chain are poor peasants who suffer "collateral damage" from military operations, including fumigation of their lands and abuse by troops, but also because as an organized movement they challenge the governments that collaborate with U.S. antidrug and antiterrorism operations.

Presidents Bush I, Clinton, and Bush II always justified military aid to Andean nations as part of the antidrug war, but counterinsurgency has always been a handmaiden of this policy (see the official U.S. policy documents in the electronic National Security Archive, www.gwu.edu/~nsarchiv). Coca cultivation in Peru's Huallaga Valley was helping to sustain the Sendero Luminoso guerrilla movement. The Drug Enforcement Agency (DEA), a police bureau, found itself conducting military operations, leading some Bush administration officials in 1989 to recommend turning the task over to regular U.S. forces. Twenty members of the U.S. Army Special Forces were deployed to help train Peruvian units.

Nowhere are human rights concerns more in conflict with U.S.-supported antidrug operations than in Colombia. Colombia's two major insurgencies, the ELN and FARC, both of which are officially considered "terrorist" organizations by Washington, finance themselves in part through protection of growers and traffickers, if not through direct involvement in trafficking. These insurgencies, as we saw in chapter 10, have their roots in political disputes going back to the immediate post–World War II era, long before the drug trade emerged as a significant part of the country's economy. Guerrilla tactics also include attacking oil and energy installations and kidnapping. The insurgents have used kidnapping to raise money and have committed other serious human rights abuses; however, their adversaries, the right-wing paramilitary forces formally grouped under the Autodefensas Unidas de Colombia (AUC), which has had strong links to the Colombian military, are even worse. In 2005, Colombian president Álvaro Uribe ushered an amnesty law through his country's Congress, pardoning paramilitary leaders, many of whom are deeply implicated in human rights atrocities and narco-trafficking. Uribe had significant success in fighting the FARC and ELN, but he may know the "enemy" too well. In 2006, an opposition Colombian senator launched an investigation of Uribe himself, uncovering evidence indicating that paramilitaries had trained on farms owned by the president and his brothers (a charge denied by Uribe). Uribe's domestic intelligence chief was accused of supplying information to the death squads to target academics and union leaders. A conservative estimate is that more than 40 union leaders were assassinated in Colombia in 2008, with more than 2,600 since 1986 (Human Rights Watch 2008).

Agreements between the United States and Latin American countries have raised an important rule-of-law issue: extraterritoriality. These agreements generally give U.S. troops legal immunity (COHA 2005b) from criminal prosecution in the host country. In 2009, the Uribe government in Colombia signed an agreement to allow the United States to locate on its territory seven military bases (euphemistically called "forward operating areas" to keep these de facto treaties from facing scrutiny in the U.S. Senate). Ultimately, Uribe's successor, Juan Manuel Santos, accepted a ruling by the Colombian Supreme Court that the agreement is unconstitutional. In 2002, the United States sought to convince Costa Rica, with Latin America's longest continuous democratic constitution, to be the host of an international law enforcement academy, successor to the School of the Americas. However, the United States would not agree to San José's conditions: (1) that only police and not military personnel would be trained there and (2) that the academy's U.S. personnel would not enjoy diplomatic immunity from prosecution for crimes under Costa Rican law. (The United States has sought immunity agreements to shield its soldiers and politicians from the International Criminal Court, which the United States rejects, despite having originally championed its creation.) In 2005, over the objection of human rights advocates, El Salvador agreed to host the academy. El Salvador's reputation could not be any more opposite that of Costa Rica. A United Nations truth commission documented in 1993 that 90 percent of the violence in El Salvador's civil war of 1980–1992 was perpetrated by government forces (COHA 2005a).

PUNTO DE VISTA: RULE OF LAW AND FIGHTING VIOLENT CRIME IN MEXICO

The following is excerpted from *Peña Nieto's Challenge: Criminal Cartels and Rule of Law in Mexico*, a report of the International Crisis Group, March 19, 2013. The full report can be found at the group's website, www.crisisgroup.org.

After years of intense, cartel-related bloodshed that has claimed tens of thousands of lives and shaken Mexico, new President Enrique Peña Nieto is promising to reduce the murder rate . . . The cartels have thousands of gunmen and have morphed into diversified crime groups that not only traffic drugs, but also conduct mass kidnappings, oversee extortion rackets and steal from the state oil industry. The military still fights them in much of the country on controversial missions too often ending in shooting rather than prosecutions. If Peña Nieto does not build an effective police and justice system, the violence may continue or worsen . . .

The development of cartels into murder squads fighting to control territory with military-grade weapons challenges the Mexican state's monopoly on the use of force in some regions. The brutality of their crimes undermines civilian trust in the government's capacity to protect them, and the corruption of drug money damages belief in key institutions. Cartels challenge the fundamental nature of the state, therefore, not by threatening to capture it, but by damaging and weakening it. The military fight-back has at times only further eroded the trust in government by inflicting serious human rights abuses. Some frustrated communities have formed armed "self-defense" groups against the cartels. Whatever the intent, these also degrade the rule of law. . . .

Within the grey world of fighting between rival cartels and security forces, there is much confusion as to who the victims of the violence are, and who killed them or made them disappear. Estimates of the total that have died in connection with the fighting over the last six years range from 47,000 to

more than 70,000, in addition to thousands of disappearances. Cartel gunmen often dress in military uniforms and include corrupt police in their ranks, so people are unsure if they are facing criminals or troops. A victim's movement is demanding justice and security. Mexico has also lost hundreds of police and army officers, mayors, political candidates, judges, journalists and human rights defenders to the bloodshed that is taking a toll on its democratic institutions.

The cartel violence began to escalate in 2004, when Vicente Fox was president and immediately after the domestic U.S. legislative ban on assault weapons expired. President Felipe Calderón launched an offensive against the criminal groups in 2006. . . . Calderón oversaw record seizures of cocaine, crystal meth and drug money, while security forces captured or killed 25 of the 37 most wanted cartel bosses. However, violence between rival criminal groups and the security forces shot up rapidly, while the army, previously one of Mexico's most respected institutions, came under scrutiny for widespread human rights abuses. The crackdown was also hindered by corruption, with police and military, as well as prosecutors, investigators and politicians being arrested for working with cartels, sometimes as killers.

Peña Nieto, who took office on 1 December 2012, has won broad consensus from the major political parties in support of a security plan. It promises to implement police and justice reforms, including overhauling a deficient judicial system and confronting the challenge of Mexico having more than 2,000 police forces that operate independently at the federal, state and municipal levels. For these reforms to succeed, the government must train police to both respect human rights and build strong cases that stand up under the new trial system. . . . Now it is essential to review how to maximize and sustain the impact. Effective police and courts are crucial to reducing impunity in the long term.

The Peña Nieto administration also needs to follow through on its announced national crime prevention plan, aimed especially at helping young people in the most violent areas. The cartels have been able to recruit tens of thousands of killers in part because poor neighbourhoods have been systematically abandoned over decades and lack sufficient schools, community centres and security—in short, they lack opportunity. There are many dedicated Mexican social workers with the experience and ability to reach the vulnerable groups if they are given resources.

While funding to help these programs is money well spent, Washington also needs to better control trafficking in guns, especially assault rifles, from U.S. suppliers, who are a principal source of arms for the cartels.

International leaders need to engage in a serious debate on counter-narcotics policies, including strategies to curtail both production and consumption. While Mexico's cartels have become diversified crime groups, they still make billions of dollars every year trafficking drugs to the U.S., money that pays for guns, killers and corruption. At the global level, it is past time to re-evaluate policies that have failed to prevent illicit drugs from maintaining dangerous levels of addiction and to reduce the corruption and violence associated with drug production and trafficking. . . .

The international community has much to learn from the efforts of the Mexican government and society to overcome these challenges. If they succeed in reducing violence, theirs can become a security model to follow instead of one to fear.

Point/Counterpoint

Is it a good idea to use military forces to fight the drug cartels?

    a. If you answered yes, how do you respond to the objections that the drug war is causing violence to solve a problem caused by U.S. consumption and that decriminalization would be more effective?

    b. If you answered no, how do you respond to the violence and corruption that seem to be connected to trafficking and to the social harm that drug addiction can cause?

For more information

For examination of why Latin American governments have grown more favorably disposed toward legalization or decriminalization of some drugs in their own countries, see "Legalize It?," *The Global Post: In Depth* (2013), www.globalpost.com/series/legalize-it. The Global Commission on Drug Policy (www.globalcommissionondrugs.org/about/), headed by former president Henrique Cardoso of Brazil, has called for reconsideration of the drug war. Among those who oppose liberalization of antidrug laws is Pope Francis, whose views are summarized at *Infosur Hoy* (http://infosurhoy.com/en_GB/articles/saii/features/main/2013/06/21/feature-01).

For Review

What are the stated objectives of the U.S. "war on drugs"? How do the objectives of this "war" and other U.S. policies conflict sometimes with support for human rights and rule of law?

Rating Human Rights Records

It can be difficult to assess any one country's human rights record. Does one examine the record in absolute or relative terms? One or a few political murders are serious enough, especially when perpetrated by the state, but few would say that the human rights record of Mexico or Venezuela in recent decades is as horrible as that of Colombia or El Salvador in the 1980s. Violations approached the level of genocide in Guatemala. An estimated 200,000 people, the majority of them Mayans, were killed in the civil strife of the 1980s in that country, the vast majority at the hands of security forces. We should look at human rights both in absolute terms, so as not to trivialize any abuse that costs even one life, and in relative terms, to keep some perspective on how countries differ from one another.

Freedom House

Freedom House (FH), an organization founded in 1941, claims to be the oldest advocate of human rights in the world. FH does criticize capitalist regimes, but during the Cold War, it consistently singled out the communist countries and leftist regimes as the worst abusers, even when they had fewer prisoners and fewer incidents of torture and political murders. The practice did not end with the Cold War. Because FH's evaluations are expressed in a numerical rating system, its ratings find their way into comparative political science more often than those of Amnesty International and Human Rights Watch, whose reports are not easily reduced to a number. How reliable are FH's ratings? FH uses reports from its contacts abroad and the judgment of its in-house experts and outside advisors to rate countries on a scale of one (best) to seven (worst) on two dimensions: political rights, which are an essential need for citizens to hold governments responsible through electoral and other constitutional mechanisms, and civil liberties, which have to do with individual freedom of conscience, expression, and so on.

Few would dispute—short of advocating the overthrow of a government—the right of individual citizens to speak and write freely, without government censorship. However, not everyone would agree with including under this mantle the "right" of media corporations to be free of government regulation of content (Miller 2005). Most large-scale private media are owned by corporations that are themselves powerful gatekeepers. "Freedom of the press belongs to the man who owns one," said the journalist A. J. Liebling. In addition, FH takes little care distinguishing regulation, which is something all countries do, from censorship. FH claims it promotes rights embodied in the Universal Declaration of Human Rights, but it does not include any of the social and economic rights embodied in that document. The Declaration includes rights to employment, decent housing, nutrition, and other "quality of life" rights, which are seen by liberal democrats as an outcome, one that might be fostered by democracy, but that is not intrinsic to democracy itself.

FH explicitly ties its conception of freedom to market economics, thereby tying democracy to a particular type of economic system. FH says its judgments are based not only on what states do but also on the actions of nonstate actors (guerrillas, death squads, etc.) "that can dramatically restrict essential freedoms in a society." FH's list of such groups does not include banks or corporations—the market, in its view, does not restrict rights. (For more information, you can visit the FH website at www.freedomhouse.org.) Its ratings can be useful, as long as we recognize that they pertain to rights as defined within liberal ideology.

FH routinely ranks Cuba with Burma, North Korea, Saudi Arabia, and Chechnya, all countries that most objective observers, whether leftist or rightist, would categorize as among the most abusive in the world. FH consistently rates Cuba at the bottom of its human rights scale—at a seven—often ranking it below Guatemala, Argentina, and a number of other countries during eras of notorious human rights abuses. In 2012, FH ranked Paraguay and Colombia both at three—"partly free"; Honduras at four, also "partly free," only one rank lower than for 2009, the year of the coup in that country; and Haiti at four, "partly free."

Not surprisingly, the Cuban government and its supporters abroad disagree. Their rebuttal calls attention to the widespread availability of health services, education, and opportunities for women that go far beyond the rest of the hemisphere, including the United States in some respects. They point out that the gap between the elites and masses in Cuba is the smallest in the hemisphere. Corruption exists, but penalties are harsh and abuses less common. Cubans have experienced no state of siege and no disappearances, unlike almost all other countries in the hemisphere. Religious denominations that refrain from political activity against the government are free to operate and even receive state subsidies.

Cuba's Committees for the Defense of the Revolution (CDRs; see chapter 10) are charged with monitoring dissidents (although their role has significantly diminished since Raúl Castro ascended to leadership in 2008). Amnesty International and Human Rights Watch severely criticized the CDRs. A *Watch Report* in 1994 included the following charge:

> Violation of the right to privacy was systematic. Tight political control was maintained through extensive monitoring of Cubans' daily lives, conducted by state-security police who often coerced or blackmailed people into becoming informants, as well as by state-sponsored "mass organizations" such as the Committees for the Defense of the Revolution Human (CDRs), which operated in neighborhoods and workplaces.
>
> (Human Rights Watch 1994)

On the other hand, the CDRs also play an important role in providing one element of effective governance: security for citizens. Mark Kruger, director of the criminal justice program at St. Louis University, attributes the very low crime rate in Cuba to the sense of community and mutual responsibility encouraged by Cuban mass organizations, especially the CDRs, in local government. "CDRs provide the glue that attaches individual community members to the larger community," says Kruger.

> Because they meet frequently and work on public projects together, CDR members know each other and are familiar with most residents on their blocks. They are aware of which block members are young and old and need checking on, which residents work during the day and are not at home, and which block members have problems in their homes that may need social support . . . Members of the neighborhood, especially older and retired persons who are home during the day, constitute the eyes of the community and watch for criminal and other inappropriate activity.
>
> (Kruger 2007: 108)

The point here is not that Freedom House ratings are meaningless or nothing more than biased propaganda. Restraints on freedom of speech and assembly are worthy of reproach. However, through the use of only liberal criteria on rights and the exclusion of other kinds of criteria, some important distinctions are lost. The FH rating system has in various years

PUNTO DE VISTA: REFORM OR ATTACK ON THE INTER-AMERICAN COMMISSION ON HUMAN RIGHTS?

In 2013, the ALBA countries proposed a set of reforms, the most controversial of which would (1) relocate the Inter-American Commission on Human Rights from Washington, DC, to a country that, unlike the United States, has ratified the 1969 American Convention on Human Rights; (2) require that annual reports be published together in a single volume, rather than allowing the one on "expression" (relating to press freedoms and freedom of speech) to be published standing alone; and (3) prohibit outside, earmarked contributions to the work of the commission and court, instead requiring that all such contributions support the work of human rights rapporteurs investigating all eight kinds of human rights issues that fall under the IACHR's jurisdiction. After intense debate, these proposals were not adopted, in part because of the unwillingness of Argentina and Brazil to support the measure. However, countries agreed to continue discussions about making reforms to the IACHR and the associated Inter-American Court for Human Rights.

The IACHR's special rapporteur for freedom of expression is the only full-time rapporteur. The other seven rapporteurs are assigned part-time to rights of, respectively, indigenous peoples, migrants, persons deprived of liberty, children, women, Afrodescendents, and human rights defenders. Each of these rapporteurs is also assigned responsibility for coverage of groups of countries, unlike the special rapporteur on freedom of expression. Also, unlike the latter, the other seven typically hold outside jobs.

Not having ratified the convention, the United States rejects the jurisdiction of the court. The U.S. contribution to the Organization of American States (OAS), like that of other countries in the region, is proportionate to the size of its economy. Were the proposals for reform to pass, it would strengthen the attempts by conservatives in the U.S. Congress who, for either reasons of fiscal restraint or claims that the OAS has become biased against the United States, want to cut or eliminate U.S. funding to the organization. In 2012, the United States contributed $48 million of the total $85 million in the OAS budget. The IACHR budget for 2012 was $7.8 million, of which $4.8 was from regular funds, $3 million from special funds. Opponents and supporters of the ALBA proposals agree that over 90 percent of funds to the special rapporteur for expression come from earmarked voluntary contributions.

The Inter-American Dialogue, a private organization based in Washington, DC, invited several individuals to comment on the ALBA reforms. Two of their positions are presented here:

Carmen Lomellin, U.S. permanent representative to the Organization of American States:

Freedom of expression is fundamental to democracy and human rights. The Inter-American Commission on Human Rights (IACHR) has improved the human and civil rights of thousands and has served for more than five decades as the hemisphere's moral conscience. It works and it is a model for other regional organizations. This is why it is so important to defend its autonomy and independence. If your conscience is bothering you, the solution is not to silence it. No government should place itself beyond international scrutiny when it comes to the protection of basic human rights and civil liberties. A stronger and more capable commission is in all our interests. None of this, however, means that a process of modernizing reflection and reform should not have taken place. This was an enormously useful exercise, and as the largest donor to the IACHR, the United States actively supported it. If the states hostile to the commission had succeeded in restricting access to outside funding, they would have undermined the important work of the IACHR, particularly the special rapporteur for freedom of expression. This would have been a clear step backward for the countries of the Western Hemisphere, a throw-back to the dark days of military dictatorships. We've seen this movie before, and we don't want to go there again. An isolated minority group of states argued that the IACHR singles them out for criticism because the financial support that the commission receives comes mostly from the United States, Canada and the European Union. There is no singling out; all countries, including ours, have been subject to scrutiny and we all have had our differences with the commission on individual cases. The answer is not to cut off funding but rather to increase it from all sources so that the work of the commission can continue in a free and independent fashion, unfettered from governmental influence.

Nathalie Cely, Ecuador's ambassador to the United States

The Inter-American Commission on Human Rights (IACHR) has played a crucial role helping to nurture and safeguard democracy in the Western Hemisphere, particularly during turbulent periods in the 1970s and 1980s. Ecuador believes that it remains crucial that members of the commission, their deliberations and all final resolutions retain their independence and autonomy. The reforms that Ecuador and others supported would not only strengthen

this autonomy, they would in fact strengthen the ability of the IACHR to fulfill its mission to protect people such as women, children and indigenous groups. Under the current IACHR funding system, seven of its eight rapporteurs are significantly underfunded, preventing them from properly protecting the rights of millions of people. Only one—the special rapporteur for freedom of expression—enjoys sufficient funding to serve full-time. In fact, it receives five times the funding as the average rapporteur. While we agree that freedom of expression is essential to the region's growth, it should not come at the expense of other equally important rights such as those of women and children. This is an inherently unjust and undemocratic system. Our proposals sought to raise the status of all eight positions to the same level as the special rapporteur and provide each with equal and sufficient funding to enable them to conduct their work fully and independently. No rapporteur would be weakened, and the IACHR as a whole would be strengthened. And no longer would individual states be allowed to wield their influence to rig the system at the expense of others. In addition, our proposal sought to require all member countries to ratify the American Convention on Human Rights, which gives the IACHR its authority, so that all agree to play by the same rules. It is unfortunate that 30 years later, certain countries still have not ratified this important convention. Fortunately, there was a consensus among the OAS members to continue ongoing discussions on these proposed reforms, and we look forward to further collaboration and debate to create a stronger, more independent and more democratic IACHR.

Point/Counterpoint

Should the IACHR be moved to one of the signatory countries? Should funding be distributed evenly through the commission to all rapporteurs—even if the United States threatens to cut off all funding in that eventuality?

a. If you answered yes to these questions, how would you respond to those who say that the real motive for proposing these changes is to weaken oversight of human rights agreements made after the most recent transitions to democracy in the region?

b. If you answered no to these questions, how do you respond to those who say that the United States picks and chooses which rights to support and not to support and that the most powerful member of the OAS has not itself ratified the treaty establishing the IACHR?

For more information

Amnesty International criticizes Venezuela's withdrawal from the IAHCR at www.amnesty-usa.org/news/news-item/venezuela-s-withdrawal-from-regional-human-rights-instrument-is-a-serious-setback. Venezuela's case is summarized at http://venezuelanalysis.com/news/10014. For a case that might cause problems for both sides on this issue, see the criticism of a recent IACHR decision in favor of mining companies and against indigenous people in Guatemala, reversing IACHR's own earlier ruling, at http://intercontinentalcry.org/inter-american-commission-on-human-rights-gives-in-to-pressure-from-guatemala.

virtually equated Cuba with North Korea. Governments practicing **ethnic cleansing**, such as Guatemala, end up with a better human rights rating than a country that has never implemented a state of siege or permitted death squads to operate.

Enforcement of human rights obligations within the hemispheric system has become somewhat contentious in recent years. In 1969, a set of international obligations known as the American Convention on Human Rights came into existence, and in 1979 the Inter-American Court on Human Rights and the Inter-American Commission on Human Rights were created to support it. (We will abbreviate only the commission as the IACHR; see www.oas.org/en/iachr/mandate/Basics/convention.asp.) The convention guaranteed civil rights but not economic and social rights, but two additional protocols afterward endorsed "second generation rights"—that is cultural, social, and economic ones.

Leaders of Venezuela and other countries in the Bolivarian Alliance for the Americas (ALBA) complain that the commission is biased by norms and institutions influenced by the United States. This might be expected from the more radical governments in the region, but the rest of Latin America has grown increasingly restive about the inadequacy of the IACHR and sympathetic to the claim that it is too influenced by the United States. Venezuela claims that the IACHR was particularly tepid in reacting to the short-lived coup against Chávez in 2002, a claim the commission denies (see Emersberger 2010; IACHR 2010). In September 2012, Venezuela formally withdrew from the Convention on Human Rights, which it had ratified in 1977; it holds that its withdrawal allows it to deny the IACHR jurisdiction after September 2013. The IACHR claims Venezuela remains obligated to the convention because of the country's membership in the Organization of American States (OAS), with which the

IACHR is affiliated. The IACHR has not made the same claim about the United States, which has never ratified the convention or the protocols but provides the lion's share of funding for the commission's operation.

For Review

What factors may cause disagreement about human rights conditions in particular countries? What can be said for and against Cuba's human rights record in the Castro era?

Progress on Law and Rights?

Few observers of Latin America believe that much progress has been made toward overcoming corruption, reducing crime, or establishing impartial judicial systems. On the other hand, it does seem that significant progress has been made in establishing respect for human rights as a principle of government—although there remain serious issues here too, of course, and significant variations across countries. Most scholars see democracy and rule of law as mutually reinforcing one another. For some, one cannot exist without the other. It is hard to believe that an effective democracy can be stabilized without more progress in all these areas, but there is a viewpoint, we have seen, that argues first for establishment of the rule of law and then democracy only later.

Discussion Questions

1.   Looking at Latin America, do you think that rule of law and democracy are inseparable from one another, or do you think it is possible to have one without the other? In particular, can one have the rule of law without democracy?
2.   In judging human rights conditions in Latin America, besides civil rights, such as freedom of speech, should we also include consideration of substantive rights, such as the right to an education?
3.   Why do you think that prison conditions are so bad (even by U.S. standards) in Latin America? Do you think it is possible for democratic governments to bring (a) crime and (b) corruption under control in the region, or might this be something only nondemocratic governments can accomplish?

Resources for Further Study

Reading: A leading study is Lynn Hammergren's *Envisioning Reform: Improving Judicial Performance in Latin America* (College Park: Pennsylvania State University, 2007). Hammergren examines the difficulties in implementing legal reform in "Latin American

Experience with Rule of Law Reform and Its Applicability to Nation-Building," *Case Western Reserve Journal of International Law* 38, no. 1 (2006): 63–93. On human rights, see Lars Schoultz's *Human Rights and United States Policy toward Latin America* (Princeton, NJ: Princeton University Press, 1981), which is particularly good on the Carter years. Martin Edwin Andersen's *Dossier Secreto* is a critical look at the Argentine Dirty War from both a human rights and a security point of view. The September/October 2011 issue of *NACLA Report on the Americas* includes several articles claiming that the human rights issue has been used politically and selectively by the right in an attempt to undermine the international reputation of leftist regimes.

Video and Film: *Cocalero* (2007) depicts human rights issues raised by the drug war in Bolivia. Journeyman Pictures offers several good films on the impact of the drug war in the Andes. See its website: www.journeyman.tv. *Landless* (2007), produced by Sonofed and available on YouTube, documents a land takeover, including the movement's interaction with law and the courts. *Dictator in the Dock* looks at the trial of former Guatemalan dictator General Efraín Ríos Montt, who was accused of crimes against humanity and genocide against the Maya Ixil people. Crime, drugs, and the lower class are all subjects of *City of God* (*Cidade de Deus*; 2002), a drama directed by Kátia Lund and Fernando Meirelles. This movie, based on a true story, tells of a dangerously violent neighborhood just outside of Rio de Janeiro, Brazil. Here, two boys grow up, one to become a photographer and one to become a drug dealer.

On the Internet: See the websites for Human Rights Watch (www.hrw.org), Amnesty International (www.amnesty.org), and the Inter-American Commission on Human Rights (www.cidh.org). The U.S. State Departments posts its annual human rights review by country on the web; the 2013 report can be found at www.state.gov/j/drl/rls/hrrpt/humanrightsreport/#wrapper. The human rights page at the University of Texas is a useful portal to the sites of human rights organizations throughout the hemisphere. See http://lanic.utexas.edu/la/region/hrights/.

PART V

Latin America in the World

FOURTH
BRICS Summit
March 29, 2012 : New Delhi

New Delhi
BRICS
2012

15 Democracy in Times of Globalization

Focus Questions

▶ Is globalization enhancing the prospects for democracy in Latin America?

▶ What challenges does globalization pose to the sovereignty of states in Latin America?

▶ What are some of the key issues in the debates about what kind of hemispheric economic integration is best suited for Latin America?

IN MARCH 2012, Brazilian judge Daniela Pereira Madeira ruled in favor of the Brazilian pharmaceutical company Cristália and annulled the patent held by Abbott Laboratories for Kaletra, a drug for treating AIDS/HIV. Cristália plans to begin producing a generic version of Kaletra. The decision was the latest (and probably not the last) in a legal battle that began in July 2005, one week after Brazil's health minister, José Saraiva Felipe, assumed his new job. Felipe found himself attempting to renegotiate access to Kaletra and other drugs that are made freely available by the Brazilian government to all who need it. The number of Brazilians taking the drug was expected to increase from 23,400 to 60,000. Felipe needed to strike a deal. Kaletra alone was absorbing a third of the health ministry's budget for antiviral medicines.

The Brazilian minister's adversary in the negotiations was a representative not of a foreign government but of a giant U.S. pharmaceutical company. Felipe's objective was not only to get a break on the price but also to obtain rights to manufacture a generic version of the drug upon expiration of Abbott's patent in 2015. He won a price reduction from Abbott, but the issue over the patent remained.

The judge ruled that allowing foreign patents to be extended beyond their initial term— a "pipeline" process, as it is known in Brazil—is not in accord with her country's constitution (New 2012). The ruling was hailed by the Brazilian Network for Integration of Peoples, which has been advocating resistance to attempts on the part of the United States, the European Union, and other developed countries to toughen protection of "intellectual property rights," as patent, trademark, and copyright laws are known. However, the Brazilian government was not solely motivated by concern for poor, HIV-positive Brazilians. Brazil wants to develop its own pharmaceutical industry. This why the country has resisted attempts by the United States and the European Union to tighten and enforce intellectual property rights in global talks to expand the **World Trade Organization (WTO)**. The minister warned that Brazil would, if necessary, go ahead and start manufacturing the drug without a license if a satisfactory agreement could not be reached. For this reason, several other **transnational** drug companies have been interested spectators (Benson 2005: B13).

In many ways, the ongoing conflict reflects the way an increasingly globalized international order seems to be testing the old rules of the game, from a time when national sovereignty trumped all. These rules, which originated in the Treaty of Westphalia back in the seventeenth century, obligate states not to intervene in the internal affairs of other territorial states. The principle was never fully respected (with good reason, in some cases), but today several significant challenges associated with globalization threaten state sovereignty:

- Information flows across borders, especially on the Internet, making censorship more difficult to enforce. Availability of social media, smartphones, and camcorders allows unmediated communication by political actors.
- Migration of undocumented workers and refugees challenges the capacity of countries to regulate population movements. The United States is building a wall along its border with Mexico, at a significant cost to friendly relationships with its southern neighbor. Mexico finds it difficult to police its borders with Guatemala.
- Climate change has unleashed natural forces that require international and not national solutions. Drug eradication policies in Colombia are poisoning rivers in Ecuador. Melting glaciers in the Andes may force hundreds of thousands of farmers to migrate across borders. Clearing of rainforests in tropical areas is contributing significantly to global warming.
- Biogenetic and other technologies can move on their own; viruses respect no borders. Brazilian and Mexican farmers find unwanted, genetically engineered crops on their land. Tourism facilitates the spread of the HIV virus in the Caribbean.
- Terrorism and the global drug trade have replaced communism as the global "threat" and have proven resilient against the power of national militaries. Illegal trafficking in drugs and people is one of the most lucrative transnational businesses, and it persists underground and resists state efforts to eradicate it.
- Human rights issues have reinforced the principle that there are crimes against humanity that take precedent over respect for sovereignty, justifying the creation of supranational judiciaries (e.g., the International Criminal Court) or humanitarian intervention to halt or prevent abuses.

In this chapter, we define **globalization** as a broad international tendency toward greater interaction of people across national boundaries of all types—economic, cultural, natural, and so on. Most commonly, globalization is associated with free flows of trade and communication among nations, but we can see already that it is a much broader phenomenon. Trade and communication technologies have lent momentum to extraordinary changes in the production of goods and services in the global economy, perhaps the most fundamental process advancing globalization overall.

The late political economist Susan Strange (1996) argued that the nation-state is being weakened by its inability to deal with widespread, growing economic inequality. But Strange has her critics. For example, Paul Haslam (1999) argues that sovereignty has never been absolute or monolithic. It changes in historical circumstance and may be getting stronger in some areas even as it weakens in others. These theoretical differences are visible in the popular media and politics. Pro-globalization theorists, who include popular commentators such as the *New York Times* columnist Thomas Friedman (2000b, 2005) and *Newsweek's* Fareed Zakaria, take the position that through increased interdependency, globalization reduces the risk of war and is key to a more prosperous global economy for all. On the other hand, a worldwide anti-globalism movement, which includes most of Latin America's largest grassroots movements (see chapter 11), is skeptical that capitalist globalization is in their economic interest, and they are loath to see national governments, where they have some influence, losing effective sovereignty in favor of distant (geographically and in terms of political distance) international organizations.

For Review

What are some of the key issues that globalization raises for Latin America? What issues about globalization are raised in particular by the dispute between Brazil and Abbott Laboratories?

Economic Globalization and Latin America

We begin to examine economic globalization out of the conviction that it is the most powerful of global tendencies, underlying many of the others to a great extent. Friedman (2000b, 2005), the *New York Times* columnist, in his widely read books *The Lexis and the Olive Tree* and *The World Is Flat*, described globalization as driven by technology and increasing interconnectedness. Friedman sees globalization as inevitable, beneficial to most people, and supportive of democracy. Countries that resist globalization, rich and poor, will lose out, for which reason he has supported various trade agreements sent to the U.S. Congress. The *Times* columnist ridicules the anti-globalization movement, saying their real name ought to be "the Coalition to Keep the World's Poor People Poor" (Friedman 2000a).

In contrast, Fatoumata Jawara and Aileen Kwa, two researchers affiliated with the London-based NGO Oxfam International, believe that the

> globalization process . . . brings increasing limitations on the ability of governments to enact policies in the interests of their own populations—even, in some cases, policies that affect trade indirectly—and effectively gives precedence to trade and international commercial interests over people and international commitments and agreements directed at their benefit.

Their conclusion is based on research and observation they did behind the scenes at the Doha Ministerial Conference of the **WTO** in November 2001. "Ministerials" are the most important venues for setting new economic global rules of the game. Jawara and Kwa conclude, "WTO decisions are taken in a way favoring the interests of the few over the many, and commercial interests over ordinary people's livelihoods" (Jawara and Kwa 2002: 5).

Economic globalization is often equated with **"free trade"**—that is, elimination of tariffs, quotas, and regulations that limit exchanges of goods and services between nations. However, trade agreements involve much more today. These agreements define the rules for protecting technologies and cultural products (e.g., patents and copyrights, as we saw in the Brazilian case just mentioned). They often prohibit a nation from treating foreign investors differently from domestic ones, limiting the range of policies (e.g., those used in the **import substitution** era) available to the state to promote national industries. These provisions also attack national laws that reserve ownership of national resources to that country's own citizens. Of course, such provisions are also binding on wealthier countries, and for this reason opposition is often voiced by unions and others concerned about the flight of manufacturing jobs from Detroit, St. Louis, and many other U.S. cities.

Thus, far from merely lowering barriers to movement of goods and service, free-trade agreements also make it easier for investments to flow over national boundaries. It is much easier today than 30 years ago for money to slip in and out of national economies. By liberating transnational capital to move with fewer restrictions, free-trade agreements facilitate the construction of an international economic system in which the manufacture of any product of any complexity (e.g., the book you are reading) may happen in several countries along what has come to be called "the global assembly line," a term taken from the title of a documentary (Gray, 1985) that noted the change early.

Economic globalization involves two different ways of reorganizing the division of labor in the world economy. One has to do with *the production and exchange of whole goods*, what most people have considered "trade" through the ages. To take a simple example, if Salvadorans produce coffee and Canadians produce ladders, and then they trade them with one another, this division of labor in the making of a whole product corresponds to the way most of us think about trade. This is mainly what the English economist David Ricardo had in mind when he put forth his theory of **comparative advantage**, arguing by way of example that Portugal and England would both benefit if the first country concentrated on production of wine, the second focused on clothing, and then the two exchanged these products with one another. This is the underlying argument that supporters of free trade make for the wider idea of "trade" we have just noted.

A second division of labor has to do with *how goods and services themselves are produced*—the *division of labor in production* itself. Adam Smith first recognized that the "wealth of nations" actually resided in the productivity of labor, which in turn depended on both technology and the way in which the labor in a society is organized. Smith's famous example involved the making of a pin. Note how elaborate the process already was nearly 250 years ago. Making a pin, he says,

> is divided into a number of branches, of which the greater part are likewise peculiar trades. One man draws out the wire, another straights it, a third cuts it, a fourth points it, a fifth grinds it at the top for receiving the head; to make the head requires two or three distinct operations; to put it on, is a peculiar business, to whiten the pins is another; it is even a trade by itself to put them into the paper; and the important business of making a pin is, in this manner, divided into about eighteen distinct operations, which, in some manufactories, are all performed by distinct hands, though in others the same man will sometimes perform two or three of them.
>
> (Smith 1766, book 1, chapter 1, paragraph 3)

As a result, Smith says, thousands more pins can be manufactured with the same amount of labor time than could be done if each person were to make the whole pin individually.

In Smith's day, factories for manufacturing items such as pins were just emerging. By the 1930s, Henry Ford had taken the idea of the division of labor in production to a new level with the assembly line, where workers performed different, specialized tasks as the product passed through different stages of production moving through the factory—and rather than a pin, the product was an automobile. Economic globalization, made possible by an information and transportation revolution, now involves a global assembly line. On the global assembly line, a product (be it a pin or an airliner) is passed not just from worker to worker but also from nation to nation, with value added along the way. The process is repeated, often 10 or 15 times, to manufacture, for example, a simple garment. Our hypothetical Canadian ladder may be the product of Canadian wood, cut into component parts and shipped out of Vancouver to Mexico for assembly, using glue manufactured by a French-owned company in Senegal, and then shipped on a Panamanian-flagged freighter to a Walmart warehouse in El Salvador—with the entire process controlled by a computer system maintained in New Delhi, India. In sum, almost anything of any complexity produced today is not produced in a single factory or country but is passed along from country to country, stage by stage, along a global assembly line.

In the next section of this chapter, we examine how this larger process of economic-integration globalization has affected Latin America's place in the division of labor in the world economy, considering four separate areas (manufacturing, agriculture, mining and energy, and tourism) that have been influenced both by new technologies (information and communications, transportation, genetic engineering, robotics, etc.) and by new markets, especially in Asia. Latin America has not entirely shaken off dependency, but (keeping in mind that this applies more to some countries than others) it has made some economic gains that are shaping political change.

For Review

Why is a "free trade" treaty or agreement today about more than just opening ports to imports? What else do such agreements involve? In general, how do Latin American countries, as part of the Global South, differ from wealthier countries in what they want from multilateral trade negotiations?

Manufacturing, Maquilas, and the Global Assembly Line

When Henry Ford "invented" the assembly line to produce Model T automobiles, his intention was to gain control over the quality of components used in making his cars and to reduce production costs by facilitating the specialization of labor (something promoted earlier by Frederick Taylor), thereby reducing the price of making a car so that his market would grow. To do this, Ford concentrated his production in large factories. Raw materials arrived at one end of his factory, and cars were driven off at the other. Although other manufacturers supplied some parts, an astounding number of components were made fully in-house, brought together in one location, in one country. Much of the raw material, such as iron for steel and coal or oil for energy, was produced in the United States as well. Other industries emulated Ford's approach, and the underlying philosophy, which included the idea that salaried workers could become a mass market for manufactured goods, came to be called "Fordism."

The global assembly line involves the first part of Ford's formula for success with a major difference. Instead of a product moving through a single factory along one conveyor belt, with workers doing specialized tasks along the way, what we now see is a process whereby the "stations" in the production process are scattered around the globe. Technological transformations in communications and transportation have enhanced the ability of corporate managers to move components from one country to another and also to control production levels (just-in-time production) to ensure that there are no bottlenecks (shortages or excess of parts) in the supply chain. In fact, unlike in the case of Fordism, it is not even necessary to own the process. Production can be divided up among factories in different parts of the world through subcontracting.

Latin America was historically integrated into the world economy as a supplier of raw materials and agricultural products. Industrialization in North America, Europe, and Japan reinforced this pattern in the **liberal modernization** era, but by World War II, the process of **import substitution industrialization** (ISI) was well underway in larger Latin American countries. Latin America's factories were modeled on Ford's way of organizing production, but the factory owners found it cheaper to import machines with older technology than to invest in research and development; also, few Latin American universities could come close to matching the scientific knowledge and practical technology developed in the north. As we have seen, ISI faltered in the 1960s and gave way to the debt-ridden "lost decade" of the 1980s, preparing the way for Latin America to move away from state-led development and toward a **neoliberal** strategy (see chapters 5 and 6). Latin America entered the new era of liberalization of the global economy with an economic infrastructure and a scientific and educational sector that had not been prepared for international competition.

Of course, not all countries in the region went through ISI. In the small and poor Central American republics, for example, little industrialization took place, and the economies continued to depend heavily on agricultural exports, such as fruit and then, after World War II, sugar, cotton, and beef. In this same period, some light manufacturing—pajamas, bras, and so on—appeared for the first time, but again, it was geared toward export markets, not meeting the needs of the local population. This trend was reinforced in 1983, when the Reagan administration promoted the Caribbean Basin Initiative, under which Central American and Caribbean countries, other than Cuba, were offered duty-free access to the U.S. market for their exports. The goal was to promote economic growth and expansion of jobs to head off revolutions.

This policy laid the basis for expansion of the *maquila* sector—factories where workers do the final assembly of consumer goods with imported components. This kind of manufacturing may not even qualify as "industrialization" since it requires little investment in equipment and technology and relies on abundant unskilled labor. Although some *maquilas* may assemble something as sophisticated and complicated as an automobile, many do little more than stitch the cover on a baseball, cut and sow cloth to make garments, or assemble electronic circuits for computers or Game Boys. Each *maquila* factory is a cog in a broader assembly line of manufacturing of clothing, electronic consumer goods, toys, and so on. Often the *maquila* is the last stop in the process. You may find a "Made in country X" label, perhaps from a Central American or Caribbean nation, on the shirt or blouse you are wearing as you read this book.

Another major step toward a global assembly line was taken in Mexico in 1965 with the establishment of the Border Industrialization Program. Mexico revised its laws to exempt American companies from customs taxes on equipment, machines, and materials brought into Mexico to produce exports back to the United States; the United States in turn reduced tariffs on these exports from Mexico. Until 1994, there were limits on how much of the production under this program could escape import taxes in the United States. Unions and companies with factories in the United States did not wish to compete with cheaper Mexican production, but this changed in 1994 with NAFTA (the North American Free Trade Agreement), described later in more detail.

Supporters of the agreement argue that the ability of U.S. companies to move facilities to Mexico keeps them competitive with cheap-labor competitors in Asia and that it has contributed to the growth of the Mexican middle class. There is some evidence for the latter, but much of the working class has slid into the ranks of the poor. Workers' wages lost 76 percent of their buying power between 1982, when reforms that paved the way for the NAFTA were first introduced, and 2012 (Esquival 2011). *Maquila* employment in Mexico rose from approximately 550,000 to 1.3 million between 1994 and 2001, but then it fell by more than 200,000 jobs in 2002 (Papademetriou et al. 2003). One reason for the fall is that other countries have adopted a similar strategy. Employment figures have continued to fluctuate, rising in the rest of the decade and then falling again with the global recession set off by the financial crisis of 2008. In 2013 workers in the manufacturing sector in Mexico were typically paid on average US$10 per hour, twice the Mexican minimum wage. A typical *maquila* worker makes about $7.50 per hour. These wages compare to a little over US$19 for a manufacturing job in the United States, but few *maquila* workers have any significant benefits, such as health insurance or social security. This trend and the global economic crisis that began in 2008 resulted in the loss of hundreds of thousands more jobs in Mexico. Chinese workers in comparable industries earn about $5 per hour, but proximity to the U.S. market and trade preferences under NAFTA keep Mexico somewhat competitive (see www.tradingeconomics.com; on *maquila* wages, see Johnson 2012).

Globalization critics contend that the global assembly line is creating a "race to the bottom." Lax environmental and labor protection, poor salaries, and harsh living conditions are fostered, they say, by the need of low-income countries to attract foreign investment with the only **comparative advantages** they have—low wages and (sometimes) raw materials (oil, wood, mineral ores, etc.). Poor conditions are characteristic of the early process of industrialization, answer the globalists. The wealthy countries went through a similar phase. However, manufacturing in the age of Fordism and ISI resulted in much of the profit and expenditure of investment (on local raw materials, machines, and labor) remaining in the host country. Would manufacturing for export based on foreign investment and cheap labor yield similar results today?

Like people in many other regions of the world, many Latin Americans have been impressed with the success of the newly industrializing countries (NICs) of Asia, which have industrialized largely by orienting production toward a world market. At least that seems to be the lesson of South Korea, China, Taiwan, Malaysia, and Thailand. Other development experts argue that the Asian Tigers did not simply open their markets and remove government from the economy to succeed. They also stressed education, have sought to limit inequality, and carried out significant land reform—all in contrast to most of Latin America (see various points of view in Dietz and Street 1987).

Brazil's vice president, Michel Temer (left), talks with China's President Xi Jinping during their meeting at the Great Hall of the People in Beijing on November 7, 2013.

It is conceivable that for the Asian Tigers, India, and a few other countries, there may be a path to a more industrialized, technologically sophisticated society. The countries best positioned in Latin America to follow this path would seem to be Brazil, because of its size, natural resources, and developing technological capacity; Chile, because of its stature as a friendly environment for foreign investment and its geographical position on the Pacific Rim; and Mexico because of its proximity to the U.S. market. On the other hand, as we have already seen, all of these countries remain highly dependent on raw material exports; all remain highly unequal (limiting the potential for internal market growth); and all have significant sectors of the population that are highly skeptical of the development model defining the path to modernity.

For Review

Economic globalization since 1980 is often associated with neoliberalisim. Why? What is meant by the "global assembly line"? How has the global assembly line been encouraged by free-trade agreements?

Fertile Profits: Agribusiness

The growth of agribusiness has raised another challenge to national sovereignty—the ability to limit the use of seeds for genetically modified (GM) crops. GM crops are produced when scientists take a gene from one living thing and insert it into the genetic structure of another. Supporters of GM food say that the technology offers ways of boosting agricultural productivity and fighting hunger, as well as producing crops more resistant to disease. Detractors say that the long-term health dangers of such foods are inadequately known. They worry that this GM farming will reduce the great variety of seeds and animals currently used by farmers. Reducing seed banks and genetic diversity will make us more vulnerable to biological hazards. Also, such technology further concentrates control of agriculture in the hands of wealthier corporations and farmers who can afford innovations that are closely protected by patents; smaller farmers and the peasantry may find themselves increasingly marginalized by large-scale, technological agribusiness.

The Southern Cone east of the Andes offers ideal soil (*mollisol*) for cultivation of corn and, especially, soy. Rising demand in Asia and Europe attracted flows of foreign capital from global agribusiness. Agribusiness and its allies argue that new technologies and their ability to move capital across national boundaries permit farmers to increase yields and feed a growing world population. However, beyond the environmental issues, the global expansion of agri-business has opened issues about "food sovereignty," the willingness and ability of countries with fertile land to regulate land use to ensure the adequate nutrition of their own people, and the side effects of agribusiness expansion include displacement of many peasants and small farmers whose production is oriented to local markets and whose relationship to the land is quite different from that of the wealthy foreign and domestic owners who live in the cities.

The GM seeds are engineered genetically to survive the herbicides and pesticides that kill weeds and pests in the fields. The herbicides are sprayed over fields using GPS coordinates, destroying the ecosystem of Paraguay's *chaco*, what was once scrub "wasteland" but also home to fast-disappearing tropical birds, armadillos, anteaters, and powerful jaguars. As of 2005, GM crops were still illegal in Brazil, but their use in the country's fast-growing export sector was expanding. During his term (2003–2011), President Luiz Inácio Lula da Silva (Lula), whose PT (Workers' Party) includes a strong environmental movement in its ranks, faced a difficult choice between keeping a promise to his environmental and indigenous supporters or harming the most dynamic growth sector in the economy—soybean exports. Brazil found itself locked in an international legal battle over the demand of the Monsanto corporation that Brazil's farm-ers pay royalties for the use of GM seeds. In 2005, one state government even went so far as to negotiate an accord on royalties with Monsanto, a response to the smuggling of GM seeds into Brazil from Argentina. The federal government found itself being challenged in international courts for failing to enforce payment of royalties for the use of the new technology.

Brazil, once dependent on exports of beef, gold, rubber, and sugar, became the largest producer and exporter of soy in the world between 1990 and 2003—only to be rapidly sur-passed by neighboring countries. Paraguay and Uruguay increased soy exports, but Argentina's production exploded and passed them all in the post-2000 era. According to IndexMundi.com, in 2013 Argentina was expected to export more than 28 million metric tons of soy, more than doubling Brazil's export of the crop, and three times what the U.S. exports.

The soy boom has encouraged **monoculture**—that is, the devotion of a large proportion of fertile land in a region to a single crop. Between 1996 and 2008, the amount of land har-vested for soy increased from 6 million to 16.7 million hectares (one hectare—10,000 square meters—equals approximately 2.5 acres). Furthermore, new agricultural technology being deployed by Argentine landowners is mostly owned and controlled by **transnational cor-porations**. The labor on these farms is provided by migrants, many from nearby Paraguay and Bolivia. The British newspaper *The Independent* reported (blog, June 2, 3013), "The soya industry is highly concentrated down to a handful of multinational firms who dominate the entire market; from the very first seed through to sowing, spraying, harvesting, post-processing, all the way to the party. This is agribusiness at its most ruthlessly efficient." The article notes that most soy imports in Britain, whose import needs require foreign cultivation of an area the size of Yorkshire, end up in feed for chickens and cattle. In other words, the concept of a "global assembly line" now extends to agriculture.

The growth of soy exports has brought new conflict between Latin America and the United States. Brazil has insisted that the United States drastically lower subsidies for its soy producers in return for Brazil's cooperation in advancing the free-trade measures in the WTO and negotiating a hemispheric free-trade accord, a major objective of U.S. foreign policy. This conflict has been magnified by U.S. energy policies to stimulate the production of ethanol, a plant-based synthetic fuel for vehicles. American subsidies are an incentive to Midwestern farmers to grow more corn, and ethanol produced from Brazilian sugar represents a serious economic threat to these farmers.

The Argentine government has reacted somewhat inconsistently to the soy boom. President Cristina Fernández Kirchner failed in her bid to raise taxes on soy exports from 35 percent to 44 percent in 2008, but even the lower rate helped fill government coffers. These revenues helped Kirchner expand spending on programs that help the poor (and her voting base) and also stimulated the economy. Although some of the wealth has trickled down, traditional employment in other sectors (fruit, livestock, forestry, etc.) has declined.

Under pressure from environmental groups and movements of small farmers and peasants, Argentina passed a law in 2011 limiting foreign ownership. The law does not apply to existing large holdings, but business news organizations greeted it as "protectionism." They more favorably look at Uruguay, which has fewer restrictions, and where 25 percent of land is foreign-owned (Colvin & Co. 2012). Kirchner, on the other hand, has attracted criticism from those the law is supposed to help because of inadequate enforcement. Argentina, like Brazil, is a federal government, and enforcement of measures to defend small landholdings and to regulate use of herbicides and pesticides depends on local governments that are often beholden to wealthy owners. In June 2013, the agricultural ministers of China and Argentina signed an agreement whereby China approved three types of soy and corn produced from genetically modified seeds, an indication that the sector will continue to expand with the blessing of the central government, despite laws restricting foreign ownership.

For Review

What kinds of environmental issues are being raised by the expansion of food exports from Latin America? How do free-trade agreements facilitate the development of export agriculture? Who benefits, and who does not benefit in the region?

Mining, Oil, and Neo-Extractivism

It could be argued that the clash between national sovereignty and economic globalization is most acute in the mining and mineral sectors. Like most of the world (but not the United

States), in Latin America the landowner's property rights extend only to the surface. What lies beneath belongs to the sovereign state. In the period of decolonization after World War II, most of the Global South, including Latin America, claimed that sovereignty meant that it could use law and the power of the state to reclaim control over natural resources—although the international pronouncements in this area always recognized the obligation to respect property rights and indemnify owners. That is, sovereignty has never been absolute when it comes to property rights, but the principle of territorial sovereignty became in this era a tool for Third World nations to force powerful foreign investors to renegotiate leases and contracts they claimed were sacrosanct under contract law and rights of property.

From the earliest days of Iberian conquest, Latin America has been prized by foreign investors for its vast mineral wealth. In the earliest days, indigenous and African labor was used to mine precious metals for export. Industrialization overseas brought increased demand for copper, iron ore, bauxite, and (later) oil. In the colonial era, the Iberian Crown insisted on a share not of the profit, but of the value of what was produced—a levy that we know today as "**royalty**," the share of production that belongs to the owner of the land. In the era of modernization (see chapter 4), Latin American governments sought to attract investment to extraction by liberalizing terms of investment. Royalties and taxes were kept low as part of the bargain.

In the populist era, governments began to drive harder bargains for access to their "natural wealth." The 1960s and 1970s saw nationalization of mines and oil fields in Chile, Venezuela, Peru, Argentina, and many other countries (Mexico had already nationalized its oil industry in 1938). The neoliberal era saw a shift in philosophy, including a return to the theory that state ownership, royalties, high taxes (even on super-profits), and regulation were counterproductive. New technologies were making possible extraction of lower grades of ore, heavier oil buried deeper below ground, and gas locked in rock formations. The capital and know-how to extract natural resources for export often required dealing with foreign companies and investors. Neoliberals also argued that states enriched by tapping into export profits would be inefficient and more subject to corruption due to "rent-seeking"—that is, elites seeking to suck at the teats of the state rather than pursue wealth through entrepreneurship.

In the 1980s, the "Lost Decade" of debt and economic stagnation, Latin American governments felt pressure from the World Bank and other agencies to privatize assets and create incentives for foreign investment. In mining and hydrocarbons, the **World Bank** laid out a blueprint (1996) that stressed the security of the property rights of mining companies, international arbitration (rather than dispute resolution in national courts), and a sliding tax scale over fixed royalty. Its recommendations included the following:

- "Security of tenure." Under a centuries-old way of doing business, the state, acting as the owner of the nation's natural wealth, maintains some bargaining power with the companies seeking to extract these resources. This also gives the state some legal authority and leverage to nationalize industries in this sector. Global mining and oil companies frequently argue that their business involves big risks and large investment, justifying security of their ownership ("tenure") of the mineral deposits themselves, not just the industry above it. In recommending "security of tenure," the World Bank sought changes in mining laws to remove any possibility of nationalization, even with compensation, thereby putting an end to the wave of nationalizations that had occurred in Third World nations, a tendency that followed decolonization of Africa, Asia, and the Middle East. Short of nationalization, countries often seek to use ownership of the subsoil to force renegotiation of contracts that were signed under the cloud of corruption or that simply took advantage of the limited knowledge of industries in the earliest periods of foreign investment. Enormous windfall profits made governments realize that they were not getting a fair share of the benefits under original contracts.

- "International dispute resolution." The World Bank's model law included eliminating the Calvo Clause, a provision by which foreign investors agree to resolve all contract disputes in the host nation's courts. Instead, under the World Bank's proposal, all legal disputes would be arbitrated in special international legal forums, one of which is provided by the Bank.

- "Clarity and transparency," in contracts. One can hardly object to better practices that might reduce corruption, but the World Bank included under this category elimination of "discriminatory" practices. That is, countries were asked to change laws giving their own citizens advantages in seeking mineral concessions. This objective has been reinforced by trade agreements prohibiting favoritism toward national investors. Under this kind of provision, a country cannot give its own companies, whether state or privately owned, advantages in order to promote the nation's ability to develop its own industry, rather than having to rely only on foreign companies for production.

- "Access to Mineral Resources," meaning the release of mineral reserves held by state-owned companies. Under this provision, state oil companies, for example, have to return unused concessions of land and minerals to the government, which would then lease them to foreign investors. Overall, the World Bank's objective was to open more land to investment.

- An "investment regime" favorable to increasing production. The World Bank model would prohibit countries from raising taxes or royalties to increase the nation's share of profits during **commodity** booms. The model also advised states to give up all rights to restrict production or exports of its natural resources. Countries would no longer be able to restrict production and export to limit supply and defend price levels. This would eliminate for mining and energy a key tool that members of the Organization of Petroleum Exporting Countries (OPEC) have used to defend the price of oil.

From the World Bank's neoliberal point of view, minerals, hydrocarbons, and nutrients in the soil are all a "free gift of nature" in the global commons; discovery ("prospecting," "exploration") takes them out of the commons, and investment plus labor gives them economic value. There are two sources of objections to this perspective. One is a position associated with environmental, indigenous, and community activists who see extraction as an unsustainable activity that generates harm and caters ultimately to a global consumer mentality. Another is the nationalist position that is mainly focused on gaining a larger share of the profits. This is sometimes called the "**neo-extractivist**" position. It is "neo" (new) because it still, as in the past, promotes extraction of natural resources for export and the generation of economic development, but it also demands that mining and agricultural exports pay higher royalties and taxes.

Indigenous groups often see themselves as stewards of nature and as advocates, in harmony with environmentalists, of a less materialist style of life—*el buen vivir*, as indigenous people in mineral-rich Andean states put it. Many indigenous groups argue that what consumers and business interests want to extract from their land is a sacred resource not to be abused. Furthermore, the nature of increasing production relies on technology that threatens the environment. Thick oil far below the surface must be emulsified (thinned) with chemicals. Small traces, much less than 1 percent, of copper ore are "leached" from massive quantities of crushed rock by chemical processes. Both practices leave water pollution and mountains or pools of hazardous waste material. The biggest threat is usually to residents of local communities, but sometimes even large property owners— for example, owners of tourist industries—may resist intrusion by large-scale mining and oil companies.

Objections to opening natural resources are also heard from nationalist sectors, and not just those on the left. Military nationalists often look at their country's natural resources as a kind of natural capital, a trove of natural wealth that can be exhausted quickly. Their attitude is that natural wealth is owned by the nation and should be exploited in its interest. Why should the profits go outside the country? Limiting production, which requires limiting the freedom of investors to use their "property" as they wish, is also a way of conserving the natural wealth for use by future generations. It is worth remembering that Latin America is littered with cases of booms that went bust. Since 1990, commodity prices have been very high, and the kinds of rules promoted by the World Bank model make it difficult for Latin Americans to capture a larger share of the super-profits that result. Hence, they seek to change tax laws, royalty rates, and other aspects of the agreements. They are open to exploitation of natural resources but want to share more fairly in the benefits.

So in effect, in the era of globalization we have at least three conflicting points of view: (1) nationalist, which prioritizes the right of the sovereign state to manage natural resources in the interest of the nation; (2) neoliberal, which prioritizes natural resources as part of the commons until discovered and worked, whereupon they become the property of the farmer, miner, or driller, regardless of nationality; (3) environmental/indigenous, which wants to restrict sovereignty for the purpose of protecting the ecosystem by restricting economic exploitation. The first two are both associated with neo-extractivism.

There were some signs of a shift away from neoliberal mining and oil policies in the 2000s. Venezuela's late president Hugo Chávez successfully reinvigorated OPEC, unilaterally raised taxes and royalties, and began to advise other countries on how to strike a better deal with foreign investors. On May 1, 2006, Bolivia's new president, Evo Morales, sent troops into Bolivia's gas and oil fields to (re)nationalize them and demand that operating companies renegotiate terms. Even neoliberal Chile began to rethink policies. In 2005, the Chilean Congress imposed a 5 percent royalty on foreign copper companies, which export two-thirds of Chile's copper but were paying virtually no significant royalties or income taxes—this in a country often called the "Saudi Arabia of copper."

Free-trade agreements can be used by foreign countries to obligate countries to submit disputes to international arbitration even when the home country of the investment is not a signatory to the agreement. For example, Exxon-Mobil and ConocoPhillips took Venezuela to the International Court for Settlements of International Disputes over a conflict regarding how much compensation was due to them for nationalization of shares of ownership in several large oil fields. Both are U.S. companies, and the United States has no free-trade treaty with Venezuela. But the Netherlands does, so the companies simply established subsidiaries in that country to serve as conduits for their investments in Venezuela (Boué 2013).

For Review

How is control over mining and oil an issue of national sovereignty for exporting countries? What is "neo-extractivism"? Why do those who use the term critically find themselves at odds with both the nationalist and the neoliberal perspective?

Tourism

Large-scale tourism has displaced commodity exports as the main source of income for many Caribbean countries. Much of the infrastructure for tourism is owned by foreign companies who export a high percentage of profits out of the host country. The United Nations estimates that of US$100 spent by a tourist in a Third World nation, only US$5 stays in the country; the rest goes mostly to tourist corporations (e.g., international hotel chains, airlines, tourist agencies, and cruise lines) based elsewhere. Mega-developments swallow beaches, mangroves, and other natural features important to the local environment. Tourists demand air conditioning, fresh linens daily, and a variety of comforts that must be imported and are not commonly available to the local inhabitants, who often find local beaches and facilities off-limits. If you take your spring break in Mexico or the Caribbean, what kind of accommodations would *you* expect?

The initial economic surge from tourism can hide long-term problems that emerge as the infrastructure begins to decay. The cruise ship industry is especially problematic for the small countries of the Caribbean and Central America. People living on cruise ships do little to spur local employment in hotels or restaurants. Cruise companies operate on the high seas beyond the reach of the state's sovereign power. Tourists tend to come from wealthier, northern nations and expect a high level of comfort during their limited vacation time. The host countries are in general among the poorest, least influential members of the world community. Their people, however, are made painfully aware of the inequalities of the global economy as they see the extravagant lifestyle of tourists on vacation. Tourism also tends to accelerate the sex trade. As Cynthia Enloe (2000) has shown, tourism advertising tends to promote destinations as subservient, using feminine stereotypes. Some governments cast a blind eye toward local escort services or marriage brokers that use the internet to advertise the availability of young women. For a fee, they will book you into a local hotel and arrange a series of "dates" with prospective wives, either poor women seeking money for their families or middle-class, educated women looking to escape from their underdeveloped homelands.

Some countries promote ecotourism as a solution to these problems. Supposedly more environmentally conscious and mindful of local development needs, ecotourism has been touted as an alternative to the exploitative type of tourism. However, a European coalition of religious clergy commented to the UN Commission on Sustainable Development,

Consumer demand for ecotourism is growing at 3–4 times the pace of regular tourism. Although much promise initially surrounded the ecotourism concept, most ecotourism today is merely a market brand, with the same damaging characteristics. In fact, ecotourism impacts can be even more acute, due to the ecologically and culturally sensitive areas targeted. As a result, most ecotourism destinations face ruin within fifteen years. Consumers, meanwhile, become desensitized to what constitutes a viable ecosystem or community.

(ECEN 2005)

Cuba has come to rely heavily on tourism, in part because of the crisis in its former key export sector, sugar (Silberman et al. 2004). The country has fared better than most in the region by regulating tourism and keeping tourist dollars in the economy. Hotel workers have health care, access to education, and other job protections. To limit the outward flow of tourism earnings, state tourism agencies operate in partnership with foreign investors. Hiring is done through the state labor ministry. However, Cubans have not escaped altogether the problems posed by tourism. Though the government and the national women's association attempt to discourage prostitution, it almost inevitably seems to follow the tourist dollar. It does not help that Cuba lures tourists with advertising campaigns designed to create nostalgia for the nightclub atmosphere and tropical stereotypes that made pre-1959 Havana the world's prime destination for a sinful vacation. Mega-tourism projects have become more common. Any visitor who cares to listen will hear environmentalists talk about the difficulties they have in limiting the impact of these projects on the local ecosystem. Until recently, the state control over tourism was justified because profits were used to subsidize Cuba's free education, health care, and other benefits. But there has always been something of a compromise here since Cubans working in the tourist trade have had more access to foreigners and their currency (e.g., tips to hotel and restaurant workers). Now, with the gradual economic liberalization launched by Raúl Castro, workers in the tourist sector are better placed, with expertise and access to foreign currency, than their countrymen and countrywomen to launch small businesses.

However, anyone who has visited Acapulco (Mexico) will find a much more unjust system of tourism than anything seen in Cuba. Acapulco's famous hotels nearly surround a bay whose splendid beaches are off-limits to most of the millions of people living in the *barrios* on the adjacent mountainsides. Well-armed police patrol the coastal road to maintain a separation between the hotels and the city neighborhoods. In the evening, the mountainsides are dotted with blazing fires—trash burning in neighborhoods lacking sanitation services. If you visit a Mexican resort for spring break, talk to some of the people who work in the markets and hotels. Ask them where they live, how far they must commute to work, what their life is like. Make your own assessment of who is benefiting from the tourist trade.

For Review

What are some of the potential benefits from tourism to countries in the Caribbean and Central American region? What are some dangers? Why has tourism become so important to Cuba, and what is positive and negative about that development?

Trade Agreements and Regional Economic Blocs

The U.S. view is that free-trade agreements not only bring economic benefits to underdeveloped countries but also strengthen democracy. In 2005 the Office of the United States Trade Representative (USTR) made this claim in a briefing for a new agreement that would tie the United States, the Dominican Republic (DR), and five Central American countries into a free-trade area (CAFTA-DR; we will simply call it "CAFTA"). It claimed,

> In the 1980s Central America was characterized by civil war, chaos, dictators, and Communist [sic] insurgencies. Today, Central America is a region of fragile democracies that need US support. Elected leaders in the region are embracing freedom and economic reform, fighting corruption, strengthening the rule of law and battling crime, and supporting America in the war on terrorism. But anti-reform forces in the region have not gone away. CAFTA is a way for America to support freedom, democracy and economic reform in our own neighborhood.
>
> (USTR 2005)

This statement is notable for its characterization of the rebellions of the 1980s as "communist" and its portrayal of a general situation of anarchy. It is also notable that the statement refers to the region as a "neighborhood," rather than a "backyard," a term once widely used, implying a relationship of neocolonialism.

Similar claims about democracy were made for the North American Free Trade Association (NAFTA) and also on behalf of a U.S.-proposed Free Trade Area of the Americas (FTAA), which would embrace the entire hemisphere and require that states be democratic. The FTAA ran into trouble at the November 2005 Summit of the Americas, where Venezuela's Chávez led an all-out assault on the idea, backed by social movements and other **Pink Tide** politicians. The idea has inched forward in the form of a series of bilateral agreements (between the United States and individual countries, such as Chile, Peru, and Colombia) and other multilateral agreements, so it is not dead but stalled—largely for the same reason we discussed previously, in regard to the WTO negotiations.

The most successful free-trade accord, which subsequently grew into a broader economic and political union, was the European Common Market (now the European Union, EU), which contributed to the region's economic recovery after World War II and made Western Europe a force to be reckoned with in global economic diplomacy. However, there are major differences between the EU and the proposed FTAA. The European nations were at comparable levels of economic development, which meant less overall displacement and relative equity among the partners in negotiation and implementation of the accord. Europeans already had achieved progressive and effective protection of workers and weaker portions of the population in the form of welfare, labor rights, and environmental protection. Unlike NAFTA and the proposed FTAA, the European integration scheme included a fund to help development of the poorest areas (e.g., Ireland, Southern Italy, and Portugal) and permitted free movement of all labor, not just skilled workers and professionals. The Common Market not only committed members to mutually lowering trade barriers but also created institutions whereby the community could represent itself as an entity in global economic talks.

NAFTA and the various bilateral trade accords between the United States and Latin America link economies at very different levels of development. To some analysts, this is an advantage, giving the underdeveloped nations access to markets, investment, and technology otherwise unavailable. In this view, these free-trade treaties will help poor countries develop, creating jobs and lifting living conditions. But critics claim that treaties linking countries at different levels of development hinder rather than promote development. The Council on Hemispheric Affairs (Birns and Schaffer 2005) argued that CAFTA's marriage of a US$12 trillion economy, with its "intrinsic advantages," to six economies that in combination amount to only US$12 billion "is like matching a major league baseball team on steroids against little leaguers and heatedly insisting that, because umpires use the same rulebook, somehow it is a fair match." In other words, the rules apply the same to all economies, rich and poor, whether or not they are able to compete effectively with one another.

Bilateral agreements were once the main instrument for linking economies to one another, but today, they are largely used to incorporate new partners into larger associations; for example, a U.S. bilateral treaty with Chile on January 1, 2005, largely grants Chile access to the U.S. market on the same terms offered to Canada and Mexico under the NAFTA of 1994.

Arguably, Chile has been the most successful Latin American country in diversifying its exports. World Bank data show that Chilean exports in mining fell from 88 percent in 1970 (mostly copper) to 43 percent in 1999. The greatest increases in exports were not in manufacturing (though this sector's exports also grew) but in timber, vegetables, fruits, seafood, wine, and dairy products. Another factor skewing the data was the fall in copper prices. Measured in tons of copper rather than export earnings, Chile exported nine times more copper ore in 1999 than it did in 1970. The problem was that the price of copper collapsed in the meantime, so mining's share of export revenues fell relative to other products. Still, there is little doubt that the policies of the Pinochet dictatorship (1973–1988) played a role in restructuring Chile's place in the world economy. In an environment of military repression and economic difficulty, the new seafood and agro-industries found workers in an army of women and of peasants displaced from the traditional *latifundia*. By the time electoral democracy was restored, these new sectors were well established. Institutional limits on democracy (see chapters 8 and 13) made it nearly impossible for elected governments to implement land reform or change the generous tax policies and leases to public lands.

Chile's "success" in adapting to globalization is often heralded as a miracle (see chapter 8), but the benefits have been sharply skewed in favor of a few, even after some redistribution of national wealth by Concertación governments since 1990. Six-day, 48-hour workweeks are common (see Schurman 2003). The minimum wage in 2003 was only US$150 a month; official unemployment hovered between 9 and 10 percent. Ten percent of the population received 50 percent of national income. Like other industries, Chile's agro-industry demands (and gets) "labor flexibility," which translates into greater freedom to lay off workers and relief from regulation. In August 2003, Chile's unions organized the country's first one-day general strike, demanding a change in the economic model. President Ricardo Lagos reacted in anger to the action, saying that it harmed Chile's image of stability and friendliness toward investment just as a major hemispheric economic summit was about to take place.

North American Free Trade Agreement (NAFTA)

NAFTA was not the first multilateral trade agreement in the region; various regional agreements, including the Andean Pact, CARICOM (an association of Caribbean states), the

Central American Common Market, and Mercosur preceded it (Mercosur originally linked Brazil, Uruguay, Paraguay, and Argentina, with Colombia, Chile, Ecuador, Peru, Guyana, and Surinam in associated status; Venezuela was added as a full member in 2013, at which time Bolivia was awaiting full membership). All these pacts were relatively weak attempts at economic integration and did not include the United States. NAFTA, which went into effect on January 1, 1994, is quite different. It stands out as the agreement that set the stage and defined the arguments for and against more recent proposals advanced by the United States.

NAFTA eliminated many regulations on foreign investment and prohibits governments from "discriminating" against those foreign investments. NAFTA prevents governments from requiring foreign investors of member nations to make local purchases of inputs (parts, services, raw materials, machines, etc.), from limiting how much profit can be exported from the country, from subsidizing national producers so that they can compete more effectively with foreign firms, and from privileging national buyers in privatization of state assets. Hence, "trade" now covers investment, even areas such as banking. The agreement also includes protection of intellectual property rights and opens the door to greater migration among professional and skilled employees, but not ordinary workers.

To gain benefits, corporations must make sure that a certain percentage of the "value added" in production of traded goods originates in one of the member countries. The idea is to prevent Japanese, European, or other investors from taking advantage of NAFTA's benefits by, for example, simply shipping products through Mexico into the United States. However, these companies too can take advantage of NAFTA by locating factories in Mexico, and many have done. *Labor Alerts*, a U.S.-based newsletter reflecting views of unions, highlighted (June 8, 1997) the plight of workers in Hyundai Corporation's factory in Tijuana, Mexico, during a 1997 strike by workers:

> While the workers assemble and weld at least 26 chassis daily, and the chassis sell for $1800 each, they make 280–360 pesos ($33–$46) weekly . . . The Han Young *maquiladora*, like most *maquiladoras* in Tijuana, pays a government-connected "union" known as the *Confederacion Regional de Obreros Mexicanos* (CROM). Workers do not participate in any meetings of the "union" and have never seen a copy of its contract with the company. It is a standard practice by the *maquiladora* industry to pay for "protection contracts" against independent organizing by workers.

After two years of strife, including a hunger strike by workers, Hyundai simply closed the plant and moved production to a different facility in the same town (Bacon 2004).

NAFTA includes an adjudication mechanism whereby a corporation or citizen can directly bring a case before an international tribunal for violation of value-added limits or abuse of copyrights. However, the treaty provides no similar recourse for violations of environmental, human rights, or labor accords. These issues are treated not in NAFTA itself but in side agreements. A study of seven labor cases by five researchers at the UCLA Center for Labor Research and Education (Delp et al. 2004: 4) found that the labor accord had helped expose serious violations that threaten the health and safety of Mexican workers and immigrant workers in the United States, but the authors also found that the accord "failed to protect workers' rights and is in danger of fading into oblivion." The researchers concluded that the labor side agreement "created a lengthy, bureaucratic process with no ability to protect workers from reprisal. To date, none of the seven cases has advanced through the first stage of the process in less than 1½ years from the time the case was submitted and two were still pending after 2½ years" (Delp et al. 2004: 7).

The story on the environmental side is similar. Stephen Mumme of the Interhemispheric Resource Center credits the Commission for Environmental Cooperation (CEC), created by a side agreement, with having shed light on many serious issues through its investigations and reports. However, Mumme argues that companies have used the antidiscrimination provisions in NAFTA to fight tougher environmental laws in particular countries. Of 20 citizen complaints submitted to the CEC for investigation after 1994, only two had even been recommended as worthy of factual investigation five years later. The CEC can only spur governments to take action; it cannot directly make policies and decisions on issues raised (Mumme 1999).

Some peasants have adapted by producing for an internal market of street vendors and community co-ops (Barkin 2006), but Mexico has experienced a serious agricultural crisis over the last two decades. Many peasants have been forced off the land by a combination of foreign competition and withdrawal of subsidies and guaranteed land rights (*ejidos*) that were repealed by the Mexican government in anticipation of NAFTA. Rural families became more dependent on money from family members working in the United States. The United States' appetite for ethanol increased demand for corn, raising prices for Mexican exports of that crop. Is this a positive development? Certainly, it improves Mexico's balance of trade and provides desperately needed export earnings, but the diversion of corn from the domestic market to exports drives up the price for this staple food in Mexico's cities. The result is something called the "tortilla wars," a conflict between consumers, Mexican farmers, and the government. To keep prices lower and avert a consumer revolt, the Mexican government opened its market to exports from the United States. This in turn hurt small Mexican farmers who are not, unlike big growers, linked to export markets through mega-companies such as Cargill, the second largest agribusiness in the world.

The Office of the U.S. Trade Representative (USTR 2004) argues that the agreement was successful because member nations' economies all grew more than 30 percent in the first 10 years. Using 1994 as a baseline for measurement, as the USTR study does, can be deceptive. The Mexican government overvalued the peso in the run-up to 1994. This was done to prevent a surge in the U.S. trade deficit with Mexico just before the U.S. Congress was to vote, and in anticipation of Mexican elections in that year. To achieve this, the government borrowed dollars heavily from abroad. After NAFTA went into effect, the government withdrew support for the peso. The subsequent "peso crisis" resulted in a drastic fall in the real wages of Mexican workers. Hence, any recovery in the Mexican economy, especially in regard to unemployment and wages, measured from 1994 is suspicious and difficult to attribute to NAFTA.

The Carnegie Endowment for International Peace, an organization generally supportive of expanded trade, issued a report (Papademetriou, et al. 2003) concluding that after 10 years, NAFTA had "produced a disappointingly small net gain in jobs" in Mexico largely because agricultural imports had reduced employment in that sector, whereas job creation in other sectors had barely kept pace. Ominously, it noted that about 30 percent of the *maquila* jobs created had been lost subsequently to even lower wage markets, including China. Real wages in Mexico remained 30 percent lower than they were before 1994 (and even lower compared to 1982, as mentioned previously), which can partly be attributed to the devaluation and to the failure of wage gains to keep pace with productivity since 1994. Carnegie also claimed, however, that, contrary to opponents' warnings, a net loss of U.S. jobs to Mexico had not materialized, nor had a race to the bottom weakened environmental protection laws. Enforcement, however, is another matter, as we have seen.

The Economic Policy Institute (EPI), which has links to unions in the United States, says that exports from *maquilas* to the United States increased from 39 percent of all Mexican exports in 1993 to 61 percent in 2002. The EPI found that there occurred a growth in the *overall* number of jobs in the United States during this period, but there was a *decline* in manufacturing jobs, and this can be attributed directly to increased exports from *maquilas*. This might not be alarming if new jobs related to exports in other sectors (technology, machines, etc.) were being added. However, the EPI says that jobs in the U.S. export sector have not kept pace with losses in manufacturing. Also, overall NAFTA reinforced a decline in wages for people with less than college degrees in the United States because employers can threaten to move plants overseas and win concessions from American workers (Scott 2003). Reviews of NAFTA in 2014, the twentieth anniversary, showed once again increased economic trade among the three countries involved, but also found that things had changed little for workers in the United States and Canada or for workers and peasants in Mexico (Aguilar 2012).

The political impact of NAFTA is hard to measure. The agreement was first proposed in Mexico by President Carlos Salinas Gortari after his election in 1988, which was marred by credible charges of fraud. The measures taken to prepare Mexico for NAFTA, similar in many ways to structural adjustment packages, had the effect of lessening patronage, the grist for the PRI's political mill that rewards and punishes voters and its affiliated groups—such as unions, neighborhood associations, credit unions, and so on. Elimination of the *ejidos*, a form of municipal ownership of land guaranteed under the 1910 constitution until it was amended by Salinas before 1994, weakened PRI support in one of its key constituencies, the peasantry (see chapter 11).

Salinas understood that NAFTA was unlikely to pass the U.S. Congress as long as Mexico remained a one-party state. Despite having been elected amid fraud, he took timid steps to open the system. His successor, Ernesto Zedillo, moved even more assertively to undermine the PRI's monopoly of power, leading to the election of Vicente Fox of the PAN in 2000. Salinas, Zedillo, and other architects of NAFTA were not politicians but bureaucrats who had never before held elective office—"technopols," in the sense discussed in chapter 12. Fox had been the president of Coca-Cola in Mexico. These technopols set out to "modernize" Mexico. Economically, this meant rolling back the state's share of the economy; politically, it meant moving toward polyarchy. Salinas's NAFTA proposal was welcomed by the George H. W. Bush administration in part because of fears about Mexico's stability and the emergence of a serious populist, leftist challenge from Cuauhtémoc Cárdenas, who believes that he was deprived of victory by the 1988 fraud (see chapter 9).

CAFTA, approved by the U.S. Congress in 2005, is even weaker on environmental and labor protection. Signers are committed only to make "strides" toward enforcement of existing codes, which are weaker than those in Mexico. As with NAFTA, CAFTA was negotiated behind closed doors and drew opposition from many social movements in the region. Demonstrators against the agreement in Guatemala, demanding a popular referendum, were met in March 2004 with violent repression. U.S. and Central American Catholic bishops announced opposition to the treaty. Strikes forced the Costa Rican government to withdraw temporarily from treaty negotiations in 2003, and the Nobel Prize–winning former president Oscar Arias, who had been expected to win a new term easily in 2006, barely survived a challenger opposed to the agreement. Arias faced a tough fight but won approval from Costa Rica's Congress. When the Honduran legislature met to ratify the agreement on March 3, 2006, demonstrators surrounded the Congress and blocked all the streets, causing the representatives to flee the building after voting their approval.

NAFTA offered Washington the opportunity to lock in place a model of development predicated on faith in a free market. It poses huge obstacles to any return to more populist economic policies and a state-centered approach to development. Although the PRD advocates renegotiating, not abandoning, NAFTA, the longer the present treaty remains in place, the more difficult it will be to change.

The Trans-Pacific Partnership

The most recent proposal for a new free-trade agreement is the Trans-Pacific Partnership (TPP), which would link together the United States, Canada, Mexico, Peru, Chile, Australia, New Zealand, Singapore, Brunei, Malaysia, Vietnam, and Japan, with provisions for other nations to join later. Together these countries account for one-third of global production. Noticeably absent from the list is China, and not by accident, since the United States has taken the lead on the proposal in part to respond to the challenge of rising Chinese investment in the Americas and growing Chinese geopolitical influence in Asia. On the other hand, U.S. officials have left open the possibility that Beijing could eventually be incorporated in the agreement. Even after 18 rounds of negotiations, beginning in 2009, it is difficult to say what the treaty will cover because the negotiations are conducted in secret. Governments involved argue that confidentiality is needed to make any progress because the talks involve delicate matters touching on many different economic interests. However, major corporations, such as Monsanto, Bank of America, and Exxon-Mobil, are formal advisors to the U.S. delegation.

Like other treaties, the TPP would aim to reduce both tariff and non-tariff barriers to trade, but once again, trade would cover much more than simply lowering customs taxes, prohibiting subsidies, and eliminating quotas. One stumbling block is intellectual property—that is, the U.S. determination to gain stronger protection over patents and copyrights. Blocking Latin American approval of a similar treaty, the Transatlantic Trade and Investment Partnership (TTIP), are not only intellectual property concerns but also the European Union's desire to maintain privileged trade and investment relations with its former colonies, most of which are in Africa and Asia.

If trade relations are not already tangled enough, it is not clear how the TPP and TTIP would coexist with other agreements in Asia and Latin America. Chile, Peru, Colombia, and Mexico have already formed a Pacific Alliance to coordinate trade policy. All four members have already forged deep economic ties through agreements with Asian countries. Mexico, with Washington's blessing, has sought to forge a common trade area among its southern states and the countries of Central America. Among the attractions for foreign investors in this region are hydroelectric resources and gold mining, a notoriously polluting extractive industry. NAFTA binds Mexico closely to the United States, which gives it privileged access to the U.S. and Canadian markets. Chile is an observer in Mercosur and does considerable business with Brazil and Argentina, but it keeps itself at arm's length from Mercosur so that it has a freer hand to negotiate agreements with countries in other parts of the world. And then there is **ALBA**, the Venezuelan initiative that offers discounts on oil and aid for cooperatives, microenterprises, and small businesses, but which also demands that countries reject the neoliberal economic model.

For Review

Describe the main features of NAFTA and give the reasons that Mexico and the United States (two of the three partner countries) sought it. What were the economic and political motivations on the Mexican side? What is the Trans-Pacific Partnership? What is the Transatlantic Trade and Investment Partnership?

Alternative Economic Integration Schemes

By 2000, three different agendas had emerged in Latin America. One was the U.S. proposal for the FTAA, based on NAFTA as a model. The second one was led by Brazil and was closer to the underlying principles in Mercosur, demanding a more rapid opening of the U.S. market. The third agenda was the Bolivarian Alliance for the Americas (**ALBA**), advanced by Venezuelan president Hugo Chávez. By May 2007, Cuba, Nicaragua, and Bolivia had joined Venezuela in ALBA, with Ecuadorian membership pending. ALBA and other Venezuelan initiatives in energy and communications have attracted support from social movements in the region. In addition, shortly before breaking with the Andean Pact in 2006, Venezuela joined Mercosur as a nonvoting member (full membership requires several years of association and approval by existing members), opening the possibility of ALBA and Mercosur becoming integrated with one another.

ALBA differs from NAFTA and the proposed FTAA in advocating social as well as economic integration, and it would institute regional economic planning, as opposed to relying purely on market mechanisms. ALBA borrows from the experience of the European Union a program for a "Compensatory Fund for Structural Convergence," which would provide developmental assistance to the poorest countries (e.g., Haiti, Bolivia, and Nicaragua) in the trade federation. ALBA also sets as a goal promotion of "endogenous development," including cooperatives and use of indigenous technologies, as an alternative to labor-intensive *maquilas*. It rejects a stricter intellectual property rights regime, especially in the area of drugs and medicines. ALBA would prioritize subsistence agriculture over export-oriented production, and it would preserve the right of government to regulate and restrict companies operating public services.

Venezuela under Chávez had some success in advancing alternative hemispheric economic integration through its oil diplomacy. Besides the preferential terms it gives to Central America and the Caribbean, Venezuela has its experience in OPEC and technical knowledge to offer other countries. Chávez advanced plans to create a hemispheric oil company formed through an association of state enterprises. Chávez also proposed to build a gas pipeline that would stretch 6,000 kilometers from Venezuela to Argentina. In addition,

Venezuela founded—initially in partnership with Argentina, Cuba, and Uruguay—Telesur, a semiprivate continental television network independent of the large, transnational media corporations. In 2009, six other South American countries followed through on the Venezuelan initiative to create the Banco del Sur (Bank of the South), a fledgling effort to provide an alternative to the IMF in times of financial crisis. In 2003 Venezuela shipped oil to Argentina to help it resist the **IMF's** attempt to impose **structural adjustment** on the Kirchner government. ALBA's most ambitious project is creation of the SUCRE, a "virtual currency" (no actual printed money, though that is envisioned for the future) that member countries of ALBA would use instead of the dollar for international transactions with one another.

In the end, whether these initiatives can prosper as alternatives to the FTAA and the neoliberal formulas advanced by Washington will depend on three factors: (1) the overall degree of prosperity in the global economy; (2) the extent to which hemispheric social movements are able to unify and advance an agenda based on the Venezuelan initiatives; and (3) Venezuela's capacity and political will to subsidize the integration scheme with its petrodollar earnings. The third factor is increasingly in doubt as President Maduro faces violent street protests from an opposition determined to force him and his party from office. In addition, Venezuela has borrowed heavily to finance its own economic projects at home and is finding it difficult to meet all of its financial obligations. And of course, there is no guarantee that oil prices will remain at the historically high levels they have achieved over the last few years.

The commitment of social movements to ALBA is predicated on its grand vision of a more autochthonous Latin American economy geared toward the poor, indigenous peoples, other people of color, women, and so on. However, Venezuela's own developmental policies and international relationships do not always coincide with the agenda of these movements. Brazilian companies are major partners in several investment projects in Venezuela that are opposed by indigenous and environmental groups. For example, a major coal-mining project (including a massive transportation and port development) threatened the already devastated ecology around Lake Maracaibo. Only after years of protest did the Venezuelan government agree to open no *new* mines—a government response welcomed by environmentalists but not necessarily the last word on a project important to the Brazilians. And other projects remain on the docket. Lines to carry electrical power from Venezuela through northeast Brazil to other parts of the continent cut through lands controlled by indigenous groups.

The United States can bring pressure through bilateral trade negotiations and has extensive resources that can be used as either carrots or sticks. The economies of a number of Latin American countries have become more deeply integrated with the U.S. economy in the past two decades. Washington's bilateral accord with Chile partially brings that country into NAFTA. Mexico is pursuing Plan Panama, a scheme to integrate its southern states with the Central American economies, thus linking CAFTA and NAFTA together. Meanwhile, the continued negotiation of the TPP and TTIP are showing that momentum for neoliberal globalization has slowed but not halted. Brazil is the key player in terms of Latin America's capacity to forge an alternative to economic integration based on neoliberal principles. It has by far the largest economy south of the United States, and its posture has been based less on opposition to free trade than on opposition to the failure of the wealthy countries to open their markets on the same terms demanded of the Global South.

We tend to analyze political trends while holding the present state of the international economy as a constant. However, we have already observed how historical changes in the global economy and political systems reverberate in Latin America. For example, the long-term deterioration of Spain's economy and the political crisis in Madrid set off by the Napoleonic Wars contributed greatly to the cause of independence. The Great Depression and World War II helped bring about import substitution and populism.

The global economic downturn that began in late 2008 was set off by a financial crisis in the United States. The trigger was a sudden collapse of a highly inflated real estate and housing market (a "bubble"), which left many banks and other financial institutions, which had gambled in risky financial speculation with mortgages, in dire straits. The crisis exposed weakness in the U.S. economy rooted also in heavy consumer debt and in borrowing to pay for wars in the Middle East and Central Asia. Deeply indebted consumers may never again be able to absorb Mexico's exports on the levels the architects of NAFTA anticipated, but the treaty limits Mexico's ability to shift to an alternative economic model built more on its domestic market or on economic relationships with other parts of the Americas and the world. In 2012–2013, there were signs that the extraordinary growth rates in China and India were slowing, dimming the prospects for the continuation of Latin America's commodity export boom.

A crisis, depending on its severity and length, could shake up the global political order in ways comparable to what happened after the 1929 stock market crash. That crisis, you will recall, contributed to major changes in Latin America's approach to development, ushering in the era of import substitution. As of April 2009, Brazil, the region's economic giant, seemed intent on working with other countries of the so-called G-20 group of large economies to work out reforms to maintain open markets, subsidize major banks (and boost funds for the IMF), and maintain the primacy of the dollar as the global currency. Venezuela, not invited to the G-20 summit of April 2009, chose, through the statements of Chávez, to align itself with Iran and other more radical nations in calling for a new international currency and replacement of the IMF with a new global financial institution more influenced by Third World nations. The problem for Chávez, of course, was that the same crisis that created opportunities to overhaul the global economic order reduced his most important diplomatic resource, oil earnings. Oil plunged from US$147 in the summer of 2008 to approximately US$35 in early 2009. Venezuela has the world's largest proven oil reserves, but production has stagnated since 2002, and expansion has been fueled largely by investment and loans from abroad, especially China. And now Chávez himself is gone, succeeded by Maduro, who does not show nearly the charisma of his patron. The peak of Venezuelan petro-diplomacy may have passed.

In 2013, Venezuela became a member of Mercosur. Although Argentina and Brazil produce oil and natural gas, neither comes close to matching Venezuela's vast reserves, and Venezuela's petrodollar-fueled market offers export opportunities for the rest of Mercosur. However, Mercosur falls far short philosophically of the "solidaristic" principles upon which ALBA is based. Just how Venezuela might reconcile the differences remains to be seen.

For Review

Where do Brazil and Venezuela coincide, and where might they disagree, on the issue of economic integration with the United States? How does ALBA differ, at least in principle, from the proposed FTAA, CAFTA, and NAFTA?

■ The Globalization of Resistance to Globalism

As we discussed in chapter 11, social movements in Latin America have generally organized in resistance to economic globalization, or at least to its neoliberal version. Groups such as *piqueteros*, the MST, and indigenous and environmental groups are mostly (but not always) resistant to opening the economy of their countries to global market forces.

Judging by the evolving patterns of investment and trade, there is little doubt that the pattern of Latin America's economic relations with the rest of the world has been changing. As Figure 15.1 suggests, the period since 1990 has been marked by a surge of foreign investment. Particularly striking is the way investment from both the traditional centers of the world economy and the "developing and transitional" economies increased in the 2000s and fell off in both cases after the 2008 global financial crisis, but then recovered mostly on the basis of investments from the latter. By 2011, Latin America was receiving almost as much foreign direct investment from developing and transitional economies as from its former providers. As Table 15.1 shows, the percentage of foreign direct investment (FDI) coming from the United States notably dropped in the second half of the 2000s, with a particularly startling drop for Brazil. Undoubtedly, decline in part is a consequence of the recession in the U.S. economy, but it is also a reflection of shifting markets.

It is worth noting, however, that the "natural resource" sectors in Spanish-speaking South America have increased their share of FDI (see Figure 15.2), which now is more than half of direct investment. Leading the way in this respect are Chinese companies in search

FIGURE 15.1   Global Flows of Foreign Direct Investment by Group of Economies (millions of dollars)

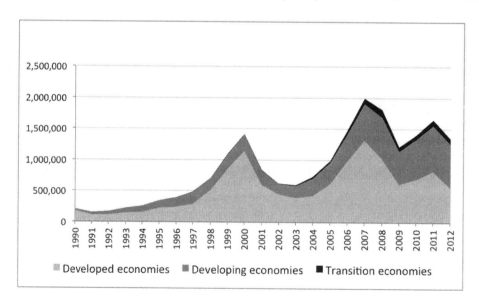

TABLE 15.1 Origins of Foreign Direct Investment (Percentages) in Latin America and the Caribbean, 2000–2010

	2000–2005					
	U.S. and Canada	EU	Latin America and Caribbean	Asia and Oceania	Other	Total
Latin America	37.8	43.2	5.3	2.6	11.1	100.0
Brazil	22.2	53.9	3.9	4.7	15.4	100.0
Mexico	58.9	33.7	1.2	2.0	4.2	100.0

	2006–2010					
	U.S. and Canada	EU	Latin America and Caribbean	Asia and Oceania	Other	Total
Latin America	28.2	40.0	8.5	6.2	17.1	100.0
Brazil	14.4	44.6	5.3	13.6	22.2	100.0
Mexico	49.4	43.3	1.4	0.9	5.0	100.0

Source: Higginbottom (2013: 191).

of raw materials both for profit and to sustain their home country's economic growth. Governments in Latin America, like those in Africa, also like the lack of strings attached to loans and aid distributed in the region. This, of course, is a mixed blessing, on the one hand demonstrating respect for the sovereignty of host countries but at the same time demonstrating little concern for international standards on rights, safety, and environment that are embedded (though not consistently) in Western aid packages. On the other hand, we should not stereotype Chinese investors; a study (Blackmore, Li, Casallas 2013) suggests that Chinese companies' record on sustainability significantly improved from their earliest efforts to enter the region.

The growth of Chinese trade with Latin America after 2000 was nothing short of remarkable. Figure 15.3 shows data only up until 2009; growth resumed after 2009. If we take into account this increase in combination with growing FDI and loans, should we conclude that Latin America is merely changing the pattern, not the essence of dependency? Certainly, Asian economies are not immune to contraction, even crisis. Loans have to be repaid, and since the terms often call for them to be repaid in the form of minerals and oil. If there were a global depression in the price of oil, copper, bauxite, and so on, the amount of raw material that Latin America must rip from its soil would go up considerably. On the other hand, Latin Americans do not depend on China's export markets excessively, at least not yet. Brazil was the only country whose exports to China in 2011 exceeded 30 percent of total exports.

FIGURE 15.2   Where Investment Goes in Latin America, by Region

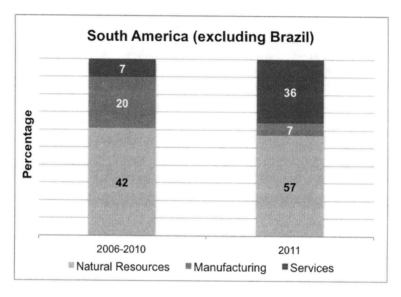

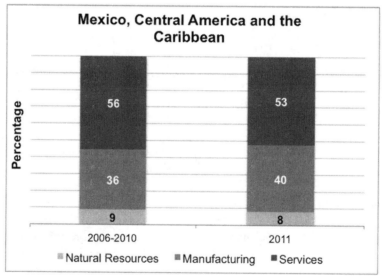

For Review

How has China's emergence as an economic power impacted Latin American economies? What are the positives and what are the negatives posed by Chinese investment in the region?

FIGURE 15.2 (Continued)

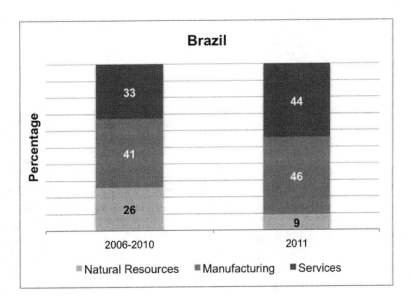

FIGURE 15.3 Growth of Latin America–China Trade Relationship

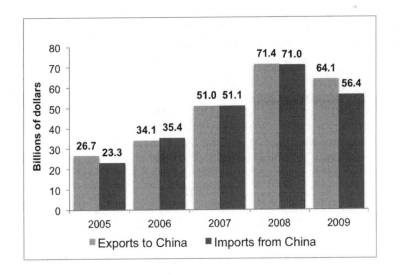

Latin America Meets the World: Separately or United?

Until the global financial crisis of 2008, further globalization—the "free market" brand, at least—seemed inevitable to many analysts. The most important formal global meetings to advance economic globalization have been the successive rounds of trade negotiations begun originally under the auspices of the General Agreement on Tariffs and Trade (GATT) and now under the **WTO** and based in Geneva. Ostensibly, these are democratic meetings where drafts are discussed in the open and decisions are made by consensus. But the process of getting to consensus and implementing agreements is heavily weighted against Latin American and other developing countries.

Jawara and Kwa's study (2002) of the 2001 conference in Doha, Qatar, uncovered a number of reasons that Latin American and other Third World nations are disadvantaged in negotiations. Larger countries may bring more than 50 delegates to these meetings, a delegation size only the largest Third World countries (e.g., Brazil) can come close to matching. Large delegations are needed because negotiations go on in hundreds of formal and informal meetings. Translations are rarely provided for small or informal meetings. Advanced "mini-ministerial" meetings, held away from Geneva, are difficult for smaller and poorer countries to attend. The United States uses aid and the prospect of bilateral trade agreements to obtain support, and it can use the withdrawal of aid to punish countries resistant to its agenda at the talks. Wealthy countries have the economic clout to make sanctions for violations work, but the poorer countries have little leverage to insist that deals be respected afterward. Hence, the wealthier countries sometimes make a concession in principle and later stonewall the development of criteria and mechanisms to put it into force.

The issues negotiated at ministerial conferences are vital to the development hopes of Latin America. These include the following:

- Elimination of tariffs and quotas. When the GATT, the predecessor of the WTO, was first adopted, Latin American countries obtained a concession that enabled them to continue with ISI. Some sectors of manufacturing continued to be protected by tariffs, quotas, and other qualifications (e.g., that foreign companies could be required to buy some of their inputs on the local market). At the time, ISI was considered, even in the wealthy countries, to be the most appropriate strategy to break economic dependency and achieve development. However, the motives of the wealthy countries were not entirely altruistic. The United States, Europe, and Japan got concessions to continue to protect their agricultural sectors with quotas and subsidies.
- When the ISI philosophy was replaced by neoliberalism, Latin America was prepared to abandon these concessions. Would the wealthy countries reciprocate? In 1986, in the Uruguay round of talks that replaced GATT with the WTO, Third World nations agreed to discuss elimination of their remaining policies protecting industry, and in exchange, the United States, Europe, and Japan agreed to put protection of agriculture up for discussion. In subsequent rounds, Third World nations found themselves giving away their exemptions but making almost no progress on agriculture. For example, Ecuador and the Central American states want to open European markets for bananas, but the Europeans privilege imports from their former colonies. Brazil wants elimination of subsidies to soybean farmers in Europe and the United States. In

2002, the United States actually increased by 62 percent the amount it subsidizes to its farmers.

- Trade in services. "Trade" is an inappropriate term here because the real objective is to facilitate foreign investment. New WTO proposals would prohibit measures to keep water, electricity, financial, and other services under national control, opening them to foreign investment. This is a sensitive issue all over Latin America. Strong popular resistance has driven foreigners out of water and other utilities in Bolivia and Argentina.

- Trade-related aspects of intellectual property rights (TRIPS). Also, as we saw in the case of the Brazilian health ministry at the beginning of this chapter, Latin American and other Third World countries want to be able to manufacture cheaper, generic versions of drugs, especially those related to treatment of HIV/AIDS. Most Latin American nations include within their territories major land preserves for biodiversity. Under pressure from indigenous movements, governments now are being pressed to insist that native peoples be compensated for their knowledge of local plants and animals, knowledge that is being exploited by international chemical, biotech, and pharmaceutical firms that want to isolate and patent active agents or "discovered" genes derived from tropic species.

- "New issues" related to transparency and standardization. Latin American states fear that proposed measures to deal with corruption will undermine sovereignty. Under the benign rubric of "standardizing customs operations" lies the possibility that governments in the region will no longer have the last say on the before-tax value of traded goods. They would thereby lose control over levels of taxation on exports and imports, a major source of revenues.

- Special and differential treatment. Like the proposal on services, this deals with the desire of wealthier nations to do away with special arrangements written into the original GATT allowing special treatment (e.g., quotas and special commercial agreements) for Third World exports. Many of these provisions were written into GATT because of the leadership of Raúl Prebisch (see chapters 5 and 6), the head of the United Nations Economic Commission for Latin America after World War II. Prebisch was skeptical that free trade would boost development and wanted the new global economic order to permit countries to implement import substitution.

Latin American countries have rarely presented a common front on these issues. At Doha in 2001, Chile, Mexico, and Costa Rica aligned with the United States, whereas Brazil, Venezuela, Cuba, and Panama led the opposition to the wealthy states' agenda. Cuba, Honduras, and the Dominican Republic are all members of the "like-minded group" of 21 Third World countries that have tried to push the WTO toward taking seriously the provision in its charter that mandates that it must not only open the global trade system but also stimulate economic development of poorer countries, so that they can compete.

The 1999 Seattle ministerial summit was shut down when tens of thousands of protestors—among whom labor and environmental groups were most prominent—disrupted the conference. In 2001, the wealthy countries thought that they had put their agenda back on track at Doha in the Arabian Gulf, a location inhospitable to protestors. At Doha, India waged a lonely fight against the First World agenda, but a surprise was in store at Cancun, Mexico, and

PUNTO DE VISTA: ARE LATIN AMERICANS GLOBAL OR "DEPENDENT"?

In 2011, Itaú Bank of Brazil, the world's fifteenth-largest bank and the largest in Latin America, began running a series of advertisements featuring photos of prominent individuals in the region from different walks of life, each one under the slogan "I Am a Global Latin American." The ad was targeted at an international audience. The bank had yet to acquire many assets outside Brazil and few outside Latin America, but the campaign was a bravado announcement of its intention to become a player in global finance, based on an optimism that Latin America in general is stepping forward.

Enrique Iglesias, former president of the Inter-American Development Bank, listed the reasons for optimism. In the 2000s the middle class increased (by 50 percent, say some experts), rates of poverty fell (to about 29 percent, comparable to about 16 percent in the United States). Growth rates slowed some in 2012 and 2013, but they still were substantially above rates in North America and Europe. These rates persisted after the onset of financial crisis in the developed West.

Gian Luca Gardini (2009), an Italian academic and European trade representative, thinks that Latin America is more wealthy, autonomous, and diplomatically independent than ever before. Gardini argues that even the most strident critics of neoliberal globalization, such as the late President Chávez of Venezuela and President Evo Morales of Bolivia, have contributed to the region's success because their criticism and promotion of ALBA had the positive impact of promoting attention to social needs and anti-poverty measures.

However, Latin America's social movements continue to express skepticism about the character of globalization in Latin America and insist that "another world is possible." One of the World Social Forum's standing principles states its "opposition to a process of globalization commanded by the large multinational corporations and by the governments and international institutions to serve their interests." It is not difficult to see vulnerabilities in Latin America's formula for success. The most significant contributor to the economic growth has been high prices for commodities, such as oil, copper, and soy. Latin America depends less on dominant trade and investment partners, but its economic well-being still depends on expansion of the economies of Asia.

Furthermore, there continue to be signs of discontent even in those countries most praised by the bankers. Chilean students have led sustained protests, joined by wide sectors of society, against the economic and social model that has produced success, at least by macroeconomic statistics. Massive protests in Brazil in 2013 broke out against that country's "celebration" of its new global economic and political muscle—that is, against the huge expenditures for the 2014 World Cup and 2016 Olympics.

One of the cardinal principles of dependency theory was the idea that Latin America's capitalists, its businesspeople, lacked the initiative and kind of entrepreneurial values—risk taking, hard work, drive to get ahead, and so on—characteristic of the bourgeoisie in the developed countries. They are "dependent" in the sense that they are not oriented to the economic development of their own societies. Cardoso and Faletto (see chapter 6) modified this theory somewhat with their notion of "associated dependent development," seeing Latin American capitalists as more dynamic than in the *dependista* view, but mainly because they find the best business opportunities by joining their business interests to those of foreign capital.

To be "global" does not necessarily mean to renounce all identity and loyalty to your own nation. To put the idea of a global Latin American bourgeoisie in some perspective, we might also think about the role of the

Chinese executives who head state-owned companies. I asked Dr. Barbara Hogenboom (interview, April 2013), a University of Amsterdam professor who has studied Chinese business practices, what motivates Chinese businessmen in their work overseas. These executives seem to be motivated, like their counterparts in private multinational companies, to gain success and wealth for themselves and their companies. However, they identify their personal and corporate success with the advancement of China. That is, although they sometimes put their company's interest ahead of their government's priorities, their pride in success of their companies and personal profit is also a pride in the success of their country.

Is there now a dynamic Latin American bourgeoisie that can sustain economic development? Is it a social class that, as Itaú's "I Am a Global Latin American" campaign suggests, is ready to lead Latin America to assume a more autonomous, less dependent relationship to the world?

Point/Counterpoint

Is the confidence in the Itaú ad campaign misplaced or prophetic?

a. If you answered "prophetic," how do you respond to those who say it is just "associated dependency" in the guise of globalization? Can the celebratory view of globalization represented by Itaú be reconciled with the more pessimistic view of Latin American social movements and the protestors?

b. If you answered "misplaced," how do you respond to evidence that Latin America has diversified its trade and investment partners and not suffered as much from the economic doldrums in the United States as in the past?

For more information

A spokesperson for Itaú explains its "Global Latin American" ad campaign on YouTube (www.youtube.com/watch?v=xKLY2c5HTIQ). Andre Gunder Frank wrote a classic argument, *Lumpenbourgeoisie and Lumpen-development: Dependency, Class and Politics in Latin America* (New York: Monthly Review Press, 1972), in which he sees the Latin American bourgeoisie as a hopeless force of progress.

a Latin American state was in the center of the action. In 2003, Brazil joined India to organize 20 other sizable Third World states into a bloc that refused to make any further concessions to the rich countries' agenda unless they agreed to commit to lowering subsidies and quotas. This time, the United States and other members of the "Quad," the group of wealthiest countries, could not break down their resistance, and the conference ended with no progress.

Anti-globalization protestors celebrated the collapse of the conference in the streets, but it should be noted that the key issue for the resisting countries was opening agriculture to free trade. At the time, Brazil's leader was Fernando Henrique Cardoso, whose policies at home were export-oriented. In reality, Brazil's position, like India's, reflected not its rejection of free trade and neoliberalism but its interest as a growing agro-exporter. Lula continued in the same vein. This suggests that we should look at each Latin American nation's economic interests in the global economy and not just the ideology of its leaders.

For Review

What are some of the global issues on which Latin America may unite in negotiations on global economic issues? What are some on which some countries diverge from one other?

Transnational Issues and Global Citizenship

We have concentrated on trade and the global assembly line, but certainly the challenges of globalization cannot be reduced to economics. Some would say that we are seeing the emergence of a "global civil society" that will replace a world where the most important political decisions are reserved for sovereign nation-states. "Transnational" (or global) issues call forth global citizenships. Here, we briefly review a few of the most important transnational issues that challenge sovereignty and raise tests for democracy.

Climate Change

Although the United States (in particular, its Congress) has refused to recognize the gravity of the situation, climate change is affecting the Americas in ways that demand—and are evoking—transnational solutions. One effect of global warming is the retreat of Latin America's glaciers in the Andes and parts of Mexico. In such tropical regions, glaciers are found only in regions three miles above sea level. Four of six glaciers in Venezuela's Andes in 1972 had disappeared by the end of the century.

Peruvian experts said in 1999 that 12 billion cubic meters of ice had melted over 27 years from glaciers in that country's Andean mountains (Lama 1999). Should this source of water disappear, deserts will advance on Peru's western slopes, and the ecosystem of the Amazon will be affected. Some of the loss can be attributed to unusual movements of the warm El Niño current, but this too may be related to global warming. The human consequences will be felt most acutely in terms of scarcer drinking water, less hydroelectric power, and more costly irrigation. In Peru, the loss of water for irrigation can be calculated as a cost of US$1 billion. People will migrate from the most affected areas, risking new kinds of international and political conflicts. Flooding and mudslides are other "natural" catastrophes that could result. Melting of glaciers and the polar ice caps threatens small Caribbean nations and low-lying coastal regions with the prospect that the sea could rise, claiming the homes of hundreds of millions of people in the next 100 years.

Water resources are a growing issue between the United States and Mexico. A water use treaty between the two countries regulates exploitation of the Río Grande (Río Bravo to Mexicans), but an increasing amount of water is taken upstream on both sides of the border, causing large parts of the river to dry up. In some years, the river does not reach its mouth on the Gulf of Mexico. Farmers near Brownsville, Texas, face ruin, but things are even worse in nearby Matamoros, Mexico. Matamoros now has no water at all for parts of each summer. Farther upstream, the river basin is heavily contaminated by industrial pollutants and overuse by Mexican residents who have migrated north within the country, seeking jobs in *maquilas* close to the U.S. border.

One likely cause of global warming is depletion of the tropical rainforests, including the Amazonian region in Brazil and Mexico's Lacondon forest in Chiapas. Called the "lungs of the world," the vegetation in the rainforest protects the earth by depleting carbon dioxide, which in turn prevents too much of this gas in the atmosphere from trapping heat on the earth—the so-called greenhouse effect. Rainforests once covered 14 percent of the earth's surface; today, they cover 6 percent. The Amazonian rainforest has been depleted by 20 percent and could, were present rates to continue, disappear in 50 years. The cause is largely economic, as the land is harvested for virgin timber (with virtually no capital invested by the landowner) and turned into cattle pastures. Poor peasants, desperate for land, follow highways cut through the forest, slashing and burning the indigenous vegetation before planting their own crops. In recent years, Brazil's booming soy-export industry has been gobbling up land. Heavy rains and flooding quickly wash the soil away after just a few harvests (Raintree Nutrition 2005).

Rainforests are biodiverse. Half the world's species of plants and animals are found in Brazil alone. Some experts think that 50,000 species a year, many of them plants with medicinal promise, are being lost. One drug, Vincristine, derived from the rainforest plant Madagascar periwinkle, has proven important in increasing the survival rate for acute childhood leukemia. Ten million Indians, guardians of knowledge about the forest, once lived in Brazil's rainforest. Today, there are only 200,000 left.

Brazilian environmentalists and sympathetic officials in the federal government have sought to reduce logging, but the country's federal structure and tradition of local rule by *coroneles* have inhibited effective enforcement. Under pressure from international environmentalists, the World Bank and other financial institutions have begun to pressure governments to take action to preserve the forests. In 2003, the Brazilian government signed an agreement with the World Bank and the World Wildlife Fund, a large international non-governmental organization (NGO), to create an "Amazon Region Protected Areas" program that would protect a network of 400 islands in the basin north of the city of Manaus. The area is larger than New York, New Jersey, and Connecticut combined; the ultimate goal of the NGO is to create a preserve the size of California. Lorenzo Carrasco, a fierce critic of such projects, accused the organizations of attempting to keep Brazilians from exploiting the region's mineral and other natural resources (AP 2005).

Loggers, ranchers, and migrant *campesinos* resent having international government organizations (IGOs) and NGOs dictate what they can do with land lying within their sovereign borders. They enjoy plenty of economic leverage because they are the key motor behind Brazil's economic growth since 1994. Soy exports are generating crucial foreign reserves needed to pay the debt and could make the country self-sufficient in vegetable oil, a staple of the diet. Some Brazilians ask why their country and other poor countries, while deeply in debt, should have to restrict development, while at the same time the most industrialized countries, especially the United States, refuse to cut down on the emission of greenhouse gases.

Not all Brazilians are merely defending an economic interest in resisting limits on exploitation of the rainforest (Figure 15.4). Many see U.S. policy in the Middle East as a grab for oil and think that the hegemon might eventually turn its attention to their part of the world. General Claudio Barbosa de Figueiredo, Brazilian commander for security in

FIGURE 15.4
Map of the Amazon Rainforest

the Amazon, argued in 2005 that behind preservation efforts lies the ultimate goal of "the internationalization of the Amazon." A poll showed that 75 percent of Brazilians believed that their country could be invaded by a foreign power to gain access to its natural resources. "The strategic axis of confrontation has shifted from East–West to North–South," argued Figueiredo. "In other words, the rich countries of the north are confronting the countries that want to develop in the south to impede this in every possible way" (Astor 2005).

Regardless of who is at fault for the disappearance of much of the world's forests, Brazilian environmentalists warn that their own country must face the consequences. Drought conditions have been worsening in recent years, and some believe that the cause is the cutting down of the country's "rain-making machine." Some worry that the rainforest may be reaching the tipping point, when damage is so extensive that it has gained a momentum of its own that will not be easily reversible.

Disease and Health

Infectious and sexually transmitted diseases are not a new feature of globalization. Many scientists believe that the Europeans brought syphilis back to their homeland from the Americas, when, as we reviewed in chapter 3, the Native American population was decimated by diseases brought by the Europeans. This process has hardly ceased. As humans from urban civilizations press further into remote areas of the tropics, the remaining indigenous populations of the Amazon basin are threatened with diseases they are biologically ill-equipped to resist. For example, in the early 1980s, approximately 450 members of the small Yora Indian population of Peru died after Shell Oil Company workers, loggers, and evangelical missionaries forced contact with the Yora community (Pantone 2008).

Another serious immediate risk in the region is from HIV/AIDS. The problem is most acute in the Caribbean, where 1.1 percent of the adult population has AIDS (HIV InSite 2008). In the early years of the new century, the population of Haiti actually began to decline, in part because AIDS afflicts fully 2.2 percent of the adult population (HIV InSite 2007). The exception is Cuba, which has a low rate of infection, in part because of an aggressive testing, education, and treatment program. Nearly 60 percent of Caribbean infections are due to unprotected heterosexual sex, whereas drug use and unprotected sex among gay men is the larger cause in other regions of Latin America.

As we have already seen, Brazil has begun an aggressive national and international campaign to secure free medicines for those diagnosed with HIV. One reason for its success is that the country has aimed to educate and provide sex workers and their clients with condoms. However, the program is in jeopardy. It seems that the Brazilian posture toward sex workers puts the country in conflict with a provision in a U.S. foreign aid program that demands vigorous prosecution and strong penalties. Prostitution is nothing more than a minor offense in Brazil. Brazil stands to lose US$40 million, 10 percent of its annual budget for fighting the disease, but the director of the program says, "Our feeling is that the manner in which U.S. aid funds were consigned would bring harm to our program from the point of view of its scientific credibility, its ethical values, and its social commitment." The American administration in charge of the program responded that receiving the aid "does require an acknowledgment that prostitution is not a good thing and to be opposed to it" (Rohter 2005).

Cuba's initial response to the HIVS/AIDS was panicked, if not homophobic. On one hand, as with all those afflicted by illness or disability, Cuba's HIV/AIDS patients have access to free medical care. However, in the 1980s the government forced diagnosed patients into sanitariums, depriving them of freedom, in part because of a homophobic prejudice that associated the disease with gays. Facing criticism, the government partially addressed its shortcomings, opening a national dialogue on homophobia and taking a new approach in slowing the epidemic. In the 1990s, the requirement that those who test positive for HIV be forced into sanitariums was lifted. Tim Holtz (1997), MD, of Doctors for Global Health, however, saw only modest progress because the availability of Cuba's extraordinary levels of care required access to the sanitariums.

In 2005, the government finally began to decentralize access to care, although the progress in establishing care through local clinics has been slow because of the cost involved. Remember, Cuba still has not fully recovered from the shock of the collapse of the Eastern European economies. On the other hand, Cuba has developed and now produces its own drugs for controlling HIV and AIDS. A study of its system in 2005 concluded,

> Cuba provides comprehensive care to all people living with the disease, and guarantees antiretrovirals (ARVs) for those needing them. Despite deep financial difficulties, treatment in Cuba, including medication, is free. In 2003, Cuba achieved universal antiretroviral therapy with domestically-manufactured ARVs for patients meeting

international clinical criteria. In 2010, over 5,600 people received ARV therapy in Cuba, more than a 10% increase from the previous year. The Cuban government estimates it costs US$6000 annually to treat each person with HIV/AIDS.

(Gorry 2005)

Migration

The migration of Latin American and Caribbean people northward has raised tensions between the United States and its neighbors. Occasionally, migration affects relationships elsewhere as well. Haitians looking for work in the Dominican Republic are frequently rounded up and deported, adversely affecting relationships between those countries. Bolivians and Paraguayans seeking work in Argentina face discrimination. The Mexican government has sought to close its border in the south, quite in contradiction to its complaints about U.S. policy. In 1969 Honduran politicians tried to deport Salvadoran immigrant workers en masse, raising tensions that led to the brief "Soccer War" of that year, superficially set off by a riot during a match.

Like iron tailings to a magnet, a relatively rich economy attracts migrants from populations living in poorer conditions nearby. In the case of Mexico and the United States, the developmental gap in terms of GDP per capita is greater than for any other two countries in the world with a common border.

Of course, a large portion of the United States is home to descendants of Mexico who lived north of the new border (80,000 in Texas alone, at the time) drawn after the Treaty of Guadalupe ended the Mexican–American War in 1848. It hardly surprises, then, that two-thirds of those who are "Hispanic" (a census designation that includes a small percentage of people of Spanish origin) are descendants of Mexicans. Altogether, in 2002, there were 37.4 million Hispanics in the United States working mostly in the service sector, skilled manufacturing, and transportation. Over one-quarter of the population of western states is Hispanic, and large populations are found in major northern cities. Rates of poverty run high among this community; one-quarter of Hispanic children live in poverty, according to the U.S. Census Population Survey for 2002.

An immediate, pressing issue for advocates of globalization and human rights is the flow of migrants outside established immigration laws, especially to the United States. For some groups, these migrants are criminals and should be called "illegal aliens," the term used by the Colorado Alliance for Immigration Reform (CAIR, http://cairo.org). CAIR denies that its motives are racist and argues that limiting immigration is a method of checking population growth and relieving pressure on resources.

The American Immigration Law Foundation (AILF), on the other hand, uses the term "undocumented workers." The AILF calculated, based on data taken from census reporters, that there are approximately 9 million undocumented workers in the United States. Of this 9 million, approximately six of every 10 are Mexicans, and two are from other parts of Latin America (especially Central America). It costs a worker typically US$2,000–US$3,000 to hire a *coyote* to smuggle them across the border. Agents for employers in North America often advance the money to the *coyote*, a practice that turns the immigrants into indentured laborers. Most are men, among whom 96 percent find employment. However, 41 percent are women, of whom 62 percent find wage employment. Women, especially those who are not employed in the wage labor force, hold the new communities together. Although this pool of labor might exert some downward pressure on wages, the jobs taken by these immigrants are usually those that other workers refuse to take, especially in agriculture, services (restaurants, hotels), and construction. Wages may be low, but some jobs that pay US$60 a day in the United States pay only US$5 in Mexico.

Groups like CAIR contend that non-legal immigrants use costly government services and are a burden on taxpayers. The U.S. counties that receive the immigrants do find their health and education systems heavily burdened by the influx of undocumented workers, but the net effect on the U.S. economy is positive. A *New York Times* investigative report (Porter 2005) estimates that undocumented workers paid US$7 billion into the Social Security Trust Fund in 2004. In addition, these workers pay sales taxes, and their employers pay into unemployment. The AILF says that in 1990, undocumented workers paid US$547 million in sales taxes in Illinois alone, and their employers paid another US$168 million. Because these workers cannot apply for social security, Medicare, or unemployment insurance, these payments represent a subsidy to these programs.

Estimates are that Mexican immigrants, legal and undocumented, sent US$4 billion to US$6 billion per year home before the 2008 economic crisis, the fourth-largest source of foreign exchange for Mexico. For El Salvador, the dollars emigrants send home constitute that country's largest source of overseas earnings. In June 2005, the Mexican Congress approved legislation making the estimated 10 million Mexican citizens living in the United States (half legally, half not, by estimates) eligible to vote, much to the dismay of immigration opponents in the United States who fear the legislation will encourage more migration northward. To discourage the election of candidates the United States opposes (e.g., López Obrador in Mexico and Ortega in Nicaragua in 2006), ambassadors from Washington warned voters that the result could be poor relationships and interruption of vital funds sent home by the family members from the north.

Supporters of NAFTA, the FTAA, CAFTA, and bilateral agreements claim that these accords will bring economic growth and jobs and thus slow the emigration of Latin Americans. Little evidence so far suggests that they are right. To staunch the flow of people, the United States has increased the deployment of technology and personnel along the border. In 2004, Congress passed legislation in the National Intelligence Reform Act (a response to the 9/11 attacks) requiring the Bush administration to add 10,000 more personnel to the Border Patrol. The border has already become highly militarized, and still the immigrants come looking for work. Walls, supplemented by barbed wire, electrified fences, and trenches, now divide populated areas along the border.

The militarization of the border and the refusal of Congress to pass legislation to create a guest worker program has become a source of tension between the United States and Mexico. President Vicente Fox was in Washington to discuss this program with President George W. Bush on September 11, 2001, and the events of that day eliminated any prospects for passage of the legislation. Anyone who has crossed the border to enter Mexico from Nogales, Arizona, or San Diego will find little obstruction moving from north to south. U.S. citizens and permanent residents easily cross back, but a long line of pedestrians and cars seeking to enter the United States slowly snakes its way on the Mexican side of the border.

In March 2006, the immigration issue in the United States exploded when Hispanic leaders, joined by other immigrant community leaders, launched massive protests against a law, passed in the House of Representatives, which would have made it a felony to live and work illegally in the United States. If passed by the Senate, the law would have made criminals out of 11 million undocumented workers. The wave of protests shocked national leaders and stalled the proposal. However, a subsequent backlash developed, including a law in Arizona requiring police to check the identification papers of people suspected of being in the United States illegally. A second immigration bill, containing a highly restrictive but still controversial "pathway to citizenship," languished in the U.S. Senate awaiting an uncertain fate in 2013.

As of 2007, only one foreign terrorist attack on the United States had originated from Latin America or the Caribbean since a group of Puerto Rican nationalists demanding independence wounded five members of Congress in 1954, when they opened fire from the gallery of the House of Representatives in Washington. The exception originated from a dictatorship supported by the United States—when the Pinochet dictatorship in Chile assassinated Allende's former foreign minister and his secretary with a car bomb in Washington. Nevertheless, since September 11, 2001, fear of terrorists infiltrating the United States from the south has increased hostility. Trade agreements are integrating economies, but not labor and people, and it is unlikely that the sovereign power of the U.S. government can cope with the magnetic force that the U.S. economy, as a regional pole of development, exercises on people.

For Review

For each of the following areas—climate change, disease, and migration—what kinds of challenges do Latin American governments face? How do these issues challenge the capacity of individual nation-states to confront them on their own?

Democracy without Sovereign Nation-States?

We have reviewed powerful forces that seem beyond the power of a nation-state—even one as powerful as the United States—to harness. Though the process of globalization seems inevitable, the particular shape that it takes and the way it affects the prospects for democracy need not necessarily follow a single, inevitable path. Democracy itself will have to become more global, meaning that international organizations will have to be made more responsive to people and their movements and not just to states.

Latin America's social movements have not rejected globalization, but most question the neoliberal version that relies on market forces and competition to generate economic growth, better living standards, and more open, transparent societies. Writers such as Thomas Friedman say globalization as fostered by the WTO, NAFTA, and other trade agreements is beneficial and inevitable. In *The Lexus and the Olive Tree*, he wrote,

> The driving idea behind globalization is free-market capitalism—the more you let market forces rule and the more you open your economy to free trade and competition, the more efficient and flourishing your economy will be. Globalization means the spread of free-market capitalism to virtually every country in the world. Therefore, globalization also has its own set of economic rules—rules that revolve around opening, deregulating and privatizing your economy, in order to make it more competitive and attractive to foreign investment.

(Friedman 2000b: 9)

Those who are known as "anti-globalization activists" think that Friedman and other enthusiasts for free trade and economic integration have spent too much time in luxury hotels or visiting the sterile enterprises of the world's high-tech zones. They have in mind a different form of globalization based on sustainable development, fair trade, and cultural diversity. In other words, these social movements insist that "another world is possible."

This chapter has no pretensions of resolving this debate, and the same can be said for the question of whether globalization will someday completely displace the norm of national sovereignty in world affairs. However, this does not mean we cannot understand the counter-vailing forces at work. We can see that economic globalization has diversified markets for Latin American exports and sources for imports and investment. We also see that Latin America has witnessed both the creation and the strengthening of trade, investment, and economic integra-tion arrangements in the hemisphere and that Latin America is increasingly engaged in trade and investment with other parts of the world. It is fair to say that recent growth, social progress, and diversification in its trade and investment partners have given Latin America some leverage in its relationship to the United States and the developed world. For the first time since the era of Bolívar, Latin American states seem to be building their own regional diplomatic institutions, lessening their political dependence on the hegemonic world power—whether that be Spain and Britain before 1900 or the United States in the twentieth century.

Discussion Questions

1. Do you see the nation-state presently growing weaker or stronger in Latin America? Why?
2. Has economic globalization, as it has unfolded thus far, strengthened or weakened democracy in Latin America?
3. Would Latin America be better off entering into a NAFTA-like agreement covering the entire hemisphere, or is some other alternative, such as ALBA or Mercosur, preferable?
4. Do you think Latin American countries should give up some sovereign control over their affairs in areas such as human rights and the environment, or should countries be allowed to retain their right to self-determination over these kinds of issues? And if you think they should yield on sovereignty, should they do so even if the United States and other wealthy countries refuse to do the same?
5. Do you agree with the Thomas Friedman quote at the end of this chapter, or is your position closer to "another world is possible"?

Resources for Further Study

Reading: The Carnegie Endowment tried with some success to make an evenhanded assessment of NAFTA's impact in *NAFTA's Promise and Reality: Lessons from Mex-ico for the Hemisphere* (2004). Thomas Friedman's *The World Is Flat: A Brief History of the Twenty-First Century* (New York: Farrar, Straus, and Giroux, 2005) offers the strongest pro-globalization argument. Manuel Castells and Roberto Laserna, in "The New Dependency: Technological Change and Socioeconomic Restructuring in Latin

America," *Sociological Forum* 4, no. 4 (1980), see technological changes and globalization constraining democracy. Michel Reid, *Forgotten Continent: The Battle for Latin America's Soul* (New Haven: Yale University Press, 2008), sees globalization as promoting democracy and finds Venezuela's President Chávez to be a threat to progress. William Robinson, *Latin America and Global Capitalism* (Baltimore: Johns Hopkins Press 2010), looks at the changing economies of Latin America and also at the resistance to neoliberal globalization.

Video and Film: *Another World Is Possible* (2008) looks at anti-globalization protests at the G8 economic summit in Genoa. *Voices from the Edge: The Favela Goes to the World Social Forum* (2005) is a Brazilian documentary. With an interesting twist on manufacturing and globalization, *The Take*, a documentary by Canadian filmmaker Avi Lewis, captures a movement in Buenos Aires that started with 30 factory workers who would not leave their factory. In protest against Argentina's Carlos Menem (claimed to be "responsible" for a grave economic collapse in 2001) and his powerful company-controlling comrades, these unemployed revolutionaries relied on their slingshots and their value of "shop-floor democracy" in a desperate struggle to get their jobs back. For more on this video, go to www.thetake.org.

On the Internet: The Carnegie study of NAFTA can also be found at http://carnegieendowment.org/2003/11/09/nafta-s-promise-and-reality-lessons-from-mexico-for-hemishphere. The World Social Forum has various sites associated with different countries, conferences, and movements. A prominent portal for the United States can be found at www.ussocialforum.net/. There are no shortages of videos on You-Tube where you can hear the views of Thomas Friedman. LANIC hosts a portal for all things NAFTA at http://lanic.utexas.edu/la/mexico/nafta/. What does a cat know about globalization and other world issues? Check out Pinky at www.pinkyshow.org/projectarchives/videos/defending-globalization-a-mission-for-the-educated-and-enlightened.

16 No One's "Backyard" Anymore

Focus Questions

▶ How have the Western Hemisphere's regional and diplomatic systems changed in recent decades?

▶ What is the future of the various intergovernmental organizations that exist in the region?

▶ To what extent has Latin America gained the ability to assert itself diplomatically in world affairs independent of the influence of the United States?

▶ Is democracy in Latin America being strengthened or weakened by U.S. foreign policy?

O N MAY 30, 2013, Edward Snowden, a contract employee for the National Security Agency, fled the United States for Hong Kong and then traveled on June 23 to Moscow. Snowden had released to news organizations, mainly *The Guardian* (London), detailed information about programs of mass surveillance of citizens in the United States and Britain, as well as embarrassing information about eavesdropping on other citizens of other countries, including European allies and friendly Latin American governments. Before he flew to Moscow, federal prosecutors indicted him on several charges, including espionage. The Kremlin, though unwilling to extradite Snowden, said it would give only temporary asylum and advised him to look elsewhere. His extradition back to the United States became a high priority for Washington, which let governments around the world know that any country granting Snowden asylum would pay a high price for its defiance of the global hegemon on this matter.

Until 2000 it was virtually unthinkable that any Latin American country, other than Cuba (and earlier in the century, perhaps Mexico), would defy the United States on a matter that Washington considered a top priority. However, by the end of July, three countries, Bolivia, Nicaragua, and Venezuela, had offered Snowden asylum, and Ecuador said it would consider an application. Ecuador's embassy in London was already sheltering Julian Assange, founder of WikiLeaks, whose publication of sensitive diplomatic documents had embarrassed many governments, including the United States. Although other Latin American countries had not offered asylum, several expressed sympathy for Snowden.

Throughout the hemisphere things took a turn for the worse for the United States when several European countries acted to force a plane carrying Bolivian president Evo Morales to land in Vienna, Austria, where his plane was kept for 14 hours while authorities sought to search it for Snowden (whether a search ever actually occurred is not clear), who they suspected was stowed away. Latin American anger now was directed with full force against the European Union and also Washington, which the region's governments suspected was behind the humiliation imposed on the region's first indigenous president.

In chapter 15, we explored how Latin America's economic relations with the world have been changing, becoming more varied and less dependent on the United States. Will its political and diplomatic relations similarly change? What impact has U.S. policy had on the democratic condition in the hemisphere?

◾ U.S. Intervention in the "Backyard"

Democracy promotion is more central to the public diplomacy of the United States today than ever before, but it also is a long-standing, moralistic component of U.S. foreign policy, closely tied to its liberal ideology. As Greg Grandin (2006) puts it, Latin America served as a "laboratory" for the global role that the United States would assume half a century later, including its policies and actions in Vietnam, Iraq, Afghanistan, and multiple locations in Latin America during the **Cold War**.

By the late 1800s, the United States had survived the Civil War and become an industrial power with formidable financial institutions of its own. In expanding westward, it displaced its own indigenous population, a form of territorial colonization justified by the idea of "Manifest Destiny"—the notion that white settlement of the supposedly empty continent was fulfillment of a God-given imperative. Along the way, the United States clashed with Mexico, annexing half of its territory in the war of 1848. By 1898, the western frontier had largely closed, just at the moment in which U.S. economic power was surging. So the question arose: was Manifest Destiny limited to the west, or should U.S. expansion flow southward? The country's entrepreneurs were already looking at that direction for new markets and investment opportunities. The war against Spain and the building of a two-ocean navy by President Theodore Roosevelt afterward demonstrated that the United States was now a commercial and military power, perhaps with an empire of its own in mind.

In the Caribbean and Central America, some elites encouraged the United States to annex their countries as new states. They remembered the lot of their brethren, the slave-owning aristocracy of Haiti who had perished in a slave revolt. They feared the same fate would befall them as Spain's power continued to deteriorate. Before the U.S. Civil War, some southern politicians saw admission of new slave states from this region as a counterweight to the admission of free states as the United States expanded westward. José Martí, the Cuban patriot who initiated the island's final war for independence from Spain, was well aware that the planters in Cuba and the Caribbean put protection of their interests above independence, and to keep them supportive of a break from Spain, he kept secret his goal of creating free, democratic societies. He was also aware of the rising power of the United States. Though he admired its innovative and popular democratic spirit, like Bolívar he also recognized its expansionist tendencies.

Martí had good reason to be concerned. Three years after he died (in 1895), the United States defeated Spain and "freed" Cuba, Puerto Rico, and other Spanish possessions.

Although freedom fighters had been waging war for decades, the United States occupied Spain's old colonies and negotiated their new status without rebel participation. Cuba was occupied for four years; Puerto Rico remains a territorial possession of the United States to this day. It is considered a "freely associated commonwealth" by the United States and a colony by the United Nations. Today, most of the island's population remains relatively evenly divided between those desiring statehood and those wishing to retain the commonwealth status. A small but vigorous independence movement regards the argument as moot, rejecting either alternative as colonialism.

The Spanish–American War of 1898 was a significant watershed in U.S. foreign policy. An explosion and the sinking of the battleship *Maine* in a harbor in Havana touched off the conflict. Rebels in Cuba (led by José Martí until his death in 1895) had been struggling to oust Spain, the "sick man of Europe," from one of its last remaining colonies. In the United States, there was a great deal of sympathy for the rebel cause, fed by propaganda in the "yellow press," mass-circulation newspapers that had emerged as a new factor in politics. At the same time, Americans held racist stereotypes similar to the ones they held about blacks in

Seattle Post-Intelligencer, 1906. Central American nations, cast again in racist stereotypes, are pacified, bringing prosperity.

the United States; they were transferred to South Americans, Caribbean people, Hawaiian natives, and Filipinos (Johnson 1980). I have provided as an example an image of Uncle Sam smiling contentedly as his "children," all depicted in racist black stereotypes from the era, sleep in bed. The image is appalling, but it reflects a historical fact, as well as a practice not entirely purged from the news media today (see, e.g., Said 1981).

U.S. troops withdrew from Cuba in 1903 but only on the condition that Cuba's constitution would recognize the Platt Amendment, passed by the U.S. Senate in 1901. Among its onerous provisions, the amendment prohibited Cuba from acquiring foreign debts and required it to lease lands to the United States for military facilities. Cuba's acquiescent rulers signed a special commercial treaty that had the effect of completely opening the sugar economy to U.S. domination. A U.S. citizen, Tomás Estrada Palma, president of Cuba in 1903, signed a lease giving the United States control "in perpetuity" over Guantánamo Bay, on the eastern tip of the island, for a naval base. After 2001, it became the site for the incarceration of prisoners taken by the United States in its Middle Eastern wars. The Platt Amendment also said, "The Government of Cuba consents that the United States may exercise the right to intervene for the preservation of Cuban independence, the maintenance of a government adequate for the protection of life, property, and individual liberty." This part of the amendment defined a neocolonial relationship that did not disappear after the amendment was abrogated in 1934.

The (Theodore) Roosevelt Corollary to the Monroe Doctrine, proclaimed in 1904, made this explicit. Roosevelt in his inauguration speech that year declared that the United States wished its "neighbors" to be "stable, orderly and prosperous" and that "any country whose people conduct themselves well can count upon our hearty friendship." But, he added,

> chronic wrongdoing, or an impotence which results in a general loosening of the ties of civilized society, may in America, as elsewhere, ultimately require intervention by some civilized nation, and in the Western hemisphere the adherence of the United States to the Monroe Doctrine may force the United States, however reluctantly, in flagrant cases of such wrongdoing or impotence, to the exercise of an international police power.

Theodore Roosevelt had risen to fame as the result of his small victory at San Juan Hill in Cuba during the Spanish–American War, an event that was hugely exaggerated by the yellow press. His words were a precursor in many ways for the theories justifying intervention into "failed states" in the contemporary world.

Roosevelt's most important direct intervention occurred in 1903, when American forces prevented Colombia's military from responding to the breakaway republic of Panama. Roosevelt ordered the action to facilitate the acquisition of the Panama Canal Zone. The canal was needed not only to serve American commercial interests but also to facilitate deployment of a two-ocean navy. Colombia had rejected the U.S. proposal to build the canal, so Roosevelt supported Panamanian rebels against Bogota. The new government

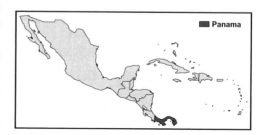

appointed a French businessman to negotiate a treaty. The Frenchman proceeded to sign an agreement that cut the new country in half, allocating "in perpetuity" a zone of U.S. control five miles wide on either side of the canal, which was completed in 1914. By 1960, Panamanian nationalist sentiment had reached the boiling point, but it took 17 more years for a new treaty to resolve the issue, returning jurisdiction over the territory to Panama at the end of 1999.

Mexico proved much more difficult to "tame" than other countries in the region. Already heightened by the loss of territory to the United States after the Mexican–American War (1846–1848), Mexican nationalism was reinforced by the revolution of 1910. The United States attempted to manipulate the outcome by backing more conservative factions. Overt military intervention included the shelling of the port of Veracruz in 1914 and the futile pursuit of the rebel Pancho Villa by U.S. troops in Mexico's northern deserts in 1917 (see chapter 9). Villa, angered by U.S. support for his rival, Venustiano Carranza, had staged a minor raid on Columbus, New Mexico, in 1916 in retaliation. His evasion of capture by General Black Jack Pershing's troops helped to make him a larger-than-life symbol of nationalist defiance, a sentiment that continues today in *corridos*, ballads that sometimes depict drug runners and *coyotes* (smugglers of migrants in the United States) as heroes. The Mexican case was an early precursor of something quite common: the United States came to regard any revolutionary movement as communist-inspired, and any regional revolution was seen to have an impact on others. The United States, born of a revolution, had become an anti-revolutionary power.

U.S. meddling in Nicaraguan affairs increased when European powers showed interest in the country as a site for a canal. American forces intervened repeatedly to prevent Nicaraguan factions favored by Europeans from gaining power. From a U.S. point of view, the political unrest was chronic and a sign of political immaturity that Americans could help alleviate. Elites in the region learned that one way to stop rival factions from consolidating power was to foment disorder and convince the United States that its vital interests were at stake. Thus, the interventions themselves contributed to unrest. In Cuba, U.S. forces intervened in 1906–1909, 1911–1912, and 1917–1922; it intervened also in the Dominican Republic (1905, 1916–1924), in Haiti (1915–1934), and in Nicaragua (1909–1933). Rival factions in countries throughout the region came to view the U.S. embassy as a resource in their own intramural disputes. The embassy in effect became a powerful player in the domestic politics of these "sovereign" nations.

The deployment of U.S. forces offshore was usually enough to influence the outcome of political conflicts— a tactic known as "gunboat diplomacy." The classic example occurred in 1908. In Venezuela, General Juan Cipriano Castro had seized power in 1899 after a period of civil war. Castro was a maverick nationalist who faced several rebellions financed by foreign interests. When General Juan Vicente Gómez, Castro's second-in-command, moved against his compatriot (who was in Europe for medical treatment), Washington deployed the American fleet offshore, a show of support for Gómez. Gómez would rule with an iron fist for 27 years and preside in the 1920s over Venezuela's first oil boom, distributing the concessions to a small circle of his family and friends who then sold them to foreign companies.

American warships stood by when General Maximiliano Hernández Martínez presided over La Matanza, the massacre of tens of thousands of Salvadoran peasants in 1934 (see chapter 10). The American force was deployed in the country's main harbor, ready to lend a hand if the Salvadoran military failed to "restore order." The Salvadoran coffee oligarchy, the Fourteen Families, and the military did not need American help to complete their grisly task. Still, in standing by, the United States made itself complicit in what became an act of genocide as Martínez's troops massacred indigenous people identified by their dress, language, and where they lived (Anderson 1971).

In neighboring Nicaragua the situation was different. American troops had landed to settle violent conflict between Liberal and Conservative elites. One of the liberal generals, José Augusto Sandino, had worked in the Mexican oil fields and absorbed some of the lessons of that revolution. Sandino was not, like Farabundo Martí, leader of the Salvadoran revolt of 1934, a communist. He was a nationalist who found the U.S. Marine intervention an affront and organized a peasant army of resistance. The American response is revealing of the relationship between democracy and intervention, setting a pattern for today's policy of "state-building" in far-flung parts of the world.

Sandino's army enjoyed popular support and could hide among the people. Between 1927 and 1933, Sandino's guerrillas inflicted a mounting toll of casualties that undermined the popularity of the war at home. The occupying force of Marines was on unfamiliar territory, both geographically and socially. The Marines complained about not being able to distinguish civilians from combatants. Today the operative word for such an enemy is "terrorists"; back then it was "bandits." Just as today, back home some Americans wondered whether it was their place to teach "democracy" to others. The public also grew weary of casualty reports. Pressure built for withdrawal. Washington decided its best strategy for stabilizing the country would be to create a professional, politically neutral army. Afterward, the planners thought, Nicaraguan elites would settle their disputes through a free and fair electoral process.

With this goal in mind, the Nicaraguan National Guard was created and trained. To command it, the U.S. Marines chose a young liberal businessman, Anastasio Somoza García, who had learned English while at school in Philadelphia. Having "Nicaraguanized" the war, the Marines left the country in 1933. The Nicaraguan state for the first time had a well-trained, well-armed force that could keep rival *caudillo* armies at bay. Sandino had said that he would negotiate an end to his resistance once the marines left the country. In 1934, he accepted an invitation to meet with Somoza, who instead ordered the assassination of the guerrilla leader. Somoza tightened his grip on power. U.S. aid ended up creating not a neutral military force but a basis for a relatively minor caudillo to create a family dynasty that lasted for 45 years, until the Sandinista revolution of 1979 (Millet 1977).

For Review

What accounts for the increase in military intervention by the United States in the twentieth century? What economic, geopolitical, and ideological motives seem to have been at work? What were the intentions, and what were the unintended consequences of intervention?

Intervention in the Cold War: Covert Operations and Democratic Breakdowns

European missions in the late nineteenth and early twentieth centuries had trained most of the military forces on the South American continent. In the period after World War II, the United States elevated the importance of its own military training and aid missions, extending them beyond the Caribbean region. In South America, the American programs had more to do with modernizing these forces and influencing their doctrines, rather than creating constabulary forces (e.g., as with the Nicaraguan National Guard). In the Cold War era, an objective of U.S. military aid was to inculcate the strategic doctrine of "national security," the phrase used to justify the creation of a large standing military and set of other institutions (the CIA, the National Security Agency, etc.; see Schoultz 1987). Throughout the Cold War, national security mainly meant "containment" of communism, though conservatives often argued that the objective should be to roll back rather than merely prevent communism's spread. In the Western Hemisphere, in effect both objectives were pursued after the Cuban Revolution—with "roll back" clearly the objective for Cuba itself.

Cuba, the Bay of Pigs, and the Economic Blockade

One reason that the United States did not invade Cuba with its own troops was the success it had achieved in removing Arbenz in Guatemala in 1954 using proxies. In 1961, former president Dwight Eisenhower, who had broken relations with Cuba just before John F. Kennedy assumed office in January 1960, bequeathed to the new president a plan hatched by the CIA to emulate its success in Guatemala. Kennedy had doubts, but rather than terminating the operation, he attempted only to reduce U.S. visibility in the project by canceling its air support. On April 17, 1961, about 1,700 Cuban exiles, trained by the CIA in Somoza's Nicaragua, landed on Cuba's south coast, expecting the local population to support them. The population remained loyal; Castro's forces moved decisively—without hindrance from the air—to crush the invasion. Ninety of the invaders were killed, the rest captured.

Invaders captured by the Cuban forces were later ransomed and returned to Miami. They became fierce, implacable enemies of Castro. In their lifetimes, they helped to create an atmosphere of fear and intimidation in Florida that kept any sizable group or institution from opposing any relaxation in U.S. pressure on Cuba. The failed invasion also greatly enhanced the legitimacy of the communist regime in Cuba and led to closer ties with the Soviet Union. The Soviets installed intermediate-range ballistic missiles, leading to the Cuban Missile Crisis of 1963. The crisis was resolved when the Soviet Union, without seeking advice or consent from Castro, agreed to pull the missiles out in exchange for a promise from Kennedy not to try another invasion and to withdraw some missiles from Turkey.

Roots of the persistently tense relationship between Havana and Washington go back to the Spanish–American War of 1898, the Platt Amendment, and the repetitive intrusion of the United States into the island's internal affairs. Still, when Fidel Castro first came to power in 1959, relations were initially good. It is difficult to sort out the sequence of events that led to the rupture in relations between Cuba and the United States. Some believe that a more enlightened U.S. policy would have prevented Castro from aligning with the Soviet Union and moderated his policies. On the other hand, Castro and his comrades were deeply influenced by the writings of Martí, who—though careful to separate his ideology from Marxism—had warned of the perfidy of wealthy Cuban elites and the hegemonic pretensions of the United States. If Fidel was not a communist, he was also not a liberal democrat. He was determined not to be one more Latin American leader who abandoned promises of social and economic renovation to win the support of the United States. As Castro began to act to break the neocolonial relationship between Cuba and the United States, things began to spiral out of control (see chapter 10).

Hundreds of thousands of Cuban civilians were mobilized into a National Revolutionary Militia, and the grassroots Committees to Defend the Revolution (CDRs) were created. After the Bay of Pigs, the likelihood of a successful counterrevolution diminished considerably, but attempts to sabotage the economy and assassinate Castro and other leaders continued under the code name Operation Mongoose, launched by the notorious U.S. general Edward Landsdale, the model for Ian Fleming's James Bond, who was known for his innovative and brutal psychological operations campaigns in Southeast Asia. In February 1962, President Kennedy imposed the embargo upon Cuba as punishment for its expropriation of U.S. properties. The sanctions include a travel ban. The ban was loosened briefly during the Carter administration, but tensions in Central America and the Soviet invasion of Afghanistan in 1979 contributed to worsening of relations again. Perhaps Cuba's revolutionary path would have led to a one-party state in any event, but U.S. policy certainly reinforced an unhealthy environment for democratic **governance** in the young regime.

Immigration policy has always been a political football in relations between the two countries. Until January 2013, when the need to get an exit visa to travel was abolished, the Cuban government sought to discourage emigration of its best-educated and most successful athletes and artists. The process of obtaining permission to emigrate was fraught with bureaucratic and political obstacles. The United States for its part sought to embarrass Cuba for restricting the free travel and emigration of its citizens but simultaneously benefited because the restrictions prevented an influx of large numbers of Cuban immigrants. In 1980, after several violent incidents in which Cuban guards prevented would-be asylum seekers from crashing into foreign embassies, Fidel Castro lost patience and announced that any Cubans who wanted to leave could do so through the port of Mariel. Cuban authorities, in an act clearly contradictory to the humanist ideals expressed by Castro himself, rounded up many prisoners and mentally ill patients and exported them through Mariel. A total of 125,000 Cubans left the island, creating a humanitarian crisis that overwhelmed U.S. authorities. The majority of those leaving, in contrast to the early exiles established in Miami, were from the lower classes and more likely to be dark-skinned. Upon arrival in the United States via a massive boatlift organized by the Miami exile community, most were imprisoned in refugee camps, some for years.

Neither Cuba nor the United States gained sympathy in the eyes of the international community. Eventually, the Reagan administration negotiated an immigration agreement intended to prevent a repetition of the event. Today, Cubans who seek to leave by rafts or other means are returned to Cuba if they are intercepted on the high seas, but should they make it to Florida, then they are granted special immigrant status, denied to other emigrants from the region. The United States continues a policy of economic pressure designed to worsen living conditions, thereby intensifying internal pressures for emigration. Meanwhile, it accepts only those eligible under the quotas and those who take the maximum risk of coming by raft or through arrangements with human traffickers.

Because U.S. laws and policy are designed to discourage not only U.S. investors but also foreign investors, the Cubans say the "embargo" is really a blockade, a violation of international law. In 1992, the U.S. Congress enacted new legislation to tighten the sanctions by prohibiting branches of American corporations based abroad from doing business in Cuba, which attracted severe criticism from the rest of Latin America. The Helms–Burton act of 1996 went even further, mandating that the U.S. government deny visas to executives of foreign companies doing business in Cuba. The act also gave Cuban Americans who lost property after the revolution the right to file for restitution in American courts—even if they were not U.S. citizens at the time of the expropriation. Ironically, the Castro government decided to translate and widely distribute the Helms–Burton Act to the Cuban population. I saw Spanish-language copies in the hands of peasants on a cooperative near Holguín. Why? Because it reinforced concerns in the island's population that Miami Cubans intended to reclaim clinics, schools, cooperatives, and housing that are now part of the fabric of life there.

In April 2009, the new U.S. administration of President Barack Obama lifted sanctions that prohibited Cuban Americans from traveling to visit relatives or sending financial support to them on the island. This initial gesture was welcomed by President Raúl Castro. At the Summit of the Americas later that month, the new U.S. president engaged in friendly conversation with President Chávez, Cuba's closest ally. In other words, there were signs that Cuban–U.S. relations might finally thaw and that the new administration would rely more on diplomacy and less on intervention in Latin America. Was a new "Good Neighbor" policy taking shape? Old habits die hard, and powerful domestic opponents in the United States remain opposed to action on Cuba. Those in favor of lifting the embargo argue that the economic sanctions allow the Cuban government to blame the United States for Cuba's economic problems, punish the Cuban people more than the government, contradict U.S. policy toward other communist countries (such as Vietnam and China), and hurt American agricultural exports. Usually, critics of the embargo claim that a policy of greater economic and cultural exchange would be more effective in promoting a "transition to democracy." The debate, we should note, is not over the propriety of the United States attempting to engineer change in a sovereign nation, or over the nature of the Cuban regime, but over what policies will most effectively undermine the current political system.

What sustains the U.S. policy? To some degree, the influence of the exile community in Florida accounts for its persistence. However, the Cuban community is becoming more diverse in its views. Ties of kinship or—for those with wealth—lost business opportunities make many Miami Cubans wish for a loosening of relations. The younger generations born in the United States bear less bitterness over the past. Recent emigrants often leave Cuba for economic opportunity rather than politics (though these are not always easily separable). However, hard-line Cuban Americans retain their grip over the politics of Dade County, some other parts of Florida, and parts of northern New Jersey. The political leadership of neither U.S. party showed much inclination to alienate this powerful lobby that can influence the outcome of presidential elections in two states that have large blocks of votes in the Electoral College, but in the 2012 election, Florida voted in the majority for the Democratic presidential candidate. The polls showed that in President Obama's successful bid for the state's electoral votes, he carried a majority of Cuban Americans.

Cuba's foreign policy often consists of a difficult balancing act between support for revolution and a need for normal relations with other countries. Just as revolutionary

Mexico was supportive of nationalist movements in Central America in the 1920s, Cuba served that role for revolutionary movements in Latin America in the 1960s. The Soviet Union was less than enthusiastic about Cuban support. Many veteran Latin American communists were reluctant to embrace a strategy that risked the party's significant political influence in established systems, but young communists and leftists throughout the hemisphere embraced Fidelismo. Nowhere were they successful in seizing power. By the 1970s, with Che Guevara killed by American-trained Bolivian commandos in 1967, Cuba had turned its attention to support African liberation movements and to mend fences with other Latin American countries. This diplomacy proved more successful in eroding the hemispheric support for U.S. policies. Nonetheless, when revolutions broke out in Central America in the 1980s, the United States was quick to see the hand of Cuba behind the unrest.

For Review

What were the original goals of the U.S. embargo/blockade of Cuba? Why did the policy persist into the early years of the Obama administration, even though it seemed to have failed in its objective of ousting the Castro regime?

Send in the Marines?

During World War II relations between the United States and Latin America were very much shaped by the goal of defeating the Axis powers. Latin America contributed economic resources, as most countries cooperated in holding down prices of raw materials needed for the war effort. Just as they did in World War I, most governments cooperated in monitoring those thought sympathetic (sometimes with good reason, often not) to the enemy countries of the Allied countries, at times depriving residents of German or Japanese descent (including their own citizens) of rights and property. Especially important was the development of cooperative arrangements among the military establishments of the region. In World War II, Brazil actually contributed troops to the Italian campaign, whereas in other cases branches of the armed forces were provided equipment and training to defend coastlines and important strategic resources.

More formal links between the United States and Latin American militaries were institutionalized in 1947 in the Inter-American Treaty of Reciprocal Assistance (known as the Río Treaty). The signatories agreed to lend mutual assistance to one another in the event of attack from an outside power, but more important, the treaty established the basis under which Latin American military officers would be influenced by training both via U.S. military missions in each country and via the attendance of Latin American officers at war colleges and other schools. Probably the best known and most targeted of these programs was the School of the Americas (now called the Western Hemisphere School for Security Cooperation) at Fort Benning, Georgia, founded in 1946. Critics called it the "School for Dictators" because of the large number of its graduates who were later associated with human rights atrocities.

Its curriculum at one time included training in torture, ostensibly to train officers to be prepared for what their enemies might practice (Gill 2004).

Direct military intervention by U.S. forces became rare in the post–World War II era, but it has happened enough to remind Latin Americans that invasion remains on the table for Washington should circumstances warrant, especially in the Caribbean. The most recent actual invasion took place in the tiny island of Granada in 1982, but probably the invasion of the Dominican Republic in 1965 is a better case study of when the United States, at least in the past, reached for the most risky policy option available, one that has been used more recently in the Middle East and Central Asia.

The Dominican Republic had suffered a U.S. Marines occupation for eight years early in the century, with U.S. forces leaving behind an American-trained National Guard upon withdrawal in 1924. As in Nicaragua with Somoza and Cuba with Batista, an ambitious young military officer established a dictatorship. Rafael Leónides Trujillo seized power in a coup in 1930 and used the Guard to turn the country into his personal family estate. He gained well-deserved notoriety for his brutality and disdain for democracy. Trujillo's anticommunism played well in the Cold War environment, but Washington was displeased by his attempts to overthrow José Figueres (1948) in Costa Rica and Rómulo Betancourt (1958) in Venezuela, both centrists opposed to communism and friendly to the United States. When Trujillo, after a series of particularly brutal acts of repression in his own country, attempted to assassinate Betancourt, the United States withdrew its support. In 1961 Trujillo's own army assassinated him, possibly with involvement of the CIA. After a year of uncertainty, Juan Bosch, Trujillo's most important opponent, returned from exile and was elected president in December 1961. Bosch began to implement reforms and develop a friendly relationship with nearby Cuba, alarming Washington, sectors of the Dominican military loyal to the deposed dictator, and the U.S.-based Gulf and Western Corporation, the largest property owner in the sugar-exporting country. In 1963, the army overthrew Bosch, but a countercoup in 1965 sought to restore the constitution and pave the way for his return to power.

President Lyndon Johnson (1963–1968), deeply embroiled in a land war against communist forces in Vietnam, invaded the Dominican Republic with 20,000 marines. They installed a compliant transitional regime that paved the way for Joaquín Belaguer, a close associate of Trujillo, to win the presidential election of 1966, heavily stacked in Belaguer's favor. By the time that Bosch finally won an election in 1978, his Revolutionary Democratic Party (PRD) was no longer a revolutionary force. Belaguer remained a powerful influence in Dominican politics until his death in 2002. The invasion ensured that no radical regime would succeed Trujillo, but it committed the United States to the support of a regime notorious for its corruption, presiding over a deeply unjust social structure. In the United States, Johnson sold the invasion as the interdiction of an international communist conspiracy, saying, "The American nations must not, cannot, and will not permit the establishment of another Communist government in the Western Hemisphere." Three years later, leaders of the Soviet Union used a very similar justification for their invasion of Czechoslovakia, putting an end to the Prague Spring (Franck and Weisband 1972). Fidel Castro announced he would support the Soviet action as a "bitter necessity."

The **bureaucratic authoritarian** regimes of the 1970s and 1980s were not installed by direct U.S. military intervention. However, the United States played a key role in fomenting destabilization in this period and also by signaling its support for the founding coups. President Johnson ordered his secretary of defense to do everything possible to help bring down populist João Goulart of Brazil in 1964. In 1976, during Gerald Ford's presidency, Secretary of State Henry Kissinger met with the Argentine foreign minister, Admiral César Augusto Guzetti, at a time when the Argentine military's Dirty War, which took 30,000 lives, was at its peak. Kissinger told Guzetti, "I have an old-fashioned view that friends ought to be supported. What is not understood in the United States is that you have a civil war. We read about human rights problems but not the context. The quicker you succeed, the better" (www2.gwu.edu/~nsarchiv/NSAEBB/NSAEBB104/, accessed August 24, 2014).

The U.S. involvement in bringing down Salvador Allende in 1973 (see chapter 7) stands out as one of the most egregious cases of antidemocratic intervention by the United States. After Allende finished a close third in the 1958 election, the United States was alarmed that he might win in 1964. With the Cuban Revolution as the background, the Kennedy administration made Chile a prime target of a new hemispheric policy, the Alliance for Progress. The idea of the Alliance was not only to train militaries and prevent a repeat of the collapse of the armed forces—that is, to avoid the kind of collapse that occurred with Batista. The purpose of the Alliance was also to encourage centrist forces to pursue an agenda of reform. One obstacle proved to be the Chilean right, which resisted change, particularly land reform. This dual track of providing military support and encouraging reform was to be practiced again in El Salvador in the 1980s.

The United States spent US$20 million to influence the 1964 vote, $8 per voter and 50 percent of the campaign spending by the winner, Christian Democrat Eduardo Frei (Robinson 1996: 157). As the 1970 elections approached, it was clear that the "threat" of an Allende victory had not been eliminated. Allende narrowly won the three-way election with 36 percent of the vote. The Chilean constitution called for Congress to choose a president if no candidate secured a majority, and in the past it had always selected the candidate with the most votes. The Nixon–Kissinger administration launched an ambitious plan to sow fear and convince the Congress to reject Allende. President Nixon ordered the CIA to "make the economy scream" to "prevent Allende from coming to power or to unseat him." Secretly, the CIA shipped weapons and ammunitions for use by a group of military officers who were to kidnap the Chilean military commander, General Rene Schneider, who opposed a coup. The idea was to blame Allende's supporters. Instead, a right-wing military faction linked to the CIA moved first to kidnap Schneider, who was killed in the attempt. In reaction the military and the country rallied behind Allende's ratification by the Congress (CIA 1970).

After Allende assumed power, the CIA believed that the Chilean military was unlikely to act immediately because of its "apolitical, constitutional" orientation (Robinson 1996: 161). Over the next three years, the U.S. government conducted a coordinated campaign on numerous fronts to bring down Allende. Tactics included subsidizing opposition media and planting false newspaper stories alleging economic shortages—inducing panic buying and real shortages. Another way to create shortages was by funneling funds to striking truck drivers. Right-wing groups were paid to put damaging spikes on highways to discourage drivers willing to work. Striking miners in the copper industry were subsidized with U.S. funds, while Washington effectively sealed off the country from international finance markets and nonmilitary aid programs. At the same time military aid was increased from US$1 million to US$15 million. The size of the U.S. military mission and intelligence activities targeting the military were increased. According to a subsequent U.S. Senate investigation, these activities included compiling names of people who would need to be detained and other contingency plans in the event of coup.

The record does suggest that the United States attempted to keep a distance from planning the coup that actually toppled Allende in 1973. William D. Rogers, who was an Assistant Secretary of State for Inter-American affairs from 1974 to 1976 and later a Secretary of State, tried to minimize U.S. involvement, arguing, "A cursory review of history suggests that had Washington done 'all it could' in Chile, it would have attempted an assassination . . . an invasion . . . an armed attack by mercenaries . . . or an attack by the U.S. military . . . Nothing close to such measures was deployed against Allende" (Rogers 2004). Here Rogers seems to defend the American role in bringing Pinochet to power by pointing out that assassinations and invasions were not deployed in Chile, though they had been used elsewhere!

Through Operation Condor, U.S. intelligence agencies cooperated with their counterparts in the dictatorships, working together to eliminate leftists. U.S. intelligence agents maintained a close relationship with Chilean general Manuel Contreras and the Chilean secret police, who were the intellectual authors of a car bomb attack that killed Orlando Letelier, a foreign minister in the Allende era, and his American assistant (Ronni Mofitt) on the streets of Washington, which was until 2001 the only actual terrorist attack ever carried out by foreign forces in Washington. When U.S. Ambassador David Popper raised concerns with Pinochet about the country's human rights record, Secretary of State Kissinger reprimanded him: "Tell Popper to cut out the political science lecture" (Bernstein 2008).

Jeane Kirkpatrick, an important official in the administration of President Ronald Reagan (1981–1988), whose academic vita included a book on Argentine politics, justified U.S. support for the military coups that ushered in the bureaucratic authoritarian states and led to the civil wars in Central America in the 1980s. After the Salvadoran army raped and murdered four American missionaries in 1980, Kirkpatrick said, "The nuns were not just nuns, they were political activists, and we should be very clear about that." When challenged to explain how she could justify tolerance of the murderous regimes in Latin America but champion policies to "roll back" communist and leftist regimes, Kirkpatrick (1979) argued that the latter sought to impose their ideology on society permanently. By contrast, she said, "authoritarian regimes" were susceptible in the long run to pressures to democratize. The distinction seemed apt to many in the Cold War, but 10 years after Kirkpatrick's assertion, the communist bloc in Eastern Europe began to crumble.

Geopolitical considerations, cultural chauvinism leavened with racism, a notion that Americans had a mission to spread civilization and democracy, and a mindset favorable to expansion (Manifest Destiny) all motivated U.S. intervention in Latin America. However, we should also recognize that many Americans dissented and articulated the country's own heritage of revolution and commitment to self-determination. Furthermore, although their actions are often inconsistent with professed policy, some American presidents have made rights and promotion of democracy a high enough priority to attract criticism from their political opponents. Franklin Roosevelt was president during several interventions, but not only did his Good Neighbor policy showed more respect for Latin America, and his New Deal policies to promote economic growth, strengthen labor rights, and institute welfare programs were admired throughout the hemisphere. Jimmy Carter failed to halt arms shipments to repressive governments in the hemisphere, but his human rights policies were nonetheless welcomed by the budding movements to defend rights in the region.

Both men had personal philosophies that at least in part motivated their initiatives, but both had other motives as well. Roosevelt thought that the Good Neighbor policy (the phrase was actually first used by his predecessor, Herbert Hoover) would help the United States open doors to increase trade with and investment in the region, especially in South America, where European influence was still strong. Carter hoped the U.S. backing of human rights would help restore American prestige and moral leadership, both badly damaged by the Vietnam War, as well as domestic scandals (especially the Watergate affair that forced Richard Nixon from the presidency). The Reagan administration did not entirely cast human rights and democracy off the agenda. Reagan's own rhetoric, casting the Soviet Union as part of an "evil empire" arrayed against democracy, embraced the selling point—useful at home and abroad—that U.S. policy was fundamentally oriented toward support of human rights and democracy.

We should not assume that Latin American militaries were always pliant tools of U.S. policy. As we reviewed in chapter 7, nationalism is a deeply embedded ethic, and it sometimes acts as a source of resistance to U.S. views on the best way to respond to leftist and revolutionary forces in the region. In some cases, such as El Salvador in the 1980s, the brutality of the officer corps (including graduates of the School of the Americas) was seen as counterproductive by their American advisors, but the Salvadorean officers were convinced that their way was most effective—just as it had been in 1935. However, there is not much doubt that the formal hemispheric military ties were meant not only to make the military a more effective fighting force but also to gain valuable political allies in a region where military intervention was quite common (Schoultz 1987: 160–190). Not surprisingly, Cuba's rebels decided that quite different doctrines would be necessary to defend the new regime from U.S. intervention. The Sandinistas too began with that assumption, but the Nicaraguan army took on a more conventional role after the defeat of the FSLN in the 1990 elections.

With the shift to the left in the region since 2000, the relationships between the U.S. military and Latin American militaries have changed, especially where more radical **Pink Tide** leaders have ascended to power. Venezuela's radical populist president Hugo Chávez decided in 2005 to change his military's fundamental doctrines. Before coming to power, Chávez was greatly interested in the theory of **asymmetric warfare**, a military doctrine regarding conflict between two powers that differ both in terms of culture and in terms of overall military strength. He could look to Cuba for an example of successful implementation of the strategy, as it played a role in discouraging direct invasion by the U.S. military (as opposed to the proxies used at the Bay of Pigs). The Pentagon estimated in 1962 that if the United States invaded Cuba, U.S. troops would suffer 18,500 casualties (www.gwu.edu/~nsarchiv/NSAEBB/NSAEBB39).

No Latin American country can expect to nearly match the power of the United States. The U.S. military budget exceeded US$560 billion for 2007 (Pentagon, intelligence agencies, other military expenditures), not including an additional US$100 billion to be spent in 2007 on the Iraq and Afghanistan wars, far surpassing that of all Latin American countries put together. Brazil leads all Latin America with less than US$15 billion. The United States is the only nuclear power in the hemisphere; by treaty, Latin America is a nuclear-free zone. So

Chávez's perspective was that any country seeking to deter possible aggression by the United States must rely on unconventional tactics. His successor, Nicolás Maduro, has maintained the new doctrine.

In July 2005, Chávez announced that the doctrine of asymmetric warfare would be formally introduced into Venezuelan operational training and military education, and he also announced the formation of a civilian militia. The Venezuelan high command was dominated by his own appointees, so the new doctrine is officially welcome, but in the long run such a shift may prove controversial within military ranks. The country that has most successfully implemented asymmetric warfare preparation is Cuba, and Havana provides military advisors. The Venezuelan opposition views formation of a militia as a step toward militarization of **civil society** and the creation of a security institution dedicated to defense of the rule of the United Socialist Party of Venezuela, not defense of the nation, and it accuses the government of intending to replicate the Cuban model. On the other hand, it would take a government with considerable confidence in its own people or an ability to exercise tight command and control over militias to arm its own people. Few Latin American governments have had either capability.

Whatever Chávez's intention, he certainly believed that changing the military's doctrine and mission was crucial to survival of his Bolivarian revolution. But Venezuela is not Cuba. Its military and civilians have cooperated in missions (social welfare programs) that have alleviated poverty, but its civic society and its military have never undergone the kind of transition, a virtually total reconstruction, that occurred in Cuba after 1959. And Chávez himself was a military man with leadership capacity and an ability to connect with ordinary soldiers. Maduro, his successor, came out to the labor movement and does not have the same stature with soldiers as his predecessor.

For Review

What was the Río Treaty? What was its stated purpose? What other value did it have for the United States? How does the doctrine of asymmetric warfare, adopted in Venezuela, differ from the kind of doctrines that most Latin American militaries assimilated during the Cold War?

The Legacy of Cold War Intervention on Latin America

During his eight years in office, Reagan aided the repressive governments of El Salvador and Guatemala and the Nicaraguan *contras* in one of the bloodiest regional conflicts of the Cold War. The death toll surpassed 70,000 political killings in El Salvador, 100,000 in Guatemala, and 30,000 in the *contra* war in Nicaragua. Certainly, the Sandinista government and the guerrillas in the other two countries were responsible for some of the violence, but in each case, responsibility for a majority of the bloodshed rested with the side supported by the

United States. Reagan said of the *contras*, "They are our brothers, these freedom fighters and we owe them our help. They are the moral equal of our founding fathers." The United States continues to maintain that its policies in this decade contributed to the establishment of democracy in the region.

The strategy in the Vietnam War, it is worth noting, was essentially the same as in El Salvador: to train and equip the South Vietnamese military forces to take over the fight against the North Vietnamese and Southern National Liberation Forces (Viet Cong), which would allow American forces to withdraw, thus "Vietnamizing" the war. The strategy, as we have seen, was first used in comparable circumstances in Nicaragua at the time of Sandino. One of the main goals of the invasion of Iraq in 2003 was not only to oust Saddam Hussein but also to substitute a **polyarchy** for his dictatorship. In both the cases, elections were organized with the twin objectives of legitimizing the U.S.-supported government and convincing Americans at home to support the war. Hence, we see a continuity of more than a century in the motives and strategies of U.S. intervention overseas.

The Central American civil wars came to an end during the administration of President George H. W. Bush (1989–1993). As Reagan's vice president he had held an important role in shaping Central American policies, especially in Honduras, which was used as a forward base of operations by the United States during the conflict. But Bush was more pragmatic than Reagan. The end of the Cold War had removed the Soviet threat from the power equation, and Cuba appeared (wrongly, it turned out) ripe to fall. European and Latin American leaders were pressuring the United States on the diplomatic front. Negotiated settlements were reached. The FMLN and FSLN each held the presidency in their respective countries, and in neither was implementing anything like their programs of the 1980s. Had Washington's project succeeded?

Throughout Central America, refugees from the violence in the countryside swelled the cities. A generation of young (mostly) men had been weaned on violence and were suddenly turned loose into society. This coincided with the emergence of a new source of violence in the form of youth gangs. These bands first emerged among boys who had grown up in refugee families in U.S. cities, especially Los Angeles, where the crack cocaine epidemic, fed in part by drug cartels linked to the *contras* and tolerated by the CIA, took early root (Webb 1999). Widespread passion for guns, alienated young men with little hope for the future, and deepening poverty all accompanied the "successful" installation of democracy in the region.

In June 2005, Amnesty International (AI) published "Guatemala: No Protection, No Justice: Killings of Women in Guatemala" (www.amnesty.org/en/library/info/AMR34/017/2005). Referring to an epidemic of murders of women, AI said, "According to Guatemalan authorities, 1,188 women and girls were murdered between 2001 and 2004. Many of the victims have been killed in exceptionally brutal circumstances. There is evidence to suggest that sexual violence, particularly rape, is a strong component characterizing many of the killings but this is often not reflected in official records." The government maintained an attitude of impunity toward the killings. Annual reports by the U.S. State Department recognize these kinds of abuses as problems and continue to harshly criticize Guatemala's human rights record, but this did not prevent Washington from supporting Guatemala over Venezuela for a temporary seat on the United Nations Security Council in 2006.

The United States and Democracy Promotion in the Western Hemisphere

Simón Bolívar had a decidedly mixed view of the United States. He once praised it as a "land of freedom and home of civic virtue." However, in Latin America he is better known for a different quotation. Dismayed that the United States had worked diplomatically to help defeat his proposed constitution, which would have made him president for life, Bolívar wrote in a letter to a British diplomat in Colombia, "The United States appears destined by Providence to plague America with misery in the name of liberty" (Bushness 1986). Bolívar's political failures had more to do with the attitudes and actions of the Creole elite than with outside intervention by the United States. Still, his prophecy has proven sadly true in many respects.

U.S. troops are less likely these days to engage in an outright invasion, but it is certainly not "off the table," as Washington likes to put it. The most recent "boots on the ground" intervention took place in Panama, in 1989. The target was Manuel Noriega, a general and power behind the scenes in the country. He was kidnapped and brought back to the United States to stand trial on drug trafficking charges. (Noriega had been an "asset" working in the employ of the CIA in the 1980s.) Before Panama, in 1982, tiny Grenada was the first invasion since the 1965 invasion of the Dominican Republic, as well as the first post–Vietnam War military operation of this type. U.S. forces are present in other ways. In recent years troops have been deployed to train or assist security forces in places such as Colombia, Mexico, and Central America.

More commonly in the post–World War II era, Washington has sought to change regimes in Latin America through destabilizing them, sometimes by funding and training proxies as insurgents, sometimes by undermining a recalcitrant country's economy while bolstering civilian opponents, and sometimes both (the "two track strategy"). The desired result is an electoral victory by the opposition, a civilian uprising, or a military coup. (An old joke in Latin America says that the United States has never experienced a coup because there is no U.S. embassy in Washington.)

The flip side of destabilization or overthrow of a government that falls into disfavor with Washington is the attempt to stabilize a new regime. William Robinson (1992, 1996) argues that the period since the U.S. defeat in Vietnam has seen greater emphasis on state-building to head off revolutionary processes and to shore up regimes installed after episodes of intervention. This has largely taken place through democracy promotion, which Robinson calls "exporting **polyarchy**." That is, Robinson, in line with those who find the **pluralist** theory of democracy wanting (see chapter 1), sees U.S. strategy as an extension of its **hegemony**—its attempt to construct a world of nation-states whose political systems are based on institutions that blunt the possibility of more direct, popular, participatory systems that may threaten **neoliberal** capitalism and **globalization** dominated by **transnational corporations.**

Democracy promotion is usually seen as a post–Vietnam War phenomenon—an effort, along with support for human rights, to recapture the high moral ground lost in the Southeast Asian conflict. However, there are precedents in American efforts to stabilize countries in the Caribbean and Central America, from the 1890s to the 1980s. Early U.S. interventions in the region sought to achieve stability with military missions to train, equip, and prepare native troops ("constabularies") to defeat insurrections, but also to assume a neutral, apolitical role in internal affairs. In theory, this would induce elites to abandon insurrection and compete for power through "democratic" means—specifically, through elections organized or promoted by the United States. The editorial cartoons in this chapter show two views of that philosophy from a pro-Sandinista, Nicaraguan newspaper (by the cartoonist Roger) mocking the United States for its sponsorship of elections in the 1980s.

Nicaraguan cartoonist Roger's view of U.S.-sponsored elections in El Salvador.

How the United States Promotes Democratization

Democracy promotion not only includes training and funding for holding elections, but also places stress on building a "civil society" consistent with the principles of a market economy and pluralist democracy—a idea taken directly from the pluralist idea that democracy requires the formation of interest groups competing with one another for political influence. One key tool in this effort has been the National Endowment for Democracy (NED), whose operations, along with those of the Office of Transition Assistance in the State Department and other programs of the U.S. Agency for International Development (AID), reveal much about Washington's approach to influencing Latin American politics in the post–Cold War era. NED was founded in 1983, according to its website (www.NED.org), "to strengthen democratic institutions around the world

PUNTO DE VISTA: WHERE DOES DEMOCRACY RANK IN U.S. FOREIGN POLICY PRIORITIES?

What follows is a thought experiment. Imagine a simple matrix (see Table 16.1) presenting stark choices on each axis: democracy versus dictatorship and capitalism versus socialism. Review the choices and rank-order the four possibilities in the matrix.

You might find the question hard to answer. What kind of democracy are we talking about in the matrix? Assume polyarchy—the pluralist variant described throughout this book. What is socialism? Indeed, socialism has many variations; so also does capitalism, which may take the form of an unregulated, free-market system or may be heavily influenced by the government, as it was in the import substitution era. You might not be sure whether a system with a strong welfare system is socialist or just a more humanistic form of capitalism. We have also seen that dictatorships can vary enormously in their degree of harshness and popularity. You have discovered what comparativists have long known: that classification risks oversimplifying reality.

Do the best you can. At the end of this chapter, return to the exercise and see whether your views have been reinforced or changed. In the Afterword, a brief conclusion to this book, I'll discuss my own views of U.S. preferences. (I generally find that many of my students do not share my answer.) What follows are some perspectives for you to consider as you decide on how to rank the outcomes.

Some radical critics contend that capitalist dictatorship is the preferred U.S. objective because dictatorships more harshly repress labor and are friendlier toward American investments. War hero General Smedley

Butler saw his military service in the Caribbean and Central America as little more than gendarmerie for business interests. In 1933, he wrote, "I spent thirty-three years and four months in active military service as a member of this country's most agile military force, the Marine Corps. I served in all commissioned ranks from Second Lieutenant to Major-General. And during that period, I spent most of my time being a high class muscle-man for Big Business, for Wall Street, and for the Bankers. In short, I was a racketeer for capitalism."

He went on,

> I helped make Mexico, especially Tampico, safe for American oil interests in 1914. I helped make Haiti and Cuba a decent place for the National City Bank boys to collect revenues in. I helped in the raping of half a dozen Central American republics for the benefits of Wall Street. The record of racketeering is long. I helped purify Nicaragua for the international banking house of Brown Brothers in 1909–1912 . . . I brought light to the Dominican Republic for American sugar interests in 1916. In China I helped to see to it that Standard Oil went its way unmolested.
>
> (www.fas.org/man/smedley .htm, accessed July 7, 2005)

On the other hand, we have seen that foreign investment in Latin America began to increase in the late twentieth century

TABLE 16.1   Support for Political and Economic Outcomes in U.S. Foreign Policy

	Capitalism	*Socialism*
Democracy	Capitalist Democracy	Socialist Democracy
Dictatorship	Capitalist Dictatorship	Socialist Dictatorship

only after the transitions to democracy took place—Chile being a key example here. And is the objective of U.S. foreign policy in the era of globalization mainly defense of American business interests, or is U.S. policy more oriented toward defense of capitalism *as a global system*? If the latter, what kind of system is best, dictatorship or democracy?

Point/Counterpoint

Based on the history and present policies of the United States, what regime, in your opinion, is the most preferred, and what is the least preferred, from the U.S. perspective?

a. If you placed support for democracy ahead of support for capitalism, how do you respond to claims that dictatorships are friendlier to big foreign corporations, restricting worker rights and remaining lax on environmental standards?

b. If you placed defense of capitalism ahead of democracy, how do you respond to those who point out that the United States supported the transitions to democracy in the most recent era of military dictatorship?

For more information

Walter LaFeber, *Inevitable Revolutions: The United States in Central America*, 2nd ed. (New York: Norton, 1993), looks closely at American policy toward many of the countries that were occupied by General Butler's forces. See also Greg Grandin, *Empire's Workshop: Latin America, the United States and the Rise of the New Imperialism* (New York: Metropolitan Books, 2006). Julia Sweig is the senior advisor for Latin America for the Council on Foreign Relations. Her task force report *Friendly Fire: Losing Friends and Making Enemies in the Anti-American Century* (New York: Public Affairs, 2006) looks at Latin America and the United States during the Cold War.

through nongovernmental efforts." In its "20th Anniversary Timeline," it lists the following Latin American activities:

- "NED assists the independent Nicaraguan daily newspaper, *La Prensa*, through the purchase of printing supplies without which the paper would have been forced to stop publication." NED proudly cites its success conducting "a wide range of activities supporting the democratic opposition in Nicaragua" in the 1980s.
- "In Chile, urgently needed support is provided by NED to a broad range of political and social forces working for peaceful transition to democracy." The organization takes credit for funding "massive civic education efforts" to encourage a democratic transition in Chile in advance of the 1988 plebiscite.
- In 1990, NED undertook a mass media voter-education project in Guatemala. In 1994, NED helped to provide funds to the Civic Alliance for election monitoring in Mexico. In 2000, support for the Civic Alliance was listed as that year's top priority.
- In 1998, it funded the Center for a Free Cuba and a journal, *Encuentro*, to support dissidents on the island.

The birth of NED coincided with revolutions that overthrew dictators supported by the United States and that subsequently took a radical turn. Revolutions in Iran in 1978 and in Nicaragua in 1979 had occurred in part because in each case a dictator (Shah Reva Pavlavi and Anastasio Somoza, respectively) had clung to power for too long. Beginning in 1983, opposition began to appear in the streets in Chile (see chapter 8), and it became clear that forces opposing Pinochet, like revolutionary forces in Iran and Nicaragua, had different visions of what the new era would look like. Hoping to replicate the success of easing out the dictator Ferdinand Marcos in the Philippines, and also to avoid another revolution in the mold of Iran and Nicaragua, the United States began to pressure the Chilean dictatorship to negotiate with the moderate political opposition. Meanwhile, NED began to fund and train sectors of society to compete with more radical unions, professional associations, women's groups, publishing houses, university associations, and so on (Robinson 1996: 157–175).

As part of its work, NED funds prominent Latin American, European, and U.S. political scientists to form teams to study "transitions to democracy," always understood as a transition to **polyarchy**. Democracy came to be valued not just for itself but as a system for preventing the radicalization of popular movements, not for empowering them. Routinely, foreign politicians are brought to the United States for workshops where this idea can be reinforced and, in the relevant cases, unity can be promoted. NED funds in Chile were also directed toward inducing unions and other groups in the *barrios*— where Communist Party influence was strong—to participate in the plebiscite.

Between 1984 and 1991, NED spent US$6.2 million (and the U.S. Agency for International Development spent an additional US$1.2 million) in Chile to help favored groups and encourage the process that led to the plebiscite of 1989 (Robinson 1996: 175; see chapter 8). The Chilean opposition was divided on whether to participate in the plebiscite and thereby accept Pinochet's 1981 constitution. U.S. aid helped ensure that the faction favoring acceptance prevailed within opposition ranks (though this seems to have been the majority position in any case). In the campaign, NED funds helped offset Pinochet's abuse of incumbency, providing money for polls and training. After victory, most of the "No" (to continuation of Pinochet's rule) forces remained together as the Concertación. The outcome was consonant with U.S. objectives: Pinochet was out of the presidency before pressures for a more revolutionary transition matured, and the Communist Party and other leftist groups were effectively marginalized. NED also played an important role in the Central American civil wars, notably in Nicaragua, where NED's support for the opposition helped it defeat the Sandinistas in the 1990 election.

NED's activities have led some governments around the world to ban foreign funding of nongovernmental organizations. The organization's funding of groups that participated in the short-lived coup against President Hugo Chávez was especially controversial. NED denies that its aid was directed toward this end, but the Venezuelan government did not see things this way. The incident led Venezuela and several other Pink Tide governments to pass legislation restricting local organizations from accepting foreign funding. This is not unlike the restrictions that the United States places on foreign funding of political parties and the requirement for foreign agents to register. However, such restrictions can be applied with a broad brush against political opponents. Not all organizations that accept funds are disloyal opponents of a government that Washington abjures.

Though the motives for funding are suspect, some organizations receiving NED money have worked in constructive ways on human rights issues and democracy. Mexico's Alianza Cívica (Civic Alliance; see chapter 9), for example, emerged as a genuine movement for clean elections. It was created in 1994 as the result of an innovative campaign to have citizens "adopt" a functionary of the state bureaucracy to audit his or her performance (Avritzer 2002: 124–129). NED monies (e.g., US$52,000 in 2003) continued to fund the Alianza after the election of Vicente Fox in the 2000 presidential election that put an end to 80 years of the PRI's monopoly. Despite this funding, Alianza was harshly critical of the Mexican election campaign of 2006 (see www.alianzacivica.org.mx), in which the U.S.-preferred candidate was victorious. As noted previously, NED played a role in the Chilean transition from military rule to electoral democracy, supporting opposition to a dictatorship.

The U.S. Department of State also operates a democracy promotion program through the Human Rights and Democracy Fund and through several separate Regional Democracy Funds. The department website states, "The United States remains committed to expanding upon this legacy until all the citizens of the world have the fundamental right to choose those who govern them through an ongoing civil process that includes free, fair, and transparent elections" (www.state.gov/j/drl/democ, accessed October 25, 2013). Funding for these programs for fiscal year 2010, the last year listed on the site, is listed at $210 million. Almost half that amount was designated for Iraq.

Democracy Promotion and the 2002 Coup in Venezuela

In the Nicaraguan case, NED supported groups in civil society as part of an overall effort to destabilize an elected regime. In the Chilean case, NED helped to force a dictator from power. What the two cases have in common is a desire to promote the pluralist version of democracy and head off more revolutionary tendencies. In the case of Venezuela, following the electoral victory of Hugo Chávez in December 1998, the NED, as highlighted on its home page (www.NED.org, accessed December 2012; now removed), spent more than US$1 million to support opposition groups in Venezuela between 1999 and 2002. Several of these organizations were directly involved in supporting the short-lived coup against Chávez in 2002. Because the Venezuelan media had promoted the coup and prematurely

celebrated its success, there exists a visual record of key leaders of NED recipients enthusiastically cheering Chávez's fall, which was reversed 48 hours later. NED was embarrassed but continues to argue that it was merely working to support a democratic **civil society** against a government showing authoritarian tendencies. NED justifies its funding to opposition groups in Venezuela by claiming that it seeks to "level the playing field" because of government support (considerable because of oil-export earnings) of the Chavista party.

After a solid majority voted "No," not to recall Chávez, he threatened to prosecute groups accepting NED funding. The Venezuelan government charged

DEMOCRACY IN VENEZUELA

MEAN SUPPORT	71%
SUPPORT 2013	87%
SATISFACTION 2013	42%

several organizations with having accepted funds illegally. One group, SUMATE ("Join Up"), had been committed to gathering signatures to force a recall of the Venezuelan president. Afterward, the organization and its leaders were charged with illegally accepting foreign money for the recall. Jorge Vivanco, of Human Rights Watch, criticized the Venezuelan government, claiming that it was persecuting "legitimate electoral activities." The charges were ultimately not pursued. Twelve years later, in 2014, some of the same organizations and leaders were at the forefront of large-scale street demonstrations calling for the ouster of President Nicolás Maduro.

The case raised some important questions about sovereignty, democracy, and civil freedoms. NED-affiliated organizations clearly receive aid from a foreign source. Was SUMATE a party or a group in civil society? The distinction is important because at the time of the recall election of 2004, it was illegal for parties, but not organizations, to accept foreign financial assistance. If it was considered a party, then, as in the United States, it could not receive funds legally. If it was part of civil society, as in the United States, it would have to report those contributions, but as long as it did not operate as a political party, it could legally accept them. SUMATE operated in a gray zone, but there is little doubt that its objective was to remove Chávez.

U.S. support is sometimes justified as "leveling the playing field" for opposition parties facing governments abusing incumbency. In Venezuela, opposition organizations claim that their members are exposed to retribution, and there is evidence that individuals who worked in legal ways to oppose the government were subject to discrimination in employment. There can be little doubt, however, that Washington would like to see regime change in oil-rich Venezuela, and its historical track record does not inspire faith in its neutrality in promoting democracy.

For Review

How does the NED define its purpose? What does it mean when NED says it supports civil society? Why do some see it as a tool of U.S. foreign policy? How has democracy promotion fit in with larger U.S. goals in regard to more radical regimes in the hemisphere? How did democracy promotion and specifically the role of the NED come into question in Venezuela during the Chávez era? How did the Chávez government react?

A Revolution in Hemispheric Diplomacy?

We are accustomed to hearing North American politicians routinely refer to U.S. support for "free markets and democracy" in the same breath, as though no other combination of political and economic systems makes sense. The United States and Latin American nations committed themselves to electoral democracy and pledged to support elected governments threatened by military coups in a Plan of Action signed at the first Summit of the Americas in Miami in December 1994. All heads of state except Fidel Castro of Cuba (who was banned from the summit at U.S. insistence) attended and signed the accords. At the summit, held at the peak of neoliberal influence in the hemisphere, the signatories also agreed to advance WTO/GATT trade negotiations and pledged to work for the Free Trade Area of the Americas (FTAA; see chapters 9 and 15).

However, in the 1990s some harbingers of change were already visible. Europeans saw U.S. policy on Central America as extremely shortsighted. The end of the Cold War was in sight. Spain and Portugal had undergone transitions to democracy by 1986 and were members of the (then) European Community; Spain in particular, as the "mother country" of most of Latin America, wished to establish a "special relationship." A group of Latin American countries (Mexico, Venezuela, Colombia and Panama) launched an initiative, much to the consternation of the Reagan administration, to bring the Central American conflicts to a close. The "backyard" mentality in the north had not disappeared, but the Caribbean no longer could be considered an American lake.

After the fall of the Berlin Wall in 1989 and the collapse of the Soviet Union in 1991, few analysts would have predicted that the power of the United States might actually decline. In fact, in at least one respect—military power—that hardly seems to have been the case. The United States has concentrated an unprecedented degree of military power and tended in the **post-9/11** era to use it unilaterally. The Center for Arms Control and Non-Proliferation (Heeley 2013) estimates that in 2012, U.S. military spending accounted for 41 percent of the world total—six times more than China, 11 times more than Russia, and 10 times more than all of Latin America and the Caribbean combined. These figures include only Pentagon spending, the war in Afghanistan, and the Energy Department's expenditures on nuclear weapons. If the CIA, spending on veterans' benefits, foreign military aid, homeland security, and interest on the part of the national debt attributable to military service were to be included, the figure would nearly double the center's estimate.

With many variations, Washington's critics see the United States as an imperial power, though some would say the nature of "empire" is different today than it was in the era of European dominance. Michael Hardt and Antonio Negri (2000) in their widely read and debated book, *Empire*, argue that a new globalized world order has emerged, one that resembles the empires of ancient Greece and Rome. As in the ancient world, the United States is a central political and military power presiding over a vast system of decentralized economic power, diffusing its cultural and political norms throughout the world.

Why are different views of "empire" relevant to Latin America's path in the world today? Consider the choice confronting the region's leaders. Should Latin Americans put the emphasis on linking their economies in a trade bloc led by the United States, or should they instead prioritize regional economic integration independent of the United States and diversification of trade and investment with Asia and Europe? Should they welcome Washington's attempts to promote liberal democracy, or should they be suspicious and insist on their sovereign right to choose a form of government most suitable to their needs? Should they develop independent security policies in areas such as the drug trade and terrorism, or should they work closely with U.S. security forces? Should they regard Washington's military dominance in the world as a security blanket or as imperialism? Does National Security Agency (NSA) surveillance help maintain U.S. control over the region, or is it part of a shield against the threat of terrorism?

Despite the record of repeated intervention in their internal affairs, most Latin Americans still see look positively at the United States (see Figure 16.1). Notice the significant drop in those expressing a good opinion of the United States during the wars in Iraq and Afghanistan, reaching a nadir of 58 percent in the last year of the Bush administration. The election of the first African descendant president, Barack Obama, seems to have restored U.S. prestige to more usual levels. However, it has become clear that in the 2000s, Latin American countries became much more pro-active in their diplomacy. While each country's interactions with the United States remained the single most important of its bilateral relations, Latin America began to interact more frequently and more independently with other parts of the world.

Some of the reasons for this shift have to do with the forces of economic globalization reviewed in the last chapter; some have to do with U.S. pre-occupation with other parts of the world; and some have to do with the enduring quest, articulated most forcefully by Bolívar and Martí, that Latin America search for unity so that it can achieve parity in its dealings with the United States.

FIGURE 16.1   Views of the U.S. in Latin America

Q. I would like to know your opinion about the following countries and potencies that I'm going to read. Do you have a very good, good, bad, or very bad opinion of (country)?
Here only "very good" and "good".

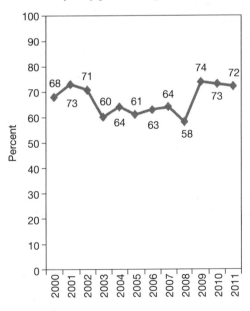
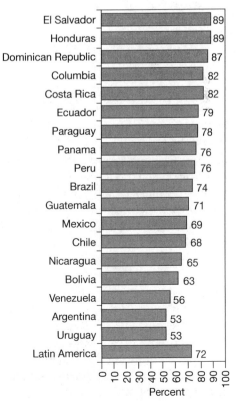

Regional trade, military, and security organizations are features on the global system of international relations. The Organization of African Unity, the European Union, and the Arab League are all examples of IGOs (intergovernmental organizations). Latin America, until recently, was the only major Third World region that lacked such an organization, whose members are exclusively drawn from a particular cultural area—unless one counts the Organization of American States (OAS). One might very well see the OAS as an IGO uniting "American states" or those in the Western Hemisphere; indeed, Pan Americanism has been expressed as an ideal by U.S. statesmen, such as Thomas Jefferson, Henry Clay, and James Monroe. Latin American leaders, such as Bolívar and Martí, have often voiced concerns about falling under the dominance of the United States. As we have seen, in the waning days of the Cold War, Latin America began to speak with a more independent voice. While strongly sympathetic to the United States in the immediate aftermath of the criminal mass slaughter of 9/11, the tendency toward unilateral use of military power by Washington and the shift leftward of electoral outcomes in the 2000s created some momentum for creation of new economic, diplomatic and security organizations where Latin Americans could act more effectively to resolve their own inter-state conflicts independent of Washington and speak with their own voice on global issues.

For Review

Why do some see U.S. influence in Latin America as having weakened in recent years? What signs are there that Latin American countries are beginning to assert more autonomy from U.S. global leadership?

The Organization of American States (OAS)

In 1948, one year after the signing of the Río Treaty creating a military cooperation between the United States and most Latin American countries, the countries of the region founded the Organization of American States (OAS), which replaced a looser association, the Pan-American Union. Bolívar's notion of Pan-Americanism envisioned Latin American unity as a bulwark against domination by the United States. The OAS, headquartered in Washington, is a hemispheric organization that is cynically called "the office of the colonies" by some Latin Americans. In 1962, the OAS adopted a resolution expelling Cuba (formally, Cuba remains a member, but without representation) and in doing so defined any state that identified itself with Marxism–Leninism as unqualified for membership. By 2010, Latin American governments were ready to readmit Cuba, but Havana had not yet expressed interest. Curiously, Washington opposed the move, it did not act to prevent the OAS from changing its posture on Cuba. Perhaps the reason is because the OAS no longer seemed to be serving the interests of the U.S. in the region.

On several occasions the OAS had provided diplomatic cover for U.S. intervention, including the 1954 intervention in Guatemala against the elected president, Jacobo Arbenz (see chapter 10). The OAS reacted ambiguously to the U.S. invasion of the Dominican Republic in 1965. The OAS supervised the election in 1962 that brought the leftist Juan Bosch to power—much to the displeasure of the United States—touching off the crisis that eventually led to the U.S. Marines invasion of 1965. Many Latin American countries objected, but faced with a *fait accompli*, the OAS decided to provide a multinational force to replace the U.S. occupation force, paving the way for elections in which Bosch was defeated.

How, then, to interpret the role of the OAS? On the one hand, the OAS force, made up of troops from six Latin American countries, allowed elections to take place and helped facilitate an end to the U.S. occupation. On the other hand, the OAS force also seemed to legitimate the U.S. invasion.

The OAS has not always conformed to Washington's lead. For example, it refused to endorse the *contra* war in Nicaragua in the 1980s, and it condemned a coup endorsed by Washington in Venezuela in 2002. The organization played an important role in bringing an end to the 1980s civil wars in Central America, one not welcomed by the Reagan administration (1981–1988). In 1989 the OAS took a stance against the U.S. invasion of Panama. Though it did not condemn the invasion, it expressed "deep regret" for the U.S. action and called for a withdrawal of troops. Two of its autonomous units, the Inter-American Commission on Human Rights and the Inter-American Court on Human Rights, have taken on an important role in adjudicating human rights disputes brought by individuals and groups of citizens against governments in the region that are signatories to the Convention on Human Rights. OAS observer missions have played key roles in highly polarized political situations—for example, in Nicaragua in 1984 and 1990 and in Venezuela in 2004.

In 2005, Latin Americans dealt U.S. diplomacy a severe setback by rejecting the U.S.-backed (Mexican) candidate to become the OAS secretary general, selecting instead Chilean José Miguel Insulza. So it could not have come entirely as a surprise when in June 2009, the United States was set back again when member states voted to readmit Cuba—though under some conditions. The **ALBA (Bolivarian Alliance for the Americas)** countries have become outspoken critics of the OAS (see, for example, the Punto de Vista on funding for the Inter-American Commission on Human Rights in chapter 14). But the OAS and Commission have vocal and powerful critics in Washington too, especially among Republican conservatives who have threatened to cut funding for the organization unless it implements sanctions against nations that, according to the Republican right, are in violation of the Inter-American Democratic Charter. This document, signed by most of the region's states in 2001, calls for the group to collectively take action against states violating the principles of representative democracy and human rights. It was signed in the waning moments of the **Washington Consensus**, and most Latin American countries see it today as too narrowly focused on liberal criteria. This has contributed to momentum for new hemispheric organizations (described in the next section) that can act independently of Washington.

The OAS faces a difficult task in adapting to the challenge of these new Latin American intergovernmental organizations that, though they lack the institutionalization and the infrastructure of the OAS, have the capacity to take positions independent of the United States and Canada. In the United States, the new generation of conservatives is suspicious of any concessions that Washington might make to international organizations. Foreign aid, which includes money for the OAS, is on their agenda for deep cuts, if not elimination. At the same time, the OAS is under pressure from its members (and not just ALBA) to put the United States under the same scrutiny on human rights and democracy as other member states. There is a possibility—a hope in some eyes, a threat in others—that the impressive OAS building, an architectural masterpiece incorporating cultural elements from all the member nations, located not far from the White House, will become merely an impressive art museum.

For Review

What is the Organization of American States? What is its purpose? Why was Cuba expelled? What challenges does the OAS face today?

New Latin American IGOs: Partners or Rivals to the OAS?

As just discussed, part of the reason for Latin American dissatisfaction with the OAS is the decline of consensus around what kinds of criteria should be used to judge democracy in human rights. Furthermore, as early as 1965, when the United States invaded the Dominican Republic, it was becoming clear to Latin Americans that the U.S. commitment to the Inter-American Democratic Charter of 1948 was highly problematic. The failure of the United States to actually place democracy ahead of its Cold War objectives eviscerated the ability of the OAS to react to interventions and coups. Of course the charter became even more of a dead letter in the period after 1968, when the majority of OAS members were under military rule. Although the commitment to democracy seemed to be restored in 2001 with an amendment of the charter, committing states to defending democratically elected governments, there is no consensus about just when a line is crossed in this respect.

Meanwhile, as we have seen, Latin America has experienced significant economic and political change, and social movements in Latin America want equality and participation considered part of the fabric of democracy. Whereas in Washington many politicians demand that the OAS take stronger action against Venezuela and the ALBA countries, Latin Americans are skeptical about the reaction of the United States to the coup in Honduras and other irregular removals of heads of state in Paraguay and Haiti. Although the most outspoken and strident complaints about U.S. policy come from the countries affiliated with **ALBA**, other Latin American states also have made clear their displeasure with Washington's attitude and policy. The U.S. defense of NSA surveillance not only of leaders but also millions of citizens of Latin America rings hollow in a region where terrorist threats against the United States are virtually nil. In the past, this kind of U.S. treatment of Latin America, the "backyard," might have been greeted with little more than a regretful shrug, but this time even countries on good terms with the United States, including Brazil, Chile, and Mexico, expressed anger.

Various new regional organizations have been created since 2005. Some focus on areas such as energy (PetroSur and PetroCaribe, both funded by Venezuela) and developmental assistance (e.g., Banco de Sur, funded mostly by Brazil and Venezuela). The three most ambitious projects for political and economic integration, all of which to some degree serve as alternatives to the OAS, are ALBA, UNASUR (Union of South American Nations), and CELAC (the Community of Latin American and Caribbean States).

- *ALBA:* **The Bolivarian Alliance for Latin America** (and the Caribbean) was founded in 2008 mainly to promote economic integration among member states, but its members (most importantly, Venezuela, Bolivia, Ecuador, and Nicaragua) have acted together on several occasions as a faction within the newer organizations (UNASUR and CELAC, described next) and also in the OAS. For example, although just about all Latin American governments individually protested the forced landing of Evo Morales's plane en route from Moscow in 2013, ALBA nations took the lead in securing resolutions in UNASUR and the OAS. In the case of the OAS, the resolution condemning the affair and demanding an explanation from European countries was adopted by consensus, with only Canada and the United States stating formally that they "cannot join consensus." Besides councils dealing with economic integration, ALBA has several councils concerned with social and political issues. ALBA members were also in discussion about forming their own defense council, and they have made some progress toward a common currency among members.
- *CELAC:* The Community of Latin American and Caribbean States was founded in December 2011. Without the formal membership of the United States and Canada, CELAC has more political space to address social and economic development issues, in particular to address needs identified and suggestions proposed by social movements. At the organization's January 2013 summit, member nations formulated a plan of

The Third Summit of the Community of Latin American and Caribbean States (CELAC) was held in Havana, Cuba, in January 2014. Like the first two in 2012 and 2013, it was virtually ignored by the U.S. media. Why do you think this was true? Is CELAC really needed, given the existence of the Organization of American States?

action, shaped in part by social movements meeting separately and by international organizations, such as the United Nations Economic Commission for Latin America. The invited movement organizations suggested free health care and education, as well as creation of a CELAC television channel. However, the summit did not address funding for such projects, nor was it resolved at the subsequent January 2014 summit.

- *UNASUR*: The Union of South American Nations was founded on May 23, 2008, at a summit of heads of state of the continental countries. As indicated in chapter 15, UNASUR has a variety of functions; among its subsidiary councils is an Electoral Council, charged with election observation. However, the most important innovation in the formation of UNASUR was that for the first time the countries on the continent established a pan-continental diplomatic organization with the capacity to address regional problems and mediate conflicts without the participation of the United States. This capacity was demonstrated in 2009 when UNASUR mediated the conflict that threatened to bring about inter-state war between Colombia on one side and Venezuela and Ecuador on the other. Despite Colombia's close relationship to the United States and the role of the U.S. military advisors, bases, and funds in its conflict with the FARC, Colombia agreed (under prodding from Brazil) to UNASUR's mediation.

Of these initiatives, UNASUR has probably advanced the furthest institutionally. The key development was the establishment of a South American Defense Council. Colombia initially was reticent to join because of its close military ties to the United States, but it joined in 2008, the year before the crisis with Venezuela and Ecuador. Although Venezuela took the lead originally in proposing UNASUR, the support of Brazil was indispensable to its success. Furthermore, President Bachelet of Chile, daughter of a general, took the lead in organizing the Defense Council's plans and first meetings.

The relatively rapid development of UNASUR in less than a decade may be attributed in part not only to the diminished (but far from extinct) **hegemony** of the United States, but also to the desire of the region's presidents to strengthen their ability to defend one another from military coups. Although Honduras is not a member of UNASUR, the organization's refusal to recognize the legitimacy of elections organized by the new government after the 2009 coup was directly at odds with U.S. policy. UNASUR also expelled Paraguay from membership (as did Mercosur) for a year after the irregular removal of elected President Lugo from power by that country's parliament. UNASUR, in contrast to the United States, characterized as a coup and condemned a police rebellion against President Rafael Correa.

UNASUR through its system of councils has institutionalized a way to give a collective voice independent of the United States, and the development of a Defense Council represents a significant departure from the security system established by the Río Treaty, with its clear reliance on U.S. military doctrine and training. It has also laid the basis for increased cooperation on a range of technical, social, and economic matters.

UNASUR does not have the institutional bureaucracy that the OAS has at its disposal, or the institutional memory. An example particularly relevant to defense of democracy is its lack of capacity and authority to carry out electoral observation. UNASUR's South American Electoral Council is made up of officials from the electoral institutions of each member nation, but it does not have a permanent institution comparable to the OAS's Department for Cooperation and Electoral Observation. Similarly, in the area of human rights, in January 2013 the organization committed itself to establishment of a permanent human rights organization, but nothing comparable to the Inter-American Commission on Human Rights and the Inter-American Court on Human Rights has been created.

ALBA speaks and acts with some coherence because of ideological similarities among its leaders, but nothing guaranties that its members will be governed indefinitely by parties or leaders who share a consensus on its principles. A change in leadership, especially in Venezuela, could jeopardize its unity, the integration plans it has set in motion, and the continuity of its membership. By contrast, both UNASUR and CELAC are composed of countries with heterogeneous leadership, bringing together the ALBA countries on the left with countries more oriented toward conservative economic and political policies.

Hugo Chávez, president of Venezuela at the time, hoped that the founding of CELAC, in combination with UNASUR, would spell the beginning of the end for the OAS. Some Latin American leaders would agree with that hope, but most today see CELAC as more an alternative to than a substitute for the OAS. Where CELAC has shown some superior capability to the OAS is in relation to other countries in the Global South. Acting on behalf of member nations, CELAC has also initiated meetings with other world regional associations, most notably the Pan African Union.

CELAC has a long way to go to establish the institutional and financial capacity to replace the OAS, but its prospects are enhanced by the overall disdain for the OAS in the United States. Should the U.S. Congress strip or drastically reduce funding (as it nearly did in 2013), CELAC (and UNASUR) might be positioned to move into the vacuum. If U.S. conservatives view CELAC with disdain, the attitude of Washington's liberal establishment can be characterized as indifference. A indication is the U.S. media's "coverage" of the founding summit of CELAC in Caracas in December 2011, which was attended by the head of government from every independent country in Latin America and the Caribbean (except Costa Rica, which sent its vice president). The meeting was almost entirely ignored by the mainstream media in the United States. The *New York Times* gave the summit one paragraph taken from a newswire.

Perhaps the most important item that the ALBA countries have on the agenda for CELAC is to establish an alternative human rights commission to replace the Inter-American Commission on Human Rights (IACHR). Leaders of the ALBA countries complain that the commission is biased by norms and institutions influenced by the United States, but their main allegation about the inadequacy of the IACHR is that it is too influenced by the United States itself. Venezuela claims that the IACHR was particularly tepid in reacting to the short-lived coup against Chávez in 2002, a claim the Commission denies (see Emersberger 2010; IACHR 2010). In September 2012, Venezuela formally withdrew from the convention, which it had ratified in 1977. The withdrawal allows Venezuela to deny the IACHR jurisdiction after September 2013. The IACHR claims Venezuela remains obligated to the convention because of its membership in OAS; the IACHR has not made the same claim about the United States.

The IACHR is unique among human rights IGOs in that citizens of member nations—28 (not the United States) of 35 nations—can directly bring complaints to the Inter-American Court, which are investigated by the IACHR for a recommendation on what action, if any, should be taken (see chapter 14). CELAC does not now possess the institutional capacity to take on such a responsibility.

The new organizations are in principle all supportive of democracy, but there remains the question of whether the political leadership in the region really wants them to promote a more profound democratic culture, or whether leaders merely seek to defend themselves more effectively from the threat of military coups and U.S. intervention. Just how committed are they to developing the capacity to respond effectively to threats to civil freedoms and **rule of law**, abuse of power, unfair elections, or concentrated power in the hands of the executive? Most elected presidents seem willing to take action to rally around colleagues threatened by security or organizations or threats from Washington, but the question remains of whether these organizations will institutionalize ways to strengthen democracy beyond defense of sovereignty and elected heads of state.

For Review

What are the most important international organizations created by Latin American countries since the end of the Cold War? What seem to be the objectives in Latin America in forming these new organizations? What are the implications of these new IGOs for the OAS?

The Foreign Policy of Latin American States: Issues and Examples

Most of this chapter has examined how U.S. foreign policy has influenced Latin America, with some emphasis on the ramifications for democracy in the region. Despite signs of some decline in U.S. influence and the expansion of economic and political ties between Latin America and other parts of the world, the gravitational weight between Latin America and the United States remains strongly pitched toward Washington. However, the relationship is not static, and each country in Latin America has particular foreign relations issues on its agenda.

As we have seen, Latin America has suffered many episodes of foreign intervention in its internal affairs, including military invasion and proxy wars sponsored by the United States. On the other hand, Latin American nations enjoy the good fortune of having little threat of war with one another. The last large, full-scale war, the Chaco War between 1932 and 1935, occurred between Bolivia and Paraguay. They disputed the Chaco region, a wilderness area but one thought (correctly, as it turned out 80 years later) to have significant energy resources. The conflict cost 100,000 lives for two of the poorest countries in the world.

Smaller-scale, shorter border conflicts have taken place and left some bitterness between the contending nations. In 1969, Honduras and El Salvador fought a five-day "Soccer War." The immediate catalyst was a riot at a soccer match between the two countries, but the tensions had built up over border issues, especially undocumented migration of Salvadorans into their less populated neighbor. Fighting broke out briefly in 1995 between Peru and Ecuador over a border dispute dating back to the independence era; can still flare the conflict led to a treaty and negotiated settlement of the dispute three years later, but tensions have not altogether disappeared. There remain simmering conflicts among several other neighbors on the continent, but at present none seem to threaten war, and the emergence of new regional diplomatic forums provides enhanced opportunity to mediate these kinds of disputes.

What follows is a broad summary of foreign policy issues for selected countries. In each case we review briefly the country's relationship with Washington and the main issues on its agenda in relations with, respectively, other parts of Latin America and the world.

Brazil

Brazil: Without a doubt, Brazil's large population, landmass, and economic resources make it the most influential country in the region. It borders on every South American nation except Chile and Ecuador. Many of those borders are ill-defined; indeed, insofar as they are marked by rivers subject to periodically heavy rains, they may shift. Whether governed by the military, by conservative or moderate presidents, or by presidents from the moderately leftist Workers' Party, Brazil has seen itself as a potential world power, and with the recent emphasis on the rise of the BRICS countries (Brazil, Russia, India, China, South Africa), the country now sees that status within its reach. Brazil's weight in hemispheric affairs is expressed in the fact that press reports sometimes use the phrase "according to Itamaraty," referring to the modernesque building in Brasilia where the Ministry of External Relations is located. As one analyst (Burges 2012) put it, "Brazil is a position to now be more of a rule maker than a rule taker."

ALBA countries have tended to take a more aggressive stance than Brazil in challenging Washington and advancing new hemispheric diplomatic and economic initiatives. In some ways, Brazil welcomes this posture, as it opens space for Itamaraty to advance its own agenda, especially on economic issues involving intellectual property (Brazil wants more technology transfer). While Venezuela, for example, takes the most militant position on relations with Iran, Brazil can more quietly and steadily assert its right as a sovereign nation to carry out economic and political relations with a regime that Washington regards as a pariah.

The Snowden affair has shaken U.S. relations with Brazil. For the first time a Latin American leader, President Dilma Rousseff, canceled a planned visit to Washington to protest not only the U.S. National Security Agency's eavesdropping on her communications, but also the refusal of the Obama administration to assure her it would not happen in the future. On the other hand, Brazil made it clear very early that it would not offer asylum to Snowden.

Brazil's relationships with neighboring countries tend to be normal, if not cordial in most respects. At times tensions emerge over economic relations with Argentina, especially when Brazil's strong currency increases its strong and consistent trade surplus with its Mercosur partner. Probably its tensest relations are with Bolivia over that country's 2006 nationalization of natural gas fields being exploited by Petrobras. However, a solution was negotiated because Bolivia needs investment from Petrobras, and Brazil needs energy for São Paolo and the rest of its dynamic southern states.

Brazil tends to criticize the imposition of sanctions by the United States on Iran. It has conducted its own negotiation on nuclear issues with the Islamic republic, much to the consternation of the United States. Perhaps to both the United States and the rest of Latin America, the most important foreign policy posture on the part of Brazil has to do with its strong support of UNASUR and CELAC. Without Brazil these organizations would be unlikely to gain eventually the stature and capacity to rival the OAS, which Itamaraty has more effectively than Venezuela, but more quietly as well, sought to marginalize.

Besides its geopolitical and economic weight, Brazil's advantage over every other Latin American state is the well-trained core of experienced diplomats who are trained and work at Itamaraty. On the other hand, some analysts (e.g., Burges 2012) think that the institution is too conservative in the sense that it defines its mission narrowly as advancing Brazilian national sovereignty, causing it to underestimate the need to seek multilateral solutions on, for example, climate issues. Itamaraty's support for multilateralism may be pragmatic, used to advance its own autonomy, not embraced as a principle.

Venezuela

Venezuela's self-identity has long been linked to advancing the ideal of Pan-Americanism found in Bolívar's writings. It also has had pretensions to exert influence over the Caribbean region. Under presidents Hugo Chávez and Nicolás Maduro, Venezuela assumed a much more assertive role in hemispheric affairs, rivaling Cuba as, from Washington's perspective, the most troublesome regime in the region. Chávez took the lead in creation of UNASUR and CELAC, though, as previously mentioned, Brazilian support has been the crucial factor in their success.

Venezuela's main leverage in hemispheric affairs comes from the petrodollars at its disposal. It has used its financial resources to fund oil-discount programs (PetroCaribe, PetroSur) and a continental satellite network, Telesur. Through its CITGO subsidiary, Venezuela even provides discounted oil to a number of poor communities in the northern United States, a reversal of the usual flow of foreign aid.

In its early years, the country's ability to carry out foreign policy initiatives was hamstrung by the attitudes of its professional foreign-service corps, made up mostly of individuals ideologically aligned with the policies of the pre-1998 era. A former ambassador to Washington told me that the content of confidential meetings held in the embassy would often find its way into the opposition media back home.

Like so many other facets of government under Chávez, control over foreign policy remained firmly in the grasp of the president. This meant that on some important issues and some lesser issues (whether to issue a visa, for example, for a visit by a dignitary), foreign ministry officials would not act before the president had spoken. Chávez was also criticized by friends, not just opponents, for verbal blasts at rival countries, in particular the United States. On the other hand, Chávez showed himself to be quite pragmatic on a number of key issues, even to the point of extraditing members of FARC guerrillas to Colombia in the face of criticism from his supporters.

In the region, Venezuela's thorniest relations are with Colombia. Tensions have periodically flared between the two countries for decades over demarcation of the boundary waters north and east of Lake Maracaibo, but Chávez never made that a high priority. Instead, it is Colombia's long-standing civil war, especially its conflict with the FARC, that has been at the center of at times highly tense relations between the two neighbors. Colombia, especially under President Álvaro Uribe, charged that Venezuela was aiding the rebels and providing shelter for them in its territory. Chávez denied the allegations. Whatever the actual relations between the Bolivarian government and the FARC, it is clear that Chávez's own sympathy for the FARC waned over time. That fact became obvious when Manuel Santos, Uribe's defense minister and successor to the Colombian presidency, sought out a more cooperative relationship. Venezuela still resents Colombia's allowing the United States to maintain seven "forward operating locations" (a euphemism for "military bases") in the country.

President Nicolás Maduro served as foreign minister before being elevated to the vice presidency in the closing months of Chávez's life. He took an especially forward role in the Middle East (and not just with oil-exporting countries) and Africa. The country has staunchly asserted its right to maintain economic and political relations with Iran, including its right to carry out economic relations in defiance of the sanctions imposed by the United States. Chávez sought to mediate early in the conflicts in Libya and Syria and accused the United States of seeking the overthrow of regimes rather than seeking a negotiated resolution. His embrace (literally) of former president Mahmoud Ahmadinejad, despite the Iranian politician's anti-Semitic utterances, was especially controversial. On the other hand, the deterioration of Libya and Syria into civil war, along with the threat that these countries might become havens for terrorist organizations, suggests that Chávez's intuitions on the conflicts were more prescient than those of Washington.

Bolivia

Under President Evo Morales, Bolivia has acquired an outsized influence in international forums because of the global welcome given to the Americas' first indigenous president. Morales has joined Ecuador's President Eduardo Correa and Maduro as the most outspoken critics of Washington. Morales's stature has enabled him to assume a strong position of advocacy in international forums on global warming. His warnings of an environmental "holocaust" and demand that countries take immediate measures to limit warming to no more than one degree (centigrade) shook up the December 2009 climate change summit in Copenhagen.

Bolivia has a long-standing concern with the fate of Bolivian immigrants in Argentina, where they have suffered discrimination and harassment. It also has a long-standing, bitter dispute with Chile over the loss to that country of its outlet to the sea, a consequence of the War of the Pacific (1879–1883). Nationalist resentment toward Chile was a factor in the successful popular resistance in 2003 to increased natural gas extraction through foreign investment, with the gas to be sent through the disputed region for export. President Morales has refused to negotiate bilaterally with Chile, as urged by the OAS, and instead opted to take the dispute to international forums.

Mexico

"So far from God, so close to the United States," Mexico has attempted to balance defense of national autonomy on some issues (restrictions on foreign investment in oil; relations with Cuba; rights of Mexican immigrants in the United States, etc.) against the reality of having a land border with a superpower in both economic and military terms. The country also benefits from a developed university system and intellectual establishment that provides key advisors for the president and also candidates for its foreign service school. However, even by Latin American standards (and in contrast to Brazil), Mexican foreign policy is concentrated in the presidency. The return of the PRI after 12 years of PAN control of the presidency has meant some shifting on what has recently been the country's most contentious issue, cooperation with the United States in the drug war. President Enrique Peña Nieto has shown wariness about allowing the U.S. security forces to actively take part in the government's efforts to subdue the drug cartels. He appointed as foreign minister a well-known critic of President Calderon's drug war policies. One of Mexico's concerns is that many of the guns fueling the drug violence are purchased in the United States, where gun control is lax. Nonetheless, Peña Nieto continues to rely on U.S. security forces for aid in antidrug enforcement.

By joining the United States and Canada in signing the NAFTA agreement, Mexico fixed its course on trade and economic integration to schemes that are consistent with neoliberal doctrine. In 2013, the two main candidates for the presidency of the **WTO** were from Brazil and Mexico, with the United States and Europe favoring Mexico. Brazil's Robert Azevedo prevailed, largely on the strength of member countries sympathetic to efforts by Brazil and other BRICS on intellectual property and access to overseas markets (see chapter 15).

Despite its economic policy orientation, Mexico has had numerous conflicts over holding the United States accountable for implementation. For example, under NAFTA, Mexican trucks were to have full access to U.S. highways, but Washington refused to implement the treaty provision. In 2009 Mexico retaliated with some tariffs. Finally in 2011, the two countries negotiated an agreement whereby Mexico would lift tariffs but accept regulations and inspections.

Mexico not only has a border issue with the United States; it also has one in the south since the country is a land bridge for Central Americans and even South American migrants seeking to enter the United States illegally. Mexico has also attempted to integrate Central America more deeply into its sphere of influence with Plan Puebla Panama, oriented toward integrating nine southern Mexico states with all of Mesoamerica and Colombia in a NAFTA-like association.

For Review

What seem to be the main issues of concern to Latin America today? Based on these four countries, how much convergence and how much divergence does there seem to be on foreign policy?

Backyard, Front Porch, or Neighbors?

In April 2013, Secretary of State John Kerry spoke to a committee of the House of Representatives about how the United States had been neglecting Latin America. He said that President Obama would soon make a trip through the region. Whatever good intentions the Secretary may have had in mind, he undermined them in his testimony by telling Congress, "The Western Hemisphere is our backyard." Perhaps it was a slip of the tongue, but perhaps it reveals what seems to be constantly in the back of the mind of most citizens of the United States.

Overall, in the second decade of the twenty-first century, one can see countervailing pulls on Latin America. On the one hand, new diplomatic institutions have given the region a more unified voice and some capacity to resolve intra-regional conflicts without relying on the United States. The diversification of trade and investment, reductions in poverty in many countries, and lack of defined policy on the part of Washington are all forces encouraging regional autonomy. Although global diversification and competition for access to Latin America's natural wealth and market open leverage for Latin America, at the same time they pull the countries at times in different directions—the northern tier toward the United States, the western regions toward Asia, and the eastern side of the continent toward Europe.

Our review of the history of U.S. intervention in Latin America certainly gives reason to suspect the motives and consistency of Washington's policies toward Latin America, yet we should be cautious about simply thinking that the United States has always supported dictatorship. Most Latin Americans, rather than reject the United States' expression of support for democracy, would simply prefer that the United States not assume it has a monopoly on what kind of politics and economic system best meets Latin American needs. Despite the resentment engendered by Washington's continued view of the region as a "backyard" and by repeated intervention in the region's internal affairs, most Latin Americans still look positively at the United States.

What we can say is that Latin Americans have found a collective voice that they lacked through most of the **Cold War**; they have laid the basis for diplomatic coordination that more closely reflects, even if it does not replicate, the ideals of Bolívar and Martí. It is unlikely that the United States can simply restore its diminished hegemony to what it was in the Cold War, but similarly, it is unrealistic, perhaps undesirable, to think that the gravitational pull of the United States, which remains a colossus in military terms and the preeminent economic power in the region, will simply disappear.

Discussion Questions

1. What has motivated U.S. foreign policy on democracy and human rights? Are democracy and human rights goals in and of themselves, or are there more imperial motives behind democracy promotion?
2. What do you think would be the most intelligent policy for the United States to take toward Cuba today? What goals would you set for that policy?
3. Do we tend to give the United States too much credit or blame for what happens in Latin America? If you had to quantify it, how much of the course of events—for better or worse—in Latin America should be ascribed to U.S. policy? None? Ten percent? Fifty percent? More? Why?
4. Would it be a good or bad development for democracy if CELAC, UNASUR, and ALBA were to entirely displace the OAS?
5. Should the Inter-American Commission on Human Rights concentrate mainly on the Washington Consensus about democracy and civil rights, or should it give equal consideration and funding to monitoring other kinds of rights?

Resources for Further Study

Reading: Larry Diamond, editor of the *Journal of Democracy* and collaborator with the U.S.-funded National Endowment for Democracy, defends pluralist democratization and worries about recent tendencies in *The Spirit of Democracy* (New York: Times

Books, 2008). A critique of "transitionology" is William Robinson's *Promoting Polyarchy: Globalization, US Intervention, and Hegemony* (Cambridge, UK: Cambridge University Press, 1996). The editorial caricatures in this chapter are among many analyzed by John J. Johnson in *Latin America in Caricature* (Austin: University of Texas Press, 1980). Christopher Sabatini does not endorse U.S. hegemony in the past, but he does think it brought some benefits and at times strengthened democracy. See his article "Will Latin America Miss U.S. Hegemony?," *Journal of International Affairs* 66, no. 2 (Spring/Summer 2013): 1–14. For a U.S. government justification of democracy programs, see *Foreign Assistance: U.S. Democracy Programs in Six Latin American Countries Have Yielded Modest Results*, GAO-03-358 (March 8, 2003). It is based on case studies of U.S. policy toward Bolivia, Colombia, El Salvador, Guatemala, Nicaragua, and Peru. NED funding of the opposition to Chávez, including groups engaged in the 2002 coup, is documented by Eva Gollinger and Saul Landau in *The Chávez Code: Cracking US Intervention in Venezuela* (Olive Branch Press, 2006).

Film and Video: A list of films (and literature) about the Guatemalan case can be found at http://depts.washington.edu/hrights/guatbib.html. *When the Mountains Tremble* (1983), about Nobel Prize winner Rigoberta Menchú, remains a classic of the genre. *Missing* (1982) is about the political disillusionment of an American father, played by Jack Lemmon, as he tries to find the truth behind the disappearance of his son in Chile during the 1973 coup. Another film, *State of Siege* (1973), by the same director, Costa Gavras, looks at American involvement in the destabilization of Uruguay. Obie Benz's *Americas in Transition* (1981) is a short, Oscar-nominated documentary describing U.S. relations with several Latin American countries in the 1970s and 1980s, including Chile, El Salvador, Guatemala, and Nicaragua.

On the Internet: The Americas Program (http://www.cipamericas.org/) at the Washington-based Center for International Policy is a valuable resource for a variety of progressive organizations' views on U.S. policy toward Latin America. The National Security Archive (www2.gwu.edu/~nsarchiv) at George Washington University is a trove of primary source material on U.S. security programs and intervention. Try searching for "Death of Che Guevara."

Afterword

Tentative Answers to Frequently Asked Questions about Democracy in Latin America

Focus Question

▶ To what extent do you agree with the broad answers I give in this afterword to the general questions raised by this book?

WHEN MOST POLITICAL scientists and political leaders in North America speak of "democracy," they mean something like Dahl's conception of **polyarchy**. Given the brutality and atrocities committed by the military dictatorships that ruled most of Latin America in the 1970s, few people who live in that region would take lightly the rights they have under this form of liberal democracy. However, we should bear in mind that polyarchies have not yet delivered the kinds of basic social and economic changes that might reverberate positively in the lives of most Latin Americans. Although some political scientists believe that globalization works against a lapse back into military authoritarianism, there is ample reason to question whether it has nurtured social and economic conditions favorable to democracy.

Advocates of polyarchy urge us to evaluate democratic conditions largely on the basis of free elections and civil rights. Some **pluralists** will acknowledge that voter participation is an indicator of democracy, but they do not agree on this issue; some political scientists think apathy means people are satisfied overall with the way things are going. Pluralists see social and economic equality as a condition favorable to democracy or as something that democracy tends to produce. Few pluralists would say that social and economic equality should be used as direct measures of how close a country comes to the democratic ideal.

By contrast, in Latin America and many other parts of the world, representative democracy has come to be questioned because, at least in part, it seems unable to address inequalities so serious that within "democratic" countries, large portions of the population seem to be excluded from any hope of attaining decent, dignified living conditions. The concentrations of wealth at both global and national levels have intensified feelings of exclusion. The reactions to these conditions can be profoundly democratic or profoundly threatening to democracy. Among the former are important experiments with participatory democracy, combined with attempts to find alternatives to neoliberal economic policies, be they simply attempts to humanize capitalism or attempts to define and construct socialist alternatives that depart radically from the failed models of the twentieth century.

How the United States responds to Latin America's search for its own path will have an impact on how these tendencies unfold. In response to the "Punto" question in chapter 16,

I would argue that the United States prefers capitalist democracy to all other forms of political economy. Although many U.S. diplomats and officials sincerely profess that Washington's main goal is supporting democracy, history suggests that concern for capitalism trumps support for democracy whenever the two conflict. The destabilizations or invasions of the elected governments of the Dominican Republic, Guatemala, Chile, and Nicaragua are just a few cases demonstrating that fact of life. U.S. pressure on Cuba, for example, contributes to maintenance of a siege mentality among many government officials and supporters, which is hardly conducive to democratic rule of any type.

Thoughts on the Democratic Condition in Latin America

From our study of Latin America, we should realize that Latin America may be the global hothouse these days for experiments with democracy. Consider some of the innovations and positive development in the last 25 years: participatory budgeting, new branches of government, workers seizing and running factories, vigorous neighborhood organizations, strong forces for social justice in religious philosophy, gains for indigenous and Afro-descendent people to the highest place in government, and well-established human rights organizations.

Democracy is experienced by people in different ways. In Latin America, we have a rich laboratory of experimentation underway, sometimes at the level of local rather than national politics. By way of conclusion, let me suggest some very tentative answers about democracy's future in Latin America.

1. *Has Latin America left military dictatorship behind for good?* Given the prevalence of arms, the threat of terrorism, and the easy resort to war by the world hegemony, it would be foolish to answer, "Definitely, yes." However, the international environment has noticeably changed. Democracy has become a norm of the international system, and barring catastrophic changes in the world (e.g., a global war or an environmental calamity), no national government will be able to escape scrutiny of its internal politics. In addition, people's movements are now linked globally into networks that allow them to exchange experiences and support one another's democratic struggles.

2. *Is the U.S. model the best form of democracy for all?* The people of the United States can take pride in our own democratic traditions, but there is much hubris in our certainty that others should adopt our political ways. We welcome delegations to study our traditions or our local governments or election system, but increasingly we take little interest in our own government and show little knowledge of political affairs. Over the past 50 years, Latin Americans have had to struggle for freedom and democracy, and these struggles have generated experiences from which we in the north should learn.

3. *Is globalization the enemy or a friend of democracy in Latin America?* Neither one—and both! Across cultures, around the world, there is evidence that most people feel that government and control over the economic forces that most shape their lives have receded from their influence. However, Latin Americans have shown a resilience in drawing on their past to invent ways of recovering control—that is, democracy-building.

I have chosen to make democracy the theme of our introduction to Latin America because despite the different conceptions of and experiences we have with democracy, few political leaders or scholars from the region would reject its legitimacy today. We need to approach understanding Latin American politics with a degree of humbleness about our own democratic shortcomings, particularly our high rate of voter abstention, the persistence of gender and racial discrimination, and the growing inequality between rich and poor. I will not leave you with a list of the many challenges and problems in the region because I have optimism that despite setbacks, the last 20 years have seen progress. The promised land of democracy, whatever it looks like, is not yet visible, but I do think Latin Americans have forged forward in ways that we in the North should study and consider for our own society.

Discussion Question

Choice, participation, and equality: Now that you are concluding this book, and probably also your classes, if you were evaluating the condition of democracy for each country of the world, would you focus, as many indices do, on factors that affect "choice," such as elections, civil rights, and markets, or would you include some attention to participation (rates of voting, extension of democracy to social and economic spheres of life) and to socioeconomic equality (wealth and income equality, for example)?

Glossary

ALBA—Bolivarian Alliance for the Americas, an alternative economic integration alliance promoted by Venezuela, which embraced Nicaragua, Bolivia, Ecuador, and several smaller Caribbean states as of 2014.

anarchism (-ist)—a philosophy that rejects the necessity of the state, seeing all forms of government as inherently repressive, by definition; mutualist anarchists stress worker democracy in the form of direct worker management of enterprises.

apartheid—state policy of white supremacy and separating the races in South Africa for most of the twentieth century.

asymmetric warfare—a military doctrine whereby a weaker power concentrates resources and develops strategies to exploit the political and military weaknesses of the larger power—for example, by preparing civilian militias, taking advantage of terrain, inflicting casualties to wear down political support for war in the strong power, and so forth.

barrio—neighborhood; usually a poor neighborhood.

Bolivarian—name adopted by Venezuela's Hugo Chávez for his own and his movement's political philosophy, which was to be based on the life and writings of the country's great independence hero, Simón Bolívar.

bourgeoisie—a French term meaning "town dwellers" that Marx used to describe the capitalist economic class as it arose out of feudalism and struggled with the landed aristocracy. Depending on the context, it can refer to capitalists, but it often is used as well to refer to the middle class in general.

Brandt Report—a 1980 report of a commission headed by former West German chancellor and social democrat Willy Brandt, calling for a series of measures to reduce the gap between rich and poor nations in the world; it was shortly afterward superseded by the rise of neo-liberal leaders, such as Ronald Reagan and Margaret Thatcher, who successfully restored the primacy of a more market-oriented approach to the global economy.

breakdown (of democracy)—the process by which populist-era democracies collapsed as a result of political polarization and inability of political elites to compromise.

broadening of democracy—the idea that democracy ought to be extended to more spheres of life beyond the affairs of government.

bureaucratic authoritarianism—a term coined by political scientist Guillermo O'Donnell to describe the type of military rule that emerged in the Southern Cone and Brazil, combining harsh military rule designed to suppress all political participation with economic policy-making by civilian technocrats.

cacerolazo—form of protest, usually by women, characterized by mass banging of empty pots.

cacique—literally, "chief." The term originally pertained to the head of an indigenous village, community, or nation but became more generally used in reference to a political strongman.

capitalism—a social and economic system characterized by private ownership of the "means of production" (factories, farms, offices, technology, etc.), allocation of goods and services by the market, and the great majority of the employees working for wages or salaries.

catch-all party—a political party that seeks to obtain votes across class lines, as opposed to class-based parties that mobilize primarily from the working class and poor.

caudillo (-ism)—a form of personalism; literally, "man on horseback," an allusion to the strongmen who achieved regional or national leadership as a result of their fighting ability and leadership qualities during the violent, anarchic nineteenth century.

charisma, charismatic—referring to authority, based on a highly personalist style by which a leader appeals to masses of people, who in turn project upon the leader the qualities of a messiah who can address their needs and desires.

checks and balances—the constitutional principle that in a democracy the danger of concentrated power can be minimized by separating and dividing power among branches of government, much like James Madison promoted and accomplished in the Constitution of the United States.

Chicago Boys—economists that, following the teachings of Milton Friedman (an economist at the University of Chicago), advocated **laissez-faire** policies to dramatically roll back the state's role in the economy.

Christian Democracy—parties that emerged after World War II as centrist parties espousing capitalism humanized by Christian social justice doctrines.

civil society—that sphere of group activity occupying associational space between the individual and family, on one hand, and government and the state on the other. In Anglo-American thought, the marketplace is often seen as friendly or even part of civil society; in Latin America, many social movements see the market as corrosive of the social solidarity needed for a strong civil society. Alternatively, civil society is seen as the network of social and economic organizations and social movements seeking to advance the interests of different groups and to influence the political attitudes of others.

clientelism—practice on the part of politicians of exchanging material benefits for support, such as votes.

cocaleros—mostly indigenous movement of peasant cultivators of the coca plant in the Andes. More specifically, the movement led originally by Evo Morales, elected president of Bolivia in 2006.

Cold War—an ideological battle in which two global, nuclear superpowers, the United States and the Soviet Union, attempted between 1945 (the end of World War II) and 1991 (with the fall of communism in Eastern Europe) to promote or impose their particular political and economic system on other countries. In many Latin American countries, dictatorships justified their seizure of or continuing in power with a "national security" argument based on the notion that communism was an alien threat.

commodity—a good produced to be sold on the market, not consumed by its maker, but also, and as used in this book, agricultural and mining products, as distinct from manufactured products.

Communism, Communists, or Communist Party—political parties that formed, usually as a faction of socialists, in the aftermath of the Russian Revolution of 1917. Communists tended to be strongest where workers, urban or rural, were paid wages. Often, they had success organizing in key sectors of the export economy. Most communist parties lost members and supporters at the end of the Cold War. The Communist Party is the governing party in Cuba today, where Fidel Castro continues to believe in the basic principles articulated by Karl Marx and Vladimir Lenin.

communitarianism—a social philosophy and/or way of life, prevalent among many indigenous peoples, though not exclusive to them, based on the idea of common ownership of property, especially the land, and sharing in both producing and distributing economic goods.

compadrazgo—the Catholic practice of assigning "godparents" to children, often used in Latin America as a way for a powerful or wealthy individual, such as a landowner, to bestow special favor on the son of a subordinate, such as the child of a peasant or employee. A form of patronage, part of a system of clientelism.

comparative advantage—an economic theory associated with the British classical economist David Ricardo, who argued in the early 1800s that free trade benefits both partners, even when one country could produce something imported more cheaply, because by freely trading what each most efficiently (the "advantages") produces, both sides benefit.

comparative politics—a subfield in political science where comparison is utilized as a way to generate theories of politics; more generally associated with the study of politics in cultures different from our own.

comparativists—those in different fields of study (history, economics, literature, etc.) who specialize in the study of other cultures and use comparison (see **comparative politics**) to do so.

core nations—rich capitalist countries that have developed economies and, according to world systems theory, exploit the nations of the periphery.

corporatism, corporatist—(1) a theory about the relationship between state and society that emphasizes a tendency for social organizations to develop a privileged relationship with government bureaucracies, undermining a central tenet of pluralism—that is, the idea that individuals can freely join and leave organizations; (2) an ideology that an activist state has a responsibility to mediate competition among social classes and groups, defending the interests of the weakest groups and looking out for the welfare of the community as a whole.

criollo, **Creole**—the colonial upper class that over time became resistant to rule by the Spanish and Portuguese authorities. When used sociologically, "Creole" has not only class but also race overtones because Creoles considered themselves white. However, because independence leaders, such as Bolívar, were usually Creoles, the term is sometimes used as a synonym for "national"—as in *comida criolla* or "national food."

debt crisis—associated with the inability of Latin American governments to make service and interest payments in dollars on loans; first became visible in 1982, when Mexico announced it did not have sufficient dollar reserves to make its payments.

deepening of democracy—the idea that besides extension of voting and citizenship rights, a strong democracy is evidenced by growing respect for rights, tolerance, rule of law, and so on.

delegative democracy—term coined by Argentine political scientist Guillermo O'Donnell to refer to the tendency of citizens to invest power in a single elected leader, leaving other aspects of democracy superficial, such as the rule of law.

deliberative democracy—a form of democracy characterized by a high degree of citizen formulation of policies, debate, and even legislation.

dependency theory (theorists)—argues that Latin American economic development has been decisively and negatively shaped by the way it is integrated into the global economy; more narrowly, it refers to the theory that Latin America has been chronically disadvantaged by its export of raw materials, said to be undervalued compared with imported manufactured goods.

devaluation—when a government weakens the national currency against others (e.g., requires more pesos to purchase each dollar) or allows the currency to weaken by removing the prior fixed rate of exchange and allowing it to float.

developmentalism, developmentalist—referring to economic views (and those who held them) that advocate state policies designed to produce economic growth through industrialization.

Dirty War—fierce repression unleashed by the Argentine military junta in 1976 against the civilian population, especially the left.

ECLA—the United Nations Economic Commission for Latin America, which developed a "structural" analysis of obstacles to development and diagnosed a chronic unfavorable balance of trade between exported raw materials and imported manufactured goods.

ejido—traditional, community- or municipality-owned land in Mexico.

encomienda—the system by which the Spanish Crown granted conquistadors and early Creole landed elites the right to work mines and land with labor owed to them by indigenous peoples. The Indians were "entrusted" (as *encomendados*) to the elites, who were expected to Christianize them and care for their souls, a responsibility taken much more seriously by the Church than by the colonial landed elite.

ethnic cleansing—a type of genocide in which an ethnic group is targeted for destruction and/or removal from territory it occupies.

excluded sector, exclusion—similar in meaning to **marginal** (see later entry) but implies that marginality is created by social and economic policies and processes and is not simply a condition generated by overpopulation.

fascism—often loosely attached to any repressive regime; historically, in Europe fascism was associated with hypernationalism, strong corporatist tendencies, militarism, and scapegoating of communists, Jews, and other minorities.

federalism—division of sovereign authority between the central government and lower jurisdictions (e.g., states). Examples include Brazil and the United States.

free trade—the goal of most recent trade treaties, the idea here is to reduce various subsidies and protectionist measures that inhibit the free flow of goods and services across national borders in accordance with supply and demand in the global market (see **comparative advantage**).

Gini coefficient—a measure of the equality of either wealth or income. Zero represents perfect equality, where all individuals or households have the same income or wealth; 100 equals perfect inequality, where one individual or household has all of the income or wealth.

globalization—broad international tendency toward free flows of trade and communication among nations; especially associated with the changes in production of goods and services made possible by the information revolution.

governance—the ability to carry out the routine tasks of government efficiently and impartially; the ability to reach decisions accepted by society in a timely, effective manner.

Great Depression—a global economic crisis that began with the collapse of the New York Stock Exchange in 1929, spread throughout the world, and did not finally end until the conclusion of World War II in 1945.

haciendas—large, traditional landed estates worked by peasants, also called *latifundia*.

hegemon, hegemonic, hegemony—referring to a form of leadership in which force is always present but usually secondary to cultural and economic power. The Italian thinker Antonio Gramsci summed it up as force plus consent. Can also be applied to dominance of a social class or group within a society or to the dominance of a country or bloc of countries in world politics.

hybrid regimes—political systems that have emerged from authoritarianism and have not completely discarded past patterns but that do show many hallmarks of pluralism; also pertains to democracies that have decayed but show many of these hallmarks. See also **illiberal democracy**.

hyperurbanization—the tendency for the population growth of cities to outstrip the services (education, transportation, sewerage, etc.) needed to support decent living conditions.

illiberal democracy—phrase coined to describe political systems with popularly elected presidents who concentrate great power around themselves and effectively limit opposition by restricting civil freedoms.

IMF—see International Monetary Fund.

import substitution industrialization (ISI)—a set of policies, including tariffs on imports and subsidies, designed to encourage domestic production of manufactured goods. Typical development strategy in the populist era.

informal sector—that part of the economy in which workers are not covered by labor laws and often scrape by on day-to-day temporary employment. Typical of this sector are the armies of small vendors who eke out a living selling toys, cosmetics, used books, DVDs, and so forth on the streets and sidewalks.

institutionalism—branch of comparative politics that emphasizes and promotes the study of constitutional arrangements, as opposed to giving primacy to cultural, social, and economic processes in understanding politics.

institutionalization—the process by which a political arrangement or organization becomes valued in and of itself and not just for whatever specific benefit or outcome it produces.

International Monetary Fund (IMF)—founded after World War II to provide stability for the world monetary market, the IMF took on the role as key negotiator on behalf of international banks during the debt crisis of the 1980s, insisting that indebted governments adopt a package of neoliberal policies in exchange for new loans.

ISI—see **import substitution industrialization**.

junta—literally, a "council." Usually refers to a collective leadership of military leaders who have installed themselves via a coup.

la raza—"the race," often meaning "new race," often equivalent to *mestizaje*.

laissez-faire—French for "let do," an economic doctrine advocating minimum government regulation of the market. Stands in contrast to the philosophy of state-led development or "state capitalism" practiced in Latin America before 1980.

latifundia—see *haciendas*.

legitimacy—the quality of ruling through consent and lawful authorization rather than force.

liberal democracy—based on the theories of John Locke and Thomas Jefferson and to some extent J. J. Rousseau, a form of democracy based on the idea of free individuals consenting to form a government based on individual freedom and rights, including the individual right to property, consent of the governed, and limited ability of government to intervene in economic affairs.

liberal modernization—referring to the period, roughly 1850–1920, when most of Latin America underwent a period of state- and nation-building, usually including the development of new export sectors stimulated by rising demand for raw materials in foreign markets; building of railroads, ports, and other facilities with foreign loans; and professionalization of the armed forces. Often overseen by liberal parties or *caudillos*.

liberalism—a political ideology that privileges individual choices and rights over those of communities or the state; defines individual choice as the essence of freedom; prefers the market over government as the preferred way of resolving economic conflict; views property rights as natural rights and an extension of individual rights; and circumscribes government power with constitutional limits and with checks and balances.

liberation theology (theology of liberation)—a Marxist-influenced religious philosophy that emerged in Latin America in the aftermath of Vatican II (1962) as a reflection on the practice of clergy committed to implementing a "preferential option for the poor."

machismo—hypermasculinity; a tendency among men to attempt to show sexual prowess through various forms of speech and behavior.

macroeconomic—pertaining to the major processes and systems that make up national and economic systems, as opposed to microeconomics, where the "firm" (company) is the unit of analysis. Gross domestic product (GDP), inflation, balance of trade, and rates of monetary exchange are examples of measures often used to study the macroeconomic situation of a country.

maquila—labor-intensive, export-oriented factories originally set up in Mexico along the border with the United States, now commonly found in the Caribbean and Central America.

marginal—see **informal sector**. People in this sector are often excluded, not by choice, from mainstream social and economic life.

marianismo—political appeal, often stereotyped, of women as nurturers, mother-figures, and reconcilers in times of conflict.

Marxism (-ist)—very broad school of thought, with many branches, associated with Karl Marx, a German philosopher who argued that ultimate political power resides in the hands of those who control the means of production (land, factories, machines, etc.) and argued that true democracy could come only after those who had to sell their labor to these owners revolted and established common ownership ("communism") of these means.

mass organizations—usually associated with revolutionary regimes, these are usually officially sanctioned as the only legitimate channels of representation. Defenders see them as instruments of participatory democracy; critics see them as instruments of corporatist control. Defenders and critics alike see them as alternatives to voluntary organizations associated with pluralism.

means of production—land, machinery, buildings, and so on used to produce other goods and services.

Mesoamerica—literally, "between the Americas" (i.e., between North and South America). Usually thought to include Panama, the countries of Central America, and Mexico, though Panama is often considered part of South America, because it was once a province of Colombia, and Mexico is often categorized as part of North America.

mestizo, mestizaje—people of mixed racial stock, mainly Indian and Hispanic. *Mestizaje* refers more broadly to the notion that Latin Americans are a "new race" with a distinct national identity.

minifundio—a small plot of land insufficient to support a family, whose members therefore seek to support themselves by working on nearby *latifundia*.

modernization theory—a general framework for understanding economic and political development as involving the transformation of traditional society and culture into a social system based on valuing individual treatment, separating religious authority from political authority, professionalizing bureaucracies, and establishing the political authority of all citizens.

monoculture—technically refers to repeated planting of a single crop in one area. More specifically, it refers to a pattern of economic dependency whereby many colonies were forced into specializing in the production of a particular commodity (rubber, cotton, sugar, hemp, coffee, etc.) for export, reducing diversity and making the population more dependent on imported goods purchased by earnings from exports.

mulato, **mulatto**—people of mixed racial stock, many African with Hispanic and/or Indian heritage.

nation-state—the main political unit in the international system that reached its apogee in the post–World War II era. Presumes the right to sovereignty is based on a people's claim to be a nation, in turn based on the idea of a shared birthright.

National Endowment for Democracy (NED)—quasi-private association of organizations linked to U.S. unions and business organizations and to political parties, funded by Congress for the ostensible purpose of supporting democracy and a strong civil society overseas, accused of intervening in support of U.S. interests abroad.

national liberation—a term that was widely adopted by African and Asian leaders in anticolonial struggles in the twentieth century. Although most of Latin America was independent at the time, post–World War II revolutionary movements adopted the term to denote their goal of achieving economic and cultural and not just political independence.

nationalism—a sense of shared identity of people in a given territory or state, built around one or more commonalities in history, language, ethnicity, religion, culture, and so on; embodied in symbols such as a flag, anthem, and literature.

neocolonialism—a "new" (neo) form of colonialism where the dominated society retains formal sovereign status.

neo-extractivism—"extractivism" refers to the historical dependence of Latin American economies on exports of raw materials "extracted" from natural resources; neo-extractivism refers to the continuation of this tendency since 1990, but often under the administration of leftist governments that have reformed the terms under which extraction takes place and the uses of the profits. However, overall the economies remain highly dependent on extractive industries.

neoliberal (-ism)—a "new" (neo) form of nineteenth-century liberalism; neoliberalism advocates a reduced role of the state in guiding economic life and increased reliance on laissez-faire. Generally, neoliberal economic philosophy is associated with structural adjustment packages mandated by the International Monetary Fund and with the Washington Consensus.

new institutionalism (-ists)—(1) school of thought among economists, focused on the importance of political institutions in fostering economic development; (2) comparative political scientists who argue for more attention to constitutions, laws, and formal political processes in regions, such as Latin America.

nongovernmental organizations (NGOs)—formally organized groups in civil society, domestic or international in nature; many domestic organizations are networked or partially funded by foreign NGOs or states.

oligarchy—a ruling class made up of a tight-knit group of wealthy elites.

organic law—a law, distinctive to the French system and influential in Latin America, that is seen as a direct outgrowth of the constitution and can be modified only by an extraordinary majority (typically three-fifths or two-thirds).

pacts—formal and informal agreements among elites to limit democracies founded after periods of authoritarian rule or at the end of severe political crisis.

Pan-Americanism—referring to the idea that all Latin Americans share a common national "American" identity that transcends the boundaries of countries.

pardo—a term used in Venezuela and some other countries, referring to people of mixed race; very similar in meaning to ***mulato***.

party system—the way that parties interact with one another and with civil society, especially in regard to the way they structure political competition.

patriarchy—a condition, which few societies have escaped, in which men hold greater power than women and also on balance hold power over women.

patrimonialism (patrimonial state)—tendency to use state resources to secure the loyalty of citizens; the exchange of material resources for loyalty.

patronage—the practice whereby politicians use their influence over government to help their friends and supporters, often thereby showing favoritism against the interests of supporters of opponents.

peon, peonage—referring to the system of forced labor whereby a peasant is perpetually exploited by a landowner through the former's perpetual indebtedness to the latter.

periphery—those countries that historically were integrated into the world system as providers of primary commodities produced by hyperexploited labor; those parts of the world that have relatively little power compared with the wealthy, core nations.

personalism—tendency in political culture to look to a strong leader, often associated with charismatic authority and ***clientelism***.

Pink Tide—the wave of victories by leftist parties and leaders that began in December 1998 with President Hugo Chávez in Venezuela. Called "pink" to distinguish these leaders and parties from "red" communists and to indicate a diversity of associated programs and social bases.

plebiscite—an election called to express the popular will on a significant issue, such as whether an existing state or constitution is legitimate or whether a particular ruler should be allowed to stay in power.

pluralist, pluralism—referring to a school of thought in political science that argues for the study of group behavior and competition among elites. Pluralism is both an empirical theory about how politics works in all societies, even dictatorships, and a normative theory about the form democracy should take (see **polyarchy**).

plurinational state—a state that recognizes not one national identity but several; recognized nations share governance and autonomy within a constitutional framework allowing for cultural diversity.

political opportunity structures—political sociologist Sidney Tarrow's concept of the degree to which social and political conditions steer the course of social movements and shape their possibility of success in achieving change.

polyarchy—term coined by Robert Dahl to describe his theory (see **pluralism**) of democracy, arguing that instead of viewing societies as one pyramidal system with elites at the apex, we ought to see multiple (poly) hierarchies in society, with competing elites at the surface. Polyarchies are characterized by several features associated with liberal democracy, most importantly constitutions requiring elites to compete for power through elections.

popular sector—refers loosely to those social classes that do not include the wealthiest strata of society. The popular sector always includes workers, peasants, and the **informal** or **excluded** population; whether or not this includes the middle class depends on who is using the term and what audience is being addressed.

populism (-ist)—the political practice of appealing for mass support by championing the cause of ordinary people against powerful elites. The period between 1930 and 1980 is considered an era of populism in Latin America, epitomized by leaders such as Juan Perón of Argentina and Getúlio Vargas of Brazil, as well as populist parties such as Venezuela's Democratic Action Party and Peru's APRA.

post-9/11 era—referring to an international system since the terrorist attacks on the Pentagon in Washington and the World Trade Center in New York.

preferential option for the poor—a principle enunciated by the leader of the Jesuit order of priests in 1968, arguing that because Latin America is poor and the home of a majority of the world's Roman Catholics, the Church has a responsibility to take the side of the poor in struggles for social and economic justice. Heavily criticized by conservative sectors of Catholicism, who say it violated the principle of a "catholic" Church that equally regards all the faithful.

proletariat—wage workers; those who sell their labor to make a living; a synonym for the "working class" in Marxist tradition, which developed in an era when most wage earners were factory workers.

proportional representation—a system of allocating seats in a legislature to parties, in principle according to the percentage of votes received in an election. Requires that seats be distributed based on results nationally or in multimember districts (i.e., more than one representative elected per district).

regime change—a change in the "order of things," usually in the relationship between state and society and in the rules of the game by which political elites compete, but in both cases short of deeper and broader revolutionary change.

rent-seeking —a tendency for private actors to seek wealth through their connections to government.

royalty—a fee paid by a company or individual to the state for the right to explore for, mine, or drill for minerals under the surface of the land. So-called because originally it was the "king's share" of such extraction.

rule of law—the condition that all citizens are treated the same under the law and can rely on the state to guarantee both justice and security for persons and property.

secularism—belief in the necessity of separating church and state, championed by Liberals against Conservatives in the nineteenth century, rarely fully implemented, the major exception being Mexico in the decades after the 1910 revolution.

social debt—the term used by some groups in Latin America to suggest that governments have as much responsibility to honor promises to finance programs that help the poor as they do to pay the debt owed to foreign banks.

social movement—loosely associated individuals or organizations that take action in resistance to common problems, in defense of common interests, or in the quest to force the government or other social actors to respond to widely supported demands.

state capitalism—often associated with import substitution, a set of policies associated with the idea that development requires active state intervention to guide and regulate market forces, even promoting state ownership of key industries in some crucial sectors.

structural adjustment—a package of policies that the International Monetary Fund typically requires of governments before granting loans (known as "special drawn rights"), including cuts in the budget, restraint on money supply, reduction of tariff protection to domestic industries, great emphasis on export, and other measures associated with neoliberal economics.

technocrats—ministers and other officials in the government bureaucracy chosen for their expertise and regarded, for that reason, as being apolitical.

third wave—a theory advanced by political scientist Samuel Huntington that for the third time in history (the first being in the 1800s, the other just after World War II) international forces are at work to reinforce a worldwide movement toward liberal democracy.

Third World—during the Cold War, the label for countries who sought to assert independence from either bloc; today refers in general to countries that have had a colonial or neocolonial past and remain underdeveloped. Always a vague term, it is believed to be obsolete by some.

totalitarianism—often seen as the opposite of democracy, this term applies to ideologies, including fascism and communism, that **pluralists** say result in an all-powerful dictatorship and eliminate the boundary between the state and **civil society**.

transition to democracy—the process of moving from dictatorship to polyarchy. Applies to many regimes in different parts of the world, but most strongly associated with the reestablishment of polyarchies in the Southern Cone and Brazil after 1980.

transnational corporations—corporations operating across national lines. Early use of this term was intended to contest the idea of a "multinational corporation," one with no loyalty to any particular nation-state. Increasingly, the terms are interchangeable, but "transnational" still connotes a more critical stance, often associated with the idea that a "transnational" capitalist class has emerged.

twenty-first-century socialism—a concept promoted by Mexican thinker Heinz Dieterich, rejecting the idea of a vanguard and critical of actual existing socialism in the twentieth century, advocating socialism based on more "horizontal" relations among social movements.

underdeveloped, underdevelopment—referring to countries that are generally poor, have not historically passed through industrialization, and generally have lower standards on various measures of human welfare (education, health, etc.). The term usually implies that countries pass through common stages in a transition to a "developed" status, though this idea is vigorously debated among comparative political specialists.

uninomial representation—a system of electing representatives, one to each district. Also known as "single-member district."

United Nations Commission on Trade and Development (UNCTAD)—originally founded as an organization to promote stability in the prices of commodities exported by Third World nations; this organization evolved in the 1980s to promote free trade and policies favorable to foreign investment.

Washington Consensus—refers to a widespread understanding among Latin American governments (excepting Cuba) that the only acceptable regime type is a pluralist democracy coupled with a free-market economy. Although various versions exist, the main features were outlined in 1990 in a speech by John Williamson, a researcher at the Institute for International Economics in Washington, DC. By 2000, the consensus was being widely questioned.

World Bank—formally, the International Bank for Reconstruction and Development, founded after World War II to finance the reconstruction of Europe and Japan, and in more recent decades a credit agency for Third World development projects too large or risky to attract private capital.

World Social Forum—annual gatherings of representatives of social movements to discuss alternatives to neoliberal globalization; originated in Porto Alegre, Brazil.

world systems theory—a broad theory about the development of the global economy associated with the theorist Immanuel Wallerstein. World systems theory categorizes nations into the wealthy nation-states of the core, or center, and those poor ones of the periphery, with a semideveloped group categorized as part of the semiperiphery. The core exploits the periphery, and this accounts in large measure for the latter's underdevelopment. However, unlike the dependency approach, world systems theory does see the possibility of nation-states moving from one category to another over time. The theory also divides world history into stages according to which nation of the core enjoys global hegemony, with general agreement that Spain dominated the 1500s, England the 1800s, and the United States the twentieth century.

World Trade Organization (WTO)—headquartered in Geneva, Switzerland; the WTO is an international organization responsible for enforcing existing global free-trade pacts and promoting an open world trade system.

References

Introduction

Borón, Atilio. 2005. "Guardianes de la democracia." Agencia Latinoamericana de Información (www.alainet .org, accessed July 22, 2010).

Castañeda, Jorge. 2006. "Latin America's Left Turn," *Foreign Affairs* (May/June, www.foreignaffairs.com/ articles/61702/jorge-g-castaneda/latin-americas-left-turn).

Chilcote, Ronald H. 1994. *Theories of Comparative Politics: The Search for a Paradigm Reconsidered* (second edition). Boulder, CO: Westview Press.

ECLAC (UN Economic Commission for Latin America and the Caribbean). 2012. "Poverty Continues to Fall in Latin America but Still Affects 167 Million People." Press release, August 12.

Ellner, Steve. 2012. "The Distinguishing Features of Latin America's New Left in Power: The Governments of Hugo Chávez, Evo Morales, and Rafael Correa." *Latin American Perspectives,* 39.96 (December): 96–114.

Grugel, Jean. 2002. *Democratization: A Critical Introduction.* New York: Palgrave.

LASA. 1984. *The Electoral Process in Nicaragua: Domestic and International Influences: The Report of the Latin American Studies Association Delegation to Observe the Nicaraguan General Election of November 4, 1984.* November 19.

Latinobarómetro. 2013. *Informe Latinobarómetro 2013 (Latin Barometer Report).* Santiago: Corporación Latinobarómetro (www.latinobarometro.org).

Lewis, Martin W. and Karen Wigen. 1997. *The Myth of Continents: A Critique of Metageography.* Berkeley: University of California Press.

Shifter, Michael. 2011. "Latin America: A Surge to the Center," *Journal of Democracy,* 22.1 (January): 107–121.

Chapter 1

Borge, Tomás. 1992. "Interview with Fidel Castro," *El Nuevo Diario* (Managua, June 4).

Buxton, Julia. 2001. *The Failure of Political Reform in Venezuela.* Aldershot, UK: Ashgate.

Castañeda, Jorge. 1993. *Utopia Unarmed: The Latin American Left after the Cold War.* New York: Alfred Knopf.

Ceresole, Norberto. 1999. *Caudillo, ejército, pueblo. El modelo venezolano o la posdemocracia. (Leader, Army, People. The Venezuelan Model or Post-Democracy).* Archived in *Venezuela Analytica* (www.analitica .com/bitblio/ceresole/caudillo.asp, accessed December 27, 2010).

Chalmers, Douglas, M. do Carmo Campello de Souza and Atilio A. Borón (eds.). 1992. *The Right and Democracy in Latin America.* New York: Praeger.

Dahl, Robert. 1971. *Polyarchy: Participation and Opposition.* New Haven, CT: Yale University Press.

De Soto, Hernando. 1989. *The Other Path: The Invisible Revolution in the Third World.* New York: Harper and Row.

Domhoff, G. William. 1967. *Who Rules America?* Englewood Cliffs, NJ: Prentice-Hall.

Farthing, Linda. 2010. "Controlling State Power: An Interview with Vice President Álvaro García Linera," *Latin American Perspectives,* 37.4 (July): 30–33.

Fukuyama, Francis. 1992. *The End of History and the Last Man.* New York: The Free Press.

Guillermoprieto, Alma. 2000. "Letter from Mexico: Enter Harpo," *New Yorker* (July 24): 30.

Huntington, Samuel. 1991. *The Third Wave: Democratization in the Late Twentieth Century.* Norman: University of Oklahoma Press.

Inglehart, Ronald and Christian Welzel. 2005. *Modernization, Cultural Change and Democracy: The Human Development Sequence.* Cambridge, UK: Cambridge University Press.

Kane, Richard F. 2005. "Brazil's Neoliberal Marxist," *Brazil Magazine* (June 15, www.brazzil.com, accessed January 31, 2007).

La Ramée, Pierre M. and Erica G. Polakoff. 1997. "The Evolution of the Popular Organizations in Nicaragua," in Gary Prevost and Harry E. Vanden (eds.), *The Undermining of the Sandinista Revolution*. London: Macmillan Press.

Lanz, Laureano Ballenilla. 1919. *Cesarismo Democrática: Estudios sobre las bases sociológicas de la constitución efectiva de Venezuela* (*Democratic Caesarism: Studies of the Sociological Bases of the Actual Venezuelan Constitution*) (edition of 1990). Caracas: Monte Avila.

Linz, Juan J. and Alfred Stepan (eds.). 1978. *The Breakdown of Democratic Regimes*. Baltimore, MD: Johns Hopkins University Press.

Linz, Juan J. and Alfred Stepan (eds.). 1996. *Problems of Democratic Transition and Consolidation: Southern Europe, South America and Post-Communist Europe*. Baltimore, MD: Johns Hopkins University Press.

Linz, Juan J. and Arturo Valenzuela (eds.). 1994. *The Failure of Presidential Democracy: The Case of Latin America*. Baltimore, MD: Johns Hopkins University Press.

McNeil, Robert. 1985. "Fidel Castro Interview, Part 2," *The MacNeil/Lehrer Newshour* (February 11).

MacPherson, C. B. 1972. *The Real World of Democracy*. New York: Oxford University Press.

Mainwaring, Scott and M. Soberg Shugart (eds.). 1997. *Presidentialism and Democracy in Latin America*. Cambridge, UK: Cambridge University Press.

Mainwaring, Scott and Timothy Scully (eds.). 1995. *Building Democratic Institutions in Latin America*. Stanford, CA: Stanford University Press.

Michels, Robert. 1915. *Political Parties: A Sociological Study of the Oligarchical Tendencies of Modern Democracy*. Trans. Eden and Cedar Paul. Glencoe, IL: The Free Press.

Mills, C. Wright. 1956. *The Power Elite*. Oxford, UK: Oxford University Press.

Munck, Gerardo L. 2004. "Democratic Politics in Latin America: New Debates and Research Frontiers," *Annual Review of Political Science,* 7: 437–462.

O'Donnell, Guillermo. 1994. "Delegative Democracy," *Journal of Democracy,* 5.1: 55–69.

O'Donnell, Guillermo, Philippe C. Schmitter and Laurence Whitehead (eds.). 1986. *Transitions from Authoritarian Rule: Tentative Conclusions about Uncertain Democracies*. Baltimore, MD: Johns Hopkins University Press.

Philip, George. 1996. "Institutions and Democratic Consolidation in Latin America," in Julia Buxton and Nicola Phillips (eds.), *Developments in Latin American Political Economy: States, Markets and Actors*. Manchester: University of Manchester Press.

Prevost, Gary and Harry E. Vanden (eds.). 1997. *The Undermining of the Sandinista Revolution*. London: Macmillan Press.

Raby, Diane. 2006. *Democracy and Revolution: Latin America and Socialism Today*. London: Verso.

Robinson, William I. 1992. *A Faustian Bargain: U.S. Intervention in the Nicaraguan Elections and American Foreign Policy in the Post-Cold War Era*. Boulder, CO: Westview Press.

Robinson, William I. 1996. *Promoting Polyarchy: Globalization, US Intervention, and Hegemony*. Cambridge, UK: Cambridge University Press.

Romero, Aníbal. 1999. "Democracias de jugete en América Latina," *Venezuela Analytica* (July 25, www.analitica.com/hispanica/8252042.asp, accessed December 9, 2010).

Ruchwarger, Gary. 1985. "The Sandinista Mass Organizations and the Revolutionary Process," in Richard Harris and Carlos Vilas (eds.), *Nicaragua under Siege*. London: Zed Books.

Stavenhagen, Rodolfo. 1966–1967. "Seven Erroneous Theses about Latin America," *New University Thought,* 4.4 (Winter): 25–37.

Stavenhagen, Rodolfo. 1974. "Dependency Theory: A Reassessment," *Latin American Perspectives,* 1.1 (Spring): 124–148.

Vilas, Carlos. 1993. "The Hour of Civil Society," *NACLA Report on the Americas,* 37 (September–October): 38–42.

Wiarda, Howard. 1981. *Corporatism and National Development in Latin America*. Boulder, CO: Westview Press.

Williamson, John. 2002. "Did the Washington Consensus Fail?" Outline of speech at the Center for Strategic & International Studies, Washington, DC, November 6.

Zakaria, Fareed. 1997. "The Rise of Illiberal Democracy," *Foreign Affairs,* 76.6 (November–December): 22–43.

Chapter 2

Ameringer, Charles. 2009. "The Socialist Impulse: Latin America in the Twentieth Century." Florida State University Press Online (http://florida.universitypressscholarship.com/view/10.5744/florida/9780813033099.001.0001/upso-9780813033099-chapter-14).

Barbados Group. 1993. "Barbados III: On Democracy and Diversity," originally in *Abya Yala News* (www.nativeweb.org/papers/statements/state/barbados3.php, accessed December 9, 2010*).

Barker, Ernest (ed., trans.). 1962. *The Politics of Aristotle*. New York: Oxford University Press.

Borge, Tomás. n.d. *My Personal Revenge* (www.geocities.com/~thinkink/war/justice.htm#books, accessed July 28, 2009).

Collier, David. 1995. "'Corporatism' in Latin American Politics," in Peter Smith (ed.), *Latin America in Comparative Perspective: New Approaches to Methods and Analysis*. Boulder, CO: Westview Press.

Declaration of Quito. 1990. Online at www.nativeweb.org/papers/statements/quincentennial/quito.php (accessed December 9, 2010).

García-Guadilla, María Pilar. 2011. "Urban Land Committees: Co-Optation, Autonomy, and Protagonism," in David Smide and Daniel Hellinger (eds.), *Venezuela's Bolivarian Democracy: Participation, Politics, and Culture under Chávez*, pp. 58–79. Durham, NC: Duke University Press.

Gender Equality Observatory. 2012. *Annual Report 2012*. New York: United Nations Economic Commission for Latin America.

Green, James. 2012. "'Who Is the Macho Who Wants to Kill Me?' Male Homosexuality, Revolutionary Masculinity, and the Brazilian Armed Struggle of the 1960s," *Hispanic American Historical Review*, 92.3 (August): 437–469.

Hellinger, Daniel. 1991. *Venezuela: Tarnished Democracy*. Boulder, CO: Westview Press.

Lustig, Nora (ed.). 1998. *Coping with Austerity: Poverty and Inequality in Latin America*. Washington, DC: Brookings Institution.

Mark, Jason. 2001. "Brazil's MST: Taking Back the Land," *Winning Campaigns*, 22.1–2.

O'Donnell, Guillermo. 1999. *Counterpoints: Selected Essays on Authoritarianism and Democratization*. South Bend, IN: University of Notre Dame.

Perón, Juan. 1950. "Mensaje a la Asamblea Legislativa." Discursos de Juan Domingo Perón. Partido Justicialista, Provincia de Buenos Aires (www.pjbonaerense.org.ar/Peron_Discursos_01051950.aspx).

Perone, Jim. 2000. "Is the Pope Capitalist?," *Laissez Faire City Times*, 4.1 (January 3, www.zolatimes.com, accessed January 21, 2002).

Schiller, Naomi. 2011. "Catia Sees You: Community Television, Clientelism, and the State in the Chávez Era," in David Smide and Daniel Hellinger (eds.), *Venezuela's Bolivarian Democracy: Participation, Politics, and Culture under Chávez*, pp. 104–130. Durham, NC: Duke University Press.

Schmitter, Philippe. 1974. "Still the Century of Corporatism?," in Schmitter and Gerhard Lembruch (eds.), *Trends toward Corporatist Intermediation*. Beverly Hills, CA: Sage.

Seligson, Mitchell and John Booth. 2009. "Predicting Coups? Democratic Vulnerabilities, the Americas-Barometer and the 2009 Honduran Crisis." Latin American Public Opinion Project, Insights Series (www.AmericasBarometer.org, accessed December 9, 2010).

Sosa Pietri, Andrés. 1998. "Venezuela, el 'Tercermundismo' y la OPEP" ("Venezuela: 'Third Worldism' and OPEC"), *Venezuela Analytica* (October).

United Nations. 1999. *Human Development Report*. New York: Oxford University Press.

Van der Hoeven, Rolph. 2000. *Poverty and Structural Adjustment: Some Remarks on Tradeoffs between Equity and Growth*. Geneva: International Labour Organization.

Wiarda, Howard. 1981. *Corporatism and National Development in Latin America*. Boulder, CO: Westview Press.

Chapter 3

Achtenberg, Emily. 2012. "Bolivia: End of the Road for TIPNIS Consulta," NACLA blog (December 13, www.nacla.org/blog/2012/12/13/bolivia-end-road-tipnis-consulta).

Anderson, Benedict. 1983. *Imagined Communities: Reflections on the Origins and Spread of Nationalism*. London: Verso Press.

Catholic News Services. 2012. "Bolivian Census to Allow Citizens to Register as Indigenous" (November 17, www.catholicsentinel.org/Main.asp?SectionID=2&SubSectionID=34&ArticleID=19873).

Crosby, Alfred, Jr. 1991. "The Biological Consequences of 1492," *NACLA Report on the Americas* (September): 6–13.

Diamond, Jared. 1997. *Guns, Germs and Steel: The Fates of Human Societies.* New York: Norton.

Dore, Elizabeth. 1991. "Open Wounds," *NACLA Report on the Americas* (September): 14–21.

Galeano, Eduardo. 2001. *The Open Veins of Latin America: Five Centuries of the Pillage of a Continent.* New York: Monthly Review Press.

Holloway, Joseph E. n.d. "Slave Resistances in Latin America," the Slave Rebellion Website (http://slaverebellion .org/index.php?page=slave-resistances-in-latin-america-2, accessed April 1, 2014).

Holston, James. 2008. *Insurgent Citizenship: Disjunctions of Democracy and Modernity in Brazil.* Princeton, NJ: Princeton University Press.

Hylton, Forrest and Sinclair Thomson. 2004. "The Roots of Rebellion: Insurgent Bolivia," *NACLA Report on the Americas,* 38.3 (November–December): 15–19.

Keen, Benjamin and Keith Haynes. 2000. *A History of Latin America* (sixth edition). Boston: Houghton Mifflin.

Lazar, Sian. 2008. *El Alto, Rebel City: Self and Citizenship in Andean Bolivia.* Durham, NC: Duke University Press.

Mann, Charles C. 2005. *1491: New Revelations of the Americas before Columbus.* New York: Alfred Knopf.

Mazano, Juan. 1996. *Autobiography of a Slave.* Detroit, MI: Wayne State University Press.

Mörner, Magnus. 1967. *Race Mixture in the History of Latin America.* Boston: Little, Brown.

Pilcher, Jeffrey M. 1998. *¡Que vivan los tamales! Food and the Making of Mexican Identity.* Albuquerque: University of New Mexico Press.

Rostow, Walt W. 1960. *The Stages of Growth: A Non-Communist Manifesto.* Cambridge, UK: Cambridge University Press.

Schroeder, Susan. 2000. "The Mexico that Spain Encountered," in Michael C. Meyer and William H. Breezley (eds.), *The Oxford History of Mexico.* New York: Oxford University Press.

Schwartz, Stuart. 2000. *Victors and Vanquished: Spanish and Nahua Views of the Conquest of Mexico.* Boston: Bedford/St. Martins.

Selverston-Scher, Melina. 2001. *Ethnopolitics in Ecuador: Indigenous Rights and the Strengthening of Democracy.* Miami, FL: North-South Center, University of Miami.

Silverblatt, Irene. 1987. *Moon, Sun and Witches.* Princeton, NJ: Princeton University Press.

Stolle-McAllister, John. 2005. "What Does Democracy Look Like?," *Latin American Perspectives,* 32.4 (July): 15–35.

Wallerstein, Immanuel. 1974. *The Modern World System: Capitalist Agriculture and the Origins of the European World Economy in the Sixteenth Century.* New York: Academic Press.

Williams, Eric. 1970. *From Columbus to Castro: The History of the Caribbean.* New York: Harper and Row.

Wilpert, Greg. 2004. "Racism and Racial Divides in Venezuela," *Venezuelanalysis.com* (January 21).

Chapter 4

Anderson, Benedict. 1983. *Imagined Communities: Reflections on the Origins and Spread of Nationalism.* London: Verso Press.

Burns, E. Bradford. 1996. *Latin America: A Concise Interpretive History* (sixth edition). Englewood Cliffs, NJ: Prentice-Hall.

de Tocqueville, Alexis. 1835/2000. *Democracy in America.* Trans. George Lawrence. Ed. J.P. Mayer. New York: Perennial Classics.

Keen, Benjamin and Keith Haynes. 2000. *A History of Latin America* (sixth edition). Boston: Houghton Mifflin Company.

Levine, R.M. 1995. *Vale of Tears: Revisiting the Canudos Massacre in Northeastern Brazil, 1893–1897.* Berkeley: University of California Press.

Loveman, Brian. 1999. *For La Patria: Politics and the Armed Forces in Latin America.* Wilmington, DE: Scholarly Resources.

Soares, José Celso de Macedo. 2009. "Coronelismo, enxada e voto," *Diario do Pernambuco* (June 18): 13B.

Ugalde, Luis. 1978. *Venezuela Repúblicana: siglo XIX.* Caracas: Centro Gumilla.

Williams, Robert G. 1994. *States and Social Evolution: Coffee and the Rise of National Governments in Central America.* Chapel Hill: University of North Carolina Press.

Chapter 5

Bergquist, Charles. 1986. *Labor in Latin America: Comparative Essays on Chile, Argentina, Venezuela, and Colombia.* Palo Alto, CA: Stanford University Press.

Burns, E. Bradford. 1993. *A History of Brazil*. New York: Columbia University Press.

Cardoso, Fernando Henrique and Enzo Faletto. 1979. *Dependency and Development in Latin America*. Berkeley: University of California Press.

Corradi, Juan. 1985. *The Fitful Republic: Economy, Society and Politics in Argentina*. Boulder, CO: Westview Press.

Drake, Paul W. 1978. *Socialism and Populism in Chile: 1932–52*. Urbana: University of Illinois Press.

Fraser, Nicholas and Marysa Navarro. 1980. *Eva Perón*. New York: Norton.

Hodges, Donald. 1976. *Argentina 1943–1976: The National Revolution and Resistance*. Albuquerque: University of New Mexico Press.

Huntington, Samuel. 1968. *Political Order in Changing Societies*. New Haven, CT: Yale University Press.

Johnson, John. 1958. *Political Change in Latin America: The Emergence of the Middle Sectors*. Palo Alto, CA: Stanford University Press.

Karl, Terry. 1994. *The Paradox of Plenty: Oil Booms and Petro-States*. Berkeley: University of California Press.

Lowy, Michael. 1987. *Notebooks for Study and Research*, vol. 6. Amsterdam: International Institute for Research and Education.

Nun, José. 1976. "The Middle Class Military Coup Revisited," in Abraham Lowenthal (ed.), *Armies and Politics in Latin America*. New York: Holmes & Meier.

Page, Joseph. 1983. *Perón: A Biography*. New York: Random House.

Perón, Juan. 1950. *Mensaje al inaugurar el Congreso nacional May 1, 1950* (*Message for the Inaugural National Congress*) (http://lanic.utexas.edu/larrp/pm/sample2/argentin/peron/500679t.html, accessed July 28, 2009).

Rostow, Walt W. 1960. *The Stages of Growth, a Non-Communist Manifesto*. Cambridge, UK: Cambridge University Press.

Stavenhagen, Rodolfo. 1974. "Dependency Theory: A Reassessment," *Latin American Perspectives*, 1.1 (Spring): 124–148.

Vilas, Carlos M. 1987. "Populism as a Strategy for Accumulation: Latin America," in Michel Lowy (ed.), *Notebooks for Study and Research*, vol. 6. Amsterdam: International Institute for Research and Education.

Weber, Maximillian. 1947. *Max Weber: The Theory of Social and Economic Organization*. Trans. A. M. Henderson and Talcott Parsons. New York: The Free Press.

Chapter 6

Amin, Samir. 1977. *Imperialism and Unequal Development*. New York: Monthly Review Press.

Armijo, Leslie Elliott and Phillippe Faucher. 2000. "We Have a Consensus: Explaining Political Support for Market Reforms in Latin America." Paper prepared for delivery at the 96th Annual Meeting of the American Political Science Association, Washington, DC, August 31–September 2.

Armstrong, Robert and Janet Shenk. 1982. *El Salvador: The Face of Revolution*. Boston: South End Press.

Cardoso, Fernando Henrique. 1977. "The Consumption of Dependency Theory in the United States," *Latin American Research Review*, 12.3: 7–24.

Cardoso, Fernando Henrique and Enzo Faletto. 1979. *Dependency and Development in Latin America*. Berkeley: University of California Press.

Cueva, Agustín. 2003 (originally 1976). "Problems of Dependency Theory" (trans. J. Villamil and C. Fortín), in Ronald H. Chilcote, *Development in Theory and Practice*. New York: Rowman and Littlefield.

da Costa, Ana Nicolaci. 2008. "In Brazil Middle Class Dreams Built on Credit," *Reuters* (July 15, www.reuters.com/article/idUSN0827980620080716, accessed December 9, 2010).

De Soto, Hernando. 1989. *The Other Path: The Invisible Revolution in the Third World*. New York: Harper and Row.

Deutsch, Karl W. 1961. "Social Mobilization and Political Development," *American Political Science Review*, 55.3 (September): 493–514.

Dos Santos, Theotonio. 1974. "Brazil: The Origins of a Crisis," in Ronald Chilcote and Joel Edelstein (eds.), *Latin America: The Struggle with Dependency and Beyond*. New York: Schenkman.

Drake, Paul W. 1978. *Socialism and Populism in Chile 1932–52*. Urbana: University of Illinois Press.

Dussel, Enrique. 1980. "Philosophy and Praxis" (provisional thesis for a philosophy of liberation), in John B. Brough et al. (eds.), *Philosophical Knowledge*. Washington, DC: Catholic University of America (www.ifil.org/Biblioteca/dussel/textos/c/1980-115.pdf, accessed July 15, 2008).

Frank, Andre Gunder. 1969. *Latin America: Underdevelopment or Revolution*. New York: Monthly Review Press.

Franko, Patrice. 1999. *The Puzzle of Latin American Economic Development*. Lanham, MD: Rowman and Littlefield.

Furtado, Celso. 1971. *La economiía latinomericana: formación histórica y problemas contemporaneous* (*The Latin American Economy: Historical Formation and Contemporary Character*). Mexico City: Siglo Veintiuno Editores.

Galeano, Eduardo. 1997. *The Open Veins of Latin America*. New York: Monthly Review Press.

Gardy, Alison. 1994. "Mexico's Political Reforms Must Begin in the Streets." *Wall Street Journal* (November 18): A19.

Hanson, Simon. 1951. *Economic Development in Latin America*. Washington, DC: Inter-American Affairs Press.

Hellinger, Daniel. 1991. *Venezuela: Tarnished Democracy*. Boulder, CO: Westview Press.

Huntington, Samuel. 1968. *Political Order in Changing Societies*. New Haven, CT: Yale University Press.

Karl, Terry. 1994. *The Paradox of Plenty: Oil Booms and Petro-States*. Berkeley: University of California Press.

Kaufman, Robert R., Harry Chernotsky and Daniel Geller. 1975. "A Preliminary Test of the Theory of Dependency," *Comparative Politics*, 7.3 (April): 303–330.

Lipset, Seymour Martin. 1960. *Political Man*. New York: Doubleday.

Martínez-Piedra, Alberto and Lorenzo L. Pérez. 1996. "External Debt Problems and the Principle of Solidarity: The Cuba Case," in *Cuba in Transition*, vol. 6. Proceedings of the Fifth Annual Meeting of the Association for the Study of the Cuban Economy (ASCE), University of Miami, Miami, FL, August 8–10.

Marx, Karl and Friedrich Engels. 1848/1948. *The Communist Manifesto*. Moscow: International Publishers.

Moguel, Julio. 1994. "Salinas' Failed War on Poverty" (interview), *NACLA Report on the Americas*, 28 (July): 38.

Osava, Mario. 2004. "Brazil's Shrinking Middle Class," *IPSNews.net* (September 21, http://ipsnews.net/africa/interna.asp?idnews=25559, accessed December 9, 2010).

Pérez, Mamerto, Sergio Schlesinger and Timothy A. Wise. 2008. *The Promise and Perils of Agricultural Trade Liberalization: Lessons from Latin America*. Washington, DC: Washington Office on Latin America.

Petras, James. 1980. *Critical Perspectives on Imperialism and Social Class in the Third World*. New York: Monthly Review Press.

Potter, Georgia Anne. 2000. *Deeper than Debt: Globalization and the Poor*. Bloomfield, CT: Kumarian Press.

Remmer, Karen. 1998. "The Politics of Neo-Liberal Economic Reform in South America, 1980–1994," *Studies in Comparative International Development*, 33.2: 3–29.

Rostow, Walt W. 1960. *The Stages of Growth, a Non-Communist Manifesto*. Cambridge, UK: Cambridge University Press.

Schumpeter, Joseph. 1947. *Capitalism, Socialism and Democracy*. New York: Harper.

Van der Molen, Paul. 2000. "After 10 Years of Criticism: What Is Left of DeSoto's Ideas?," *Cadastral and Land Administrative Perspectives* (www.fig.net/pub/fig2012/papers/ts07b/TS07B_vandermolen_5503.pdf).

Wachtel, Howard. 1977. "A Decade of International Debt," *Theory and Society*, 9.3: 504–518.

Wallerstein, Immanuel. 2004. *World-Systems Analysis: An Introduction*. Durham, NC: Duke University Press.

World Bank. 1996. *World Debt Tables 1994–1995*. Washington, DC: World Bank.

Chapter 7

Allende, Salvador. 2000. "Last Words Transmitted by Radio Magallanes," in James Cockroft (ed.), *Salvador Allende Reader: Chile's Voice of Democracy*. New York: Ocean Press.

Cockroft, James. 1996. *Latin America: History, Politics and U.S. Policy* (second edition). Chicago, IL: Nelson-Hall.

Diamint, Rut. 2002. "Civilians and the Military in Latin American Democracies," *Disarmament Forum*, 2: 15–24.

Dominguez, Jorge I. and Abraham Lowenthal (eds.). 1996. *Constructing Democratic Governance: The New South American Democracies*. Baltimore, MD: Johns Hopkins University Press.

Dos Santos, Theotonio. 1974. "Brazil: The Origins of a Crisis," in Ronald Chilcote and Joel Edelstein (eds.), *Latin America: The Struggle with Dependency and Beyond*. New York: Schenkman.

Drake, Paul W. 1978. *Socialism and Populism in Chile 1932–52*. Urbana: University of Illinois Press.

Huntington, Samuel. 1968. *Political Order in Changing Societies*. New Haven, CT: Yale University Press.

Huntington, Samuel. 1991. *The Third Wave: Democratization in the Late Twentieth Century*. Norman: University of Oklahoma Press.

Janowitz, Morris. 1964. *The Military in Political Development of New Nations.* Chicago, IL: University of Chicago Press.

Kaufman, Robert R. 1972. *The Politics of Latin Reform in Chile, 1950–1970: Public Policy, Political Institutions, and Social Change.* Cambridge, MA: Harvard University Press.

Lasswell, Harold. 1936. *Politics: Who Gets What, When and How.* Chicago, IL: University of Chicago.

Linz, Juan J. and Alfred Stepan (eds.). 1978. *The Breakdown of Democratic Regimes* (4 vols.). Baltimore, MD: Johns Hopkins University Press.

Loveman, Brian. 1999. *For La Patria: Politics and the Armed Forces in Latin America.* Wilmington, DE: Scholarly Resources Press.

Loveman, Brian and Thomas M. Davies Jr. 1997. *The Politics of Antipolitics in Latin America.* Wilmington, DE: Scholarly Resources Press.

Millet, Richard. 1977. *Guardians of the Dynasty.* New York: Orbis Books.

Norden, Deborah. 2003. "Democracy in Uniform: Chávez and the Venezuelan Armed Forces," in Steve Ellner and Daniel Hellinger (eds.), *Venezuelan Politics in the Chávez Era: Class Polarization and Conflict.* Boulder, CO: Lynn Rienner.

Nordlinger, Eric A. 1970. "Soldiers in Mufti: The Impact of Military Rule Upon Economic and Social Change in the Non-Western States," *American Political Science Review,* 64.3 (December): 1131–1148.

Nun, José. 1976. "The Middle Class Military Coup Revisited," in Abraham Lowenthal (ed.), *Armies and Politics in Latin America.* New York: Holmes & Meier.

O'Donnell, Guillermo. 1973. *Modernization and Bureaucratic–Authoritarianism: Studies in South American Politics.* Berkeley: University of California Press.

O'Donnell, Guillermo. 1978. "Permanent Crisis and the Failure to Create a Democratic Regime: Argentina, 1955–66," in Linz and Stepan (eds.), *The Breakdown of Democratic Regimes: Latin America.* Baltimore, MD: Johns Hopkins University Press.

Perlmutter, Amos. 1977. *The Military and Politics in Modern Times.* New Haven, CT: Yale University Press.

Pye, Lucien. 1962. "Armies in the Process of Political Modernization," in John J. Johnson (ed.), *The Role of the Military in Underdeveloped Countries.* Princeton, NJ: Princeton University Press.

Roxborough, Ian, Phil O'Brien and Jackie Roddick. 1977. *Chile: The State and Revolution.* London: Macmillan Press.

Sánchez, Alan. 2011. "Costa Rica: An Army-less Nation in a Problem-Prone Region." Council on Hemispheric Affairs (www.coha.org/costa-rica-an-army-less-nation-in-a-problem-prone-region).

Sartori, Giovanni and Giacomo Sani. 1983. "Polarization, Fragmentation, and Competition in Western Democracies," in Hans Daalder and Peter Mair (eds.), *Western European Party Systems: Continuity and Change.* Berkeley, CA: Sage Publications.

Sigmund, Paul E. (ed.). 1970. *Models of Political Change in Latin America.* New York: Praeger.

Stepan, Alfred. 1971. *The Military in Politics: Changing Patterns in Brazil.* Princeton, NJ: Princeton University Press.

Valenzuela, Arturo. 1978. *The Breakdown of Democratic Regimes: Chile.* Baltimore, MD: Johns Hopkins University Press.

Winn, Peter. 1989. *Weavers of Revolution: The Yarur Workers and Chile's Road to Socialism.* New York: Oxford University Press.

Zenteño, Raúl Benítez (ed.). 1977. *Clases sociales y crisis política en américa latina* (*Social Classes and Political Crisis in Latin America*). Mexico City: Siglo Veintiuno.

Chapter 8

Andersen, Martin Edwin. 1993. *Dossier Secreto: Argentina's Desaparecidos and the Myth of the Dirty War.* Boulder CO: Westview Press.

Avritzer, Leonardo. 2002. *Democracy and the Public Space in Latin America.* Princeton, NJ: Princeton University Press.

Castañeda, Jorge. 1993. *Utopia Unarmed: The Latin American Left after the Cold War.* New York: Alfred Knopf.

Friedman, Elizabeth. 2000. *Unfinished Transitions: Women and the Gendered Development of Democracy in Venezuela.* University Park, PA: Penn State Press.

Garretón, Manuel. 1986. "The Political Evolution of the Chilean Military Regime and Problems in the Transition to Democracy," in O'Donnell, Schmitter and Whitehead (eds.), *Transitions from Authoritarian Rule: Latin America.* Baltimore, MD: Johns Hopkins University Press.

Huntington, Samuel. 1991. *The Third Wave: Democratization in the Late Twentieth Century.* Norman: University of Oklahoma Press.

Keck, Margaret. 1992. *The Workers' Party and Democratization in Brazil.* New Haven, CT: Yale University Press.

Latinobarómetro. 2013. *Informe Latinobarómetro 2013* (*Latin Barometer Report*). Santiago: Corporación Latinobarómetro (www.latinobarometro.org.)

Levitt, Steven and Stephen J. Dubner. 2005. *Freakonomics: A Rogue Economist Explores the Hidden Side of Everything.* New York: William Morrow/HarperCollins.

Mallinder, Louise. 2009. *Uruguay's Evolving Experience of Amnesty and Civil Society's Response.* Belfast: Queen's University, Institute of Criminology and Criminal Justice.

Moulian, Tomás. 2002. *Chile Actual: Anatomía de un mito* (*Chile Today: Anatomy of a Myth*). Santiago: LOM Ediciones.

O'Donnell, Guillermo and Philippe C. Schmitter. 1986. *Transitions from Authoritarian Rule: Tentative Conclusions about Uncertain Democracies.* Baltimore, MD: Johns Hopkins University Press.

O'Donnell, Guillermo, Philippe C. Schmitter and Laurence Whitehead (eds.). 1986a. *Authoritarian Rule: Comparative Perspectives.* Baltimore, MD: Johns Hopkins University Press.

O'Donnell, Guillermo, Philippe C. Schmitter and Laurence Whitehead (eds.). 1986b. *Transitions from Authoritarian Rule: Latin America.* Baltimore, MD: Johns Hopkins University Press.

O'Donnell, Guillermo, Philippe C. Schmitter and Laurence Whitehead (eds.). 1986c. *Transitions from Authoritarian Rule: Southern Europe.* Baltimore, MD: Johns Hopkins University Press.

Oppenheim, Lois Hecht. 1993. *Politics in Chile: Democracy, Authoritarianism, and the Search for Development.* Boulder, CO: Westview Press.

Osava, Mario. 2004. "The Struggle to Pry Open Brazil's Military Archives" (www.antiwar.com/ips/osava .php?articleid=3859, accessed August 12, 2004).

Przeworski, Adam. 1986. "Some Problems in the Study of the Transition to Democracy," in O'Donnell, Schmitter and Whitehead (eds.), *Transitions from Authoritarian Rule: Comparative Perspectives.* Baltimore, MD: Johns Hopkins University Press.

Rettig Commission. 2000. Report of the Chilean National Commission on Truth and Reconciliation (www.usip.org/sites/default/files/resources/collections/truth_commissions/Chile90-Report/Chile90-Report.pdf).

Trigona, Marie. 2006. "Recuperated Factories in Argentina: Reversing the Logic of Capitalism," *Znet* (March 27).

Welzel, Christian. 2009. "Theories of Democratization," in Christian Haerpfern et al. (eds.), *Democratization.* New York: Oxford University Press (www.worldvaluessurvey.org/wvs/articles/folder_published/publication_579/files/OUP_Ch06.pdf).

Chapter 9

Avritzer, Leonardo. 2002. *Democracy and the Public Space in Latin America.* Princeton, NJ: Princeton University Press.

Burns, E. Bradford and Julie A. Charlip. 2002. *Latin America: A Concise Interpretive History* (seventh edition). Upper Saddle River, NJ: Prentice Hall.

Camp, Roderic Ai. 1999. *Politics in Mexico: The Decline of Authoritarianism.* New York: Oxford University Press.

Collier, George A. (with Elizabeth Lowery Quaratiello). 1999. *Land and the Zapatistas: Rebellion in Chiapas* (second edition). Oakland, CA: Food First.

Coronil, Fernando. 1997. *The Magical State: Nature, Money and Modernity in Venezuela.* Chicago, IL: University of Chicago Press.

Crozier, Michel, Samuel Huntington and Joji Watanuki. 1975. *The Crisis of Democracy.* New York: The Trilateral Commission.

Cyr, Jennifer. 2013. "Political Parties and the State in Post-Collapse Venezuela and Bolivia." Paper delivered at the XXXI International Congress of the Latin American Studies Association, Washington, DC, May 29–June 1.

Ellner, Steve and Daniel Hellinger (eds.). 2003. *Venezuelan Politics in the Chávez Era: Class Polarization and Conflict.* Boulder, CO: Lynne Rienner.

Foweracker, Joe and Ann Craig (eds.). 1990. *Popular Movements and Political Change in Mexico.* Boulder, CO: Lynne Rienner.

Handelman, Howard. 1997. *Mexican Politics: The Dynamics of Change.* New York: St. Martin's Press.

Hellinger, Daniel. 1991. *Venezuela: Tarnished Democracy.* Boulder, CO: Westview Press.

Hellinger, Daniel. 2003. "Political Overview: The Breakdown of Puntofijismo," in Steve Ellner and Daniel Hellinger (eds.), *Venezuelan Politics in the Chávez Era.* Boulder, CO: Lynne Rienner.

Huntington, Samuel. 1968. *Political Order in Changing Societies.* New Haven, CT: Yale University Press.

Jones, Bart. 2007. *Hugo! The Hugo Chávez Story from Mud Hut to Perpetual Revolution.* Hanover, NH: Steerforth Press.

Karl, Terry Lynn. 1986. "Petroleum and Political Pacts: The Transition to Democracy in Venezuela," in Guillermo O'Donnell, Philippe Schmitter and Laurence Whitehead (eds.), *Transitions from Authoritarian Rule: Latin America.* Baltimore, MD: Johns Hopkins University Press.

La Botz, Dan. 1995. *Democracy in Mexico: Peasant Rebellion and Political Reform.* Boston: South End Press.

Langston, Joy. 2006. "The Birth and Transformation of the Dedazo in Mexico," in Gretchen Helmke and Steven Levitsky (eds.), *Informal Institutions and Democracy: Lessons from Latin America.* Baltimore, MD: Johns Hopkins University Press.

Levine, Daniel. 1978. "Venezuela since 1958: The Consolidation of Democratic Politics," in Juan J. Linz and Alfred Stepan (eds.), *The Breakdown of Democratic Regimes: Latin America,* pp. 82–109. Baltimore, MD: Johns Hopkins University Press.

Levy, Daniel and Gabriel Székely. 1983. *Mexico: Paradoxes of Stability and Change.* Boulder, CO: Westview.

McCoy, Jennifer and David Myers (eds.). 2006. *The Unraveling of Democracy in Venezuela.* Baltimore, MD: Johns Hopkins University Press.

Merrill, Tim and Ramón Miró, eds. 1996. *Mexico: A Country Study.* Washington: GPO for the Library of Congress (http://countrystudies.us/mexico/).

Meyer, Michael C. and William H. Beezley. 2000. *The Oxford History of Mexico.* New York: Oxford University Press.

Middlebrook, Kevin J. 1986. "Political Liberalization in an Authoritarian Regime," in Guillermo O'Donnell, Philippe C. Schmitter and Laurence Whitehead (eds.), *Transitions from Authoritarian Rule: Latin America,* pp. 123–147. Baltimore, MD: Johns Hopkins University Press.

Mommer, Bernard. 2002. *Global Oil and the Nation State.* Oxford, UK: Oxford Institute for Energy Studies.

NACLA (North American Congress on Latin America). 1994. *Mexico Out of Balance,* 38.1 (July–August).

Orme, William A. Jr. 1996. *Understanding NAFTA: Mexico, Free Trade and the New North America.* Austin: University of Texas Press.

Padgett, L. Vincent. 1966. *The Mexican Political System.* Boulder: University of Colorado.

Pilcher, Jeffrey M. 1998. *¡Que vivan los tamales! Food and the Making of Mexican Identity.* Albuquerque: University of New Mexico Press.

Pzeworski, Adam. 1986. "Some Problems in the Study of the Transition to Democracy," in O'Donnell, Schmitter and Whitehead (eds.), *Transitions from Authoritarian Rule: Comparative Perspectives.* Baltimore, MD: Johns Hopkins University Press.

Rey, Juan Carlos. 1972. "El sistema de partidos venezolanos" ("The Venezuelan Party System"), *Politeia,* 1: 135–175.

Ruiz, Ramón Eduardo. 2000. *On the Rim of Mexico: Encounters of the Rich and Poor.* Boulder, CO: Westview Press.

Shirk, David A. 2005. *Mexico's New Politics: The PAN and Democratic Change.* Boulder, CO: Lynne Rienner.

Womack, John Jr. 1968. *Zapata and the Mexican Revolution.* New York: Vintage Books.

Chapter 10

Anderson, Thomas P. 1971. *Matanza: El Salvador's Communist Revolt of 1932.* Lincoln: University of Nebraska Press.

Arendt, Hannah. 1963. *On Revolution.* New York: Viking Press.

Armstrong, Robert and Janet Shenk. 1982. *El Salvador: The Face of Revolution.* Boston: South End Press.

Barry, Tom and Deb Preusch. 1986. *The Central America Fact Book.* New York: Grove Press.

Brenner, Philip, William M. LeoGrande, Dona Rich and Daniel Siegel. 1989. *The Cuba Reader: The Making of a Revolutionary Society.* New York: Grove Press.

Castro Ruz, Fidel. 1991. "Fidel Castro on Unity, Upcoming Party Congress," Castro Speech Data Base, University of Texas at Austin (www1.lanic.utexas.edu/project/castro/db/1991/19910606.html, accessed July 27, 2009).

CHRN (Colombia Human Rights Network). 2001. "An Overview of Recent Colombian History" (colhrnet .igc.org/timeline.htm, accessed December 9, 2010).

De la Fuente, Alejandro. 2001. *A Nation for All: Race, Inequality, and Politics in Twentieth-Century Cuba.* Chapel Hill: University of North Carolina Press.

Debray, Regis. 1967. *Revolution in the Revolution.* London: Penguin Books.

Doyle, Kate and Michael Kornbluth. 1997. "CIA and Assassinations: The Guatemala 1954 Documents," National Security Electronic Archive Briefing Book, no. 4 (www.gwu.edu/~nsarchiv/NSAEBB/ NSAEBB4/, accessed December 9, 2010).

Goldstone, Jack A., Ted Robert Gurr and Farrokh Moshini. 1991. *Revolutions of the Late Twentieth Century.* Boulder, CO: Westview Press.

Hinckle, Warren and William Turner. 1981. *The Fish Is Red: The Story of the Secret War against Castro.* New York: HarperCollins.

Jonas, Susanne. 1991. *The Battle for Guatemala: Rebels, Death Squads and U.S. Power.* Boulder, CO: Westview Press.

Lauria-Santiago, Aldo. 1999. *An Agrarian Republic: Commercial Agriculture and the Politics of Peasant Communities in El Salvador.* Pittsburgh, PA: University of Pittsburgh Press.

Machiavelli, Niccolo. 1947. *The Prince.* Ed. T. G. Bergin. New York: Appleton Century Crofts.

Martí, José. 1999. "Letter to Manuel Mercado," in Deborah Schoonaka and Mirta Muñiz (eds.), *The José Martí Reader.* New York: Ocean Press.

Matthews, Herbert. 1957. "Before the Year Ended, He Said, He Would Be a Hero or a Martyr. Interview with Fidel Castro," *New York Times* (February 24): 1A.

Millet, Richard. 1977. *Guardians of the Dynasty.* New York: Orbis Books.

Pérez, Louis A. 1988. *Cuba: Between Revolution and Reform.* New York: Oxford University Press.

Prevost, Gary and Harry E. Vanden (eds.). 1996. *The Undermining of the Sandinista Revolution.* London: Macmillan Press.

Robinson, William. 1992. *A Faustian Bargain: U.S. Intervention in the Nicaraguan Elections and American Foreign Policy in the Post-Cold War Era.* Boulder, CO: Westview Press.

Roman, Peter. 2003. *People's Power: Cuba's Experience with Representative Government.* Lanham, MD: Rowman and Littlefield.

Chapter 11

Alexander, Robin and Dan La Botz. 2014. "A Workers' Defeat—For Now." *NACLA Report on the Americas* (Spring): 49–53.

Azicri, Max. 2000. *Cuba Today and Tomorrow: Reinventing Socialism.* Gainesville: University of Florida Press.

Barber, Benjamin. 1969. "Conceptual Foundations of Totalitarianism," in Barber, Michael Curtis, and Carl Friedrich (eds.), *Totalitarianism in Perspective,* pp. 3–52. New York: Praeger.

Barry, Tom and Deb Preusch. 1986. *The Central America Fact Book.* New York: Grove Press.

Bergquist, Charles. 1986. *Labor in Latin America: Comparative Essays on Chile, Argentina, Venezuela, and Colombia.* Stanford, CA: Stanford University Press.

Berins Collier, Ruth and David Collier. 1991. *Shaping the Political Arena.* Princeton, NJ: Princeton University Press.

Burbach, Roger. 2002. "'Throw Them All Out': Argentina's Grassroots Rebellion," *NACLA Report on the Americas,* 34.1: xxx.

Conaghan, Catherine. 2011. "Rafael Correa and the Citizens' Revolution," in Steve Levitsky and Kenneth M. Roberts (eds.), *The Resurgence of the Latin American Left,* pp. 260–282. Baltimore, MD: Johns Hopkins University Press.

Crozier, Michael, Samuel Huntington and Joji Watanabi. 1975. *The Crisis of Democracy.* New York: New York University Press.

Cusicanqui, Silvia Rivera. 2004. "The Roots of Rebellion: Reclaiming the Nation," *NACLA Report on the Americas,* 38.3 (November–December): 19–23.

Cypher, James M. 2014. "Energy Privatized: The Ultimate Neoliberal Triumph," *NACLA Report on the Americas* (Spring): 27–31.

De Soto, Hernando. 1989. *The Other Path: The Invisible Revolution in the Third World.* New York: Harper and Row.

Hellinger, Daniel. 1996. "Venezuelan Democracy and the Challenge of the *Nuevo Sindicalismo*," *Latin American Perspectives,* 23 (Summer): 110–131.

Holmes, Jennifer and Sheila Amin Gutiérrez de Piñeres. 2006. "The Illegal Drug Industry, Violence and the Colombian Economy: A Department Level Analysis," *Bulletin of Latin American Research,* 25.1 (January): 104–118.

Hylton, Forest and Sinclair Thomson. 2003. "The Roots of Rebellion: I. Insurgent Bolivia," *NACLA Report on the Americas,* 38 (November–December): 15–19.

Ikawa, Daniela. 2009. "The Right to Affirmative Action in Brazilian Universities," *The Equal Rights Review,* 3: 28–37.

Keck, Margaret. 1992. *The Workers' Party and Democratization in Brazil.* New Haven, CT: Yale University Press.

LaFeber, Walter. 1993. *Inevitable Revolutions: The United States in Central America.* New York: Norton.

Portes, Alejandro and Kelly Hoffman. 2003. "Latin American Class Structures: Their Composition and Change during the Neoliberal Era," *Latin American Research Review,* 38.1 (February): 41–77.

Rodríguez, Roberto. 1996. "Before Canseco—Early History of Latinos in Baseball Full of Hits and Runs around the Colorline," *Black Issues in Higher Education* (April 18): 18–19.

Roman, Peter. 2003. *People's Power: Cuba's Experience with Representative Government.* Lanham, MD: Rowman and Littlefield.

Rosenburg, Tina. 1987. "Death Watch in Mexico: Labor Boss Fidel Velazquez," *The Nation,* 24 (April 18).

Sagas, Ernesto. 1993. "A Case of Mistaken Identity: Antihaitianismo in Dominican Culture," *Latinamericanist,* 29.1: 1–5.

Schneider, Ben Ross. 2004. *Business Politics and the State in Twentieth-Century Latin America.* Cambridge, UK: Cambridge University Press.

Senzek, Alva. 1997. "Entrepreneurs Who Become Radicals," *NACLA Report on the Americas,* 30.4 (January–February): 28.

Swanger, Joanna. 2007. "Feminist Community Building in Ciudad Juarez: A Local Cultural Alternative to the Structural Violence of Globalization," *Latin American Perspectives,* 34.2 (March): 108–123.

Tarrow, Sidney. 1994. *Power in Movement.* Cambridge, UK: Cambridge University Press.

Thompson, E. P. 1966. *The Making of the English Working Class.* New York: Vintage Books.

Tilly, Charles. 1978. *From Mobilization to Revolution.* Reading, MA: Addison-Wesley.

United Nations Office on Drugs and Crime. 2008. *Elementos Orientados para las Políticas Públicas sobre Drogas en la Subregión.* Lima, Peru (www.unodc.org/documents/peru/ElementosOrientadores-Peru-June08.pdf).

U.S. Senate. 1975. "Covert Action in Chile, 1963–1973." Staff Report of the Senate Select Committee on Intelligence Activities. Washington, DC: U.S. Government Printing Office.

Womack, John Jr. 1968. *Zapata and the Mexican Revolution.* New York: Vintage Books.

Chapter 12

Alcoñiz, Isabella and Melissa Scheier. 2007. "The MTL Piqueteros and the Communist Party in Argentina," *Latin American Perspectives,* 34.2: 157–171.

Barber, Benjamin. 1984. *Strong Democracy: Participatory Politics for a New Age.* Berkeley: University of California Press.

Castañeda, Jorge. 2006. "Latin America's Left Turn," *Foreign Affairs,* 85.3 (May–June): 28–43.

Domínguez, Jorge. 1997. *Technopols: Freeing Politics and Markets in Latin America.* University Park, PA: Pennsylvania State University Press.

Duverger, Maurice. 1972. *Party Politics and Pressure Groups: A Comparative Introduction.* New York: Thomas Crowell.

Gramsci, Antonio. 1971. *Selections from the Prison Notebooks.* Trans. Quinton Hoare and Geoffrey Nowell Smith. New York: International Publishers.

Harris, Richard. 1993. "The Nicaragua Revolution: A Postmortem," *Latin America Research Review,* 28.3: 197–213.

Hellinger, Daniel. 2005. "When 'No' Means 'Yes': Electoral Politics in Bolivarian Venezuela," *Latin American Perspectives,* 32.3: 8–32.

Landi, Oscar. 1995. "Outsiders, Nuevos Caudillos y Media Polítics," in Perelli et al. (eds.), *Partidos y Clase Política en América Latina en los 90 (Parties and Political Class in Latin America in the 90s).* Costa Rica: Instituto Interamericano de Derechos Humanos.

Lewis, Norman. 1989. *God against the Indians.* New York: McGraw-Hill.

MacPherson, C. B. 1965. *The Real World of Democracy.* New York: Oxford University Press.

Mainwaring, Scott. 1995. "Brazil: Weak Parties, Feckless Democracy," in Mainwaring and Tim Scully (eds.), *Building Democratic Institutions: Party Systems in Latin America.* Stanford, CA: Stanford University Press.

PBS (Public Broadcast System). 2001. *The Commanding Heights: The Battle for the World Economy.* New York: A Touchstone Book.

Pecci, Gioacchino. 1891. *Rerum Novarum.* Papal Encyclical. Vatican City.

Prevost, Gary and Harry E. Vanden (eds.). 1996. *The Undermining of the Sandinista Revolution.* London: Macmillan Press.

Putnam, Robert D. (ed.). 2002. *Democracies in Flux: The Evolution of Social Capital in Contemporary Society.* New York: Oxford University Press.

Quandt, Midge. 2007. "The Left in Latin America Today" (www.quandt.com, accessed April 22, 2007).

Rial, Juan. 1995. "Percepciones sobre las instituciones democràticas y los medios de comunicación" ("Perceptions about Democratic Institutions and the Means of Communication"), in Perelli et al. (eds.), *Partidos y Clase Política en América Latina en los 90 (Parties and Political Class in Latin America in the 90s).* Costa Rica: Instituto Interamericano de Derechos Humanos.

Tangeman, Michael. 1995. *Mexico at the Crossroads: Politics, the Church, and the Poor.* New York: Orbis Books.

Womack, John Jr. 1968. *Zapata and the Mexican Revolution.* New York: Vintage Books.

Zamora, Rubén. 1997. "Democratic Transition or Modernization? The Case of El Salvador since 1979," in Jorge Domínguez and Marc Lindenberg (eds.), *Democratic Transitions in Central America.* Gainesville: University of Florida Press.

Chapter 13

Ames, Barry. 2002. *The Deadlock of Democracy in Brazil.* Ann Arbor: University of Michigan Press.

Astor, Michael. 2008. "Brazil's President Says G-8 No Longer Relevant," *Associated Press* (November 16).

Avritzer, Leonardo. 2002. *Democracy and the Public Space in Latin America.* Princeton, NJ: Princeton University Press.

Barry, Tom and Deb Preusch. 1986. *The Central America Fact Book.* New York: Grove Press.

Broadman, H. G. and F. Recanatini. 1999. *Seeds of Corruption: Do Market Institutions Matter?* Washington, DC: World Bank. Working Paper 2368.

Brown, Nathan J. (ed.). 2011. *The Dynamics of Democratization: Dictatorship, Development, and Diffusion.* Baltimore, MD: Johns Hopkins University Press.

Buxton, Julia. 2001. *The Failure of Political Reform in Venezuela.* Aldershot, UK: Ashgate.

Cameron, Maxwell A., Eric Hershberg and Kenneth E. Sharpe (eds.). 2012. *New Institutions for Participatory Democracy in Latin America: Voice and Consequence.* New York: Palgrave-MacMillan.

Carothers, David. 2002. "The End of the Transition Paradigm," *Journal of Democracy,* 13.1: 5–21.

Cary, John. 2002. "Parties, Coalitions and the Chilean Congress in the 1990s," in Scott Morgenstern and Benito Nacif (eds.), *Legislative Politics in Latin America,* pp. 222–253. Cambridge, UK: Cambridge University Press.

Coppedge, Michael. 1994. *Strong Parties and Lame Ducks: Presidential Partyarchy and Factionalism in Venezuela.* Stanford, CA: Stanford University Press.

Corrales, Javier. 2006. "Hugo Boss: How Chavez Is Refashioning Dictatorship for a Democratic Age," *Foreign Policy* (January–February): 33–40.

Craig, Ann L. and Wayne A. Cornelius. 1995. "Houses Divided: Parties and Political Reform in Mexico," in Scott Mainwaring and Timothy R. Scully (eds.), *Building Democratic Institutions: Party Systems in Latin America.* Stanford, CA: Stanford University Press.

Crisp, Brian. 2000. *Democratic Institutional Design: The Powers and Incentives of Venezuelan Politicians and Interest Groups.* Palo Alto, CA: Stanford University Press.

Diamond, Larry. 2005. "The State of Democratization at the Beginning of the 21st Century," *Journal of Diplomacy,* 6 (Winter–Spring): 13–18.

Dilla Alfonso, Haroldo. 2006. "Cuban Civil Society: Future Directions and Challenges," *NACLA Report on the Americas,* 39.4: 37–42.

Global Development Research Center. n.d. "Understanding the Concept of Governance" (www.gdrc.org/u-gov/governance-understand.html, accessed July 28, 2009).

Hammergren, Lynn. 2008. "Twenty-Five Years of Latin American Judicial Reforms: Achievements, Disappointments, and Emerging Issues," *Whitehead Journal of Diplomacy and International Relations* 9.1 (Winter–Spring): 89–104.

Hawkins, Kirk A. 2010. *Venezuela's Chavismo and Populism in Comparative Perspective.* New York: Cambridge University Press.

Herman, Edward S. and Frank Brodhead. 1984. *Demonstration Elections: U.S.-Staged Elections in the Dominican Republic, Vietnam, and El Salvador.* Boston: South End Press.

Huntington, Samuel. 1968. *Political Order in Changing Societies.* New Haven, CT: Yale University Press.

La Botz, Dan. 2012. "Mexico's Labor Movement after the Elections: A House Still Divided," *NACLA Report on the Americas,* 45.1 (Winter): 34–37.

LASA (Latin American Studies Association). 1984. *Report of the Latin American Studies Association Delegation to Observe the Nicaraguan General Election of November 4, 1984. LASA Forum* (Fall).

Levitsky, Steven. 2000. "The 'Normalization' of Argentine Politics," *Journal of Democracy,* 11.2: 56–69.

Maher, Stephen. 2012. "Elections, Imperialism, Socialism, and Democracy: Coups and Social Change in Latin America," *NACLA Report on the Americas,* 45.1 (Winter): 56–58.

Mainwaring, Scott and M. Soberg Shugart (eds.). 1997. *Presidentialism and Democracy in Latin America.* Cambridge, UK: Cambridge University Press.

McCarthy, Michael M. 2012. "The Possibilities and Limits of Politicized Participation: Community Councils, Coproduction, and *Poder Popular* in Chávez's Venezuela," in Maxwell A. Cameron, Eric Hershberg and Kenneth E. Sharpe (eds.), *New Institutions for Participatory Democracy in Latin America: Voice and Consequence,* pp. 123–148. New York: Palgrave-MacMillan.

McCoy, Jennifer and David Myers (eds.). 2004. *The Unraveling of Representative Democracy in Venezuela.* Baltimore, MD: Johns Hopkins University Press.

Morgenstern, Scott and Benito Nacif (eds.). 2002. *Legislative Politics in Latin America.* Cambridge, UK: Cambridge University Press.

Munck, Gerardo L. 2004. "Democratic Politics in Latin America: New Debates and Research Frontiers," *Annual Review of Political Science,* 7: 437–462.

Mustapic, Ana Maria. 2002. "Oscillating Relations: President and Congress in Argentina," in Scott Morgenstern and Benito Nacif (eds.), *Legislative Politics in Latin America,* pp. 23–47. Cambridge, UK: Cambridge University Press.

Neto, Octavio Amorim. 2002. "Presidential Cabinets, Electoral Cycles and Coalition Discipline," in Scott Morgenstern and Benito Necif (eds.), *Legislative Politics in Latin America.* Cambridge, UK: Cambridge University Press.

O'Donnell, Guillermo. 1994. "Delegative Democracy," *Journal of Democracy,* 5.1: 55–69.

Plattner, Marc F. 1998. "Liberalism and Democracy: Can't Have One without the Other," *Foreign Affairs* (March–April): 171–180.

Roman, Peter. 2003. *People's Power: Cuba's Experience with Representative Government.* Lanham, MD: Rowman and Littlefield.

Saney, Isaac. 2004. *Cuba: A Revolution in Motion.* London: Zed Books.

Von Mettenheim, Kurt and James Malloy (eds.). 1998. *Deepening Democracy in Latin America.* Pittsburgh, PA: University of Pittsburgh Press.

Wei, Pan. 2006. "Toward a Consultative Rule of Law Regime in China," in Suisheng Zhao (ed.), *Debating Political Reform in China: Rule of Law vs. Democratization.* Armonk, NY: M. E. Sharpe.

Zakaria, Fareed. 1997. "The Rise of Illiberal Democracy," *Foreign Affairs* (November–December): 22–42.

Chapter 14

Amnesty International. 2002. "El Salvador: 10th Anniversary of Peace Accords, Still No Justice." AI Index: AMR 29/001/2002 (January 16, www.amnestyusa.org).

Amnesty International. 2006. "Mexico: Killings and Abductions of Women in Ciudad Juarez and the City of Chihuahua—The Struggle for Justice Goes On." AI Index: AMR 41/012/2006 (February 20, www.amnestyusa.org, accessed August 28, 2007).

Barry, Tom. 2005. "Southcom Generals Say 'Not in Our Backyard,'" *Updater,* Americas Program, International Relations Resource Center (www.americaspolicy.org, accessed June 20, 2006).

Bremer, Catherine. 2007. "Once Quiet Towns Engulfed by Mexican Drugs War," *Reuters* (July 18).

CIP (Center for International Policy). 2006. "Plan Colombia: Six Years Later," *International Policy Report* (www.ciponline.org/colombia/0611ipr.pdf, accessed July 28, 2009).

COHA (Council on Hemispheric Affairs). 2005a. *Too Close for Comfort: El Salvador Ratchets Up Its U.S. Ties.* Washington, DC: Council on Hemispheric Affairs, July 19.

COHA (Council on Hemispheric Affairs). 2005b. *Washington Secures Long-Sought Hemispheric Outpost, Perhaps at the Expense of Regional Sovereignty.* Washington, DC: Council on Hemispheric Affairs, July 20.

Cruz, José Miguel. 2010. "Police Misconduct and Democracy in Latin America." *AmericasBarometer Insights,* 33.

Emersberger, Joe. 2010. "IACHR Rehashes Debunked Claims about Venezuela," *Venezuelanalysis.com* (May 6, http://venezuelanalysis.com/analysis/5337, accessed August 10, 2013).

Gender Equality Observatory. 2012. *Annual Report 2012.* New York: United Nations Economic Commission for Latin America.

Human Rights Watch. 1994. "Cuba: Stifling Dissent in the Midst of Crisis." Washington, DC: Human Rights Watch, February 1.

Human Rights Watch. 2008. "Colombia: Not a Time for a Trade Deal." Washington, DC: Human Rights Watch, November 20.

IACHR. 2010. "Democracy and Human Rights in Venezuela." Inter-American Commission on Human Rights (www.cidh.oas.org/countryrep/Venezuela2009eng/VE09CHAPIENG.htm, accessed August 10).

Issa, Daniela. 2007. "Praxis of Empowerment: *Mística* and Mobilization in Brazil's Landless Rural Workers' Movement," *Latin American Perspectives,* 34.2 (March): 124–138.

Kaufman, Robert. 1972. *The Politics of Land Reform in Chile 1950–1970: Public Policy, Political Institutions, and Social Change.* Cambridge, MA: Harvard University Press.

Kawell, JoAnn. 2002. "Drug Economies of the Americas," *NACLA Report on the Americas,* 36.2 (September–October): 25–26.

Kruger, Mark H. 2007. "Community Based Crime-Control in Cuba," *Contemporary Justice Review,* 10.1 (March): 101–114.

Lacey, Marc. 2007. "Drug Gangs Use Violence to Sway Guatemala Vote," *New York Times* (August 4): A1.

Latinobarómetro. 2005. *Informe Latinobarómetro 2006* (*Latin Barometer Report*). Santiago: Corporación Latinobarómetro (www.latinobarometro.org).

Latinobarómetro. 2012. *Informe Latinobarómetro 2012* (*Latin Barometer Report*). Santiago: Corporación Latinobarómetro (www.latinobarometro.org.)

Lauria-Santiago, Aldo. 1999. *An Agrarian Republic: Commercial Agriculture and the Politics of Peasant Communities in El Salvador.* Pittsburgh, PA: University of Pittsburgh Press.

Miller, Jamie. 2003. *The Intellectual, Economic, Ludicrous Whisperings of God.* Mennonite Central Committee (www.mcc.org/globalizationconsultations/latin_america/miller.html, accessed June 1, 2007).

Miller, John. 2005. "Free, Free at Last," *Dollars and Sense* (www.dollarsandsense.org/archives/2005/0305miller.html, accessed October 4, 2008).

O'Donnell, Guillermo. 1998. "Polyarchies and the (Un)Rule of Law in Latin America," in Juan Méndez, O'Donnell and Paulo Sérgio Pinheiro (eds.), *The Rule of Law and the Underprivileged in Latin America.* Notre Dame, IN: University of Notre Dame Press (www.march.es/ceacs/publicaciones/working/archivos/1998_125.pdf, accessed December 9, 2010).

PAHO (Pan American Health Organization). 1999. *Statistics on Homicides, Suicides, Accidents, Injuries, and Attitudes toward Violence* (www.paho.org/English/AD/DPC/NC/violence-graphs.htm, accessed July 28, 2009).

Phillips, Tom. 2006. "Blood Simple," *Observer* (London, September 17): 27.

Putnam, Robert. 1993. *Making Democracy Work: Civic Traditions in Modern Italy.* Princeton, NJ: Princeton University Press.

Putnam, Robert D. (ed.). 2002. *Democracies in Flux: The Evolution of Social Capital in Contemporary Society.* New York: Oxford University Press.

Schor, Miguel. 2003. "The Rule of Law and Democratic Consolidation in Latin America." Paper prepared for delivery at the 2003 Meeting of the Latin American Studies Association, Dallas, TX, March 27–29.

Transparency International. 2005. *Global Corruption Barometer 2004* (www.globalcorruptionreport.org/gcr, accessed December 9, 2010).

UNDP. 2012. *Anticorruption Programs in Latin America and the Caribbean.* New York: United Nations Development Programme.

UNODC. 2014. *Global Study on Homicide.* New York: United Nations Office on Drug and Crime.

U.S. Department of State. 2004. *Country Reports on Human Rights Activities.* Washington, DC: U.S. Department of State.

Webb, Gary. 1999. *Dark Alliance: The CIA, the Contras and the Crack Cocaine Explosion.* New York: Seven Stories Press.

Chapter 15

Aguilar, Julián. 2012. "Twenty Years Later NAFTA Remains a Source of Tension," *New York Times* (December 7).

AP (Associated Press). 2005. "Stealing the Rainforest," *Associated Press* (July 4).

Astor, Michael. 2005. "Brazilians Suspect Foreigners Covet Amazon Rainforest," *Associated Press* (May 18).

Bacon, David. 2004. *The Children of NAFTA: Labor Wars on the U.S./Mexican Border.* Berkeley: University of California Press.

Barkin, David. 2006. "Building a Future for Rural Mexico," *Latin American Perspectives,* 33.2 (March): 132–140.

Benson, Todd. 2005. "Brazil Says Deal on Drug Isn't Assured," *New York Times* (July 16): B13.

Birns, Larry and Sarah Schaffer. 2005. "CAFTA and Its Discontents," *Council on Hemispheric Affairs* (May 31, www.coha.org/2005/05/31/cafta-and-its-discontents, accessed July 22, 2007).

Blackmore, Emma, Danning Li and Sara Casallas. 2013. *Sustainability Standards in China-Latin America Trade.* London: International Institute for Environment and Development (http://pubs.iied.org/pdfs/16544IIED.pdf).

Boué, Juan Carlos. 2013. *Enforcing Pacta Sun Servanda? Conoco-Phillips and Exxon-Mobil versus the Bolivarian Republic of Venezuela and Petróleos de Venezuela.* Working Papers Series 2, no. 1. Centre of Latin American Studies, University of Cambridge.

Colvin & Co. 2012. "Protectionism in Argentina Threatens Foreign Ownership," *Farmland Forecast* (May 14; http://farmlandforecast.colvin-co.com/2012/05/14/protectionism-in-argentina-threatens-foreign-investment.aspx).

Delp, Linda, Marisol Arriaga, Guadalupe Palma, Haydee Urita and Abel Valenzuela. 2004. *NAFTA's Side Agreement: Fading into Oblivion?* Los Angeles, CA: UCLA Center for Labor Research and Education.

Dietz, Henry and James Street (eds.). 1987. *Latin America's Economic Development: Institutionalist and Structuralist Perspectives.* Boulder, CO: Lynne Rienner.

ECEN. 2005. Report. European Christian Environmental Network (report no longer online).

Enloe, Cynthia. 2000. *Bananas, Beaches, and Bases: Making Feminist Sense of International Politics.* Berkeley: University of California Press.

Esquivel, Gerardo. 2011. "The Dynamics of Income Inequality in Mexico since NAFTA." *Economía,* 12.1 (Fall): 155–179.

Friedman, Thomas. 2000a. "The Coalition to Keep the World's Poor People Poor," *New York Times* (April 14).

Friedman, Thomas. 2000b. *The Lexus and the Olive Tree: Understanding Globalization.* New York: Farrar, Straus, and Giroux.

Friedman, Thomas. 2005. *The World Is Flat: A Brief History of the Twenty-First Century.* New York: Farrar, Straus, and Giroux.

Gardini, Gian Luca. 2009. *Latin America in the 21st Century: Nations, Regionalism, Globalization.* London: Zed Books.

Gorry, Connor. 2005. "Cuba's National HIV/AIDS Program." *MEDICC Review,* 13 (April 2011): 5–8.

Gray, Lorraine (director). 1985. *The Global Assembly Line* (motion picture). New Day Films.

Haslam, Paul. 1999. "Globalization and Effective Sovereignty: A Theoretical Approach to the State in the International Political Economy," *Studies in Political Economy,* 58 (Spring): 41–68.

Higginbottom, Andy. 2013. "The Political Economy of Foreign Investment in Latin America: Dependency Revisited." *Latin American Perspectives,* 40.3 (May): 184–206.

HIV InSite. 2007. "Haiti." University of California, San Francisco (http://hivinsite.ucsf.edu/global?page=cr02-ha-00, accessed April 23, 2009).

HIV InSite. 2008. "Caribbean." University of California, San Francisco (hivinsite.ucsf.edu/global?page=cr02-00-00, accessed April 23, 2009).

Holtz, Timothy. 1997. "Summary of Issue of HIV-AIDS in Cuba" (www.cubasolidarity.net/cubahol2.html, accessed July 28, 2009).

Jawara, Fatoumata and Aileen Kwa. 2002. *Behind the Scenes at the WTO: The Real World of International Trade Negotiations.* London: Zed Books.

Johnson, Tim. 2012. "Mexico's 'Maquiladora' Labor System Keeps Most Mexicans in Poverty," *McClatchy DC* (June 17, www.mcclatchydc.com/2012/06/17/152220/mexicos-maquiladora-labor-system.html, accessed October 25, 2013).

Lama, Abraham. 1999. "Glacial Snow Disappearing in the Andes," *InterPress Service,* July 24 (ipsnews.net, accessed December 10, 2010).

Mumme, Stephen. 1999. "NAFTA's Environmental Side Agreement: Almost Green?," *Borderlines,* 9 (www.irc-online.org, accessed April 26, 2006).

New, William. 2012. "Brazil HIV Drug Patent Ruling Allows Generics, Sends Pipeline Process into Doubt," *Intellectual Property Watch* (March 21, www.ip-watch.org/2012/03/21/brazil-hiv-drug-patent-ruling-allows-generics-sends-pipeline-process-into-doubt).

Pantone, Dan James. 2008. "Uncontacted Amazon Indians in Peru" (www.amazon-indians.org/Uncontacted-Amazon-Indians-Peru.html, accessed July 28, 2009).

Papademetriou, Demetrios, John Audley, Sandra Polaski and Scott Vaughan. 2003. *NAFTA's Promise and Reality: Lessons for the Hemisphere.* Washington, DC: Carnegie Endowment for International Peace.

Porter, Eduardo. 2005. "Illegal Immigrants Are Bolstering Social Security with Billions," *New York Times* (April 5): xx.

Raintree Nutrition. 2005. "Welcome to the Rainforest" (www.rain-tree.com, accessed July 28, 2009).

Rohter, Larry. 2005. "Prostitution Puts U.S. and Brazil at Odds on AIDS Policy," *New York Times* (July 25): A1.

Schurman, Rachel. 2003. "Fish and Flexibility: Working in the New Chile," *NACLA Report on the Americas,* 37.1: 36–37.

Scott, Robert. 2003. *The High Price of Free Trade.* Washington, DC: Economic Policy Institute. Briefing Paper No. 147.

Silberman, Jonathan, Martín Koppel and Mary-Alice Waters. 2004. "Radical Reorganization and Cutback of Cuba's Sugar Industry," *The Militant,* 68.5 (February 9, www.themilitant.com/2004/6805/680550.html, accessed December 10, 2010).

Smith, Adam. 1766. *Inquiry into the Nature and Causes of the Wealth of Nations.* London: Methuen (www.bibliomania.com/2/1/65/112/frameset.html, accessed December 10, 2010).

Strange, Susan. 1996. *The Retreat of the State: The Diffusion of Power in the World Economy.* Cambridge, UK: Cambridge University Press.

USTR. 2004. *NAFTA: A Decade of Success.* Washington, DC: Office of the U.S. Trade Representative (www.ustr.gov/Document_Library/Fact_Sheets/2004/NAFTA_A_Decade_of_Success.html, accessed November 2, 2009).

USTR. 2005. *CAFTA: Facts.* Washington, DC: Office of the U.S. Trade Representative.

World Bank. 1996. *A Mining Strategy for Latin America and the Caribbean.* Washington, DC: World Bank. Technical Paper No. 345.

Chapter 16

Anderson, Thomas. 1971. *Matanza: El Salvador's Communist Revolt of 1932.* Lincoln: University of Nebraska Press.

Avritzer, Leonardo. 2002. *Democracy and the Public Space in Latin America.* Princeton, NJ: Princeton University Press.

Bernstein, Adam. 2008. "Obituary: David Potter, 95; Ambassador to Chile during Pinochet Era," *Washington Post* (July 31): B7.

Burges, Sean. 2012. "Is Itamaraty a Problem for Brazilian Foreign Policy?," *Política Externa,* 21.3: 133–148 (in English at http://anclasblog.files.wordpress.com/2013/01/2012-2013-english-seria-o-itamaraty-um-problema-para-a-policc81tica-externa-brasileira.pdf).

Bushness, David. 1986. "Simón Bolívar and the United States: A Study in Ambivalence," *Air Force Review* (July–August, www.airpower.maxwell.af.mil/airchronicles/aureview/1986/jul-aug/bushnell.html, accessed December 27, 2010).

CIA (U.S. Central Intelligence Agency). 1970. *Report of CIA Chilean Task Force Activities, 15 September to 3 November 1970.* National Security Archives (November 18, www.gwu.edu/~nsarchiv/NSAEBB/NSAEBB8/ch01-01.htm, accessed April 27, 2009).

Emersberger, Joe. 2010. "IACHR Rehashes Debunked Claims about Venezuela," *Venezuelanalysis.com* (May 6, http://venezuelanalysis.com/analysis/5337, accessed August 10, 2013).

Franck, Thomas and Edward Weisband. 1972. *Word Politics: Verbal Strategy among the Superpowers.* New York: Oxford University Press.

Gill, Leslie. 2004. *The School of the Americas: Military Training and Violence in the Americas*. Durham, NC: Duke University Press.

Grandin, Greg. 2006. *Empire's Workshop: Latin America, the United States and the Rise of the New Imperialism*. New York: Metropolitan Books.

Hardt, Michael and Antonio Negri. 2000. *Empire*. Cambridge, MA: Harvard University Press.

Heeley, Laicie. 2013. *U.S. Defense Spending versus Global Defense Spending*. The Center for Arms Control and Non-Proliferation (March 13, http://armscontrolcenter.org/issues/securityspending/articles/2012_topline_global_defense_spending).

Herman, Edward S. and Frank Brodhead. 1984. *Demonstration Elections: U.S.-Staged Elections in the Dominican Republic, Vietnam, and El Salvador*. Boston: South End Press.

IACHR. 2010. *Democracy and Human Rights in Venezuela*. Inter-American Commission on Human Rights (www.cidh.oas.org/countryrep/Venezuela2009eng/VE09CHAPIENG.htm, accessed August 10).

Johnson, John J. 1980. *Latin America in Caricature*. Austin: University of Texas Press.

Kirkpatrick, Jeane. 1979. "Dictatorships and Double Standards," *Commentary Magazine*, 68.5 (November): 34–45.

Millet, Richard. 1977. *Guardians of the Dynasty*. New York: Orbis Books.

Robinson, William I. 1992. *A Faustian Bargain: U.S. Intervention in the Nicaraguan Elections and American Foreign Policy in the Post-Cold War Era*. Boulder, CO: Westview Press.

Robinson, William I. 1996. *Promoting Polyarchy: Globalization, US Intervention, and Hegemony*. Cambridge, UK: Cambridge University Press.

Rogers, William. 2004. "Fleeing the Chilean Coup: The Debate over U.S. Complicity," *Foreign Affairs*, 83.1 (January–February): 160–165.

Said, Edward W. 1981. *Covering Islam*. New York: Pantheon.

Schoultz, Lars. 1987. *National Security and United States Policy toward Latin America*. Princeton, NJ: Princeton University Press.

Webb, Gary. 1999. *Dark Alliance: The CIA, the Contras and the Crack Cocaine Explosion*. New York: Seven Stories Press.

Credits

Introduction

p. 6   Data from Latinobarometro.com
p. 7   Data from Latinobarometro.com
p. 8   Data from Latinobarometro.com
p. 15   © iStockphoto.com/KURL

Chapter 1

p. 21   Getty Images
p. 26   http://members.aol.com/DrDeSart/1010/modelsofdem.html (accessed July 2007, no longer available at this address)
p. 28   Inglehart and Welzel (2005): 176
p. 42   Latin Content/Getty Images

Chapter 2

p. 53   Latinobarometer 2013
p. 55   Economic Commission for Latin America and the Caribbean (ECLAC), on the basis of special tabulations of data from household surveys conducted in the respective countries
p. 63   © Shutterstock (left)
p. 63   © Shutterstock (right)
p. 70   *Cartoons from Nicaragua: The Revolutionary Humor of Roger*, Managua: Committee of U.S. Citizens Living in Nicaragua (1984), p. 31

Chapter 3

p. 75   APF/Getty Images
p. 82   WikiCommons, Courtesy University of California-Bakersfield
p. 91   © iStockphoto.com/rambo182

Chapter 4

p. 111   © iStockphoto.com/KURL
p. 122   Library of Congress

Chapter 5

p. 134   © Shutterstock
p. 139   WikiCommons, Caras y Caretas 2236, Accessed 23 May 2014

Chapter 6

p. 159   Rostow (1960)
p. 164   Getty Images

Chapter 7

p. 191   *Galtieri-Credit:* Gamma-Keystone via Getty Images;
p. 191   *Pinochet-Credit:* Gamma-Rapho via Getty Images;
p. 191   *Figueiredo-Credit:* Getty Images;
p. 191   *Fernandez-Credit:* iStockphoto;
p. 191   *Bachelet-Credit:* AFP/Getty Image;
p. 191   *Rousseff-Credit:* AFP/Getty Images
p. 201   Getty Images
p. 222   Latinobarómetro 2013

Chapter 8

p. 248   AFP/Getty Images
p. 249   AFP/Getty Images

Chapter 9

p. 254   Time & Life Pictures/Getty Images (left); Joe Raedle/Newsmakers/Liaison Agency (right)

Chapter 10

p. 305   Getty Images, WikiCommons, Grupo Cinteupiltzin CENAR El Salvador

Chapter 11

p. 317   LatinContent/GettyImages
p. 333   AFP/Getty Images

Chapter 12

p. 377   AFP/Getty Images

Chapter 13

p. 392   Reprinted with permission of the Center for Economic and Political Research (CEPR) (top)
p. 392   Reprinted with permission of the Center for Economic and Political Research (CEPR) (bottom)
p. 393   Reprinted with permission of the Center for Economic and Political Research (CEPR)
p. 413   LatinContent/Getty Images

Chapter 14

p. 422   Latinobarometer 2010-2011
p. 423   Latinobarometer 2013
p. 426   Latinobarometer 2013
p. 429   AFP/Getty Images
p. 432   Latinobarometer 2013

Chapter 15

p. 449   Getty Images
p. 474   UN Economic Commission for Latin America
p. 476   UN Economic Commission for Latin America
p. 477   UN Economic Commission for Latin America
p. 484   © iStockphoto.com/KURL

Chapter 16

p. 493   Johnson (1980: 199)

p. 508   *From Cartoons from Nicaragua: The Revolutionary Humor of Roger,* Managua: Committee of U.S. Citizens Living in Nicaragua (1984: 37)

p. 515   Latinobarometer 2011

p. 519   AFP/Getty Images

Index

Page numbers in italic format indicate figures and tables.